FROMMER'S

BUDGET TRAVEL GUIDE

COSTA RICA, GUATEMALA & BELIZE ON $35
3RD EDITION

by Karl Samson
with Jane Aukshunas

D1411613

MACMILLAN • USA

About the Authors: Karl Samson lives in the Pacific Northwest, but likes to escape that region's rainy winters by heading south to sunny Central American countries. *Frommer's Costa Rica, Guatemala & Belize* was his first guidebook to the region. When at home he spends his time working on two Frommer guides to the Northwest as well as other books. **Jane Aukshunas,** who agreed to travel the world when she married Karl Samson, has become the organizational wizard of the several books the two have now written together.

Macmillan Travel

A Prentice Hall Macmillan Company
15 Columbus Circle
New York, NY 10023

ISBN 0-671-88369-0
ISSN 1051-6859

Design by Robert Bull Design
Maps by Ortelius Design

Special Sales
Bulk purchases (10+ copies) of Frommer's Travel Guides are available to corporations at special discounts. The Special Sales Department can produce custom editions to be used as premiums and/or for sales promotion to suit individual needs. Existing editions can be produced with custom cover imprints such as corporate logos. For more information write to: Special Sales, Prentice Hall, 15 Columbus Circle, New York, NY 10023

Manufactured in the United States of America

CONTENTS

LIST OF MAPS

WHAT THE SYMBOLS MEAN

 FROMMER'S FAVORITES—hotels, restaurants, attractions, and entertainments you should not miss

 SUPER-SPECIAL VALUES—really exceptional values

 FROMMER'S SMART TRAVELER TIPS—hints on how to secure the best value for your money

IN HOTEL AND OTHER LISTINGS

The following symbols refer to the standard amenities available in all rooms:

A/C air conditioning   TV television   TEL telephone
MINIBAR refrigerator stocked with beverages and snacks

The following abbreviations are used for credit cards:

AE American Express   DISC Discover   EU Eurocard
CB Carte Blanche   ER enRoute   MC MasterCard
DC Diners Club   V VISA

CHAPTER 1

GETTING TO KNOW COSTA RICA

Costa Rica in Spanish means "Rich Coast," which was a misnomer when gold-hungry Spaniards named the country nearly 500 years ago. They found little gold or silver and few Indians to convert and enslave; what they did find was a land of rugged volcanic peaks blanketed with dense forests. Costa Rica was ignored for centuries, but today it is beginning to live up to its name—a name that might rightfully be "Costas Ricas" since it has two coasts, one on the Pacific and one on the Caribbean. Along these coasts are some of the most beautiful beaches in Central America, and this translates into dollars as resort developments spring up along the shores. The dense forests and rugged mountain ranges that cover much of Costa Rica are also bringing in unexpected revenues. To reduce its national debt, Costa Rica agreed to set aside hundreds of thousands of acres of undisturbed forests as national parks and wildlife preserves. With tropical forests around the world disappearing at an alarming rate, concerned individuals and groups are flocking to Costa Rica to visit and study its pristine wilderness areas.

Costa Rica, bordered by the troubled nations of Nicaragua and Panama, is also a relative sea of tranquillity in a region of turmoil. For more than 100 years, the country has enjoyed a stable democracy; in fact, there isn't even a standing army here, something that Costa Ricans are very proud of. Former president Oscar Arias Sanchez was awarded the Nobel Peace Prize for his work in implementing a Central American peace plan. With political stability, an educated populace, and vast areas of wilderness, Costa Rica today is a rich coast, indeed.

1. GEOGRAPHY, HISTORY & POLITICS

GEOGRAPHY

Bordered on the north by Nicaragua and on the southeast by Panama, Costa Rica (19,530 square miles) is only slightly larger than Vermont and New Hampshire combined. Within this area are more than 750 miles of coastline on both the Caribbean Sea and the Pacific Ocean. Much of the country is mountainous, with three major ranges running from northwest to southeast. Among these mountains are several volcanic peaks, some of which are still active. Between the mountain ranges there are fertile valleys, the largest and most populated of which is the Central Valley. With the exception of the dry Guanacaste region, much of Costa Rica's coastal area is hot and humid and covered with dense rain forests. The earliest Spanish settlers found the climate much more amenable in the highlands, and to this day most of the population lives in this region.

80 km
0 ████████ 50 mi

N

Lake Nicaragua

La Cruz
Santa Cecilia

Santa Elena Bay

Murciélagos Islands
Santa Rosa National Park

CORDILLERA DE GUANACASTE

Upala

Los Chiles

35

Golfo de Papagayo

Rincón de la Vieja
Rincón de la Vieja National Park

Caño Negro Lake

San Raphael de Guatuso

Guayabo

Lake Cote

6

Río Cote

4

Playa Hermosa
Playa Coco
Playa Ocotal
Playa Pan de Azucar
Playa Potrero
Playa Flamingo
Playa Brasilito
Playa Conchal
Playa Grande
Playa Tamarindo

Liberia

Pan American Hwy.

Río Tempisque

Belén

Tamarindo

Santa Cruz

Playa Junquillal

160

21

Nicoya

Puerto Moreno

18

Tilarán
Lake Arenal

142

Cañas

Monteverde

CORDILLERA DE TILARAN

Fortuna

Arenal Volcano

Juntas

Monteverde Cloud Forest Reserve

1

Chira Island

Hojancha

Playa Nosara

Nosara

160

Puntarenas

23

Playa Garza
Playa Sámara

Sámara

Nicoya Peninsula

Playa Naranjo

Golfo de Nicoya

Paquera

Tambor

160

34

Playa Tambor

Montezuma
Playa Montezuma

Playa de Jeoó
Jacó

Cabo Blanco Nature Preserve

Pacific

Ocean

Coco Island National Park

9147

COSTA RICA

REGIONS IN BRIEF

The Central Valley The Central Valley is characterized by rolling green hills between 3,000 and 4,000 feet above sea level, where the climate has been described as "eternal spring." The rich volcanic soil of this region makes it ideal for growing almost anything, especially coffee. The country's earliest settlements were in this area, and today the Central Valley is a densely populated area laced with good roads and dotted with small towns. Surrounding the Central Valley are high mountains, among which are four volcanic peaks. Two of these, Poás and Irazú, are still active and have caused extensive damage over the past two centuries. Much of the mountainous regions to the north and to the south of the capital of San José have been declared national parks to protect their virgin rain forests from logging.

Guanacaste and the Nicoya Peninsula This northwestern region of Costa Rica is the driest part of the country and has been likened to west Texas. The area has one of the last remnants of tropical dry forest left in Central America. Because the forest gives way to areas of savannah in Guanacaste, this is Costa Rica's "Wild West," where cattle ranching is the primary occupation. The Nicoya Peninsula is also the site of many of Costa Rica's sunniest and most popular beaches.

The Northern Zone This region lies to the north of San José and includes rain forests, cloud forests, Arenal Volcano (the country's most active volcano), Braulio Carillo National Park, and numerous remote lodges. Because this is one of the few regions of Costa Rica without any beaches, it primarily attracts people interested in nature. The northern zone also attracts windsurfers to Arenal Lake, which boasts some of the best windsurfing in the world.

The Central Pacific Coast The central Pacific Coast is the most easily accessible coastline in Costa Rica, and consequently boasts the greatest number of beach resorts and hotels. Jacó Beach is primarily a charter company destination attracting Canadian and German tourists, while Manuel Antonio caters to people seeking a bit more tranquillity and beauty. This region is also the site of the highest peak in Costa Rica—Mount Chirripó—where frost is common.

The Caribbean Coast Most of the Caribbean Coast is a wide, steamy lowland laced with rivers and blanketed with rain forests and banana plantations. The northern region of this coast is accessible only by boat or small plane and is the site of Tortuguero National Park, which is known for its nesting sea turtles and riverboat trips. The southern half of the Caribbean Coast has several beautiful beaches, and as yet has few large hotels.

The South Pacific Coast This is one of Costa Rica's most remote and undeveloped regions. Much of the area is protected in Corcovado and La Amistad national parks. This is a hot, humid region characterized by rain forests and rugged coastlines.

DATELINE

- **13,000 B.C.** Earliest record of human inhabitants in Costa Rica.
- **1,000 B.C.** Olmec people from Mexico arrive in Costa Rica, searching for rare blue jade.
- **1,000 B.C.– A.D. 1400** City of Guayabo inhab-
  (continues)

HISTORY & POLITICS

EARLY HISTORY Little is known of Costa Rica's history prior to its colonization by Spanish settlers. The pre-Columbian Indians who made their home in this part of Central America never developed the large cities or advanced culture that flowered farther north in what would become Guatemala, Belize, and Mexico. However, from scattered excavations around the country, primarily in the northwest, ancient artifacts have been unearthed that indicate a strong sense of aesthetics. Beautiful gold and jade jewelry, intricately carved grinding stones, and artistically painted terra-cotta ware point toward a highly skilled, if not large, population. The most enigmatic of these ancient relics are carved stone balls, some measuring several yards across and weighing many tons, that have been found along the southern Pacific Coast. The purpose of these stone spheres remains a mystery: Some archeologists say that they may have been boundary markers; others think that they were celestial references. Still other scientists now claim that they are not man-made at all, but rather are natural geological formations.

In 1502, on his fourth and last voyage to the New World, Christopher Columbus anchored just offshore from present-day Limón. Whether it was he who gave the country its name is open to discussion, but it was not long before the inappropriate name took hold. The earliest Spanish settlers found that, unlike the Indians farther north, the native population of Costa Rica was unwilling to submit to slavery. Despite their small numbers and scattered villages, they fought back against the Spanish. However, the superior Spanish firepower and the European diseases that had helped to subjugate the populations farther north conquered the natives. But when the fighting was finished, the settlers in Costa Rica found that there were no more Indians left to force into servitude. The settlers were forced to till their own lands, an exercise unheard of in other parts of Central America. Few pioneers headed this way; they settled instead in Guatemala, where there was a large native work force. Costa Rica was nearly forgotten, as the Spanish crown looked elsewhere for riches to plunder and souls to convert.

It didn't take long for Costa Rica's few Spanish settlers to head for the hills, where they found rich volcanic soil and a climate that was less oppressive than in the lowlands. Cartago, the colony's first capital, was founded in 1563, but it would not be until the 1700s that more cities were founded in this agriculturally rich region. In the late 18th century, the first coffee plants were introduced, and because these plants thrived in the highlands, Costa Rica began to develop its first cash crop. Unfortunately, it was a long and difficult journey transporting the coffee to the Caribbean Coast and thence to Europe, where the demand for coffee was growing.

FROM INDEPENDENCE TO THE PRESENT

In 1821, Spain granted independence to its colonies in Central America. Costa Rica joined with its neighbors to form the Central American Federation, but in 1938 it withdrew to form a new nation and pursue its own interests, which differed considerably from those of the other Central American nations. By the mid-1800s, coffee was the country's main export. Land was given free to anyone willing to plant coffee on it, and plantation owners soon grew wealthy and powerful, creating Costa Rica's first elite class. Coffee plantation owners were powerful enough to elect their own representatives to the presidency.

This was a stormy period in Costa Rican history, and in 1856 the country was invaded by William Walker, a soldier of fortune from Tennessee who had grandiose dreams of presiding over a slavery state in Central America. Prior to his invasion of Costa Rica, he had invaded Baja California and Nicaragua. The people of Central America were

DATELINE

ited by as many as 10,000 people.

• **1502** Columbus discovers Costa Rica in September, landing at what is now Limón.

• **1519–1561** Spanish explore and colonize Costa Rica.

• **1563** City of Cartago founded in Central Valley.

• **1737** San José founded.

• **Late 1700s** Coffee introduced as a cash crop.

• **1821** On September 15, Costa Rica, with the rest of Central America, gains independence from Spain.

• **1823** Capital moved to San José.

• **1848** Costa Rica proclaimed an independent republic.

• **1856** Battle of Santa Rosa; Costa Ricans defeat U.S.-backed proslavery advocate William Walker.

• **1870s** First banana plantations formed.

• **1889** First election is won by an opposition party, establishing democratic process in Costa Rica.

• **1899** The United Fruit Company is founded by railroad builder Minor Keith.

• **1948** After civil war, Costa Rican army is abolished.
(continues)

DATELINE

• **1987** President Oscar Arias Sanchez awarded the Nobel Peace Prize for orchestrating the Central American Peace Plan.

outraged by the actions of this man, who actually had backing from U.S. president James Buchanan. Costa Ricans, led by their own president, Juan Rafael Mora, marched against Walker and chased him back to Nicaragua. Walker eventually surrendered to a U.S. warship in 1857, but in 1860 he attacked Honduras, claiming to be the president of that country. The Hondurans soon captured and executed Walker.

Until 1890 coffee growers had to transport their coffee either by ox cart to the Pacific port of Puntarenas or by boat down the Sarapiquí River to the Caribbean. In the 1870s a progressive president proposed a railway from San José to the Caribbean Coast to facilitate the transport of coffee to European markets. It took nearly 20 years for this plan to reach fruition and more than 4,000 workers lost their lives constructing the railway, which passed through dense jungles and rugged mountains on its journey from the Central Valley to the coast. It was under the direction of the project's second chief engineer, Minor Keith, that a momentous deal was made with the government of Costa Rica: In order to continue the financially strapped project, Keith had struck on the idea of using the railway right-of-way (land on either side of the tracks) as banana plantations. The export of this crop would help to finance the railway, and in exchange Keith would get a 99-year lease on 800,000 acres of land with a 20-year tax deferment. In 1878 the first bananas were shipped from Costa Rica, and in 1899 Keith and a partner formed the United Fruit Company, a company that would eventually become the largest landholder in Central America and cause political disputes and wars throughout the region.

In 1889 Costa Rica held what is considered the first free election in Central American history. The opposition candidate won the election, and the control of the government passed from one political party to another without bloodshed or hostilities. Thus Costa Rica established itself as the region's only true democracy. In 1948 this democratic process was challenged by former president Rafael Angel Calderón, who lost a bid for a second term in office by a narrow margin. Calderón, who had the backing of communist labor unions, refused to yield the country's leadership to the rightfully elected president, Otilio Ulate, and a civil war ensued. Calderón was eventually defeated. In the wake of this crisis, a new constitution was drafted; among other changes, it abolished Costa Rica's army so that such a war could never happen again.

Peace and democracy have become of tantamount importance to Costa Ricans since the civil war of 1948. When Oscar Arias Sanchez was elected president in 1986, his main goal was to seek a solution to the ongoing war in Nicaragua, and one of his first actions was to close down contra bases inside Costa Rica. In 1987 Arias won the Nobel Peace Prize for initiating a Central American peace plan aimed at settling the war in Nicaragua.

Costa Rica's 100 years of nearly uninterrupted democracy have helped make it the most stable economy in Central America. This stability and adherence to the

---

IMPRESSIONS

Below us, at a distance of perhaps two thousand feet, the whole country was covered with clouds. . . . the more distant clouds were lifted, and over the immense bed we saw at the same time the Atlantic and Pacific Oceans. . . . This was the grand spectacle we had hoped. . . . It is the only point in the world which commands a view of two seas . . .
—J. L. STEPHENS, *INCIDENTS OF TRAVEL IN CENTRAL AMERICA, CHIAPAS AND YUCATAN,* 1841

democratic process are a source of great pride to Costa Ricans. They like to think of their country as a "Switzerland of Central America," not only because of its herds of dairy cows but also because of its staunch position of neutrality in a region that has been torn by nearly constant civil wars and revolutions for more than 200 years.

2. CULTURAL & SOCIAL LIFE

ART   Though the pre-Columbian cultures of Costa Rica were small compared to those of the Mayas, Aztecs, and Incas, they did leave the country with an amazing wealth of artistically designed artifacts. Gold and jade jewelry, painted terra-cotta pots, and carved stone sculptures and grinding stones from this period can be seen in several San José museums. Since the Spanish conquest, Costa Rica's artists have followed European artistic styles. The Museo de Arte Costarricense exhibits works by the country's better-known artists of the last 400 years.

ARCHITECTURE   The pre-Columbian peoples of Costa Rica left few signs of their habitation. The excavations at Guayabo, little more than building foundations and paved streets, are the country's main archeological site. Numerous earthquakes over the centuries have destroyed most of what the Spanish built. One such earthquake, in 1910, halted the construction of a cathedral in Cartago, the ruins of which are now a peaceful park in the middle of town. The ruins of another church, the oldest in Costa Rica, can be found near the village of Ujarrás in the Orosi Valley. This church was built in 1693 and abandoned in 1833 when the village was flooded. The central plaza in Heredia has a historic church built in 1796, and also on this square is an old fortress tower known as El Fortín.

RELIGION   Costa Ricans on the whole are devout Roman Catholics. The patron saint of Costa Rica is Nuestra Señora de Los Angeles (Our Lady of the Angels) who has a Byzantine-style church dedicated to her in Cartago. In the church is a shrine that contains a tiny figure of La Negrita, the Black Virgin, to whom miraculous healing powers have been attributed. The walls of the shrine are covered with a fascinating array of tiny silver images left as thanks for cures effected by La Negrita. August 2 is the day dedicated to her, when thousands of people walk from San José to Cartago in devotion to this powerful statue.

THE PEOPLE   When the first Spaniards arrived in Costa Rica, the small Indian population was further reduced by wars and disease until they became a minority. Consequently, most of the population of Costa Rica today is of pure Spanish descent, and it is not at all surprising to see blond Costa Ricans. However, there are still some remnant Indian populations on reservations around the country. On the Caribbean Coast, there is also a substantial population of English-speaking black Creoles who came over from Jamaica to work on the railroad and in the banana plantations. They have never moved far inland, preferring the humid lowlands to the cool Central Valley. For the most part, these different groups coexist without friction.

Costa Ricans, who are also known as *Ticos,* have a high literacy rate. Women constitute nearly 50% of the work force, and there is a large, working middle class; the gross disparity between rich and poor that you see in other Central American countries is not found here.

PERFORMING ARTS & EVENING ENTERTAINMENT   One of the very first things that Costa Ricans did with their newfound coffee wealth in the mid-19th century was to build an opera house. Today that opera house is known as the Teatro Nacional and hardly a night goes by that some performance isn't held in the stately theater.

IMPRESSIONS

We, the people of Costa Rica, believe that peace is much more than the absence of hostility among men and nations. . . . To us peace is the only ideal that, once achieved, will give us the right to call ourselves . . . human beings.
—OSCAR ARIAS SANCHEZ, FORMER COSTA RICAN PRESIDENT AND NOBEL PEACE PRIZE LAUREATE

However, despite San José's interest in classical music, mariachi, marimba, and salsa music have a firm grip on the hearts of all Ticos. In San José there are several 24-hour restaurants where mariachi and marimba music can be heard live and for free at any hour of the day or night. Discos specializing in salsa music are also common throughout the country. And down on the Caribbean Coast, reggae and soca music are also popular.

SPORTS & RECREATION Soccer is the national sport of Costa Rica, but baseball, polo, squash, and handball also are popular. As yet, golf has not caught on in Costa Rica; there are fewer than half a dozen golf courses in the country. Sportfishing, however, is very popular, and the waters in and around Costa Rica abound with tarpon, sailfish, and marlin. There are fishing tournaments throughout the year and fishing boats for hire on both coasts. Surfing is another sport that has caught on in a big way in Costa Rica. There are excellent surfing waves at various points on both coasts.

3. FOOD & DRINK

Very similar to other Central American cuisines, Costa Rican food is not especially memorable. Perhaps this is why there is so much international food available throughout the country. However, if you really want to save money, you'll find that Costa Rican food is always the cheapest food available. It is primarily served in *sodas,* Costa Rica's equivalent of diners.

FOOD
MEALS & DINING CUSTOMS

Rice and beans are the basis of Costa Rican meals. At breakfast, they're called *gallo pinto* and come with everything from eggs to steak to seafood. At lunch or dinner, rice and beans go by the name *casado* (which also means "married"). A casado usually comes with a cabbage-and-tomato salad, fried plantains (a type of banana), and a meat dish of some sort.

Dining hours in Costa Rica are flexible: Many restaurants in San José are open 24 hours, a sign that Ticos are willing to eat at any time of the night or day. However, expensive restaurants tend to open for lunch between 11am and 2pm and for dinner between 6pm and midnight.

THE CUISINE

Appetizers *Bocas* are served with drinks in most bars. Often the bocas are free, but even if they aren't, they're very inexpensive. Popular bocas include *gallos* (stuffed tortillas), *tamales,* and *ceviche.*

Soups Black bean soup, *sopa negra,* is a creamy soup with a poached or boiled egg soaking in the broth. It is one of the most popular of Costa Rican soups and shows up on many menus. *Olla de carne* is a delicious soup made with beef and several local vegetables, including *chayote, ayote, yuca,* and plantains, all of which have textures and flavors similar to various winter squashes. *Sopa de mondongo* is made with tripe, the stomach of a cow, which some love and others find disgusting.

Sandwiches and Snacks   Ticos love to snack, and there are a large variety of tasty little sandwiches and snacks available on the street, at snack bars, and in sodas. *Arreglados* are little meat-filled sandwiches, as are *tortas,* which are served on little rolls with a bit of salad tucked into them. *Gallos* are tortillas stuffed with meat, beans, or cheese. Tacos, tamales, and empanadas also are common.

Meat   Costa Rica is beef country, one of the tropical nations that has converted much of its rain-forest land to pastures for raising cattle. Beef is cheap and plentiful, although it may be a bit tougher than you are used to. Spit-roasted chicken is also very popular here and is surprisingly tender.

Seafood   Costa Rica has two coasts, and as you would expect, there is plenty of seafood available everywhere in the country. *Corvina* (sea bass) is the most commonly served fish, and it is prepared innumerable ways, including as ceviche, a sort of marinated salad.

Vegetables   On the whole, you will find vegetables surprisingly lacking in the meals you are served in Costa Rica. The standard vegetable with any meal is a little pile of shredded cabbage topped with a slice or two of tomato. For a much more satisfying and filling salad, order *palmito* (heart of palm salad). Hearts of palm are considered a delicacy because an entire palm tree must be cut down to extract the heart. The heart consists of many layers of leaves wrapped around one another. These leaves are chopped and served with other fresh vegetables with a salad dressing on top. If you want something more than this, you'll have to order a side dish such as *picadillo,* a stew of vegetables with a bit of meat in it. Most people have a hard time thinking of *plátanos* (plantains) as vegetables, but these giant relatives of bananas require cooking before they can be eaten and are served as a side dish. Yuca (manioc root) is another starchy staple vegetable of Costa Rica.

One more vegetable worth mentioning is the *pejibaye,* a form of palm fruit that looks like a miniature orange coconut. Boiled pejibayes are frequently sold from carts on the streets of San José. When cut in half, a pejibaye reveals a large seed surrounded by soft, creamy flesh and looks a bit like an avocado.

Fruits   Costa Rica has a wealth of delicious tropical fruits. The most common are mangos (season begins in May), papayas, pineapples, and bananas. Other less-known fruits include the *marañon,* which is the fruit of the cashew tree and has orange or yellow glossy skin; the *granadilla* (passion fruit); the *mamón chino,* which Asian travelers will immediately recognize as the rambutan; and the *carambola* (star fruit). When ordering *ensalada de fruita* in a restaurant, make sure that it is made with fresh fruit and does not come with ice cream and gelatin cubes.

Desserts   *Queque seco,* which literally translates as "dry cake," is the same as pound cake. *Tres leches* cake, on the other hand, is so moist you almost need to eat it with a spoon. *Flan de coco* is a sweet coconut flan.

DRINKS

WATER & SOFT DRINKS   Although water in most of Costa Rica is said to be safe to drink, visitors often become ill shortly after arriving in Costa Rica. Play it safe and stick to bottled water, which is readily available. *Aqua mineral,* or simply *soda,* is sparkling water in Costa Rica. Most major brands of soft drinks are also available.

Frescos, a bit like milk shakes, are my favorite drinks in Costa Rica. They are usually made with fresh fruit and milk or water. Among the more common fruits used are bananas, papayas, blackberries (*moras*), and pineapples. Some of the more unusual frescos are *horchata* (made with rice flour and a lot of cinnamon) and *pinolillo* (made with roasted corn flour). Order *un fresco de leche sin hielo* if you are trying to avoid untreated water.

BEER, WINE & LIQUOR   Costa Rica bottles several brands of beer, all of which are quite inexpensive. Heineken also is available. Costa Rica distills a wide variety of liquors, and you'll save money by ordering these instead of imported brands. Imported wines are available at fairly high prices in the better restaurants throughout the country. You can save a bit of money by ordering South American wines. Café Rica

❓ DID YOU KNOW . . . ?

- Costa Rica has the oldest democracy in Central America.
- San José, the capital, is farther south than Caracas, Venezuela.
- Costa Rica has no army, navy, air force, or marine corps.
- Costa Rica has 10% of the butterfly species in the world—more than the entire African continent has—as well as more than 1,200 varieties of orchids and more than 800 species of birds.
- Isla del Coco, the largest uninhabited island in the world, is part of Costa Rica.
- You can see both the Caribbean Sea and the Pacific Ocean from the top of Costa Rica's Mount Chirrippó.
- During an *arribada* more than 15,000 sea turtles may nest on the same beach over a period of only a few nights.
- In the rain forests of the Osa Peninsula it sometimes rains as much as 200 inches per year.

and Salicsa are two coffee liqueurs made in Costa Rica; the former is very similar to Kahlua, and the latter is a cream coffee liqueur.

4. RECOMMENDED BOOKS & FILMS

BOOKS

GENERAL *The Costa Ricans* (Prentice Hall, 1987), by Richard, Karen, and Mavis Biesanz, is a well-written account of the politics and culture of Costa Rica. To learn more about the life and culture of Costa Rica's Talamanca Coast, an area populated by Afro-Caribbean people, pick up a copy of *What Happen, A Folk-History of Costa Rica's Talamanca Coast* (Publications in English, 1993) by Paula Palmer. Or, for a look at the perspective of the indigenous people of the Talamanca region, read *Taking Care of Sibo's Gifts: An Environmental Treatise from Costa Rica's Kekoldi Indigenous Reserve* (Editorama, 1993) by Palmer, Sanchez, and Mayorga.

The Costa Rica Reader (Grove Press, 1989), edited by Marc Edelman and Joanne Kenen, is a collection of essays on Costa Rican topics. For insight into Costa Rican politics, economics, and culture, this weighty book is invaluable. *Costa Rica, A Traveler's Literary Companion* (Whereabouts Press, 1994), edited by Barbara Ras and with a forward by Oscar Arias Sánchez, is a collection of short stories by Costa Rican writers and is organized by region.

NATURAL HISTORY *Costa Rica National Parks* (Editorial Heliconia, Fundacion Neotropica, 1988), by Mario A. Boza, is a beautiful picture book of Costa Rica's national parks. *Costa Rica's National Parks and Preserves* (The Mountaineers, 1993), by Joseph Franke, is similar but with fewer photos and more text.

Dr. Donald Perry's fascinating *Life Above the Jungle Floor* (Don Perro Press, 1991) is an account of Perry's research into the life of the tropical rain-forest canopy. Perry is well known for the cable car network he used for studying the canopy.

Lessons of the Rainforest (Sierra, 1990), edited by Suzanne Head and Robert Heinzman, is a collection of essays by leading authorities in the fields of biology, ecology, history, law, and economy who look at the issues surrounding tropical deforestation. *A Guide to the Birds of Costa Rica* (Christopher Helm Ltd., 1991), by F. Gary Stiles and Alexander Skutch, is an invaluable guide to identifying the many birds you may see during your stay. Other interesting natural history books include *Sarapiquí Chronicle* (Smithsonian Institution Press, 1991), by Allen Young; *Costa Rica Natural History* (University of Chicago Press, 1983), by Daniel Janzen; and *Butterflies of Costa Rica* (Princeton University Press), by Philip DeVries.

FILM

1492—Conquest of Paradise (1993), starring Gerard Depardieu, is the story of Christopher Columbus's discovery of the Americas and was filmed at several locations in Costa Rica, including the Pacific and Caribbean coasts, Jacó and Limón.

CHAPTER 2

PLANNING A TRIP TO COSTA RICA

Costa Rica is one of the fastest growing tourist destinations in the Americas, and as the number of people visiting Costa Rica has increased, so too has the need for pretrip planning. When is the best time to go to Costa Rica? The cheapest time? Should I rent a car? What will that cost? Where should I go in Costa Rica? What are the hotels like? How much should I budget for my trip? These are just a few of the important questions that this chapter will answer for you so you can be prepared when you arrive in Costa Rica.

---

1. INFORMATION, ENTRY REQUIREMENTS & MONEY

SOURCES OF INFORMATION

In the United States, you can get information on Costa Rica by contacting the **Costa Rica Brochure Service** (tel. toll free 800/327-7033), a representative of the **Costa Rican Tourist Board (I.C.T., or Instituto Costarricense de Turismo)** in the United States.

Once you are in Costa Rica, you'll find an I.C.T. information desk at Juan Santamaría Airport (on the left just past the Customs counters). If you don't yet have a room reservation, the helpful staff here will call around to try to find you one. The main tourist information center is beneath the Plaza de la Cultura, Calle 5 between Avenida Central and Avenida 2 (tel. 222-1090 or 223-8423) in downtown San José.

ENTRY REQUIREMENTS

SECURING & RENEWING YOUR U.S. PASSPORT Passport applications are available from authorized post offices, clerks of court, or passport agencies. It is also possible to request an application—Form DSP-11 for a new passport or DSP-82 for a renewal—by mail, from Passport Services, Office of Correspondence, Department of State, 1425 K St. NW, Washington, DC 20522-1075. The back of the application gives the addresses of 13 agencies that can process the applications, including Boston, Chicago, Honolulu, Houston, Los Angeles, Miami,

New Orleans, New York City, Philadelphia, San Francisco, Seattle, Stamford, Conn., and Washington, D.C. Be forewarned that lines are long in these agencies, and you can get a passport more quickly and easily from a post office or courthouse. (Processing usually takes four weeks in either case.)

The passport application must be accompanied by proof of U.S. Citizenship: an old passport, a certified copy of your birth certificate complete with registrar's seal, a report of birth abroad, or naturalized citizenship documents. In addition, a driver's license, employee identification card, military ID, or student ID card with photo is acceptable.

The application must be accompanied by two identical recent two- by two-inch photos, either color or black-and-white with a white background. Look in the *Yellow Pages* of your telephone book for places that take passport photos and expect them to be expensive (up to $9 for two).

First-time applicants age 18 and older pay $65 ($55 plus a $10 first-time processing fee); under 18 and the fee is $40 ($30 plus a $10 first-time fee). Parents or guardians may apply for children under 13, presenting two photos for each child. Children 14 years and older must apply in person. Anyone 16 years or older who has an expired passport issued no more than 12 years ago may reapply by mail, submitting the old document with new photos and pink renewal form DSP-82. You must send a check or money order for $55; there is no additional processing fee. Adult passports are valid for 10 years; children's passports, for 5 years.

If your passport is lost or stolen, you must submit form DSP-64 in person to reapply. There is a $10 processing fee.

The booklet "Your Trip Abroad" (publication no. 044-000-02335-1) provides general information about passports and is available for $1.25 per copy from the U.S. Government Printing Office, Superintendent of Documents, P.O. Box 371954, Pittsburgh, PA 15250-7954 (tel. 202/783-3238 8am to 4pm eastern time; fax 202/512-2250).

For recorded passport information, or to report a lost or stolen passport, call 202/647-0518.

DOCUMENTS FOR ENTRY INTO COSTA RICA If you are a citizen of the **United States, Canada, Great Britain,** or **Northern Ireland,** you may visit Costa Rica for a maximum of 90 days. No visa is necessary, but you must have a valid passport (U.S. citizens can use an original certified birth certificate and a driver's license, though this is an inconvenience when cashing traveler's checks, renting a car, or returning to the United States). If you are a citizen of the **Republic of Ireland,** a visa, valid passport, and round-trip ticket are required, and you can stay for only 30 days. Citizens of **New Zealand** or **Australia** need a valid passport, but no visa to enter Costa Rica, and can stay for 30 days. If you want to extend your visa, you will need to apply to the Department of Immigration with your passport.

If you overstay your visa or entry stamp, you will have to pay around $50 for an exit visa. If you need to get an exit visa, talk to a travel agent in San José. They can usually get the exit visa for you for a small fee. If you want to stay longer than the validity of your entry stamp or visa, the easiest thing to do is cross the border into Panama or Nicaragua for 72 hours and then reenter Costa Rica on a new entry stamp or visa.

If you need a visa or have other questions about Costa Rica, you can contact any of the following Costa Rican embassies: in the **United States,** 2114 S St. NW, Washington, DC 20008 (tel. 202/234-2945); in **Canada,** 135 York St., Suite 208, Ottowa, Ontario K1N 5T4 (tel. 613/562-2855); in **Great Britain,** 14 Lancaster Gate, London, England W2 3LH (tel. 71-723-1772). Residents of Northern Ireland use the embassy in London. There are no embassies in Australia or New Zealand.

MONEY

CURRENCY/CASH The unit of currency in Costa Rica is the colón (¢). The colón is divided into 100 centimos. There are coins of 50 and 100 centimos and 1, 2,

THE COLÓN, THE U.S. DOLLAR & THE BRITISH POUND

In early 1994 there were approximately 148 colónes to the American dollar, or 223 colónes to the British pound. However, because the colón has been in a constant state of devaluation, expect this rate to have changed somewhat by the time you arrive. Because of this devaluation and the accompanying inflation, this book lists prices in U.S. dollars only.

Colónes	U.S. $	U.K. £	Colónes	U.S. $	U.K. £
5	0.035	0.02	1,000	7.0	4.0
10	0.07	0.04	5,000	35.0	20.0
25	0.175	0.1	10,000	70.0	40.0
50	0.35	0.2	25,000	175.0	100.0
75	0.525	0.3	50,000	350.0	200.0
100	0.7	0.4	75,000	525.0	300.0
200	1.4	0.8	100,000	700.0	400.0
300	2.1	1.2	200,000	1,400.0	800.0
400	2.8	1.6	300,000	2,100.0	1,200.0
500	3.5	2.0	500,000	3,500.0	2,000.0
750	5.25	3.0	1,000,000	7,000.0	4,000.0

5, 10, and 20 colónes. There are notes in denominations of 50, 100, 500, 1,000, and 5,000 colónes. You might also encounter a special issue 5-colon bill that is a popular gift and tourist souvenir. It is valid currency, although it sells for much more than its face value.

TRAVELER'S CHECKS   Traveler's checks can be readily changed at hotels and banks. The exchange rate at banks is sometimes slightly higher than at hotels, but it can take a very long time to change money at a bank, and therefore it is not recommended.

CREDIT CARDS   Major international credit cards accepted readily at hotels throughout Costa Rica include American Express, MasterCard, and VISA. The less expensive hotels tend to take cash only. Many restaurants and stores also accept credit cards. Before paying for a hotel with your credit card, check to see if the policy is to charge extra (from 5% to 8%) for credit cards.

WHAT THINGS COST IN SAN JOSÉ	U.S. $
Taxi from the airport to the city center	12.00
Local telephone call	.03
Double at Hotel Herradura (very expensive)	$125.00
Double at Hotel Grano de Oro (moderate)	$69.00
Double at Hotel Bienvenido (budget)	$19.00
Lunch for one at Café de Teatro Nacional (moderate)	9.50
Lunch for one at Soda La Central (budget)	3.50
Dinner for one, without wine, at El Balcon de Europa (expensive)	16.50
Dinner for one, without wine, at La Cocina de Leña (moderate)	12.25
Dinner for one, without wine, at Pollos Gallo Pinto (budget)	5.45
Bottle of beer	.85

	US$
Coca-Cola	.85
Cup of coffee	.60
Roll of ASA 100 Kodacolor film 24 exposures	5.85
Admission to the Jade Museum	Free
Movie ticket	2.05
Ticket at Teatro Melico Salazar	4.05

2. WHEN TO GO — CLIMATE, HOLIDAYS & EVENTS

CLIMATE　Costa Rica is a tropical country and has distinct wet and dry seasons. However, some regions are rainy all year and others are very dry and sunny for most of the year. Temperatures vary primarily with elevation, not with season. On the coasts it is hot all year, while up in the mountains, it can be cool at night any time of year. In the highest elevations (10,000 to 12,000 feet), frost is common.

Average Monthly Temperatures and Rainfall in San José

	Jan	Feb	Mar	Apr	May	June	July	Aug	Sept	Oct	Nov	Dec
Temp (°F)	66	66	69	71	71	71	70	70	71	69	68	67
Temp (°C)	19	19	20.5	21.5	21.5	21.5	21	21	21.5	20.5	20	19.5
Days of Rain	1	0	1	4	17	20	18	19	20	22	14	4

Generally speaking, the rainy season (or "green season," as the tourism industry has begun calling it) is from May to mid-November. Costa Ricans call this wet time of year their winter. The dry season, considered summer by Costa Ricans, is from mid-November to April. In Guanacaste, the dry northwestern province, the dry season lasts several weeks longer than in other places. Even in the rainy season, days often start sunny, with rain falling in the afternoon and evening. On the Caribbean coast, especially south of Limón, you can count on rain all year round, although this area gets less rain in September and October than the rest of the country gets. The best time of year to visit is in December and January, when everything is still green from the rains, but the sky is clear. However, advantages to traveling to Costa Rica in the rainy season are that prices are lower, the country is greener, and there are fewer tourists. Rain doesn't usually fall all day long, and when it does, it's a good opportunity to climb into a hammock and catch up on your reading.

HOLIDAYS　Because Costa Rica is a Roman Catholic country, most of its holidays and celebrations are church related. The major celebrations of the year are Christmas, New Year's, and Easter, which are all celebrated for several days. Keep in mind that Holy Week (Easter Week) is the biggest holiday time in Costa Rica and many families head for the beach (this is the last holiday before school starts). Also there is no public transportation on Holy Thursday or Good Friday. Official holidays in Costa Rica include: January 1 (New Year's Day), March 19 (St. Joseph's Day), Thursday and Friday of Holy Week, April 11 (Juan Santamaría's Day), May 1 (Labor Day), June 29

(Saints Peter and Paul's Day), July 25 (annexation of the province of Guanacaste), August 2 (Virgin of Los Angeles's Day), August 15 (Mother's Day), September 15 (Independence Day), October 12 (Discovery of America), December 8 (Immaculate Conception of the Virgin Mary), December 25 (Christmas Day), December 31 (New Year's Eve).

COSTA RICA
CALENDAR OF EVENTS

The major celebrations are Christmas, New Year's, and Easter, which are all celebrated for several days. Holy Week (Easter Week) is the biggest holiday in Costa Rica and many families head to the beach. There is no public transportation on Holy Thursday or Good Friday.

JANUARY

☐ **Fiesta of Santa Cruz,** Santa Cruz, Guanacaste. A religious celebration honoring the Black Christ of Esquipulas (a famous Guatemalan statue) featuring folk dancing, marimba music, and bullfights. Mid-January.

FEBRUARY

☐ **Fiesta of the Diablitos,** Rey Curré village near San Isidro de El General. Boruca Indians wearing wooden devil and bull masks perform dances representative of the Spanish conquest of Central America. Fireworks displays, Indian handcrafts market. Date varies.

MARCH

☐ **Dia del Boyero (Oxcart Drivers' Day),** San Antonio de Escazú. Colorfully painted oxcarts parade through this suburb of San José, and local priests bless the oxen. Second Sunday.

APRIL

☐ **Holy Week (week before Easter),** Religious processions are held in cities and towns throughout the country. Dates vary from year to year (between late March and early April).

JULY

☐ **Fiesta of the Virgin of the Sea,** Puntarenas. A regatta of colorfully decorated boats carrying a statue of Puntarenas's patron saint. A similar festival is held at Playa del Coco. Saturday closest to July 16.
☐ **Annexation of Guanacaste Day,** Liberia. Tico-style bullfights, folk dancing, horseback parades, rodeos, concerts, and other events in celebration of this region becoming part of Costa Rica. July 24.

AUGUST

☐ **Dia de San Ramon,** San Ramon. More than two dozen statues of saints from various towns are brought to San Ramon where they are paraded through the streets. August 31.
☐ **Fiesta of the Virgin of Los Angeles,** Cartago. This is the annual pilgrimage day of the patron saint of Costa Rica, and many people walk from San José to the basilica in Cartago. August 2.

OCTOBER

☐ **Limón Carnival,** Limón. A smaller version of Mardi Gras complete with floats and dancing in the streets. Commemorates Columbus's discovery of Costa Rica. Week of October 12.

DECEMBER

☐ **Festejos Populares,** San José. Bullfights, a horseback parade (El Tope), a carnival with street dancing and floats, and an amusement park at the fairgrounds in Zapote. On the night of December 31, there is a dance in the Parque Central. Last week of December.

☐ **Fiesta de los Negritos,** Boruca. Boruca Indians celebrate the feast day of their patron saint, the Virgin of the Immaculate Conception, with costumed dances and traditional music. December 8.

☐ **Las Posadas,** throughout the country. Children and carolers go door to door seeking lodging to reenact Joseph and Mary's search for a place to stay. Starting December 15.

3. HEALTH, INSURANCE & OTHER CONCERNS

HEALTH   Vaccinations   No vaccinations are required for a visit to Costa Rica, Guatemala, or Belize, unless you are coming from an area where yellow fever exists. However, because sanitation is generally not as good as it is in developed countries, you may be exposed to diseases for which you may wish to get vaccinations: typhoid, polio, tetanus, and infectious hepatitis (gamma globulin). If you are planning to stay in major cities, you stand little risk of encountering any of these diseases, but if you venture out into remote regions of the country, you stand a higher risk.

Malaria is found in the lowlands on both coasts. Although it is rarely found in urban areas, it is still a problem in remote wooded regions, and in 1993 there was a malaria outbreak in Playa de Jacó. Malaria prophylaxes are available, but several have side effects and others are of questionable effectiveness. Consult your doctor or your local health board as to what is currently considered the best preventative treatment for malaria. Be sure to ask whether a recommended drug will cause you to be hypersensitive to the sun. Because malaria-carrying mosquitoes only come out at night, you should do as much as possible to avoid being bitten by mosquitoes after dark. If you are in a malarial area, wear long pants and long sleeves, use insect repellent, and sleep under a mosquito net or burn mosquito coils (similar to incense, but with a pesticide). Of greater concern may be an outbreak of dengue fever that occurred in 1993. Dengue fever is similar to malaria and is spread by a daytime mosquito. This mosquito seems to be most common in lowland urban areas, and Liberia and Limón were the worst-hit cities. If you should develop a high fever accompanied by nausea, diarrhea, or vomiting during or shortly after a visit to Costa Rica, consult a physician and explain that you have been in a country with both malaria and dengue fever. Many people are convinced that taking B-complex vitamins daily will help prevent mosquitos from biting.

Costa Rica has been relatively free from the cholera epidemic that has spread through much of Latin America in recent years. This is largely due to an extensive public awareness campaign that has promoted good hygiene and increased sanitation. Your chances of contracting cholera while you're here are very slight. However, it is still advisable to avoid *ceviche,* a raw seafood salad, if it has any shellfish in it. Shellfish are known carriers of cholera.

Riptides   Many of Costa Rica's beaches have riptides, strong currents that can drag swimmers out to sea. A riptide occurs when water that has been dumped on the shore by strong waves forms a channel back out to open water. These channels have strong currents. If you get caught in a riptide, you can't escape the current by swimming toward shore; that is the equivalent of trying to swim upstream in a river. To break free of the current, swim parallel to shore until you are out of the riptide before trying to swim to shore.

INSURANCE Before leaving on your trip, contact your health-insurance company and find out whether your insurance will cover you while you are away. If not, look into travel health-insurance policies. You may also want to consider trip insurance to cover cancellations or loss of baggage. If you have homeowner's or renter's insurance, you may be covered against theft and loss while you are on vacation. Be sure to check this before taking out additional insurance. Some credit cards provide trip insurance when you charge an airline ticket, but be sure to check with your credit card company. If you decide that your current insurance is inadequate, you can contact your travel agent for information on various types of travel insurance, including insurance against cancellation of a prepaid tour. The following companies offer various types of travel insurance: **Teletrip** (Mutual of Omaha), P.O. Box 31685, Omaha, NE 68131 (tel. toll free 800/228-9792); **Wallach and Co., Inc.,** P.O. Box 480, Middleburg, VA 22117-0480 (tel. toll free 800/237-6615); or **Access America, Inc.,** P.O. Box 90315, Richmond, VA 23286-4991 (tel. toll free 800/424-3391 or 800/284-8300).

4. WHAT TO PACK

CLOTHING Costa Rica is a tropical country, so to stay comfortable, bring lightweight, natural-fiber clothing. In the rainy season, umbrellas, not raincoats (which are too hot), are necessary. Nights at any time of year can be cool in San José and the mountains, so bring a sweater or jacket. Good walking shoes are also a must. If you will be traveling to exceptionally humid areas, such as the Osa Peninsula or the Caribbean Coast, you might consider bringing nylon shorts and a nylon tank top, as these fabrics can be washed and dried quickly.

OTHER ITEMS A bathing suit is a must and insect repellent is invaluable. Sunscreen, an absolute necessity, is available in Costa Rica but is more expensive than in the United States. Be sure to have waterproof sunscreen if you plan to go rafting. Bring plenty of film and spare batteries for your camera. A water-filter straw, available in camping supply stores, is a convenient way to be sure you always have purified water to drink. A Swiss army knife almost always comes in handy at some point, as do earplugs, and a small sewing kit. Bring along a couple of plastic bags of different sizes to keep your camera and other items dry in the event of a sudden rainstorm.

5. TIPS FOR THE DISABLED, SENIORS, SINGLES, FAMILIES & STUDENTS

FOR THE DISABLED In general, there are few handicapped-accessible buildings in Costa Rica. In San José, sidewalks are crowded and uneven. Few hotels offer handicapped-accessible accommodations, and there are neither public buses nor private vans for transporting disabled individuals. It is difficult for a person with disabilities to get around in Costa Rica.

Mobility International USA, P.O. Box 10767, Eugene, OR 97440 (tel. 503/343-1284) is a membership organization that promotes international educational exchanges for people of all disabilities and ages. For a $20 membership, you can receive their quarterly newsletter and access to their referral service ($10 newsletter only). Also available is a video tape that recounts the story of two exchange groups between Costa Rica and the United States.

FOR SENIORS Many airlines now offer senior-citizen discounts, so be sure to ask about these when making reservations. Due to its temperate climate, stable government, low cost of living, and friendly *pensionado* program, Costa Rica is popular with retirees from North America. If you would like to learn more about retiring in Costa Rica, contact the **Costa Rican Pensionado Office** in San José (tel. 506/223-1733 extension 244 or 264).

Elderhostel, 75 Federal St., Boston, MA 02110 (tel. 617/426-7788), offers very popular study tours to Costa Rica. To participate in an Elderhostel program, either you or your spouse must be at least 60 years old. Bird-watching and lectures on Costa Rican culture and history are two of the more interesting aspects of these trips.

FOR SINGLES You'll pay the same penalty here that you would elsewhere: Rooms are more expensive if you aren't traveling in a pair. If you are looking for someone to travel with, **Travel Companions Exchange**, P.O. Box 833, Amityville, NY 11701-0833 (tel. 516/454-0880), provides listings of possible travel companions categorized under such headings as special interests, age, education, and location. It costs a minimum of $36 for a six-month membership and subscription to the service. A newsletter subscription alone costs $24 for six months.

FOR FAMILIES Hotels in Costa Rica occasionally give discounts for children under 12 years old, and sometimes children under 3 or 4 years are allowed to stay for free.

FOR STUDENTS Costa Rica is the only country in Central America with a network of hostels that are affiliated with the International Youth Hostel Federation. Ask at the **Toruma Youth Hostel,** Avenida Central between Calles 29 and 31, San José (tel. 224-4085) for information on hostels around the country. In San José, there is also a student travel agency: **OTEC,** Edificio Ferencz, 2nd floor, Calle 3 between Avenidas 1 and 3, 275 meters north of the National Theater (tel. 255-0554 or 222-0866). If you already have an **international student identity card,** you can use your card to get discounts on airfares, hostels, national and international tours and excursions, car rentals, and store purchases. If you don't have one, stop by the OTEC office with a passport or other identification that shows you are under 35 years old, proof of student status, and 2 passport photos; for about $10, they'll prepare an ID card for you.

Students interested in a working vacation in Costa Rica should contact the **Council on International Educational Exchange (C.I.E.E.),** 205 E. 42nd St., New York, NY 10017 (tel. 212/661-1414 or 212/661-1450). This organization also issues student identity cards and has offices all over the United States. They also publish *Smart Vacations: The Traveler's Guide to Learning Adventures Abroad* (St. Martin's Press, 1993), a directory of companies, organizations, and schools offering educational travel programs.

6. ALTERNATIVE/ADVENTURE TRAVEL

LANGUAGE PROGRAMS

There are several schools in the San José area that offer Spanish-language courses, and many people come to Costa Rica with the intention of learning Spanish. Courses are of varying length and intensiveness, and often include cultural activities and day excursions. The Spanish schools can also arrange for homestays with a middle-class Tico family, an experience that will help you to speak only Spanish in your daily life. Classes are intensive and often one-on-one. Listed below are some of the larger and more popular Spanish-language schools, with approximate costs. Contact the schools for the most current price information.

Forester Instituto Internacional, Apdo. 6945-1000, San José (tel. 506/225-3155, 225-0135, or 225-1649; fax 506/225-9236), is located 75 meters south of the Automercado in the Los Yoses district of San José. Prices for a 4-week language course range from about $500 without homestay to about $900 with homestay.

Central American Institute for International Affairs (ICAI), Apdo. 10302, San José (tel. 506/233-8571; fax 506/221-5238), offers a 4-week Spanish-language immersion program, along with a homestay, for $895. In the United States, contact the Language Studies Enrollment Center, P.O. Box 5095, Anaheim, CA 92814 (tel. 714/527-2918; fax 714/826-8752).

Centro Lingüístico Conversa, Apdo. 17-1007, Centro Colón, San José (tel. 506/221-7649; fax 506/233-2418), provides a most attractive environment for studying Spanish at its El Pedregal farm 10 miles west of San José. A 4-week course here, including room and board, costs $1,340 for one person and $2,530 for a married couple.

Costa Rican Language Academy, Avenida Central across from Calle 25B and the Pizza Hut (Apdo. 336-2070), San José (tel. 506/233-8914 or 221-1624; fax 506/233-8670), offers three, four, or five hours of Spanish instruction in 1- to 4-week packages. Four hours per day for four weeks will cost $900, including homestay.

Instituto Interamericano de Idiomas (Intensa), Calle 33 between Avenidas 5 and 7 (Apdo. 8110-1000), San José (tel. 506/224-6353 or 225-6009; fax 506/253-4337), offers 2- to 4-week programs. A 4-week, 4-hour-per-day program with homestay costs $845.

Instituto Universal de Idiomas, Apdo. 751-2150, Moravia (tel. 506/257-0441 or 233-2980; fax 506/223-9917), is located on Avenida 2 at the corner of Calle 9. Conveniently located, it charges $750 for a 4-week course (only three hours per day) with homestay.

La Escuela Idiomas D'Amore, Apdo. 67, Quepos (tel. 506/777-1143, 777-0543, or in the United States, 213/851-2739 or 414/781-3151), is situated in the lush surroundings of Manuel Antonio. Four weeks of classes for four hours per day costs $550; with homestay the cost is $785.

ECOTOURISM & ADVENTURE TRAVEL

Ecotourism (from the term "ecological tourism") is the word these days in Costa Rica. With the growing awareness of the value of tropical forests and the interest in visiting rain forests, dozens of lodges and tour companies have sprung up to cater to tourists interested in enjoying the natural beauties of Costa Rica. These lodges are usually located in out-of-the-way locations, sometimes deep in the heart of a forest and sometimes on a farm with only a tiny bit of natural forest. However, they all cater to environmentally aware people with an interest in nature. Horseback riding, rafting, kayaking, hiking, and bird-watching are among the popular activities offered. Most such lodges are out of our budget, but you may want to splurge on one while you are down here.

Some U.S. tour operators that offer adventure tour packages to Costa Rica include **International Expeditions Inc.,** One Environs Park, Helena, AL 35080 (tel. 205/428-1700, or toll free 800/633-4734); **Journeys International, Inc.,** 4011 Jackson Road, Ann Arbor, MI 48103 (tel. 313/665-4407, or toll free 800/255-8735); **Mountain TraveloSobek,** 6420 Fairmount Avenue, El Cerrito, CA 94530 (tel. 510/527-8100, or toll free 800/227-2384); **Wilderness Travel,** 801 Allston Way, Berkeley, CA 94710 (tel. 510/548-0420, or toll free 800/368-2794); **Overseas Adventure Travel,** 349 Braodway, Cambridge, MA 02139 (tel. 617/876-0533, or toll free 800/221-0814); and **Costa Rica Connection,** 75 Oso Street, San Luis Obispo, CA 93401 (tel. 805/543-8823, or toll free 800/345-7422).

In addition to the above-mentioned companies, many environmental organizations, including the Sierra Club, Nature Conservancy, Smithsonian Institution, and the Audubon Society also offer trips to Costa Rica.

There are also dozens of tour companies in San José that offer nature-related tours. Among the most popular multiday soft adventure trips in Costa Rica are trips to

Tortuguero National Park (lowland Caribbean rain forests and rivers), white-water rafting trips, trips to Monteverde or another cloud forest area, and trips to the Osa Peninsula (lowland Pacific rain forest and beaches).

These tours are sometimes held only when there are enough interested people or on set dates, so it pays to contact a few companies to find out what they might be doing during your visit. For information on day trips out of San José, see the "Easy Excursions" section of Chapter 3. The following is a list of some of the larger companies offering adventure- or eco-travel trips:

Costa Rica Expeditions, Calle Central and Avenida 3, Apdo. 6941, San José (tel. 506/257-0766 or 222-0333; fax 506/257-1665), offers tours to Monteverde Cloud Forest Reserve, Tortuguero National Park, and Corcovado National Park, as well as white-water rafting trips and other excursions.

Costa Rica Sun Tours, Apdo. 1195-1250, Escazú (tel. 506/255-2011 or 255-3418; fax 506/255-4410) specializes in small country lodges for nature-oriented travelers.

Geotur, Apdo. 469 Y-1011, San José (tel. 506/234-1867; fax 506/253-6338), offers tours of Braulio Carrillo National Park, Carara Biological Reserve, and other destinations.

Pura Natura, Avenida 7 between Calle 1 and Calle Central (Apdo. 7126-1000), San José (Tel. 506/255-0011 or 255-2055; fax 506/255-2155), offers 1- to 5-day hiking, mountain-biking, and horseback riding trips that are among the most adventurous of any available in Costa Rica.

If your interest is in rafting or sea kayaking, contact **Rios Tropicales,** Apdo. 472-1200, Pavas (tel. 506/233-6455; fax 506/255-4354). This company operates several 1- to 10-day raft trips, as well as sea-kayaking and mountain-biking trips.

Tikal Tour Operators, Apdo. 6398-1000, San José (tel. 506/257-1480; fax 506/223-1916), offers rafting, diving, and volcano trips and visits to Braulio Carrillo National Park, Rincón de la Vieja National Park, Monteverde, and other parks.

FISHING

Costa Rica offers some of the best fishing in the Americas. Among the game fish along the country's two coasts are tarpon, snook, marlin, and sailfish. There is also good fishing for rainbow bass in Lake Arenal. In the regional chapters I have mentioned sports fishing companies in various locations. However, if you want to learn more about fishing in Costa Rica and arrange a fishing vacation, contact **Sportfishing Costa Rica,** Apdo. 115-1150, La Uruca (tel. 506/238-2726 or 238-2729).

7. GETTING THERE

BY PLANE

It takes between three and seven hours to fly to Costa Rica from most U.S. cities, and as Costa Rica becomes more and more popular with North American travelers, more flights are being added. The following airlines currently serve Costa Rica.

American Airlines (tel. toll free 800/433-7300) flies from Miami and Dallas/Fort Worth. **Aviateca** (Guatemalan) (tel. toll free 800/327-9832) flies from Los Angeles, Houston, Miami, and New Orleans. **Continental** (tel. toll free 800/231-0856) flies from Houston. **Lacsa** (Costa Rican) (tel. 800/225-2272) flies from New York, Miami, New Orleans, Los Angeles, and San Francisco. **Mexicana** (tel. toll free 800/531-7921) flies from New York, Denver, Miami, Dallas/Fort Worth, San Antonio, San José (California), and San Francisco. **Taca** (El Salvadoran) (tel. toll free 800/535-8780) flies from Los Angeles, San Francisco, Chicago, Houston, New Orleans, Miami, Washington, and New York. **United Airlines** (tel. toll free 800/241-6522) and **Aero Costa Rica** (tel. toll free 800/237-6274) both fly from Miami.

From Europe, you can take **Iberia** from Spain or **LTU International Airways** from Germany. Coming from the U.K., you can take American Airlines or Continental to Miami and then onward to San José, Costa Rica. You can also fly British Airways or Delta to Miami and then transfer to a different airline, or Delta Airlines.

REGULAR AIRFARES   In recent years airfares have been very unstable. Such instability makes it difficult to quote an airline ticket price. APEX (advance purchase excursion) ticket prices seem to be similar with each airline, but first-class ticket prices can have a wide variation. At press time, an APEX ticket or coach ticket from New York to San José was running between $650 and $790; from Los Angeles between $570 and $730. First class from New York was about $1,680; and from Los Angeles was about $2,100. On rare occasions, special fares may be offered at rock-bottom prices, but don't count on it.

Regardless of how much the cheapest ticket costs when you decide to fly, you can bet it will have some restrictions. It will almost certainly be nonrefundable, and you may have to pay within 24 hours of making a reservation. You'll likely have to buy the ticket in advance (anywhere from one week to 30 days). You will also likely have to stay over a weekend and limit your stay to 30 days or less.

TICKET BROKERS/CONSOLIDATORS   You can shave a little bit off these ticket prices by purchasing your ticket from what is known as a ticket broker or consolidator. These ticketing agencies sell discounted tickets on major airlines; although the tickets have as many, and sometimes more, restrictions as an APEX ticket, they can help you save money. You'll find ticket brokers' listings—usually just a column of destinations with prices beside them—in the Sunday travel sections of major city newspapers. You'll almost never get the ticket for the advertised price, but you will probably get it for less than the airline would sell it to you.

BY BUS

Bus service runs regularly from both Panama City, Panama, and Managua, Nicaragua. From Panama City it is a 20-hour, 900-kilometer trip; buses leave Panama City daily at 8pm. For more information, call the **Tica Bus Company** (tel. 506/221-8954 or 221-9229). From Managua it is 11 hours and 450 kilometers to San José. Buses leave Managua Monday through Saturday at 6:30am or 7am. For more information, call the Tica Bus Company, above, or **Sirca Company** (tel. 506/222-5541 or 223-1464).

Ⓕ FROMMER'S SMART TRAVELER: AIRFARES

1. Check the ticket brokers' ads in the Sunday travel sections of major-city newspapers. These tickets can be $100 to $200 cheaper than the lowest standard airfares.
2. Keep tuned in to fare wars. Ticket prices to Central American destinations are sometimes cut drastically. If your schedule is flexible, you may be able to save quite a bit of money.
3. Try getting a discounted ticket from your departure city to one of the Central American gateway cities (Miami, New Orleans, Houston, or Los Angeles), and combine this with a discount ticket from one of those cities on to Costa Rica.
4. Shop all the airlines that fly to Costa Rica, including the small Central American airlines that travel agents don't usually check.
5. You'll usually save money if you take a "milk run" (flight that makes several stops) rather than a direct flight.
6. Always ask for the lowest-priced fare, which will usually be a mid-week departure.

BY CAR

It is possible to travel to Costa Rica by car, but it can be difficult, especially for U.S. citizens. The Interamerican Highway (also known as the Panamerican Highway) passes through El Salvador, Honduras, and Nicaragua after leaving Guatemala and before reaching Costa Rica. All three of these countries can be problematic for travelers because of the continuing internal strife and visa formalities. If you do decide to undertake this adventure, take the gulf coast route from the border crossing at Brownsville, Texas, as it involves traveling the least number of miles through Mexico. Don't drive at night because of the danger of being robbed by bandits.

Contact **Sanborn's Insurance Company,** 2009 S 10th St., McAllen, TX 78501 (tel. 210/686-0711). They can supply you with trip insurance for Mexico and Central America—some insurance is not available after you leave the United States—and an itinerary. Sanborn's also has branches at other U.S./Mexico border crossings.

If you want to consult a good guidebook, look up *Drive the Pan-Am Highway to Mexico and Central America* by Audrey and Raymond Pritchard, available through P.O. Box 526770, Miami, FL 33152.

PACKAGE TOURS

It is sometimes cheaper to purchase an airfare-and-hotel package rather than buy an airline ticket only. This is especially true if airfares happen to be in a high period and if you will be traveling with a companion. The best way to find out about these package tours is to contact a travel agent.

Some companies that specialize in travel to Costa Rica include **Costa Rica Experts,** 3166 North Lincoln Avenue, Chicago, IL 60657 (tel. 312/935-1009) and **Tour Tech,** 17780 Fitch Street, Suite 110, Irvine, CA 92714 (tel. toll free 800/882-2636). Some Canadian companies specializing in tours to Costa Rica include **Via Nova-America,** 4571 Rue St. Denis, Montréal, P.Q. H2J 214 (tel. 514/847-9279) and **Onisac International,** 221-2002 Quebec Avenue, Saskatoon, Sask. S7K 5G6 (tel. 306/652-4410).

Once you are in Costa Rica, there are dozens of tour companies that will arrange overnight and longer tours to remote lodges that cater to ecotourists. For information on some of these companies, see the Alternative/Adventure Travel section above.

8. GETTING AROUND

BY PLANE

Surprisingly, flying is one of the best ways to get around Costa Rica. Because the country is quite small, the flights are short and not too expensive. The domestic airlines of Costa Rica are **Sansa,** Calle 24 between Avenida Central and Avenida 1 (tel. 233-3258 or 233-0397), which offers a free shuttle bus from their downtown office to the airport, and **Travelair** (tel. 232-7883 or 220-3054), which charges more for flights to the same destinations but is popular because it is more reliable. Flights last between 20 and 50 minutes. Travelair operates from Pavas Airport, 4 miles from San José, and Sansa operates from the Juan Santamaría International Airport.

In the high season, between December and May, be sure to book reservations well in advance. If you plan to return to San José, buy a round-trip ticket as they tend to be less expensive than two one-way tickets.

BY BUS

This is by far the best way to visit most of Costa Rica. Buses are inexpensive, well maintained, uncrowded, and they go nearly everywhere. There are three types of buses: local buses are the cheapest and slowest. They stop frequently and are generally a bit dilapidated. Express buses run between San José and most beach towns and major cities. However, beach-bound buses sometimes only operate on weekends and holidays. A few luxury buses and minibuses drive to destinations frequented by foreign tourists. For details on how to get to various destinations from San José, see the "Getting There" heading of each section in the regional chapters. You should also be sure to pick up a current bus schedule from a Tourist Information Office in San José once you arrive in Costa Rica.

BY CAR

CAR RENTALS   Renting a car in Costa Rica is not something to be entered into lightly. Costa Rica has the second highest accident rate per capita in the world. In addition, since all rental cars in Costa Rica bear special license plates, they are readily identifiable to thieves. Nothing is ever safe in a car in Costa Rica, although parking in guarded parking lots helps. The tourist plates also signal police that they can extort money from unwary tourist motorists. Never pay money directly to a police officer who stops you for any traffic violation. Before driving off with a rental car, be sure that you inspect the exterior and point out to the rental company representative every tiny scratch, dent, tear, or any other damage. It is a common practice with Costa Rican car-rental companies to claim that you owe payment for damages the company finds when you return the car.

On the other hand, renting a car allows you much greater freedom to explore remote areas of the country. Several people have written to me to say that they feel visitors should always rent four-wheel-drive vehicles. I have always rented a regular car, and though there are roads I can't drive down, I have always managed to get around just fine (including to Monteverde).

Avis, Budget, Hertz, National, and **Thrifty** car-rental agencies all have offices in Costa Rica. You will save somewhere between $35 and $75 per week on a car rental if you make a reservation in your home country at least one week before you need the car. The least-expensive car from National rents for about $230 per week, plus insurance (total of around $320), in San José, but if you book this same car in advance in the U.S., you can get it for $194 per week, plus insurance (total of around $285). See the "Getting Around" section of the San José chapter for details on renting a car in San José. Cars can also be rented in Quepos, Jacó, and Limón.

GASOLINE   Regular gasoline is what is most readily available in Costa Rica. Most rental cars take regular. When going off to remote places, try to have as full a gas tank as possible—in very small towns, you can sometimes get gasoline from enterprising families who sell it by the liter from their houses. Look for hand-lettered signs that say "gasolina."

ROAD CONDITIONS   Most roads are in fairly good condition, with the exception of unpaved roads in the rainy season, which can be rutted, slippery, and difficult to negotiate. If possible, before you rent a vehicle, find out about the road conditions to see if it is necessary to have four-wheel-drive to get to your destination. Some paved roads are badly potholed, so stay alert for the invisible pothole hiding in the shadows. An especially bad example is the road from San Isidro de General to Cartago over the Cerro de la Muerte. Route numbers are rarely used on road signs in Costa Rica.

DRIVING RULES   To rent a car in Costa Rica, you must be at least 21 years old and have a valid driver's license and a major credit card. A foreign driver's license is valid for the first three months that you are in Costa Rica. Use of seat belts is required for driver and passengers. Motorcyclists must wear a helmet. Highway police use radar, so keep to the speed limit. Speeding tickets can be charged to your credit card for up to a year if they are not paid before leaving.

MAPS   Car-rental agencies and the I.C.T. information centers (see "Information, Entry Requirements & Money" at the beginning of this chapter) at the airport and in downtown San José have adequate road maps. Other sources in San José are **The**

Bookshop, Avenida 1 between Calles 1 and 3 (tel. 221-6847), **Libreria Lehmann,** Avenida Central between Calles 1 and 3 (tel. 223-1212), and **Jimenez & Tanzi,** Calle 3 between Avenidas 1 and 3 (tel. 233-8033).

BREAKDOWNS If your car should break down and you are unable to get it off the road, check to see if there is a reflective triangle in the trunk. If not, place a pile of leaves and/or tree branches in the road 100 feet on either side of the car to warn approaching drivers.

BY FERRY

There are four different ferries operating across the Gulf of Nicoya. Three are car ferries: one across the Rio Tempisque, one from Puntarenas to Playa Naranjo, and one from Puntarenas to Paquera. The passenger ferry runs from Puntarenas to Paquera. For more detailed information, see the Puntarenas and appropriate Nicoya Peninsula sections in this book.

HITCHHIKING

Although buses go to most places in Costa Rica, they can be infrequent in the remote regions, and consequently local people often hitchhike to get to their destination sooner. If you are driving a car, people will frequently ask you for a ride. If you are hitching yourself, keep in mind that if a bus doesn't go to your destination, there probably aren't too many cars going there either. Good luck.

9. SUGGESTED ITINERARIES

HIGHLIGHTS

The following are the main tourist destinations in Costa Rica: 1) San José; 2) Manuel Antonio National Park; 3) Jacó Beach; 4) the beaches of the Nicoya Peninsula; 5) Monteverde Cloud Forest Reserve (or another cloud-forest region); 6) Tortuguero National Park; 7) Irazú Volcano; 8) Poás Volcano; 9) Arenal Volcano and Arenal Lake; 10) the Osa Peninsula; 11) jungle lodges throughout the country; 12) Cahuita/Puerto Viejo; and 13) Dominical.

PLANNING YOUR ITINERARY

IF YOU HAVE ONE WEEK

Day 1: Visit the museums and the National Theater in San José.
Day 2: Make an excursion to the Orosi Valley, Lankester Gardens, and Irazú Volcano.
Days 3 and 4: Travel to Monteverde (or another cloud forest region) and spend a day exploring the cloud forest.
Days 5 and 6: Head to one of the many Pacific Coast beaches.
Day 7: Return to San José.

IF YOU HAVE TWO WEEKS

Day 1: Visit the museums and National Theater in San José.
Days 2 and 3: Make an excursion to the Orosi Valley, Lankester Gardens, and Irazú Volcano one day and go rafting on the other.
Days 4 and 5: Travel to Monteverde (or another cloud forest area) and explore the cloud forest.
Days 6 and 7: Travel to Lake Arenal to see the eruptions of Arenal Volcano, soak in some hot springs, and maybe go to Caño Negro National Wildlife Refuge.
Day 8: Explore Rincon de la Vieja or Santa Rosa National Park.

Days 9, 10, 11, and 12: Spend these days relaxing on a beach or perhaps exploring the Corcovado Peninsula.

Days 13 and 14: Fly to Tortuguero National Park and spend a day there, returning the next day by boat and bus.

IF YOU HAVE THREE WEEKS

If you have three weeks, you can spend more time on the beach, perhaps several different beaches. With this much time, you can easily visit both coasts. You could also do trips to two or three different remote lodges in different parts of the country. You might also consider doing a week-long cruise along the Pacific Coast.

THEMED CHOICES

The most common choice for a themed vacation in Costa Rica is to make it a **naturalist tour** by visiting as many of the national parks and private nature reserves as you can in the amount of time available. Another possible theme would be to sample as many of the different **beaches** as you can.

10. ENJOYING COSTA RICA ON A BUDGET

Although Costa Rica is now one of the most expensive countries in Central America, it still offers the budget traveler a lot of options. Room rates have been escalating rapidly in the past few years, but there are still great bargains to be had throughout the country. Meal costs continue to be low. If you travel by bus, you'll find it's very cheap to explore Costa Rica, and even if you choose to fly, you'll find that airfares, though no longer the incredible bargain they were a few years ago, are still a good deal.

THE $35-A-DAY BUDGET

The premise of this book is that you can enjoy Costa Rica, Guatemala, and Belize on a budget of $35 per day per person. This budget covers lodging and three meals a day but does not cover travel expenses, museum admissions, cost of souvenirs, and so forth. If you are willing to stay in the lowest-budget accommodations recommended in this book, you should easily be able to include all your transportation expenses and many other costs in your $35 a day. However, there are some places where most hotel room rates have risen above our budget range. In these places you may want to consider either splurging, visiting in the off season, or skipping that spot all together.

This is roughly how I break down daily costs: $18 per person (based on double occupancy) for a room, $3 for breakfast, $5 for lunch, and $9 for dinner. Many hardy travelers actually get by on about $15 per day. However, a $35 daily budget should allow you to live quite well. For those who prefer a bit more luxury, I have listed some hotels and restaurants that are worth the extra bucks.

SAVING MONEY ON ACCOMMODATIONS

Best Budget Bets Your best way to save money on accommodations in Costa Rica is to choose carefully where you want to go. If you are heading to a beach resort that primarily has expensive rooms and you want one of the handful of budget rooms in town, book early (everybody wants those cheap rooms). Montezuma and Puerto Viejo are the backpackers' hangouts in Costa Rica these days. If you plan to stay around for several weeks or longer, look into renting a house or apartment by the week or month. For young travelers, there are a number of **IYHF**-affiliated hostels in Costa Rica.

Seasonal and Other Discounts During the rainy season, many hotels,

FROMMER'S FAVORITE COSTA RICA EXPERIENCES

A Night at San José's Teatro Nacional Built in the late 19th century with money raised through a tax on coffee exports, this classic opera house is still staging the best cultural performances in the country.

A Day of White-Water Rafting Costa Rica offers some of the best white-water rafting opportunities in the world. The water is warm, the mountains are green, and the rapids are as rough as you want.

Cruising the Tortuguero Canals North of Limón, on the Caribbean coast, there are no roads, only canals through the wilderness. A boat trip through the canals to Tortuguero National Park is as thrilling as exploring the Amazon.

A Hike Through a Cloud Forest The mountain-top cloud forests of Costa Rica are home to an amazing diversity of plants and animals, including the resplendent quetzal, one of the world's most beautiful birds.

Bird Watching Almost anywhere in Costa Rica, you are likely to see colorful and unfamiliar birds. The sight of a quetzal or a scarlet macaw are enough to turn anyone into an avid bird-watcher.

Hiking Through the Rain Forest There are rain forests all over Costa Rica and all of them are fascinating. A walk through one of these forests with a knowledgeable guide can teach you much about rain-forest ecology.

Swimming on Deserted Beaches Costa Rica has 735 miles of coastline, which means it isn't too difficult to find a stretch of beach with nearly no one else on it. No matter what your taste in beaches, you're sure to find one to match your dreams.

Soaking in the Hot Springs at Tabacón This is actually a hot river that flows down off of Arenal Volcano. The crystal-clear water flows through a lush, forested valley.

especially those at the beaches, offer substantial discounts. Some beach hotels also have weekly rates.

SAVING MONEY ON MEALS

Best Budget Bets The cheapest place to eat in Costa Rica will always be a soda, the equivalent of a diner in the United States. The food might not be great, but the prices can't be beat. If you like rice and black beans, you can save even more money. Ticos eat rice and beans (with something else on the side) at every meal, and it's always cheap.

Other Money-Saving Strategies Quite a few hotels in Costa Rica come with kitchenettes, especially those at the beaches. If you visit the local market and fix your own meals, you can save considerably. I try to buy as much and as many different types of tropical fruits as I can when I'm here. You might want to consider buying a little immersion heating coil and a Costa Rican reusable drip-coffee bag. With these two items and a cup, you can make your own fresh coffee every morning.

SAVING MONEY ON SIGHT-SEEING & ENTERTAINMENT

Best Budget Bets Museum admissions in San José are already so low that there is no need to worry about special discounts (there aren't any). Much of the entertainment in San José is free; marimba bands play daily outside the National

Theater, and it doesn't cost anything to enjoy the bands at La Esmeralda or the Soda Palace. Even tickets to performances at the National Theater are quite inexpensive.

SAVING MONEY ON SHOPPING

Costa Rica doesn't have the wide variety of traditional handcrafts that neighboring countries have (in fact, many Guatemalan crafts and textiles are sold in Costa Rica), so if you're including Guatemala on your trip to Central America, I suggest that you save your money to spend there. However, there are a few good buys in Costa Rica.

Best Buys One of Costa Rica's best buys is **coffee.** The air in the streets around the San José market is redolent with the smell of roasting coffee beans. The best place to buy coffee is in market roasters or supermarkets. Avoid the tourist shops, which charge almost as much as you would pay back home. When buying coffee be sure to buy only bags labeled *100% puro;* otherwise, you will get coffee that has already had sugar added to it (that's the way they like it down here).

Other good buys in Costa Rica are gold and silver reproductions of pre-Columbian **jewelry,** which you'll find in shops all over San José. You'll also find tropical hardwoods carved into all manner of jewelry, bowls, figurines, and knickknacks. Some are quite expensive, others are quite reasonably priced, but all are beautiful.

Markets Every town in Costa Rica has a market, and these are the best places to buy fresh fruits and vegetables. Some markets, such as the one in San José, also sell souvenirs and countless other useful items. Take a look in one of the kitchen utensil stalls; you'll probably find dozens of interesting and inexpensive little gadgets. Be sure to keep close tabs on your money at all times because markets are notorious haunts of pickpockets.

Bargaining You should always try to bargain in markets and with street vendors. It's expected and can save you quite a bit. Tourist prices are always higher, so if you are shopping for souvenirs (especially on the Plaza de Cultura in San José), bargain hard.

SAVING MONEY ON TRANSPORTATION

See "Getting Around" above.

SAVING MONEY ON SERVICES & OTHER TRANSACTIONS

Tipping Tipping is not necessary in restaurants, where a 10% service charge is almost always added to your bill (along with 11% tax). If service was particularly good, you can leave a little at your own discretion, but it is not mandatory. Porters and bellhops get around 60¢ per bag. Taxi fares must be negotiated prior to getting into a taxi, and therefore tips are unnecessary.

Money Changing and Credit Cards Although it is illegal to change money on the black market (which offers a slightly better rate than the banks do), it is possible to change money in many hotels and avoid the service charge that banks charge. However, most hotels offer a lower exchange rate than you'll get at a bank. By using your credit card to pay hotel and restaurant bills, you can lock in that day's official exchange rate and avoid having to pay bank service charges on changing money. However, many hotels apply a surcharge on bills paid with a credit card. Always check on this before paying.

Telephone Calls You can save money on phone calls home by using a USA Dial-Direct or similar operator. See "Telephone, Telex and Fax" below for details.

 COSTA RICA

American Express American Express (tel. 223-3644) has a counter in San José at the Banco de San José on Calle Central between Avenidas 3 and 5. It's open Monday to Friday from 8am to 4pm.

Business Hours   Banks are usually open Monday to Friday from 9am to 3pm. Offices are open Monday to Friday from 8am to 5pm (closed for two hours at lunch). Stores are open Monday to Saturday from 9am to 7pm (many close for an hour at lunch). Bars are open until 1 or 2am. Many restaurants stay open 24 hours, while others close between meals.

Camera/Film   Most types of film, except Kodachrome, are available. However, prices are higher than in the U.S.

Climate   See "When to Go" in this chapter.

Country Code   The country code for Costa Rica is 506.

Crime   See "Safety," below.

Currency   See "Information, Entry Requirements & Money" in this chapter.

Customs   You can bring in half a kilo of tobacco products, three liters of liquor, and two cameras duty-free.

Documents Required   See "Information, Entry Requirements & Money" in this chapter.

Driving Rules   See "Getting Around" in this chapter.

Drug Laws   Drug laws in Costa Rica are strict, so stay away from marijuana and cocaine. You'll also need a prescription from a doctor or lab results to have a prescription filled in Costa Rica.

Drugstores   A drugstore in Costa Rica is a *farmacia*. You'll find at least one in nearly every town.

Electricity   The standard in Costa Rica is the same as in the United States: 110 volts.

Embassies and Consulates   The following are all in San José: **United States Consulate,** in front of Centro Commercial, road to Pavas (tel. 220-3939); **Canadian Embassy,** Calle 3 and Avenida Central (tel. 255-3522); **British Embassy,** Paseo Colón between Calles 38 and 40 (tel. 221-5566).

Emergencies   For an **ambulance** call 221-5818; to report a **fire** call 118; to contact the **police** call 117, or 127 outside cities.

Etiquette   Ticos tend to dress conservatively and treat everyone very respectfully. Both sexes shake hands.

Hitchhiking   This is permitted and is fairly common. If you're trying to get to remote parks or volcanoes, however, there usually isn't much traffic on such roads. Buses, which are quite inexpensive, go almost everywhere in the country.

Holidays   See "When to Go" in this chapter.

Information   See "Information, Entry Requirements & Money" in this chapter.

Language   Spanish is the official language of Costa Rica. *Berlitz Latin-American Spanish Phrasebook and Dictionary* (Berlitz Guides, 1992) is probably the best phrase book to bring with you.

Laundry   Laundromats are few and far between in Costa Rica, more common are expensive hotel laundry services. For listings of laundromats, see individual city and town sections.

Liquor Laws   Alcoholic beverages are sold every day of the week throughout the year, with the exception of the two days before Easter and the two days before and after a presidential election.

Mail   Mail to the U.S. takes about one week. A letter or postcard to the U.S. costs 30¢. A post office is called a *correo* in Spanish. You can get stamps at the post office, newsstands, or gift shops in large hotels. If you are sending mail to Costa Rica it can take as much as a month to get to the more remote corners of the country. Plan ahead. Also, many hotels now have mailing addresses in the U.S. Always use this address when writing from North America or Europe.

Maps   The Costa Rican National Tourist Bureau (I.C.T.), (see "Information, Entry Requirements & Money," in this chapter) can usually provide you with maps of both Costa Rica and San José. Other sources in San José are The Bookshop, Avenida 1 between Calles 1 and 3 (tel. 221-6847), Libreria Lehmann, Avenida Central between Calles 1 and 3 (tel. 223-1212), and Jimenez & Tanzi, Calle 3 between Avenidas 1 and 3 (tel. 233-8033).

Newspapers/Magazines There are three Spanish-language dailies in Costa Rica and one English-language weekly, the *Tico Times*. In addition, you can get *Time, Newsweek,* and several U.S. newspapers at bookstores and hotel gift shops in San José.

Passports See "Information, Entry Requirements & Money" in this chapter.

Pets If you want to bring your cat or dog, be sure it has current vaccinations against rabies and distemper, and take along the documentation to prove it.

Police The number to call for the Policía de Transito is 227-7150 or 227-8030.

Radio/TV There are about 10 TV channels, plus satellite TV from the U.S. and more than 100 AM and FM radio stations.

Restrooms These are known as *sanitarios* or *servicios sanitarios*. They are marked *damas* (women) and *hombres* or *caballeros* (men).

Safety Though most of Costa Rica is very safe, it is known for its pickpockets. Never carry a wallet or anything of value in pants pockets or in a day pack on your back. A woman should keep a tight grip on her purse (keep it tucked under your arm). Don't leave valuables in your hotel room.

Because all rental cars have special plates, they are easily spotted by thieves who know that such cars are likely to be full of expensive camera equipment, money, and so on. Don't ever leave anything of value in a car parked on the street, not even for a moment. In fact, don't park a car on the street in Costa Rica, especially in San José; there are plenty of public parking lots around the city. Public intercity buses are also frequent targets of stealthy thieves. Never check your bags into the hold of a bus if you can avoid it. If this cannot be avoided, keep your eye on what leaves the hold any time the bus stops. If you put your bags in an overhead rack, be sure you can see the bag at all times. Try not to fall asleep.

Taxes Hotels charge 14.3% tax, and restaurants charge 11% tax. There is an airport departure tax of $6.75.

Telephone, Telex and Fax Costa Rica has an excellent phone system, with a dial tone similar to that heard in the U.S. As of March 1993, all phone numbers in Costa Rica have seven digits. If you run across an old six-digit number, check the phone book or try calling the operator to find out what the new number is. There is one telephone book for all of Costa Rica which includes both white pages and yellow pages. A pay phone costs 5 colónes (2¢) and most phones take 5, 10, or 20 colón coins, though some take 5 colón coins only. For making calling-card and collect calls, you can reach an AT&T operator by dialing 114, MCI by dialing 162, Sprint by dialing 163, Bell by dialing 161, and a Costa Rican operator by dialing 0 (pay phones require deposit of coins). The Costa Rican telephone system allows direct international dialing but it is expensive. You can make international phone calls, as well as send telexes and faxes, from the I.C.E. office, Avenida 2 between Calle 1 and 3. Open daily from 7am to 10pm.

The Western Union office (tel. 257-1150) is on Calle 9 between Avenidas 2 and 4. Radiográfica (tel. 287-0087) at Calle 1 and Avenida 5 has telex, telegram, and fax service.

Time Costa Rica is on Central Standard Time, six hours behind Greenwich Mean Time.

Tipping See "Saving Money on Services and Transactions" in this chapter.

Tourist Offices See "Information, Entry Requirements & Money" in this chapter. Also see specific cities.

Visas See "Information, Entry Requirements & Money" in this chapter.

Water Though the water in San José is said to be safe to drink, outside of this city, water quality varies. Because many tourists do get sick within a few days of arriving in Costa Rica, I recommend avoiding ice and sticking to bottled drinks as much as possible.

SAN JOSÉ

San José is a city built on coffee. This is not to say that the city runs on bottomless pots of java. San José was built on the profits of the coffee export business. Between the airport and downtown you pass by coffee farms, and glancing up from almost any street in the city, you can see, on the volcanic mountains that surround San José, a patchwork quilt of farm fields, most of which are planted with the *grano de oro* (golden bean), as it is known here. San José was a forgotten backwater of the Spanish empire until the first shipments of the local beans made their way to the sleepy souls in Europe late in the 19th century. Soon, San José was riding high on this vegetable gold. Coffee planters, newly rich and craving culture, imposed a tax on themselves in order to build the Teatro Nacional, San José's most beautiful building. Coffee profits also built the city a university. Today, you can smell the coffee roasting as you wander the streets near the central market, and in any café or restaurant, you can get a hot cup of sweet, milky *café con leche* to remind you of the bean that built San José.

Why does coffee grow so well around San José? The Central Valley, in which the city sits, has a perfect climate. At 3,750 feet above sea level, San José enjoys springlike temperatures year-round. It is this pleasant climate and the beautiful views of lush green mountainsides that make San José a memorable city to visit. When those views have you longing to get out in the country, you'll find that it's extremely easy to get out of the city. Within an hour or two, you can climb a volcano, go white-water rafting, hike through a cloud forest, or stroll through a butterfly garden.

1. FROM A BUDGET TRAVELER'S POINT OF VIEW

Budget Bests None of the city's museums charge much in the way of admission; the Jade Museum and the Gold Museum, which are probably the two most impressive museums in Costa Rica, are absolutely free.

Public buses are another of San José's great bargains at only 10¢, and taxis are quite inexpensive, although you must agree on a price before you get in.

WHAT'S SPECIAL ABOUT SAN JOSÉ

Museums

- ☐ The Gold Museum, the largest collection of pre-Columbian gold jewelry and ornaments in the Americas.
- ☐ The Jade Museum, an equally impressive collection of pre-Columbian jade artifacts and jewelry.
- ☐ The National Museum, an excellent collection of pre-Columbian artifacts.

Parks/Gardens

- ☐ Lankester Gardens, near Cartago, with hundreds of species of orchids on display.

Religious Shrines

- ☐ The basilica in Cartago, with a statue of the Virgin of Los Angeles that is said to heal the sick.
- ☐ Also in Cartago, the ruins of a church that have been turned into a park.

Natural Spectacles

- ☐ Two volcanoes near San José with roads to their rims.

After Dark

- ☐ San José's Teatro Nacional, a stately old opera house with performances almost nightly.

Zoos

- ☐ The Serpentarium, a reptilian zoo with dozens of Costa Rica's poisonous snakes on display.
- ☐ Spirogyra Butterfly Garden, the Butterfly Farm, and the Butterfly Paradise, three butterfly gardens around the San José area.
- ☐ Zoo Ave, a private bird zoo near Alajuela.

Shopping

- ☐ Fresh-roasted Costa Rican coffee, available very inexpensively.

Activities

- ☐ A myriad of active day trips, including white-water rafting, horseback riding, forest hikes, biking trips, hot-air ballooning, and many others, are offered from San José.

☐ El Pueblo, a shopping, dining, and entertainment complex with nearly a dozen bars, discos, nightclubs, and even a roller-skating rink.

When it comes to dining, your best bet for saving money is to look for a soda, which serves inexpensive Costa Rican–style meals. But no visit to San José would be complete without having at least one meal at the Gran Hotel's patio buffet (which isn't that expensive by U.S. standards), overlooking the National Theater and all the activity of Plaza de la Cultura.

What's Worth Paying For   By all means splurge and buy a ticket for a performance at the **National Theater** (Teatro Nacional). Although you can get a seat for as little as $2 or $3, live it up, hobnob with the elite of Costa Rica (but be sure to look the part). At most it might cost you $15 or $20 to hear the national symphony or see a touring opera company.

You're likely to be bombarded with offers to take this tour or that excursion, but most of them can be done just as easily and at a fraction of the cost on public transport. What you should spring for is a trip to **Tortuguero National Park** if you are interested in seeing nesting sea turtles or visiting a remote jungle. If you've never been **white-water rafting,** you won't find a better place to try a 1-day excursion than San José, and if you dream of spending a day exploring remote islands surrounded by turquoise waters, take one of the day-long cruises around the **Gulf of Nicoya.**

2. ORIENTATION

ARRIVING

BY PLANE   **Juan Santamaría International Airport** (24-hour airport information tel. 441-0744) is located near the city of Alajuela, about 20 minutes to downtown San José. A taxi into town will cost around $12, and a bus only 40¢. The Alajuela–San José buses run frequently and drop you on Avenida 2 between Calle 12 and Calle 14. There are several car-rental agencies located at the airport, although if you are planning on spending a few days in San José, a car is a liability. If you are planning on heading off to the beach immediately, it is much easier to pick up your car here than at a downtown office. You'll find the car-rental offices and the bus and taxi stands up the stairs and to the left after you clear Customs.

You have several options for **changing money** when you arrive at the airport. You can get colónes at the money-changing kiosk just before the Immigration desks. There is also a bank in the departures hall. It's open Monday through Friday from 9am to 2pm. When the banks are closed, there are usually official money changers (with badges) working inside the terminal. Outside the terminal, you may also be approached by unofficial money changers.

BY BUS   If you arrived in Costa Rica overland and are coming to San José for the first time by bus, where you disembark depends on where you are coming from. Bus companies have their offices all over downtown San José. To find out where you will be dropped off, see the "Getting There" information that heads the descriptions of destinations outside San José.

TOURIST INFORMATION

There is an **I.C.T. (Instituto Costarricense de Turismo)** desk at Juan Santamaría International Airport, open daily from 8am to 9pm, where you can pick up maps and brochures before you head into San José. You'll find the desk on the left just beyond the Customs inspection counters. The main tourist information center is at the Plaza de la Cultura, on Calle 5 between Avenida Central and Avenida 2 (tel. 222-1090). This office is open Monday through Friday from 9am to 5pm and Saturday from 9am to 1pm.

CITY LAYOUT

MAIN ARTERIES & STREETS   Downtown San José is laid out on a grid. *Avenidas* (avenues) run east and west, while *calles* (streets) run north and south. The center of the city is at **Avenida Central and Calle Central.** To the north of Avenida Central, the avenidas have odd numbers beginning with Avenida 1; to the south, they have even numbers beginning with Avenida 2. Likewise, calles to the east of Calle Central have odd numbers, and those to the west have even numbers. The main downtown artery is Avenida 2, which merges with Avenida Central on either side of the downtown area. West of downtown, Avenida Central becomes Paseo Colón, which ends at Sabana Park and feeds into the highway to Alajuela, the airport, and the Pacific Coast. East of downtown, Avenida Central leads to San Pedro and then to Cartago and the Interamerican Highway heading south. Calle 3 will take you out of town to the north and put you on the road to the Caribbean Coast.

FINDING AN ADDRESS   This is one of the most confusing aspects of visiting San José in particular and Costa Rica in general. There are no street addresses, at least not often. Addresses are given as a set of coordinates such as "Calle 3 between Avenida Central and Avenida 1." It is then up to you to locate the building within that block, keeping in mind that the building could be on either side of the street. Many addresses include additional information, such as the number of meters or *varas* (an old Spanish measurement roughly equal to a yard) from a specified intersection or some other well-known landmark. These landmarks are what become truly confusing for visitors to the city because they are often landmarks only if you have lived in the neighborhood all your life. The classic example of this is the Coca-Cola, one of the most common landmarks used in addresses in the blocks surrounding San José's main market. It refers to a Coca-Cola bottling plant that once stood in this area. Unfortunately, the edifice is long gone, but the address descriptions remain. In outlying neighborhoods, addresses can become long directions such as "50 meters south of the old church, then 100 meters east, then 20 meters south." Luckily for the visitor, most downtown addresses are straightforward. Oh, if you're wondering how mail deliverers manage, you'll be reassured to know that nearly everyone in San José uses a P.O. box. This is called the *apartado* system and is abbreviated **Apdo.** on mailing addresses.

NEIGHBORHOODS IN BRIEF

San José is sprawling. Today it is divided into dozens of neighborhoods known as *barrios*. Most of the listings in this chapter fall within the main downtown area, but there are a few outlying neighborhoods you will need to know about.

Downtown   This is San José's busiest area and is where you'll find most of the city's museums. There are also many tour companies, restaurants, and hotels downtown. Unfortunately, traffic noise and exhaust fumes make this one of the least pleasant parts of the city. Streets and avenues are usually bustling and crowded with pedestrians and vehicular traffic.

Barrio Amon/Barrio Atoya   These two neighborhoods are the site of the greatest concentration of historic buildings in San José, and in the past few years, enterprising entrepreneurs have been renovating the old buildings and turning them into hotels. If you're looking for character and don't mind the noise and exhaust fumes, this neighborhood makes a good base for exploring the city.

Paseo Colón   Paseo Colón, a wide boulevard west of downtown, is an extension of Avenida Central and ends at Sabana Park. There are several good, small hotels and numerous excellent restaurants in this neighborhood. This is also where many of the city's rental-car agencies have their offices. Because this area is really part of downtown, I have not treated it as a separate area in the hotel and restaurant listings.

San Pedro/Los Yoses   Located east of downtown San José, this neighborhood is home to the University of Costa Rica. There are numerous college-type bars and restaurants all around the edge of the campus and several good restaurants and small hotels.

Escazú   Located in the hills west of San José, Escazú is a suburb with a small-town atmosphere. Although it's only 15 minutes from San José by taxi, it seems much farther away because of its relaxed atmosphere. Many bed and breakfast establishments are located here.

3. GETTING AROUND

BY BUS   Bus transportation around San José is cheap—the fare is usually less than 15¢. The most important buses are those running east and west along Avenida 2 and

Avenida 3. The Sabana-Cementerio bus runs from Sabana Park to downtown and is one of the most convenient buses to use. San Pedro buses will take you out of downtown heading east. You'll find a bus stop for the outbound Sabana-Cementerio bus across the street from Costa Rica Expeditions on Avenida 3 near the corner of Calle Central. These buses don't run very frequently, and their stops are far apart. Considering this and the congestion on Avenida 3, you'll find that it is generally easier to walk to your destination if it is closer than Sabana Park. Buses are always boarded from the front, and the bus drivers can make change. Be especially mindful of your wallet, purse, or other valuables since pickpockets often work the crowded buses. The Alajuela–San José buses that run in from the airport cost 40¢.

BY TAXI   Although taxis in San José have meters (*marías*), the drivers sometimes refuse to use them, so occasionally you'll have to negotiate the price. However, always try to get them to use the meter first. The official rate at the time of writing is around 55¢ for the first kilometer and around 25¢ for each additional kilometer. If you have a rough idea of how far it is to your destination, you can estimate how much it should cost from these figures. You'll find taxis in front of the National Theater (high prices) and around the Parque Central at Avenida Central and Calle Central. Taxis in front of hotels usually charge more than others. You call also get a cab by calling 235-9966 or 254-5847.

ON FOOT   Downtown San José is very compact. Nearly everyplace you might want to go is within an area 15 blocks by 4 blocks. Because of the traffic congestion, you'll often find it faster to walk than to take a bus or taxi. Avenida Central is a pedestrians-only street for several blocks around Calle Central.

BY MOTORCYCLE   Motorcycles rent for about the same amount as cars, $35 a day or $210 a week. Due to poor road conditions and the difficulty of driving in Costa Rica, they are not recommended unless you are an experienced rider. Companies renting motorcycles include **Moto Rental,** Avenida 1 between calles 30 and 32 (tel. 257-1065), and **La Aventura Rent a Moto,** Avenida 10 at Calle 8 (tel. 233-6629).

BY CAR   It will cost you around $40 per day to rent a car in Costa Rica, unless you make a reservation before you leave home. If you do decide to rent a car, and pick it up in downtown San José, be prepared for some very congested streets. The following international companies have offices in San José: **Avis Rent A Car,** Avenida las Américas, Sabana Norte (tel. toll free in the U.S. 800/331-1212; tel. at airport 442-1321; tel. in downtown San José 232-9922); **Budget Rent A Car,** Calle 30 and Paseo Colón (tel. toll free in the U.S. 800/527-0700; tel. at airport 441-4444; tel. in downtown San José 223-3284); **Dollar Rent A Car,** Avenida 1 between calles 26 and 28 (tel. toll free in the U.S. 800/800-4000; tel. in downtown San José 257-1585); **Hertz Rent A Car,** Paseo Colón at Calle 38 (tel. toll free 800/654-3131; tel. at airport 221-1818; tel. in downtown San José 223-5959); **National Car Rental,** Calle 36 and Avenida 7 (tel. toll free 800/227-7368; tel. at airport 441-6533; tel. in downtown San José 233-4044); **Thrifty Car Rental,** Calle 3 at Avenida 13 (tel. toll free 800/367-2277; tel. in downtown San José 255-4141).

You will save somewhere between $35 and $75 per week on a car rental if you make a reservation in your home country at least one week before you need the car. The least-expensive National car available rents for about $230 per week, plus insurance (total of around $320) in San José, but if you book this same car in advance from the United States, you can get it for $194 per week, plus insurance (total of around $285). Though it is possible at some rental-car agencies to waive the insurance charges, you will have to pay all damages before leaving the country if you are in an accident. Even if you do take the insurance, you will have a deductible of between $500 and $750. At some agencies you can pay additional insurance to buy down the deductible.

There are dozens of other rental car agencies in San José, including the following: **Adobe Rent A Car,** Calle 7 between avenidas 8 and 10 (tel. 221-5425); **Hola! Rent A Car,** west of Hotel Irazú, La Uruca, San José (tel. 231-5666); **Elegante Rent A Car,** Calle 10 between avenidas 13 and 15 and Paseo Colón at Calle 34 (tel.

233-8605 or toll free 800/582-7432); and **Tico Rent A Car,** Calle 10 between avenidas 13 and 15 or Paseo Colón between calles 24 and 26 (tel. 222-8920 or 223-9642).

FAST
SAN JOSÉ

Airlines Don't forget to reconfirm your return flight. Here are the numbers in San José of the international airlines: Aero Costa Rica (tel. 234-6013), American Airlines (tel. 257-1266), Aviateca (tel. 255-4949), Continental (tel. 233-0266), Iberia (tel. 221-3311), Lacsa (tel. 231-0033), LTU (tel. 257-2990), Mexicana (tel. 222-1711), Taca (tel. 222-1790), and United (tel. 220-4844).

American Express American Express (tel. 223-3644) has a counter in the Banco de San José on Calle Central between avenidas 3 and 5. It's open Monday to Friday from 8am to 4pm.

Babysitters Your only chance for a babysitter in San José is to check with your hotel.

Bookstores The Bookshop, Avenida 1 between calles 1 and 3 (tel. 221-6847) has a wide selection of English-language newspapers, magazines, and books; it's open Monday to Saturday from 9am to 7pm and Sunday from 9am to 3pm. For used books in English, stop by Book Traders (tel. 255-0508), open Monday to Saturday from 9am to 5pm. It's located above the Pizza Hut on Avenida 1 between calles 3 and 5, and has another location (which is open on Sundays) just down the street on Avenida 1 between calles 5 and 7.

Car Rentals See "Getting Around" in this chapter.

Climate See "When to Go" in Chapter 2.

Crime See "Safety" below.

Currency Exchange The best thing to do is to change money at your hotel. If they can't do this for you, they can direct you to a private bank where you won't have to stand in line for hours. Avoid changing money on the street.

Dentist If you need a dentist while in San José, your best bet is to call your embassy, which will have a list of recommended dentists.

Doctor Contact your embassy for information on doctors in San José.

Drugstores Farmacia Fischel, Avenida 3 and Calle 2, is across from the main post office (tel. 223-0909). Open Monday to Saturday from 8am to 7pm.

Embassies and Consulates United States Consulate, in front of Centro Comercial, road to Pavas (tel. 220-3939 or, after 4pm, 220-3127); **Canadian Embassy,** Calle 3 and Avenida Central (tel. 255-3522); **British Embassy,** Paseo Colón between calles 38 and 40 (tel. 221-5566).

Emergencies In case of **fire** dial 118; for the **police** dial 117; for an **ambulance** dial 128 or 221-5818.

Eyeglasses Optica Jiménez, Avenida 2 and Calle 3 (tel. 222-0233 or 233-4417), is open Monday to Saturday from 8am to noon and 2 to 6pm.

Hairdressers/Barbers El Toque Nuevo, Avenida 2 between calles 1 and 3 in Edificios Los Arcados (tel. 222-0877), is open Monday to Saturday from 9am to 7pm. It services both men and women.

Holidays See "When to Go" in Chapter 2.

Hospitals Clinica Biblica, Avenida 14 between Calle Central and Calle 1 (tel. 223-6422 or, for emergencies, tel. 257-0466), is conveniently located close to downtown and has several English-speaking doctors.

Information See "Tourist Information" above in this chapter.

Laundry/Dry Cleaning Sixaola, Avenida 2 between calles 7 and 9 (tel. 221-2111), open Monday to Friday from 7am to 6pm and Saturday from 8am to 1pm, is one of the only places downtown to get clothes cleaned. Unfortunately, their prices are quite high. Ask at your hotel—most offer a laundry service, though these too are expensive.

Libraries The National Library is at the corner of Avenida 3 and Calle 15.

Lost Property   If you lose something in San José, consider it gone.

Luggage Storage/Lockers   Most hotels will store luggage for you while you are traveling around the country. Sometimes there is a charge for this service.

Newspapers/Magazines   The *Tico Times* is Costa Rica's English-language weekly paper and serves both the expatriate community and tourists. You can also get the *International Herald Tribune, USA Today, Time,* and *Newsweek,* among other English-language publications. You'll find these publications in hotel gift shops and in bookstores selling English-language books.

Photographic Needs   Film is very expensive in Costa Rica, so bring as much as you will need. You can buy film and other photographic equipment at Dima, Avenida Central between calles 3 and 5 (tel. 222-3969), which is open Monday to Friday from 9am to 5pm and Saturday from 8am to noon. I recommend that you wait until you get home to have your film processed.

Police   Dial 117 for the police.

Post Office   The main post office (*correo*) is on Calle 2 between avenidas 1 and 3. It's open Monday to Friday from 7am to 10pm, and Saturday 8am to noon for purchasing stamps. For mailing packages, hours are Monday to Friday 8am to 5pm.

Radio/TV   There are about 10 TV channels, plus satellite TV from the U.S. There are dozens of AM and FM radio stations in San José.

Religious Services   The *Tico Times* has a listing of churches in San José. You can also ask at the tourist office for a list of the city's churches, or ask at your hotel. The following are a number of suggestions for English-language services: Episcopal Church of the Good Shepherd (tel. 222-1560); reformed Jewish services at B'Nai Israel (tel. 225-8561); Catholic mass at the International Chapel of St. Mary at the Hotel Herradura complex; Christian Fellowship services (tel. 228-0594); International Baptist Church (tel. 224-9424); Quaker services (tel. 233-6168).

Restrooms   These are known as *sanitarios* or *servicios sanitarios*. They are marked *damas* (women) and *hombres* or *caballeros* (men).

Safety   Never carry anything you value in your pockets or purse. Pickpockets and purse slashers are rife in San José, especially on public buses, in the markets, or near a hospital. Leave your passport, money, and other valuables in your hotel safe, and only carry as much as you really need when you go out. If you do carry anything valuable with you, keep it in a money belt or special passport bag around your neck. Day packs are a prime target of brazen pickpockets throughout the city. Also be advised that the Parque Central is not a safe place for a late-night stroll.

Other precautions include walking around corner vendors, not between the vendor and the building. The tight space between vendor and building is a favorite spot for pickpockets. Never park a car on the street, and never leave anything of value in a car, even if it's in a guarded parking lot. Don't even leave your car by the curb in front of a hotel while you dash in to check on your reservation. With these precautions in mind you should have a safe visit to San José.

Shoe Repairs   Ask at your hotel for the repair shop nearest you.

Taxes   All hotels charge 14.3% tax. Restaurants charge 11% tax and add on a 10% service charge, for a total of 21% more on your bill. There is an airport departure tax of $6.75.

Taxis   See "Getting Around" above in this chapter.

Telegrams/Telexes   You can send telegrams and telexes from the I.C.E. office on Avenida 2 between calles 1 and 3 (open daily from 7am to 10pm) or from the Western Union office (tel. 257-1150) on Calle 9 between avenidas 2 and 4.

Telephones   Pay phones are not as common in San José as they are in North American cities. When you do find one, whether on the street or in a restaurant or hotel lobby, it may take coins of various denominations or it may take only 5 colón coins. A call within the city will cost 5 colónes. Pay phones are notoriously unreliable, so it may be better to make calls from your hotel, though you will likely be charged around 100 colónes per call.

Useful Telephone Numbers   For the exact **time,** call 112.

Water   The water in San José is said to be perfectly fine to drink. Residents of the city will swear to this. However, frequent complaints about intestinal illnesses by tourists make me a bit skeptical about San José's water. If you want to be cautious, drink bottled water and *frescos* made with milk instead of water. *Sin hielo* means "no ice."

Weather   The weather in San José (including the Central Valley) is usually temperate, never getting extremely hot or cold. May to November is the rainy season, though the rain usually falls in the afternoon and evening.

4. WHERE TO STAY

As the capital of Costa Rica, San José has a wide variety of hotels, ranging from luxury resorts to budget pensions charging only a few dollars a night. However, these two extremes are the exceptions, not the norm. The vast number of hotels, and the best deals, are to be found in the $30-to-$90 price range. Within this range you'll find restored homes that have been turned into small hotels and bed-and-breakfasts. You will also find modern hotels with swimming pools and exercise rooms, and older downtown business hotels. When considering where to stay in San José, you should take into consideration how long you plan to stay, and what you expect to do while you're here.

Downtown hotels, of which many are in beautifully restored homes, though convenient to museums, restaurants, and shopping, are often very noisy. Many people are also bothered by the exhaust fumes downtown. If you want cleaner air and a more peaceful night's sleep, consider staying in the Paseo Colón area. If you have rented a car, I recommend that you don't stay at a downtown hotel because parking is often expensive and the traffic congestion is trying, to say the least.

In the past few years, dozens of bed-and-breakfast inns have opened up around the San José area. Most are in residential neighborhoods that are quieter, though less convenient, than downtown locations. You can find out about many B&B's by contacting the **Costa Rica Bed & Breakfast Group** (tel. 506/223-4168 or 228-9200).

A word about laundry service at hotels: Laundry is charged by the piece and prices are ludicrous. Just a quick tally of my wife's and my dirty clothes came up with something like $75 for a load of laundry. Rinse out your own clothes if possible, or take them to a laundromat.

Please keep in mind that the 14.3% hotel room tax, which adds quite a bit to the price of a room, is not included in rates listed below.

DOWNTOWN SAN JOSÉ

DOUBLES FOR LESS THAN $25

GRAN HOTEL CENTROAMERICANO, Avenida 2 between calles 6 and 8 (Apdo. 3072-1000), San José. Tel. 506/221-3362. 45 rms (all with bath). TEL

$ Rates: $17.30 single; $21 double; $25.20 triple; $29.05 quad. No credit cards.

Though *"gran"* in name only, and not to be confused with the nearby landmark Gran Hotel Costa Rica, this hotel is located at the back of a shopping arcade only two blocks from the terminal for airport buses, which makes the hotel a good choice if you will be arriving late in the evening. Rooms are small and dark but generally clean.

N

ACCOMMODATIONS:
Coffee Garden Inn **36**
Gran Hotel Centroamericano **13**
Hotel Bienvenido **11**
Hotel Cacts **7**
Hotel Diplomat **14**
Hotel Don Carlos **31**
Hotel Dunn Inn **29**
Hotel Fortuna **18**
Hotel Grano de Oro **5**
Hotel Johnson **12**

Hotel Petite Victoria **6**
Hotel Ritz and
   Pensión Continental **19**
Hotel Santo Tomas **27**
Joluva Guesthouse **28**
Pensión American **16**
Pensión Costa Rica Inn **32**
Pensión de la Cuesta **34**
Toruma Youth Hostel **37**

DINING:
Amstel Grill Room **26**

Café Parisien **21**
Café de Teatro Nacional **22**
El Balcon de Europa **33**
Le Casa del Lago **2**
La Cocina de Leña **30**
La Esmeralda **24**
La Masia de Triquel **1**
La Perla **17**
The Lobster's Inn **10**
Machu Pichu Bar
   and Restaurant **3**

Manolo's Restaurante **15**
Pasteleria Francesa
   Boudsocq **4**
Pollos Gallo Pinto **35**
Restaurante Campesino ◆
Soda B y B **23**
Soda Coppelia **8**
Soda Vishnu **20**
Sus Antojos **9**

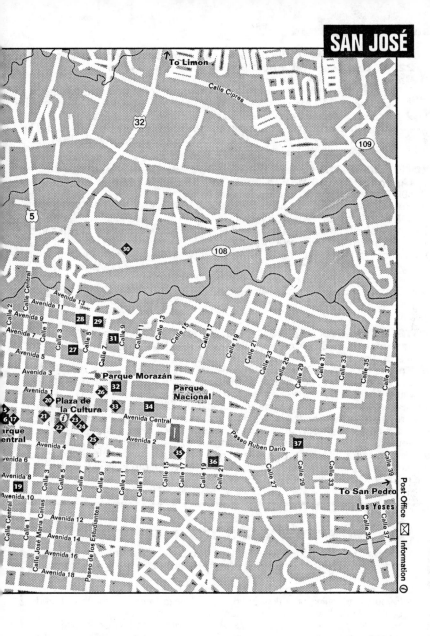

SAN JOSÉ

To Limón

Calle Cipres

32

109

5

30

108

Calle Central
Avenida 13
Calle 2
Avenida 11
Avenida 9
Calle 3
28 29
Avenida 7
Calle 5
Calle 9
Calle 11
Calle 13
Avenida 5
31
Calle 7
Calle 15
Calle 17
27
Avenida 3
Calle 19
Parque Morazán
Avenida 1
32
26
Parque Nacional
Calle 21
Calle 23
Calle 25
Calle 29
Calle 31
Calle 33
Calle 35
Calle 37
20 **Plaza de la Cultura**
33
34
5
17
21
6
_i_
23 24
22
Avenida Central
arque entral
25
Avenida 2
Paseo Ruben Dario
37
Avenida 4
35
enida 6
Calle 3
Calle 5
Calle 7
Calle 9
Calle 11
Calle 13
Calle 15
Calle 17
36
Calle 19
Calle 2
Calle 27
Calle 29
Calle 33
Calle 39
Avenida 8
19
Avenida 10
Calle Central
To San Pedro
Los Yoses
Calle 35
Calle 37
Calle 1
Calle José María Cañas
Avenida 12
Paseo de los Estudiantes
Avenida 14
Avenida 16
Avenida 18

Post Office ⊠ Information ⓘ

HOTEL BIENVENIDO, Calle 10 between avenidas 1 and 3 (Apdo. 389-2200), San José. Tel. 506/221-1872. 48 rms (all with bath).

$ Rates: $14.85 single; $21.75 double; $32.60 triple. No credit cards.

This very basic hotel is one of the most popular in the city with travelers on a tight budget. The rooms are clean, though a bit dark, and there is always ample hot water. The hotel was created from an old movie theater, and there are still a few architectural details remaining from the building's former incarnation. This place fills up by early afternoon in the high season, so call ahead for a reservation and ask for a quiet room in the back.

HOTEL JOHNSON, Calle 8 between Avenida Central and Avenida 2a (Apdo. 6638-1000), San José. Tel. 506/223-7633 or 223-7827. Fax 506/222-3683. 57 rms, 3 suites (all with bath).

$ Rates: $12.45–$15.60 single; $15.60–$17.65 double; $18.70–$20.80 triple; $27 suite (for five). DC, MC, V.

The lobby of this large, centrally located hotel is on the second floor. You'll find the hotel patronized primarily by Costa Rican businesspeople and families, but it is a good choice for any budget traveler. In the lobby there is a television and several lounge chairs, and on each of the residence floors above there is a sitting area. The rooms have tile floors and open onto a narrow air shaft that lets in a bit of light and noise from other rooms. Bathrooms are relatively clean and roomy. Most rooms come with twin beds (you might want to test a few beds if you're picky about mattresses).

HOTEL RITZ AND PENSIÓN CONTINENTAL, Calle Central between avenidas 8 and 10 (Apdo. 6783-1000), San José. Tel. 506/222-4103. Fax 506/222-8849. 27 rms (5 with bath).

$ Rates: $6.40–$11.60 single without bath, $16.75 single with bath; $11.20–$17.80 double without bath, $22.05 double with bath; $14.65–$24.40 triple without bath, $27.70 triple with bath. AE, MC, V.

These two side-by-side budget hotels are under the same management and together have rooms to fit most budget travelers' needs. There is even a travel agency and tour company on the first floor, so you can arrange all of your travels around Costa Rica without leaving the hotel. Rooms vary greatly in size and comfort levels, but all tend to be dark and a bit musty. Bathrooms are a bit old and showers have showerhead heaters that just barely work. If the first room you see isn't to your liking, just ask to see another in a different price category.

Ⓕ FROMMER'S SMART TRAVELER: HOTELS

1. Always remember to ask what the total cost of a room will be with the taxes added in. Currently the room tax is a whopping 14.3%, which adds a sizable chunk to your hotel bill.
2. Visit in the rainy season (May to November) when rates are usually lower.
3. If you are traveling on a tight budget, consider taking a room with a shared bath, which will save you a considerable amount of money.
4. You'll also save money if you take a room with a fan instead of one with air-conditioning. In most parts of the country, a fan is really all that's necessary, and air-conditioned rooms often have problems with mildew.
5. To avoid a frantic hotel search, make a reservation for your first night in town, especially if you're arriving after dark.
6. Keep your eyes open for new hotels; the tourism industry is booming in Costa Rica and newer hotels often offer good values.
7. Always ask for a room away from the street if you are staying in downtown San José. Traffic noise here can be horrendous.

PENSIÓN AMERICAN, Calle 2 between Avenida Central and Avenida 2 (Apdo. 4853-1000), San José. Tel. 506/221-4171 or 221-9799. 35 rms (none with private bath).
$ Rates: $6.20 single; $12.40 double. No credit cards.
This is an old favorite with Central American backpack travelers. The rooms are dark, the beds are old and uncomfortable, and the walls are paper thin, but still, the hotel stays full with hardy young travelers looking to save a few bucks.

DOUBLES FOR LESS THAN $35

COFFEE GARDEN INN, 75 meters east of the northeast corner of the Corte Suprema de Justicia, San José. Tel. 506/221-6191. 6 rms (all with shared bath).
$ Rates (including Tico breakfast): Dec–Mar $34.30 single, $40 double; Apr–Nov $22.85 single, $28.60 double. No credit cards.

This newer home was recently converted into a bed-and-breakfast inn, and though none of the guest rooms have private bathrooms, this lack is made up for by the presence of a small swimming pool in the back garden. You just won't find a hotel with a pool for this little money anywhere else in San José. There is also a small bar and restaurant, so you have all the amenities of a bigger hotel under this one small roof. Rooms are fairly basic, but antiques in public areas lend the B&B a touch of class. This place is popular with students and other younger travelers.

HOTEL CACTS, 2845 Avenida 3 between calles 28 and 30 (Apdo. 379-1005), San José. Tel. 506/221-2928 or 221-6546. Fax 506/221-8616. 18 rms (14 with private bath).
$ Rates (including continental breakfast): $31.05 single with bath; $31.05 double without bath, $35 double with bath; $39 triple without bath, $45.05 triple with bath. No credit cards.

This is one of the most interesting and unusual budget hotels I've ever seen, housed in an attractive tropical contemporary home on a business and residential street. You reach the reception area via a flight of outside steps that lead past a small garden area. Once inside, you are in a maze of halls on several levels (the house is built on a slope). My favorite room is the huge bi-level family room with its high beamed ceiling. The Cacts has been in the midst of an ambitious expansion for several years now and by the time you arrive you may find a rooftop terrace dining area and quite a few more rooms in various price ranges.

HOTEL FORTUNA, Avenida 6 between calles 2 and 4 (Apdo. 7-1570), San José. Tel. 506/223-5344. Fax 506/223-2743. 30 rms (all with bath). TEL
$ Rates: $21.05 single; $27.55 double; $37.75 triple; $43.05 quad. AE, MC, V.
Located only two blocks from the Parque Central, the Fortuna has a vague Chinese theme. The second-floor rooms are sunny and warm, and the first-floor rooms are cooler and darker. The brightness of the rooms makes this place feel much more cheery than other hotels, despite the lack of carpeting.

JOLUVA GUESTHOUSE, 936 Calle 3B between avenidas 9 and 11, San José. Tel. 506/223-9901 or (in the U.S.) 619/298-7965. Fax 619/294-2418. 8 rms (6 with private bath). TV
$ Rates (including continental breakfast): $28.60 single without private bath, $34.30 single with private bath; $34.30 double without private bath, $45.75 double with private bath. MC, V.
Though you can find less expensive hotels, there are few in this price range that offer the old-fashioned architectural detail of the Joluva. There are old tile and hardwood floors throughout and high ceilings (and in one room, beautiful plasterwork on the

ceiling). However, the rooms are small and a bit dark, with windows that open into a covered courtyard. The breakfast room has skylights, which help brighten it a bit.

PENSIÓN COSTA RICA INN, 154 Calle 9 between avenidas 1 and 3 (Apdo. 10282-1000), San José (In the U.S.: P.O. Box 59, Arcadia, LA 71001). Tel. 506/222-5203 or (in Canada) 318/263-2059 or toll free (in the U.S.) 800/637-0899. Fax 506/223-8385. 35 rms (all with bath).
$ Rates: $26.30 single; $32.60 double; $43.45 triple. MC, V.
Although most of the rooms are rather small and dark, this little hotel is still very popular, especially with young travelers. If you're a light sleeper, this is definitely not the place for you. The walls are typical of those in old Costa Rican wood buildings—paper thin. There's a small bar that always seems to have a handful of young foreigners hanging around as well as a TV lounge with plenty of couches. The rooms are situated off small courtyards down a maze of narrow hallways. Recommended for those who like to stay out late.

DOUBLES FOR LESS THAN $45

HOTEL DIPLOMAT, Calle 6 between Avenida Central and Avenida 2 (Apdo. 6606-1000), San José. Tel. 506/221-8133 or 221-8744. Fax 506/233-7474. 29 rms (all with bath). TEL
$ Rates: $29.15 single; $42.30 double. AE, MC, V. **Parking:** Nearby.
It's easy to miss the entrance to this hotel. Watch for it on the east side of the street. The lobby is narrow, and the front door is fairly nondescript. The carpeted rooms are rather small but comfortable nonetheless, and some rooms on the upper floors have nice views of the mountains. The tiled baths are clean, and the water is hot. The hotel's restaurant serves meals priced from $2 for a sandwich to $15 for a lobster dinner.

PENSIÓN DE LA CUESTA, 1332 Cuesta de Nuñez, Avenida 1 between calles 11 and 15, San José. Tel. 506/255-2896. Fax 506/223-2272. 8 rms (none with private bath).
$ Rates (including continental breakfast): $28.60 single; $40 double. MC, V.
⭐ Though these prices may seem a bit steep for a room without a private bathroom, this little bed-and-breakfast is definitely worth considering. It is owned by an artist from the Guanacaste province of Costa Rica, and original artwork abounds. The building itself is a classic example of a tropical wood-frame home and has been painted an eye-catching pink with blue and white trim. The rooms are a bit dark and are very simply furnished, but there is a very sunny and cheery sunken lounge area in the center of the house. You'll find this hotel on the hill leading up to the Parque Nacional.

A HOSTEL

TORUMA YOUTH HOSTEL, Avenida Central between calles 29 and 31, San José. Tel. 506/224-4085. 105 beds (all with shared bath).
$ Rates (including continental breakfast): $6.20–$9.45 per person per night with an IYHF card; $7.65–$10.80 without IYHF card. No credit cards.
This attractive old building, with its long veranda, is the largest hostel in Costa Rica's system of official youth hostels. Although it is possible to find other accommodations around town in this price range, any such room would not likely be as clean. Also, the atmosphere here is convivial and will be familiar to anyone who has hosteled in Europe. The large lounge in the center of the building has a high ceiling and a great deal of light. The dorms have four to six beds per room. There is an inexpensive restaurant adjacent to the hostel, and if you want, you can store luggage here for 35¢ per day.

WORTH THE EXTRA BUCKS

HOTEL DON CARLOS, 779 Calle 9 between avenidas 7 and 9, San José (In the U.S.: Dept. 1686, P.O. Box 025216, Miami, FL 33102-5216). Tel. 506/221-6707. Fax 506/255-0828. 25 rms, 6 suites.
$ Rates (including continental breakfast): $45.75–$57.15 single; $57.15–$68.60 double. AE, MC, V. **Parking:** Nearby.

Located in a historic residential neighborhood only blocks from the business district, the Don Carlos hints at the days of the planters and coffee barons. Bronze statues of *campesinos* stand outside the front door of the hotel, which was once a Costa Rican president's mansion. Inside the lobby, you'll find pre-Columbian stone reproductions, as well as orchids, ferns, palms, and parrots. Most of the rooms are quite large, and each is a little different from the others. The gift shop here is one of the largest in San José and is the best in the country. The complimentary breakfast, as well as moderately priced meals, are served in the Pre-Columbian Lounge. Many people can't tolerate the traffic noises here, so, if you're a light sleeper, be forewarned.

HOTEL DUNN INN, Calle 5 and Avenida 11 (Apdo. 1584-1000), San José. Tel. 506/222-3232 or 222-3426. Fax 506/221-4596. 27 rms, 1 suite.
$ Rates (including continental breakfast): $52.30 single or double; $63.75 triple; $102.05 suite. V. **Parking:** Nearby.

Located in the Barrio Amon historic neighborhood, the Dunn Inn is among the better small hotels in the area. Part of the hotel is housed in a century-old mansion, while other rooms are in a new wing. This hotel offers quiet sophistication at reasonable rates. The courtyard of the old mansion has been partially covered and turned into the dining room and bar, which, if you have a room directly above, can be a bit noisy at night. Orchids and bromeliads hang from the brick walls, and a fountain bubbles away beside a huge philodendron vine. Some of the rooms have the original hardwood flooring and some are carpeted. The new wing has some very nice rooms with exposed brick walls.

HOTEL PETITE VICTORIA, Paseo Colón, Costado Oeste Sala Garbo, San José. Tel. 506/233-1812 or 233-1813. Fax 506/233-1938. 15 rms (all with bath).
$ Rates: May–Nov $45 single, $55 double; Dec–Apr $55–$85 single, $60–$85 double. AE, MC, V. **Parking:** Free.

One of the oldest houses in San José, this tropical Victorian home was once the election campaign headquarters for Oscar Arias Sánchez, Costa Rica's former president who won a Nobel Peace Prize. Today, after extensive remodeling and restoration, it is an interesting little hotel that offers a historic setting at moderate rates. The big front porch is perfect for sitting and taking in the warm sun, while inside, a circular banquette sits in the middle of a tile-floored lobby. Guest rooms have high ceilings and fans to keep the air cool and tiled bathrooms. Inside, walls are made of wood, so noise can be a bit of a problem. Tour arrangements and a laundry service are also offered. When I last visited, there were plans to add several new less-expensive rooms with shared bathrooms.

HOTEL SANTO TOMAS, Avenida 7 between calles 3 and 5, San José. Tel. 506/255-0448. Fax 506/222-3950. 20 rms.
$ Rates (including continental breakfast): $56.60–$85.75 single; $62.90–$97.15 double; $97.15–$108.60 triple (5% discount on entire stay after 3 consecutive days). Credit cards accepted for room reservation guarantee only. **Parking:** Nearby.

Even though it is on an otherwise nondescript street, this converted mansion is a real jewel inside. Built around 100 years ago by a coffee baron, the house was once slated to be bulldozed in order to build a parking lot. Under the direction of American Thomas Douglas, the old mansion has been restored to its former grandeur. In the guest rooms you'll find exquisitely crafted antique reproduction furnishings made here in Costa Rica. The hardwood floors throughout most of the hotel are original. The rooms vary in size, but most are fairly large. There are skylights in some bathrooms, and queen-size beds throughout. Maps of Costa Rica hang on the walls of all the guest rooms so you can get acquainted with the country. There are a couple of patio areas, as well as a television lounge and combination breakfast room and outdoor bar. A laundry service and baggage storage room are available.

HOTEL GRANO DE ORO, Calle 30 –251, between avenidas 2 and 4, 150 meters south of Paseo Colón (Apdo. 1157-1007, Centro Colón), San José (In the U.S.: P.O. Box 025216-36, Miami, FL 33102-5216). Tel. 506/255-3322. Fax 506/221-2782. 35 rms, 2 suites. TV TEL SAFE
$ Rates: $73.15–$91.45 single; $78.90–$97.15 double; $131.45 suite. AE, MC, V (add 6% surcharge). **Parking:** Free.

⭐ San José boasts dozens of old homes that have been converted into hotels, but few offer the luxurious accommodations or professional service that can be found at the Grano de Oro. Located on a quiet side street off of Paseo Colón, this small hotel offers a variety of room types to fit most budgets and tastes. Personally, I like the patio rooms, which have French doors opening onto private patios. However, if you want a room with plenty of space, ask for one of the deluxe rooms, which have large, modern tiled baths with big tubs. Throughout all the guest rooms, you'll find attractive hardwood furniture, including old-fashioned wardrobes in some rooms. For additional luxuries, you can stay in one of the suites, which have whirlpool tubs. The hotel's patio garden restaurant serves excellent international meals and some of the best desserts in the city, and when it comes time to relax you can soak in a hot tub or have a drink in the rooftop lounge, which has a commanding view of San José.

5. WHERE TO EAT

San José has an amazing variety of restaurants serving cuisines of the world in all price ranges, and you won't pay much for even the best meal in town. However, for the best deals around, head to a *soda*, the equivalent of a diner in the U.S., where you can get good, cheap, and filling Tico food. Rice and beans are the staples here and show up at breakfast, lunch, and dinner. Rice and beans are called *gallo pinto* when served for breakfast and may come with anything from fried eggs to steak. At lunch and dinner those very same rice and beans are called a *casado,* (which also means "married") and are served with a salad of cabbage and tomatoes, fried bananas, and steak, chicken, or fish. Gallo pinto might cost $2, and a casado might cost $2.70.

Another favorite of Ticos, and tourists, is the *fresco.* A fresco is a bit like a fresh-fruit milk shake without the ice cream; and when made with mangos, papayas, bananas, or any of the other delicious tropical fruits of Costa Rica, it is pure ambrosia. Frescos are also made with water (*con agua*), but these are not nearly as good as those made with milk (*con leche*).

DOWNTOWN

MEALS FOR LESS THAN $6

LA CASA DEL LAGO, at north end of lake in Sabana Park. No phone.
   Cuisine: COSTA RICAN. **Reservations:** Not accepted.
$ Prices: $1.50–$3.05. No credit cards.
   Open: Tues–Sun 11am–5pm.
On Sundays this little restaurant and the patio outside are filled with Tico families

enjoying their day in the park. It's not surprising, because the view here, of the lake, a large fountain, and Pico Blanco in the distance, is one of the best views in the city. Another advantage is that it is close to the Museum of Art and makes a good stop for finger foods such as burgers or fried chicken, or something more substantial such as a casado, fish with garlic, or pork chops. Counter service is fast, and they serve interesting *naturales* (fruit juices) such as naranjilla (a small citrus fruit) or mora (blackberry).

LA ESMERALDA, Avenida 2 between calles 5 and 7. Tel. 221-0530.
   Cuisine: COSTA RICAN. **Reservations:** Not necessary.
$ **Prices:** Entrees $3.55–$7.80. AE, DC, MC, V.
   Open: Mon–Sat 11am–5am.

No one should visit San José without stopping in at La Esmeralda at least once, the later at night the better. This is much more than just a restaurant serving Tico food: It is the Grand Central Station of Costa Rican mariachi bands. In fact mariachis and other bands from throughout Central America and Mexico hang out here every night waiting for work. While they wait they often serenade diners in the cavernous open-air dining hall of the restaurant. Friday and Saturday nights are always the busiest, but you'll probably hear lots of excellent music any night of the week. The classic Tico food is quite good. Try the coconut flan for dessert.

LA PERLA, Avenida 2 and Calle Central. Tel. 222-7492.
   Cuisine: INTERNATIONAL. **Reservations:** Not accepted.
$ **Prices:** Entrees $1.30–$7.45. MC, V.
   Open: Daily 24 hours.

It's easy to walk right past this place (I did) the first time you try to find it. The entrance is right on the corner looking across to Parque Central, and the restaurant itself is a little bit below street level. This place isn't long on atmosphere but the food is good and the portions are large. The special here is paella, a Spanish rice-and-seafood dish for only $5.60. Other good choices are *sopa de mariscos,* which is a seafood soup with mussels and clams in a delicious broth, or *huevos à la ranchera,* which is prepared a bit differently than in Mexico and makes a filling meal any time of the night or day. Be sure to try a delicious *refresco,* made with water or milk and fresh fruit whirred in a blender. *Mora* (blackberry) is my favorite.

PASTELERIA FRANCESA BOUDSOCQ, Calle 30 at Paseo Colón. Tel. 222-6732.
   Cuisine: PASTRIES. **Reservations:** Not necessary.
$ **Prices:** $1.05–$2.75. No credit cards.
   Open: Mon–Sat 8am–7pm, Sun 8am–6:30pm.

Ticos love their pastries, and bakeries and pastry shops abound all over San José. However, this little place on Paseo Colón is one of the best I've found. They have savory meat-filled pastries that make good light lunches as well as plenty of unusual sweets that are great afternoon snacks. There are only a couple of tables here.

POLLOS GALLO PINTO, One block south of the National Museum (Calle 17 between avenidas 2 and 6). Tel. 257-4437.
   Cuisine: COSTA RICAN. **Reservations:** Not accepted.
$ **Prices:** Entrees $1.35–$5.45.
   Open: Daily 11am–10pm.

Jorge Zuñiga, owner of this family-run restaurant, made a great success of his former eating establishment, Restaurante Campesino, and now brings his touch to Pollos Gallo Pinto. What's the big attraction? Chickens roasted over coffee-root fires, enticing you with their mouth-watering fragrance. And that's not all—accompanying each order of tender bird (which comes in quarter-, half-, and whole-chicken servings) are crunchy salads, french fried potatoes, refried beans, and little homemade tortillas with that wood-smoked flavor. Even if you aren't very hungry, the food here is sure to whet your appetite.

RESTAURANTE CAMPESINO, Calle 7 between avenidas 2 and 4. Tel. 222-1170.

   Cuisine: COSTA RICAN. **Reservations:** Not accepted.

$ **Prices:** Whole chicken $5.05; half chicken $2.65. MC, V.

   Open: Daily 10am–midnight.

This little restaurant serves delicious chicken, which is not surprising since chicken is just about all they serve and thus they have had time to perfect its cooking. The secret of this delectable chicken is in the wood fire over which it is roasted. Depending on how hungry you are, you can get a quarter, half, or full chicken; and you might also try the palmito (heart of palm) salad. You can't miss this place—watch for the smoking chimney high above the roof, or at street level watch for the window full of chickens roasting over an open fire.

SODA B y B, Calle 5 and Avenida Central. Tel. 222-7316.

   Cuisine: COSTA RICAN. **Reservations:** Not accepted.

$ **Prices:** Sandwiches $1–$3.10; breakfast $1.15–$2.25. MC, V.

   Open: Mon–Fri 8:30am–10pm, Sat 9am–10pm.

Located on the corner across from the Tourist Information Center on the Plaza de la Cultura, this spot is popular with downtown shoppers and office workers. Service is good, prices (and noise level) are low, and the food is surprisingly good for a sandwich shop. Slide into a high-backed wooden booth and order the *chalupa de pollo B y B.* It's a sort of tostada piled high with chicken salad and drenched with sour cream and guacamole.

SODA COPPELIA, Paseo Colón between calles 26 and 28. Tel. 223-8013.

   Cuisine: COSTA RICAN. **Reservations:** Not accepted.

$ **Prices:** Entrees $1.70–$3.15. No credit cards.

   Open: Mon–Sat 8am–7pm.

If you're looking for a filling, cheap, and quick breakfast in the Paseo Colón area, I recommend this soda. You'll find it near the movie theater. The wooden booths and a few tables on a covered walkway (noisy) are frequently full of local businesspeople because the meals are so reasonably priced, such as steak for $2.90. For lighter fare, try the burgers, sandwiches, or some of the good-looking pastries such as flaky empanadas or carrot bread.

SODA VISHNU, Avenida 1 between calles 1 and 3. Tel. 222-2549.

   Cuisine: VEGETARIAN. **Reservations:** Not accepted.

 FROMMER'S SMART TRAVELER: RESTAURANTS

1. Always remember that an 11% tax and 10% service charge are added to the price of dinner. Your total bill will be 21% higher than the prices you saw on the menu.

2. If you want to save money, eat at *sodas,* the Costa Rican equivalent of a diner. *Gallo pinto* is the national breakfast and is always quite cheap, while *casados* offer similar flavors and savings at lunch and dinner.

3. Keep an eye on the bar tab. Liquor and wine are pricey, while beer is as cheap as soft drinks.

4. Always ask what *frescos* a restaurant has. These are fresh fruit drinks the likes of which you will rarely ever find at home.

$ Prices: Entrees $1.05–$2.95. No credit cards.
Open: Mon–Sat 7am–9pm, Sun 9am–7pm.

Vegetarians may find themselves eating all their meals at this bright and modern natural foods eatery. There are booths for two or four people and photo murals on the walls. At the cashier's counter you can buy natural cosmetics, honey, and bags of granola. However, most people just come for the filling *plato del dia* that includes soup, salad, veggies, an entree, and dessert for around $2.10. There are also bean burgers and cheese sandwiches on whole-wheat bread. There is another Vishnu around the corner on Calle 3 between Avenida Central and Avenida 1.

MEALS FOR LESS THAN $12

AMSTEL GRILL ROOM, Avenida 1 and Calle 7. Tel. 222-4622.

Cuisine: CONTINENTAL/COSTA RICAN. **Reservations:** Not necessary.
$ Prices: Appetizers $2.05–$12.20; entrees $5.60–$16.90. AE, MC, V.
Open: Daily 6:30–11am, 11:30am–3pm, 6–10pm.

Ask anyone in San José for a restaurant recommendation and this hotel dining room is always near the top of the list. For years the Grill Room has maintained its high standards. The atmosphere is one of quiet sophistication with white-jacketed waiters moving unobtrusively between the tables, making sure that everyone is happy. Businesspeople and well-dressed matrons are the primary customers, but tourists in more casual attire receive the same careful attention. Lunch here is a real bargain and the most popular meal of the day. For between $4.90 and $6.45 you can order the special of the day or the deluxe special of the day, which may include entrees such as corvina meunière or sirloin steak. Soup or salad and a dessert round out the meal. Should you choose to order à la carte, try one of the choice steaks of Costa Rican beef or fresh shrimp.

CAFÉ DE TEATRO NACIONAL, Teatro Nacional, Avenida 2 between calles 3 and 5. Tel. 223-4488.

Cuisine: CONTINENTAL. **Reservations:** Not necessary.
$ Prices: Sandwiches and soups $2.50–$4.65; entrees $5–$8.35. MC, V.
Open: Mon–Sat 11am–6pm.

This is one of my favorite places to eat in all of San José. Even if there is no show at the Teatro Nacional during your visit, you can enjoy a meal or a cup of coffee here and soak up the neoclassical atmosphere. The theater was built in the 1890s from the designs of European architects, and the art nouveau chandeliers, ceiling murals, and marble floors and tables are purely parisienne. There are changing art displays by local artists to complete the tres chic café atmosphere. The menu includes such continental dishes as quiche, Hungarian goulash, and wiener schnitzel, but the main attractions here are the specialty cakes and tortes which are displayed in a glass case. Ice cream dishes are raised to a high art form here with names such as passionate love and spaghetti ice cream. The ambience is classic French café, but the marimba music drifting in from outside the open window will remind you that you are still in Costa Rica.

CAFÉ PARISIEN, Gran Hotel Costa Rica, Avenida 2 between calles 1 and 3. Tel. 221-4011.

Cuisine: INTERNATIONAL. **Reservations:** Not necessary.
$ Prices: Sandwiches $1.90–$5.10; appetizers $1.50–$6.65; entrees $5.50–$18.25. AE, MC, V.
Open: Daily 24 hours.

The Gran Hotel Costa Rica is hardly the best hotel in San José, but it does have a picturesque patio café right on the Plaza de la Cultura. A wrought iron railing, white columns, and arches create an old-world atmosphere, and on the plaza all around the café, marimba bands perform and vendors sell handcrafts. It's open 24 hours a day and there is almost no hour when there isn't something interesting going on in the plaza. Stop by for the breakfast buffet ($6.75–$8.15) and fill up as the plaza's vendors set up their booths; peruse the *Tico Times* over coffee while you have your shoes polished; or simply bask in the tropical sunshine while you sip a beer. Lunch and dinner buffets are also offered for about $8.80.

LA COCINA DE LEÑA, El Pueblo. Tel. 255-1360.
Cuisine: COSTA RICAN. **Reservations:** Not necessary.
$ Prices: Entrees $5.40–$18.95. AE, DC, MC, V.
    Open: Daily lunch 11:30am–3pm, dinner 6–11:30pm.

Located in the unusual El Pueblo shopping, dining, and entertainment center, La Cocina de Leña (The Wood Stove) has a rustic feel to it. There are stacks of firewood on shelves above the booths, long stalks of bananas hanging from pillars, tables suspended by heavy ropes from the ceiling, and most unusual of all—menus printed on paper bags. Though almost every restaurant in Costa Rica offers *tipico* meals, few serve the likes of green banana or heart of palm *ceviche*. After such unusual appetizers you might wonder what could come next. Perhaps oxtail stew served with *yuca* and *platano* might appeal to you; if not there are plenty of steaks and seafood dishes on the menu. *Chilasuilas* are delicious tortillas filled with fried meat. Black bean soup with egg is a Costa Rican standard and is well done here, and the corn soup with pork is equally satisfying. For dessert there is *tres leches* cake as well as the more unusual sweetened *chiverre,* which is a type of squash that looks remarkably like a watermelon.

MACHU PICHU BAR AND RESTAURANT, Calle 32 between avenidas 1 and 3. Tel. 222-7384.
Cuisine: PERUVIAN/CONTINENTAL. **Reservations:** Accepted.
$ Prices: Appetizers $1.70–$9.30; entrees $3.50–$11.50. No credit cards.
    Open: Daily 8am–10pm.

Located just off Paseo Colón near the Kentucky Fried Chicken, Machu Pichu is an unpretentious little restaurant that has become one of the most popular places in San José. The menu is primarily seafood (especially sea bass), and consequently most dishes tend toward the upper end of the menu's price range, but all are well worth the price. The soups are good, and several of my favorite entrees are *causa Limeña,* which is lemon-flavored mashed potatoes stuffed with shrimp, *aji de gallina,* a dish of chopped chicken in a fragrant cream sauce, and octopus with garlic butter. Be sure to ask for one of the specialty drinks.

MANOLO'S RESTAURANTE, Avenida Central between calles 0 and 2. Tel. 221-2041.
Cuisine: COSTA RICAN. **Reservations:** Not necessary.
$ Prices: $3–$9.15. MC, V.
    Open: Daily 11am–10pm upstairs; 24 hours downstairs.

Upstairs on a busy corner on Avenida Central, you'll find this roomy restaurant popular with Ticos and tourists alike. You can view the action in the street below, or catch the live folk dance performance that is staged nightly. The open kitchen serves up steaks and fish, but there is also a popular buffet that includes several tipico dishes such as plantains and black bean soup for $5.10. Downstairs you'll find Manolo's Churreria, a good place for a quick sandwich—and they have espresso.

SUS ANTOJOS, Paseo Colón between calles 26 and 28 (across from Ambassador Hotel). Tel. 222-9086.
Cuisine: MEXICAN. **Reservations:** Not necessary.
$ Prices: Entrees $2.25–$7.45. AE, MC, V.
    Open: Daily 11:30am–10pm.

Located down some steps in the Paseo Colón neighborhood, this cozy place serves a dozen types of tacos, or *antojitos* (little bits to mix and match), and you can watch the cook making tortillas and grilling meats on the huge griddle in the open kitchen. We tried *chilasquiles de pollo,* chicken baked with a layer of cheese, tomato, and sour cream, and *entremes ranchero,* a little bit each of steak, pork chops, salad, beans and guacamole, and both were tasty and well prepared. One of the renowned margaritas is a good accompaniment to just about anything on the menu.

WORTH THE EXTRA BUCKS

EL BALCON DE EUROPA, Calle 9 between avenidas Central and 1. Tel. 221-4841.
   Cuisine: CONTINENTAL. **Reservations:** Recommended.
$ Prices: Appetizers $4.40–$5.10; entrees $5.10–$15.35. No credit cards.
   Open: Sun–Fri noon–10pm.
Open since 1908, El Balcon de Europa is one of San José's most popular restaurants. What attracts people from all walks of life to this restaurant is outstanding service, gourmet Italian food, and cheese. You may have noticed a lack of cheese in other parts of Costa Rica, but not here. The centerpiece of the restaurant is a table covered with imported European cheeses (at room temperature) and an array of fresh-baked desserts. Take a seat and immediately a basket of two types of bread and bread sticks arrives, accompanied by a sample plate of cheeses. There are many different pastas on the menu served in a variety of tasty sauces, mostly cream-based. For an entree, try the unusual piccatine al limone, a paper-thin steak cooked in lemon sauce. To accompany your meal there is a limited selection of wines from Europe, California, and South America.

THE LOBSTER'S INN, Paseo Colón at Calle 24 (opposite Mercedes Benz). Tel. 223-8594.
   Cuisine: SEAFOOD. **Reservations:** Not necessary.
$ Prices: Appetizers $3.20–$18.20; entrees $6.60–$22.25. AE, DC, MC, V.
   Open: Lunch Mon–Sat 11am–3pm, dinner Mon–Sat 5:30–10:30pm, Sun 11am–10:30pm.
Located on Paseo Colón in a neighborhood where there are other restaurants of similar quality, this one stands out for its delicious seafood, which is fresh off the restaurant's own fishing fleet. One taste of the cream of shrimp soup, which comes loaded with shrimp, will prove it. Try shrimp en brochette, or choose from about 10 different preparations of corvina (seabass), including corvina with plenty of garlic or in a caper sauce. A specialty is the (very large) lobster dinner. The red tablecloths, heavy colonial furniture, and hanging ferns are rather formal, brightened by aquariums full of large fish—carp, gars, and oscars (to look at, not to eat). Portions are generous and the service, by waiters in red ties and cummerbunds, is friendly and thoughtful. To end your meal, choose from a cart full of cordials. Occasionally there is live music in the evening.

LA MASIA DE TRIQUEL, Corner Avenida 2 and Calle 40, across from the Parque del Largo Hotel. Tel. 221-5073 or 232-3584.
   Cuisine: SPANISH. **Reservations:** Recommended on weekends.
$ Prices: Appetizers $3.50–$14.90; entrees $6.10–$21.65. AE, DC, MC, V.
   Open: Lunch Tues–Sat noon–2pm, dinner Tues–Fri 6:30–11pm, Sat 7–11pm, Sun noon–4pm.
Located in an aging white stucco house only a block from Parque la Sabana, La Masia de Triquel is San José's finest Spanish restaurant. Service is extremely formal and the clientele comes from the city's upper crust. Though Costa Rica is known for its beef, here you'll also find such meats as lamb, quail, and rabbit. Seafood dishes include the usual shrimp and lobster but also squid and octopus. However, there is really no decision to be made when perusing the menu; start with a big bowl of gazpacho and then spend the rest of the evening enjoying all the succulent surprises you'll find in a big dish of paella.

ESCAZÚ

MEALS FOR LESS THAN $12

EL CHÉ, 100 meters south of the Escazú/Santa Ana crossroad. Tel. 228-1598.

Cuisine: STEAK. **Reservations:** For large groups.

$ Prices: Appetizers $1.40–$4.40; entrees $6.70–$8.80. AE, MC, V.

Open: Lunch Mon–Fri noon–3pm, dinner Mon–Fri 6–11pm, Sat–Sun 11am–11pm.

This small neighborhood place is owned by a former Argentinian who likes to play '60s rock n' roll music in his restaurant. Charcoal broiled *lomita* (sirloin steak) is the raison d'être for this place. The steak is so tender that you can cut it with a fork (possibly because of the secret marinade). While waiting for your very fine steak, order some mouth watering appetizers such as parsley/garlic sauce that you can pile onto crunchy french bread, pickled onions, a spicy and flavorful *chorizo* (sausage), or a heart of palm salad. Enjoy your meal outside on the patio or indoors in a comfortable atmosphere with red tablecloths and candles.

SPECIALTY DINING

STREET FOOD   On almost every street corner in downtown San José you'll find a fruit vendor. If you're lucky enough to be in town between April and June you can sample more varieties of mangoes than you ever knew existed. I like buying them already cut up in a little bag. They cost a little more this way but you don't get nearly as messy. Be sure to try a green mango with salt and chili peppers. That's the way they seem to like mangoes best in the steamy tropics—guaranteed to wake up your taste buds.

Another common street food that you might be wondering about is called *pejibaye,* a bright orange palm nut about the size of a small apple. They are boiled in big pots on carts. You eat them in much the same way you would an avocado, and they taste a bit like squash.

LATE NIGHT/24 HOURS   San José has quite a few all-night restaurants including **La Perla, La Esmeralda,** and **Café Parisien,** all of which are described above. Another popular place, which is almost exclusively for men, is the **Soda Palace** on Avenida 2 and Calle 2 (see the "Evening Entertainment" section for more information).

6. ATTRACTIONS

Though most visitors try to get out of San José as quickly as possible because of its smog and congestion, there are quite a few attractions here in the city to keep you busy for a couple of days, and if you start doing day trips out of the city, you can spend several more days in the area.

SUGGESTED ITINERARIES

IF YOU HAVE ONE DAY   Start your day on the Plaza de la Cultura. Visit the Gold Museum (if it is a Friday, Saturday, or Sunday) and see if you can get tickets for a performance that night at the Teatro Nacional. From the Plaza de la Cultura stroll up Avenida Central to the Museo Nacional. After lunch head over to the Jade Museum if you have the energy for one more museum. After all this culture, a stroll through the chaos of the Mercado Central is in order. Try dinner at La Cocina de Leña before going to the Teatro Nacional. After the performance you absolutely must swing by La Esmeralda for some live mariachi music before calling it a day.

IF YOU HAVE TWO DAYS   Follow the itinerary above on the first day. On day two visit the Serpentarium or the Spirogyra Butterfly Garden, do a bit of shopping, and then head out Paseo Colón to the Museo de Arte Costarricense.

IF YOU HAVE THREE DAYS   Follow the itinerary for two days outlined above. On day three, head out to Irazú Volcano, Orosi Valley, Lankester Gardens, and Cartago. Start your day at the volcano and work your way back toward San José.

IF YOU HAVE FIVE DAYS   Follow the itinerary for three days outlined above. Then spend days four and five on other excursions from San José. You can go white-water rafting, hiking in a cloud forest, or horseback riding for a day if you are an active type. If you prefer less strenuous activities, try a cruise around the Gulf of Nicoya and a trip to the Rain Forest Aerial Tram.

THE TOP ATTRACTIONS

MUSEO DE ARTE COSTARRICENSE, Calle 42 and Paseo Colón, East Sabana Park. Tel. 222-7155 or 222-7932.
   This small museum at the end of Paseo Colón in Sabana Park was formerly an airport terminal. Today, however, it houses a collection of works in all media by Costa Rica's most celebrated artists. On display are many exceptionally beautiful pieces in a wide range of artistic styles, demonstrating how Costa Rican artists have interpreted the major European artistic movements. In addition to the permanent collection of sculptures, paintings, and prints, there are regular temporary exhibits. If the second floor is open during your visit, be sure to go up and have a look at the conference room's unusual bas-relief walls, which chronicle the history of Costa Rica from pre-Columbian times to the present with evocative images of the people.
   Admission: $2.05; Sun free (donation is suggested).
   Open: Daily 10am–5pm. **Bus:** Sabana-Cementerio.

MUSEO DE JADE MARCO FIDEL TRISTAN [Jade Museum], Avenida 7 between calles 9 and 9B, 11th floor, INS Building. Tel. 223-5800, ext. 2584.
   Among the pre-Columbian cultures of Mexico and Central America, jade was the most valuable commodity, worth more than gold. This modern museum displays a huge collection of jade artifacts from throughout Costa Rica's pre-Columbian archeological sites. Most of the jade pieces are large pendants that were parts of necklaces and are primarily human and animal figures dating from 330 B.C. to A.D. 700. There is also an extensive collection of pre-Columbian poly-chromed terra-cotta vases, bowls, and figurines. Particularly fascinating is a vase that incorporates real human teeth, and a display that shows how jade was imbedded in human teeth for decorative reasons.
   Admission: Free.
   Open: Mon–Fri 8am–3:30pm. **Bus:** Any bus to downtown.

MUSEO DE ORO BANCO CENTRAL [Gold Museum], Calle 5 between Avenida Central and Avenida 2. Tel. 223-0528.
   Located directly beneath the Plaza de la Cultura, this unusual underground museum houses one of the largest collections of pre-Columbian gold in the Americas. On display are more than 20,000 troy ounces of gold in more than 2,000 objects. The sheer number of small gold pieces can be overwhelming, however, the unusual display cases and complex lighting system show off every piece to its utmost. This museum also includes a gallery for temporary art exhibits and a numismatic and philatelic museum.
   Admission: Free.
   Open: Fri 1–5pm, Sat–Sun 10am–5pm. **Bus:** Any bus to downtown.

MUSEO NACIONAL DE COSTA RICA, Calle 17 between Avenida Central and Avenida 2. Tel. 257-1433.

Costa Rica's most important museum is housed in a former army barracks that was the scene of fighting during the civil war of 1948. You can still see hundreds of bullet holes on the turrets at the corners of the building. Inside this traditional Spanish-style courtyard building, you will find displays on Costa Rican history and culture from pre-Columbian times to the present. In the pre-Columbian rooms, you'll see a 2,500-year-old jade carving that is shaped like a seashell and etched with an image of a hand holding a small animal. Among the most fascinating objects unearthed at Costa Rica's many small archeological sites are *metates* or grinding stones. This type of grinding stone is still in use today throughout Central America. However, the ones on display here are more ornately decorated than those that you will see anywhere else. A separate vault houses the museum's small collection of pre-Columbian gold jewelry and figurines. In the courtyard, you'll see some of Costa Rica's mysterious stone spheres.

Admission: 70¢.

Open: Tues–Sat 8:30am–4:30pm, Sun 9am–4:30pm. **Bus:** San Pedro.

MUSEO NACIONAL DE CIENCIAS NATURALES "LA SALLE," across from the southwest corner of Parque la Sabana. Tel. 232-13016.

Before heading out to the wilds of the Costa Rican jungles, you might want to stop by this natural history museum and find out more about the animals you might be seeing. There are stuffed and mounted anteaters, monkeys, tapirs, and many others. The collection includes animals from all over the world as well. There are also 1,200 birds and 12,500 insects displayed. A collection of 13,500 seashells is another highlight.

Admission: 70¢ adults, 35¢ children.

Open: Mon–Fri 8am–3pm, Sat 8am–noon, Sun 9am–4pm. **Bus:** Escazú or Pavas from Avenida 1.

MUSEO DE ENTOMOLOGIA, University of Costa Rica, School of Music, San Pedro. Tel. 253-5323, ext 5042.

The tropics have produced the world's greatest concentration and diversity of insects, and here at this small museum, you can see more than one million mounted insects from around the world. The butterfly collection is the star attraction here, and many you may recognize during walks around the Costa Rican countryside.

Admission: $2.05.

Open: Mon–Fri 1–4:45pm. **Bus:** San Pedro from Avenida 2 between calles 5 and 7.

MORE ATTRACTIONS

PARQUE ZOOLÓGICO SIMÓN BOLÍVAR, Avenida 11 and Calle 11. Tel. 233-6701.

I don't think I have ever seen a sadder zoo than this little park tucked away beside the polluted Río Torres. It is a shame that a country that has preserved so much of its land in national parks would ignore this zoo. The cages here are only occasionally marked, and many are dirty and small. The collection includes Asian, African, and Costa Rican animals. For many years, there have been plans to build a new zoo with more modern displays, but as yet nothing has happened.

Admission: 55¢.

Open: Daily 8am–4pm. **Bus:** Any bus to downtown, then walk.

SERPENTARIUM, Avenida 1 between calles 9 and 11. Tel. 255-4210.

The tropics abound in reptiles and amphibians, and the Serpentarium is an excellent introduction to all that slithers and hops through the jungles of Costa Rica. The live snakes, lizards, and frogs are kept in beautiful large terrariums that simulate their natural environments. Poisonous snakes make up a large part of the collection with the dreaded fer-de-lance pit viper eliciting the most gasps from enthralled visitors. Also fascinating to see are the tiny, brilliantly colored poison arrow frogs. Iguanas and Jesus Christ lizards are two of the more commonly spotted of Costa Rica's reptiles, and both are represented here. This little zoological museum is

well worth a visit, especially if you plan to go bashing about in the jungles. It will help you identify the numerous poisonous snakes you'll want to avoid.
Admission: $2.05.
Open: Daily 9am–6pm. **Bus:** Any bus to downtown.

SPIROGYRA BUTTERFLY GARDEN, 100 meters east and 100 meters south of El Pueblo Shopping Center, Tel. 222-2937.
Butterflies have been likened to self-propelled flowers, so it comes as no surprise that butterfly gardens are becoming all the rage throughout the tropics these days. If you'd like to find out why, drop in here at Spirogyra. Though this butterfly garden is smaller and less spectacular than the Butterfly Farm, it is a good introduction to the life cycle of butterflies. You'll find Spirogyra near El Pueblo, a 30-minute walk from the center of San José.
Admission: $4.
Open: Wed–Mon 9am–4pm. **Bus:** Calle Blancos from Calle 3 and Avenida 5.

ATTRACTIONS OUTSIDE OF SAN JOSÉ

THE BUTTERFLY FARM, in front of Los Reyes Country Club, La Guácima de Alajuela. Tel. 438-0115.
At any given time, you may see around 30 of the 80 different species of butterflies raised at this butterfly farm south of Alajuela. The butterflies live in a large enclosed garden similar to an aviary and flutter about the heads of visitors during tours of the gardens. When we visited we saw glittering blue morphos and a butterfly that mimics the eyes of an owl. In the demonstration room you'll see butterfly eggs, caterpillars, and pupae. Among the latter, there are cocoons trimmed in a shimmering gold color and cocoons that mimic a snake's head in order to frighten away predators. The farm also offers a bee tour during which you can observe bees at work in glass observation hives.
Admission: $9 adults, $4 children ages 4–12, $6 students. Group rates available.
Open: Daily 9am–5pm. **Bus:** San Antonio/Ojo de Agua on Avenida 1 between calles 20 and 22.

CAFÉ BRITT FARM, north of Heredia on the road to Barva. Tel. 260-2748.
Though bananas are the main export of Costa Rica, people are far more interested in the country's second most important export—coffee. Café Britt is one of the leading brands of coffee here, and the company has put together an interesting tour and stage production at its farm 20 minutes outside of San José. Here, you'll see how coffee is grown. You'll also visit the roasting plant to learn how a coffee "cherry" is turned into a delicious roasted bean. Tasting sessions are offered for the visitor to experience the different qualities of coffee. There is also a store here where you can buy very reasonably priced coffee. Call the above number for the tour, which includes pickup at your hotel.
Admission: $15 adults, $7.50 children under age 12.
Open: Tours Dec–Apr, daily 9am, 11am, and 3pm; May–Oct, Mon–Sat 10am, Sun 10am and 12pm. Store open daily 8am–5pm.

LANKESTER GARDENS, Paraíso de Cartago, Tel. 551-9877.
There are more than 1,200 varieties of orchids in Costa Rica, and no less than 800 species are on display at this botanical garden in Cartago province. Created in the 1940s by English naturalist Charles Lankester, the gardens are now administered by the University of Costa Rica. The primary goal of the gardens is to preserve the local flora, with an emphasis on orchids and bromeliads. Paved trails wander from open sunny gardens into shady forests. In each environment, different species of orchids are in bloom. There are free guided tours, or you can wander on your own.
Admission: $2.05.
Open: Daily 8am–3pm. **Bus:** Cartago bus from San José, then Paraíso bus from the south side of the Central Park in Cartago.

MUSEO JOYAS DEL TROPICO HUMEDO (Jewels of the Rain Forest), 100 meters east of the cemetery of Santo Domingo de Heredia. No phone.
Far more than just another bug collection, this exhibit takes the position that insects are works of art, tiny tropical jewels. The displays are artistically arranged and include more than 50,000 arthropods (including thousands of different butterflies) collected from around the world by former Oregon biologist Richard Whitten and his wife Maggie.
Admission: $4.05 adults, 70¢ children under age 12.
Open: Tues–Sun 9am–1pm and 2–5pm. **Bus:** At Calle 1 between avenidas 7 and 9, take the Heredia/Tibás/Santo Domingo bus, then taxi from Santo Domingo.

ZOO AVE, La Garita, Alajuela. Tel. 433-9140.
Dozens of scarlet macaws, several different species of toucans, and other brilliantly colored birds from Costa Rica and around the world make this place an exciting one to visit. Bird-watching enthusiasts will be able to get a closer look at birds they may have seen in the wild. Look out for the 12-foot-long crocodile.
Admission: $4.75.
Open: Daily 9am–5pm. **Bus:** Catch an Alajuela bus on Avenida 2 between calles 12 and 14. In Alajuela, transfer to a bus for Atenas and get off at Zoo Ave before you get to La Garita.

WALKING TOUR — DOWNTOWN SAN JOSÉ

Start: Plaza de la Cultura.
Finish: Plaza de la Cultura.
Time: Allow a full day for this tour, though most of your time will be spent touring the three museums mentioned.
Best Time: Friday, when the maximum number of museums will be open.
Worst Time: Monday, when some museums may be closed.

Because San José is so compact, it is possible to visit nearly all of the city's major sites in a single day's walking tour. Begin your tour on the Plaza de la Cultura, perhaps after having breakfast at the Gran Hotel Costa Rica.

Begin by walking to the:

1. **Teatro Nacional,** which faces the entrance to the Gran Hotel Costa Rica. Be sure to take a walk around inside this baroque masterpiece. The café here is another great place to have a meal or a pastry and coffee. Next door is the:
2. **Gold Museum,** which is built beneath the Plaza de la Cultura to the left of the Teatro Nacional. This museum houses the largest collection of pre-Columbian gold in Central America. From the Gold Museum, walk two blocks west on Avenida 2 to reach the:
3. **National Cathedral,** a neoclassical structure with a tropical twist. The roof is tin, and the ceiling is wood. A statue of the Virgin Mary is surrounded by neon stars and a crescent moon. Diagonally across the street is the:
4. **Melico Salazar Theater.** This theater has an impressive pillared facade, though the interior is not nearly as ornate. Continue west on Avenida 2 and turn right on Calle 6. In two blocks, you will be in the:
5. **Mercado Central,** a fragrant (not necessarily pleasantly so) district of streets crowded with produce vendors. A covered market, with its dark warren of stalls, takes up an entire block and is the center of activity. Beware of pickpockets in this area. Head back toward the Teatro Nacional on Avenida 1, and in seven blocks you will come to an excellent place for lunch.

REFUELING STOP One of the best lunches in San José is at the **Amstel Grill Room,** Avenida 1 and Calle 7. White-jacketed waiters attend to your every

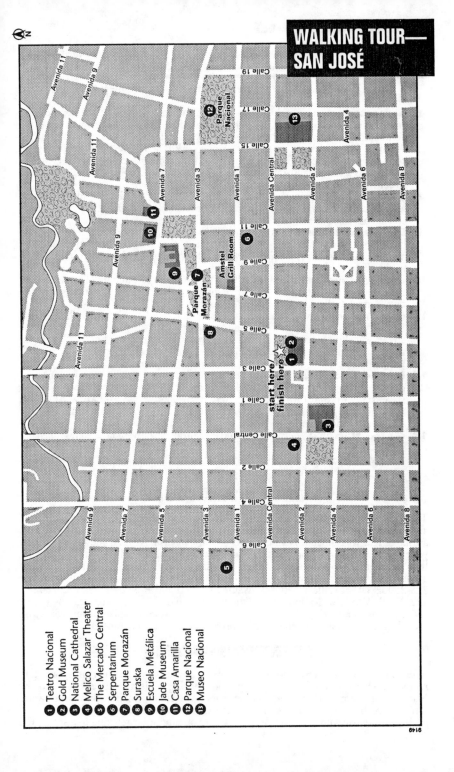

WALKING TOUR—
SAN JOSÉ

① Teatro Nacional
② Gold Museum
③ National Cathedral
④ Melico Salazar Theater
⑤ The Mercado Central
⑥ Serpentarium
⑦ Parque Morazán
⑧ Suraska
⑨ Escuela Metálica
⑩ Jade Museum
⑪ Casa Amarilla
⑫ Parque Nacional
⑬ Museo Nacional

start here/
finish here

need. The cuisine is American, Continental, and Costa Rican, and the prices are reasonable.

After lunch head over to the corner of Avenida 1 and Calle 9 where you'll find the:

6. **Serpentarium.** This indoor zoo offers a fascinating look at the reptiles and amphibians of Costa Rica and other parts of the world. When you leave the Serpentarium, head north on Calle 9 and you will come to:

7. **Parque Morazán,** a classically designed park that was restored to its original configuration in 1991. This is a good place for people-watching. At the center of the park is a large bandstand modeled after a music temple in Paris. Across the street from the west side of the park you'll find:

8. **Suraska,** a handcrafts shop with a good selection of products made from local woods, ceramics, and jewelry. Retrace your steps back to the far side of the park and across the street to the north, you will see the:

9. **Escuela Metálica,** Avenida 5 and Calle 9, which is one of the most unusual buildings in the city. It is made of metal panels that are bolted together, and was manufactured in Europe late in the 19th century. One block north, on Avenida 7, you'll come to the:

10. **Jade Museum,** which is located in a high-rise office building. The cool, dark exhibit halls are filled with jade pendants, and there are also great views of the city. Across Calle 11 from the Jade Museum is the:

11. **Casa Amarilla,** which is an attractive old building that now houses the Ministry of Foreign Affairs. This building, along with the park directly across the street, was donated to Costa Rica by Andrew Carnegie. From here walk back up the hill (east) to Calle 15 and turn right. Ahead of you, at the corner of Avenida 3, you will see the:

12. **Parque Nacional,** which has an impressive monument to the nations that defeated Tennessean William Walker's attempt to turn Central America into a slave state in the 19th century. Across Avenida 1 is a **statue of Juan Santamaría,** who gave his life to defeat Walker. If you continue south on Calle 17, you will find the:

13. **Museo Nacional,** between Avenida Central and Avenida 2. This museum houses Costa Rica's largest collection of pre-Columbian art and artifacts. After touring the museum, you need only head west on Avenida Central or Avenida 2 and in seven blocks you will be back at the Plaza de la Cultura.

ORGANIZED TOURS

There are literally dozens of tour companies operating in San José, and the barrage of advertising brochures can be quite intimidating. There really isn't much reason to take a tour of San José since it is so compact—you can easily visit all the major sites on your own. However, if you want to take a city tour, which will run you about $18, here are some companies: try **Otec Tours,** Edeficio Ferencz, Calle 3 between avenidas 1 and 3, Apdo. 323-1002, San José (tel. 255-0554, 222-0866, or 24-hour line 225-2500); **TAM,** Calle 1 between Avenida Central and Avenida 1 (tel. 222-2642 or 222-2732); **Vic-Vic Tours,** Calle 3 between avenidas 5 and 7 (tel. 233-3435); or **Swiss Travel Service,** (tel. 231-4055), which has several offices around San José including in the lobbies of the Hotel Corobici and the Hotel Amstel.

SPORTS/RECREATION

Sabana Park, formerly San José's airport, is the city's center for sports and recreation. Here you'll find everything from jogging trails and soccer fields to the National Stadium. For information on horseback riding, hiking, and white-water rafting trips from San José, see "Easy Excursions" at the end of this chapter.

If you like to swim and would like to spend an afternoon relaxing in a spring-fed swimming pool, head out to **Ojo de Agua,** which is just beyond the airport near Alajuela. The crystal-clear waters are cool and refreshing, and even if it seems a bit chilly in San José, it is always several degrees warmer out here. Admission is 70¢ and there are express buses from San José Monday through Saturday both in the morning and in the afternoon. These buses depart from Avenida 1 between calles 20 and 22.

7. SAVVY SHOPPING

In Costa Rica, you probably won't be overwhelmed with the desire to buy things the way you might be in other countries that have indigenous handcrafts, but there are a few interesting and unique items to buy. For lack of their own handcrafts, Costa Ricans do a brisk business of selling crafts and clothes imported from Guatemala.

THE SHOPPING SCENE

Shopping in San José centers around the parallel streets of Avenida Central and Avenida 2, from about Calle 14 in the west to Calle 13 in the east. For several blocks east of the Plaza de la Cultura, Avenida Central is a pedestrian-only street where you'll find store after store of inexpensive clothes for men, women, and children. Most shops in the downtown shopping district are open from Monday to Saturday from about 8:30am to noon and from about 2 to 6pm. You'll find that some shops close for lunch while others remain open. When you do purchase something, you'll be happy to find that there is no sales tax.

There are several markets around downtown San José, but by far the largest is the **Mercado Central,** which is located between Avenida Central and Avenida 1 and calles 6 and 8. Inside this dark maze of stalls you'll find all manner of vendors. Although this is primarily a food market, you can find a few vendors selling Costa Rican souvenirs. Be especially careful about your wallet or purse because this area is frequented by very skillful pickpockets. All the streets surrounding the Mercado Central are jammed with produce vendors selling from small carts or loading and unloading trucks. It is always a hive of activity, with crowds of people jostling for space on the streets. In the hot days of the dry season, the aromas can get quite heady.

International laws prohibit purchasing endangered wildlife—visitors to Costa Rica should not buy any wildlife or plants, even if it is legal. The Audubon Society does not tolerate the sale of any kind of sea turtle products (including jewelry), wild birds, lizard or snake skin, coral, or orchids (except those grown commercially).

Just in case you discover when you get home that the photos you took on your trip don't capture the beauty of Costa Rica, you might want to buy one of the picture books on Costa Rica mentioned in the "Recommended Books" section of Chapter 1.

BEST BUYS

MARKETS

MERCADO CENTRAL, Between Avenida Central and Avenida 1 and calles 6 and 8. No phone.
This rabbit warren of a market sells primarily food, but you can also find some interesting local household goods, tools, and the usual souvenirs. A good place for people-watching, but also keep an eye on your wallet or purse. On Sundays, only a few vendors are open.

COFFEE

Two words of advice—buy coffee. Buy as much as you can carry. Coffee is probably the best shopping deal in all of Costa Rica. Although the best Costa Rican coffee is supposedly shipped off to North American and European markets, it is hard to beat coffee that is roasted right in front of you. Though Café Britt is the big name in Costa Rican coffee, it is also the most expensive. For good flavor and value, visit **Café Trebol,** on Calle 8 between Avenida Central and Avenida 1. Be sure to ask for whole beans; Costa Rican grinds are too fine for standard coffee filters. Best of all is the price: One pound of coffee sells for very little! If you should happen to buy prepackaged coffee in a supermarket in Costa Rica, be sure the package is marked *puro;* otherwise, it will likely be mixed with a good amount of sugar—the way Ticos like it.

HANDCRAFTS

If your interest is in handcrafts, there are many places for you to visit. The most appealing artisan's market is the daily one on the Plaza de la Cultura. Prices here tend to be high and bargaining is necessary, but there are some very nice items for sale. If you prefer to do your craft shopping in a flea-market atmosphere, head over to **La Casona** on Calle Central between Avenida Central and Avenida 1.

ANNEMARIE SOUVENIR SHOP, Calle 9 between avenidas 7 and 9. Tel. 221-6063.

Tucked into the lobby of the Hotel Don Carlos, this shop has an amazing array of wood products, leather goods, papier mâché figurines, paintings, books, cards, posters, and jewelry, to mention just a few of the things you'll find here. Don't miss this shopping experience.

ATMÓSFERA, Calle 5 between avenidas 1 and 3. Tel. 222-4322.

This place has high-quality Costa Rican arts and crafts, from naive paintings and sculpture to skilled turned-wood bowls. It consists of several small rooms on two floors, so be sure to explore every nook and cranny—you'll see stuff here that is not available anywhere else in town.

LA GALERÍA, Calle 1 between Avenida Central and Avenida 1. Tel. 221-3436.

This small store features some of the best of modern Costa Rican handcrafts. There is a fine selection of wood carvings and gold and silver pre-Columbian jewelry reproductions, paintings and prints with Latin American themes, metalware, and rugs. The little boxes and bowls of native Costa Rican hardwoods are particularly attractive.

MERCADO DE ARTESANOS CANAPI, Calle 11 and Avenida 1. Tel. 221-3342.

The most unusual crafts for sale here are the brightly painted miniature oxcarts that are almost the national symbol. These oxcarts are made in the small town of Sarchí, which is mentioned under "Easy Excursions" in this chapter. This store also carries a wide variety of typical Costa Rican handcrafts, including large, comfortable woven rope hammocks; reproductions of pre-Columbian gold jewelry and pottery bowls; coffee-wood carvings; and many other wood carvings from rare Costa Rican hardwoods.

SURASKA, Calle 5 and Avenida 3. Tel. 222-0129.

If you haven't been impressed with the quality of Costa Rican handcrafts, save your money for a visit to this store. Among the selections here are ceramics, mobiles, and jewelry. Of particular note are the wood carvings of North American artist Barry Biesanz, who turns out exquisite pieces of finely worked hardwood. Be forewarned, however, that these pieces are expensive.

8. EVENING ENTERTAINMENT

To find out about the entertainment scene in San José, pick up a copy of the *Tico Times* (English) and *La Nacion* (Spanish). The former is a good place to find out where local expatriates are hanging out; the latter's "Viva" section has extensive listings of everything from discos to movie theaters to live music.

THE PERFORMING ARTS

TEATRO NACIONAL, Avenida 2 between calles 3 and 5. Tel. 221-1329.

Financed with a self-imposed tax on coffee exports, this grand baroque theater was completed in 1897. Muses representing Music, Fame, and Dance gaze off into the distance from the roof, while statues of Beethoven and Calderón de la Barca flank the entrance. The lobby is simple and elegant. Marble floors, frescoes, and gold-framed Venetian mirrors offer cultured Ticos a grand foyer in which to congregate prior to performances by the National Symphony Orchestra, ballet companies, opera companies, and all the other performers who keep this theater busy almost every night of the year. Within the hall itself, there are three tiers of seating amid an elegant gilt-and-plasterwork decor, and of course the wealthy patrons have their private box seats. Marble staircases are lined with sculptures; the walls are covered with murals and changing art exhibits. The symphony season begins in late April, shortly before the start of the rainy season, and continues until November.

Open: Mon–Sat 9am–noon and 1:30–5pm.
Prices: Tour tickets $2.40; tickets for performances $1.35–$6.10; purchasers of cheaper tickets must use side entrance. **Bus:** Sabana-Cementerio.

TEATRO MELICO SALAZAR, Avenida 2 between Calle Central and Calle 2. Tel. 221-4952.

Just a few blocks away from the Teatro Nacional, and directly across the street from the Parque Central, is this 1920s neoclassical theater. Though the facade is far more impressive than the interior, it is still a grand old theater. "Fantasia Folclórico," which features modern dance, pantomime, and traditional dances that together tell the history of Costa Rica, is staged every Tuesday night at 8pm. The box office is open daily from 9am to noon and from 2 to 8pm.

Prices: $4.05–$10.15. **Bus:** Sabana-Cementerio.

THE CLUB & MUSIC SCENE

Salsa is the music of young people in San José, and on any weekend you can join the fun at half a dozen or more high-decibel nightclubs around town. The "Viva" section of *La Nacion* newspaper has weekly performance schedules. A couple of performing groups (*grupos*) to watch for are "Marfil" and "Los Brillanticos."

The best place to sample San José's nightclub scene is in El Pueblo, a shopping, dining, and entertainment complex done up like an old Spanish village. It's just across the river to the north of town. The best way to get here is by taxi. Within the alleyways that wind through El Pueblo are a dozen or more bars, clubs, and discos. **Cocoloco** (tel. 222-8782) and **Discoteque Infinito** (tel. 233-0988) are El Pueblos' two main discos. **Manhattan** is a piano bar, and the **Tango Bar** is just what its name implies.

LIVE MUSIC

AKELARE, Calle 21 between avenidas 4 and 6. Tel. 223-0345.

This popular club is located in a renovated old house near the National Museum. There are many rooms in which to check out the action, as well as a garden out back. There are frequent live music performances by hot Costa Rican groups.

LA ESMERALDA, Avenida 2 between calles 5 and 7. Tel. 221-0530.

A sort of mariachi Grand Central Station, La Esmeralda is a cavernous open-air restaurant and bar that stays open 24 hours a day. In the evenings, mariachi bands park their vans out front and wait to be hired for a moonlight serenade or perhaps a surprise party. While they wait, they often wander into La Esmeralda and practice their favorite melodies. If you've never been serenaded at your table before, this place is a must.

KEY LARGO, Calle 7 between avenidas 1 and 3. Tel. 221-0277.

Housed in one of the most beautiful old buildings in San José, Key Largo is elegant and expensive and the best-known nightclub in Costa Rica. It's worth a visit just to see the interior of the building, but be forewarned—this is known as San José's number one prostitute hangout.

DISCOS

SALSA 54, Calle 3 between avenidas 1 and 3. No phone.
A place to go to watch expert salsa dance, and try some yourself. You might even run into a Latin dance class here.

LAS TUNAS, Sabana North, 500 meters west of I.C.E. office. Tel. 231-1802.
This happening place serves Mexican food and barbecue, but where it really cooks is in the bar and discotheque, where live Costa Rican pop music is featured weekly.

THE BAR SCENE

The best part of the varied bar scene in San José is something called a *boca,* the equivalent of a *tapa* in Spain, a little dish of snacks that arrives at your table when you order a drink. In most bars, the bocas are free; but in some, where the dishes are more sophisticated, you'll have to pay for the treats. Also, with the exception of Key Largo, drinks are very reasonably priced at 85¢ to $3.40.

CHARLESTON, Avenida 4 between calles 7 and 9. Tel. 255-3993.
Jazz lovers will enjoy this relaxed bar, which has a 1920s theme. Great recorded jazz music plays on the stereo all day and night. There are occasional live bands.

EL CUARTEL DE LA BOCA DEL MONTE, Avenida 1 between calles 21 and 23. Tel. 221-0327.
This very popular bar is reputed to have the best bocas in San José, although you'll have to pay for them. Their cocktails are also famous. Just look around and see what sort of amazing concoctions people are drinking and ask for whichever one strikes your fancy.

SODA PALACE, Calle 2 and Avenida 2. Tel. 221-3441.
Mostly a men's hangout, this dingy but brightly lit bar hardly lives up to its name, but it is a Costa Rican institution. It opens directly onto busy Avenida 2 and is open 24 hours a day. Men of all ages sit at the tables conversing loudly and watching the world pass by. You never know what might happen at the Palace. Mariachis stroll in, linger for a while, then continue on their way. Legend has it that the revolution of 1948 was planned right here.

RIO, Avenida Central, Los Yoses. Tel. 253-5088.
This bar and restaurant is close to the University of Costa Rica and consequently attracts a younger clientele. Rio is always packed to overflowing at night with the wealthy and the wanna-be's of San José.

RISA'S BAR, Calle 1 between Avenida Central and Avenida 1. Tel. 223-2803.
This second-floor bar is in a beautiful old building in the heart of downtown San José. There's a big dug-out canoe over the bar, but the exposed brick walls and U.S. rock videos give Risa's a very North American urban atmosphere. The music is loud!

MORE ENTERTAINMENT

MOVIE THEATERS At most movie theaters in downtown San José, the screens are huge and movies are shown in English with Spanish subtitles. Check the "Viva" section of *La Nacion* or the *Tico Times* for movie listings and times. Tickets are between $1.75 and $2.

GAMBLING CASINOS   Gambling is legal in Costa Rica, and there are casinos at virtually every major hotel. In most of these hotel casinos, you'll need to get dressed up; but at the casino in the lobby of the Gran Hotel Costa Rica, at Calle 3 between Avenida Central and Avenida 2, on the Plaza de la Cultura, there doesn't seem to be any dress code.

9. NETWORKS & RESOURCES

FOR STUDENTS   The University of Costa Rica is located north of the church in San Pedro, which is an eastern suburb of San José. If you're looking to meet other college students check with the university administrative office or try hanging out in some of the many bars in this neighborhood.
 Ask at the **Toruma Youth Hostel,** Avenida Central between calles 29 and 31 (tel. 224-4085) in San José for information on hostels around Costa Rica. There is also a student travel agency: **OTEC,** Edificio Ferencz, 2nd floor, Calle 3 between avenidas 1 and 3, 275 meters north of the National Theater (tel. 255-0554 or 222-0866) where you can get an **international student identity card** for discounts on airfares, hostels, national and international tours and excursions, car rentals, and store purchases.

FOR GAY MEN & LESBIANS   The **International Gay and Lesbian Association** (tel. 234-2411) is a place to contact for information and weekly meetings.

FOR WOMEN   Feeling safe   Costa Rican men may occasionally hiss at you (an attention-getting device) on the street, but if you ignore them they will leave you alone. On the whole, Ticos are very well mannered.
 Organizations   **Casa de la Nueva Mujer** (House of the New Woman) is a meeting place, pension, and a place to hang out. It also offers Spanish courses and specialized trips for women visiting Costa Rica. Tours include day trips to such places as Irazú Volcano and multiday trips to Santa Rosa National Park. It is 250 meters north and 100 meters east of La Cosecha market on Sabanilla's main street (tel. 225-3784).
 Accommodations   Women visitors can stay at **Casa de la Nueva Mujer** (see above) for less than $10 a night.

FOR SENIORS   **Elderhostel,** 75 Federal St., Boston, MA 02110 (tel. 617/426-7788), offers very popular study tours to Costa Rica. To participate in an Elderhostel program, either you or your spouse must be at least 60 years old.

10. EASY EXCURSIONS

San José makes an excellent base for exploring the beautiful Meseta Central and the surrounding mountains, and in fact it is possible to explore much of the country on day tours from here. Probably the best way to make the most of these excursions is on guided tours, though if you rent a car, you'll have greater independence. Guided tours are expensive, however (generally around $65 or $70), so must be considered a splurge if you're traveling on a budget. There are also some day trips that can be done by public bus. Below is information on many of the day tours that are offered by tour companies in San José. I have arranged these by type of activity. In addition to the tours listed below, there are many other tours, some of which combine two or three different activities or destinations. Companies offering a wide variety of primarily nature-related day tours out of San José include **Costa Rica Expeditions** (tel. 257-0766 or 222-0333), **Costa Rica Sun Tours** (tel. 255-3418), **Geotur** (tel. 234-1867 or 224-1899), **Otec Tours** (tel. 255-0554 or 222-0866), and **Swiss Travel Service** (tel. 231-4055).

Before signing on for a tour of any sort, find out how much time is spent in transit and eating lunch and how much time is actually spent doing the primary activity. I've had a complaint about the Carara Biological Reserve tours, which spend most of their time on the road or in Jacó Beach. Most tours include transportation and one or two meals.

RECREATIONAL DAY TRIPS

BICYCLING   Narrow mountain roads with spectacular views make for some great, though strenuous, bicycling in Costa Rica. **Rios Tropicales** (tel. 233-6455) offers a day-long mountain-bike trip to Tapantí National Park. Most of this ride is downhill, and there are numerous opportunities to bird-watch and explore nature trails. The cost is $70. Rios Tropicales also offers multi-day biking and rafting trips. When I was last in Costa Rica, the **Costa Verde Inn** (tel. 228-4080) in Escazú had just begun offering downhill volcano rides. These rides start at the top of Poás Volcano and roll for 18 kilometers down the slopes of the volcano. The tour costs $65.

CRUISES   Several companies offer cruises to remote islands in the Gulf of Nicoya, and these excursions include gourmet buffet meals and stops at deserted (until your boat arrives) beaches. Companies offering these trips include **Calypso Tours** (tel. 233-3617), **Bay Island Cruises** (tel. 239-4951 or 239-4952), **Costa Sol Tropical Cruises** (tel. 239-2000), **Sea Ventures** (tel. 257-2904 or 257-3097), and **Fantasia** (tel. 255-0791). The cruises cost $70 and include transportation from San José to Puntarenas and back. Most of these companies also offer various sunset cruises and dinner cruises. Calypso Tours also offers catamaran sailing trips around the Gulf of Nicoya for $79.

A FLOWER FARM   If you're a flower fancier and would like to visit a tropical flower farm, contact **Adventours of Costa Flores** (tel. 220-1311). Costa Flores is the largest tropical flower farm in the world and grows more than 600 varieties of tropical flowers. Strikingly beautiful heliconias are the main produce of this farm. A trip to the farm costs $70.

HIKING   If you do not plan to visit Monteverde or one of Costa Rica's other cloud forest reserves, consider doing a day tour to a cloud forest. Guided hikes through these misty high-altitude forests provide an opportunity to visit one of the tropics' most fascinating habitats. Bird-watching and a chance to learn about the ecology of the cloud forest are the main attractions of these trips. One of the most popular and highly recommended hiking tours is to the Los Angeles Cloud Forest Reserve. This tour is operated by **Hotel Villablanca** (tel. 228-4603) and includes a 3-hour guided walk through the cloud forest. The cost is $70. Hiking tours through the cloud forest on Barva Volcano are offered by **Jungle Trails** (tel. 255-3486) for $75 per person. This trip offers a chance to see the resplendent quetzal. Another cloud forest day hike is offered by **Senderos de Iberoamérica** (tel. 255-2859). This trip takes you to the Los Juncos Biological Reserve for a total of five hours of guided walks. The cost is $70.

HORSEBACK RIDING   If you enjoy horseback riding, you have your choice of many fascinating locations near San José for day-long trips. The going rate for a day trip out of San José to go horseback riding is around $70 per person for a 4-hour guided ride. **L.A. Tours** (tel. 221-4501) offers rides through pastures and along the beach. **Sacramento Horseback Ride** (tel. 237-2116 or 237-2441) offers rides through mountain forests and pastures. Great view! **Viajes Alrededor del Mundo** (tel. 221-3060 or 222-5005) offers a trip through the cloud forest on the flank of Poás Volcano. The ride visits two different waterfalls.

PRE-COLUMBIAN RUINS Though Costa Rica lacks such massive pre-Columbian archeological sites as can be found in Guatemala or Honduras, it does have Guayabo National Monument, a small excavated town, which today is but a collection of building foundations, cobbled streets, and the like. **Senderos de Iberoamérica** (tel. 255-2859) offers trips to the monument to see Costa Rica's most extensively excavated pre-Columbian archeological site. The tour costs $70.

RAFTING, KAYAKING & RIVER TRIPS Cascading down from Costa Rica's mountain ranges are dozens of tumultuous rivers, several of which have become very popular for white-water rafting and kayaking. For between $65 and $90, you can spend a day rafting through lush tropical forests. Longer trips are also available. Some of the more reliable rafting companies are **Costa Rica Expeditions** (tel. 257-0766); **Rios Tropicales** (tel. 233-6455), and **Costaricaraft** (tel. 225-3939). If I had to choose just one day trip to do out of San José, it would be a white-water rafting trip. Rios Tropicales also offers sea kayaking trips in Curú Bay ($85) and three different sea kayaking trips from Manuel Antonio (see Chapter 6 for details on these latter trips).
   There are also some raft and boat trips on calmer waters. These trips usually focus on the wildlife and scenery along the river. **Panamericana de Viajes** (tel. 223-4567) offers a leisurely float, during which you'll have ample opportunities to photograph the Tarcoles River's many crocodiles. The trip costs $75.
   Uno Travel Services (tel. 253-7589 or 253-6759) offers tours that include a boat trip down the Sarapiquí River. The scenery along this river is a combination of rain forest and farms. These tours also include a stop at either Poás Volcano ($95 per person) or Arenal Volcano ($115 per person). You can also kayak the Sarapiquí River. Trips are offered by **Rancho Leona**, La Virgen de Sarapiquí, Heredia (tel. 761-1019). For $80 you get a day of kayaking plus two nights' lodging in shared accommodations (bunks) at the ranch's private hostel. Lunch on the day of your kayak trip is included in the price, but other meals are not. Be sure to ask about getting there when making a reservation.

RAIN FOREST AERIAL TRAM By the time you arrive in Costa Rica, you should be hearing all about the Rainforest Aerial Tram. The tramway was under construction on a private reserve bordering Braulio Carillo National Park when we were last in Costa Rica. The tramway is the dream of rain forest researcher Dr. Donald Perry, whose cable-car system through the forest canopy at Rara Avis helped him to spend years studying and writing about that little-known yet most important aspect of the rain forest environment. The tramway will take visitors on a 90-minute ride through the rain forest tree tops, where they will have a chance to glimpse the complex web of life that makes these forests so unique. The cost for tours, including transportation from San José, is expected to be around $70. Check with any tour operator in San José to find out more about this excursion.

TRAIN EXCURSIONS For many years the most popular excursion from San José was the so-called jungle train that chugged from San José to Limón amid rugged and remote scenery. This train no longer operates, but a section of the track is still used for a railroad excursion known as the **Banana Train.** This excursion is operated by **Swiss Travel Service** (tel. 231-4055) and includes a tour of a banana plantation and a short trip in restored narrow-gauge railway cars. The **Green Train** is a similar excursion operated by **TAM Tours** (tel. 222-2642 or 222-2732). Either trip will cost you $70.

VOLCANO TRIPS Poás, Irazú, and Arenal volcanoes are three of Costa Rica's most popular destinations. For more information on the Arenal Volcano, see Chapter 5, and for more information on Poás and Irazú, see below. Numerous tour companies in San José offer trips to all three volcanoes, and though the trips to Poás and Irazú take only a half day, the trips to Arenal take all day. I don't recommend these latter trips because you arrive when Arenal is hidden by clouds and leave before the night's darkness shows off the volcano's glowing eruptions. Tour companies offering trips to Poás and Irazú include **Costa Rica Expeditions** (tel. 257-0766 or 222-0333), **Costa Rica Sun Tours** (tel. 255-3418), **Otec Tours** (tel. 255-0554 or 222-0866), and **Swiss Travel Service** (tel. 231-4055). Prices range from $28 for a half-day trip to $55 for a full-day trip.

CARTAGO, THE OROSI VALLEY & IRAZÚ VOLCANO

Located about 15 miles southeast of San José, Cartago is the former capital of Costa Rica. Founded in 1563, it was Costa Rica's first city. Irazú Volcano rises up from the edge of town, and although it is quiescent these days, it has not always been so peaceful. Earthquakes have damaged Cartago repeatedly over the years, so that today there are few colonial buildings left standing. However, in the center of the city are the ruins of a large church that was destroyed in 1910, before it was ever finished. Construction was abandoned after the quake, and today the ruins are a neatly manicured park.

Cartago's most famous building, however, is the **Basílica de Nuestra Señora de Los Ángeles** (the Basilica of Our Lady of the Angels), which is dedicated to the patron saint of Costa Rica and stands on the east side of town. Within the walls of this Byzantine-style church is a shrine containing the tiny figure of La Negrita, the Black Virgin, which is nearly lost amid its ornate altar. This statue was found at a spring that now bubbles up at the rear of the church on the right side. Miraculous healing powers have been attributed to La Negrita, and over the years thousands of pilgrims have come to the shrine seeking cures for their illnesses and difficulties. The walls of the shrine are covered with a fascinating array of tiny silver images left as thanks for cures effected by La Negrita. Amid the plethora of diminutive arms and legs, there are also hands, feet, hearts, lungs, eyes—and, peculiarly, guns, trucks, and planes. August 2 is the day dedicated to La Negrita. On this day thousands of people walk from San José to Cartago in devotion to this powerful statue.

If you'd like to soak in a warm-water swimming pool, head 4 kilometers south of Cartago to Aguas Calientes. A few kilometers east of Cartago, you'll find Lankester Gardens, a botanical garden known for its orchid collection. See "Attractions," above, for details.

Buses for Cartago leave San José frequently from Calle 5 and Avenida 18. The length of the trip is 45 minutes; the fare is about 45¢.

Located 32 kilometers north of Cartago, 11,260-foot-tall Irazú Volcano is one of Costa Rica's more active volcanoes, although at this time it is dormant. It last erupted on March 19, 1963, on the day that President John F. Kennedy arrived in Costa Rica. The eruption showered ash on the Meseta Central for months after, destroying crops and collapsing roofs but enriching the soil. There is a good paved road right to the rim of the crater, where a desolate expanse of gray sand nurtures few plants and the air smells of sulfur. If you arrive early enough, you may be treated to a view of both the Pacific Ocean and the Caribbean Sea. Clouds descend by noon, so schedule your trip up here as early in the day as possible. From the parking area, a short trail leads to the rim of the volcano's two craters, their walls a maze of eroded gullies feeding onto the flat floor far below. This is a national park and is officially open only from 8am to 4pm, but there is nothing to stop you from visiting earlier. Don't forget to wear warm clothes—it's cold up at the top. In the busy season, an admission of $1.35 is charged.

Buses leave for Irazú Volcano Saturday, Sunday, and holidays from Avenida 2 between calles 1 and 3 (in front of the Gran Hotel Costa Rica). The fare is around $4.90 and the trip takes about 1½ hours. To make sure the buses are running, phone 272-0651. If you are driving, head northeast out of Cartago toward San Rafael, then continue driving uphill toward the volcano, passing the turnoffs for Cot and Tierra Blanca en route.

The Orosi Valley, southeast of Cartago and frequently visible from the top of Irazú, is called the most beautiful valley in Costa Rica. The Reventazón River meanders through this steep-sided valley until it collects in the lake formed by the Cachí Dam. There are scenic overlooks near the town of Orosi, which is at the head of the valley, and in Ujarrás, which is on the banks of the lake. Near Ujarrás are the ruins of Costa Rica's oldest church, whose tranquil gardens are a great place to sit and gaze at the surrounding mountains. Across the lake is a popular recreation center, called Charrarra, where you'll find a picnic area, swimming pool, and hiking trails. In the town of Orosi itself is a colonial church built in 1743. A small museum here displays religious artifacts.

It would be difficult to explore this whole area by public bus, since this is not a densely populated region. However, there are buses from Cartago to the town of Orosi. During the week, these buses run every half hour and leave from a spot one block east and three blocks south of the church ruins in Cartago. Saturday and Sunday, a bus runs every hour from the same vicinity and will drop you at the Orosi lookout point. The trip takes 30 minutes, and the fare is 30¢. If you are driving, take the road to Paraíso from Cartago, head toward Ujarrás, continue around the lake, then pass through Cachí and on to Orosi. From Orosi, the road leads back to Paraíso. There are also guided day tours of this area from San José.

POÁS VOLCANO

This is another active volcano accessible from San José in a day trip. It is 58 kilometers from San José on narrow roads that wind through a landscape of fertile farms and dark forests. As at Irazú, there is a paved road right to the top. The volcano stands 8,800 feet tall and is located within a national park, which preserves not only the volcano but also dense stands of virgin forest. Poás's crater is nearly a mile across and is said to be the second-largest crater in the world. Geysers in the crater sometimes spew steam and muddy water 600 feet into the air, making this the world's largest geyser. There is an information center where you can see a slide show about the volcano, and marked hiking trails through the cloud forest that rings the crater. About 20 minutes from the parking area, along a forest trail, is an overlook onto beautiful Botos Lake, which has formed in one of the volcano's extinct craters.

Because the sulfur fumes occasionally become dangerously strong at Poás, the park is sometimes closed to the public. Before heading out for the volcano, contact the tourist office to make sure that the park is open. The admission fee is $1.35.

There is an excursion bus on Sunday leaving from Calle 12 and avenidas 2 and 4 at 8:30am and returning at 2:30pm. The fare is $3.65 for the round trip. The bus is always crowded, so arrive early. Other days, take a bus to Alajuela, then a bus to San Pedro de Poás. From there you will have to hitchhike or take a taxi ($20 round trip), which makes this alternative as costly as a tour. All the tour companies in San José offer excursions to Poás, although they often don't arrive until after the clouds have closed in. If you're traveling by car, head for Alajuela and continue on the main road through town toward Varablanca. Just before reaching Varablanca, turn left toward Poasito and continue to the rim of the volcano.

HEREDIA, ALAJUELA, GRECIA, SARCHÍ & ZARCERO

All of these cities and towns are northwest of San José and can be combined into a long day trip, perhaps in conjunction with a visit to Poás Volcano.

Heredia was founded in 1706. On its central park stands a colonial church dedicated in 1763. The stone facade leaves no questions as to the age of the church, but the altar inside is decorated with neon stars and a crescent moon surrounding a statue of the Virgin Mary. In the middle of the palm-shaded park is a music temple, and across the street is the tower of an old Spanish fort. Of all the cities in the Meseta Central, this is the only one that has even the slightest colonial feeling to it.

Alajuela is one of Costa Rica's oldest cities and is located only 19 kilometers from San José. Although it is an attractive little city filled with parks, there isn't much to see or do here. The **Juan Santamaría Historical Museum**, Avenida 3 between Calle Central and Calle 2 (tel. 442-1838), commemorates Costa Rica's national hero, who gave his life defending the country against a small army led by William Walker, a U.S. citizen who invaded Costa Rica in 1856. Open Tuesday through Sunday 8am to 6pm; admission is free.

From Alajuela, a narrow, winding road leads to the town of **Grecia,** which is noteworthy for its unusual metal church, painted a deep red with white gingerbread trim. The road to Sarchí is to the right as you go around the church.

Sarchí is Costa Rica's main artisan's town. It is here that the colorfully painted miniature oxcarts you see all over Costa Rica are made. Oxcarts such as these were once used to haul coffee beans to market. Today, though you may occasionally see oxcarts in use, most are purely decorative. However, they remain a well-known symbol of Costa Rica. In addition to miniature oxcarts, many other carved wooden souvenirs are made here. There are dozens of shops in the town, and all have similar prices. The other reason to visit Sarchí is to see its unforgettable church. Built between 1950 and 1958, the church is painted pink with aquamarine trim and looks strangely like a child's birthday cake.

Beyond Sarchí, on picturesque roads lined with cedar trees, you will find the town of **Zarcero.** In a small park in the middle of town is a menagerie of topiary sculptures (sculpted shrubs) that includes a monkey on a motorcycle, people and animals dancing, and an ox pulling a cart. It is well worth the drive to see this park.

The road to Heredia turns north off the highway from San José to the airport. To reach Alajuela from Heredia, take the scenic road that heads west through the town of San Joaquín. To continue on to Sarchí, it is best to return to the highway south of Alajuela and drive west toward Puntarenas. Turn north to Grecia and then west to Sarchí.

TURRIALBA

This attractive little town 53 kilometers east of San José is best known as the starting and ending point for popular white-water rafting trips. However, it is also worth a visit if you have an interest in pre-Columbian history or botany. **Guayabo National Monument** is one of Costa Rica's only pre-Columbian sites that is open to the public. It's located 19 kilometers northeast of Turrialba and preserves a townsite that dates to between 1000 BC and AD 1400. Archeologists believe that Guayabo may have had a population of as many as 10,000 people, but there is no clue yet as to why the city was eventually abandoned shortly before the Spanish arrived in the New World. Excavated ruins at Guayabo consist of paved roads, aqueducts, stone bridges, and house and temple foundations. There are also grave sites and petroglyphs. The monument is open daily from 8am to 3pm, and admission is $1.35.

Botanists and gardeners may want to pay a visit to the **Center for Agronomy Research and Development (CATIE),** which is located 5 kilometers southeast of Turrialba on the road to Siquerres. This center is one of the world's foremost facilities for research in tropical agriculture. Among the plants on CATIE's 2,000 acres are hundreds of varieties of cacao and thousands of varieties of coffee. The plants here have been collected from all over the world. In addition to trees used for food and wood products, there are also plants grown strictly for ornamental purposes. CATIE is open Monday through Friday from 7am to 4pm. For information on guided tours, phone 556-6431.

While you are in the area, don't miss an opportunity to spend a little time at **Turrialtico** (tel. 556-1111) an open-air restaurant and small hotel high on a hill overlooking the Turrialba Valley. The view from here is one of the finest in the country, with the lush green valley far below and volcanoes in the distance. Meals are quite inexpensive and a room will cost you only $20. This place is popular with rafting companies.

CHAPTER 4

GUANACASTE & THE NICOYA PENINSULA

Guanacaste province, in northwestern Costa Rica, is the nation's sunniest and driest region. The rainy season here starts later and ends earlier, and even the dry season is more dependably sunny than in other parts of the country. Combine this climate with a coastline that stretches from the Nicaraguan border to the southern tip of the Nicoya Peninsula and you have an equation that equals beach bliss. Beautiful beaches abound along this coastline. Some are pristine and deserted, some are lined with luxury resort hotels, and others are backed by little villages where you can still get a room for under $30. These beaches vary from long, straight stretches of sand to tiny coves bordered by rocky headlands. Whatever your passion in beaches, you're likely to find something that comes close to perfection.

There is, however, one caveat. During the dry season, the hillsides of Guanacaste turn browner than the chaparral of southern California. Dust from dirt roads blankets the trees in many areas and the vistas are far from tropical. However, if you can't tolerate the least bit of rain on your holiday in the sun, the beaches up here are where you'll want to be.

Guanacaste is also Costa Rica's Wild West, a dry landscape of cattle ranches and *sabaneros* (cowboys), a name that derives from the Spanish word for grassland. If it weren't for those rain-forest clad volcanoes in the distance, you might swear you were in Texas. However, Guanacaste hasn't always looked this way. At one time this land was covered with a dense, though fairly dry, forest that was cut for lumber. The land was then turned into pasturelands for cattle. Today that dry tropical forest exists only in remnants preserved in several national parks. Up in the mountains, in Rincón de la Vieja National Park, not only will you find forests and wildlife, but you'll also find hot springs and bubbling mudpots.

---

1. LIBERIA

232 kilometers NW of San José; 133 kilometers NW of Puntarenas

GETTING THERE By Air The airstrip in Liberia was recently expanded to accommodate commercial international flights, but at the time of publishing, flights were not yet going into Liberia.

By Bus Express buses leave San José eight times daily from Calle 14 between

WHAT'S SPECIAL ABOUT GUANACASTE & THE NICOYA PENINSULA

Beaches

- ☐ Playa Conchal, which is formed from crushed seashells.
- ☐ Playa Flamingo, one of the whitest beaches on this coast.
- ☐ The beaches of Ostional National Wildlife Refuge (not far from Nosara), almost always deserted.

Parks/Gardens

- ☐ Rincón de la Vieja, site of numerous hot springs, steam vents, and bubbling mudpots.
- ☐ Santa Rosa and Guanacaste national parks, which include some of the last tropical dry forest in Central America.
- ☐ Cabo Blanco Absolute Nature Preserve, with its howler monkeys and deserted beaches.

Natural Spectacles

- ☐ Every year, hundreds of thousands of turtles lay their eggs on beaches in Santa Rosa National Park.
- ☐ Nesting turtles on Playa Grande, near Tamarindo.

Activities

- ☐ Sportfishing for billfish off the northwest coast.
- ☐ Scuba diving around the Bat Islands.
- ☐ Rafting float trips on the Corobicí River.
- ☐ Hot surfing at Tamarindo and at Witch's Rock in Santa Rosa National Park.

---

avenidas 1 and 3. Duration: 4 hours. Fare: $3.60. From Puntarenas, buses leave four times daily. Duration: 2 hours. Fare: $2.10.

By Car   Take the Interamerican Highway west out of San José, and follow the signs for Nicaragua. It takes about four hours to get to Liberia.

DEPARTING   The Liberia bus station is 200 meters north and 100 meters east of the main intersection on the Interamerican Highway. To reach Monteverde take any San José bus leaving before 1pm. Get off at the Río Lagarto bridge and catch the 3:15 Puntarenas–Santa Elena bus.

ESSENTIALS   There is a small tourist information center (tel. 666-1606) three blocks south of the modern white church on Liberia's central park. The center is open Monday through Saturday from 9am to 5pm.

Orientation   The highway passes slightly to the west of town. At the intersection with the main road into town, there are several hotels and gas stations. If you turn east into town, you will come to the central square in less than a kilometer.

Founded in 1769, Liberia is the capital of Guanacaste province, and though it can hardly be considered a bustling city, it does have the distinction of having the most colonial atmosphere of any city in the country. Narrow streets are lined with old adobe homes, many of which have ornate stone accents on their facades.

Liberia is best looked upon as a base for exploring this region. From here it is possible to do day trips to nearby beaches and three national parks. Several moderately priced hotels are located on the outskirts of Liberia at the intersection of the Interamerican Highway and the road out to the Nicoya Peninsula and its many beaches.

WHAT TO SEE & DO

To find out more about what there is to see and do in this region, first stop by the tourist information center. While you're here gathering information, you can quickly tour the center's little museum of Guanacaste culture. The emphasis is on the life of the sabanero.

North of Liberia, you'll find three national parks, though only two of them currently have any facilities for visitors. **Santa Rosa National Park** is about 30 kilometers north of Liberia on the Interamerican Highway. The park, which covers the Santa Elena Peninsula, has both historic and environmental significance. Santa Rosa was Costa Rica's first national park and was founded to preserve La Casona, an old hacienda that played an important role in Costa Rican independence. Today, however, the park is best known for its remote, pristine beaches, which are sometimes accessible by four-wheel-drive vehicle but usually can only be reached by hiking 13 kilometers. **Playa Nancite** is known for its *arribadas* (mass egg-layings) of olive ridley sea turtles, which come ashore to nest by the tens of thousands each year in October. Nearby **Playa Naranjo** is best known for its perfect surfing waves. On the northern side of the peninsula is the even more remote **Playa Blanca.** In the dry season, this beach can be reached by way of the village of Cuajiniquil if you have a four-wheel-drive vehicle.

Rincón de la Vieja National Park, which has its main entrance 25 kilometers northeast of Liberia down a badly rutted dirt road, is an area of geothermal activity. Fumaroles, geysers, and hot pools cover part of this park, creating a bizarre other-worldly landscape. In addition to hot springs and mudpots, there are waterfalls, a lake, and a volcanic crater to be explored. The bird-watching here is excellent, and the views out across the pasturelands to the Pacific Ocean are stunning.

Leisurely raft trips (no white water) are offered by **Safaris Corobici** (tel. 669-1091) about 40 kilometers south of Liberia. They have 2-hour ($35), 3-hour ($43), and half-day ($60) trips that are great for families and bird-watchers. Along the way you may see howler monkeys, iguanas, caiman, coatimundis, otters, toucans, parrots, and many other species of birds.

If you want to tour the surrounding countryside with a guide, contact **CATA Tours** (tel. 669-1026) in nearby Cañas. This company offers boat tours down the Bebedero River to Palo Verde National Park, which is best known for its migratory bird populations. They also lead a horseback trip up through the cloud forest on Miravalles Volcano, which is north of Cañas.

WHERE TO STAY

IN TOWN

Doubles for Less Than $25

HOTEL GUANACASTE, 25 meters west and 100 meters south of the bus station, Liberia, Guanacaste. Tel. 506/666-2287. Fax 506/666-0085. 27 rms (all with private bath).
$ Rates: $11.95 single; $16.20 double; $20.80 triple. V.

This very economical little hotel is primarily a hostel-type establishment catering to young travelers on a tight budget. In addition to the simply furnished rooms, there's a basic soda serving cheap Tico meals. The management here can help arrange trips to nearby national parks and tell you about other interesting budget accommodations, including campgrounds, in the area. You'll find this basic hotel around the corner from the Hotel Bramadero.

Doubles for Less Than $45

NUEVO HOTEL BOYEROS, Apdo. 85, Liberia, Guanacaste. Tel. 506/666-0722. Fax 506/666-2059. 60 rms (all with private bath). A/C
$ Rates: $31.40 single; $43.66 double; $49.05 triple. AE, MC, V.
You'll find this hotel just before the main Liberia intersection on the Interamerican

Highway. Arches with turned-wood railings and a red-tile roof give the two-story motel-style building a Spanish feel. In the courtyard of the hotel are two pools—one for adults and one for children—and a *rancho* bar/snack bar. All the rooms have a private balcony or patio overlooking the pool and gardens. The furniture is getting old and worn, but if you're just in town for one night, you shouldn't be too uncomfortable. The small restaurant serves meals for between $3.45 and $6.10.

HOTEL BRAMADERO, Carretera Interamericana, Liberia, Guanacaste. Tel. 506/666-0371. Fax 506/666-0203. 25 rms (all with private bath).

$ Rates: $16.05–$22.45 single; $23.15–$33.30 double; $27.50–$38.50 triple (higher prices are for A/C rooms). AE, MC, V.

The rates at this motel-style place are good, and the rooms are clean though cramped and very simply furnished. Some rooms can be a bit musty, so ask to see a couple. Behind the restaurant is the hotel's small pool, which can be noisy on weekends. At the front of the hotel, there is a large open-air restaurant and bar, which gets a lot of traffic noise and serves filling meals.

Worth the Extra Bucks

HOTEL EL SITIO, Liberia, Guanacaste. Tel. 506/666-1211. 52 rms (all with private bath). TV TEL

$ Rates: $36–$52 single; $51.45–$74.30 double. AE, DC, MC, V.

Located about 80 yards west of the fire station on the road to Santa Cruz and the beaches, this is one of Liberia's most upscale hotels. Throughout the hotel, there are red-tile floors and original paintings of local Guanacaste scenes on the walls. All the rooms are carpeted, and most rooms are very clean. Unfortunately, the air conditioners can be noisy, so you might want to stick with a fan. The pool area is shady (a welcome relief from the strong Guanacaste sun). Beside the pool, there is a rancho-style bar/restaurant. Other amenities and services include horseback riding, bike rentals, a children's play area, whirlpool tub, tour arrangements, and car rental desk.

NEAR RINCÓN DE LA VIEJA NATIONAL PARK

Doubles for Less Than $35

SANTA CLARA LODGE, Apdo. 17, Quebrada Grande de Liberia, Guanacaste. Tel. 506/666-0085 or 221-1000. Fax 506/666-0475. 7 rms (all with shared bath), 1 cabin (with private bath).

$ Rates: $13–$20 single without bath; $26–$30 double without bath, $37.50 double with bath; $39–$40 triple without bath, $46 triple with bath. Meals are an additional $14 per person per day. No credit cards.

Santa Clara Lodge is located on a working dairy farm in the foothills of the mountains, and with its shady grounds on the banks of a small river, the setting is quite tranquil. Rooms are simply furnished, and meals are filling Tico fare. There is even a pool. You can also hike through fields and forests to hot springs and four different waterfalls. Guided hikes ($7) and horseback rides ($10 to $20) can be arranged. It is also possible to camp here. To reach the lodge, head north from Liberia for about 23 kilometers and turn right on the road to Qhebrada Grande. In Quebrada Grande, turn right at the soccer field and continue for another 4 kilometers. You can arrange free transportation from Liberia to the lodge if you phone in advance.

Doubles for Less Than $45

RINCÓN DE LA VIEJA MOUNTAIN LODGE, Apdo. 114-5000, Liberia, Guanacaste. Tel. 506/685-5422, 666-2369, or 225-1073. Fax 506/666-0473. 24 rms (17 with private bath).

$ Rates: $16 single without bath, $18–$22 single with bath; $32 double without bath, $36–$44 double with bath. Meals are an additional $24 to $28 per person per day. MC, V.

⭐ This is the closest lodge to Las Pailas mudpots and the Azufrale hot springs, and it feels very remote. The polished-wood main lodge looks like a cross between a ranch hacienda and a mountain cabin. There's a long veranda set with chairs, and inside a small lounge and dining room. The rooms with shared baths are quite small, but those with private baths have lots of space. These latter rooms have cement floors and hammocks on their verandas. The lodge offers numerous day-long tours either on foot or on horseback. Transportation from Liberia can be arranged at additional cost. If you are driving, follow the directions to the Hacienda Lodge Guachepelin and continue driving for another 7 kilometers, passing the turnoff for the park entrance.

WHERE TO EAT

You don't have too many choices for dining in Liberia, so your hotel dining room is certainly going to be the most convenient.

RESTAURANTE PÓKOPÍ, 100 meters west of the gas station on road to Santa Cruz. Tel. 666-1036.
   Cuisine: CONTINENTAL. **Reservations:** Not necessary.
$ Prices: Entrees $2.05–$10.15. AE, MC, V.
   Open: Sun–Thurs 10am–10pm, Fri–Sat 10am–midnight.
It doesn't look like much from the outside, but this tiny restaurant has a surprising amount of class inside. An even more pleasant surprise is the unusual (for rural Costa Rica) variety of continental dishes on the menu. Order one of their delicious daiquiris while you peruse the menu, which is on a wooden cutting board. You have your choice of dolphin (the fish, not the mammal) prepared five different ways, pizza, chicken cordon bleu, chicken in wine sauce, and other equally delectable dishes.

RESTAURANT RINCÓN COROBICI, Interamerican Highway, 4 kilometers north of Cañas. Tel. 669-0303.
   Cuisine: COSTA RICAN/INTERNATIONAL. **Reservations:** Not accepted.
$ Prices: Appetizers $1.45–$6.10; entrees $3.05–$17.60. MC, V.
   Open: Daily 8am–10pm.
⭐ The open-air dining room and deck here overlook a beautiful section of the Corobici River. The sound of rushing water tumbling over the rocks in the riverbed is soothing accompaniment to the simple but filling meals. The whole fried fish is the number one choice here, though they also have steaks, lobster, shrimp, and sandwiches. This restaurant, located 35 kilometers south of Liberia, makes an ideal lunch stop if you are heading to or from Liberia or have just done a rafting trip on the Corobici River. Be sure to try the fried yucca chips.

2. PLAYA HERMOSA & PLAYA PANAMÁ

258 kilometers NW of San José; 40 kilometers SW of Liberia

GETTING THERE   By Bus   Express buses leave San José daily at 3:30pm from Calle 12 between avenidas 5 and 7. Duration: 5 hours. Fare: $8.50. Alternatively, you can first take a bus to Liberia (see above for details) and then take a bus from Liberia to Playa Hermosa or Playa Panamá. Buses leave Liberia for these two beaches twice daily. Duration: 45 minutes. Fare: $1.10.

By Car   Follow the directions for getting to Liberia, then head west toward Santa

Cruz. Just past the village of Comunidad, turn right. In about 11 kilometers you will come to a fork in the road. Take the right fork. It takes about five hours from San José.

DEPARTING   The bus to San José leaves daily at 5am. Buses to Liberia leave Playa Panamá twice daily, stopping in Playa Hermosa a few minutes later. Ask at your hotel where to catch the bus.

ESSENTIALS   Orientation   There are no real towns here, just a few houses and hotels on and near the beach. You will come to Playa Hermosa first, followed by Playa Panamá a few kilometers later on the same road.

Playa Hermosa means "beautiful beach," which is a very appropriate name for this crescent of sand. Surrounded by dry rocky hills, this curving gray sand beach is long and wide and rarely crowded, despite the presence of the Condovac La Costa condominium development on the hill at the north end of the beach. Fringing the beach is a swath of trees that stay surprisingly green right through the dry season. The shade provided by these trees is a big part of this beach's appeal. It gets hot here and some shade is always appreciated at the beach. At both ends of the beach, rocky headlands jut out into the surf, creating tide pools at their bases.

Beyond Playa Hermosa, you'll find the even more secluded and appealing Playa Panamá. This big bay is bordered by a shady forest. However, at the time of my last visit there were a couple of big resorts under construction here.

WHAT TO SEE & DO

In the middle of the Playa Hermosa, you'll find **Aqua Sport** (tel. 670-0050), the tourist information and water-sports equipment rental center for Playa Hermosa. Kayaks, sailboards, canoes, bicycles, beach umbrellas, snorkel gear, and parasails are all available for rental at fairly reasonable rates. This is also where you'll find the local post office, public phones, and a restaurant. Up at the north end of the beach, you'll find the **Virgin Diving** dive shop (tel. 670-0472) where you can rent equipment ($10 for mask, snorkel, and fins; $24 for regulator, B.C., and tank), arrange dive trips ($55 for a two-tank dive), and take scuba classes ($295 for an open-water course). Either beach is usually good for swimming, though Playa Panamá is slightly more protected.

WHERE TO STAY

DOUBLES FOR LESS THAN $35

CABINAS PLAYA HERMOSA, Apdo. 117, Liberia, Guanacaste. Tel./fax 506/670-0136. 20 rms (all with private bath).
$ Rates: $15.55 single; $31.10 double. No credit cards.

⭐ This little hotel tucked away under shady trees and surrounded by green lawns is run by Italians who make sure that their guests enjoy the quiet vacation they dreamed about before leaving home. Rooms, though rather dark, are only a few steps from the beach. Horseback riding and boat trips can be arranged. The open-air restaurant has a rustic tropical feel to it, with unfinished tree trunks holding up the roof. Seafood and homemade pasta are the specialties here. Menu prices range from $4.75 to $10.15. To find the hotel, turn left at the first road into Playa Hermosa. The hotel's gate is just after the curve.

WORTH THE EXTRA BUCKS

CABINAS SULA-SULA, Playa Panamá, Guanacaste. Tel. 506/670-0492 or 253-0728. 6 rms (all with private bath).
$ Rates: $68.60–$85.75 for one to six people. Campsites: $3.05 per person per night. MC, V.

By the time you visit Playa Panamá, the latest big resorts will likely have opened and this quiet beach will have changed its character completely, but if you are looking for economical accommodations with plenty of space and lots of cool shade, Cabinas Sula-Sula is just the ticket. However, the rates here aren't that great unless you have three or more people. The rooms are fairly basic, though they do have kitchenettes and fans. Because of the trees, there is good bird-watching. If you have a tent you can camp out here and have access to showers and toilets.

EL VELERO HOTEL, Playa Hermosa, Guanacaste. Tel. 506/670-0330.
   Fax 506/670-0310. 14 rms (all with private bath).
$ Rates: $40–$64 single; $59.45–$75.45 double. MC, V.
   This small hotel is located right on the beach and has its own small swimming pool. White walls and polished tile floors give El Velero a Mediterranean flavor. The guest rooms are large and most have high ceilings. The hotel has its own restaurant, which offers a good selection of fish and shrimp dishes in the $7.80-to-$12.20 range. Various tours, horseback riding, and fishing trips can be arranged through the hotel.

WHERE TO EAT

AQUA SPORT, on the beach. Tel. 670-0450.
   Cuisine: CONTINENTAL. **Reservations:** Not accepted.
$ Prices: Main dishes $3.40–$18.95. MC, V.
   Open: Daily 9am–9pm (noon–9pm in rainy season).
Part of the Aqua Sport market and equipment rental shop is a small open-air restaurant with tables of polished hardwood. The beach is only steps away, and the atmosphere is very casual. The food, however, is much better than what you would expect from such a place. The focus is on continental—with paella for $13.50, grilled lobster for $18.90, and shrimp à la diabla for $8.15.

3. PLAYA DEL COCO & PLAYA OCOTAL

253 kilometers NW of San José; 35 kilometers W of Liberia

GETTING THERE   By Bus   An express bus leaves San José at 10am daily from Calle 14 between avenidas 1 and 3. Duration: 5 hours. Fare: $3.85. From Liberia, buses leave six times daily. Duration: 45 minutes. Fare: $1.10.

By Car   Follow the directions for getting to Liberia and Playa Hermosa, but take the left fork instead. It takes about five hours from San José.

DEPARTING   The bus for San José leaves daily at 9:15am. Buses for Liberia leave five times daily.

ESSENTIALS   Orientation   Playa del Coco is a small but busy beach town with most of the hotels and restaurants right on the water. Playa Ocotal is south of Playa del Coco on a dirt road that leaves the main road just before the beach. Playa Ocotal is a collection of vacation homes and hotels, and has one bar on the beach.

This is one of the most easily accessible of the Guanacaste beaches, with a paved road right down to the water, and has long been a popular destination with middle-class Ticos from San José. Unfortunately, most of the hotels right in town are quite run-down, and the water doesn't look too clean (this is a busy fishing port). The crowds that come here like their music loud and constant and their beer icy cold, so if you're in search of a quiet retreat, stay away.
   The beach, with its grayish brown sand, is quite wide at low tide and almost nonexistent at high tide. Trash is a bit of a problem right in town. However, if you walk down the long curving beach to the north of town, you're bound to find a nice

clean spot to unfold your blanket. Better still, if you have a car, head over to Playa Ocotal, which is a couple of kilometers down a dirt road. This is a tiny pocket of a cove bordered by high bluffs and is quite beautiful.

WHAT TO SEE & DO

There is not much to do here except lie on the sand, hang out in the sodas and bars, or go to the discos. If you're interested, you might be able to join a soccer match (the soccer field is in the middle of town). Over at nearby Playa Ocotal there are often volleyball games by the soda on the beach. It's also possible to arrange horseback rides; ask at your hotel.

Mario Vargas Expeditions (tel. 670-0351) rents scuba-diving and snorkeling equipment, offers scuba classes, and leads dives. A two-tank dive will run you $55; snorkeling equipment is $8 a day; a PADI open-water course is $300. Similar rates are offered by **Rich Coast Diving** (tel. 670-0176).

WHERE TO STAY

DOUBLES FOR LESS THAN $25

ANEXO LUNA TICA, Apdo. 67, Playa del Coco, Guanacaste. Tel. 506/ 670-0279. Fax 506/670-0392. 16 rms (all with private bath).
$ Rates: $20.30 single or double; $28.40 quad. No credit cards.
These basic rooms are just across the street from the beach and though they are pretty spartan, they are among the better budget rooms in town. You'll find the cabinas south of the soccer field at the quieter end of town. A few of the rooms have air conditioning. Don't confuse this place with the older (and even more basic) Cabinas Luna Tica across the street.

CABINAS CHALE, Playa del Coco, Guanacaste. Tel. 506/670-0036 or 235-6408. Fax 506/670-0303. 21 rms (all with private bath).
$ Rates: $22.35 single; $24.10 double; $27.85 triple. No credit cards.
Located down a dirt road to the right as you are coming into town, this small hotel is quite a bit better than those right on the beach and is also much quieter. The rooms are simply furnished with double beds, overhead fans, tile floors, and refrigerators. Some larger rooms have just been added and these are a bit nicer than the older rooms. There is a spartan, screen-walled bar that is open only during the busy season (November to April) and a small pool on a raised patio in back.

COCO PALMS HOTEL, Apdo. 188-5019, Playa del Coco, Guanacaste. Tel. 506/670-0367. Fax 506/670-0117. 20 rms (all with private bath).
$ Rates: $20.30 single; $23.65–$27.05 double; $30.40 triple. DC, MC, V.
This hotel is, by far, the best deal in Playa del Coco. The hotel is located about a block from the beach and overlooks the soccer field. The large guest rooms have tile floors, double beds, ceiling fans, and modern bathrooms with bamboo accents. Window seats, big picture windows (unfortunately with no view), wall sconces, vanities, and pastel colors round out the decor. There's a pool and rancho-style bar in the back walled garden area. An open-air restaurant completes the picture.

WORTH THE EXTRA BUCKS

HOTEL LA FLOR DE ITABO, Apdo. 32, Playa del Coco, Guanacaste. Tel. 506/670-0292 or 670-0011. 18 rms, 8 apts (all with private bath). A/C
$ Rates: $51.45–$68.60 single; $51.45–$74.30 double; $108.60 apartment for 1 to 4 people. AE, DC, MC, V.
This is the most luxurious of the hotels right in Playa del Coco, and though it is not on the beach, the pool is large and the grounds are lushly planted. With fewer than two dozen rooms, service here is reliably good. The rooms are spacious (especially the

bungalows), attractively decorated with wood carvings and Guatemalan textiles, and situated in beautiful two-story houses. Italian dishes are the specialty of the restaurant, with prices ranging from $6.10 to $10.15 for entrees. The bar is a popular hangout with sport fishermen. There is even a small casino here. In addition to a pool, the hotel has a volleyball court, children's play area, and a small park.

HOTEL VILLA CASA BLANCA, Apdo. 176, Playa del Coco, Guanacaste. Tel. 506/670-0448. 10 rms (all with private bath).
$ Rates: $45.75–$51.45 single; $57.15–$62.90 double; $68.60–$74.30 triple. MC, V (add 6% surcharge).

With friendly, helpful owners, beautiful gardens, and attractive rooms, this bed-and-breakfast inn is my favorite spot in the area. The inn is located in a new development and is built in the style of a Spanish villa. All the guest rooms have their own distinct character, and though some are a bit cramped, there are others that feel quite roomy. One room has a canopy bed and a beautiful bathroom with step-up bath. A little rancho serves as open-air bar and breakfast area, and beside this is a pretty little lap pool with a bridge over it. Villa Casa Blanca also represents several rental houses and condos in the area.

WHERE TO EAT

There are dozens of cheap, open-air restaurants at the traffic circle in the center of town. These restaurants serve Tico standards, with the emphasis on fried fish. Prices are quite low. For better food try the following two places. For views, you can't beat the restaurant at Hotel El Ocotal.

HELEN'S, 100 meters south of the ice factory. Tel. 670-0221.
Cuisine: COSTA RICAN/SEAFOOD. **Reservations:** Not accepted.
$ Prices: Main dishes $4.05–$10.15. No credit cards.
Open: Daily 11am–11pm.

There was no sign yet for this out-of-the-way place when we were last there, but by the time you arrive in town, Helen will probably have put one up. This is a local favorite, and because Helen's husband is a fisherman, the seafood is always absolutely fresh. The ceviche comes in a big bowl and is enough for a meal. Be sure to try the lobster soup if it's on the menu.

EL RANCHO DE OCOTAL, Playa Ocotal. No phone.
Cuisine: INTERNATIONAL. **Reservations:** Not accepted.
$ Prices: Sandwiches and main dishes $2.40–$7.50.
Hours: Daily 8am–10pm.

This open-air restaurant near the beach at Playa Ocotal specializes in wood-oven pizzas but is also popular for its swimming pool. You can order a meal or just a drink and use the pool for as long as you like. There are also steaks and seafood on the menu.

4. PLAYAS FLAMINGO, POTRERO & BRASILITO

280 kilometers NW of San José; 66 kilometers SW of Liberia

GETTING THERE **By Bus** Express buses leave San José twice daily from the corner of Calle 20 and Avenida 3. Duration: 6 hours. Fare: $5.10. Alternatively, there are buses from this same San José station to Santa Cruz five times daily. Duration: 5 hours. Fare: $3.40. From Santa Cruz, there are buses to Playas Flamingo, Brasilito, and Potrero twice daily. Duration: 1½ hours. Fare: $1.50.

By Car The most direct route is by way of the Tempisque River ferry. Take the

Interamerican Highway west from San José, and 47 kilometers past the turnoff for Puntarenas, turn left for the ferry. After crossing the Tempisque River, follow the signs for Nicoya, continuing north to Santa Cruz. About 16 kilometers north of Santa Cruz, just before the village of Belen, take the turnoff for Playas Flamingo, Brasilito, and Potrero. After another 20 kilometers, take the right fork to reach these beaches. The drive takes about six hours.

On Fridays and Saturdays, when beach traffic is heavy, it is often quicker to drive all the way north to Liberia and then come back south, thus avoiding the lines of cars waiting to take the ferry. This also applies if you are heading back to San José on a Sunday.

DEPARTING   Express buses to San José leave Playa Potrero twice daily, stopping a few minutes later in Playa Brasilito and Playa Flamingo. Ask at your hotel where the best place is for catching the bus. Buses to Santa Cruz also leave twice daily. If you are heading north toward Liberia, get off the bus at Belen and wait for a bus going north.

ESSENTIALS   Orientation   These three beaches are strung out over several miles of roads. Playa Flamingo is down a side road, while the villages of Brasilito and Potrero are right on the main road.

These three beaches were among the first in Costa Rica to attract international attention, and today Playa Flamingo is the most highly developed beach on this stretch of coast. This isn't surprising when you see the blue water and narrow strand of white sand that is Playa Flamingo or the pink, crushed-shell beach of nearby Playa Conchal. The views from Playa Potrero are beautiful, and in Brasilito, budget travelers have a chance at some fun in the sun without spending a fortune. The rugged coastline here, with little, rocky islands offshore, is particularly memorable.

On Playa Brasilito you will find one of the only two real villages in the area. The soccer field is the center of the village, and around its edges you'll find a couple of little *pulperías* (general stores). There's a long stretch of beach, and though it is of gray sand, it still has a quiet, undiscovered feel to it (at least on weekdays). Playa Brasilito is becoming popular both with Ticos and budget travelers from abroad.

Only a few miles away and at the opposite end of the scale is the luxury resort beach called Playa Flamingo. This is one of Costa Rica's top resort beaches, with luxury hotels, a marina, retirement and vacation homes, and, best of all, one of the only white-sand beaches in the area. In fact, the old name for this beach was Playa Blanca, which made plenty of sense. When the developers moved in, they needed a more romantic name, so it became Playa Flamingo, even though there are no flamingos. You'll probably want to spend plenty of time on this beautiful beach even if you can't afford to stay here. There is little shade along this beach, so be sure to use plenty of sunscreen and bring an umbrella if you can.

If you continue along the road from Brasilito without taking the turn for Playa Flamingo, you will soon come to Playa Potrero. The sand here is a brownish gray, but the beach is long, clean, and deserted.

WHAT TO SEE & DO

Though Playa Flamingo is the prettiest beach in this area, Playa Potrero tends to have the gentlest surf, and therefore is the best swimming beach. Playa Conchal, which is known for its beach of crushed pink seashells (and dangerous riptides), is a short walk south of Brasilito. The water at Playa Brasilito is often fairly calm, which makes it another good swimming choice.

The Flamingo Marina Resort Hotel & Club tel. 233-8056 or 257-1431 has a dive shop that offers open-water courses for $280 and two-tank dive trips for $60, and at the Marina Flamingo Yacht Club, there is the **Quicksilver Dive Shop** (tel. 654-4010, ext 177), which offers similar rates. In Playa Brasilito, there is **Costa Rica Diving** (tel. 654-4021).

If you're interested in fishing for marlin or sailfish, contact the Flamingo Marina Resort Hotel & Club, which offers full-day fishing trips for between $550 and $895. Another option is to contact **Blue Marlin Sport Fishing** (tel. 654-4043) which offers trips at competitive rates.

If you'd rather stay on dry land, you can arrange a horseback ride with **Jalisco Tours** (tel. 654-4106). They charge around $10 per hour for their rides.

WHERE TO STAY

DOUBLES FOR LESS THAN $35

CABINAS CONCHAL, Playa Brasilito (Apdo. 185-5150, Santa Cruz), Guanacaste. Tel. 506/654-4257. 7 rms (all with private bath).
$ Rates: Nov–Mar $20.30–$27.05 single, $27.05 double, $33.80 triple; Apr–Oct $13.55 single, $20.30 double, $27.05 triple. No credit cards.
Located on the south edge of Brasilito, Cabinas Conchal consists of several yellow buildings inside a walled compound. The stucco and stone construction gives the buildings a bit of character. Some rooms have just a double bed, while others have a double and a pair of bunk beds. Table fans help keep the rooms cool.

CABINAS CRISTINA, Playa Potrero (Apdo. 121, Santa Cruz), Guanacaste. Tel. 506/654-4006. 5 rms (all with private bath).
$ Rates: $23.30 single; $28.60 double; $35.30 triple; $41.95 quad. No credit cards.
⭐ This little place is located on Playa Potrero across the bay from Playa Flamingo and a few kilometers north of Brasilito. Although Cabinas Cristina isn't right on the beach, it's still a great value in this area of high-priced hotels. The rooms are spacious and very clean and have kitchenettes. On the veranda there are large rocking chairs. There is a small pool in the middle of a grassy green yard and a thatched-roof palapa. Playa Potrero is a five-minute walk down a dirt road, and Restaurant La Perla is only 50 yards away (see "Where to Eat" below).

HOTEL BRASILITO, Playa Brasilito, Santa Cruz, Guanacaste. Tel./fax 506/654-4237. 15 rms (all with private bath).
$ Rates: $16.90 single; $23.65 double. No credit cards.
Ⓢ This hotel, right in Brasilito and just across a sand road from the beach, offers basic, small rooms that are generally quite clean. There's also a bar and big open-air restaurant serving economical meals. This is the best value in town, though the building across the street seems to be a disco, which means don't plan on going to bed early on the weekends. The hotel also rents snorkeling equipment, bicycles, body boards, and horses.

WORTH THE EXTRA BUCKS

HOTEL SUGAR BEACH, Apdo. 90, Playa Pan de Azucar, Guanacaste. Tel. 506/654-4242 or (in the U.S.) 307/733-4692. Fax 506/654-4329 or (in the U.S.) 307/733-1058. 26 rms (all with private bath).
$ Rates: Nov–Mar $74.30 single or double without A/C, $102.90 single or double with A/C; Apr–Oct $62.90 single or double without A/C, $80.05 single or double with A/C. AE, MC, V.
⭐ Just as the name implies, the Hotel Sugar Beach is located on a white-sand beach—one of the few in the area—and is on a small cove surrounded by rocky hills. Unfortunately, the hills become very brown and desolate in the dry season (which is when most tourists come to visit). Most of the rooms have air conditioning, tile floors, wicker furniture, beautiful carved doors, and big bathrooms that together add up to first-class comfort. The rooms without air conditioning are the oldest and most basic and are the least expensive. The dining room has a panoramic

vista of ocean, islands, and hills. There are daily specials with prices from $6 to $13.50 for entrees. Scuba diving and snorkeling trips, horseback riding, and fishing boat charters can be arranged.

LONG-TERM STAYS & CAMPING

If you plan to be here for a while or are coming down with friends or a large family, you might want to consider renting a house. They rent for anywhere between $100 and $300 per day in the high season (slightly less in the low season). For information and reservations, contact **Sea View Rentals,** Apdo. 77, Santa Cruz, Guanacaste (tel. 506/654-4007; fax 506/654-4009).

If you're interested in camping, talk to Alvaro Chinchilla at Hal's American Bar & Grill. He was about to open up a campground nearby when I last visited and expected to charge $2 per person per night.

WHERE TO EAT

MEALS FOR LESS THAN $6

HAL'S AMERICAN BAR & GRILL, between the turnoff for Playa Flamingo and Playa Potrero. Tel. 654-4213.
Cuisine: INTERNATIONAL. **Reservations:** Not accepted.
$ Prices: $6.50–$10. MC.
Open: Daily 3:30–11pm.
If you've been down in Costa Rica for a while and long for a familiar meal and setting, try Hal's. Not only can you get a pizza or burger, but you can play a round of miniature golf before or after your meal. Pasta, burgers, steaks, and roast chicken are the staples, but there is also a long list of side orders that includes such offerings as stuffing, roast peppers, buffalo wings, and a Greek salad. A round of miniature golf costs $2.70 for adults and $1.35 for children. The restaurant operates a shuttle bus to Playa Flamingo.

MARIE'S, Playa Flamingo near the Flamingo Marina Hotel. Tel. 654-4136.
Cuisine: INTERNATIONAL/SEAFOOD. **Reservations:** Not accepted.
$ Prices: Appetizers $1.35–$5.40; main dishes $4.40–$16.90. MC, V.
Open: Daily 7am–9pm. Closed Tues May–Sept.
Right in the middle of all the luxury hotels at Playa Flamingo is a great little place for a snack or a full dinner. The menu is primarily sandwiches and other lunch foods, but on the blackboard behind the bar you'll find daily specials such as mahi-mahi (called dorado down here) and, from August to December, lobster and conch. You'll also find such Tico favorites as casados and ceviche. Be sure to try the three-milks cake, which just might be the moistest cake on earth.

RESTAURANT LA PERLA, Playa Potrero, at the corner near Cabinas Cristina. No phone.
Cuisine: AMERICAN/COSTA RICAN. **Reservations:** Not accepted.
$ Prices: All meals $1.35–$2.35. No credit cards.
Open: Daily 6am–10pm.
La Perla, an unusual open-air restaurant with chain-link fencing for walls, is primarily the local community center but also serves up decent breakfasts and lunches. You can chat with Perlita, the resident parrot, while you wait for your meal.

MEALS FOR LESS THAN $12

AMBERES, Playa Flamingo near the Flamingo Marina Hotel. Tel. 654-4001.
Cuisine: CONTINENTAL. **Reservations:** Recommended in high season.
$ Prices: Appetizers $5.75–$6.10; main dishes $5.40–$16.90. MC, V.
Open: Daily 6:30–10pm.

This is the happening spot in Flamingo. Not only is it the most upscale restaurant outside of a hotel, but it also boasts a bar, disco, and even a tiny casino. You can come here for dinner and make it an evening. Fresh fish served either meunière or provence style are two of the best dishes on the menu. One drawback is that they play their music way too loud at dinner. Luckily the open-air disco doesn't get cranking until 10pm.

5. PLAYA TAMARINDO

295 kilometers NW of San José; 73 kilometers SW of Liberia

GETTING THERE By Air Sansa (in San José: tel. 233-0397, 233-5330, or 233-3258) flies to Tamarindo daily. Duration: 40 minutes. Fare: $52 each way. Travelair (tel. 220-3054 or 232-7883) also flies to Tamarindo daily. Duration: 6am flight takes 50 minutes; 9:30am flight takes 1 hour and 40 minutes. Fare: $66 one way, $114 round trip.

By Bus An express bus leaves San José daily at 4pm from Calle 20 between avenidas 1 and 3. Duration: 6 hours. Fare: $4.65. Alternatively, you can catch a bus to Santa Cruz from this same station and then take a bus from Santa Cruz to Tamarindo. Buses leave San José for Santa Cruz five times daily. Duration: 5 hours. Fare: $3.40. Buses from Santa Cruz to Tamarindo leave six times daily. Duration: 1½ hours. Fare: $1.60. Another express bus leaves San José daily at 3:30pm from Calle 14 between avenidas 3 and 5. Duration: 5½ hours. Fare: $4.65. If you are coming from Liberia, you can take a Santa Cruz or Nicoya bus (which run almost hourly) and get off in Filadelfia or Belén, and wait for the next Tamarindo-bound bus. However, since buses to Tamarindo are infrequent, you may have a long wait.

By Car The most direct route is by way of the Tempisque River ferry. Take the Interamerican Highway west from San José, and 47 kilometers past the turnoff for Puntarenas, turn left toward the ferry. After crossing the Tempisque River, follow the signs for Nicoya, continuing north to Santa Cruz. About 16 kilometers north of Santa Cruz, just before the village of Belén, take the turnoff for Tamarindo. In another 20 kilometers, take the left fork for Playa Tamarindo. The drive takes about six hours.

On Fridays and Saturdays, when beach traffic is heavy, it is often quicker to drive all the way north to Liberia and then come back south, thus avoiding the lines of cars waiting to take the ferry. This also applies if you are heading back to San José on a Sunday.

DEPARTING Sansa and Travelair fly to San José daily. Buses leave for San José twice daily.

ESSENTIALS Orientation The unpaved road leading into town runs parallel to the beach and dead-ends just past Cabinas Zully Mar. There are a couple of side roads off this main road and most new hotels are to be found on these side roads.

Tamarindo is a long, wide swath of white sand that curves gently from one rocky headland to another. Behind the beach are low, dry hills that can be a very dreary brown in the dry season but instantly turn green with the first brief showers of the rainy season. Several small and inexpensive hotels have made Tamarindo one of the most popular beaches on this coast. A sandy islet offshore makes a great destination if you are a strong swimmer; if you're not, it makes a great foreground for sunsets. Because of the strong waves here, Tamarindo is popular with surfers.

Nearby is Playa Grande, one of the last nesting sites for the giant leatherback turtle, which is the largest turtle in the world. This beach is usually too rough for swimming, but there are often great surfing waves.

WHAT TO SEE & DO

Tamarindo is a long beach and though it can be great for swimming at times, it is often too rough. You also have to be careful when and where you swim on Tamarindo Beach. There are rocks just offshore in several places, some of which are exposed only at low tide. An encounter with one of these rocks could be nasty. Also, you should avoid swimming near the estuary mouth where the currents can carry you out away from the beach. If you want to try some surfing or other water-sports activity, drop by **Iguana Surf** (tel. 654-4019), which is up the road toward the Hotel Pasatiempo and then down a side road a bit. These folks rent snorkeling equipment ($10.15 per day), boogie boards ($6.75 per day), sea kayaks ($10 per hour), and surfboards ($20 per day). You can also rent similar equipment, as well as bicycles, beach chairs, umbrellas, and mats, at slightly lower rates from **Tamarindo Tour/Rentals** (tel. 654-4078), which is located on the right as you come into town. Both places are open daily.

The leatherback sea turtles nest between August and February on Playa Grande, and during this time there are night tours to see nesting turtles. The tours cost around $11.85 per person. Only a few guides are licensed to operate these tours and all groups are required to use only red-light flashlights. No flash photography is allowed because any sort of light can confuse the turtles and prevent them from laying their eggs. Before going on one of these tours, make sure that your guide will be following all precautions aimed at protecting the turtles.

Papagayo Excursions (tel. 680-0859 or 680-0652), which has its office at the Hotel Tamarindo Diria, offers sportfishing trips during the peak billfish season between mid-April and August. Rates are $250 to $450 for a half day and $350 to $700 for a full day for the boat. **Tamarindo Sportfishing** (tel. 654-4090) offers half-day trips for between $250 and $500 and full-day trips for between $350 and $800.

Through Papagayo Excursions, you can also arrange to go horseback riding. Two-hour guided rides are $25. This company also offers 2-hour boat tours of the nearby estuary for $25 per person and two-tank scuba diving trips for $60. Estuary tours, which head back into the mangrove swamp near Tamarindo, are offered by several companies around town. Ask at your hotel, and you should be able to arrange one of these trips for under $13.

WHERE TO STAY

In addition to hotels listed below, there's a private campground across from the Tamarindo Turicentro on the outskirts of town.

DOUBLES FOR LESS THAN $25

CABINAS MARIELOS, Playa Tamarindo, Guanacaste. Tel. 506/654-4041. 14 rms (all with private bath).
$ Rates: $13.90 single; $23.20 double; $27.05 triple. No credit cards.
This place is located down a palm-shaded driveway across the road from the beach. Rooms are clean and fairly new, though small and simply furnished. There are tile floors and wooden chairs on the patios. The bathrooms have no door on them but are otherwise quite acceptable. There is even a kitchen that guests can use. The garden provides a bit of shade.

DOUBLES FOR LESS THAN $35

CABINAS ZULLY MAR, Tamarindo, Guanacaste. Tel. 506/226-4732. 27 rms (all with private bath).
$ Rates: $20.30 single; $25.25–$39.75 double; $30.55–$46.25 triple. No credit cards.
The Zully Mar has long been a favorite of budget travelers staying in Tamarindo. The newer rooms, which are in a two-story white-stucco building with a wide curving

staircase on the outside, have air conditioning and are the more comfortable. The doors to these guest rooms are particularly interesting; they're hand carved with pre-Columbian motifs. There are also high ceilings with fans, tile floors, a long veranda, and large bathrooms. The older rooms, though smaller, are also clean and pleasant.

HOTEL POZO AZUL, Playa Tamarindo, Santa Cruz, Guanacaste. Tel. 506/680-0147 or 654-4280. 27 rms (all with private bath).

$ Rates: $29.35–$37.10 single, double, or triple; $46.35 quad. No credit cards.

This is one of the first hotels you spot as you drive into Tamarindo. It's on the left side of the road and therefore is not on the beach. There isn't much shade on the grounds, but there are swimming pools for adults and kids. In the 17 rooms with air conditioning, there are also hot plates, refrigerators, tables and chairs, and large windows. Some rooms have covered parking to keep your car out of the blistering heat. In recent years, the Pozo Azul has become a surfer hangout.

WORTH THE EXTRA BUCKS

HOTEL EL MILAGRO, Playa Tamarindo, Guanacaste (Apdo. 145, Santa Cruz-5150). Tel. 506/441-5102. Fax 506/441-8494. 32 rms (all with private bath).

$ Rates (including continental breakfast): $45.70–$57.15 single or double with fan; $57.15–$68.60 single or double with A/C. AE, MC, V.

This attractive little hotel is on the edge of town across the road from the beach. Each room has a wall of louvered doors that can be opened up to give the room plenty of air. These doors open onto small semicircular patios. Rooms are comfortable and have high ceilings. Pretty gardens and some big old shade trees make El Milagro a pleasant place. The restaurant serves excellent continental dishes, and there is a swimming pool with swim-up bar. Various tours and excursions can also be arranged.

PUEBLO DORADO HOTEL, Playa Tamarindo, Guanacaste (Apdo. 1711-1002, San José). Tel./fax 506/222-5741. 27 rms (all with private bath). A/C

$ Rates: $45.75 single; $57.15 double; $68.60 triple. AE, MC, V.

This two-story, blindingly white hotel has a central garden courtyard and looks a bit like a Los Angeles apartment building. There's a small pool at the back of the garden and above the pool is an open-air restaurant and bar serving meals in the $4-to-$8 range. Guest rooms are done in white tile and have big bathrooms and double beds. In the guest rooms and elsewhere around the hotel there are huge stone masks (reproductions of pre-Columbian stone carvings) mounted on the walls. This hotel offers one of the best deals in Tamarindo if you want a place with air conditioning and a swimming pool.

WHERE TO EAT

MEALS FOR LESS THAN $6

FIESTA DEL MAR, at the end of the road. No phone.

Cuisine: STEAK/SEAFOOD. **Reservations:** Not accepted.

$ Prices: Main dishes $3.95–$8.80. MC, V.

Open: Daily 11am–11pm.

Located across the circle from the beach, the Fiesta del Mar specializes in steaks and seafood cooked over a wood fire. Try the grilled steak in garlic sauce for $8.80 or the whole fried fish for $4.75. The open-air dining area is edged with greenery, and has a thatch roof, so it feels very tropical. There is also live marimba music several nights a week.

PANADERIA JOHANN, on the road into town. No phone.

Cuisine: BAKERY. **Reservations:** Not accepted.

$ Prices: $2–$9. No credit cards.

Open: Daily 6am–8pm.

⭐ There are always fresh-baked goodies at this Belgian-run bakery on the outskirts of Tamarindo, although what you might find on any given day is never certain. Possibilities include croissants, pizzas, chocolate eclairs, and different types of bread. A whole pizza goes for around $9. If you are heading out to the beach for the day, be sure to stop by and pick up some bread or pastries. There are a few tables out back where you can eat your pizza.

RESTAURANT ZULLY MAR, at the end of the road. No phone.
   Cuisine: COSTA RICAN. **Reservations:** Not accepted.
$ **Prices:** Meals $3.40–$16.90. No credit cards.
   Open: Daily 7am–10pm.
This restaurant, opposite the hotel of the same name, is right on the beach at the end of the road that leads into Tamarindo. It's a basic Tico-style open-air restaurant, but the food is good, and the view can't be beat. Sit and watch the boats bob in the swells just offshore while you dine on fresh fish sauteed in garlic. The bar is a popular hangout with locals and tourists.

MEALS FOR LESS THAN $12

COCONUT CAFE, on the left as you come into town. No phone.
   Cuisine: INTERNATIONAL. **Reservations:** Not accepted.
$ **Prices:** Appetizers $3.40–$6.80; main dishes $6.45–$19.60. No credit cards.
   Open: Daily 6–10pm.

⭐ On the left as you come into town, you'll find one of Tamarindo's more atmospheric restaurants. A thatch roof, wicker furniture, and a raised deck all add up to a gringo fantasy of the tropics, but isn't that what you came down here for anyway? The Coconut Cafe serves some of the most imaginative food in town, including such dishes as red chicken curry, mahi-mahi macadamia, shrimp brochettes, and fondue. However, because the menu changes daily, you can expect other, equally enticing dishes when you visit. The drawback here is that the dusty road is only a few feet away.

EL MILAGRO, on the left as you enter town. Tel. 654-4042.
   Cuisine: CONTINENTAL/COSTA RICAN. **Reservations:** Not necessary.
$ **Prices:** Appetizers $1.55–$3.05; main dishes $5.40–$21.65. AE, MC, V.
   Open: Daily 7am–11pm.
Lush gardens and wide terraces make this the most attractive restaurant in town, and you might even be able to go for a swim in the adjacent pool if you're so inclined. Reproductions of pre-Columbian stone statues stand in the gardens and the bar has carved wood columns. On those rare occasions when it is raining, you can retreat to one of the indoor dining rooms. Though the emphasis here is on seafood, you'll also find such unexpected offerings as beef fondue, fried Camembert, and banana flambé.

---

6. PLAYA JUNQUILLAL

30 kilometers W of Santa Cruz; 20 kilometers S of Tamarindo.

GETTING THERE   By Bus   An express bus leaves San José daily at 2pm from the corner of Calle 20 and Avenida 3. Duration: 5 hours. Fare: $5.31. Alternatively, you can take a bus to Santa Cruz (see above under "Playas Flamingo, Brasilito & Potrero" for details) and then take a bus from Santa Cruz to Playa Junquillal. Duration (Santa Cruz to Playa Junquillal): 1½ hours. Fare: $1.60.

By Car   Take the Interamerican Highway from San José, and 47 kilometers past the turnoff for Puntarenas, turn left toward the Tempisque ferry. After crossing the Tempisque River, continue north through Nicoya to Santa Cruz. In Santa Cruz, head west 14 kilometers to the town of 27 de Abril, which is where the pavement ends. From here it is another 18 kilometers to Playa Junquillal.

DEPARTING   The express bus to San José leaves Playa Junquillal daily at 5am. There is also a bus to Santa Cruz daily at the same time.

ESSENTIALS   Playa Junquillal is a long windswept beach backed by rolling hills and pastures. The hotels mentioned here are all along the main road.

Playa Junquillal (pronounced hoong-key-*awl*) is a long windswept beach that, for most of its length, is backed by grasslands. This gives it a very different feel from other beaches on this coast. There is really no village to speak of here, so if you're heading out this way, plan on getting away from it all. Once here, your options for what to do are limited to whatever is on offer at your chosen hotel. However, the long beach is good for strolling and the sunsets are superb.

WHAT TO SEE & DO

Other than walking the beach, swimming (when the surf isn't too strong), and exploring tide pools, there isn't much to do here, which is just fine with me. This beach is ideal for anyone who just wants to relax without any distractions. Bring a few good books. Actually, the larger hotels here—Antumalal, Iguanazul, and Villa Serena—all offer plenty of activities and facilities, including volleyball, swimming pools, tennis courts, even a disco at Hotel Antumalal. Sportfishing trips can also be arranged at most hotels. At the Iguanazul, guests can rent bicycles or mopeds, which are both good ways to get up and down this beach.

WHERE TO STAY & EAT

DOUBLES FOR LESS THAN $35

HIBISCUS HOTEL, Playa Junquillal, (Apdo. 163-5150, Santa Cruz), Guanacaste. Tel. (in Alajuela) 506/441-2282. 5 rms (all with private bath).
$ Rates: Dec–Apr $17.15–$34.30 single, $17.15–$45.75 double, $51.45 triple; May–Nov $17.15–$32 single or double. No credit cards.
Though the accommodations here are very simple, the French owner makes sure that everything is always clean and in top shape. The grounds are pleasantly shady, and the beach is just across the road. The least expensive room is quite small and has only cold water, but in this hot climate, you really don't need the hot water that the more expensive rooms offer.

HOTEL EL CASTILLO DIVERTIDO, Playa Junquillal, Guanacaste. Tel. (in Santa Cruz) 506/680-0015. 7 rms (all with private bath).
$ Rates: Dec–Apr $35–$40 double; May–Nov $28 double. No credit cards.
Quite a few people have moved to Costa Rica from around the world in hopes of living out fantasy lives impossible in their home countries. This fanciful hotel is just such a creation. Built by a young German, the hotel is a tropical rendition of a classic medieval castle (well, sort of). Ramparts and a turret with a rooftop bar certainly grab the attention of passersby. Guest rooms here are fairly small, though rates are also some of the lowest in the area.

WORTH THE EXTRA BUCKS

HOTEL ANTUMALAL, Playa Junquillal, Guanacaste (Apdo. 49-5150, Santa Cruz). Tel./fax 506/680-0506. 23 rms (all with private bath).
$ Rates: Dec–Apr $80.05 single, $91.45 double, $102.90 triple; May–Nov $51.45 single, $57.15 double, $62.90 triple. AE, DC, MC, V.
Located at the end of the road, the Antumalal is set amid shady grounds and lush gardens that create a world of tropical tranquillity. Guest rooms are all in duplex buildings with stucco walls and beautiful murals on inside walls. Out front you'll find a big patio with a hammock, while inside there are brick floors,

colorful Guatemalan bedspreads, and big bathrooms. The dining room is housed under a huge, high-peaked rancho and has a menu that includes plenty of good inexpensive Italian dishes. The swimming pool, with its swim-up bar, is only a few steps from the beach. Other facilities include a tennis court, exercise room, and minigolf course. There's even a small disco here. Horseback riding, fishing charters, and scuba trips are all offered as well.

IGUANAZUL HOTEL, Playa Junquillal (Apdo. 130-1550, Santa Cruz), Guanacaste. Tel./fax 506/680-0783. 24 rms (all with private bath).

$ Rates: Dec–Apr $54.30 single, $68.60 double, $82.30 triple; May–Nov $40 single, $51.45 double, $59.45 triple. AE, MC, V.

Though the gravel road leading up to this hotel doesn't make Iguanazul seem too promising, once you step through the entry and see the resortlike pool, you may well be captivated, as my wife and I were. Set on a windswept grassy bluff above a rocky beach, Iguanazul is far from the madding crowd. Guest rooms are beautifully decorated with basket lamp shades, wicker furniture, red-tile floors, high ceilings, and blue-and-white tile bathrooms. This is definitely a spot for sun worshippers who like to have a good time, and the clientele tends to be young and active. The pool is large, there's a volleyball court, and the bar plays lively classic rock throughout the day. You can rent horses, bicycles, mopeds, and boogie boards, and there are board games, table tennis, and karaoke music in the evenings.

7. PLAYA SÁMARA

35 kilometers S of Nicoya; 245 kilometers W of San José.

GETTING THERE By Air Sansa (in San José: tel. 233-0397, 233-3258, or 233-5330) flies to Carillo (15 minutes south of Sámara) daily. Duration: 1 hour and 45 minutes. Fare: $46 each way. Travelair (in San José: tel. 220-3054 or 232-7883) also flies to Carillo daily. Duration: 55 minutes. Fare: $58 one way, $100 round trip.

By Bus An express bus leaves San José daily at noon from Calle 14 between avenidas 3 and 5. Duration: 6 hours. Fare: $5.55. Alternatively, you can take a bus from this same San José station to Nicoya and then catch a second bus from Nicoya to Sámara. Buses leave San José for Nicoya eight times daily. Duration: 6 hours. Fare: $4.85. Buses leave Nicoya for Sámara and Carillo Monday through Friday at 3pm and Saturday and Sunday at 8am. Duration: 2 hours. Fare: $1.65 (Sámara) and $2.20 (Carillo).

By Car Follow the directions for Playa Junquillal above, but in Nicoya, follow the signs south on a road that is paved for a few kilometers but that then turns into an unpaved road under construction (or destruction as it often seems to be).

DEPARTING The express bus to San José leaves daily at 4am. Buses for Nicoya leave Monday through Friday at 6am and Saturday and Sunday at 2pm. Buses leave Nicoya for San José six times daily.

ESSENTIALS Sámara is a busy little town at the bottom of a steep hill. The main road heads straight into town, passing the soccer field before coming to an end at the beach.

Sámara is a pretty beach on a horseshoe-shaped bay, and because the beach is fairly easily accessible by bus or car, Sámara is popular with Tico families for a little weekend beach partying. A small rocky island and steep cliffs on the far side of the bay together make this a very attractive spot, and the beach is long and wide. The calm waters of the bay here are perfect for swimming because the rocks across the mouth of the bay break the waves. Directly behind the main beach is a wide, flat valley that stretches inland and to the north.

WHAT TO SEE & DO

The main activities here in Playa Sámara seem to be hanging out in the sodas and dancing into the early morning hours. One disco here even has rooms right off the dance floor, or is it a hotel that has a disco right outside the guest room doors. Whichever it is, no one there goes to sleep until the disco shuts down.

You'll find that the beach is nicer and cleaner down at the south end near Las Brisas del Pacífico hotel. For fewer crowds, head south to Playa Carillo, a long, flat beach about 15 minutes from Sámara.

Spelunkers may want to visit **Barra Honda National Park,** which is 62 kilometers northeast of Playa Sámara on the road to the Tempisque ferry. Here there is an extensive system of caves.

WHERE TO STAY

DOUBLES FOR LESS THAN $35

CABINAS BELVEDERE, Playa Sámara, Guanacaste (George Salina Cortes, Galleria Musical, Second Level, San José). No phone. 2 rms, 3 cabins (all with private bath).
$ Rates (including continental breakfast): $23.20 single; $30.95 double. No credit cards.
These tropical Swiss chalets are ranged across the hillside across the street from the Hotel Marbella on the inland edge of town. The two rooms are rather small and are in the main house, adjacent to the hotel's restaurant, which has a good view of the Pacific. However, I like the miniature, thatched-roof chalets, which have porches and more space.

WORTH THE EXTRA BUCKS

HOTEL LAS BRISAS DEL PACÍFICO, Playa Sámara, Guanacaste (Apdo. 129-6100, Ciudad Colón). Tel./fax 506/680-0876 or (in San José) 233-9840. 27 rms (all with private bath).
$ Rates: $51.45–$91.45 single or double; $68.60–$108.60 triple. AE, MC, V.
Located on the same road as the Marbella, this hotel is set amid shady grounds right on the beach and backs up to a steep hill. Most of the rooms are up a long, steep flight of stairs at the top of the hill. These hilltop rooms have large balconies and walls of glass that take in the views. However, they also can get very hot and stuffy if you don't opt for an air-conditioned room. At the base of the hill, there are rooms in stucco duplexes with tile roofs and patios. These rooms have cold-water showers only. There is also a second pool and restaurant at the top of the hill. The main dining room is a breezy open-air restaurant surrounded by lush garden plantings. The menu changes daily but entree prices range from $6.50 to $8.50.

HOTEL MARBELLA, Playa Sámara, Guanacaste (Edificio Cristal, Avenida 1a, San José). Tel./fax 506/233-9980. 14 rms, 6 apts (all with private bath).
$ Rates: Nov–Mar $40 single, $48–$51.45 double, $57.15 triple, $68.60 apt.; Apr–Oct $20.60 single, $32 double, $40 triple, $57.15 apt. AE, MC, V.
Though it is a bit of a walk to the beach and the immediate surroundings are none too appealing, this small German-run hotel is properly tropical in decor. You'll find the Marbella just around the corner from the main road into town. Guest rooms are fairly large and have red-tile floors and woven mats for ceilings. There are open closets and modern bathrooms with hot water. The apartments are a good choice for families or long-term stays. There's a small swimming pool in a gravel courtyard and a second-floor dining room and bar. All the rooms have a balcony or porch, though not necessarily a view. The dining room menu focuses on seafood. Prices are in the $6-to-$15 range.

WHERE TO EAT

There are numerous inexpensive sodas in Sámara, and most of the hotels have their own dining rooms. My favorite place to eat is the dining room at Las Brisas. In town, try the following:

COLOCHOS BAR, on the main street through town. Tel. 680-0445.
Cuisine: COSTA RICAN/INTERNATIONAL. **Reservations:** Not accepted.
$ **Prices:** Appetizers $2.05–$3.40; main dishes $3.40–$16.90. No credit cards.
Open: Daily 11am–10pm.

This open-air rancho restaurant on the main street through town offers a great selection of seafoods. There are four different types of ceviche, lobster dishes, paella, and plenty of shrimp plates. Prices are very reasonable and portions are large.

8. PLAYA NOSARA

55 kilometers SW of Nicoya; 266 kilometers W of San José.

GETTING THERE   By Air   Sansa (in San José: tel. 233-0397, 233-3258, or 233-5330) flies to Nosara daily. Duration: 1 hour and 10 minutes. Fare: $46 each way. Travelair (in San José: tel. 220-3054 or 232-7883) also flies to Nosara daily. Duration: 1 hour and 15 minutes. Fare: $58 one way, $100 round trip.

By Bus   An express bus leaves San José daily at 6:15am from Calle 14 between avenidas 3 and 5. Duration: 7 hours. Fare: $6.90. Alternatively, you can take a bus from San José to Nicoya (see above under "Playa Sámara" for details) and then catch a second bus from Nicoya to Nosara. A bus leaves Nicoya for Nosara daily at 1pm. Duration: 2 hours. Fare: $1.80.

By Car   Follow the directions above for getting to Playa Sámara, but watch for a fork in the road a few kilometers before you reach that beach. The right-hand fork leads, in another 22 kilometers, to Nosara. The roads out here are in horrendous shape, although some sections are in the process of being paved.

DEPARTING   The bus to San José leaves daily at 1pm. The bus to Nicoya leaves daily at 6am. Buses leave Nicoya for San José daily at 4, 7:30, and 9am, noon, and 2:30 and 4pm.

ESSENTIALS   The village of Nosara is about 5 kilometers inland from the beach, while most of the hotels listed here are on the beach itself. If you need a taxi, phone 680-0857.

Playa Nosara is actually several beaches, almost all of which are nearly deserted most of the time. Because the village of Nosara is several kilometers from the beach, and because the land near the beach has been turned into a large spread-out resort community, Nosara has been spared the sort of ugly, uncontrolled growth characteristic of Sámara or Flamingo. All of the hotels are spread out and most are tucked away down side roads. In fact, on first arriving here, it's hard to believe there are any hotels around at all. Nosara has long been popular with North American retirees, who have hidden their homes among all the trees that make Nosara one of the greenest spots on this coast.

WHAT TO SEE & DO

There are several beaches at Nosara, including the long, curving Playa Guiones, Playa Nosara, and, my personal favorite, diminutive **Playa Pelada**. This latter is a short white-sand beach lined with sea grasses and mangroves. However, there isn't too much sand at high tide, so you'll want to hit the beach when the tide's out. At either end of the beach there are rocky outcroppings that contain tide pools at low tide. Surfing and bodysurfing are both good here. Because the village of Nosara is several miles inland, these beaches are clean and quiet.

Most of the hotels in the area can arrange **fishing charters** for around $250 a half day or $400 for a full day. These rates are for one to four people. You can also contact Pesca Bahia Garza (tel. 680-0856) and arrange a fishing trip.

Bird-watchers should get in touch with Estrella del Pacífico hotel, which offers a 3-hour bird-watching trip to the mangrove swamps of the Río Nosara. The cost is $23.65 per person. For about the same price, you can also take a night tour to nearby Playa Ostional to watch **nesting olive ridley sea turtles.** These turtles come ashore by the thousands in a mass egg-laying phenomenon known as an *arribada*. These arribadas take place 4 to 10 times between July and November, with each arribada lasting between 3 and 10 days. Consider yourself very lucky if you should happen to be around during an arribada. Even if it is not turtle nesting season, you may want to look into going up to Playa Ostional. During the dry season you can usually get there in a regular car, but during the rainy season, you'll need four-wheel-drive. This beach is part of Ostional National Wildlife Refuge, at the northwest end of which is India Point, a spot known for its tide pools and rocky outcrops.

WHERE TO STAY

DOUBLES FOR LESS THAN $25

CABINAS CHOROTEGA, Nosara, Guanacaste. Tel. 506/680-0836. 10 rms (4 with private bath).
$ Rates: $6.80 single; $13.55 double. No credit cards.
Located on the outskirts of Nosara village, Cabinas Chorotega is about 5 kilometers from the beach, so you'll need to have some sort of transportation if you stay here and want to go to the beach. The rooms are very basic but clean, and the rooms with private bath are a particularly good value. Some rooms have more windows and are quite a bit brighter than others, so have a look at a couple of rooms if you can.

WORTH THE EXTRA BUCKS

ESTANCIA NOSARA, Playa Nosara (Apdo. 37, Bocas de Nosara), Guanacaste. Tel./fax 506/680-0378. 10 rms (all with private bath).
$ Rates: $45.75 single; $52.60 double; $61.75 triple; $70.90 quad. MC, V.
Although this hotel is a mile or so from the beach, it's set amid shady jungle trees and has a swimming pool and tennis court, which together make Estancia Nosara a good value. The guest rooms are in two buildings and have red-tile floors, kitchenettes, high ceilings, overhead fans, and showers with hot water. There's a large open-air restaurant serving moderately priced meals. Use of the tennis court will cost you $5 an hour, and horses ($8 per hour) and bikes ($7 per day) can also be rented. A full day of fishing for up to four people will cost $400 for the boat.

RANCHO SUIZO LODGE, Playa Nosara (Apdo. 14, Bocas de Nosara), Guanacaste 5233. Tel. 506/255-0011. Fax 506/255-2155. 10 rms (all with private bath).
$ Rates: Nov–Apr $29 single, $40 double; May–Oct $25 single, $30 double. No credit cards.
Though this pleasant little lodge is not located right on the beach, the waves are just a 5-minute walk down a trail. The guest rooms, which are fairly small, are in several little cabins across a foot bridge from the parking area. However, despite the size, the rooms are comfortable and have double beds, bamboo furniture, porches, and big windows. Bathrooms have tiled showers with cold water only. Inexpensive breakfasts and dinners are served in the restaurant. Various tours can be

arranged through the hotel, and bikes ($10 per day), horses ($10 per hour), and fishing boats ($250 per half day) can all be hired. The hotel also has aviaries full of exotic birds. Peace and quiet are the main offering here.

WHERE TO EAT

MEALS FOR LESS THAN $6

DOÑA OLGA'S, on the beach at Playa Pelada. No phone.
   Cuisine: COSTA RICAN. **Reservations:** Not accepted.
   $ Prices: Main dishes $1.70–$16.90. No credit cards.
   Open: Daily 6:30am–10pm.
Little more than a roof with some tables under it, Olga's is still the most popular restaurant in Nosara. Gringos and Ticos alike hang out here savoring fried fish casados, sandwiches, and breakfasts that include huge plates of bacon. On the weekends the cavernous structure beside the restaurant becomes a lively disco.

---

9. PLAYA MONTEZUMA

166–184 kilometers W of San José (not including the ferry ride);
36 kilometers SE of Paquera; 54 kilometers S of Naranjo

GETTING THERE   By Bus and Ferry   If you are traveling from San José by public transportation, it will take you two buses and a ferry ride to get to Montezuma. This can require spending a night in Puntarenas, so don't plan on heading out this way unless you have plenty of time. Buses leave San José for Puntarenas daily every 30 minutes between 5am and 7pm from the corner of Calle 12 and Avenida 9. Duration: 2 hours. Fare: $2.60. From Puntarenas take the *lancha* (tel. 661-2830), which leaves from the pier behind the market twice daily (three times on Monday and Friday). This passenger launch should not be confused with the two car ferries that also leave from Puntarenas. Duration: 1½ hours. Fare: $1.70. The bus south to Montezuma will be waiting to meet the lancha when it arrives in Paquera. Duration: 1½ hours. Fare: $2.85.

By Car   Take the Interamerican Highway from San José to Puntarenas and catch either the Naranjo ferry or the Paquera ferry, which is operated by the Barceló company and has been surrounded with controversy since it began operating. You'll probably have to arrive the night before and put your car in line to assure a space on a ferry the next morning. The Naranjo ferry leaves five times daily. Duration: 1½ hours. Fare: $8.80 for cars, $1.25 for adults, and 70¢ for children. The Naviera Tambor ferry to Paquera leaves three times daily. Duration: 1½ hours. Fare: $11.50 for cars; $2.05 for adults, $4.75 for adults in first class; $1.05 for children, $2.70 for children in first class. Montezuma is about 3 hours south of Naranjo and 1½ hours south of Paquera. These roads are mostly gravel, with a few short paved sections. Be prepared for some rough riding.

DEPARTING   The Paquera bus leaves twice daily (three times on Monday and Friday) and meets the Paquera lancha. Total duration: 3½ hours. Total fare: $4.55. The car ferry from Paquera leaves three times daily. The car ferry from Naranjo leaves five times daily.

ESSENTIALS   There is a tourist information desk in a little kiosk in the center of the village. The bus stops at the end of the road into the village. From here, hotels are scattered up and down the beach and around the village's few sand streets. Motorcycles can be rented in the center of town for $40 per day (plus a $500 deposit).

Before I first came to Montezuma, I had heard different opinions about this beach at the southern tip of the Nicoya Peninsula. Some budget travelers thought it was the best beach in Central America. Other people, those who prefer a few more amenities, thought it would be a great beach in a few years, when it had some decent accommodations and restaurants. After spending some time there myself, I have to agree with all of them. Montezuma has its charms and its drawbacks, not least of which is a problem with untreated sewage flowing onto the village's main beach from some of the establishments in the village. Unfortunately, Montezuma has gained popularity far faster than local restaurants and hotels can cope with the growing sanitary needs. This problem is further aggravated by the large numbers of people who camp on the beach. There is a severe shortage of rooms here, despite the fact that people seem to be building hotels as fast as they can. If you don't show up with reservations, you better have a tent or hammock. And even if you do manage to get a room in the village, don't expect to go to sleep early; a disco and a bar, side by side, blast their respective music for hours on end. Head out of town if peace and tranquillity are what you're seeking.

On the other hand, the water here is a gorgeous royal blue, though the waves can occasionally be too rough for casual swimming and you need to be aware of stray rocks at your feet. Be sure you know where the rocks are before doing any bodysurfing. In either direction from Montezuma are a string of sandy coves separated by outcroppings of volcanic rock that form tide pools.

WHAT TO SEE & DO

Mostly you just hang out on the beach, hang out in a restaurant, hang out in a bar, or hang out in front of the disco. However, if you're interested in more than just hanging out, head for the **waterfall** just south of town. This waterfall is one of those tropical fantasies where water comes pouring down into a deep pool. It's a popular spot, but it's a bit of a hike up the stream. There are actually a couple of waterfalls up this stream, but the upper falls are by far the more spectacular. You'll find the trail to the falls just over the bridge south of the village (near Las Cascadas restaurant).

Several people around the village rent **horses** for around $5 an hour, though most people choose to do a 4-hour horseback tour for $20 to $25. These latter rides usually go to a waterfall 8 kilometers north of Montezuma. This waterfall cascades straight down into the ocean. You can also ride a horse to Cabo Blanco. Luis, whose rental place is down the road that leads north through town to the beach, is a reliable source for horses, as are Armando, Ana, and José, all of whom can be contacted through El Sano Banano. In the center of the village, there is a rental center where you can rent bicycles ($8.15 per day) and boogie boards ($4.75 per day).

As beautiful as the beaches around Montezuma are, the beaches at **Cabo Blanco Nature Reserve,** 11 kilometers south of the village, are, in many people's opinion, even more beautiful. Located at the southernmost tip of the Nicoya Peninsula, Cabo Blanco preserves a nesting site for brown pelicans, magnificent frigate birds, and brown boobies. The beaches are backed by lush tropical forest that is home to howler monkeys that are often seen (and heard!). You can hike through the preserve's lush forest right down to the deserted, pristine beach. There are usually shared taxis heading out this way in the morning. The fare is $5 per person.

Five-hour tours to **Tortuga Island** are available for $23.65, which is a considerable savings over similar trips offered by companies in San José, although the trips out of San José include a gourmet lunch that isn't a part of trips from Montezuma.

WHERE TO STAY

DOUBLES FOR LESS THAN $15

HOTEL EL TUCAN, Montezuma, Cobano de Puntarenas. Tel. 506/661-1122, ext. 284. 10 rms (all with shared bath).
$ Rates: $6.10 single; $10.15 double. No credit cards.
This small two-story hotel is on the road south to Cabo Blanco and is located just

around the corner from the main road into town. Rooms are small and Spartan but generally clean.

HOTEL MOCTEZUMA, Montezuma, Cobano de Puntarenas. Tel. 506/ 661-1122, ext. 258. 22 rms (15 with private bath).
$ Rates: $5.80 single without bath, $10.45 single with bath; $10.85 double without bath, $17.80 double with bath. V.

Located right in the center of the village across the street from the disco, the Hotel Moctezuma offers basic but clean rooms with fans. Some of the rooms are upstairs from the hotel's noisy bar and restaurant. If you like to go to sleep early, try to get a room at the back of the hotel's building across the street instead. The walls here don't go all the way to the ceiling, which is great for air circulation but lousy for privacy.

PENSIÓN ARENAS, Montezuma, Cobano de Puntarenas. No phone. 14 rms (all with shared bath).
$ Rates: $4.65–$5.60 single; $9.25–$11.15 double.

This is the backpacker's first choice in Montezuma. If they haven't got a room for you, you can pitch a tent or hammock on the sand in front of the pension. Rooms are split between an old wooden house and a newer cement building. The end rooms on the second floor are probably the best because they catch the breezes. However, most rooms have fans. This place is about as basic as it gets in Costa Rica, though there are toilet seats.

DOUBLES FOR LESS THAN $25

HOTEL LA AURORA, Montezuma, Cobano de Puntarenas. Tel./fax 506/ 661-2320. 6 rms (3 with private bath).
$ Rates (including breakfast): Dec–Mar $20 single or double without bath, $25 single or double with bath; Apr–Nov $15 single or double without bath, $20 single or double with bath. No credit cards.

Just to the left as you enter the village of Montezuma, you'll see this large white house. The rooms are arranged around the spacious second-floor porch, which has a small library of books, some hammocks and comfortable chairs, and flowering vines growing up the walls. In fact there are vines all over La Aurora, which gives it a tropical yet gothic feel. Guest rooms have wooden walls that don't go all the way to the ceiling. There is also a kitchen available to guests, and lunch and dinner are served.

DOUBLES FOR LESS THAN $35

AMOR DE MAR, Montezuma, Cobano de Puntarenas. Tel. 506/ 661-1122, ext. 262. 12 rms (8 with private bath). 1 cabin.
$ Rates: $25 single or double with shared bath; $35–$45 single or double with private bath; $50 single or double in cabin. No credit cards.

It would be difficult to imagine a more idyllic spot in this price range. With its wide expanse of neatly trimmed grass sloping down to the sea, tide pools (one of which is as big as a small swimming pool), and hammocks slung from the mango trees, this is the perfect place for anyone who wants to do some serious relaxing. The owners, who have young children, love to have other families as guests and there's always a cheerful family atmosphere. However, couples and individuals will also enjoy a stay at Amor de Mar. The big porch on the second floor of the main building makes a great place to sit and read or gaze out to sea. Breakfast is served and the homemade whole-wheat French bread is excellent.

LOS MANGOS, Montezuma, Cobano de Puntarenas. Tel. 506/661-1122, ext. 259. 10 rms (6 with private bath), 10 bungalows.
$ Rates: Dec–Mar $25 single, double, or triple without bath, $35 single, double, or triple with bath, $50 single, double, or triple bungalow; Apr–Nov rates are slightly lower. V.

✪ This hotel takes its name from the many mango trees on the grounds and was the first hotel in Montezuma to have its own swimming pool. Located south of town near Amor de Mar, Los Mangos has bungalows as well as rooms. The latter are fairly basic and are in an older building close to the road. However, it is the octagonal bungalows built of Costa Rican hardwoods that are the most attractive accommodations. Beside the pool is a large rancho-style restaurant and bar serving inexpensive meals.

WORTH THE EXTRA BUCKS

EL SANO BANANO, Montezuma, Cobano de Puntarenas. Tel. 506/661-1122, ext. 272. Fax 506/661-2320. 12 cabins, 3 rms (all with private bath).

$ Rates: Dec–Mar $40–$50 single or double; Apr–Nov $30–$40 single or double. AE, MC, V.

✪ El Sano Banano is a 10-minute walk up the beach to the left as you enter the village, and from the front porch of your cabin, you can sit and listen to the waves crashing on the beach a few feet away. There are two types of cabins here—octagonal hardwood Polynesian-style buildings and white ferro-cement geodesic domes that look like igloos—as well as three standard rooms in the main building. All the rooms are set amid a lush garden. One thing you should know is that the showers, though private, are outside of the cabins among the trees. Why not? Please do not try to drive up the beach. Seclusion and quiet are the main offerings of this place and cars would ruin the atmosphere. If you don't want to carry all your bags, you can leave some of your stuff at the Sano Banano restaurant in the village.

WHERE TO EAT

In addition to the restaurants listed below, Montezuma also has a great little ice cream stand called La Esquina Dulce. It's in front of the Mediterraneo Ristorante and serves its own homemade ice cream in tropical fruit flavors.

LAS CASCADAS, on the road to Cabo Blanco. No phone.
   Cuisine: COSTA RICAN/SEAFOOD. **Reservations:** Not accepted.
$ Prices: Main dishes $3.40–$9.80. No credit cards.
   Open: Daily 9am–9pm.
This little open-air restaurant is built on the banks of the stream just outside of the village and takes its name from the nearby waterfalls. The short menu sometimes includes fresh fish fillets, whole red snapper, or shrimp in *salsa ranchera*. This is such a pleasant spot, you could sit for hours beneath the thatched roof listening to the stream rushing past.

MEDITERRANEO RISTORANTE, to the left of the disco. No phone.
   Cuisine: ITALIAN. **Reservations:** Not accepted.
$ Prices: Main dishes $5.10–$8.10. No credit cards.
   Open: Daily 6–10:30pm.
If you're craving Italian food, this is the place to find it in Montezuma. The open-air restaurant is beneath an old house just back from the beach, and there are only a few tables. Arrive early if you want to be sure of getting a seat, this place is popular. The seafood spaghetti is great.

EL SANO BANANO, on main road into village. Tel. 661-1122, ext. 272.
   Cuisine: VEGETARIAN. **Reservations:** Not accepted.
$ Prices: Main dishes $2.30–$5.10. No credit cards.
   Open: Daily 7am–10pm.
✪ Delicious vegetarian meals including nightly specials, sandwiches, and salads are the specialty of this ever-popular Montezuma restaurant. You can even order a sandwich with cheese from the cheese factory in Monteverde. The day's menu specials are posted on a blackboard out front early in the day so you can be savoring the thought of dinner all day. Any time of day or night, the yogurt-fruit shakes are fabulous. El Sano Banano also shows videos nightly.

CHAPTER 5

THE NORTHERN ZONE

The northern zone, roughly defined here as the area north of San José and between Guanacaste province on the west and the lowlands of the Caribbean Coast on the east, is a naturalist's dream come true. There are rain forests and cloud forests, jungle rivers, and an unbelievable diversity of birds and other wildlife. In addition to its reputation for muddy hiking trails and crocodile-filled rivers, the northern zone also claims one of the best windsurfing spots in the world (on Lake Arenal, which is free of crocodiles by the way) and Costa Rica's most active volcanoes. Arenal Volcano, when free of clouds, puts on spectacular nighttime light shows and by day is reflected in the waters of nearby Lake Arenal. Adding a touch of comfort to a visit to the northern zone are several hot springs that vary in their levels of luxury.

1. PUERTO VIEJO DE SARAPIQUÍ

82 kilometers N of San José; 102 kilometers E of La Fortuna

GETTING THERE **By Bus** Express buses leave San José eight times daily from Avenida 11 between Calle Central and Calle 1. If you are heading to La Selva, Rara Avis, or El Gavilán lodges, be sure you are on a bus going through Las Horquetas. Duration: 3 hours. Fare: $3.75.

By Car The Guápiles Highway, which leads to the Caribbean Coast, heads north out of downtown San José on Calle 3 before heading east. Turn north before reaching Guápiles on the road to Río Frio and continue north through Las Horquetas, passing Rara Avis, La Selva, and El Gavilán Lodge, before reaching Puerto Viejo. An alternative route goes through Heredia, Barva, Varablanca, and San Miguel before reaching Puerto Viejo. This is a more scenic route, but the road is in very bad condition in certain stretches. If you want to take this route, head west out of San José and then turn north to Heredia and follow the signs for Varablanca.

DEPARTING Express buses for San José leave Puerto Viejo seven times daily. Buses leave Las Horquetas for San José four times daily.

ESSENTIALS Puerto Viejo is a small town at the center of which is the soccer field. If you continue past the soccer field on the main road and stay on the paved road, you will come to the Sarapiquí River and the dock where you can look into arranging a boat trip.

The Sarapiquí region, named for the river that drains this area, lies at the foot of the Cordillera Central mountain range. To the west is the rain forest of Braulio Carillo

WHAT'S SPECIAL ABOUT THE NORTHERN ZONE

Natural Spectacles
- Arenal Volcano, an active volcano with a large artificial lake at its base. The eruptions put on amazing nighttime light shows.
- Resplendent quetzals, among the world's most beautiful birds, can be seen in the cloud forests.

Parks/Gardens
- Caño Negro National Wildlife Refuge has one of Costa Rica's largest concentrations of wading birds.
- Arenal Botanical Gardens are filled with tropical flowers, as well as butterflies and hummingbirds.

- Monteverde Cloud Forest Reserve, one of the most famous natural areas in Costa Rica.

Activities
- Soaking in the hot river at Tabacon, on the flanks of Arenal Volcano.
- World-class sailboarding on Arenal Lake.
- Fishing for rainbow bass in Arenal Lake.
- Boat and kayak trips on the Sarapiquí River.

National Park, and to the east are Tortuguero National Park and Barra del Colorado National Wildlife Refuge. In between these protected areas lie thousands of acres of banana, pineapple, and palm plantations. It is here that you can see the great contradiction of Costa Rica. On one hand the country is known for its national parks, which preserve some of the largest tracts of rain forest left in Central America, but on the other hand, nearly every acre of land outside of those parks has been clear-cut and converted into plantations (and the cutting is still continuing).

Within the remaining rain forests, there are several lodges that attract naturalists (both amateur and professional) who are interested in learning more about the rain forest. Two of these lodges, La Selva and Rara Avis, have become well known around the world for the research that has been done on their surrounding reserves.

WHAT TO SEE & DO

For the adventurous, Puerto Viejo is a jumping-off point for trips down the Sarapiquí River to Tortuguero and Barra del Colorado on the Caribbean Coast. **Boat trips** can be arranged at the Hotel el Bambú. A boat for three people will cost you $100 to Oro Verde Lodge and back, $200 to Tortuguero, and $250 to Barra del Colorado. Alternatively, you can head down to the town dock on the bank of the Sarapiquí and see if you can arrange a less expensive boat trip on your own. A trip down the Sarapiquí, even if it's only for an hour or two, provides opportunities to spot crocodiles, caiman, monkeys, sloths, and dozens of bird species.

Another option is to do a **kayak trip** down the Sarapiquí. These trips are offered by **Rancho Leona**, La Virgen de Sarapiquí, Heredia (tel. 761-1019), a small kayaking center and guest house on the banks of the Sarapiquí River in the village of La Virgen. The trips are done as a package that includes two nights' lodging (very basic dormitory accommodations) and an all-day kayak trip that includes some basic instruction, and lunch on the river. The cost for the trip is $75 per person. No experience is necessary and the river is very calm. Other more extensive trips and trips for experienced kayakers can be arranged.

All of the lodges listed below arrange excursions throughout the region, including boat trips on the Sarapiquí, guided hikes in the rain forest, and horseback or mountain-bike rides.

WHERE TO STAY & EAT

DOUBLES FOR LESS THAN $25

MI LINDO SARAPIQUÍ, Puerto Viejo, Sarapiquí. Tel. 506/766-6281 or 766-6074. 6 rms (all with private bath).
$ Rates: $12.25 single; $20.80 double; $24.30 triple. MC, V.
This little family-run hotel is in the center of town overlooking the soccer field. The comfortable and clean rooms are on the second floor, above the large restaurant and bar.

NEARBY PLACES TO STAY

WORTH THE EXTRA BUCKS

EL GAVILÁN LODGE, Apdo. 445-2010, San José. Tel. 506/234-9507.
Fax 506/253-6556. 16 rms (all with private bath).
$ Rates (including breakfast): $45.75 single; $68.60 double; $102.90 triple. MC, V.
⭐ Located on the banks of the Sarapiquí River just south of Puerto Viejo on the road to Río Frío, El Gavilán is surrounded by 250 acres of forest reserve (secondary forest) and a 25-acre garden planted with lots of flowering ginger and orchids. Guest rooms are simply furnished, but do have fans and hot water, and there are always fresh flowers. The rooms in the main building are fairly basic, but do have huge bathrooms with two sinks. Other rooms are in rustic duplexes with cement floors. Tico meals are served buffet style, and there are always plenty of fresh fruits and juices (no alcohol is served, so bring your own). Lunch and dinner each cost $8. There's a kilometer-long nature trail here at the lodge, and guided hikes through the forest ($15 per person), horseback rides ($15 per person), and river trips ($20 per person) can all be arranged.

ORO VERDE STATION, Apdo. 7043-1000, San José. Tel. 506/233-6613. Fax 506/223-7479. 14 rms (8 with private bath).
$ Rates: $28.75–$34.50 single; $46–$57.50 double; $58.65–$75.90 triple. AE (San José office only).
Surrounded by nearly 20,000 acres of private reserve (3,000 acres of which is virgin forest) and bordering the Barra del Colorado National Wildlife Refuge, the Oro Verde Station is primarily a facility for researchers and students but is also open to the public. The nearest road is 30 miles away, so the lodge can only be reached by boat. The lodge's several high-peaked thatched-roof buildings lend a very tropical air to the facilities. Guest rooms are fairly basic, as you might expect at a research facility, and meals are often less than memorable. Both lunch and dinner are in the $5-to-$15 range. There are plenty of hiking trails, and river trips and guided hikes can be arranged at additional cost.

RARA AVIS, Apdo. 8105-1000, San José. Tel./fax 506/253-0844. 20 rms (10 with private bath).
$ Rates (including transportation from Horquetas, guided hikes, and three meals daily): $51.45 single with shared bath, $85.75–$97.15 single with private bath; $102.90 double with shared bath, $171.45 double with private bath. MC, V.
⭐ Once the exclusive stomping grounds of scientists and students, Rara Avis was made famous by the pioneering canopy research of Dr. Donald Perry, who first erected his famous canopy cable-car system in the rain forest here at Rara Avis. Though Perry's canopy cable car is no longer here, the rain forest research facility is still a fascinating place to visit. To get to Rara Avis, you must first travel to the village of Horquetas, which is between Guapiles and Puerto Viejo de Sarapiquí. In Horquetas, you are met by a tractor that takes four hours to cover the 15 kilometers to

the first of Rara Avis's two lodges. The ride, over a road made of logs, is excruciatingly uncomfortable and very hard on the back. The Waterfall Lodge is by far the more comfortable and has rustic rooms and a wraparound porch. The more economical El Plastico Lodge is much more Spartan. Meals are basic Tico-style dishes. Rara Avis is adjacent to Braulio Carillo National Park, and together the two have many miles of trails for you to explore. More than 320 species of birds have been sighted here.

2. ARENAL VOLCANO & LA FORTUNA

140 kilometers NW of San José; 61 kilometers E of Tilarán

GETTING THERE By Bus Buses leave San José for La Fortuna three times daily from Calle 16 between avenidas 1 and 3. Duration: 4½ hours. Fare: $3.30. Alternatively, you can take a bus to Ciudad Quesada from the same location in San José and then take a local bus from Ciudad Quesada to La Fortuna. Ciudad Quesada buses leave San José daily every hour from 5am to 7:30pm. Duration: 3 hours. Fare: $2.20. Buses leave Ciudad Quesada for La Fortuna six times daily. Duration: 1 hour. Fare: $1.10.

By Car There are several routes to La Fortuna from San José. The most popular is to head west on the Interamerican Highway and then turn north at Naranjo, continuing north, through Zarcero, to Ciudad Quesada. From Ciudad Quesada, one route goes through Jabillos while the other goes through Muelle. This latter route is the better road. Alternatively it is a little quicker to go first to Alajuela and then head north to Varablanca and then to San Miguel, where you turn west toward Río Cuarto and Aguas Zarcas. From Aguas Zarcas, continue west through Muelle to the turnoff for La Fortuna. Travel time either way is around three hours. A new route from San Ramon (west of Naranjo) north through Tigra, though unpaved, is very scenic.

DEPARTING There are buses to San José five times daily. Buses to Ciudad Quesada leave seven times daily. From there you can catch one of the hourly buses to San José. There are also buses to Tilarán, at the northern end of Lake Arenal, twice daily.

ESSENTIALS Fortuna is only a few streets wide, with almost all the hotels, restaurants, and shops clustered along the main road. There are several small information and tour booking offices across the street from the soccer field.

U ntil 1937, when the mountain just west of La Fortuna was first scaled, no one ever dreamed that it might be a volcano. Gazing up at the cinder-strewn slopes of Arenal Volcano today, it is hard to believe that people could not have recognized this perfectly cone-shaped volcano for what it is.

In July of 1968 the volcano, which had lain dormant for hundreds of years, erupted with sudden and unexpected violence. The nearby village of Tabacón was destroyed and nearly 80 of its inhabitants were killed. Since that eruption more than a quarter century ago, 5,358-foot-high Arenal Volcano has been Costa Rica's most active volcano. Frequent powerful explosions send cascades of red-hot lava rocks tumbling down the western slope of the volcano. During the day, the lava flows steam and rumble. However, it is at night that the volcano puts on its most mesmerizing show. If you should be lucky enough to be here on a clear night, you will see the night sky turned red by lava spewing from Arenal's crater. In the past few years, the forests to the south of the volcano have been declared Arenal National Park.

Lying at the foot of this natural spectacle is the tiny farming community of La

Fortuna. In recent years, this town has become a center for volcano watchers from around the world. There are several budget hotels in La Fortuna, and it is here that you can arrange night tours to the best volcano-viewing spot.

WHAT TO SEE & DO

The first thing you should know is that you can't climb Arenal Volcano. It is not safe because of the constant activity, and several foolish people who have ignored this warning have lost their lives. Watching Arenal's constant eruptions is the main activity in La Fortuna and is best done at night when the orange lava glows against the starry sky. Though it is possible to simply look up from the middle of town and see Arenal erupting, the view is better from the west side of the volcano, about 17 kilometers distant. If you have a car, you can drive to the viewing area, but if you have arrived by bus, you will need to take a tour. These night tours, which cost $6.75, are offered through every hotel in town and at several tour offices on the main street.

To learn more about Arenal Volcano and volcanoes in general, try to catch the evening slide show at the **Eco-Trust Information Center** (tel. 479-9186) next to the Vaca Muca Restaurant, 1 kilometer west of La Fortuna. These slide shows are held Tuesday, Thursday, and Saturday evenings at 6 and 8pm. This info center also includes a free museum of volcanology and has a small collection of local pre-Columbian artifacts. The center is open Tuesday through Saturday from 10am to 6pm and Sunday from 10am to 4pm.

There are also a few activities to keep you busy during the day. The first thing you might do is hike out to the **Río Fortuna waterfall.** It's about 5½ kilometers outside of town in a lush jungle setting. There is a sign in town to indicate the road that leads out to the falls, and as you hike along this road, you'll probably be offered a lift. If this seems like too much exercise, you can rent a horse and guide for four hours for $13.55. You can arrange this ride through your hotel or through **Pura Vida** (tel. 479-9045). Another good ride is up to **Cerro Chato,** an extinct side cone on the flank of Arenal. There is a pretty little lake up here. Ask at your hotel about this trip. It should cost you around $13.50.

When you've finished your ride or hike, you'll probably want a soak in a hot spring. If so, head 12 kilometers west of La Fortuna to Tabacón, where a hot river flows down off the slopes of Arenal Volcano. At Tabacón, you can luxuriate at the **Tabacón Hot Spring Resort** (tel. 233-0780 in San José), where there are several hot pools, hot waterfalls, sun decks, a restaurant and bar, and a great view of the volcano. The resort is open daily from 10am to 11pm and charges $9.50 admission. Alternatively, you can cross the road and walk down a gravel driveway to a less luxurious and more natural stretch of this hot river. Here you'll pay only $1.70 to soak away your aches and pains.

You can also arrange a tour to the **Venado Caverns,** which are a 45-minute drive from La Fortuna. You'll see plenty of stalactites, stalagmites, and other limestone formations, of course, but you'll also see bats and cave fish. Tours cost $20.30 per person and are offered by Pura Vida in La Fortuna. You can also go rafting with **Rafting Safaris** (tel. 479-9076), which offers half-day raft float trips for $40 per person. Bird-watching and croc-spotting are good on these trips.

La Fortuna is also the best place from which to make a day trip to the **Caño Negro National Wildlife Refuge.** This vast network of marshes and rivers is 100 kilometers north of La Fortuna near the town of Los Chiles. This refuge is best known for its amazing abundance of bird life, including roseate spoonbills, jabiru storks, herons, and egrets, but you can also see caiman and crocodiles here. Keep in mind that the main lake here dries up in the dry season, which reduces the number of wading birds to be seen. Pura Vida in La Fortuna offers tours to Caño Negro for $33.80 per person.

WHERE TO STAY

In addition to the budget hotels listed below, there is Los Lagos campground 1 kilometer east of Tabacón and another campground 2 kilometers west of La Fortuna.

DOUBLES FOR LESS THAN $25

HOTEL FORTUNA, La Fortuna, San Carlos. Tel. 506/479-9197. 7 rms (all with private bath).
$ Rates: $8.50 single; $17.05 double; $25.50 triple. No credit cards.

Located one block south of the gas station, this small hotel is dark and very basic, but the rooms are clean and the prices are great. Try to get a second-floor room; these are a bit brighter than those on the ground floor. There is an open-air restaurant at the front of the hotel.

HOTEL SAN BOSCO, 200 meters north of the gas station, La Fortuna, San Carlos. Tel. 506/479-9050. Fax 506/479-9109. 27 rms (all with private bath).
$ Rates: $14.10–$29.95 single; $24.40–$44.10 double; $29.10–$48.50 triple. V.
Located a block off La Fortuna's main street, the San Bosco has two styles of rooms. The older, cheaper rooms are small and dark and have cement floors. However, the newer rooms are much more attractive and have stone walls, tile floors, ceiling fans, reading lights, and benches on the veranda in front. Up on the top floor, there is an observation deck for volcano viewing.

DOUBLES FOR LESS THAN $35

HOTEL LAS COLINAS, 150 meters south of the National Bank, La Fortuna, San Carlos. Tel./fax 506/479-9107. 21 rms (all with private bath).
$ Rates: $15.45 single; $28.70 double; $35.70 triple. MC, V.
This modern three-story building in the center of town offers clean, modern rooms. However, you'll need to be in good shape if you stay in one of the third-floor rooms which have the best views. The stairs are very steep. There are a few rooms on the ground floor, but they don't even have windows to the outside and so are very dark. My favorite room is the one with the balcony and the view of Arenal Volcano.

WORTH THE EXTRA BUCKS

ALBERGUE BURÍO, Apdo. 1234-1250, Escazú. Tel./fax 506/479-9076 or 228-6623. 8 rms (all with private bath).
$ Rates (including continental breakfast): Dec–Apr $22.90 single, $45.75 double; May–Nov $17.15 single, $34.30 double; $11.50 for students. MC, V.
This small lodge is on the main road through La Fortuna, though it is set back from the street behind some shops and is a bit difficult to spot. There is a grassy garden, a small breakfast room, and the owners are very helpful. Guest rooms have big windows and lots of polished hardwood and are attractively decorated with lace curtains. This hotel also operates as a youth hostel and consequently offers lower rates for students. You can arrange various tours here at the Burío, including night tours to see the volcano, trips to Tabacón hot springs, and fishing trips on Lake Arenal.

LAS CABAÑITAS RESORT, Apdo. 5-4417, La Fortuna, San Carlos. Tel./fax 506/479-9091. 30 cabins (all with bath).
$ Rates: Dec–Apr $68.60 single, $74.30 double; May–Nov (including breakfast and dinner) $63.75 single, $81.10 double. AE, MC, V.

Located 8 kilometers east of town, these rustic mountain cabins are the place to stay if you want the best view of Arenal Volcano. Most of the cabins face the volcano and have little porches where you can sit and enjoy the show by day or night. Each cabin is built of varnished hardwoods and has a beautiful floor, a high ceiling, louvered walls to let in the breezes, a king bed, a modern tile bathroom down a few steps from the sleeping area, and rocking chairs on the porch. There is a small swimming pool with a snack bar beside it and also a larger, full-service restaurant. Note that in the off season, the hotel includes breakfast and dinner in the room rates. Various tours can be arranged through the hotel.

NEARBY PLACES TO STAY
WORTH THE EXTRA BUCKS

ARENAL OBSERVATORY LODGE, Costa Rica Sun Tours, Apdo. 1195-1250, Escazú. Tel. 506/255-2011. Fax 506/255-4410. 10 rms (all with private bath).
$ Rates (including breakfast and dinner): $68.60 single; $102.90 double. AE, MC

⭐ This rustic lodge was originally built for the use of volcanologists from the Smithsonian Institution, but is today open to the public as well. The lodge is only 2½ miles from the volcano and is built on a high ridge, which gives it the best view of any of the local lodges. Some of the rooms, as well as the dining room, have superb views of the volcano. Surrounding the lodge is the Arenal Forest Preserve, which includes thousands of acres of forest and many kilometers of trails. To reach this lodge, you'll need a four-wheel-drive vehicle. There are two river crossings (including the Río Agua Caliente) to make on the 9-kilometer gravel road to the lodge.

---

3. TILARÁN & LAKE ARENAL

200 kilometers NW of San José; 20 kilometers NW of Monteverde; 70 kilometers SE of Liberia

GETTING THERE   By Bus   Express buses leave San José for Tilarán four times daily from Calle 14 between avenidas 9 and 11. Duration: 4 hours. Fare: $3.10. There are also morning and afternoon buses from Puntarenas to Tilarán. Duration: 3 hours. Fare: $1.75. From Monteverde (Santa Elena), there is a bus daily at 7am. Duration: 3 hours. Fare: $1.10.

By Car   From San José, take the Interamerican Highway west toward Puntarenas and then continue north on this road to Cañas. In Cañas, turn east toward Tilarán. The drive takes 4 hours. If you are thinking of heading up this way from La Fortuna, be aware that the road is unpaved, in very bad shape, and entails several stream crossings. The road should not be tried in a regular car except during the dry season.

DEPARTING   Direct buses to San José leave four times daily. Buses to Puntarenas leave twice daily. The bus to Monteverde (Santa Elena) leaves daily at 12:30pm. Buses to the town of Nuevo Arenal, on the far side of the lake, leave three times daily. Buses to Cañas, where you can catch buses north or south along the Interamerican Highway, leave six times daily. Buses for La Fortuna, at the south end of Lake Arenal, leave twice daily.

ESSENTIALS   Tilarán is about 5 kilometers from Lake Arenal. All roads into town lead to the central park, which is Tilarán's main point of reference for addresses. If you need to change money, check at one of the hotels listed here. If you need a taxi to get to a lodge on Lake Arenal, phone 695-5324.

Lake Arenal, a man-made lake with an area of 33 square miles, is the largest lake in Costa Rica and is surrounded by rolling hills that are partly pastured and partly forested. At the opposite (south) end of the lake from Tilarán lies the perfect cone of Arenal Volcano. The volcano's barren slopes are a stunning sight from here, especially when reflected in the waters of the lake. The north side of Lake Arenal is a dry region of rolling hills and pastures, distinctly different from the lusher landscape near La Fortuna at the south end.

People around here used to curse the winds, which often come blasting across this end of the lake at 60 knots or greater. However, since the first sailboarders caught wind of Lake Arenal's combination of warm fresh water, high winds, and a spectacular view, things have been changing quickly. Though the town of Tilarán is still little more than a quiet farm community, out along the shores of the lake, hotels are proliferating. Even if you aren't a rabid boardhead (fanatical sailboarder), you still might enjoy hanging out by the lake in hopes of catching a glimpse of Arenal volcano.

The lake's other claim to fame is its rainbow bass fishing. These fighting fish are known in their native South America as *guapote* and are large members of the cichlid family. Their sharp teeth and fighting nature make them a real challenge.

WHAT TO SEE & DO

If you want to try windsurfing, you can rent equipment from **Tilawa Windsurfing Center** (tel. 695-5050 or 695-5666), which has its facilities on one of the lake's few accessible beaches, about 8 kilometers from Tilarán on the road around the west end of the lake. Windsurfers rent for $35 to $45 per day and lessons are also available. On the other side of the lake you'll find the new **Tico Wind** (fax 695-5387), which rents equipment for $45 per day or $250 per week between November and April. If you'd rather stay on dry land, the folks at Tilawa can arrange for you to rent a horse for $10 per hour.

Up above Lake Arenal on the far side of the lake from Tilarán, you'll find the beautiful little heart-shaped **Coter Lake.** This lake is surrounded by forest and has good swimming, picnicking, and some trails. A taxi to Coter Lake will cost around $12. Continuing south on the road around the lake will bring you to the town of Nuevo Arenal, where the pavement ends. If you continue another 4 kilometers on this road, you will come to the **Arenal Botanical Gardens** (tel. 695-5266, ext. 273), which is open Wednesday through Sunday from 9am to 5pm and charges $3.40 admission. This private garden was started only in 1991 but is already quite beautiful. Not only are their many tropical plants and flowers to be seen, but there are always butterflies and hummingbirds in the gardens.

If you want to try your hand at fishing for rainbow bass, contact **J.J.'s Fishing Tours** (tel. 695-5825). A half-day fishing trip will cost between $30 and $100 per person, depending on the number of people in your party. If you'd just like to go for a boat ride on the lake, check at **Xiloe Lodge** (tel. 259-9192 or 229-0161).

WHERE TO STAY
DOUBLES FOR LESS THAN $15

CABINAS MARY, costado sur del parque, Tilarán, Guanacaste. Tel. 506/695-5479. 16 rms (11 with private bath).
$ Rates: $5.05 single with shared bath, $7 single with private bath; $10.05 double with shared bath, $12.40 double with private bath. No credit cards.
Located right on Tilarán's large and sunny central park, Cabinas Mary is a very basic but fairly clean hotel. It's upstairs from the restaurant of the same name and has parking in back. Rooms are large and have plenty of windows. You even get hot water here, which is a surprise at this price. The restaurant downstairs is a gringo hangout. It's open daily from 7am to 10pm; meals cost between $3 and $6.

DOUBLES FOR LESS THAN $45

CABINAS EL SUEÑO, Tilarán, Guanacaste. Tel. 506/695-5347. 12 rms (all with private bath).
$ Rates: $16.20 single; $26.92 double; $31.40 triple. MC, V.
Right in the middle of this small town, Cabinas El Sueño is a simple two-story hotel, but it is clean and bright, and the management is friendly. There is parking in back of the hotel and a small courtyard complete with fountain on the second floor of the building. Downstairs there's a restaurant and bar.

CHALET NICHOLAS, Apdo. 72-5710, Tilarán, Guanacaste. No phone. Fax 506/695-5387. 3 rms (all with private bath).
$ Rates (including full breakfast): $44.60 double. No credit cards.

✪ This friendly, American-owned bed-and-breakfast is located 2 kilometers west of the town of Nuevo Arenal and sits on a hill above the road. There are great views from the garden, and one of the three rooms has a view of Arenal Volcano out the window. The modern home is set on three acres and has pretty flower gardens, an organic vegetable garden, and an aviary full of toucans and other colorful birds. Behind the property stretch acres of forest through which you can hike in search of birds, butterflies, orchids, and other tropical beauties. The upstairs loft room is the largest room and has its own deck. Owners John and Catherine Nicholas go out of their way to make their guests feel at home.

ROCK RIVER LODGE, Apdo. 2907-1000, San José. Tel. 506/235-9348 or 222-4547. Fax 506/297-1364 or 221-3011. 6 rms (all with private bath).
$ Rates: $40 single or double. No credit cards.

✪ Set high on a grassy hill above the lake, Rock River Lodge is popular with sailboarders. The guest rooms are housed in a long, low lodge set on stilts. Walls and floors are made of hardwood and there are bamboo railings along the veranda. Wind chimes let you know when the winds are up. Rooms have double beds (with mosquito nets) and bunk beds. Though fairly simple, this is one of the most attractive lodges in the area. However, it's a long walk down to the lake (and back up). Meals in the open-air dining room will cost you around $25 per person per day.

WORTH THE EXTRA BUCKS

HOTEL TILAWA, Apdo. 92, Tilarán, Guanacaste. Tel. 506/695-5050, 695-5666, or (in the U.S.) toll free 800/851-8929. Fax 506/695-5766. 28 rms (all with private bath).
$ Rates (including breakfast): $54 single; $71 double; $87 triple. AE, MC, V.

✪ Built to resemble the Palace of Knossos on the island of Crete, the Hotel Tilawa is an avid windsurfer's dream brought to reality. The American owners have for many years run a windsurfing center on Lake Arenal. The hotel sits high on the slopes above the lake and has a sweeping vista down the lake. Unusual colors and an antique paint effect make the hotel look as though it has been weathered by the ages. Guest rooms have dyed cement floors, Guatemalan bedspreads, and big windows. Some rooms have kitchenettes. Hotel amenities include a swimming pool and tennis court. There is a bar, as well as a moderately priced restaurant. The Tilawa can arrange not only windsurfing but mountain biking, horseback riding, fishing trips, and excursions around the lake.

VILLAS ALPINO, Apdo. 7-5710, Tilarán, Guanacaste. No phone. Fax 506/695-5387. 5 cabins (all with bath).
$ Rates: Dec–Apr $57.15 single, double, or triple; May–Nov $45.72 single, double, or triple. No credit cards.

Built by a Dutch windsurfer, these cozy cabins have great views and all the conveniences of apartments. The refrigerator in the kitchen even comes stocked with four beers and some coffee. The kitchens have two walls of windows that make the cabins fairly cheery. There are also picture windows beside the beds and small porches out front to let you maximize your vista-viewing time. There are Guatemalan bedspreads, and in the bathroom, you'll find a river-rock wall and window seat and a brick-tile floor. Keep in mind that it's a long way down to the lake, so you'll need to have your own car if you plan to stay here. You'll find Villas Alpino on the east side of the lake.

WHERE TO EAT

If you are staying in Tilarán, there are numerous inexpensive eateries, including restaurants at Cabinas Mary and Cabinas El Sueño, both of which are mentioned above. Also, around the corner from Cabinas Mary is El Lugar, a popular restaurant and bar that is definitely worth checking out. If you are staying outside of town, you'll likely be eating in your hotel's dining room since there are few restaurants around the shores of the lake. Worth mentioning is Equus BBQ, an open-air restaurant in front of Xiloe Lodge. Equus specializes in roast chicken and steaks. If you are staying near Nuevo Arenal, try the following restaurant.

RESTAURANT LAJAS, on the main street through town. Tel. 695-5266.
   Cuisine: COSTA RICAN. **Reservations:** Not accepted.
$ Prices: Main dishes $2.05–$3.75. No credit cards.
   Open: Daily 5am–10pm.
This surprisingly fancy little restaurant is one of the best values in Costa Rica. There are red tablecloths on every table, waiters in bow ties, and a wall of mirrors to make the tiny dining room look larger than it really is, but these are only the incidentals. The real reason to eat here is for good Tico cooking at rock-bottom prices. The deal of the day is always the casado.

4. MONTEVERDE

167 kilometers NW of San José; 82 kilometers NW of Puntarenas

GETTING THERE By Bus Express buses leave San José Monday through Thursday at 2:30pm and Saturday and (December through April) Sunday at 6:30am from Calle 14 between avenidas 9 and 11. Duration: 3½ hours. Fare: $5.85. There is also a daily bus at 2:15pm from Puntarenas to Santa Elena, which is only a few kilometers from Monteverde. The bus stop in Puntarenas is across the street from the main bus station. Duration: 2½ hours. Fare: $2.40. There is a daily bus from Tilarán (Lake Arenal) at 1pm. Duration: 3 hours (40 kilometers!). Fare: $1.10. One other option is to take Costa Rica Expeditions' (tel. 257-0766) van from San José. You must have a reservation. Fare: $35 each way.

By Car Take the Interamerican Highway toward Puntarenas and follow the signs for Nicaragua. About 31 kilometers past the turnoff for Puntarenas, watch for the Río Lagarto bridge. It takes about 2¼ hours to this point. Take the dirt road to the right just before the bridge. From this turnoff, it's another 38 kilometers (1½ to 2 hours) to Monteverde. The going is very slow because the road is so bad. Many people are told that this road is not passable without four-wheel drive, but I have been driving it for years, albeit in the dry season, in regular cars. Just don't try it in the rainy season unless you have four-wheel drive. Be sure you have plenty of gas in the car before starting up to Monteverde.

DEPARTING The express bus to San José leaves Tuesday, Wednesday, and Thursday at 6:30am; Friday, Saturday (December through April), and Sunday at 3pm. The bus from Santa Elena to Puntarenas leaves daily at 6am. To reach Liberia, take the 6am Santa Elena–Puntarenas bus and get off at the Río Lagarto bridge, where the bus reaches the paved road. You can then flag down a bus bound for Liberia (almost any bus heading north). The Santa Elena–Tilarán bus leaves daily at 7am.

ESSENTIALS Orientation As you approach Santa Elena, take the right fork in the road if you are heading directly to Monteverde. If you continue straight, you will come into the village of Santa Elena, which has the Puntarenas bus stop, a health clinic, bank, general store, and a few simple restaurants and budget hotels. There is also a small information center (tel. 645-5137). It's located across the street from the Hotel El Tucan and is open Monday through Saturday from 9am to noon and from 1 to 6pm.
   Monteverde, on the other hand, is not a village in the traditional sense of the word. There is no center of town, only dirt lanes leading off from the main road to various farms. This main road has signs for all the hotels and restaurants mentioned here and dead-ends at the reserve entrance.

A taxi (tel. 645-5071) between Santa Elena and either the Monteverde Cloud Forest Biological Reserve or the Santa Elena Forest. Reserve will cost around $7. Count on $4 to $6 from Santa Elena to the lodge in Monteverde.

It is not surprising that the name Monteverde (Spanish for "Green Mountain") was chosen for this area. That is exactly what you find up here at the end of a long, rutted dirt road that passes through mile after mile of often dry, brown pasture lands. All of those pastures you pass through were once covered with dense forest, but now only small pieces of that original forest remain.

The village of Monteverde was founded in the 1950s by Quakers from the United States who wished to leave behind the constant fear of war and the obligation to support continued militarism through U.S. taxes. They chose Costa Rica because it was committed to a nonmilitaristic economic path. Although Monteverde's founders came here to farm the land, they recognized the need to preserve the rare cloud forest that covered the mountain slopes above their fields, and to that end they dedicated the largest adjacent tract of cloud forest as the **Monteverde Cloud Forest Biological Reserve.**

If you have an interest in the environment and are planning a trip to Costa Rica, you have no doubt already heard of Monteverde. Perched on a high mountain ridge, this tiny, scattered village and cloud forest reserve are well known both among scientific researchers and ecotravelers. Cloud forests are a mountaintop phenomenon. Moist warm air sweeping in off the nearby ocean is forced upward by mountain slopes, and as the moist air rises, it cools, forming clouds. The mountain tops of Costa Rica are almost daily blanketed in dense clouds, and as these clouds cling to the slopes, moisture condenses on forest trees. This constant level of moisture has given rise to an incredible diversity of life forms and a forest in which every square inch of space has some sort of plant growing on it. Within the cloud forest, the branches of huge trees are draped with epiphytic plants—orchids, ferns, bromeliads. This intense botanic competition has created an almost equally diverse population of insects, birds, and other wildlife. Monteverde Reserve covers 26,000 acres of forest, including several different life zones that are characterized by different types of plants and animals. Within this small area are more than 2,000 species of plants, 320 bird species, and 100 different species of mammals. It is no wonder that the reserve has been the site of constant scientific investigations since its founding.

The reserve was originally known only to the handful of researchers who came here to study different aspects of life in the cloud forest. However, as the beauty and biological diversity of the area became known outside of university circles, casual visitors began arriving. For many, the primary goal was a chance to glimpse the rare, elusive, resplendent quetzal, a bird once revered by the pre-Columbian peoples of the Americas. As the numbers of visitors began to grow, lodges began opening. Word spread, more lodges opened, and so on. Today Monteverde is a prime example of too many people chasing after the same little piece of nature. However, despite the hordes of ecotourists traipsing the trails of Monteverde, it is still a beautiful place and offers a glimpse into the life of one of the world's most threatened ecosystems. I urge you, though, to seriously consider visiting another cloud forest area in an effort to lessen the impact of tourism on Monteverde. Other places you could visit include the Los Angeles Cloud Forest Reserve (a day trip from San José) or the Tapantí National Wildlife Refuge, which has several nearby lodges. At either of these places you will find far fewer crowds and better chances of seeing resplendent quetzals.

WHAT TO SEE & DO

At $15.20 per person, the reserve's tours are expensive, especially after you pay the $8.10 reserve entrance fee, but I strongly recommend that you go with a guide. On one of the reserve's official guided 2-to-3-hour hikes (or with a guide hired through your hotel), you can see far more than you could on your own. I've been into the reserve twice in the same morning—once on my own and once with a guide—and with the guide I saw much more and learned much more about cloud forests and their inhabitants. On the other hand, while alone I saw a rare bird, a guan, that I didn't see when walking the trails with a dozen or more rather noisy visitors.

The preserve is open daily from 7am to 4pm. Because only 100 people are allowed into the preserve at any one time, you may be forced to wait for a while before being allowed in. However, if you stop by the office the afternoon before you want to visit, you can usually get tickets for early the next morning. Rubber boots are available at the reserve entrance and rent for less than $1. The trails here are very muddy, so these boots are a very good idea.

Perhaps the most famous resident of the cloud forests of Costa Rica is the quetzal, a robin-sized bird with iridescent-green wings and a ruby-red breast, which has become extremely rare because of habitat destruction. The male quetzal also has two long tail feathers that make it one of the most spectacular birds on earth. The best time to see quetzals is early to midmorning, with February through April (mating season) being the easiest months to spot these magnificent birds.

Other animals that have been seen in Monteverde include jaguars, ocelots, and tapirs. After the quetzal, Monteverde's most beautiful resident was the golden toad (*sapo dorado*). However, owing to several years of low precipitation, the golden toad seems to have disappeared from the forest, which was its only known home in the entire world. There has been speculation that the toad was adversely affected by a natural drought cycle, the disappearing ozone layer, or acid rain. Photos of the golden toad abound in Monteverde, and I'm sure you'll be as saddened as I was by the disappearance of such a beautiful creature.

Hiking opportunities can also be found outside the reserve boundaries. You can avoid the crowds at Monteverde by heading 5 kilometers north from the village of Santa Elena to the 900-acre **Santa Elena Forest Reserve.** There are 8 kilometers of hiking trails as well as an information center. The **Bajo Tigre Trail,** which starts from near the CASEM artesan's shop in Monteverde, is a 2-mile-long trail that's home to several different bird species that are not usually found within the reserve. The trail is open daily from 8am to 4pm. There is a $2.70 charge to hike this privately owned and maintained trail. You can also go on guided 3-hour hikes at the **Reserva Sendero Tranquilo** (tel. 645-6032), which has 200 acres of land, two-thirds of which is in virgin forest. This reserve is located up the hill from the cheese factory, charges $11.50 for its tours, and is open daily from 5am to 2pm seasonally. At **Finca de Aves,** which is open daily from 7am to 5pm, there are hiking trails through primary and secondary forest on 43 acres. More than 100 species of birds have been seen here. Admission is $5. Guided night tours are another fascinating way to experience the world of the cloud forest. These tours are offered by most area hotels or can be arranged by phoning 645-5118. Glowworms, walking sticks, and luminescent fungi are among the flora and fauna to be seen at night.

When you feel like you've had enough hiking, you might want to try exploring the area on horseback. Most of the hotels here can arrange horseback rides with a guide for between $7 and $10 per person per hour. You can also contact **Meg's Riding Stables** (tel. 645-5052), which offers 3-hour guided rides for $34.

To learn more about Monteverde, stop in at the **Monteverde Conservation League** (tel. 645-5003) office, which is located across the street from the gas station and is open Monday through Friday from 8am to noon and 1 to 5pm. They also sell T-shirts and cards here, and proceeds go to help purchase more land for the Bosque Eterno de Los Niños (Children's Eternal Forest).

You can glimpse part of the area's history at **El Trapiche,** an old-fashioned sugar mill where an ox-driven mill can be demonstrated if you make prior arrangements. El Trapiche is open daily from 10am to 7pm, and admission is $2. You'll find the mill 1½ kilometers north of Santa Elena on the road to Tilarán.

Because the vegetation in the cloud forest is so dense, most of the forest's animal residents are rather difficult to spot. If you were unsatisfied with your sightings, even with a naturalist guide leading you, you might want to consider attending a slide show of photographs taken in the reserve. These slide shows are presented by the **Hummingbird Gallery** (tel. 645-5030) daily at 9:30am and 4:30pm. Admission is $3.40. There are also similar slide shows at the **Monteverde Lodge** several nights a week.

You'll find the Hummingbird Gallery just outside the reserve entrance. Hanging from trees around the gallery are several hummingbird feeders that attract more than seven species of these avian jewels. At any given moment, there might be several dozen hummingbirds buzzing and chattering around the building. Inside, you will, of course, find a lot of beautiful color photos and postcards of hummingbirds and other Monteverde nature scenes. The gallery is open daily from 8:30am to 4:30pm.

Birds are not the only colorful fauna in the Monteverde cloud forest. Butterflies abound here, and the **Butterfly Garden,** located near the Pensión Monteverde Inn, displays many of Costa Rica's most beautiful species. Besides the hundreds of preserved and mounted butterflies, there are also gardens and a greenhouse full of live butterflies. The garden is open daily from 9:30am to 4pm, and the admission is $5 for adults and $2.45 for children, which includes a guided tour. The best time to visit is between 11am and 1pm, when the butterflies are most active.

If you're in the mood to do some shopping, stop in at **CASEM,** which is on the right just past Restaurant El Bosque. This crafts cooperative sells embroidered clothing, T-shirts, posters and postcards with photos of the local flora and fauna, their own Monteverde coffee, and many other items to remind you of your visit to Monteverde. CASEM is open Monday through Saturday from 8am to 5pm, and on Sunday from 10am to 4pm (closed Sundays May through October). Between November and April, you can also visit the **Sarah Dowell Watercolor Gallery,** which is up the hill from the cheese factory and sells paintings by this local artist.

WHERE TO STAY
DOUBLES FOR LESS THAN $15

PENSIÓN EL PINO, Monteverde, Puntarenas. Tel. 506/645-5130. 5 rms (all with shared bath).
$ Rates: $5.75 single; $11.45 double; $17.15 triple. No credit cards.
These rooms are about as basic as they come. They are slightly larger than those at the Pensión Manakin next door and have red-tile floors. Some rooms have double beds and others have bunk beds. No meals are available here, so you'll have to walk down the road a little ways to the nearest restaurant. You'll find this *pensión* just off the main road about a third of the way from Santa Elena to the reserve.

PENSIÓN FLOR MAR, Apdo. 10165-1000, San José. Tel. 506/645-5009. Fax 506/645-5011. 13 rms (3 with private bath).
$ Rates (including three meals): $25.15 single without bath, $28.60 single with bath; $50.30 double without bath, $57.15 double with bath. No credit cards.

S The Flor Mar was one of the first lodges to open in Monteverde and initially catered almost exclusively to professors and students doing scientific research in the reserve. Study groups are still the bulk of the Flor Mar's business, but casual visitors are also welcome, though the accommodations are very basic. The rooms are very simply furnished, which means bunk beds in some rooms. However, this lodge is close to the park entrance, which is a definite plus if you don't have a car. The dining room is large and rather dark, but there is a much more appealing lounge in the lower of the lodge's two main buildings. Note that the rates here include all your meals.

PENSIÓN MANAKIN, Apdo. 11-5655, Santa Elena, Monteverde, Puntarenas. Tel. 506/645-5080. 15 rms (6 with private bath).
$ Rates: $5.75 single without bath, $17.15 single with bath; $11.45 double without bath, $22.90 double with bath. No credit cards.
Though most of the rooms here are merely tiny cubicles with bunk beds and cement floors, the rooms with private baths are a bit better. These rooms have carpeting and

clean tile bathrooms. You'll find this *pensión* about a third of the way from Santa Elena to the reserve.

DOUBLES FOR LESS THAN $25

HOTEL EL TUCAN, Santa Elena, Puntarenas. Tel. 506/645-5017. 14 rms (7 with private bath).
$ Rates: $7.75 single without bath, $11.60 single with bath; $15.45 double without bath, $23.20 double with bath. No credit cards.
This very basic hotel is located on the edge of Santa Elena (on the back road from the village's main street to the road to Monteverde). Though the rooms without bath are only slightly larger than closets, they are fairly clean. Rooms with private bathrooms are in a separate building and are slightly larger. Costa Rican–style meals are served. Keep in mind that this hotel is 5 kilometers from the reserve. If you don't have a car, taxis to and from the reserve are going to add to your expenses.

PENSIÓN MONTEVERDE INN, Apdo. 10165-1000, San José. Tel. 506/ 645-5156. 10 rms (all with private bath).
$ Rates: $9.15 single; $18.30 double. No credit cards.
Of the numerous budget lodgings in the area, this one has the most pleasant surroundings. Located next to the Monteverde Butterfly Garden, the Monteverde Inn is a couple of hundred yards off the main road on a small farm. Owner David Savage and his family have operated this simple rustic lodge for years. The rooms are small and come with two twin beds or a double bed. Hardwood floors keep the rooms from seeming too Spartan. It's a bit of a walk up to the park entrance, but once you reach the main road, you can try hitching a ride. Horse rentals here are $5 per hour, and economical meals are available.

DOUBLES FOR LESS THAN $35

EL BOSQUE, Apdo. 1165-1000, San José. Tel./fax 506/645-5129. 20 rms (all with private bath).
$ Rates: $20 single; $28 double; $34 triple; $38 quad. V.
Hidden down the hill behind El Bosque restaurant (on the main road to the preserve) is one of Monteverde's best values. Though the rooms are very basic, they are clean, fairly large, and have high ceilings, picture windows, and double beds. The cement floors and simple furnishings are what help keep the rates down. Tico standards and international dishes are served in the hotel's restaurant, with prices ranging from $3.05 to $12.20. The hotel also has a camping area ($2.70 per person per night).

CABINAS EL GRAN MIRADOR DE SAN GERARDO, Monteverde, Puntarenas. Tel. 506/661-3750 (leave message). Fax 506/661-3505. 5 cabins (none with private bath), 12 dorm beds.
$ Rates: $9.15 per person in the dorm; $20.60 single; $28.60 double. No credit cards.
If you're looking for a bit more adventure and rusticity than is offered at any of the lodges in Monteverde or Santa Elena, give these friendly folks a call. The rustic wooden cabins and dormitory building are all very simply furnished, though the cabins do have great views of Arenal Volcano (when it's clear). Here's the catch: For most of the year, you'll have to spend three hours on horseback to reach these cabins. Only during the driest months, from February to May, is it possible to drive a car to the cabins. The cabins are a long way from the Monteverde Cloud Forest Reserve, but they are close to the Santa Elena Rainforest Reserve.

WORTH THE EXTRA BUCKS

HOTEL BELMAR, Monteverde, Puntarenas. Tel. 506/645-5201. Fax 506/645-5135. 32 rms (all with private bath).
$ Rates: $45.75 single; $57.15 double. Discounts sometimes available in low season. No credit cards.

★ You'll think that you're in the Alps when you stay at this beautiful Swiss chalet–style hotel. Set at the top of a grassy hill, the Belmar has stunning views all the way to the Nicoya Gulf and the Pacific Ocean. Afternoons in the dining room or lounge are idyllic, with bright sunlight streaming in through a west-facing wall of glass that provides a grandstand seat for spectacular sunsets. Most of the guest rooms come with wood paneling, French doors, and little balconies that open onto splendid views. Meals usually live up to the surroundings and run between $18 and $21 per person per day. The Belmar is up a road to the left of the gas station in Monteverde.

EL SAPO DORADO, Apdo. 10165-1000, San José. Tel./fax 506/645-5010. 20 rms (all with private bath).
$ Rates: $56.60 single; $69.15 double; $81.75 triple. No credit cards.

★ Located up a steep hill from the main road between Santa Elena and the preserve, El Sapo Dorado (named for Monteverde's famous golden toad) offers attractive cabins with good views. The cabins are built of hardwoods and are surrounded by a grassy lawn. Big windows let in lots of light, and high ceilings keep the rooms cool during the day. The older cabins also have fireplaces, which are a welcome feature on chilly nights. The hotel's restaurant serves some of the best food in Monteverde (see below for details). To find the hotel and restaurant, watch for the sign on the main road to the preserve.

WHERE TO EAT

Most lodges in Monteverde have their own dining rooms, and these are the most convenient places to eat. However, there are also a few restaurants scattered along the road between Santa Elena and Monteverde. Two inexpensive places worth mentioning are the **Pizzeria de Johnny** near the Hotel Heliconia and the **Soda Cerro Verde** across from the gas station. Most people have their lodge pack them a bag lunch, but you can also piece together your own lunch. Stop in at **Stella's Bakery** (across from the CASEM gift shop) for some fresh bread, cake, or cookies. Stella's is open daily from 6am to 6pm and has a small café serving pizza and light meals. Next, stop by the **Monteverde Cheese Factory** and pick up some of the best cheese in Costa Rica. The cheese factory is open Monday through Saturday from 7:30am to 4pm and on Sunday from 7:30am to 12:30pm.

LA CASCADA, off main road near the gas station. Tel. 645-5128.
Cuisine: INTERNATIONAL. **Reservations:** Not accepted.
$ Prices: Complete meals $6.10–$13.20. V.
Open: Tues–Sun 6–10pm.
This unusual restaurant is set back a bit from the main road and looks out on a waterfall, though it also looks out on what appears to have once been a rock quarry. There is even a small waterfall inside the large open-air restaurant. This has recently become the hangout for Monteverde and, as unlikely as it sounds, offers dancing to recorded music after nine o'clock each night. Meals are comparable to what is served at most area lodges.

EL SAPO DORADO, off the Santa Elena–Monteverde road. Tel. 645-5010.
Cuisine: INTERNATIONAL. **Reservations:** Not accepted.
$ Prices: Appetizers $1.35–$4.60; entrees $6.60–$12.20. No credit cards.
Open: Daily 7–10am, noon–3pm, 6–9pm.
Located high on a hill above the main road, El Sapo Dorado provides great sunsets and good food for accompaniment. The menu here is a little bit more imaginative than at most restaurants in Monteverde, which makes this restaurant well worth a visit even if you miss the sunset. A recent menu included such dishes as grilled corvina, fettuccini in peanut-squid sauce, and filet mignon in a pepper-cream sauce. In addition to a large, formal dining room, there is a patio that's a great spot for lunch or an early dinner.

CHAPTER 6

THE CENTRAL PACIFIC COAST

The central Pacific Coast offers several of the most easily accessible beaches in Costa Rica. These vary in character from the Miami-style beachfront promenade of Puntarenas to the fun-in-the-sun Canadian-charter-flight hotels of Jacó to the jungle-clad hillsides of Manuel Antonio and Dominical. The climate here is considerably more humid and the landscape much greener than farther north. Jacó and Manuel Antonio are Costa Rica's two most developed beaches, while Puntarenas, a former seaport, offers the most urban beach setting in the country.

1. PUNTARENAS

130 kilometers W of San José; 113 kilometers S of Liberia; 60 kilometers N of Jacó Beach

GETTING THERE By Bus Express buses leave San José daily every 30 minutes between 5am and 7pm from the corner of Calle 12 and Avenida 9. Duration: 2 hours. Fare: $2.60.

By Car Head west out of San José on the Interamerican Highway, passing the airport and Alajuela, and follow the signs to Puntarenas. The drive takes about 1½ hours.

By Ferry See the "Playa Montezuma" section of Chapter 4 for information on crossing to Puntarenas from the Nicoya Peninsula.

DEPARTING The main Puntarenas bus station is a block east of the Hotel Imperial, which is in front of the old main dock on the Paseo de los Turistas. Buses to San José leave daily every 30 minutes between 5am and 7pm. The bus to Santa Elena leaves daily at 2:15pm from a stop across the railroad tracks from the main bus station. Buses to Quepos (Manuel Antonio) leave twice daily. A bus leaves for Liberia daily at 5:30pm.
See the "Playa Montezuma" sections of Chapter 4 for information on taking ferries to the Nicoya Peninsula.

ESSENTIALS Orientation Puntarenas is built on a long, narrow sand spit that stretches 3 miles out into the Gulf of Nicoya and is only five streets wide at its

WHAT'S SPECIAL ABOUT
THE CENTRAL PACIFIC COAST

Beaches
☐ Manuel Antonio National Park, three idyllic beaches set amid jungle-clad hills.
☐ Playade Jacó Beach, an inexpensive resort area with many deserted beaches nearby.
☐ Dominical, great surfing, and not far away, pretty beaches and tide pool area.

Natural Spectacles
☐ The views of mountains, jungle, and sea from the hills of Manuel Antonio.
☐ Waterfalls, reached by horse from Dominical.

Activities
☐ Sportfishing out of Quepos.
☐ A day-long cruise around the Gulf of Nicoya.
☐ Sea-kayak trips near Quepos and Manuel Ántonio.
☐ Hiking up Mount Chirripó.
☐ Surfing at Playa de Jacó Beach and Playa Hermosa.

Parks
☐ Carara Biological Reserve, a transitional forest between wet and dry regions.

widest. The ferry docks for the Nicoya Peninsula are near the far end of the town, as are the bus station and market. The north side of town faces an estuary, while the south side faces the mouth of the gulf. The Paseo de los Turistas is on the south side of town, beginning at the pier and extending out to the point. If you need a taxi, phone 661-0053 or 663-0250. Car rentals are available from Discovery Rent-a-Car (tel. 661-0328).

Puntarenas, a 10-mile-long spit of sand jutting into the Gulf of Nicoya, was once Costa Rica's busiest port, but a while back it was replaced by nearby Puerto Caldera, a modern containerport facility. Since losing its port, the city has been struggling to attract more tourists. To that end the city built a sewage treatment plant to clean up the water, and Puntarenas now has the only beach-cleaning machine in Costa Rica. With a good highway leading all the way from San José, Puntarenas can be reached in an hour and a half, which makes it the closest beach to San José, at least in traveling time if not in actual mileage.

Because Puntarenas is a city, this beach has a very different character from any other beach in Costa Rica. The beach itself, a long, straight stretch of sand with gentle surf, is backed for most of its length by the Paseo de los Turistas, a promenade that is ideal for strolling. Across a wide boulevard from the Paseo are hotels, restaurants, bars, discos, and shops. It's all very civilized, though the preponderance of cement gives it too much of an urban feel for my tastes. The views across the Gulf of Nicoya and the sunsets here are quite beautiful, and there is almost always a cooling breeze blowing in off the water. All around town you'll find unusual old buildings, reminders of the important role Puntarenas once played in Costa Rican history. It was from here that much of the Central Valley's coffee crop was once shipped, and while the coffee barons in the highlands were getting rich, so too were the merchants of Puntarenas.

If you're in Costa Rica for only a short time and want to get in some time on the beach, Puntarenas is a good option. You can even do it in a day trip from San José. Likewise, if you are looking for a base from which to visit national parks up and down the Pacific Coast, Puntarenas is one of your best bets. From here you can head north to the national parks in Guanacaste or south to Carara Biological Reserve. Also, if you are heading out to any of the beaches at the southern end of the Nicoya Peninsula, you'll be passing through Puntarenas to catch one of the three ferries. Puntarenas is most popular as a weekend holiday spot for Ticos from San José and is at its liveliest on the weekends.

WHAT TO SEE & DO

Take a walk along the Paseo de los Turistas and notice how similar this side of town is to a few Florida towns 50 years ago. If you want to go swimming, the ocean waters are now said to be perfectly safe. Alternatively, you can head out to the end of the peninsula to the **Balneario Municipal,** the public pool. It is huge, has a great view (albeit through a chain-link fence), and is surrounded by lawns and gardens. Entrance is only 85¢ for adults and 50¢ for children. The pool is open Tuesday through Sunday from 9am to 4pm. If the beach right in the city doesn't appeal to you, head back down the spit to the **Playa Doña Ana,** a popular beach park with picnic tables and a restaurant.

Puntarenas isn't known as one of Costa Rica's prime **sportfishing** ports, but there are usually a few charter boats available. Check at your hotel or at the Hotel Colonial. Rates are usually between $300 and $400 for a half day and between $500 and $600 for a full day. These rates are for up to four people.

The most popular water excursions from Puntarenas are **yacht cruises** among the tiny uninhabited islands of the Guayabo, Negritos, and Pájaros Islands Biological Reserve. These cruises include a gourmet seafood buffet and a stop at beautiful and undeveloped Tortuga Island, where you can swim, snorkel, and sun. The water is a clear blue, and the sand is bright white. Several San José–based companies offer these excursions, with round-trip transportation from San José, but if you are already in Puntarenas, you may be able to get a discount. **Calypso Tours** (tel. 233-3617), **Costa Sol Tropical Cruises** (tel. 239-2000), and **Fantasy Fun Cruise** (tel. 255-0791) are just three of the companies that offer similar tours and will pick you up at your hotel in San José. The price for one of these trips is $70 (or slightly less if leaving from Puntarenas). These companies also offer sunset cruises with live music, snacks, and a bar. Calypso also offers sailing excursions on their catamaran *Star Chaser.*

WHERE TO STAY

DOUBLES FOR LESS THAN $25

HOTEL AYI CON, 50 meters south of the market (Apdo. 358), Puntarenas. Tel. 506/661-0164 or 661-1477. 44 rms (22 with private bath).
$ Rates: $5.25 single without bath, $7.30 single with bath; $10.05 double without bath, $14.50 double with bath. No credit cards.

Centrally located near the market and the ferryboat docks, the Ayi Con is your basic low-budget Tico hotel. It's above a row of shops in a very busy shopping district of Puntarenas and is frequented primarily by Costa Ricans. Backpackers will find that this is probably the best and the cleanest of the cheap hotels in Puntarenas. If you're just passing through and have to spend a night in town, this place is convenient and acceptable.

HOTEL IMPERIAL, Paseo de los Turistas, frente al Muelle (Apdo. 65), Puntarenas. Tel. 506/661-0579 or 661-0600. 30 rms (10 with private bath).
$ Rates: $11.35 single without bath, $13.70 single with bath; $22.75 double without bath, $27.30 double with bath; $25.90 triple without bath, $31.30 triple with bath. No credit cards.

The Imperial, despite its name, is as basic as hotels get in Costa Rica and would hardly be worth mentioning if not for its atmosphere. Located directly across from the old main dock, the hotel is a weather-beaten, green wooden building that certainly must have seen its share of sailors in days past. The architecture is classic tropical colonial, with high ceilings, wide halls, and wooden walls that don't go all the way to the ceiling (to keep the air circulating). In the middle of the large building, there is a narrow courtyard garden that has seen better days. Light sleepers may want to find lodgings somewhere else.

DOUBLES FOR LESS THAN $45

HOTEL LA PUNTA, 100 meters south of the ferry terminal, Barrio El Carmen (Apdo. 228), Puntarenas. Tel. 506/661-0696. 13 rms (all with private bath).

$ Rates: $27.05 single; $34.75 double; $43.30 triple; $51 quad ($6.75 extra for A/C). AE, DC, MC, V.

This modest hotel is located out at the far end of the Puntarenas peninsula near the car ferry dock, which makes it a great choice for anyone heading over to the Nicoya Peninsula with a car. A covered sidewalk leads from the street to the open-air bar/restaurant that also serves as reception area. If you can overlook the mismatched sheets on the beds and the occasional stuffiness, the rooms here are generally acceptable. They all have fans, and a couple also have air conditioning. Try to get a room with a balcony. There's also a small pool out back.

HOTEL TIOGA, Paseo de los Turistas (Apdo. 96-5400), Puntarenas. Tel. 506/661-0271, or (in San José) 255-3115. Fax 506/661-0127 or (in San José) 255-1006. 46 rms (all with private bath). A/C

$ Rates (including breakfast): $34–$50.90 single; $42.50–$63.70 double (lower rates in off season). AE, MC, V.

This 1950s modern-style hotel is Puntarenas's old standard on the Paseo de los Turistas. The beach is right across the street and there are plenty of restaurants within a short walk. When you walk through the front door, you enter a courtyard with a pool. Rooms vary in size, and some come with cold-water showers only, so if you must have hot water, be sure to request it. The larger rooms are very attractive and have modern bathrooms. There is a cafeteria and bar on the second floor and a breakfast room and lounge on the fourth floor. You'll be able to look out across the water as you enjoy your complimentary breakfast.

WORTH THE EXTRA BUCKS

HOTEL LAS BRISAS, Paseo de los Turistas (Apdo. 83-5400), Puntarenas. Tel. 506/661-4040. Fax 506/661-1487. 19 rms (all with private bath). A/C

$ Rates: $34.30 single; $57.15 double; $68.60 triple (discounts in the off-season). AE, MC, V.

Out near the end of the Paseo de los Turistas, you'll find a very clean hotel with large air-conditioned rooms, a small pool out front, and the beach right across the street. All the rooms have tile floors, double or twin beds, and small tables. Large picture windows keep the rooms sunny and bright during the day. The hotel's small open-air dining room serves some of the best food in town with the emphasis on continental dishes. The bouillabaisse is excellent. It's worth staying here just to enjoy the food.

HOTEL PORTO BELLO, Apdo. 108, Puntarenas. Tel. 506/661-1322 or 661-2122. Fax 506/661-0036. 34 rms (all with private bath). A/C TEL

$ Rates: Dec–Apr $51.45 single, $68.60 double, $80 triple; May–Nov $36.60 single, $46.90 double, $68.60 triple. AE, MC, V.

Located on the landward end of town, the Porto Bello is a weekend escape for wealthy Ticos. The stucco walls of the hotel are almost blindingly white, tempered by the lush overgrown garden that surrounds the buildings. Most of the rooms have high ceilings, red-tile floors, attractive teak-and-cloth headboards, and balconies or patios that are often hidden by the shrubbery. There are pools for adults and kids, with a poolside bar, and even a small beach. You can hire a water taxi for a spin around the bay or book an all-day cruise to some of the remote and picturesque islands out in the gulf. The open-air restaurant is breezy and cool, and grilled meats and seafood are the specialties—with entrees ranging in price from $6 to $20.25.

WHERE TO EAT

Your hotel restaurant is likely going to be the best place to eat. At the Porto Bello, the grilled steaks are particularly good. Another option is to pull up a table at one of the half-dozen open-air snack bars along the Paseo do los Turistas. They have names like Soda Rio de Janeiro and Soda Acapulco and serve sandwiches, drinks, ice cream, and other snacks. Sandwiches are priced at around a dollar.

LA CARAVELLE, frente al mar calles 21 y 23, Paseo de los Turistas. Tel. 661-2262.
    Cuisine: FRENCH. **Reservations:** Suggested in high season and on weekends.
$ **Prices:** Appetizers $2.40–$3.05; entrees $5.30–$15.20. DC, MC, V.
    Open: Wed–Sat noon–3:30pm, 6–10pm; Sun noon–10pm.

For more than 15 years, La Caravelle has been serving Puntarenas fine French dinners amid an eclectic café atmosphere. The restaurant's walls are decorated with a curious assortment of paintings, as well as a carousel horse, that together give La Caravelle a very playful feel. The menu, however, is strictly traditional French, with such flavorful and well-prepared dishes as tenderloin with a bourguignonne sauce or a tarragon béarnaise. There are quite a few good seafood dishes, as well as a salade niçoise. There's a good assortment of both French and Chilean wines to accompany your meal, though prices are rather high (as they are all over Costa Rica).

READERS RECOMMEND

La Ostra, four blocks west of the Hotel Porto Bello. Tel. 661-0272. "... the best restaurant in Costa Rica is in Puntarenas—La Ostra—splendid service, fine food, and the best fresh coconut custard I've ever had."—John Sinning Jr., Davenport, Iowa

---

2. JACÓ BEACH

108 kilometers W of San José; 60 kilometers S of Puntarenas

GETTING THERE **By Bus**   Express buses leave San José twice daily from Calle 16 between avenidas 1 and 3. Duration: 2½ hours. Fare: $2.30. From Puntarenas, you can catch Quepos-bound buses twice daily and get off in Jacó. Duration: 1 hour. Fare: $1.60. Buses returning from Quepos to San José also stop in Jacó. These buses leave Quepos four times daily. Duration: 2½ hours. Fare: $1.65.

By Car   There are two main routes to Jacó. The easier, though longer, route is to take the Interamerican Highway west out of San José and get off at the Puntarenas exit. From here, head south on the Costanera, the coast road. Alternatively, you can take the narrow and winding, though more scenic, old highway, which turns off the Interamerican Highway just west of Alajuela near the town of Atenas. This highway meets the Costanera a few kilometers west of Orotina.

DEPARTING   The Jacó bus station is at the north end of town about 50 yards off the main road near the Hotel El Jardin. Buses for San José leave twice daily. Buses bound for Quepos stop in Jacó five times daily.

ESSENTIALS **Orientation**   Jacó Beach is a short distance off the southern highway. One main road runs parallel to the beach and it is off this road that you will find most of the hotels and restaurants. You'll find a coin-operated laundry, open daily from 8am to noon and 1 to 8pm, opposite the I.C.E. building on the main drag. You can rent a car from Elegante (tel. 643-3224) for about $50 per day. There's a bank in the middle of town on the main road. Botiquín Garabito, the town's pharmacy, is down the street from the bank. There is a gas station out by El Bosque restaurant at the south end of town. The health center and post office are at the Municipal Center at the south end of town, across from El Naranjal restaurant. A public phone office, from which you can make international calls, is located in the I.C.E. building on the main road. This office is open Monday through Saturday from 8am to noon and from 1 to 5pm.

If you're looking for a cheap place to spend a week in the sun, Jacó Beach is currently the top choice in Costa Rica. Charter flights arrive weekly from Montreal and Toronto, and consequently many of the hotels here are owned by Canadians, some of whom speak French and Spanish but little English. Jacó is also now gaining popularity with Germans, so if English is your native tongue, you may find yourself in a distinct minority here. This is the most touristy beach in Costa Rica and is a prime example of what happens when rapid growth hits a beach town. With no master plan and few building codes in effect, Jacó is now a hodgepodge of big and small hotels, cheap eateries, souvenir shops, and lots of cinder-block walls. However, on the outskirts of town and close to the beach there is still plenty of greenery to offset the excess of cement along the town's main street. In fact, this is the northernmost beach on Costa Rica's Pacific Coast that actually has a tropical feel to it. The humidity is palpable and the lushness of the tropical forest is visible on the hillsides surrounding town. In hotel gardens, flowers bloom profusely throughout the year.

WHAT TO SEE & DO

Unfortunately, the water here has a nasty reputation for riptides, as does most of the water of Costa Rica's Pacific Coast. Even strong swimmers have been known to drown in the powerful rips. Storms far offshore often cause huge waves to pound on the beach, making it impossible to go into the water at all. You'll have to be content with the hotel pool (if your hotel has one) most of the time.

After you've spent some time on Playa de Jacó, you might want to visit some of the other nearby beaches, of which there are several. Playa Esterillos, 22 kilometers southwest of Jacó, is long and wide and almost always nearly deserted. Playa Hermosa, 10 kilometers southeast of Jacó, where sea turtles lay eggs from July to December, is also well known for its great surfing waves. Playa Herradura, about 6½ kilometers northwest of Jacó, is ringed by lush hillsides and has a campground and a few very basic cabinas. All of these beaches are beautiful and easily reached by car or bicycle (if you've got plenty of energy).

The same waves that often make Playa de Jacó unsafe for swimming make this beach the most popular in the country with gringo surfers. In addition, there are a couple of other excellent **surfing** beaches nearby—Playa Hermosa and Playa Escondida. Those who want to challenge the waves can rent surfboards for $2.50 an hour and boogie boards for $1.50 an hour. If you'd rather do a bit of sailing on a Sunfish, check with **Cross Cruises** at the Hotel Copacabana down near the beach in the center of town. This company charges $15 an hour or $50 for half a day. They also offer sailing lessons and beach chair and umbrella rentals.

At several places along the main road, you can rent a bike for $6.75 per day. Surfboards are also available. If you're interested in doing some sportfishing, contact **Viajes Jaguar** (tel. 643-3242), which has its office in an older house next door to the phone office on the main road through town. A half-day fishing trip for four people will cost $300 and a full day will cost $450. Scuba divers can arrange dive trips through Viajes Jaguar, where a two-tank dive is a pricey $80 ($100 with equipment rental). They also rent snorkeling gear for $10 a day.

For nature lovers, the **Carara Biological Reserve,** 15 kilometers north of Jacó, has several miles of trails. There is a loop trail that takes about an hour and another trail that is open only to tour groups. Among the wildlife you might see here are caimans, coatimundis, armadillos, pacas, peccaries, river otters, kinkajous, and, of course, hundreds of species of birds. The reserve is open daily from 8am to noon and from 1 to 4:30pm daily. Admission is $1.35. There are several companies offering tours to Carara Biological Reserve for around $30. Check at your hotel or contact **Fantasy Tours** (tel. 643-3231 or 643-3383) or **San José Travel** (tel. 643-3258).

Horseback riding tours are also very popular. These trips give you a chance to get away from all the development in Jacó and see a bit of nature. Contact Fantasy Tours, **Unicornio Ranch** (tel. 643-3019), **Sanchez Madrigal Bros.** (tel. 643-3203), or **AFA Tours** (tel. 643-3215) to make a reservation. Tours lasting three to four hours cost around $25 to $30.

If you will be spending your entire Costa Rican visit in Jacó but would like to see some other parts of the country, you can arrange tours through the local office of San José Travel. This company offers day tours to various destinations around the country. Another local tour company, **Explorica** (tel. 643-3586), offers similar tours. Rates range from $50 to $70 for day trips.

There are several discos in Jacó. Most convenient is the **Disco La Central** (tel. 643-3067), which is right on the beach near the east end of town. The disco is complete with flashing lights and a mirrored ball in a huge open-air hall. **Upe!** (tel. 643-3002), out on the road to the airport, is another local favorite. Both are open Thursday through Sunday with a very low admission and reasonably priced drinks.

WHERE TO STAY

DOUBLES FOR LESS THAN $35

CABINAS ALICE, 100 meters south of the Red Cross, Playa de Jacó, Puntarenas. Tel. 506/643-3061 or 237-1412. 22 rms (all with private bath).
$ Rates: $30.90 single or double; $38.65–$50.25 triple. MC, V.
Cabinas Alice, though a small and modest Tico-run place, is one of the best values in Jacó. The rooms are in the shade of large old mango trees, and the beach is right outside the gate. Rooms here vary in age, so have a look at a couple if you can. The largest rooms are those with kitchens. The rooms in back each come with a carved wooden headboard and matching nightstand, a tile floor, a large shower, and even potted plants. The other rooms are pretty basic, with nothing but a double and a single bed. The road down to Cabinas Alice is across from the Red Cross center. The small dining room serves inexpensive seafood.

CABINAS LAS PALMAS, Playa de Jacó, Puntarenas. Tel./fax 506/643-3005. 23 rms (all with private bath).
$ Rates: $20.45–$47.90 single; $23.85–$47.90 double; $29.50–$59.90 triple. No credit cards.
Although all the rooms here are acceptable, the newer ones are a bit nicer. Some rooms come with refrigerators, hot plates, kitchen sinks, laundry sinks, and tables with four chairs, so you can set up housekeeping and stay a while. All the rooms have tile floors and very clean bathrooms, and most have two double beds. There are lots of flowers in the garden, and the location down a narrow lane off the main road makes Las Palmas a quiet place. If you're coming from San José, take the Jacó exit from the Costanera and go straight through the first (and only) intersection you come to. Take a right on the narrow lane just past Cabinas Antonio.

CHALET SANTA ANA, Playa de Jacó, Puntarenas. Tel. 506/643-3233. 8 rms (all with private bath).
$ Rates: $15.50 single; $27.05 double or triple. No credit cards.
Located at the quiet east end of the beach across from the Hotel Jacofiesta, Chalet Santa Ana is a small, two-story building. Though it is rather basic, the guest rooms sleep up to five people and half of them have kitchenettes. There's even carpeting in

the rooms, and walls are of varnished wood. The second-floor rooms have the added advantage of high ceilings and a large veranda with chairs. Though the surroundings are not too attractive, this is a good deal for Jacó.

HOTEL ZABAMAR, Playa de Jacó, Puntarenas. Tel. 506/643-3174. 20 rms (all with private bath).
$ Rates: $23.20–$30.95 single; $27.05–$34.75 double; $38.65–$54.10 triple. Discounts for week stays. V.

The Zabamar is set back a little from the beach in an attractively planted compound. The older rooms have red-tile floors, small refrigerators, ceiling fans, hammocks on their front porches, and showers in enclosed, private patios. There are also 10 newer rooms with air conditioning. There are even *pilas* (laundry sinks) in little gravel-and-palm gardens behind the older rooms. Some rooms have rustic wooden benches and chairs. The shallow swimming pool stays quite warm. Surfers get a 10% discount and will appreciate the size of the older, less expensive rooms. Prices for everyone are lower from April 15 to December 15. A little open-air bar/restaurant serves inexpensive seafood and burgers.

DOUBLES FOR LESS THAN $45

FLAMBOYANT HOTEL, Apdo. 18, Playa de Jacó, Puntarenas. Tel. 506/ 643-3146. 8 rms (all with private bath).
$ Rates: $34.30–$45.75 single; $40–$45.75 double. No credit cards.

The Flamboyant doesn't quite live up to its name, but it is still a good value. The rooms are arranged around a small swimming pool, and you are only a few steps from the beach. All the rooms are spacious and have kitchenettes, though otherwise the furnishings are quite simple. You'll find the Flamboyant down a narrow lane from the Flamboyant Restaurant, which is on the main road in the middle of Jacó.

HOTEL BOHIO, Playa de Jacó. Tel. 506/643-3017. 8 rms, 7 apts (all with private bath).
$ Rates: Dec–Apr $20.30 single, $38.50 double; May–Nov $13.50–$16.90 single, $27.05–$30.40 double. No credit cards.

Popular with a young crowd, the Bohio has a slightly run-down air about it, but the rooms are still quite acceptable. Little care is paid to the garden, but there is a small pool and a thatched-roof bar and restaurant right on the beach. Each room has two double beds, a ceiling fan, a refrigerator, a kitchenette, and a bar. Recommended for groups of young people who plan to stay for a while.

HOTEL EL JARDIN, Playa de Jacó, Puntarenas. Tel./fax 506/643-3050. 7 rms (all with private bath).
$ Rates (including continental breakfast): Dec–Apr $38 single or double; May–Nov $43.45 single or double. MC, V.

Though this hotel's namesake garden is nothing to write home about, the hotel does offer economical rates, comfortable rooms, and friendly French-speaking management. This combination seems to have made El Jardin one of the more popular small hotels in Jacó. The guest rooms are large and clean and have big bathrooms as well. There is a small pool in the center of the garden. You'll find this hotel at the far west end of the beach, near the San José bus stop.

CAMPING

There are several campgrounds in or near Jacó Beach. **Madrigal,** at the south end of town at the foot of some jungly cliffs, is my favorite. The campground is right on the beach and has a bar/restaurant that is open from 7am to midnight. **El Hicaco,** in town and close to the beach, is right next door to an open-air disco, so don't expect much sleep if you stay here. Campsites are around $1.50 per night.

WORTH THE EXTRA BUCKS

HOTEL CLUB DEL MAR, Apdo. 107-4023, Playa de Jacó, Puntarenas. Tel. 506/643-3194. 16 rms (all with private bath).
$ Rates: Nov–Apr $77.75–$99.45 single or double; May–Oct $34.30–$62.90 single or double. MC, V.

Because of its location, friendly owners, and attractively designed new rooms, this is my favorite Jacó Beach hotel. The Club del Mar is at the far eastern end of the beach where the rocky hills meet the beach. The newest rooms have green-tile floors, pastel bedspreads, fascinating custom-made lampshades, tile bathroom counters, and private patios. Older rooms are almost as attractive and have Guatemalan throw rugs, bamboo furniture, kitchens, and huge picture windows. There's a small swimming pool and a first-class restaurant. Owner Philip Edwardes is the chef and prepares such dishes as lemon chicken and chateaubriand. The conviviality and helpfulness of Edwardes and his wife Marilyn are what make a stay here so enjoyable. The Edwardeses also arrange horseback rides, raft trips, and various other tours.

HOTEL COCAL, Apdo. 54, Playa de Jacó, Puntarenas. Tel. 506/643-3067 or (in the U.S.) 313/732-8066. Fax 506/643-3082. 29 rms (all with private bath).
$ Rates: $45.72 single; $62.90 double; $80 triple. Lower rates in off season. AE, MC, V.

This is a surprisingly elegant little hotel. The buildings here are done in colonial style, with arched porticos surrounding a courtyard that contains two medium-size pools, a few palapas for shade, and a thatched-roof bar. Each guest room has a tile floor, a double and a single bed, a desk, and a porch or balcony. However, the furniture is a bit old and has seen better days. The rooms with ocean views get the best breezes. The Cocal is on one of the nameless streets leading down to the beach from the main road through Jacó. Watch for its sign in the middle of town. There are two dining rooms here with the best view from the upstairs dining room. Service is generally quite good, and so is the food. Prices range from $5.75 to $17.25 for entrees. No children are allowed at this hotel.

VILLAS MIRAMAR, Playa de Jacó, Puntarenas. Tel. 506/643-3003. 10 rms (all with private bath).
$ Rates: Dec–Apr $54.10 single or double, $65.70 triple; May–Nov $38.65 single, double, or triple. MC, V.

Located down a narrow lane off the main road through town, the Miramar is about 100 feet from the beach, though it also has its own small pool surrounded by a terrace. There is a snack bar by the pool and barbecues in the gardens in case you'd like to grill some fish or steaks. Guest rooms sport a Spanish architectural style with arched doorways, wrought-iron wall lamps, and red-tile floors throughout. There are large patios and all the rooms have kitchenettes. The apartments vary in size; the largest can sleep up to six people.

NEARBY PLACES TO STAY & DINE

DOUBLES FOR LESS THAN $25

CABINAS VISTA HERMOSA, Playa Hermosa de Jacó, Jacó, Puntarenas. Tel. 506/224-3687. 6 rms (all with private bath).
$ Rates: $15.50 single; $23.20 double; $34.75 quad. No credit cards.

This little cabina place just south of Jacó was recently taken over by new Italian owners, and changes are under way. Though the rooms are pretty basic, they're right on Playa Hermosa. Because this beach is popular with surfers, that's who you'll often find staying here. All the rooms have kitchens, and those on the second floor have a nice view of the waves from the front veranda. There is even a little above-ground pool here, and a rancho contains a table-tennis table. Right next door is a hip little restaurant under separate management. Big old trees provide some welcome shade.

WORTH THE EXTRA BUCKS

PUNTA LEONA HOTEL & CLUB, Apdo. 8592-1000, San José. Tel. 506/231-3131 or 661-1414. Fax 506/232-0791. 92 rms, 73 apts (all with private bath).
$ Rates: $51.80 single; $61.80–$77.30 double; $74.20–$162.20 for 4–8 people. AE, DC, MC, V.

This gated resort and residential community 10 kilometers north of Jacó boasts some of the most impressive hotel grounds in Costa Rica. Rain forest, white-sand beaches (two of them totaling four miles), and a rocky promontory jutting out into the Pacific all add up to drama rarely encountered in Costa Rican resorts. The resort is at the end of a gravel road that passes through dense primary rain forest before arriving at the grassy lawns that sprawl beneath huge old trees. The least expensive rooms are standard hotel rooms in Spanish-style buildings with red-tile roofs and white stucco walls. In addition to these rooms, there are a variety of different apartments, including some unusual little chalets. Restaurant León Marino serves a variety of Costa Rican and international dishes at moderate prices. There are also three beach bars and a disco on the property. Scuba lessons and rental equipment are available. Two swimming pools, a boutique, and a super market round out the facilities here.

TERRAZA DEL PACIFICO, Playa Hermosa de Jacó (Apdo. 168), Jacó, Puntarenas. Tel. 506/643-3222, 643-3444, 643-3424, or (in the U.S.) 212/213-2399 or 213-1838. 43 rms (all with private bath). A/C TV TEL
$ Rates: $51.45 single; $57.15 double. AE, MC, V.

It may be a bit out of town, but the Terraza del Pacifico is the best beachfront hotel in the Jacó area. Located at the north end of Playa Hermosa, which is just over the hill to the south of Jacó Beach, this hotel seems to have done everything right. Rooms are built so that they all have ocean views, and in the middle of the hotel complex is a circular pool with a swim-up bar. Red-tile roofs and white walls give the buildings a very Mediterranean look. Every guest room has either a patio or balcony. The hotel's restaurant is located right on the beach and serves good Italian food.

WHERE TO EAT

Many of the accommodations in Jacó come with kitchenettes, and if you want to save money on meals, I advise shopping at the local supermercado and fixing your own. One of the best restaurants in town is the dining room at the **Hotel Cocal.** The menu includes such dishes as chateaubriand for two, wiener schnitzel, and pepper steak.

MEALS FOR LESS THAN $12

EL BOSQUE, 27 yards south of the gas station. Tel. 643-3009.
Cuisine: INTERNATIONAL. **Reservations:** Suggested on weekends.
$ Prices: Appetizers $2.55–$12.50; entrees $4.05–$13.20. MC, V.
Open: Tues–Sun 10:30am–9:30pm.

Located on the highway leading south to Manuel Antonio, El Bosque (The Forest) is set amid shady mango trees. The dining room itself is a small open-air building with hanging fern baskets and nests of oropendula birds used as decorations. The furnishings are heavy colonial reproductions. Shrimp or lobster is a pricey $13.20, but you can get a delicious corvina filet for only $4.05. If you are not in the mood for seafood, you can order steak or chicken. There is also a long list of fresh juices and fruit shakes from which to choose. El Bosque makes a great meal stop if you are on your way back from Manuel Antonio.

FLAMBOYANT RESTAURANT, on the main road east of the telephone office. Tel. 643-3023.
   Cuisine: COSTA RICAN/INTERNATIONAL. **Reservations:** Not accepted.
$ **Prices:** Appetizers $2.40–$11.50; entrees $3.75–$14.90. MC, V.
   Open: Thurs–Tues 11am–5pm, 6–10:30pm.
Though it is located right on Jacó's busy main road and can be rather noisy, the Flamboyant is still one of the better restaurants in town. Seafood is the specialty here, of course, and you can get jumbo shrimp in garlic butter or a whole red snapper. However, if you are absolutely crazy about seafood, try the bountiful seafood platter. If you're not in the mood for fish, try the pepper steak or some meaty pork chops.

RESTAURANT GRAN PALENQUE, next to the Jacó Beach Hotel. Tel. 643-3419.
   Cuisine: COSTA RICAN/SEAFOOD. **Reservations:** Not necessary.
$ **Prices:** Appetizers $3.40–$5.10; main dishes $5.75–$8.15. MC, V.
   Open: Tues–Sun 11am–10:30pm.
Gran Palenque is set amid spacious and shady grounds where palm trees rustle in the breeze. The large restaurant is a huge thatch-roofed, open-air structure, and there is a smaller but similar building housing the restaurant's bar. This latter is right on the edge of the beach, which is only steps away. Both have unobstructed views of the ocean. With the inclusion of such Spanish specialties as paella and *zarzuela,* the menu is a bit more than the standard seafood-and-steaks Tico menu. All the dishes are well prepared and the prices are quite reasonable.

RESTAURANT OCEANO PACIFICO, west of the Hotel Jacó Beach. Tel. 643-3116.
   Cuisine: COSTA RICAN/INTERNATIONAL. **Reservations:** Not accepted.
$ **Prices:** Main dishes $3.05–$10.85. No credit cards.
   Open: Mon–Fri 10am–10pm, Sat 6am–10pm, Sun 6am–3pm.
If you follow the main road through town all the way west (past the San José bus stop), you'll come to this little open-air restaurant. Come during the day and you'll have a view of a steep, jungly hillside across an estuary. Weekends can be a bit noisy here because there is a pool right beside the restaurant. However, the view is great and the food is good and inexpensive. Try the palmito (heart of palm) appetizer, it's a Tico treat that you don't often find up north. If you like submarine sandwiches, try the Costa Rican version, which is called a *lápiz* (pencil). The dinner menu is primarily seafood.

3. MANUEL ANTONIO

140 kilometers SW of San José; 69 kilometers S of Jacó Beach

GETTING THERE   By Air   Sansa (in San José: tel. 233-0397, 233-3258, or 233-5330) flies to Quepos daily. Duration: 20 minutes. Fare: $27 each way. Travelair (tel. 220-3054 or 232-7883) also flies daily. Duration: 20 minutes. Fare: 35 one way, $60 round-trip. Travelair also has flights to Quepos from Golfito and Palmar Sur.

By Bus   Express buses to Manuel Antonio leave San José three times daily from Calle 16 between avenidas 1 and 3. Duration: 3½ hours. Fare: $5.60. Regular buses to Quepos leave San José four times daily. Duration: 5 hours. Fare: $3.40. Buses leave Puntarenas for Quepos twice daily. Duration: 3½ hours. Fare: $3.10. Buses leave Jacó for Quepos five times daily. Duration: 2½ hours. Fare: $1.65.

By Car   From San José, take the Interamerican Highway west to the Puntarenas turnoff and head south on the Costanera, the coastal road through Jacó. This is an excellent road until south of Puerto Caldera. From there until south of Jacó, the potholes are killers. At Parrita, 44 kilometers past Jacó, the pavement gives out completely and you spend the next 25 kilometers bumping along a potholed, washboarded, muddy gravel road. Needless to say, the driving is slow. An alternative is to take the narrow and winding old highway, which turns off the Interamerican Highway just west of Alajuela near the town of Atenas and joins the Costanera near Orotina, just in time to catch the worst of the potholes.

DEPARTING   Sansa (in Quepos: tel. 777-1170) flies to San José daily and also has flights to Palmar Sur and Puerto Jiménez. Travelair also flies to San José daily and has flights to Palmar Sur and Golfito. The airport is a taxi ride outside of town.

The Quepos bus station is in the market, which is two blocks east of the water and one block north of the road to Manuel Antonio. Express buses leave three times daily (four times on Sunday). Local buses that take five hours leave four times daily. In the busy winter months, get your ticket several days in advance. Buses for Puntarenas leave three times daily. Any bus headed for San José or Puntarenas will let you off in Playa de Jacó.

ESSENTIALS   Orientation   Quepos is a dusty little port town at the mouth of the Boca Vieja Estuary. After crossing the bridge into town, take the lower road (to the left of the high road). In two blocks, turn left and you will be on the road to Manuel Antonio.

Getting Around   A taxi between Manuel Antonio and Quepos, or vice versa, costs around $3. You'll usually get a better price if you have your hotel call the taxi. Also, if you do have the hotel call you a cab, remember to take only the taxi you've been told is coming for you.

The bus from Quepos to Manuel Antonio takes 15 minutes and departs daily at 5:40, 7, 8, 9:30, 10:30, and 11:30am and 12:30, 2, 3, 4, 5, 7, and 10pm. The bus returns 20 minutes later. Fare: 30¢.

You can also rent a car from Elegante Rent A Car (tel. 777-0115) for around $50 a day. If you should be driving a car, never leave anything of value in it. Car break-ins are commonplace here. There are now children who offer to watch your car for a small price when you leave it outside the park entrance. Take them up on the offer if you want to avoid damage to your car by thieves trying to find out what's in your trunk.

Fast Facts   You'll find Julieanne's Laundry Service around the corner from the Restaurant Isabel. It's open Monday through Friday from 7:30 to 11:30am and from 2 to 6pm. They charge $2.05 per kilo with a 2-kilo minimum. There's a pharmacy called Botica Quepos on the corner of the main street where you make the turn for Manuel Antonio (tel. 777-0038). Open daily from 7am to 6pm.

No other beach in Costa Rica has received more international attention than Manuel Antonio. What is it about Manuel Antonio that has given it such an international reputation? Simply that it is one of the most beautiful locations in the entire country. Gazing down on the blue Pacific from high on the mountainsides of Manuel Antonio, it is almost impossible to hold back a gasp of delight. Offshore rocky islands dot the vast expanse of blue. In the foreground the rich deep green of the rain forest sweeps down to the water. It is this superb view that hotels at Manuel Antonio sell, and this view that enchants both those who have only seen photos and those who have been here for a visit.

Of course there is also the national park itself, which though it covers fewer than 1,700 acres is one of the most popular national parks in the country and is the site of three nearly perfect little beaches. These beaches are connected by a trail that meanders through the rain forest between the beach and the mountains that rise quickly as you head inland from the water. However, **Manuel Antonio National Park** was created not because it had beautiful beaches but because its forests are home to the endangered squirrel monkey, three-toed sloths, purple-and-orange crabs, and hundreds of other species of birds, mammals, and plants. This stretch of coast has been almost entirely transformed into plantations, so this little rocky outcrop of forests is the region's last stronghold of nature.

However, in the past few years rampant development and ever-growing crowds of beach-goers have turned what was once a peaceful and pristine spot into an area of hastily built, overpriced hotels, packed parking areas, and noisy crowds that make seeing any wildlife almost an impossibility. Manuel Antonio has become completely overburdened with adoring throngs. The stream that forms the boundary of the park and through which park visitors must wade has become polluted with garbage and human waste. On weekends the beaches are packed with people and the discos blare their music until early morning, drowning out the sounds of crickets and frogs that once lulled visitors to sleep here. A shanty town of snack shacks lines the road just outside the park, marring the beauty of this area.

Quepos, where most of the area's budget hotels are to be found, was once a quiet banana port. The land to the north was used by Chiquita to grow its bananas. However, a disease wiped out the banana plantations, and now the land is planted with oil palm trees. To reach Quepos by road, you must pass through miles and miles of these oil-palm plantations. Today Quepos is changing its image from that of shipping port to that of cluttered and dirty tourist boom town.

Despite these caveats, Manuel Antonio is still a beautiful spot, and if you plan your visit, you can avoid many of the problems that detract from its appeal. If you avoid the peak months from December to March, you will avoid the crowds. If you must come during the peak months, try to avoid weekends, when the beach is packed with families from San José. Visit the park early in the morning, and you can leave when the midday crowds show up.

WHAT TO SEE & DO

The road from Quepos dead-ends at the long Playa Espadilla (Espadilla Beach), which is just outside the park. This beach is often too rough for casual swimming but can be perfect for board surfing and bodysurfing. To reach the park itself, you must cross a small, polluted stream that is little more than ankle-deep at low tide but can be knee- or even waist-deep at high tide. Just after crossing the stream you will have to pay the park entrance fee of $1.35. Playa Espadilla Sur is the first beach you come to within the park boundaries. You can walk along this soft sand beach or follow a trail through the forest behind the beach. At the far end there is a short connecting trail to Playa Manuel Antonio, which is sometimes clear enough to offer good snorkeling. A branch trail from this beach leads up and around Punta Catedral (Cathedral Point), where there are some spectacular views. If you take this trail, wear good shoes. Cathedral Point is one of the best places to spot monkeys, though you are more likely to see the white-faced monkey than the rare squirrel monkey. From Playa Manuel Antonio (the second beach) there is another, slightly longer, trail to the third beach, Puerto Escondido. There is a blowhole on this beach that sends up plumes of spray at high tide. Beyond here, at Punta Serrucho, there are some sea caves. Two other trails wind their way inland from the trail between Playa Manuel Antonio and Puerto Escondido. The park is open daily from 7am to 4pm.

If you're staying in Quepos and don't want to go all the way over the hill to the park, you can swim and lounge at **Nahomi,** Quepos's public swimming pool. You'll find this pool on a tiny peninsula at the end of the road that parallels the water. Admission is $1.05 and the pool is open daily from 9am to 7pm.

If your tropical fantasy is to **ride a horse** down a beach between jungle and ocean, contact Stable Equus (tel. 777-0001), which charges $30 for a 2-hour ride. Planes Turisticos Nahomi (tel. 777-0161) offers an all-day tour that includes horseback riding as well as a boat trip around the Isla Damas estuary. The trip costs $65. If you'd like a guide to take you through the national park, contact Alberto (tel.

777-0413), who charges $25 for a 3-hour **hike. Kayaking** trips among the rocky islets of Manuel Antonio National Park or up the nearby Isla Damas estuary are offered by Rios Tropicales (tel. 777-0574). They charge $65 for a full-day paddle around the estuary (includes lunch at La Tortuga restaurant) or through the national park (with a picnic on the beach). They also offer half-day trips for $35, and **white-water rafting** trips on the nearby Río Naranjo ($65 to $70 full day or $45 half day). Rafting trips are usually only offered between June and November, when the water level in the river is high enough. Rios Tropicales also rents sea kayaks on Playa Espadilla. **Rainforest Expeditions & School** (tel. 777-1170) offers rafting trips on both the Río Naranjo and the Río Savegre and charges $65 to $75 for a full-day trip. This company also offers dive trips for $70 and guided all-day hikes for $45. The *Byblos I* (tel. 777-0411) does 7½-hour **cruises** that include lunch, fishing, and snorkeling for $80 per person.

Quepos is one of Costa Rica's **sportfishing** centers, and sailfish, marlin, and tuna are all common in these waters. If you're into sportfishing and happen to be here between December and April, contact La Buena Nota (tel. 777-0345), where you can arrange a fishing charter for around $300 per day. Other companies to try include JP Tours (tel. 777-1613); Tours Cambute (tel. 777-0082); and Sportfishing Costa Rica (tel. 777-0505).

If you're looking for **souvenirs,** try La Buena Nota, which is on the left just over the bridge as you enter Quepos (tel. 777-0345). This little shop is jam-packed with all sorts of beach wear, souvenirs, and U.S. magazines and newspapers, and also acts as an informal information center for the area. If you'd like to find out about renting a house, this is a good place to ask.

The **market** (two blocks in from the main road into town) sells lots of delicious fruit. If you're doing your own cooking, this is the place to shop. Super Quepos is a general store on the main street, near the corner where you turn to head out to Manuel Antonio.

The main **evening entertainment** at Manuel Antonio is the disco that appears after dark at Restaurant Mar y Sombra. You can also hang out at the Vela-Bar, which is up the road to the left just before you reach Manuel Antonio and seems to be popular with gay men. The bar at the Barba Roja restaurant is another good place to hang out and meet people. If you are staying in Quepos, check out the Disco Arco Iris, which is across the bridge from town and is built over the water.

WHERE TO STAY
DOUBLES FOR LESS THAN $25

CABINAS PISCIS, Apdo. 219, Quepos. Tel. 506/777-0046. 6 rms (all with private bath).

$ Rates: Dec–Apr $23.20 single or double, $27.05 triple or quad; May–Nov $19.35 single or double, $23.20 triple or quad. No credit cards.

If you want to be within walking distance of the park but out of earshot of the discos' booming speakers, and you don't want to spend a lot of money, this is one of the only choices you have. The rooms are basic but clean, and the management is very friendly. The beach is just a hundred yards or so down a forest trail. You'll find Cabinas Piscis on the beach side of the road just before you reach the bottom of the hill and Manuel Antonio.

CABINAS VELA-BAR, Apdo. 13, Manuel Antonio, Quepos. Tel. 506/ 777-0413. Fax 506/777-1071. 9 rms, 1 apt, 1 house (all with private bath).

$ Rates: $12.60–$33.15 single; $22.90–$72 double; $49.15–$81.15 triple; $73.15 quad. AE, MC, V.

You'll find this unusual little hotel up the dirt road that leads off to the left just before the end of the road to Manuel Antonio National Park. There's a wide variety of room choices in various price ranges at Vela-Bar. If you're on a budget, you can stay in a tiny room, or, if you have more money to spend, you can opt for a spacious one-bedroom house that has tile floors and arched windows. The open-air restaurant/bar is deservedly very popular. Prices range from $5.10 to $11.50 for entrees.

HOTEL CECILIANO, Quepos. Tel. 506/777-0192. 20 rms (11 with private bath).
$ Rates: $15.45 single without bath, $23.20 single with bath; $19.75 double without bath, $27.05 double with bath. No credit cards.

This is one of Quepos's best low-budget hotel choices. The rooms, though dark, are as clean as you'll find anywhere in town, and the management is friendly. You'll find the Ceciliano about a block before the Hotel Quepos, which happens to be operated by the daughter of the owner of the Ceciliano.

HOTEL MALINCHE, Quepos. Tel./fax 506/777-0093. 28 rms (all with private bath).
$ Rates: $9.15–$34.30 single; $17.15–$40 double. V.

The Hotel Malinche is located on the first street to your left as you come into Quepos. You can't miss the hotel's arched brick entrance. Inside you'll find bright rooms with louvered windows but no screens, so be sure to buy some mosquito coils (mosquito-repelling incense coils, available in general stores) before night falls. The rooms are small but have hardwood floors and clean bathrooms. The more expensive rooms have air conditioning and carpets.

HOTEL QUEPOS, Apdo. 79, Quepos. Tel. 506/777-0274. 29 rms (9 with private bath).
$ Rates: $9.65 single without bath, $11.60 single with bath; $19.35 double without bath, $23.20 double with bath. No credit cards.

Located in Quepos, across from the soccer field, this little budget hotel is both comfortable and clean. There are hardwood floors, ceiling fans, a large, sunny TV lounge, and even a parking lot and laundry service. The management is very friendly, and downstairs from the second-floor hotel is an interesting souvenir shop and a charter fishing office.

DOUBLES FOR LESS THAN $45

CABINAS PEDRO MIGUEL, Manuel Antonio, Quepos. Tel. 506/777-0035. 14 rms (all with private bath).
$ Rates: $23.20 single; $30.95 double; $61.80 triple. No credit cards.

Located a kilometer out of Quepos on the road to Manuel Antonio (across from Plinio), these cabinas are very basic (cement floors and cinder-block walls), but at least they're out of town and surrounded by forest. The second-floor rooms are newer and cleaner, and there's even a glimpse of the water from the veranda. One of the rooms is huge and has an entire wall of screen that looks out into the trees. During the high season there is restaurant serving barbecued steaks and various salads. There's a tiny swimming pool that sometimes has water in it.

HOTEL SULA BYA BA, Apdo. 203, Quepos. Tel. 506/777-0547. 9 rms (all with private bath).
$ Rates: Dec–Apr $32 single, $40 double, $51.45 triple; May–Nov slightly lower rates. AE, MC, V.

You're still a long way from the beach when you stay at the Sula Bya Ba, but the artistic decor and atmosphere make this one of the most interesting hotels at Manuel Antonio. Rooms are large and seem to be a hybrid of pueblo and Japanese motifs. The doors are reminiscent of shoji screens, and there are opaque windows around the showers, which make the bathrooms quite bright. Color schemes are very soothing and there are works of art on display in all the rooms. Breakfast is available.

WORTH THE EXTRA BUCKS

APARTOTEL EL COLIBRI, Apdo. 94, Manuel Antonio, Quepos. Tel. 506/777-0432. 10 rms (all with private bath).

$ Rates: Dec–Apr $56 single, $68 double, $79 triple; May–Nov $30 single, $40 double, $50 triple. V.

If you have dreams of a secluded, tranquil retreat where you can laze in a hammock and watch hummingbirds sipping nectar from crimson flowers, this hotel is for you. The eight elegant rooms are set amid a garden that would have kept Monet happy for years. Narrow paths wind up a hill through lush vegetation, and each of the cozy duplex rooms has a king-size bed with Guatemalan bedspread, high ceiling with overhead fan, and French doors that lead to a patio. The spacious patios have hammocks, tables and chairs, and barbecues. There are even rooms with beautiful kitchenettes with blue-and-white-tile counters and espresso makers. A couple of older rooms close to the road are not as nice as the others.

LA COLINA, Apdo. 191, Quepos. Tel. 506/777-0231. 5 rms (all with private bath).

$ Rates (with continental breakfast): Dec–Apr $29 single, $40 double; May–Nov $18 single, $25 double. V.

This casual little bed-and-breakfast is operated by two men from Quebec who moved down to Manuel Antonio a few years ago and converted this house into a B&B. Though the rooms are fairly small, they are very stylishly decorated. There are black-and-white-tile floors, louvered French doors, and despite the small size of the rooms, a good writing desk. Outside each room there are some chairs on the patio. Breakfast is served in your room or on the patio and might consist of a crepe or pancake and coffee.

COSTA VERDE, Apdo. 106-6350, Quepos. Tel. 506/777-0584 or 777-0187. Fax 506/777-0506. 30 rms (all with private bath).

$ Rates: Dec–Apr $68.60–$102.90 single or double; May–Nov $45.75–$80 single or double. AE, DC, MC, V.

The guest rooms at Costa Verde have long been some of my favorite in the area. With their screen walls, they seem to sum up the sensual climate of the tropics. No need for walls when they only keep out the breezes. The original rooms are the least expensive and are quite pleasant. All the rooms have ocean views, kitchenettes, and balconies. There's a very pretty little pool set into the hillside and up above the pool is an open-air restaurant that looks into the forest, where sloths are sometimes seen. Costa Verde is about halfway down the hill to Manuel Antonio and has good views.

HOTEL CASITAS ECLIPSE, Manuel Antonio, Quepos. Tel./fax 506/777-0408 or (in the U.S.) 619/753-6827. 10 casitas (all with private bath). A/C

$ Rates: Nov 15–Apr 15 $74.30 single or double, $97.15–$114.30 casita with one bedroom, $171.45 casita with two bedrooms; Apr 16–Nov 14 $45.75 single or double, $57.15–$68.60 casita with one bedroom, $102.90 casita with two bedrooms. V.

Located close to the top of the hill between Quepos and Manuel Antonio, these beautiful *casitas* (little houses) are some of the most boldly styled structures in Manuel Antonio. Each casita is basically a miniature Mediterranean villa. All are painted a blinding white, which is contrasted by red roof tiles. The casitas are very comfortable and attractive inside. There are tile floors, built-in banquettes, high ceilings, and full kitchens. Each sleeps up to five people and has a big patio. The small second-floor rooms are the cheapest, but if you have friends or family with you, the one-bedroom apartments are also a good value. There are no ocean views here, but there is a swimming pool. A poolside snack bar serves breakfast as well as bar drinks.

HOTEL MIRADOR DEL PACIFICO, Apdo. 164, Quepos. Tel./fax 506/777-0119. 20 rms, 3 villas (all with private bath).

$ Rates (including continental breakfast): Dec–Apr $62.90–$85.75 single or double; villas $114.30 double, $148.60 quad (villa rates do not include breakfast). AE, MC, V (add 6% surcharge).

Located 200 yards up the road from the Hotel Plinio, this lodge is set amid shady trees on a steep hillside. From the hotel's verandas you can look out over the forest to the ocean far below. Guest rooms have a Central American touch, with Guatemalan rugs, place mats on the bedside stands, and paintings by local artists. The newest rooms overlook the pool. The German owner has had a fascination with cable cars for years and has built one of his own. It carries guests to a restaurant/bar at the top of the property. From here there is a magnificent view of the mountains, forests, and ocean.

HOTEL PLINIO, Apdo. 71, Quepos. Tel. 506/777-0055. Fax 506/777-0558.

6 rms, 6 suites (all with private bath).

$ Rates (including full breakfast): Dec–Apr $40–$45.75 single, $57.15–$62.90 double, $74.30–$91.45 suite; May–Nov lower rates available. AE, MC, V.

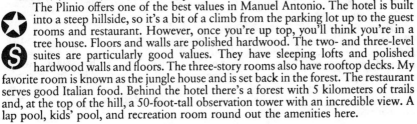

The Plinio offers one of the best values in Manuel Antonio. The hotel is built into a steep hillside, so it's a bit of a climb from the parking lot up to the guest rooms and restaurant. However, once you're up top, you'll think you're in a tree house. Floors and walls are polished hardwood. The two- and three-level suites are particularly good values. They have sleeping lofts and polished hardwood walls and floors. The three-story rooms also have rooftop decks. My favorite room is known as the jungle house and is set back in the forest. The restaurant serves good Italian food. Behind the hotel there's a forest with 5 kilometers of trails and, at the top of the hill, a 50-foot-tall observation tower with an incredible view. A lap pool, kids' pool, and recreation room round out the amenities here.

READERS RECOMMEND

Hotel California, Quepos. Tel. 506/777-0595. "We stayed at the Hotel California for a week. This new hotel offered many advantages. . . . Overall, the place was quiet, friendly, and inexpensive ($40 to $60 double). Our stay in this hotel made us appreciate this part of the country." —Nicole Lemire, Montreal, Quebec, Canada

WHERE TO EAT

For the cheapest meals around, head to one of the dozen or so open-air shacks just before the entrance to the park. The standard Tico menu prevails with prices in the $2.70 to $8.10 range. Though these little places lack atmosphere, they do have a view of the ocean.

MEALS FOR UNDER $6

GEORGE'S AMERICAN BAR, on road to Manuel Antonio, 100 meters from the dike. No phone.

Cuisine: MEXICAN/AMERICAN. **Reservations:** Not accepted.

$ Prices: All dishes $2.05–$4.05. No credit cards.

Open: Mon–Sat 8am–10pm.

If you are in Quepos and want a cheap and familiar meal, drop in at George's. To find this little place, just watch for the sign with the stars and stripes and the eagle. This is a gringo hangout and serves such comfort foods as hamburgers, brownies, burritos, guacamole, and even a mahimahi burger con queso. There's also a full bar and occasional live music.

LA TORTUGA, Isla Damas. No phone.

Cuisine: SEAFOOD. **Reservations:** Not accepted.

$ Prices: Main dishes $3.40–$10.80. V.

Open: Daily 9am–8pm.

This is a floating restaurant, and though it is just a basic Tico hangout, it is an experience worth searching out. To reach it, you must first drive north out of town toward Jacó Beach. Watch for the Complejo Turistico sign and turn west for another mile or so. When you reach the water, you'll find a boatman waiting to take you out to the restaurant, which is a large converted boat. If there is no boatman around, flash your lights and beep your horn; someone will soon come for you. The menu is primarily fish, and the owner seems to always have the very best catches of the day. For just what you'd pay in town, you get great seafood, a boat ride, and a view across the estuary to the forested mountains beyond.

MEALS FOR UNDER $12

BARBA ROJA, Quepos-Manuel Antonio Rd. Tel. 777-0331.
   Cuisine: SEAFOOD/CONTINENTAL. **Reservations:** Suggested in high season.
   $ Prices: Appetizers $2.35–$5.10, entrees $5.50–$15.60; sandwiches $2.35–$3.05. No credit cards.
   Open: Tues–Sun 7:30am–10:30pm.
The Barba Roja has one of the best views around, which alone would make it worth a few visits. However, it also has good food and a lively atmosphere. Take a seat at the counter, and you can sit for hours gazing out at the view. Local art hangs on the walls, and there is even a gallery attached to the restaurant. On the blackboard there are daily specials such as grilled fish steak served with a salad and baked potato. For breakfast there is delicious whole-wheat french toast, and for lunch, there are a number of different sandwiches.

KAROLA'S, Quepos-Manuel Antonio Road. Tel. 777-0424.
   Cuisine: SEAFOOD/CONTINENTAL. **Reservations:** Not accepted.
   $ Prices: Appetizers $2.55–$3.75; entrees $4.75–$14.20. No credit cards.
   Open: Thurs–Tues 7am–10pm.
★ The steep driveway leading down to this open-air restaurant is within a few feet of the Barba Roja parking lot but is easily overlooked. The restaurant itself is across a footbridge and is set against a jungle-covered hillside. If you are here during the day, you can see the ocean far below. Grilled seafoods are the specialty here, but they also do peel-and-eat shrimp with a great house sauce. Desserts, such as lemon chiffon pie, are good, and you can order margaritas by the pitcher.

PLINIO RESTAURANT, 1 kilometer out of Quepos toward Manuel Antonio. Tel. 777-0055.
   Cuisine: ITALIAN/GERMAN. **Reservations:** Recommended in high season.
   $ Prices: Appetizers $2.70–$6.45; entrees $5.45–$9.50. MC, V.
   Open: Daily 7–10am and 5–10pm.
★ This is the most popular restaurant in Manuel Antonio, and the open-air dining area is three stories above the parking lot, so be prepared to climb some steps before you get to eat. The basket of bread that arrives at your table shortly after you sit down is filled with delicious treats, and the menu is full of tempting dishes. Italian is the primary cuisine here, but you may also encounter some German specials. Some of my favorite dishes include the spaghetti with pesto and the broccoli-and-cauliflower parmigiana. There's also a great antipasto plate that includes prosciutto, salami, and cheese.

RESTAURANT VELA-BAR, 100 meters down side road near park entrance. Tel. 777-0413.
   Cuisine: INTERNATIONAL. **Reservations:** Not accepted.
   $ Prices: Appetizers $2.05–$6.10; entrees $5.10–$11.50. AE, MC, V.
   Open: Daily 7am–10am, 11:30am–2:30pm, 5:30–11pm (closed at lunch June–Nov).
The Vela-Bar is a small and casual place that serves some of the more creative cookery in Manuel Antonio. Seafood and vegetarian meals are the specialties here, and the most interesting dishes are almost always the specials posted on the blackboard. A typical day's choices might include fish in sherry or wine sauce. As the name implies, this is also a bar.

4. DOMINICAL

29 kilometers SW of San Isidro; 42 kilometers S of Quepos;
160 kilometers S of San José

GETTING THERE   By Bus   To reach Dominical, you must first go to San Isidro de El General or Quepos. Buses for San Isidro de El General leave San José daily every hour from 5:30am to 5pm from Calle 16 between avenidas 1 and 3. Leave no later than 9:30 if you want to catch the 1:30 bus to Dominical. Duration: 3 hours. Fare: $3.25. From San Isidro de El General, buses leave for Dominical at 7am and 1:30 and 3pm. The bus station for Dominical is one block south of the main bus station and two blocks west of the church. Duration: 1½ hours. Fare: $1.85. From Quepos, buses leave twice daily. Duration: 2 hours. Fare: $2.10.

By Car   From San José, head south (toward Cartago) on the Interamerican Highway. Continue on this road all the way to San Isidro de El General, where you turn right and head down toward the coast. The entire drive takes about five hours.

DEPARTING   Buses leave Dominical for San Isidro de El General twice daily, but you'll have to catch the morning bus if you want to get to San José that same day. Buses to Quepos also leave twice daily. Buses leave San Isidro for San José every hour from 5:30am to 5pm.

ESSENTIALS   Dominical is a small village on the banks of the Barú River. The village is to the right after you cross the bridge and centers around the soccer field and general store, where there is a public telephone.

The road south from Quepos to Dominical leads through mile after mile of flat oil-palm plantations, but here, 60 kilometers south of Manuel Antonio, the mountains once again meet the sea. From Dominical south, the rugged coastline is dotted with tide pools and tiny coves. Dominical itself is the largest village in the area and has several small lodges both in town and along the road to the south. The village enjoys an enviable location on the banks of the Río Barú, which at this point, just before emptying into the ocean, becomes a wide lagoon. There is good bird-watching along the banks of the river. Over the past few years Dominical has become something of a surfers' hangout.

WHAT TO SEE & DO

Because the beach right in the village of Dominical is unprotected and at the mouth of a river, it is often much too rough for swimming. However, you can go for a swim in the lagoon at the mouth of the Río Barú, or head down the beach a few kilometers to the little sheltered cove at Roca Verde. If you have a car, you can continue driving south, exploring beaches as you go. At the village of Uvita, 16 kilometers south of Dominical, you'll reach the northern end of the **Ballena Marine National Park,** which protects a coral reef that stretches from Uvita south to Playa Piñuela and includes the little Isla Ballena, which is just off shore. This park is named for the whales that are often sighted close to shore in the winter.

Although the beaches stretching south from Dominical should be beautiful enough to keep most people content, there are lots of other things to do. Several local farms offer horseback tours through forests and orchards, and at some of these farms you can even spend the night. **Hacienda Barú** (tel. 771-1903, leave message) offers several different hikes and tours, including a walk through mangroves and along the river bank (good bird-watching), a rain-forest hike through 200 acres of virgin jungle, an all-day trek from beach to mangrove to jungle that includes a visit to some Indian petroglyphs, an overnight camping trip, and a combination horseback and hiking tour. Tour prices range from $12.50 to $60 if there is only one person. The more people there are in your group, the lower the per-person rate (maximum six people per tour). Hacienda Barú can also help you arrange various hikes and horseback rides on other nearby farms.

Finca Brian y Milena, Apdo. 2-8000, San Isidro de El General (tel. 771-1903, leave message), offers day and overnight trips to their farm in the hills outside of Dominical. Here you can bird-watch, explore the tropical rain forest, and visit a working farm where tropical fruits, nuts, and spices are grown. If you stay for several nights, you can visit the Santo Cristo or Diamante waterfalls by horseback or on foot. Rates range from $30 for a day trip for one person ($40 for two) to $190 for two people for five days and nights. Horse rentals are additional.

Down near Uvita there are several beautiful waterfalls that make wonderful destinations for hikes or horseback rides. Ask at Uvita's Soda Cocotico for Jorge Díaz, who leads people to the **Emerald Pools Falls,** which are a great place to go for a swim.

Reel & Reelease (tel. 771-1903, leave message) offers fishing charters. A full-day fishing trip for four will cost $425, for two people the cost is $275. Half-day trips are $250 for two people and $375 for four people.

WHERE TO STAY

In addition to the places listed here, if you continue south another 16 kilometers, you'll find a campground on Playa Ballena and a couple of basic cabina places in Uvita.

DOUBLES FOR LESS THAN $25

CABINAS NAYARIT, 200 meters west of Rancho Coco, Dominical. Tel. 506/771-1878. 13 rms (all with private bath).
$ Rates: Dec–Apr $23.20–$46.35 single or double; May–Nov $15.50–$30.95 single or double. No credit cards.

Wedged between the mouth of the Río Barú and the beach, there are several sandy lanes lined with simple houses and some cabina places, of which the Cabinas Nayarit are the best. There are several styles of rooms here including older ones with fans and lots of beds (cramped), older rooms with air conditioning, and (most expensive) newer rooms with air conditioning, skylights, carved wooden headboards, and jalousie windows.

ROCA VERDE, Dominical. Tel. 506/771-2490. 12 rms (7 with private bath).
$ Rates: $7.75 single, double, or triple without bath; $19.35 single or double with bath; $23.20 triple with bath. No credit cards.

Though Roca Verde is a couple of miles south of town, it does have a restaurant where you can get inexpensive meals. The setting is superb—on a little cove with rocks and tide pools at the near end. The cheaper rooms are very basic, with wooden walls, a fan, one small window, and a couple of beds. The shared toilets and showers are comparable to what you might find at a campground. The more expensive cabins have private baths and a decidedly tropical feel. There's a disco every Saturday night at Roca Verde's open-air restaurant/bar. Be prepared to party.

DOUBLES FOR LESS THAN $35

ALBERGUE WILLDALE, Dominical. Tel. 506/771-1903 (leave message). 7 rms (all with private bath).
$ Rates: $22.90 single; $28.60 double; $34.30 triple. No credit cards.

The Albergue Willdale is located directly across from the soccer field and is by far the friendliest place in Dominical. Directly behind the lodge is the river, where you can go swimming, fishing, or paddling around. The owners of this lodge will gladly fill you in on all there is to do in the area. The rooms are large and have big windows and patios. There are reading lights, fans, hot water, and attractive Mexican bedspreads. If you are interested in staying for a while, the owners also rent a very comfortable house (with a pool) up in the hills for $120 a night.

BELLA VISTA, Dominical (c/o Selva Mar, Apdo. 215-8000, San Isidro de El General). Tel. 506/771-1903. Fax 506/771-0060. 4 cabins (all with private bath).

$ Rates (including breakfast): $17.15–$22.90 single; $34.30–$45.75 double. No credit cards.

Bella Vista means "beautiful view" and that is exactly what you get when you stay at one of these rustic little cabins high in the hills south of Dominical. The owners here are very friendly and the location is superb. Transportation between Dominical and Bella Vista is $10 per person each way. Simple meals are served ($3 for lunch, $5 for dinner), though one of the cabins also has its own kitchen. The favorite activity here is an all-day horseback ride through the rain forest to a beautiful waterfall ($40 per person).

DOUBLES FOR LESS THAN $45

CABAÑAS ESCONDIDAS, Apdo. 364, San Isidro de El General (in the U.S.: c/o Selva Mar, AAA Express, 1641 NW 79th Ave., Miami, FL 33126). Tel. 506/771-1903. 6 rms (all with private bath).

$ Rates (including breakfast): $40 single or double; $51.45 triple. No credit cards.

Most mornings will find guests here meditating on the porch of their cabin or doing tai chi chuan in the garden, and the owners of these cabañas encourage such pursuits. The cabins are situated high on a hill overlooking the Pacific Ocean and are all very secluded. Several are done in a beautiful Japanese style with shoji screens and stone walls. Most are quite a hike from the parking area, so travel light. Down below is a beautiful little cove, and surrounding the lodge are 80 acres of farmland and virgin rain forest. Tours of the forest can be arranged for $10 to $15 per person. You'll find Cabañas Escondidas about 6 kilometers south of Dominical. Because lunch and dinner are not always available, you'll need a car if you stay here.

HOTEL RIO LINDO, Dominical. Tel. 506/771-2009. Fax 506/771-1725. 10 rms (all with private bath).

$ Rates: Dec–Apr $23.20 single, $38.65 double, $46.35 triple; May–Nov slightly lower rates. No credit cards.

This is one of the newest hotels in Dominical and is located just across the bridge where the road turns into the village. Rooms here are simple but clean and all have ceiling fans. The upstairs rooms are definitely the better choice here. These rooms are larger and have nicer furnishings and better ventilation. Adjacent to the hotel is the Restaurant Maui, a moderately priced place that seems to keep the stereo blaring all day long.

WORTH THE EXTRA BUCKS

PUNTA DOMINICAL, Apdo. 196-8000, San Isidro de El General. Tel./fax 506/771-1903. 4 cabins (all with private bath).

$ Rates: $40 single; $51.45 double; $62.90 triple; $68.60 quad; $85.75 large cabin for one to six people. No credit cards.

Located about 5 kilometers south of Dominical on a rocky point, this place has a stony cove on one side and a sandy beach on the other. The cabins and restaurant are set among shady old trees high above the surf and have excellent views of both coves. The best views are to be had from the cabins higher up the hill, but all have good views. The cabins, built on stilts and constructed of dark polished hardwood, all have big porches with chairs and hammocks. Screened and louvered walls are designed to catch the breezes. The hotel's open-air restaurant, which specializes in seafood, is the best in Dominical. Entree prices range from $3.75 to $14.90.

WHERE TO EAT

Right in town, there's the **Soda Laura,** which serves basic Tico meals and has a nice view of the river mouth. Prices range from $1.70 to $6.75. Other options right in

Dominical include **Jungle Jim's,** a gringo hangout and sports bar, and the **Bar Maui.** The latter two places have meals for between $3.50 and $15. However, if you want the best food in the area, head south of town to the dining room at **Punta Dominical.**

5. SAN ISIDRO DE EL GENERAL

120 kilometers SE of San José; 123 kilometers NW of Palmar Norte; 29 kilometers NE of Dominical

GETTING THERE By Bus Express buses leave San José twice daily from Calle 16 between avenidas 1 and 3. Duration: 3 hours. Fare: $3.25. There are also buses from Puerto Jiménez to San Isidro twice daily. Duration: 5 hours. Fare: $4.50. Buses from Golfito to San José also stop in San Isidro. These buses leave twice daily. Duration: 5 hours. Fare: $6.15.

By Car It is a long and winding road from San José to San Isidro. The section of the Interamerican Highway from San José to San Isidro is one of the most difficult sections of road in the country. Not only are there the usual car-eating potholes, but you must also contend with driving over the 11,000-foot-high Cerro de la Muerte (Mountain of Death), which the I.C.T. (Costa Rican Tourism Institute) would like to rename Buenavista (Beautiful View). This aptly named mountain (in either case) is legendary for its dense afternoon fogs, blindingly torrential downpours, steep drop-offs, constant switchbacks, and breathtaking views. In other words, drive with care. And bring a sweater; it's cold up at the top. It'll take you about three hours to get to San Isidro.

DEPARTING Buses for San José leave daily every hour between 5:30am and 5pm. Buses to Dominical leave three times daily. Buses to Golfito leave three times daily. Buses to Puerto Jiménez leave twice daily.

ESSENTIALS Downtown San Isidro is just off of the Interamerican Highway. The main bus station is two blocks west of the north end of the central park.

San Isidro de El General is the largest town in this region and is located on the Interamerican Highway in the foothills of the Talamanca Mountains. Though there isn't much of anything to do right in town, this is the jumping-off point for trips to Chirripó National Park. This is also the transfer point if you are coming from or going to Dominical.

WHAT TO SEE & DO

At 12,412 feet in elevation, Mount Chirripó is the tallest mountain in Costa Rica, and because of the great elevations within **Chirripó National Park,** temperatures often go well below freezing. If you are headed up this way, come prepared for chilly weather. The elevation and low temperatures here have produced a very different sort of environment from the rest of Costa Rica. Above about 10,000 feet, only stunted trees and shrubs can survive in regions known as *paramos*. If you are driving the Interamerican Highway between San Isidro and San José, you will pass through the paramo on the Cerro de la Muerte (Mountain of Death).

Hiking up to the top of Mount Chirripó is one of Costa Rica's great adventures. On a clear day (usually in the morning), you can see both the Pacific Ocean and the Caribbean Sea from the summit. You can do this trip fairly easily on your own if you have brought gear and are an experienced backpacker. It will take you around four days to hike from the park entrance to the peak and back down again. For much of the way you'll be hiking through cloud forests that are home to the resplendent quetzal. These cloud forests are cold and damp, so come prepared for rain and fog. To reach

Chirripó National Park from San Isidro, catch a bus to San Gerardo de Rivas at 5am or 2pm. Buses return to San Isidro at 7am and 4pm. Park admission is $1.35. If you'd like to do the trip with a guide, contact **Chirripó Trekking Adventures** (tel. 254-4811 or 254-6096).

WHERE TO STAY & EAT
DOUBLES FOR LESS THAN $25

HOTEL CHIRRIPÓ, south side of church, San Isidro de El General. Tel. 506/771-0529. 46 rms (20 with private bath).
$ Rates: $6 single without bath, $9.65 single with bath; $10.30 double without bath, $15.90 double with bath; $23.80 triple with bath. V.
This budget hotel is about the best you'll find right in San Isidro and is located on the central square within a couple of blocks of all the town's bus stations. Rooms vary considerably. Some have windows (and street noise), and some have no windows (or street noise). Stay away from the rooms in front, since these are the noisiest. There's a restaurant at the front of the lobby.

EN ROUTE TO SAN JOSÉ

Between San Isidro de El General and San José, the Interamerican Highway climbs to its highest point in Costa Rica and crosses over the Cerro de la Muerte. This area has recently acquired a newfound importance as one of the best places in Costa Rica to see resplendent quetzals in the wild. March, April, and May are nesting season for the quetzals, and this is usually the best time to see them. However, in this area, it is usually possible to see them year-round.

WORTH THE EXTRA BUCKS

ALBERGUE DE MONTAÑA SAVEGRE, kilometer 80 Carretera Interamericana Sur, San Gerardo de Dota (Apdo. 482, Cartago). Tel. 506/771-1732. 14 cabins (all with private bath).
$ Rates (including three meals): $57.15 per person. V.
⭐ This working apple and pear farm has recently acquired quite a reputation for itself as one of the best places in the country to see quetzals. The farm has long been popular as a weekend vacation and picnicking spot for Ticos, but now people from all over the world are searching out the rustic lodge. The rooms here are quite basic, but if you're serious about bird-watching this shouldn't matter. Hearty Tico meals are served, and if you want to try your hand at trout fishing, you might luck into a fish dinner. You'll find this lodge 9 kilometers down a dirt road off the Interamerican Highway.

FINCA DE EDDIE SERRANO-MIRADOR DE QUETZALES, kilometer 70 Carretera Interamericana Sur, Tres de Junio de Dota. No phone. 8 rms (all with shared bath).
$ Rates (including three meals): $28.60 per person. No credit cards.
This very rustic lodge, which overlooks a beautiful valley, hadn't yet opened when I last visited, but was very close. Construction is of slab boards and most of the rooms are tiny cubicles with bunk beds. Meals are served in the building's central lounge area where there is a wood stove to take the chill off the high-altitude nights (the lodge is at 8,450 feet). This place is definitely for younger bird-watchers who don't mind very basic accommodations. The Serrano family is very helpful and friendly, though little English is spoken. They offer guided hikes and night tours ($6.80 per person for two to three hours), though you can often see quetzals right from the lodge itself.

CHAPTER 7

THE SOUTHERN ZONE

The heat and humidity are more than many people can handle, but this remote southern region of Costa Rica is one of the country's most beautiful and wild areas. Lush forested mountains tumble into the sea, streams still run clear and clean, and scarlet macaws squawk raucously in the treetops. However, this beauty does not come easy, you must have plenty of time (and/or money) and a desire for a bit of adventure if you want to explore this region. Because there are few roads, the most fascinating spots can only be reached by small plane or boat, though hiking and four-wheeling will also get you into some memorable surroundings.

Because the south is such a long drive from San José (about eight hours), it has been the last area of Costa Rica to open up to tourism. There are still relatively few places to stay down here, but that is, of course, changing almost weekly. With the opening of a duty-free port at Golfito, even Ticos are discovering this region.

1. DRAKE BAY

145 kilometers S of San José; 32 kilometers SW of Palmar

GETTING THERE By Plane   The closest airport to Drake Bay is in Palmar Sur. Sansa (tel. 233-0397, 233-3258, or 233-5330) has flights to Palmar Sur Monday through Saturday. Duration: 1½ hours. Fare: $46 each way. Travelair (tel. 220-3054 and 232-7883) has flights to Palmar Sur daily. Duration: 55 minutes. Fare: $58 one way, $100 round-trip.

By Bus   Express buses leave San José six times daily from Avenida 18 between calles 2 and 4. Duration: 5 hours. Fare: $4.30. You can also catch a Golfito-bound bus from this same station and get off in Palmar Norte. Once in Palmar Norte, find out when the next bus goes to Sierpe. If it doesn't leave for a while, you'll have to take a taxi.

By Taxi and Boat   Once you arrive at either the Palmar Norte bus station or the Palmar Sur airstrip, you'll need to take a taxi (or bus) to the village of Sierpe. The fare should be between $10 and $15. A seat on a boat from Sierpe downriver to Drake Bay will cost you another $15.

DEPARTING   Have your lodge arrange your boat trip back upriver to Sierpe. Also be sure to have the lodge arrange a taxi to meet you in Sierpe for the trip to Palmar Sur or Palmar Norte. If you're on a budget, you can take the late-morning public bus from

WHAT'S SPECIAL ABOUT
THE SOUTHERN ZONE

Beaches
- ☐ Drake Bay, where there are miles of small deserted beaches backed by rain forest.
- ☐ Playa Zancudo, a budget traveler's dream come true, and good swimming too.
- ☐ Playa Pavones, with what may be the longest surfable waves in the world.

Great Towns/Villages
- ☐ Golfito, an old banana-shipping port complete with company housing and jungle-covered hills on the edge of town.

Parks/Gardens
- ☐ Corcovado National Park on the Osa Peninsula, one of Costa Rica's most remote national parks.

- ☐ The Wilson Botanical Gardens, which are planted with an amazing variety of tropical plants from around the world.
- ☐ Caño Island Biological Reserve, with pre-Columbian archeological sites and great diving.

Natural Spectacles
- ☐ The largest population of scarlet macaws in Costa Rica is to be found on the Osa Peninsula.

Activities
- ☐ Hiking the beaches and rainforests of Corcovado National Park.
- ☐ Bird watching at Drake Bay.
- ☐ Sportfishing out of Drake Bay and in the Sierpe River.

Sierpe to Palmar Norte. In the two Palmars you can make onward plane and bus connections. Most buses headed north go to San José, and almost any bus headed south will take you to Golfito.

ESSENTIALS   Because Drake Bay is so remote and only accessible by water or chartered plane, it is almost imperative that you have a reservation before arrival. The lodges listed here are scattered along several kilometers of coastline.

Drake Bay, named for Sir Francis Drake, who is believed to have anchored here in 1579, is a small bay on the northern coast of the Osa Peninsula. Little more than a collection of lodges catering to naturalists, anglers, scuba divers, and assorted vacationers, the bay can only be reached by boat or chartered plane, which makes it one of the more remote destinations in Costa Rica. Because of the bay's remoteness, there has been little development here. Accommodations vary from tents on wooden platforms and cement-walled cabinas to very comfortable lodges.

Emptying into the bay is the tiny Río Agujitas, which acts as a protected harbor for small boats and is a great place to do a bit of canoeing or swimming. It is here in the Río Agujitas that many of the local lodges dock their boats. Stretching south from Drake Bay are miles of deserted beaches. Adventurous explorers will find tide pools, spring-fed rivers, waterfalls, forest trails, and some of the best bird-watching in Costa Rica.

South of Drake Bay lay the wilds of the Osa Peninsula and Corcovado National Park. This is one of Costa Rica's most beautiful regions, yet it is also one of its least accessible. Corcovado National Park covers about half of the peninsula and contains the largest virgin lowland rain forest in Central America. Take note of the operative words here—rain forest. It does, indeed, rain here. In fact, some parts of the peninsula receive more than 250 inches per year.

WHAT TO SEE & DO

Beaches, forests, and solitude are the main attractions of Drake Bay, with **Corcovado National Park** being the area's star attraction. The Osa Peninsula is home to an unbelievable variety of plants and animals: more than 140 species of mammals, 267 species of birds, and 117 species of amphibians and reptiles. Some of the animals you can expect to see include several species of monkeys, coatimundis, scarlet macaws, parrots, and hummingbirds. The tallest tree in Costa Rica, a 230-foot-tall silk-cotton tree, is located within the park, as is Costa Rica's largest population of scarlet macaws. Other inhabitants here include jaguars, tapirs, sloths, and crocodiles. If you're lucky, you might even see one of the region's *osas*. Though the word means "bear" in Spanish, in this case it refers to the giant anteaters that live on the peninsula.

Around Drake Bay and within the national park there are many miles of trails through rain forests and swamps, down beaches, and around rocky headlands. All of the lodges listed below offer guided excursions into the park. It is also possible to begin a hike around the peninsula from Drake Bay. Within the park camping is allowed and there are several ranger stations where you can get a dorm bed and a meal. To find out more about hiking and camping in Corcovado National Park, contact the park headquarters in Puerto Jiménez (see below for details) or the national parks headquarters in San José at Avenida 9 between calles 17 and 19 (tel. 233-6701).

Excursions you can arrange at local lodges include guided hikes ($15 to $55), trips to Caño Island ($40 to $110), horseback rides ($35 to $55), sportfishing ($240 to $450 for a full day for 3 or 4 people), and boat tours of the nearby mangrove swamp ($50). Drake Bay Wilderness Camp seems to have the lowest tour prices, which makes it a good choice of place to stay.

One of the most popular excursions from Drake Bay is a trip out to **Caño Island,** a biological reserve, for a bit of exploring and snorkeling or scuba diving. The island is located about 12 miles offshore from Drake Bay and was once home to a pre-Columbian culture about which little is known. A trip to the island will include a visit to an ancient cemetery, and you'll also be able to see some of the stone spheres that are commonly believed to have been carved by the people who once lived in this area. The island is most unique for its geological isolation: due to plate tectonics, the island has remained separate from the rest of Central America for more than 40 million years. The dominant tree species on the island is the huge cow or milk tree, which produces a milky sap that can be drunk. The coral reefs just offshore teem with life and are the main reason most people come here. Trip prices vary depending on whether you plan to snorkel or scuba dive.

WHERE TO STAY & EAT

I have chosen to list nightly room rates at the following lodges. However, all but the least expensive couple of places do most of their business as package trips that include several nights' lodging, all meals, transportation, and tours. If you intend to do several tours while you are here, be sure to ask about these packages.

DOUBLES (WITH MEALS) FOR LESS THAN $70

ALBERGUE JINETES DE OSA, Drake Bay, Peninsula de Osa. No phone. 5 rms (all with shared bath).
$ Rates (including three meals): $30 single; $60 double; $90 triple. No credit cards.
Though the rooms here are small and dark, this is still one of the nicer budget places at Drake Bay. The wooden construction of the building and the long veranda almost directly above the beach are what give this lodge the edge over others in its class. It is also the closest budget place to the nearly deserted beaches south of the Río Agujitas. Basic Tico-style meals are served in a small open-air dining room.

CABINAS CECILIA, Drake Bay, Peninsula de Osa. No phone. 5 rms (2 with private bath).
$ Rates (including three meals): $25 single; $50 double. No credit cards.

This is about as cheap as it gets at Drake Bay. Though Cecilia's cabinas, housed in a cinder-block bunker, are rather stark, there is a long veranda and a nice view of the bay. Rooms vary in size, and some have bunk beds, while others have twin or double beds. Other than the beds, there is no furniture in the rooms. Meals are served in a separate open-air dining room a short distance from the cabinas.

CORCOVADO ADVENTURE TENT CAMP, Drake Bay, Peninsula de Osa.
Tel. 506/238-2726. Fax 506/260-4434. 10 tents (all with shared bath).
$ Rates (with three meals): $60 double. No credit cards.
If you don't mind camping, this place, midway between the lodges at Drake Bay and Marenco Biological Reserve, is a good inexpensive choice. The tents are quite large and are set on wooden decks, and a good swimming beach is only a few yards away. The large dining room serves simple meals with an emphasis on fresh seafood. Various tours are available and there are kayaks and snorkeling gear available for rent. The setting here is much more appealing than that of the two inexpensive lodges in the village.

WORTH THE EXTRA BUCKS

COCALITO LODGE, Apdo. 63, Palmar Norte, Osa Peninsula. No phone in Costa Rica. Tel. (in Canada) 519/782-4592. Fax (in Costa Rica) 506/786-6150 or 786-6335. 6 rms (all with private bath).
$ Rates (including three meals): Dec–Apr $50–$65 single, $100–$130 double; May–Nov $38.50–$50 single, $77–$100 double. No credit cards.
The owners of this little place right on the beach south of La Paloma Lodge are gringos who have been living here for years. Their choice of this remote alternative lifestyle has translated into a rustic and casual beachfront lodge that attracts primarily a younger crowd. Some of the rooms are a bit cramped and dark, but there are also larger and more expensive cabinas that offer plenty of room. Cocalito's greatest attraction is that it is right on a beautiful little cove bordered on both ends by rocky outcrops. The lodge's dining room offers excellent meals, with many ingredients from the owners' organic garden.

DRAKE BAY WILDERNESS CAMP, Apdo. 98-8150, Palmar Norte, Osa.
Tel./fax 506/771-2436. 4 tents (all with shared bath), 21 rms (all with private bath).
$ Rates (including three meals): Tents $50.30 single, $100.60 double; rooms $75.45 single, $150.90 double, $226.35 triple. MC, V.
This is one of the most convenient and best located of the lodges at Drake Bay. It backs onto the Río Agujitas and fronts onto the Pacific, though because it is on a rocky spit, there isn't a good swimming beach right here. The lodge offers a variety of accommodations of different ages and styles. Budget travelers can opt for a large tent, while those seeking more comfort can ask for one of the new rooms. These newer rooms have ceiling fans, verandas, and good mattresses on the beds. The older rooms, though smaller, are also comfortable. The family-style meals are filling, with an emphasis on fresh seafood and fresh fruits.

LA PALOMA LODGE, Apdo. 97-4005, San Antonio de Belén, Heredia
Tel./fax 506/239-0954 or 239-2801. 5 rms, 5 cabins (all with private bath).
$ Rates (including three meals): Rooms $85.75 single, $137.20 double, $205.75 triple; cabins $171.45 double, $257.20 triple. May–Nov 15, rates are 10% lower. No credit cards.
Bird-watchers will find no better place to stay in Drake Bay. Situated on a hill that can leave the out-of-shape a bit winded, La Paloma offers expansive ocean views. The main lodge building is a huge open-air thatched structure with a long veranda. Over in one corner is a sitting area that makes for a pleasant place to meet other lodge guests. Unfortunately the beach is down at the bottom of the hill, and the trail can be very muddy. However, for my money, the cabins here at La Paloma are the best buys in the area. The two older cabins are my favorites simply for their spaciousness and seclusion. Four screen walls keep you in touch with nature and

let the ocean breezes blow through. There is electricity in the evenings for those who like to stay up late reading. However, if you're like me, you'll want to get up at dawn to watch the early-morning birds. These cabins, as well as the newer ones, are built on stilts and have large verandas that look into the trees and shrubs, which are all alive with beautiful birds. The rooms, though much smaller, are still very attractive and have good views from their verandas. All the cabins and rooms have hammocks on their verandas. There are also canoes, kayaks, and snorkeling equipment for rent.

NEARBY PLACES TO STAY

HOTEL PARGO, Sierpe. Tel. 506/788-8111. 10 rms (all with private bath).
$ Rates: $15.45–$20.10 single; $21.70–$26.30 double. No credit cards.
This is the only hotel in Sierpe, and it is located right at the dock from which boats leave to head down river to Drake Bay. So, if you are on your way to Drake Bay and expect to arrive in Sierpe late in the day (when no boats are heading downriver), this is where you should spend the night. Rooms are fairly large, though basically furnished, and are clean. The higher prices are for rooms with air conditioning, however there are also ceiling fans in all the rooms. There is an inexpensive open-air restaurant adjacent to the hotel.

---

2. PUERTO JIMÉNEZ

35 kilometers W of Golfito by water (90 kilometers by road);
85 kilometers S of Palmar Norte.

GETTING THERE   By Plane   Sansa (tel. 233-0397, 233-3258, or 233-5330) has flights Monday, Wednesday, and Friday. The flight stops at Quepos and Palmar Sur en route. Duration: 1 hour and 25 minutes. Fare: $52 each way.

By Bus   Express buses leave San José twice daily from Calle 12 between avenidas 7 and 9. Duration: 8 hours. Fare: $7.70. Buses from San Isidro to Puerto Jiménez leave twice daily. These buses leave from next to the church in San Isidro. Duration: 5 hours. Fare: $4.50.

By Boat   There is daily passenger launch service from Golfito to Puerto Jiménez at noon. The boat leaves from the municipal dock. Duration: 1½ hours. Fare: $2.70. It's also possible to charter a water taxi from Golfito to Puerto Jiménez for around $30 for two people.

By Car   Take the Interamerican Highway east out of San José (through San Pedro and Cartago) and just continue south on this road. In three hours or so, you'll pass through San Isidro de El General. In another three hours or so, take the turnoff for La Palma and Puerto Jiménez. This road is paved for a ways but at Rincon turns to gravel. The last 35 kilometers are slow and rough, and if it's the rainy season, too muddy for anything but a four-wheel-drive vehicle.

DEPARTING   Buses to San José and San Isidro leave Puerto Jiménez daily from the main street. The launch to Golfito leaves from the public dock.

ESSENTIALS   Puerto Jiménez is a dirt-laned town on the southern coast of the Osa Peninsula. The public dock is down the road at the north end of the soccer field. The bus stop is in the center of town. There are several general stores here.

Puerto Jiménez, located on the east side of the Osa Peninsula is about as sleepy a little town as you'll find in Costa Rica. A couple of gravel streets, the ubiquitous soccer field, and a block of general stores, sodas, butcher shops, and bars. On first glance it is hard to imagine anything ever happening here, but looks are often deceiving. Signs in English on walls around town advertise a variety of tours, with most of the excursions being to nearby Corcovado National Park. The national park has its headquarters here, and this town makes an excellent base or starting point for exploring this vast wilderness. Puerto Jiménez is also somewhat of a boom town in the style of the U.S.'s Wild West. There's gold in them thar hills! Gold miners use Puerto Jiménez as an outpost, stocking up on staples before heading out to work their claims and cashing in their finds every time they come to town.

WHAT TO SEE & DO

Though a few gringos have, over the years, come to Puerto Jiménez to try their luck at gold panning, the primary reason for coming here these days is to arrange a visit to **Corcovado National Park.** Within a couple of hours by four-wheel-drive vehicle, there are several entrances to the park. However, there are no roads into the park, so once you reach any of the entrances, you'll have to start hiking. Exploring Corcovado National Park is not something to be undertaken lightly. The biggest problems of overnight backpacking trips through the park are the heat and humidity. Frequent rain storms cause the trails to be quite muddy, and should you choose the alternative of hiking on the beach, you will have to plan your hiking around the tides. Often there is no beach at all at high tide. Be sure to pick up a tide table at the park headquarters office in Puerto Jiménez. You'll find the headquarters one block over from the main street (toward the water) at the end of town near the soccer field (tel. 735-5036).

Coming around from the south, you can enter the park at the La Leona ranger station, which has a campground, some very basic dormitory accommodations, and a cantina. It is 3 kilometers to La Leona from Carate, which is the end of the dirt road from Puerto Jiménez. Alternatively, you can travel to El Tigre, about 14 kilometers by dirt road from Puerto Jiménez, where there is another ranger station, campground, and cantina. Trails from El Tigre only go a short distance into the park. From the Los Patos ranger station, which is reached from the town of La Palma north of Puerto Jiménez, there is a 19-kilometer trail through the park. This latter trail leads to Sirena, a ranger station and research facility. Frequented primarily by scientists studying the rain forest, Sirena has basic accommodations, a cantina, a campground, and a landing strip used by charter flights. From Sirena it is 16 kilometers along the beach to La Leona and 25 kilometers along the beach to San Pedrillo, the northern entrance ranger station, which also has a campground and cantina. From San Pedrillo it is another 9 kilometers to Marenco Biological Reserve and about 14 kilometers to Drake Bay. Park admission is $1.35 per person. Campsites in the park are $2.10 per person per night. A dorm bed will run you $2.70, and meals are around $13.50 per day.

If you're not into hiking in the heat, you can charter a plane in Puerto Jiménez to take you to Carate, Sirena, Drake Bay, or even Tiskita Lodge, which is across the gulf. Contact Saeta (735-5060).

If you're interested in doing some billfishing or deep-sea fishing, check around the public dock for notices of people with charter boats. Rates are usually around $400 for a full day or $300 for a half day.

WHERE TO STAY

IN TOWN

Doubles for Less Than $25

CABINAS MARCELINA, Puerto Jiménez. Tel. 506/735-5007. 6 rms (all with private bath).
$ Rates: $6.20–$7.75 single; $10.80–$13.90 double; $13.90–$16.30 triple. No credit cards.

Located a block off Puerto Jiménez's main street, these basic rooms are a good choice for anyone on a shoestring budget. The owner keeps the tile-floored rooms clean and there is surprisingly little mildew (always a problem in cinder-block buildings). Bathrooms are basic but adequate.

CABINAS PUERTO JIMÉNEZ, 50 meters north of Bar y Restaurant El Rancho, Puerto Jiménez. Tel. 506/735-5090 or 735-5152. 6 rms (all with private bath).
$ Rates: $7.75 single; $15.45 double; $23.15 triple. No credit cards.

⑤ This basic little place is located right on the waterfront at the north end of the soccer field. The exterior of the building, with its varnished wood, is much more appealing than the rooms themselves. Though large, the guest rooms have cement floors and are very basic. However, they are generally clean and are the best choice in town for budget travelers.

Double for Less Than $45

AGUA LUNA, in front of the public dock, Puerto Jiménez. Tel. 506/735-5033, 735-5034, or 735-5108. 3 rms (all with private bath). A/C TV TEL
$ Rates: $38.65 single, double, or triple. V.

Though there are only three rooms here, they offer the most luxury of any of the in-town lodgings in Puerto Jiménez. Agua Luna is located right at the foot of the town's public dock and backs to a mangrove forest. The most surprising feature in each of these rooms is the huge bathroom, which includes both a shower and a tub facing a picture window that looks into the mangroves. There are double and twin beds in the rooms, and on the tiled veranda out front, you'll find hammocks for lounging. There isn't much landscaping here, just a gravel parking area.

HOTEL MANGLARES, Apdo. 55-8203, Puerto Jiménez de Golfito. Tel. 506/735-5002. Fax 506/735-5121. 10 rms (all with private bath).
$ Rates: $28.60 single; $34.30 double. MC, V.

✪ Bird-watchers will want to make this their base in Puerto Jiménez. The hotel is on the edge of the mangrove forest, and some of the rooms can only be reached by an elevated walkway through the mangroves. The trees, and several bird feeders, assure good bird-watching. Though the rooms in front are a bit small and can be musty, the rooms in back are very attractive, and surprisingly don't cost extra. These latter rooms are surrounded by an attractive garden as well as mangroves. All the rooms have fans to keep you cool, and there is a restaurant serving inexpensive Tico standards.

AROUND THE OSA PENINSULA

Worth the Extra Bucks

BOSQUE DEL CABO WILDERNESS LODGE, Apdo. 2907-1000, San José. Tel. 506/222-4547 or 222-7738. Fax 506/221-3011. 4 cabins (all with private bath).
$ Rates (including three meals): $85.75 single; $125.75 double; $171.45 triple. No credit cards.

✪ This simple yet tasteful lodge is located 500 feet above the water at the southern tip of the Osa Peninsula. The lodge is surrounded by 300 acres of land that the owners purchased in order to preserve a piece of the rain forest. The thatched-roof cabins are attractively furnished and are set amid beautiful gardens. Meals are well prepared and filling and usually feature fruits grown here on the premises. There's a trail down to a secluded beach that has some tide pools. Surfing is a popular activity here, as are hiking and horseback riding. Trips to the national park or out fishing can be arranged. It will cost you around $14 for a taxi out here.

CORCOVADO LODGE TENT CAMP, Costa Rica Expeditions, P.O. Box 6941-1000, San José. Tel. 506/257-0766 or 222-0333. Fax 506/257-1665. 20 tents (all with shared bath).

$ Rates (including three meals): $48.35 single; $79.55 double. Package rates available. AE, MC, V.

Costa Rica Expeditions' Corcovado Lodge Tent Camp is beyond the end of the rough road around the south end of the peninsula and is built on a low bluff right above the beach. Behind the tent camp, forested mountains rise up, and just a few minutes' walk away is the entrance to Corcovado National Park. Accommodations are in large tents pitched on wooden decks. Each tent has two twin beds, a table, and a couple of folding chairs on the front deck. Toilets and showers are a short walk away. Meals are served in a large screen-walled dining room. Services at the lodge include guided walks and boat excursions both into the national park and out to Caño Island. Unless you fly or boat in, you'll need a four-wheel-drive vehicle to get out here, and even then, it's a 30-minute walk from the end of the road.

WHERE TO EAT

BAR RESTAURANT AGUA LUNA, 25 meters north of the public pier. Tel. 735-5034.
  Cuisine: COSTA RICAN. **Reservations:** Not accepted.
$ Prices: Main dishes $3.40–$10.15. No credit cards.
  Open: Daily 9am–11pm.
The first restaurant you come to after arriving in Puerto Jiménez by boat is also the best restaurant in town. Little more than a collection of thatch *ranchos* (the equivalent of Mexican *palapas*) set amid shady gardens, Agua Luna has a nice view of the water. The bar is popular and the music is always loud so don't expect a quiet, romantic dinner for two. Seafood is plentiful and prices for fish dinners are low even for Costa Rica, so enjoy.

SODITA CAROLINA, on the main street. No phone.
  Cuisine: COSTA RICAN. **Reservations:** Not accepted.
$ Prices: $2.35–$6.75. No credit cards.
  Open: Daily 6am–10 or 11pm.
This is Puerto Jiménez's budget travelers' hangout and also serves as an unofficial information center. The walls are plastered with notices for tours to the national park and information on hiring taxis, guides, and planes. Once again seafood is the way to go. They've got good fried fish as well as a variety of ceviches. The black bean soup is usually good, and the casados are filling and cost less than $3. If you need a place to stay, ask here. When I last visited, they were building some cabinas behind the restaurant. The rate should be under $15 for a double room.

---

3. GOLFITO

87 kilometers S of Palmar Norte; 337 kilometers S of San José

GETTING THERE   By Plane   Sansa (tel. 233-0397, 233-3258, or 233-5330) has flights to Golfito Monday through Saturday. Duration: 45 minutes. Fare: $52. Travelair (tel. 220-3054 and 232-7883) has flights to Golfito daily. The flight stops in Quepos and Palmar Sur en route. Duration: 1 hour and 25 minutes. Fare: $66 one way, $114 round-trip.

By Bus   Express buses leave San José three times daily from Avenida 18 between calles 2 and 4. Duration: 8 hours. Fare: $6.15.

By Boat   A passenger launch leaves Puerto Jiménez, on the Osa Peninsula, daily at 6am. Duration: 1½ hours. Fare: $2.70. You may also be able to hire a boat to take you across the Golfo Dulce to Golfito. However, you're likely to have to pay quite a bit ($50 to $75) for such a service.

By Car   It is a straight shot down the Interamerican Highway south from San José to Golfito. However, it is a long and arduous road. In the eight hours it takes to drive the 337 kilometers from San José, you'll pass over the Cerro de la Muerte (Mountain of Death), which is infamous for its dense fog, torrential downpours, and gargantuan potholes.

DEPARTING   Sansa flies to San José Monday through Saturday and Travelair flies daily, with a stop in Quepos en route. Buses leave for San José daily from near the municipal dock. The launch to Puerto Jiménez leaves daily from the municipal dock.

ESSENTIALS   You can rent a car or four-wheel-drive Isuzu Trooper from Golfito Rent A Car, Avenida 6 between calles 7 and 9 (tel. 257-3747, 257-3727, or, after 6pm, 257-3707). If you need to change money, you can do so at the gas station in the middle of town. Golfito Centro (tel. 775-0449, Fax 775-0506), on the upper main street in Golfito, is a combination informal information center and real estate office. Drop by to find out about new lodges in the area, horseback riding trips, jungle tours, fishing trips, and boat rentals and tours.

This old banana port is set on the north side of the Golfo Dulce and is at the foot of lush green mountains. The setting alone is beautiful enough to make this one of the most attractive cities in the country, but Golfito also has an undeniable charm all its own. Sure, the area around the municipal park is kind of seedy, but if you go a little bit farther along the bay, you come to the old United Fruit Company housing. Here you'll find well-maintained wooden houses painted bright colors and surrounded by neatly manicured gardens. It's all very lush and green and clean, an altogether different picture than is painted by most port towns in this country. These old homes are experiencing a sort of renaissance as they become small hotels catering to shoppers visiting the adjacent duty-free shopping center.

WHAT TO SEE & DO

There isn't a whole lot to do in Golfito other than make connections to other places. You can walk or drive through town admiring the United Fruit Company buildings, drop in at one of the souvenir shops, or have a drink overlooking the gulf. However, because this area is gaining in popularity, more tourist-oriented activities are becoming available. Check the bulletin boards in restaurants to see what sort of tours or activities are available when you arrive. When I was last in town, **El Jardín Restaurant** (tel. 775-0235) was renting open-deck sea kayaks for $35 per day. However, they had plans to move across the gulf to Puerto Jiménez.

To arrange jungle tours, horseback rides, boat rentals, and fishing trips, check with **Golfito Centro** (tel. 775-0449), which has its office on the upper road through downtown Golfito.

The waters off Golfito offer some of the best sportfishing in Costa Rica, and if you'd like to try hooking into a marlin or sailfish, contact Steve Lino at **Golfito Sportfishing** (tel. 288-5083) or **Leomar Sportfishing & Diving** (tel. 775-0230) which offer fishing trips for between $350 and $550.

About 30 minutes by boat out of Golfito, you'll find **Casa Orchidia,** a private botanical garden. Two-hour tours of the garden cost $5 per person with a minimum of four people. You'll also have to hire a boat to get out here, which should cost you around $75 for the trip and waiting time. If you have a serious interest in botanical gardens, consider an excursion to **Wilson Botanical Gardens** (tel. 773-3278), which are located in the town of San Vito, about 65 kilometers to the northeast. The gardens are owned by the Organization for Tropical Studies and include more than 2,000 species of tropical plants from around the world. There are many beautiful and unusual flowers amid the manicured grounds here. If you'd like to stay the night here, there are rustic rooms and cabins. Rates, including three meals, are $55 per person in the rooms and $75 per person in the cabins. You'll find the gardens about 6 kilometers before San Vito. To get here from Golfito, drive back out to the Interamerican Highway and continue south toward Panama. In Ciudad Neily, turn north.

WHERE TO STAY

DOUBLES FOR LESS THAN $15

CASA BLANCA LODGE, 300 meters south of the Depósito Libre, Golfito. Tel. 775-0124. 7 rms (all with private bath).
$ Rates: $5.45 single; $10.90–$16.25 double; $27.05 triple or quad. No credit cards.

In the old United Fruit Company neighborhood near the airport, there are many pretty old houses surrounded by attractive, neatly manicured gardens. Several of these old homes have been turned into inexpensive hotels catering to shoppers visiting the free port. This is one of the nicer of these small family-run hotels. The upstairs rooms are more attractive and more comfortable than the rooms on the ground floor, which tend to be dark and musty.

DOUBLES FOR LESS THAN $35

GOLFO AZUL, Barrio Alameda, 300 meters south of the Depósito Libre, Golfito. Tel. 506/775-0871. Fax 506/775-0832. 24 rms.
$ Rates: $23.90 single or double, $26.50 triple; $46.20 single to quad with air-conditioning. MC, V.

Located in the old United Fruit Company neighborhood, the Golfo Azul offers a quiet location amid the most attractive part of Golfito. Many of the people who stay here are Ticos in town to shop at the nearby Depósito Libre (Free Port). However, anyone will appreciate the clean rooms. The smallest rooms are cramped, but there are larger rooms, some with high ceilings that make them feel even more spacious. Rooms have either fans or air-conditioning. The hotel's restaurant is housed in an older building. Meals are quite reasonably priced.

LAS GAVIOTAS HOTEL, Apdo. 12-8201, Golfito. Tel. 506/775-0062. Fax 506/775-0544. 18 rms, 3 cabañas (all with private bath).
$ Rates: $30.55–$43.70 single or double; $39.20–$50.65 triple; $53.35 cabaña. AE, MC, V.

If you want to be right on the water, this is your best (and only) choice in Golfito. Situated a short taxi ride out of town on the road that leads out to the Interamerican Highway, Las Gaviotas has long been the hotel of choice on the Golfo Dulce. Guest rooms, which are set amid attractive gardens, all face the ocean, and though they are quite large, they're a bit Spartan. There are small tiled patios in front of all the rooms, and the cabañas have little kitchens. There's also a small pool and a large open-air restaurant that looks out over the gulf.

WORTH THE EXTRA BUCKS

HOTEL SIERRA, Apdo. 37, Golfito (or Apdo. 5304-1000, San José). Tel. 506/775-0666 (506/233-9693 or 224-3300 in San José). Fax 506/775-0087 (506/224-3399 in San José). 72 rms (all with private bath). TV TEL A/C
$ Rates: $44.60 single; $53.50 double; $60.95 triple. AE, DC, MC, V.

Located right beside the airstrip, the Hotel Sierra has become the hotel of choice of people flying in and out of Golfito. It offers the most luxurious accommodations in town, with a courtyard swimming pool, aviaries full of squawking macaws, and a big dining room and bar. The building is constructed to be as open and breezy as possible, though the guest rooms also have modern air conditioners. Covered walkways connect the hotel's various buildings, and lots of tropical plants and cages full of birds lend an exotic flavor to the surroundings. The swimming pool is fairly large and even has a swim-up bar. Prices in the main dining room are fairly moderate. A casino and tour operator round out the facilities at the hotel.

PUNTA ENCANTO, Golfito (in the U.S.: Dick or Jackie Knowles, P.O. Box 481, Chautauqua, NY 14722). Tel. (in the U.S.: toll free 800/543-0397). Fax 506/775-0373, box 28. 9 rms (all with private bath).

$ Rates (including three meals): $108.60 single; $148.60 double; $188.60 triple. No credit cards.

✪   This small lodge is a 30-minute boat ride up the bay from Golfito, and if you stay for a minimum of three nights, there is no charge for the transfers to and from Golfito. The star attraction here is the lodge's deserted beach, which is great for swimming. Surrounding the lodge are acres and acres of rain forest. The guest rooms are simply furnished, though comfortable, and have views of the water. Meals, a combination of Tico and American favorites, are served family style. The lodge can also arrange tours of the nearby Casa Orchidia Botanical Gardens, trips up the Esquinas River to go bird- and monkey-watching, and fishing charters. This charmingly casual lodge offers a tranquil getaway for anyone who is looking for tropical solitude.

WHERE TO EAT

JARDIN CERVECERO ALAMEDAS, 100 meters south of the Depósito Libre. Tel. 775-0126.

Cuisine: COSTA RICAN/SEAFOOD. **Reservations:** Not necessary.

$ Prices: Appetizers $2.05–$8.80; entrees $2.40–$8.80. MC, V.

Open: Tues–Sat 7am–midnight (Dec–Mar open daily).

If you are staying at the Hotel Sierra, Golfo Azul, or any of the other hotels up near the Depósito Libre, this should be your first choice of where to eat. The restaurant is located underneath an old house that is built on stilts. White chairs and dark green tablecloths provide a sort of fern-bar feel, while outside, real tropical gardens surround the house. There are great deals on seafood here, including a long list of ceviches. The only drawback here is that they tend to play the stereo too loud.

POLLO FRITO RANCHERO, 30 meters north of the public dock. No phone.

Cuisine: COSTA RICAN/INTERNATIONAL. **Reservations:** Not accepted.

$ Prices: All dishes 85¢–$6.75. No credit cards.

Open: Daily 11am–10pm.

If you like the atmosphere at the Samoa but are on a rock-bottom budget, try this smaller rancho almost next door. You get a view of the water from the small tables, and you can fill up on burgers or fried chicken.

SAMOA DEL SUR, 100 meters north of the public dock. Tel. 775-0233.

Cuisine: CONTINENTAL. **Reservations:** Not necessary.

$ Prices: Appetizers $2.70–$10.15; entrees $4.05–$16.90. AE, MC, V.

Open: Daily 8am–2am.

✪   It's hard to miss the Samoa del Sur. It's that huge circular rancho just north of the public dock. This oversize jungle structure seems out of place in a town where cinder blocks are the preferred construction material, but its tropical atmosphere is certainly well appreciated. The restaurant's biggest surprise, however, is its extensive menu of familiar continental and French dishes such as onion soup, salade niçoise, fillet of fish meunière, and paella. There are also pizzas and spaghetti. There's a good view of the gulf, which makes this a great spot for a sunset drink or dinner. Later in the night, you can work up a sweat at the adjacent Disco Loco.

---

4. PLAYA ZANCUDO

19 kilometers S of Golfito (by boat); 35 kilometers S of Golfito (by road).

GETTING THERE   By Boat   Water taxis can be hired in Golfito to make the trip out to Playa Zancudo. However, trips depend on the tides and weather conditions, with morning trips being more common. Currently it costs $6.75 per person for a water taxi, with a minimum charge of $20.30. Alternatively, there is a passenger launch from the municipal dock in Golfito Monday, Wednesday, and Friday at 8am. Because the schedule sometimes changes, be sure to ask in town for the current schedule. Duration: 45 minutes. Fare: $1.35.

By Bus   There is no regularly scheduled bus service to Zancudo.

By Car   If you've got a four-wheel-drive vehicle, you should be able to make it out to Zancudo even in the rainy season, but be sure to ask in Golfito before leaving the paved road. A four-wheel-drive taxi will cost around $20 from Golfito. It takes about two hours when the road is in good condition.

DEPARTING   The public launch to Golfito leaves at 6am Monday, Wednesday, and Friday from the dock near the school in the center of Zancudo. Current departure time is 6am. If you're heading to either Pavones of the Osa Peninsula next, contact Zancudo Boat Tours, which is sometimes willing to make the trips to these two places. They charge $10.15 per person with a minimum charge of $30.40 for either trip.

ESSENTIALS   Zancudo is a long, narrow peninsula (sometimes only 100 yards or so wide) at the mouth of the Río Colorado. On one side is the beach, and on the other is a mangrove swamp. There is only one road that runs the length of the beach, and it is along this road, spread out over several kilometers, that you will find the hotels mentioned here. It's about a 30-minute walk from the public dock near the school to the popular Cabinas Sol y Mar.

Playa Zancudo is one of Costa Rica's main backpacker hangouts, which means basically that there are plenty of cheap rooms, some cheap places to eat, and lots of other young gringos around. These factors alone are enough to keep Zancudo jumping through the winter months. The beach itself is long and flat and, because it is protected from the full force of Pacific waves, relatively good for swimming. However, it is certainly not one of the most beautiful beaches in the country. Behind the beach, which disappears at high tide, are piles of driftwood and plastic flotsam and jetsam. There is a splendid view across the Golfo Dulce, though, and the sunsets are hard to beat. Because there is a mangrove swamp directly behind the beach, mosquitoes here can be a problem. Be sure to bring insect repellent.

WHAT TO SEE & DO

The main activity at Zancudo is relaxing, and folks take it seriously. There are hammocks at almost every lodge, and if you bring a few good books, you can spend quite a few hours swinging slowly in the tropical breezes. Sure there's a bar that doubles as a disco, but people are more likely to spend their time just hanging out in restaurants meeting like-minded folks.

If you're feeling more energetic, consider a boat tour. Susan and Andrew Robertson, who rent out two small houses here in Zancudo, also operate **Zancudo Boat Tours** (tel. 775-0353 and leave a message). Excursions they offer include a trip up the Coto River to bird- and wildlife-watch, snorkeling trips, and trips to the Casa Orchidia botanical garden. Tour prices range from $15 per hour for two people to $25 per hour for four people.

WHERE TO STAY

DOUBLES FOR LESS THAN $15

CABINAS ZANCUDO, Playa Zancudo, Golfito. Tel. 506/773-3006 or 773-3027. 20 rms (all with private bath).
$ Rates: $10.15–$13.50 single or double. No credit cards.

This is your basic Tico weekend beach getaway. The rooms are small, dark, and musty. There's no cross ventilation, and half of the rooms are in a building facing the back wall of another building. Weekends are crowded and can be noisy, especially in the dry season. However, if you don't have much money to spend, this is a good choice. There's also a restaurant/bar here.

DOUBLES FOR LESS THAN $35

CABINAS SOL Y MAR, Apdo. 87, Playa Zancudo, Golfito. Tel. 506/775-0353. Fax 506/775-0373. 4 rms (all with private bath).
$ Rates: Dec 1–Apr 30 $34.30–$40 single or double; May 1–Nov 30 $28.60–$34.30. No credit cards.

⭐ Though owners Bob and Monika Hara have only four rooms, they have for several years been the most popular lodging in Zancudo. Two of the rooms are modified geodesic domes with tile floors, verandas, and tin roofs. The bathrooms have unusual showers that consist of a tiled platform surrounded by smooth river rocks. The bathrooms also have translucent roofs that flood the rooms with light. The other two rooms are larger and newer but aren't as architecturally interesting. You'll have to decide between space and character. There is an adjacent open-air restaurant that is the best and most popular place to eat in Zancudo. Seafood dishes are the specialty here and prices are very reasonable.

LOS COCOS, Apdo. 88, Golfito. Tel. 506/775-0353 (and leave a message). 2 cabins.
$ Rates: $30 per night; $500–$600 per month. No credit cards.
Though owners Susan and Andrew Robertson prefer to rent their two small houses by the month, in a pinch they'll rent by the night. Set under the trees near Cabinas Sol y Mar (which is the contact for Los Cocos), these two houses are old banana plantation housing that the Robertsons salvaged and rebuilt here. Each house has a big veranda, a bedroom, and a large eat-in kitchen. Bathrooms are down a few steps in back and have hot water. If you plan to stay in Zancudo for a while, you'll certainly appreciate the refrigerator and hot plate.

HOTEL LOS ALMENDROS, Apdo. 41, Playa Zancudo, Golfito. Tel. 506/775-0515. 10 rms (all with private bath).
$ Rates: $22.90 single; $34.30 double; $45.75 triple. V.
Though this simple lodging up at the north end of Zancudo is primarily a fishing lodge, it is also one of the more comfortable and attractive places in town. The rooms all look out onto a bright green lawn of soft grass with the waves crashing on the beach a few steps beyond. The rooms have hardwood floors, small clean bathrooms, ceiling and floor fans, and small verandas. There is a small restaurant that, of course, specializes in fresh fish. The lodge offers many different types of fishing excursions.

WHERE TO EAT

The best restaurant in Zancudo is at Cabinas Sol y Mar. The small open-air spot is also a popular hangout for resident gringos as well as travelers.

5. PLAYA PAVONES

40 kilometers S of Golfito

GETTING THERE **By Bus** There is a bus to Pavones from Golfito daily at 2pm. Duration: 3½ hours. Fare: $1.80.

By Car If you have a four-wheel-drive vehicle, you should be able to get to Pavones even in the rainy season, but be sure to ask in Golfito before leaving the paved road. A four-wheel-drive taxi from Golfito to Pavones will cost between $30 and $40. It takes around 3 hours from Golfito.

DEPARTING The bus to Golfito leaves daily. Ask in the village for the current departure time.

ESSENTIALS Pavones is a tiny village with few amenities and no electricity.

If you are a serious surfer, you have already heard about Playa Pavones. The wave here is reputed to be the longest rideable wave in the world. It takes around six feet of swell to get this wave cranking, but when the surf's up, you're in for a long, long ride. So long, in fact, that it's easier to walk back up the beach to where the wave is breaking than it is to paddle back.

WHAT TO SEE & DO

Other than surfing when the surf is up and swimming when its not, there isn't a whole lot to do. You can walk the beach, swing in your hammock, or if you feel energetic, go for a horse ride.

WHERE TO STAY & EAT

CASA IMPACT, Apdo. 133, Golfito. Tel. 775-0637. 5 rms (all with private bath).

$ Rates (including three meals): $40 single; $80 double. No credit cards.

Casa Impact is an octagonal house with four simple rooms plus a separate cabin. Most of the clientele is surfers, and of course there are surfboards for rent. You can also rent horses, for $10 per hour, or a sea kayak. Meals include fresh juices, pizzas, and freshly baked breads and cakes. Electricity here is provided by photovoltaic cells.

CHAPTER 8

THE CARIBBEAN COAST

Though this was the coast that Christopher Columbus discovered in 1502 and christened Costa Rica (Rich Coast), it has until recently remained *terra incognita*. It was not until 1987 that the Guápiles Highway opened between San José and Limón. Prior to that the only routes down to this region were the famous jungle train (which is no longer in operation) and the narrow, winding road from Turrialba to Siquirres. More than half of this coastline is still inaccessible except by boat or small plane. This inaccessibility has helped preserve large tracts of virgin lowland rain forest, which are now set aside as Tortuguero National Park and Barra del Colorado National Wildlife Refuge. These two parks, on the northern reaches of this coast, together form one of Costa Rica's most popular destinations with ecotravelers. Of particular interest are the sea turtles that nest along this stretch of coast.

So remote was the Caribbean Coast from Costa Rica's population center in the Central Valley that it developed a culture all its own. Until the 1870s, there were few non-Indians in this area. However, when Minor Keith built the railroad to San José and began planting bananas, he brought in black laborers from Jamaica to lay the track and work the plantations. These people were well adapted to the hot, humid conditions of these lowlands and established fishing and farming communities up and down the coast. Today dreadlocked Rastafarians, reggae music, Creole cooking, and the English-based patois of this Afro-Caribbean culture give this region a distinctly Jamaican flavor. Many visitors find fascinating this striking contrast with the Spanish-derived Costa Rican culture. However, in beach towns such as Cahuita and Puerto Viejo, some visitors see only a drug-and-surf culture, and there is no denying that surfing and partying are a way of life for many people, local and visitor alike, in these two towns. Though you need not participate in such activities, if this lifestyle is offensive to you, consider heading to one of the many beaches on the Pacific Coast.

1. TORTUGUERO NATIONAL PARK

250 kilometers NE of San José

GETTING THERE **By Air** Sansa (tel. 233-0397, 233-3258, or 233-5330) flies Tuesday, Thursday, and Saturday. Duration: 65 minutes (Tortuguero). Fare: $41. Travelair (tel. 220-3054 and 232-7883) flies daily. Duration: 55 minutes (Tortuguero). Fare: $51 one way, $88 round-trip. Many of the lodges in this area operate charter flights as part of their package trips.

By Boat Though flying to Tortuguero is convenient if you have only a limited amount of time, the boat trip through the canals and rivers of this region is the highlight of any visit to Tortuguero. All of the more expensive lodges listed below operate boats and will make all arrangements for your trip through the canals. However, if you are coming up here on the cheap and plan to stay at one of the less

WHAT'S SPECIAL ABOUT THE CARIBBEAN COAST

Beaches

☐ Long, nearly deserted beaches both north and south of the village of Cahuita. There's also a coral reef here.

☐ Miles of beaches and blue water south of Puerto Viejo.

Natural Spectacles

☐ The Tortuguero canals, which will make you feel like you're exploring deep in the Amazon.

Parks

☐ Tortuguero National Park, known for the turtles that lay their eggs on the beaches.

☐ Cahuita National Park, with forest trails, deserted beaches, and a coral reef.

Activities

☐ Surfing the Salsa Brava in Puerto Viejo.

☐ Snorkeling among the coral and clear water south of Puerto Viejo.

☐ Guided walks through the Bribri indian reservation and elsewhere around Puerto Viejo.

☐ Fishing for tarpon and snook in Tortuguero and Barra del Colorado.

Regional Food and Drink

☐ Run-down soup, a coconut-based favorite of the Caribbean coast's Creole residents.

☐ Home-made fresh cocoa candies from the cacao trees around Puerto Viejo.

---

expensive lodges or at a budget cabina place in Tortuguero, you will have to arrange transportation yourself. In this, you have a couple of options.

In Cahuita, a small beach town south of Limón, Cahuita Tours (tel. 758-1515, ext. 232) will arrange round-trip boat transportation for around $60. This price also includes transportation from Cahuita to the dock in Moín, which is the port just outside of Limón. Alternatively, you can go directly to Moín yourself and try to find a boat on your own. You should be able to negotiate a fare of between $40 and $60 depending on how many people you can round up to go with you. One boat captain to check with is Modesto Wilson (tel. 226-0986) who owns a boat named *Francesca*. Laura's Tropical Tours (tel. 758-2410) also offers boat tours to Tortuguero from Moín. The trip from Moín to Tortuguero takes between three and four hours.

It is also possible to travel to Tortuguero by boat from Puerto Viejo de Sarapiquí (see Chapter 5). From this town, expect to pay $200 to $250 for a boat to either destination. Check at the public dock in Sarapiquí or ask at the Hotel El Bambú.

DEPARTING The airstrip is a couple of kilometers north of Tortuguero village. Be sure to have your return flight arranged before you arrive. These flights stay full.

ESSENTIALS Tortuguero National Park is one of the most remote locations in Costa Rica. There are no roads into this area, so all transportation is by boat or plane. Most of the lodges are spread out over several kilometers to the north of the village of Tortuguero. The Tortuguero National Park entrance and ranger station is at the south end of Tortuguero village. In the center of the village is an information kiosk that outlines the cultural and natural history of this region. Turtle nesting season is mid-June through mid-September, and this is the most popular time to visit Tortuguero.

The name Tortuguero is a reference to the giant Atlantic green sea turtles (*tortugas*) that nest each year on the beaches of this region every year between July and September. The chance to see nesting sea turtles is what attracts many people to this remote region, but the trip here is equally interesting. This stretch of coast is connected to Limón, the Caribbean Coast's only port city, by way of a series of rivers and canals that parallel the sea, often only 100 yards or so from the beach. This aquatic highway is lined for most of its length with dense rain forest that is home to howler monkeys and three-toed sloths, toucans and great green macaws. A trip up the canals is akin to cruising the Amazon, though on a much smaller scale.

North of Tortuguero is Barra del Colorado National Wildlife Refuge. This area is better known among anglers than with naturalists. The waters at the mouth of the Río Colorado offer some of the best tarpon and snook fishing in the world.

WHAT TO SEE & DO

First of all, let me say up front that you don't come to this area for the beaches. Though they are long and deserted, the surf is usually very rough and the river mouths have a nasty habit of attracting sharks that feed on the many fish that live there. What you can do here is explore the **rain forest,** both on foot and by boat, and if you're here between July and September, watch **sea turtles nesting** at night. All of the lodges listed below, with the exception of the Cabinas Ribersai in Tortuguero village, offer various hikes, night tours, and boat trips through the canals. See the individual lodge listings for rates on these tours. If you are coming up here on a package trip, you will likely have already arranged your excursions before arriving. All of the lodges along this coast also offer **fishing** trips and fishing packages. If you want to try your hand at reeling in a monster tarpon, it will generally cost you between $30 and $35 per hour, including a boat, guide, and tackle.

Tortuguero village is a tiny collection of houses connected by footpaths. In the center of the village you'll find a kiosk that has information on the cultural and natural history of this area. On the south side of the village, you'll find the headquarters for **Tortuguero National Park.** Within this section of the park there are several trails. Admission to the park is $1.35, and camping is allowed here at the ranger station for a small fee.

In the village, you can rent dugout **canoes,** known here in Costa Rica as *cayucos.* You can also find people with boats who will take you on tours through the canals. There are a couple of souvenir shops here in the village—the Jungle Shop (which donates 10% of its profits to local schools) and Paraíso Tropical Gift Shop.

WHERE TO STAY & DINE

Though the room rates below appear quite high, keep in mind that the package trips include round-trip transportation (which amounts to around $100 per person) and all meals.

DOUBLES FOR LESS THAN $35

CABINAS RIBERSAI, Barra Tortuguero, Limón. Tel. 506/710-6716. 4 rms (all with bath).

$ Rates: $15 single; $25 double. MC, V.

Though these rooms are tiny and cramped, they're the best in town. They sit off by themselves near the soccer field on the south side of the village and are very close to the beach. Two of the rooms have double beds and two have bunk beds. Luckily they all have fans. You can find out about the rooms at the Abastecador Riversan, a general store that is just south of the national park information kiosk.

EL MANATEE LODGE, Tortuguero, Limón. Tel. 506/288-1828. 5 cabins (all with private bath).

$ Rates: $40 double. No credit cards.

S If you'd like to have a Tortuguero jungle lodge experience, but can't afford one of the expensive places, this is your next best choice. This lodge is located across the canal and about a kilometer north of Tortuguero village. The young owners live here and have slowly built the lodge themselves over the years. The rooms are fairly basic, but there are new fixtures in the bathrooms and warm water. Breakfast ($4) and dinner ($6) are available. Canal tours and turtle-watching walks are $10 per person for two hours, and there are canoes that can be rented for $5. Transportation up here and back can be arranged in Moin near Limón for $50 to $60 round-trip. Piece it all together and you come up with a 3-day, 2-night trip with tours, meals, and transportation from Limón for around $250 for two people!

WORTH THE EXTRA BUCKS

HOTEL ILAN-ILAN, Apdo. 91-1150, San José. Tel. 506/255-2262 or 255-2031. Fax 506/255-1946. 20 rms (all with private bath).

$ Rates (transportation and all meals): $344–$454 double, 2 days/1 night; $454–$686 double, 3 days/2 nights. AE, MC, V.

Named after a fragrant tropical flower that grows on the hotel grounds, the Ilan-Ilan is on the opposite side of the canal from the beach. Guest rooms are fairly basic, though large, and are all angled toward the canal so they each get a bit of breeze. Screened windows front and back, and overhead fans also help keep the rooms cool. Tico meals are served in the small screen-walled dining room, and there is a bar where you can meet other guests. There are bilingual guides to point out wildlife and answer questions both during the boat trip to the lodge and during outings through the canals and (in season) to the beach at night to watch sea turtles laying their eggs. The lodge also has several acres of forest land through which there are several kilometers of trails. The higher room rates include one-way air travel.

JUNGLE LODGE, Apdo. 1818-1002, San José. Tel. 506/233-0133 or 233-0155. Fax 506/222-0778. 34 rms (all with private bath).

$ Rates (including transportation and all meals): $284 single, 3 days/2 nights; $436 double, 3 days/2 nights; $552 triple, 3 days/2 nights. AE, DC, MC, V.

Located just south of Ilan-Ilan on the same side of the river and about a kilometer from Tortuguero National Park, the Jungle Lodge offers rooms in wooden buildings raised up above the ground. There are long verandas where you can sit and bird-watch or just listen to the forest. Most rooms have windows on two sides to let the breezes through. Wooden floors and walls give these rooms an attractive, tropical look. Simple but filling meals such as fried chicken or fish with rice and beans are served buffet-style in a screen-walled dining hall. Tours, led by bilingual guides, include boat trips through the canals, a visit to Tortuguero village, a hike through the forest, and (in season) trips to the beach to watch sea turtles lay their eggs. Optional canoe tours and night tours are also available for $10 and $15 respectively.

LAGUNA LODGE, Apdo. 344, San Pedro, San José. Tel./fax 506/225-3740. 14 rms (all with private bath).

$ Rates (including transportation and all meals): $438 double, 3 days/2 nights. MC, V.

This is one of the newest and smallest lodges in the area and is located 2 kilometers north of Tortuguero village on the beach side of the canal. Because this lodge is fairly new, the gardens are not yet very developed and so the grounds look a bit barren. However, the rooms are all very attractive, with wood walls, waxed hardwood floors, and tiled bathrooms with screened upper walls to let in air and light. Each room also has a little veranda. There's a small screen-walled dining room that serves tasty meals. A little covered deck has been built over the water, and there is even a tiny beach area on the river. Several different optional tours are available.

MAWAMBA LODGE, Apdo. 10050-1000, San José. Tel. 506/223-7490, 223-2421, or 222-5463. Fax 506/255-4039. 36 rms (all with private bath).

$ Rates (including transportation and all meals): $438–$538 double, 3 days/2 nights. AE, MC, V.

Located about 500 meters north of Tortuguero village on the beach side of the canal, Mawamba is a good choice for anyone who would like to be able to wander this isolated stretch of beach at will. Rooms have unvarnished wood floors, twin beds, and table fans, and the showers have cold water only. However, there are wide verandas and plenty of hammocks around for anyone who wants to kick back. Meals are above average for Tortuguero and might include pasta with lobster or chicken in béchamel sauce. You can dine either in the screened-in dining room or out on the patio. Tours included in the rates include a 4-hour boat ride through the canals and a guided forest hike. Optional tours include a night hike ($15) and fishing trips ($30 per hour for two people).

2. LIMÓN

160 kilometers E of San José

GETTING THERE   By Bus   Express buses leave San José daily every hour on the hour between 5am and 7pm from the corner of Avenida 3 between calles 19 and 21. Duration: 2½ hours. Fare: $2.70–$3.25 (deluxe).

By Car   The Guápiles Highway heads north out of San José on Calle 3 before turning east and passing close to Barva Volcano and through Braulio Carillo National Park en route to Limón. The drive takes about 2½ hours. Alternatively, you can take the old highway, which is equally scenic, though slower. This highway heads east out of San José on Avenida Central and passes through San Pedro before reaching Cartago. From Cartago on, the road is narrow and winding and passes through Paraíso and Turrialba before descending out of the mountains to Siquirres where the old highway meets the new. This route will take you to Limón in 4 hours or more.

DEPARTING   Express buses leave for San José almost hourly between 6am and 8pm. The bus stop for these buses is one block east and half a block south of the municipal market. Buses to Cahuita and Puerto Viejo leave from in front of Radio Casino, which is one block north of the municipal market. Buses to Punta Uva and Manzanillo, both of which are south of Puerto Viejo, leave Limón twice daily.

ESSENTIALS   Orientation   Nearly all addresses in Limón are measured from the market or from Parque Vargas, which is at the east end of town. The stop for buses out to Playa Bonita is just around the corner to the north of the Cahuita bus stop.

It was just offshore from present-day Limón that Christopher Columbus is believed to have anchored in 1502, on his fourth and last voyage to the New World. Though he felt this was potentially a very rich land and named it Costa Rica, it never quite lived up to his expectations. However, the spot where he anchored has proved over the centuries to be the best port on the Caribbean Coast. It was from here that the first shipments of bananas headed to North America in the late 19th century. Today, Limón is a busy port city that ships millions of pounds of bananas northward every year.

WHAT TO SEE & DO

There is little to see or do here in Limón. You can take a seat in Parque Vargas downtown along the seawall and watch the city's citizens go about their business. Take a walk around town if you're interested in architecture. When banana shipments built this port, many local merchants erected elaborately decorated buildings, several of which have survived the city's many earthquakes. If you want to get in some beach time while you're here in Limón, hop in a taxi or a local bus and head north to Playa Bonita, a small public beach park. Although the water isn't very clean and I don't recommend swimming, the setting is more attractive than downtown. This beach is popular with surfers.

The biggest event of the year in Limón, and one of the most fascinating festivals in Costa Rica, is the annual **Carnival,** which is held for a week around Columbus Day (October 12). For this one week of the year, languid Limón shifts into high gear for a nonstop bacchanal orchestrated to the beat of reggae, soca, and calypso music. During the revelries, residents of the city don costumes and take to the streets in a dazzling parade of color. If you want to experience this carnival, make hotel reservations early.

WHERE TO STAY & EAT

DOUBLES FOR LESS THAN $35

HOTEL ACON, Avenida 3 and Calle 3 (Apdo. 528), Limón. Tel. 506/758-1010. Fax 506/758-2924. 39 rms (all with private bath). A/C TEL
$ Rates: $24.95 single; $32.55 double; $38.50 triple. AE, MC, V.
This older in-town choice is the best you can do in Limón. The rooms, all of which are air-conditioned (almost a necessity in this muggy climate), are clean and have two twin beds and a large bathroom. The restaurant on the first floor just off the lobby is a cool, dark haven on steamy afternoons, highly recommended for lunch or as a place to beat the heat. Prices range from $2.85 to $11.50. The second-floor discotheque stays open late on weekends, so don't count on a quiet night.

PARK HOTEL, Avenida 3 between calles 1 and 3, Limón. Tel. 506/758-3476 or 758-2400. Fax 506/758-4364. 31 rms (all with private bath).
$ Rates: $11.10–$17.30 single; $19.30–$23.45 double. V.
You can't miss this pink, yellow, and turquoise building across the street from the fire station. It's certainly seen better years, but in Limón there aren't too many choices. What makes this place memorable is it's aging tropical ambience, so don't expect clean-and-new. Be sure to ask for a room on the ocean side of the hotel because these are brighter, quieter, and cooler than those on the side of the hotel that faces the fire station. The large sunny dining room off the lobby serves standard Tico fare.

WORTH THE EXTRA BUCKS

CABINAS COCORI, Playa Bonita (Apdo. 1093), Limón. Tel. 506/758-2930. 6 apartments (all with private bath).
$ Rates: $45.75–$57.15 for 1–5 people. MC, V.
Located on the water just before you reach Playa Bonita, these apartments command a fine view of the cove and crashing surf. The grounds are in need of landscaping, but the rooms are quite nice. A two-story white building houses the apartments, each of which has a kitchenette with hot plate and refrigerator, two bedrooms, and a bathroom. A long veranda runs along both floors. Staying at this location is far preferable to staying in town. You can get here by bus or taxi. When I was last in town, the Cocori was undergoing a major expansion.

---

3. CAHUITA

200 kilometers E of San José; 42 kilometers S of Limón

GETTING THERE By Bus Express buses leave San José three times daily from Avenida 11 between Calle Central and Calle 1. Duration: 4 hours. Fare: $6.35. Alternatively, you can take a bus to Limón (see above for details) and from there take a bus to Cahuita. These latter buses leave Limón four times daily from in front of Radio Casino, which is one block north of the municipal market. Duration: 1 hour. Fare: 85¢ to $1.30.

By Car Follow the directions above for getting to Limón, and, as you enter the outskirts of Limón, watch for a paved road to the right (it's just before the railroad tracks). Take this road south to Cahuita.

DEPARTING   Express buses from Sixaola (on the Panama border) stop in Cahuita three times daily en route to San José. However, these buses are almost always full. To avoid standing in the aisle all the way to San José, take a bus first to Limón, and then catch a Limón–San José bus. Buses to Limón leave five times daily. Buses headed from Limón to Puerto Viejo stop in Cahuita four times daily.

ESSENTIALS   Orientation   Three roads lead into town from the highway. The first road leads to the north end of Playa Negra; the second roads leads to the south end of Playa Negra; and the third road leads into the center of town. Buses usually take the road that leads into the heart of town and drop their passengers at the Salon Vaz bar. If you come in on the bus and are staying at a lodge on Playa Negra, head a mile out of town on the street that runs between Salon Vaz and the small park. The village's main street dead-ends at the entrance to the national park.

You can arrange to have laundry done at Moray's, which is one of the two tour companies in town. The post office, located where the road to Playa Negra curves north, is open Monday to Friday from 8 to 5pm. You can change money at Cahuita Tours.

Cahuita is one of the most laid-back villages you'll find anywhere in Costa Rica, and if you spend any time here, you'll likely find yourself slipping into a heat-induced torpor that affects anyone who ends up here. The gravel streets are almost always deserted, and the social heart of the village is the front porch of the Salon Vaz, Cahuita's main bar and disco. The village traces its roots to Afro-Caribbean fishermen and laborers who settled in this region in the mid-1800s, and today the population is still primarily English-speaking blacks whose culture and language set them apart from other Costa Ricans.

The main reason people come to Cahuita, other than the laid-back atmosphere, are the miles of beaches stretching both north and south from town. The beaches to the south, as well as the forest behind them, and the coral reefs beneath the waters offshore are all part of **Cahuita National Park.** It is here that you will find one of Costa Rica's few coral reefs. However, silt and pesticides washing down from nearby banana plantations are taking a heavy toll on this reef.

WHAT TO SEE & DO

You'll immediately feel the call of the long curve of beach that stretches south from the edge of town. This beach is glimpsed through the trees from Cahuita's sun-baked main street and extends a promise of relief from the heat. You can walk on the beach itself or follow the trail that runs through the forest just behind the beach. The best place to swim is beyond the Peresoso (Lazy) River, a few hundred yards inside the park. The trail behind the beach is great for bird-watching, and if you're lucky, you might see some monkeys or a sloth. The loud whooping sounds you hear off in the distance are the calls of howler monkeys. Nearer at hand, you are likely to hear crabs scuttling about amid the dry leaves on the forest floor. The trail behind the beach stretches a little more than 4 miles to Puerto Vargas at the southern end of the park. At Puerto Vargas, you'll find a white-sand beach, the park headquarters, and a campground. The reef is off the point just north of Puerto Vargas. The national park is open daily from dawn to dusk. Admission is $1.35 and the camping fee is $2.05 per person per day.

Outside the park, the best place for swimming is Playa Negra. If you want to find out where the best diving spots are, I suggest a snorkeling trip by boat. There are two companies running boats out to the reef. **Moray's** (tel. 758-1515, ext. 216), on the road to Playa Negra near the post office, charges $16.90 with gear. Snorkeling gear alone rents for $4.05 per day. Moray's also rents bicycles ($4.75 per day) and arranges boat trips to Tortuguero ($60). **Cahuita Tours & Rentals** (tel. 758-1515, ext. 232), around the corner on the village's main street, charges the same price for boat trips.

Snorkeling gear rents for $5.10 per day. You can also rent surfboards ($6.75 per day), boogie boards ($5.40 per day), and bicycles ($6.75 per day). Cahuita Tours also arranges various tours including trips to Tortuguero ($60) and to the Bribri Indian reservation ($20.30).

Brigitte (watch for the sign on Playa Negra) rents horses for $5.10 per hour and offers 4-hour guided horseback rides (you must have prior experience) for $25.70. Bird-watchers who have a car should head north 9 kilometers to the **Aviarios del Caribe** bed-and-breakfast lodge, where canoe tours of the Estrella Estuary are available. Nearly 300 species of birds have been sighted in the immediate area. Canoe trips cost $25 per person.

At Restaurant Vaz and a couple of other places around the village, you can pick up a copy of Paula Palmer's *What Happen, A Folk-History of Costa Rica's Talamanca Coast* (Publications in English, 1993). The book is a history of the region based on interviews with many of the area's oldest residents. Much of it is in the traditional Creole language, from which the title is taken. It makes fun and interesting reading.

For evening entertainment, the **Salon Vaz** in the center of town is the place to spend your nights (or days, for that matter) if you like cold beer and very loud reggae and soca music. At night the back room of this bar becomes a very lively disco.

WHERE TO STAY

DOUBLES FOR LESS THAN $25

CABINAS ATLANTIC SURF, Cahuita, Limón. No phone. 6 rms (all with private bath).
$ Rates: $11.60 single; $15.50 double; $19.35 triple. No credit cards.
These small but attractive rooms are a great choice for budget travelers. The rustic, varnished wood walls and floors and small porches of these rooms make them a cut above most budget rooms in town. There are fans and tiled showers and Adirondack chairs on the porches. The upstairs rooms have high ceilings but still get pretty warm. The Atlantic Surf is down the lane beside the Cabinas Sol y Mar.

CABINAS RHODE ISLAND, Cahuita, Limón. Tel. 506/758-1515, ext. 264. 11 rms (all with private bath).
$ Rates: $7.45–$10.30 single; $11.45–$17.15 double. No credit cards.
S These newer cinder-block rooms are down the lane beside the Cabinas Sol y Mar. The rooms are on the left, but the owners live in the house across the street. The rooms are very basic, but they're clean and have a tiled veranda. You're within 100 yards of the park entrance if you stay here.

CABINAS SOL Y MAR, Cahuita, Limón. Tel. 506/758-1515, ext. 237. 11 rms (all with private bath).
$ Rates: $15.50–$19.35 single or double; $18.35–$22.20 triple. No credit cards.
The nicer, and more expensive, rooms here are the ones upstairs, which have more light and catch more of the breezes, an important factor in these hot, humid, and cloudy climes. However, all the rooms are large, quite clean, and have fans. There isn't much decor, but you're only steps from the park entrance and the beach. Because of the nearby restaurants, it can be a little noisy here at night.

CABINAS VAZ, Cahuita, Limón. Tel. 506/758-1515, ext. 218. 14 rms (all with private bath).
$ Rates: Dec–Apr $15.45 single, $19.35 double, $23.20 triple; May–Nov $11.60 single, $15.45 double, $19.35 triple. No credit cards.
Only steps from the park entrance, Cabinas Vaz is one of the more popular places in town, especially with folks from San José, which means that it can get pretty noisy on the weekends. Most of the rooms are in an L-shaped building behind the Restaurant Vaz, though there are also a few located directly above the restaurant. I recommend asking for a room as far from the restaurant as possible because the tape player blares from dawn until late at night. The large rooms are simple but clean and have fans.

These folks have another 10 rooms out on the highway, though these rooms are used primarily by tour groups.

SURF SIDE CABINS, Apdo. 360, Limón. Tel. 506/758-1515, ext. 246.
   23 rms (all with private bath).
$ Rates: $15.45–$23.20 single or double. No credit cards.
Despite its name, this hotel is not right on the water; however, it is one of the nicer places in Cahuita. All the rooms are clean and have jalousie windows that let in a lot of light and air. The hotel does actually have a few rooms close to the water, but these rooms are always in high demand. The restaurant is popular with locals and can get noisy at times. Prices for Tico meals range from $2.70 to $12.15. The hotel management can be rather unfriendly at times.

DOUBLES FOR LESS THAN $35

ALBY LODGE, Apdo. 840, Limón. No phone. 4 cabins (all with private bath).
$ Rates: $34.30 single, double, or triple. No credit cards.
Located about 150 yards down the lane to the right just before you reach the park entrance, the Alby Lodge is a fascinating little place hand-built by German owners Yvonne and Alfons Baumgartner. Though these four small cabins are close to the center of the village, they are surrounded by a large lawn and feel secluded. The cabins are all quintessentially tropical with thatch roofs, mosquito nets, hardwood floors, big shuttered windows, tile bathrooms, and a hammock slung on the front porch. You won't find more appealing rooms in this price range.

CABINAS TITO, 250 metros suroeste de G.A.R., Cahuita, Limón. Tel.
   506/758-1515, ext. 286. 6 cabins (all with private bath).
$ Rates: Dec–Apr $34.30 double; May–Nov $17.15–$22.90 double. No credit cards.
Located down a grassy path off of the road to Playa Negra, these little cabins are quiet and comfortable. They're surrounded by a shady yard, and the owner's old Caribbean wood-frame house is to one side. The cabins are made of cement block with tin roofs, but they have tile floors and front porches with a couple of chairs. Two of the cabins have little refrigerators, and at least one has a tiled wall and wicker headboard. The good value and pleasant surroundings have made this place quite popular.

SEASIDE JENNY'S, Cahuita, Limón. Tel. 506/758-1515, ext. 256. 9 rms (all with private bath).
$ Rates: Dec–Apr $27.05–$30.95 single or double, $32.50–$36.35 triple; May–Nov $19.35–$23.20 single or double, $24.75–$20.90 triple. No credit cards.
Located 200 yards straight ahead (toward the water) from the bus stop, Jenny's place has been popular for years. The newer rooms are some of the best in town in this price range. Best of all they're right on the water, so you can go to sleep to the sound of the waves. All of the rooms have shuttered windows, and on their porches there are sling chairs and hammocks. The more expensive rooms are on the second floor and have a better view and high ceilings. There are a couple of rooms in an older building, which is not nearly as nice as the newer building.

WORTH THE EXTRA BUCKS

AVIARIOS DEL CARIBE, Apdo. 569-7300, Limón. No phone. Fax 506/758-4459. 5 rms (all with private bath).
$ Rates (including full breakfast): $68.60 double. No credit cards.
If you prefer bird-watching to beaching, this is the place for you. The B&B is 9 kilometers north of Cahuita and is located on the edge of a small river delta, and within the immediate area, nearly 300 species of birds have been spotted. The house is built on stilts and is surrounded by a private wildlife sanctuary. The guest rooms are all large and comfortable and have fans, tile floors, potted plants, fresh flowers, and modern bathroom fixtures. In the lounge you'll find a fabulous mounted insect collection, as well as terrariums that house live snakes and poison-

arrow frogs. Lunch and dinner are also available. Canoe trips through the delta are the main attraction here.

CABINAS ATLANTIDA, Cahuita, Limón. Tel. 506/758-1515, ext. 213. 30 rms (all with private bath).
$ Rates (including continental breakfast): Dec 16–Apr 15 $52 single, $57 double, $64 triple; May–Nov $46 single, $51 double, $57 triple. AE, MC, V.

Set amid lush gardens and wide green lawns, the Atlantida is one of my favorite hotels in Cahuita. You'll find it beside the soccer field out by Playa Negra, about a mile out of town. The guest rooms are done in a style reminiscent of local Indian architecture, with thatched roofs and pale yellow stucco walls. Although only breakfast is included in the rates above, you can also order lunch and dinner. The meals are served in a rancho dining room. Dinners are primarily continental style dishes and are some of the best in town, though they are only available to hotel guests. Several different tours can be arranged. The beach is right across the street, and the hotel also has a small pool.

CHALET HIBISCUS, Apdo. 943, Limón. No phone. Fax 506/758-1543 or 758-0652. 1 house, 2 cabinas (all with private bath).
$ Rates: Dec–Apr $51.45 cabina (single or double), $102.90 house (1–6 people); May–Nov $45.75 cabina, $85.75 house. No credit cards.

Although it is about 2 kilometers from town on the road along Playa Negra, the Chalet Hibiscus is well worth the journey. The house has two bedrooms and sleeps up to six people. There is hardwood paneling all around, a full kitchen, hot water, red-tile floors, and even a garage. A spiral staircase leads to the second floor, where you'll find hammocks on a balcony that looks over a green lawn to the ocean. The attractive little cabinas have wicker furniture and walls of stone and wood. If you ever wanted to be marooned on the Mosquito Coast, this is the place to live out your fantasy. There's even a swimming pool. The chalet is both simple and elegant; the setting, serene and beautiful.

MAGELLAN INN, Plaza Víquez, Cahuita. Fax 506/758-0652. 6 rms (all with private bath).
$ Rates (including continental breakfast): $51.45 single; $62.90 double; $74.30 triple. DC, MC, V.

⭐ This small inn is out at the far end of Playa Negra (about 2 kilometers north of Cahuita) and is the most luxurious hotel in the area. The six large rooms are all carpeted and have French doors, vertical blinds, big tiled bathrooms with hardwood counters, and king-size beds with attractive bedspreads. Each room has its own tiled veranda with an overhead fan and bamboo chairs. There is a combination bar/lounge and breakfast room that has Oriental-style rugs and wicker furniture. However, most memorable are the hotel's sunken pool and garden, both of which are built into a crevice in the ancient coral reef that underlies this entire region.

WHERE TO EAT

If you'd like to try some of the local foods, check out the little shack just before the bridge leading into the national park. The folks here sell meat and vegetable turnovers (called patties), delicious coconut tarts, various stews with coconut rice, and a refreshing tamarind drink. Also, several women cook up pots of various local specialties and sell them from the front porch of Salon Vaz (the disco) on Friday and Saturday nights. A full meal will cost you about $2.50. For snacks, there is a tiny bakery on the left side of the main road as you head toward Playa Negra. The coconut pie, brownies, ginger snaps, banana bread, and corn pudding are all delicious. Prices range from 55¢ to 75¢.

MEALS FOR LESS THAN $6

MARGARITAVILLE, Playa Negra Road 2 kilometers north of Cahuita near Cabinas Cocal. No phone.

Cuisine: INTERNATIONAL. **Reservations:** Not accepted.
$ Prices: Complete meal $4.05–$4.75. No credit cards.
Open: Daily 7–10am, noon–2pm, and 6–9pm.

There's only one dish served each night at this little restaurant, but if you drop by ahead of time and make a special request, the friendly owner may try to accommodate you. However, if you're an adventurous eater, I'm sure you'll enjoy whatever is coming from the kitchen, which might be a local Creole dish made with coconut milk or roasted chicken or eggplant lasagne. All the breads are home baked, and there are great sandwiches at lunch. The tables here are set up on the porch of an old house and they all have a view of the ocean through the trees. It's all very mellow, definitely not to be missed.

PIZZERIA EL CACTUS, on the road from the south end of Playa Negra to the highway. No phone.
Cuisine: ITALIAN. **Reservations:** Not accepted.
$ Prices: Pizza or spaghetti $3.35–$6.10. No credit cards.
Open: Tues–Sun 4–9pm.

There are only a few tables at this small open-air restaurant, so be sure to arrive early if you have your heart set on pizza. Try the pizza Cahuita, which is made with tomatoes, mozzarella, salami, red peppers, olives, and oregano. There's also one made with hearts of palm. The pizzas are just the right size for one hungry person. Also on the menu are seven types of spaghetti, salads, and ice cream.

MEALS FOR LESS THAN $12

BRIGITTE'S RESTAURANTE, Playa Negra Road north of Cabinas Atlantida. No phone.
Cuisine: SWISS/CREOLE. **Reservations:** Not accepted.
$ Prices: Main dishes $3.75–$7.45. No credit cards.
Open: Thurs–Tues 8am–10pm.

Brigitte is from Switzerland but she's been in Cahuita for quite a few years, so her menu includes an eclectic blend of cuisines. You can get good Creole soups with cow's tail and cow's feet, but you can also get a steak with mushroom sauce. There are good salads and home-baked breads as well. You never know what might show up as the daily special. The restaurant is located at the back of a house just off the Playa Negra Road. Just follow the signs.

RESTAURANT EDITH, by the police station. Tel. 758-1515, ext. 248.
Cuisine: SEAFOOD. **Reservations:** Not accepted.
$ Prices: Main dishes $3.40–$11.50. No credit cards.
Open: Mon–Sat 7am–noon, 3–6pm, and 7–10pm; Sun 4–10pm.

Miss Edith is a local lady who decided to start serving up home-cooked meals to all the hungry tourists hanging around. While Miss Edith's daughters take the orders, Mom cooks up a storm out back. The menu, when you can get ahold of it, is long, with lots of local seafood dishes and creole combinations such as yuca in coconut milk with meat or vegetables. Though the Creole cooking is great, if you don't get here very early (before 6pm), you may have to wait an hour for your meal. Miss Edith's place is at the opposite end of town from the park entrance and is just around the corner from the main street.

4. PUERTO VIEJO

200 kilometers E of San José; 55 kilometers S of Limón

GETTING THERE   By Bus   Express buses to Puerto Viejo leave San José daily at 3pm (also at 8am on Saturday and Sunday) from Avenida 11 between Calle Central and Calle 1. Duration: 5 hours. Fare: $6.10. Alternatively, you can catch a bus to Limón (see above for details), and then transfer to a Puerto Viejo–bound bus in Limón. These latter buses leave four times daily from in front of Radio Casino, which is one block north of the municipal market. Duration: 1½ hours. Fare: 85¢–$1.30.

By Car To reach Puerto Viejo, continue south from Cahuita for another 16 kilometers. Watch for a gravel road that forks to the left from the paved highway. This road will take you into the village after another 5 kilometers.

DEPARTING Express buses leave Puerto Viejo for San José daily at 7am (also at 3:30pm on Saturday and Sunday). Buses for Limón leave three times daily (twice on Sunday). Buses to Punta Uva and Manzanillo leave Puerto Viejo twice daily. There are also northbound buses that stop in Home Creek, out on the highway 5 kilometers from Puerto Viejo, three times daily. If you can get to Home Creek, you can catch one of these buses.

ESSENTIALS Orientation The gravel road in from the highway runs parallel to Playa Negra just before entering the village of Puerto Viejo, which has all of about six dirt streets. The sea will be on your left and forested hills on your right as you come into town. Public phones are located at Hotel Maritza and Pulpería Manuel Leon. The nearest bank is in Bribri, about 10 kilometers away.

Though Puerto Viejo is even smaller than Cahuita, it has an even more lively atmosphere due to the many surfers who come here from around the country and around the world to ride the village's famous Salsa Brava wave. For nonsurfers, there are also some good swimming beaches, and if you head still farther south, you will come to the most beautiful beaches on this coast. The waters down in this region are some of the clearest anywhere in the country and there is good snorkeling among the coral reefs.

WHAT TO SEE & DO

Most people who show up in this remote village have only one thing on their mind—**surfing.** Just offshore from the village park is a shallow reef where powerful storm-generated waves sometimes reach 20 feet. These waves are the biggest and most powerful on the Atlantic coast. Even when the waves are small, this spot is recommended only for very experienced surfers because of the danger of the reef. For swimming, head out to Playa Negra, along the road into town, or to the beaches south of town where the surf is much more manageable.

If you aren't a surfer, there isn't much else for you to do here. The same activities that prevail in Cahuita are the norm here as well. Read a book, take a nap, or walk on the beach. However, if you have more energy, you can rent a bicycle or a horse (watch for signs) and head down the beach toward Punta Uva.

You should be sure to stop in at the **Association Talamanqueña de Ecoturismo y Conservacion** (ATEC) office across the street from the Soda Tamara. This local organization is concerned with preserving both the environment and the cultural heritage of this area and promoting ecologically sound development in the region. They publish and sell *Coastal Talamanca, A Cultural and Ecological Guide,* a small booklet packed with information about this area. They also offer quite a few different tours. There are half-day walks that focus on nature and either the local African-Caribbean culture or the indigenous Bribri culture. These walks pass through farms and forests, and along the way you'll learn about local history, customs, medicinal plants, and Indian mythology as well as have an opportunity to see sloths, monkeys, toucans, and other wildlife. There are four different walks through the Bribri Indians' Kekoldi Reserve. There are also more strenuous hikes through the primary rain forest. ATEC also offers snorkeling trips to the nearby coral reefs and fishing trips in dugout canoes. There are also bird walks, night walks, and overnight treks. The local guides who lead these tours are a wealth of information and make a hike through the forest a truly educational experience. Half-day walks (and night walks) are $11.70 and full-day walks are $19.45. A half day of snorkeling or fishing is $15.55. The ATEC office is open Tuesday through Saturday from noon to 6pm and Sunday from 8am to noon.

To learn more about the culture of the local Bribri Indians, look for a copy of *Taking Care of Sibö's Gifts,* which was written by Paula Palmer, Juanita Sánchez, and Gloria Mayorga.

If you continue south on the coast road from Puerto Viejo, you will come to a couple of even smaller villages. Punta Uva is 8 kilometers away, and Manzanillo is about 15 kilometers away. There is a trail along the beach from Barra Cocles to Manzanillo, a distance of about 10 kilometers. Another enjoyable hike is from Monkey Point to Manzanillo (about 5½ kilometers). There is a reef offshore from Manzanillo that is good for snorkeling. Still farther south is the Manzanillo-Gandoca Wildlife Refuge, which extends all the way to the Panamanian border. Within the boundaries of the reserve live manatees and crocodiles and more than 350 species of birds. On the reserve's beaches, four species of sea turtles nest between March and July.

WHERE TO STAY

DOUBLES FOR LESS THAN $15

CABINAS JACARANDA, Puerto Viejo, Limón. No phone. 4 rms (1 with private bath).
$ Rates: $11.60 single without bath; $13.95 double without bath, $19.35 double with bath; $23.20 triple with bath. No credit cards.

This basic backpackers' special has a few nice touches that set it apart from the others. The floors are cement, but there are mats, with Japanese paper lanterns covering the lights and mosquito nets hanging over the beds. The Guatemalan bedspreads add a dash of color and tropical flavor, as do the tables made from sliced tree trunks. If you are traveling in a group, you'll enjoy the space and atmosphere of the big room. The Garden Restaurant, adjacent to the rooms, serves the best food in town.

DOUBLES FOR LESS THAN $25

CABINAS BLACK SANDS, Puerto Viejo, Limón. Tel. 506/758-3844 (leave message). 3 rms (all with shared bath).
$ Rates: $19.35 single or double; $57.15 for 6 people. No credit cards.
The owners of this rustic beachside thatch house are refugees from chilly Wisconsin. They offer basic accommodations in a secluded spot on a long black-sand beach. The three rooms are all in a single rustic thatched-roof building, which has a communal kitchen and dining-room table. It's wonderfully tranquil out here, and though it's a long walk to the nearest restaurant, there is a general store nearby where you can buy groceries for doing your own cooking. If arriving by bus, be sure to get off at the Pulperia Violeta before the road reaches the beach. Otherwise it's a long walk from the bus stop in town.

CASA VERDE, Puerto Viejo, Limón. Tel. 506/758-0854 or 758-3844 (leave message). 8 rms (4 with private bath).
$ Rates: $13.15 single without bath, $28.60 single with bath; $19.35 double without bath, $28.60 double with bath. No credit cards.
This little hotel is located on a side street on the south side of town. The older rooms, with shared bath, are in an interesting building with a wide, covered breezeway between the rooms and the showers and toilets out in back. The front and back porches of this building are hung with hammocks. The newer rooms are behind the house next door and are a bit larger than the older rooms. These new rooms have high ceilings, tile floors, and a veranda.

HOTEL PURA VIDA, Puerto Viejo, Limón. No phone. 7 rms (all with shared bath).

$ Rates: $12.40 single; $19.35 double; $22.50 triple. No credit cards.

You'll find the Pura Vida around the corner from Cabinas Jacaranda and facing the soccer field. This pink and pale green cement and wood building is a sprawling structure with several cool and breezy covered patios. The second floor, where most of the guest rooms are located, has a veranda on three sides. Guest rooms have high ceilings, fans, and sinks, though the clean tiled bathroom is down the hall. Walls are made of wood, so sounds carry. Down in the shade of the patios there are hammocks for those who want to laze away the days.

DOUBLES FOR LESS THAN $35

CABINAS CHIMURI, Puerto Viejo, Limón. Tel. 758-3844 (leave message). 4 cabins (all with shared bath).

$ Rates: $25.15–$37.75 single, double, or triple; $37.75 quad. No credit cards.

If you don't mind being a 15-minute walk from the beach and are accustomed to camping, you may enjoy this rustic lodge. It's built in traditional Bribri Indian–style with thatched-roof A-frame cabins in a forest setting, and rooms are very basic. It's a short stroll down a trail from the parking lot to the lodge buildings, and there are other trails on the property as well. The lodge runs several different hiking trips into the rain forest and the adjacent Bribri Indian Kekoldi Reserve. If arriving by bus, be sure to get off at the trail to Cabinas Chimuri before the road reaches the beach.

ESCAPE CARIBEÑO, Puerto Viejo, Limón. Tel. 506/758-3844. 12 rms, 1 apt (all with private bath).

$ Rates: $30 single; $35.05 double; $38 triple; $40–$55 quad; $60 apartment (1–3 people). MC, V.

Located just outside of Puerto Viejo on the road to Punta Uva, Escape Caribeño consists of 12 little white cabins with brick pillars and tiled patios. Clerestory windows, vertical blinds, and rather fancy hardwood furniture give these cabins the aesthetic edge over many area places in this price range. There are reading lamps by the beds and small refrigerators in every room. The attractive gardens have been planted with bananas and palms. It's a 5-minute walk into town or out to a beautiful beach that has a small island just offshore.

HOTEL MARITZA, Puerto Viejo, Limón. Tel. 506/758-3844. 14 rms (all with private bath).

$ Rates: $22.15 single or double; $26.30 triple. V.

This very basic hotel is behind a popular restaurant, which also happens to have one of the only public phones in town. The rooms are fairly new and have fans and hot water. There's nothing in the way of a garden here, though, so don't expect any tropical ambience.

WORTH THE EXTRA BUCKS

EL PIZOTE, Apdo. 230-2200, Coronado. Tel. 506/758-1938 or 229-1428. Fax 506/229-1428. 8 rms (all with shared bath), 6 bungalows, 1 casita (all with private bath).

$ Rates: $35.45 single without bath, $85.75 single with bath; $52.60 double without bath, $85.75 double with bath; $68.60 triple without bath, $101.75 triple with bath; $114.30 casita single, double, or triple. MC, V.

This comfortably rustic lodge would be ideal for anyone who wants to get away from it all. Located about 500 meters outside of town, El Pizote is set back across the road from a long black-sand beach. The rooms are in two beautiful, unpainted wooden buildings and have polished wood walls, double beds, and beautiful bathrooms with huge screen windows looking out on dense jungle. For activity, there are hiking trails in the adjacent forest and a volleyball court. You can also rent snorkeling and scuba equipment and sea kayaks. The restaurant serves breakfast ($8) and dinner ($14.50). There is a set menu each evening, which might be lobster with broccoli or an equally delectable fish plate. If arriving by bus, ask the bus driver to let you off at the entrance to the lodge. If you're looking for someplace more rustic, ask about their jungle lodge.

NEARBY PLACES TO STAY
DOUBLES FOR LESS THAN $45

PLAYA CHIQUITA LODGE, Avenida 2 between calles 17 and 19 (Apdo. 7043-1000), San José. Tel. 506/233-6613. Fax 506/223-7479. 11 rms (all with private bath).
$ Rates: $28.60 single; $40 double; $51.45 triple. AE, V (accepted only at the San José office).

This place just oozes jungle atmosphere and is sure to please anyone searching for a steamy retreat on the beach. Set amid the shade of large old trees a few miles south of Puerto Viejo (watch for the sign), the lodge consists of unpainted wooden buildings set on stilts and connected by wooden walkways. Rooms are dark and cool with wide-board floors and paintings by local Indian artists. The top of the bathroom wall is only screen so you can gaze out into the jungle as you shower. A short trail leads down to a private little swimming beach with tide pools and beautiful turquoise water. Meals here cost from $2 to $12 and choices range from spaghetti to lobster.

WORTH THE EXTRA BUCKS

LAS PALMAS RESORT, Edificio Cristal, 5th floor, Avenida 1 between calles 1 and 3 (Apdo. 6942-1000), San José. Tel. 506/255-3939. Fax 506/255-3737. 40 rms (all with private bath).
$ Rates (including breakfast): $45 single; $56 double; $81 triple. AE, DC, MC, V.
Located five miles south of Puerto Viejo in the village of Punta Uva, Las Palmas Resort is one of the only true beachfront hotels in the area. The beach here stretches for miles, and when the water is calm, snorkeling is good among the coral just offshore. Guest rooms are clean and comfortable, though not very attractive. Basically what you're paying for here is the location, not the atmosphere or decor. The open-air restaurant serves moderately priced Tico and continental meals, with an emphasis on lobster and seafood. Additional amenities include a small swimming pool and a tennis court. Various tours and horseback rides can be arranged through the hotel. There's also a dive shop that gives lessons, leads trips, and rents equipment.

WHERE TO EAT

To really sample the local cuisine, you need to look up a few local ladies. **Miss Dolly** bakes bread (especially banana) and ginger biscuits, and she sometimes fixes Caribbean meals, but you have to ask a day in advance. **Miss Sam** makes pineapple rolls, plantain tarts, and bread. **Miss Daisy** makes pan bon, ginger cakes, patties (meat-filled turnovers), and coconut oil (for tanning). Ask around for these folks and someone will direct you to them. If you get the chance, try some rundown soup, a spicy coconut-milk soup made with anything the cook can run down.

MEALS FOR LESS THAN $6

SODA TAMARA, on the main road through the village. No phone.
Cuisine: COSTA RICAN. **Reservations:** Not accepted.
$ Prices: Main dishes $2.40–$5.45. No credit cards.
Open: Wed–Mon 7am–9pm.
This little Tico-style restaurant has long been popular with budget-conscious travelers and has an attractive setting for such an economical place. There's a small patio dining area in addition to the main dining room, which is a bit dark. At the counter inside, you'll find homemade cocoa candies and unsweetened cocoa biscuits. These are made

by several local ladies. Unfortunately, the town's cacao trees are being killed by a blight.

MEALS FOR LESS THAN $12

CAFE PIZZERIA CORAL, on the road to the soccer field. No phone.
Cuisine: PIZZA. **Reservations:** Not accepted.
$ Prices: Pizza $3.65–$6.80; pasta $4.05–$4.75. No credit cards.
Open: Tues–Sun 7–11am and 6–9:30pm.
Though the owner here is from El Salvador, she cooks a great pizza. She also bakes great chocolate cake! Some of the goodies not to be missed are the pumpkin soup, the tomato and green peppercorn pizza (the peppercorns are grown locally), the summer wine (a bit like sangría), and of course the chocolate cake (though the key lime pie is good too). You'll find the Cafe Pizzeria Coral about two blocks from the water in the center of the village.

GARDEN RESTAURANT, Cabinas Jacaranda. No phone.
Cuisine: CARIBBEAN/ASIAN. **Reservations:** Not accepted.
$ Prices: Appetizers $2.20–$2.70; entrees $4.40–$5.75. No credit cards.
Open: Thurs–Mon 5:30–9pm.
Located a couple of blocks from the water (near the soccer field), this restaurant serves the best food in Puerto Viejo and some of the best in all of Costa Rica. The co-owner and chef is from Trinidad by way of Toronto and has created an eclectic menu that is guaranteed to please. You'll find such surprising offerings as chicken saté (a Thai dish), yakitori (Japanese), and Jamaican jerk chicken. There are also lots of delicious fresh juices. Many of the ambrosial desserts are made with local fruits, and there are also such delights as ginger spice cake and macadamia chocolate torte. Every dish is garnished with flowers.

NEARBY PLACES TO EAT
MEALS FOR LESS THAN $12

EL DUENDE FELIZ, on the main road, Punta Uva. No phone.
Cuisine: ITALIAN. **Reservations:** Not accepted.
$ Prices: Appetizers $2.75–$6.45; entrees $5.10–$12.20. No credit cards.
Open: Sat–Wed 11am–2pm and 6–9pm, Thurs–Fri 6–9pm.
Isn't it reassuring to know that even in the middle of nowhere, you can get a plate of spaghetti or a pizza? El Duende Feliz is on the outskirts of Punta Uva village and serves a wide selection of authentic Italian dishes. Seafood shows up quite a bit, of course. Depending on the day's catch, you can get seafood spaghetti or pizza with clams, among other dishes. There are also steaks and plenty of pasta dishes. You can even finish off your meal with a scoop of gelato and an espresso.

NATURALES, on the main road, Punta Uva. No phone.
Cuisine: SWISS/CONTINENTAL. **Reservations:** Not accepted.
$ Prices: Main dishes $3.75–$12.50. No credit cards.
Open: Fri–Wed 4–10pm.
Located south of Playa Chiquita on the road to Punta Uva, Naturales is built into a hillside at the top of a steep flight of 48 steps. From this tree house–like vantage point there is a great view of the water and the surrounding forests. Every day there's a different menu. You may find the likes of beef fondue or homemade pastas. If you order a day in advance, you can have special meals prepared. There are also a couple of rooms for rent here for $21 per night (double).

CHAPTER 9

GETTING TO KNOW GUATEMALA

1. **GEOGRAPHY, HISTORY & POLITICS**
- **DATELINE**
2. **ART, ARCHITECTURE & LITERATURE**
- **DID YOU KNOW . . . ?**
3. **CULTURAL & SOCIAL LIFE**
4. **FOOD & DRINK**
5. **RECOMMENDED BOOKS & FILMS**

Guatemala: The very name sounds exotic as it rolls off the tongue. Even though it is possible to drive there by way of Mexico, Guatemala seems worlds away. The name conjures up images of lost cities in the steamy jungle and colorfully clothed Mayan Indians. These are here, yes, but there is more. Guatemala is also a country rich in Spanish history, the history of the Conquest. Colonial architecture—with its arches, porticos, stucco walls, and cobblestone streets—has been preserved in the city of Antigua, once the capital of all Central America. Ruins of churches, monasteries, and universities have become parks, giving the late 20th century a glimpse of the greatness of Central America in earlier times.

With nearly 50% of the population claiming Indian ancestry and clinging to ancient customs and costumes, Guatemala is culturally fascinating. Spanish is the official language, but ancient Indian languages such as Quiché and Mam are still spoken in the highlands. Primitive rituals and masked dances are the last vestiges of the once-great Mayan culture.

Guatemala has been called "the land of eternal spring" because of the nearly perfect weather that the highlands enjoy throughout the year. It was this gentle climate that first attracted Spanish settlers, and today it is this same climate (and the stunning setting) that attracts tourists from all over the world to Lake Atitlán, which is encircled by volcanoes and which many claim is the most beautiful lake in the world. Why, then, has Guatemala not become overrun with tourists? Politics. Central America in the last 20 years became a terra incognita for citizens of the United States. Civil wars, revolutions, death squads, and communist guerrillas throughout the narrow strip of land connecting North and South America made the headlines and stopped the once-growing flow of tourists to the region. Guatemala, suffering plenty of its own internal strife, became one of those places that only soldiers of fortune and journalists wanted to visit.

But things have changed in Guatemala, and things remain the same. Ancient cultures with ties to the mysterious Mayan civilization of more than 1,000 years ago survive, although these Indian peoples continue to struggle, sometimes violently, for land reform and a better standard of living. There is still occasional guerrilla activity in remote regions of Guatemala, but these are generally far from anyplace a tourist would likely venture. Every year, more tourists discover Guatemala's highlights: the ancient Mayan ceremonial center of Tikal; Antigua, once the capital of Central America; the stunning vistas of Lake Atitlán; and the fascinating Indian cultures and crafts of the Guatemalan highlands. From the jungled plains of El Petén to the volcanoes of the Sierra Madre, Guatemala offers a diversity of natural beauty unrivaled anywhere in Central America.

1. GEOGRAPHY, HISTORY & POLITICS

GEOGRAPHY

Guatemala is the northernmost country of Central America, bordered on the north and west by Mexico; on the south by the Pacific Ocean, El Salvador, and Honduras; and on the east by the Caribbean Sea and Belize. Covering 42,000 square miles, Guatemala is roughly the size of the state of Tennessee. Stretching from northwest to southeast are several volcanic mountain ranges that form the backbone of the country.

To the south of the mountains lies the Costa Sur, the South Coast, a narrow strip of plains. To the northeast is El Petén, a vast, jungle-covered rolling plain. This is the most remote and least developed region of Guatemala and was at one time the heart of the Mayan culture.

HISTORY

The earliest Mayan culture dates back to the Pre-Classic Period from 300 B.C. to A.D. 100, but it did not fully flower until the Classic Period (A.D. 200 to 925). By A.D. 600 the Mayas were the most important culture in Mesoamerica. The advanced culture of Teotihuacan was declining, while the Mayas were rising intellectually and artistically to a height never before reached by the natives of the New World. In Guatemala and the Yucatán peninsula, the Mayas built magnificent ceremonial centers; carved intricate hieroglyphic stelae; and developed superior astronomical, calendrical, and mathematical systems.

Then in the Late Classic Period, around A.D. 790, the Mayan civilization began to decline. Over the next 40 to 100 years, one village after another was abandoned, until by the end of the 9th century, the last chapter of this brilliant civilization was closed. Why? No one is certain. Was it the population explosion? The misuse of land? The northern barbarians who were roaming Mesoamerica? Whatever the reason, the Post-Classic Period, from A.D. 900 up to the Spanish Conquest, shows the loss of splendor and the beginning of a polity of class systems (priests, merchants, and serfs), government regulation and taxation, trade guilds, and a primitive but productive agriculture.

In 1519 Hernán Cortés conquered Mexico, and in 1523 he sent his chief lieutenant, Pedro de Alvarado, to explore the region of Guatemala. Alvarado led an expedition against the Quiché people (then the most powerful and wealthy tribe in Guatemala). In the words of a 16th-century Spanish historian, Alvarado was "reckless, merciless and impetuous, lacking in veracity if not common honesty, but zealous and courageous." It wasn't long before Alvarado had conquered the indigenous peoples and was named representative of the sovereign power of Spain. He set about establishing a typical Spanish colonial empire, founding cities and towns throughout Central America, and converting the Indians to Catholicism. But unlike Mexico, Central America did not yield vast amounts of gold and silver for the conquerors and was thus somewhat of a disappointment. Many of the Spaniards stayed on, however, to carve out large plantations using the Indians as laborers.

DATELINE

- **200 B.C.** Earliest record of inhabitants at Mayan city of Tikal.
- **A.D. 600–A.D. 900** Mayan civilization reaches its zenith.
- **1523** Pedro de Alvarado, under command from Hernán Cortés, marches into Guatemala with an army of Spanish and Indian troops.
- **1524** Iximché becomes the first Spanish capital of Guatemala and is renamed Santiago (St. James).
- **1527** The capital is moved to the Valley of Almolonga at the foot of Agua Volcano and given the name of Santiago.
- **1541** Pedro de Alvarado dies from injuries sustained when a horse falls on him. His second wife, Doña Beatriz, proclaims herself captain general, becoming the first female head of a

(continues)

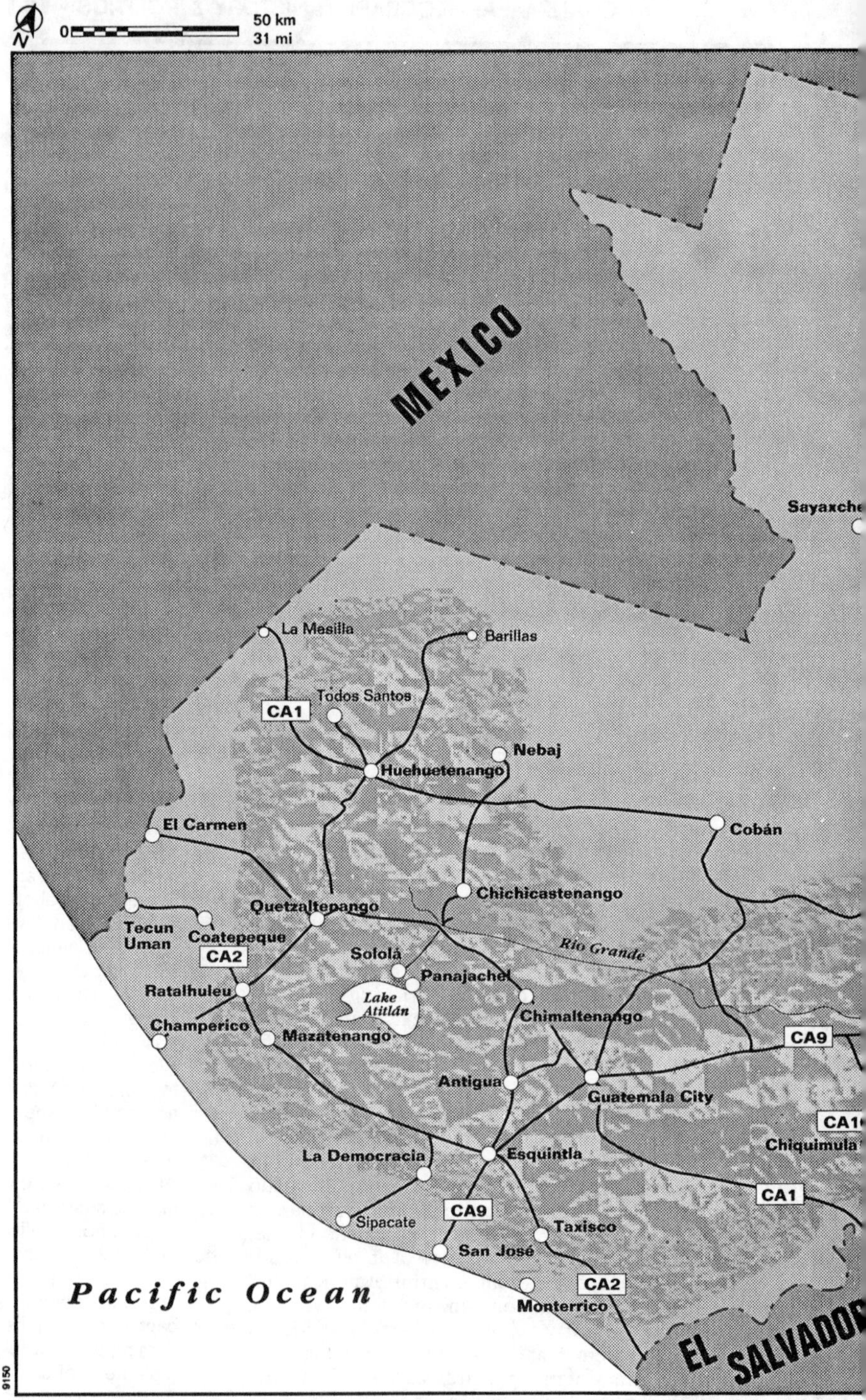

N
0
50 km
31 mi
MEXICO
Sayaxche
La Mesilla
Barillas
Todos Santos
CA1
Nebaj
Huehuetenango
El Carmen
Cobán
Chichicastenango
Quetzaltepango
Tecun Uman
Coatepeque
CA2
Río Grande
Sololá
Panajachel
Ratalhuleu
Lake Atitlán
Chimaltenango
Champerico
Mazatenango
CA9
Antigua
Guatemala City
Chiquimula
La Democracia
Esquintla
CA1
Sipacate
CA9
Taxisco
San José
CA2
Monterrico
Pacific Ocean
EL SALVADOR
9150

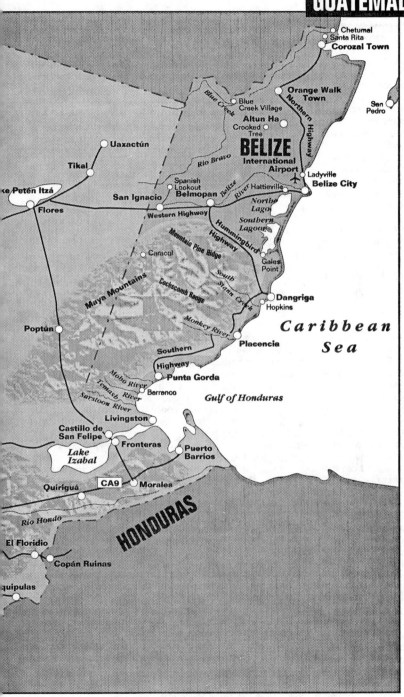

Chetumal
Santa Rita
Corozal Town

Orange Walk Town

Blue Creek Village

Blue Creek

Northern Highway

San Pedro

Uaxactún

Altun Ha
Crooked Tree

BELIZE
International Airport

Tikal

Rio Bravo

Ladyville
Belize City

ke Petén Itzá

Spanish Lookout
Belmopan

Belize River

Hattieville

San Ignacio

Flores

Western Highway

Northe Lago

Southern Lagoon

Hummingbird Highway

Mountain Pine Ridge

Gales Point

Caracol

South Stann Creek

Cockscomb Range

Dangriga
Hopkins

Maya Mountains

Caribbean Sea

Poptún

Monkey River

Placencia

Southern Highway

Moho River

Punta Gorda

Temash River

Barranco

Gulf of Honduras

Sarstoon River

Livingston

Castillo de San Felipe

Fronteras

Puerto Barrios

Lake Izabal

Quiriguá

CA9

Morales

Rio Hondo

HONDURAS

El Floridio

Copán Ruinas

quipulas

The Spanish made their first capital at Iximché, a Cakchiquel Maya city; after forming an alliance with the Cakchiquels they renamed the city Santiago (St. James). In 1527, they built a new capital at the foot of Agua volcano in the Almolonga Valley. This city, also called Santiago, lasted only until 1541 when it was destroyed by a flood. In 1543, the capital was moved a few miles away to what was thought a safer location in the Panchoy Valley. Once again the city was called Santiago (de los Caballeros). This city, now known as Antigua, was a religious and cultural center even before it became the capital. The friars established universities and monasteries, building grand edifices to rival any in colonial Mexico or Peru. Between 1543 and 1773, the city flourished and the city's population rose to 55,000. From Santiago, the Spanish governed a vast dominion that stretched from southern Mexico to Costa Rica.

However, this capital, too, was ill fated. Between 1543 and 1717 it suffered numerous floods, earthquakes, and fires. Then, in 1773, a series of devastating earthquakes virtually destroyed the city, and in 1775, the capital was moved once again—this time to the Ermita Valley. This new capital, now known as Guatemala City, proved just as prone to natural catastrophes as the three previous cities, but it has remained the capital.

Early in the 19th century, Guatemalan and other Central American leaders followed the lead of other Latin American states and declared their independence from Spain. The captain-general of Guatemala became the chief executive. But in Mexico the empire of Agustín Iturbide had been formed, and conservative Guatemalan leaders voted for annexation to the empire. This political arrangement didn't last. A republican Federation of Central American States was formed in 1823. The federation lasted some 15 years but was continually torn by internecine battles, both political and military. By 1840 Central America had taken the political form it has today, and political struggles were confined to the large towns. As a result, except for Guatemala City and the provincial capitals, "progress" is a stranger to much of the country, leaving it untouched and incredibly beautiful.

POLITICS

Throughout its history, Guatemala has been subjected to tumultuous political upheavals. Even before the Spanish Conquest, the various Indian tribes of the highlands had been constantly at war. When Pedro de Alvarado marched into the country with his armies, he utilized these feuds to his advantage, playing one tribe against the other and eventually conquering the entire country. During the colonial period, priests from various Catholic sects were busy converting (and virtually enslaving) the Indian population that remained after the wars, and European diseases took their toll (between 75% and 90% of the native population was lost after the Conquest). The church and the wealthy Spanish landowners thus had a ready, if unwilling, work force at their command. They used this conscripted work force to make themselves wealthy.

Pure Spanish blood is rare in Guatemala today, but the Ladino population, which is descended from marriages of Indians and Spaniards, are firmly in control of the government. Those of Indian ancestry (generally defined as anyone who wears traditional attire and farms on subsistence plots) have almost no power. Although Guatemala is ostensibly a democracy (with elections held every four years), the military wields a great deal of power. Throughout the past 100 years, the military has often taken control of government, suspending the constitution as necessary to maintain its power. There is a great disparity between the rich and the poor. Wealthy landowners own nearly all of the land in the country, with peasants forced to farm small plots on the least productive land. This disparity has led to constant conflicts for nearly 200 years as the liberal parties have tried to wrest power from the wealthy and the church.

Today there is still guerrilla activity throughout much of Guatemala, but on a relatively small scale. The guerrillas, primarily poor rural Indians from the highlands and left-wing intellectuals, continue to demand land reform.

DATELINE

owned company and the largest landowner in Guatemala, to lose much of its land.

• **1954** CIA–backed Guatemalan exiles invade Guatemala from Honduras and overthrow government.

• **1950s–Present** Scattered guerrilla activity continues.

2. ART, ARCHITECTURE & LITERATURE

ART The Mayas, who reached a cultural peak around A.D. 600, have left an amazing legacy of intricately beautiful works of art. Stone carvings, pottery, and gold and jade jewelry give us some idea of the high level of artistic ability reached by this ancient culture. The stylized figures depicted on many works of Mayan art are actually historical records. Through these images, archeologists have been able to deduce a great deal about Mayan culture. The Museum of Archeology and Ethnology in Guatemala City has the most outstanding collection of pre-Columbian art in all of Central America, and the Popul Vuh Museum, also in Guatemala City, has a smaller but equally interesting collection.

ARCHITECTURE As long ago as 200 B.C., the Mayas were building at Tikal, an ancient religious center in the remote Petén region of Guatemala. Today the hundreds of pyramids, temples, and palaces that have been excavated make this one of the great archeological finds of the New World. Using limestone, the Mayas at Tikal erected one pyramid after another, often building directly on top of previously existing structures. Many of these buildings incorporated what has come to be known as the Mayan, or corbeled, arch. Although not a true arch (a keystone is not used), the Mayan arch allowed ancient architects to build structures entirely of stone, structures that have withstood the ravages of time and today are a testament to the architectural skills of Mesoamerica's greatest civilization. In 1979, Tikal was declared a "World Cultural and Natural Monument" by UNESCO.

With the Spanish Conquest came an entirely new form of architecture: Moorish influences, interpreted by Spanish architects, were incorporated into the many colonial cities erected by the Spanish throughout Guatemala. Unfortunately, Guatemala is a land of volcanic activity and is subject to earthquakes of devastating magnitude, so much of the country's colonial architecture has been destroyed over the years. However, the city of Antigua, once the capital of all Central America, although destroyed several times by earthquakes and floods, still preserves its colonial heritage. It was named a "Heritage of Humanity" by UNESCO in 1979. At one time, the city was the grandest in all the Americas, but after the devastating earthquake of 1773 many of the most grandiose churches, universities, and convents were destroyed. Today the ruins of these buildings have been turned into parks and museums, giving

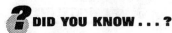

DID YOU KNOW . . . ?

- Tikal is the largest excavated Mayan ruin.
- Antigua was once the capital of all of Central America.
- There is a town on the Caribbean Coast where the people are predominantly black, with English as their mother tongue.
- The quetzal, described as the most beautiful bird in the world, is the national bird of Guatemala.
- Manatees live in the Río Dulce, a river that drains into the Caribbean Sea.
- The United Fruit Company was once the largest landholder in Guatemala.
- The Indians of the Guatemalan highlands still practice rituals passed down from the ancient Mayas.
- Lake Atitlán was formed by the crater of a giant extinct volcano.
- Guatemala City is the fourth capital of Guatemala; the others were destroyed by earthquakes, volcanic eruptions, and floods.

Antigua much of its charm. Regulations prohibiting obtrusive signs and advertising help the city retain its 17th-century atmosphere. There are literally dozens of colonial and colonial-style buildings of architectural interest here.

Guatemala City, on the other hand, has few historical buildings since over the years the city's colonial buildings were destroyed by earthquakes. Guatemala City's most architecturally noteworthy buildings are those of the Centro Cívico and the Centro Cultural Miguel Angel Asturias, constructed in the 1950s and 1960s. The facades of the former buildings are covered with murals, while the latter is designed to resemble the superstructure of a luxury cruise ship.

LITERATURE The single most significant piece of literature produced in Guatemala is the *Popol Vuh,* a history of the Quiché people written in the Mayan language sometime shortly after the Conquest. Although the original accordian-pleated codex is housed in a museum in Dresden, Germany, there is a beautiful reproduction in the Popol Vuh Museum in Guatemala City. It is an exact copy in every detail, down to the type of tree used to produce the paper. The book consists of both Mayan glyphs and small, colorful paintings. The original was discovered in the early 18th century in Chichicastenango and was translated into Spanish. Numerous editions of the *Popol Vuh* are now available in both Spanish and English and offer fascinating reading.

In 1992, Rigoberta Menchú, a Guatemalan woman of indigenous descent, won a Nobel Prize. Menchú, in writings such as *I, Rigoberta Menchú,* has spoken out for the rights of the indigenous people of Guatemala and has given these people an international voice. Another Guatemalan Nobel laureate, Miguel Angel Asturias, is known and loved for his novels and translations into Spanish of ancient Indian legends. Otto René Castillo is a revolutionary poet whose works are unavailable in Guatemala but are popular outside the country.

3. CULTURAL & SOCIAL LIFE

Guatemalan cultural life is decidedly stratified. The population of the country is almost evenly divided between the indigenous peoples (Indians) and the *ladinos* (those who can trace their ancestry to Spain). However, these are becoming very loose terms. Today an Indian who moves to the city and gives up his or her traditional dress in favor of North American or European fashions becomes a ladino; an Indian who becomes wealthy and gives up farming also may be labeled a ladino, as may any Indian who is educated. The term *indigeno* has come to refer almost exclusively to the poor peasants who cling to their traditional ways and still farm the rugged mountains of the Guatemalan highlands.

Down on the Caribbean Coast is yet a third culture, that of the English-speaking blacks who migrated from Jamaica in the 18th century. These people have nothing in common with the rest of Guatemala's population and maintain their isolation in the small town of Lívingston, which can be reached only by boat. In Lívingston, the sound of the marimba band, ubiquitous in the rest of the country, is replaced by reggae music from the Caribbean islands and, increasingly, by rap music from the United States.

RELIGION, MYTH & FOLKLORE   The melding of ancient Mayan traditions and religious beliefs with Roman Catholicism has created a singular form of Catholicism that is filled with obscure rituals and the worship of Mayan gods thinly disguised as saints. The Mayan religion was pantheistic, and many of the gods demanded human

GUATEMALAN TERMS
ARCHEOLOGICAL

Corbeled arch   False arch used in construction of Mayan buildings

Stela[e]   Stone with carved figures (usually of warriors, princes, or kings) and glyphs, erected as a record of a historic event

Preclassic Period   Mayan period from 300 B.C. to A.D. 300

Early Classic Period   Mayan period from A.D. 300 to 600

Late Classic Period   Mayan period from A.D. 600 to 900

Postclassic Period   Mayan period from A.D. 900 to the Conquest

MUSIC & DANCE

Marimba   Instrument related to the xylophone and also the music performed on this instrument—the most popular music in Guatemala

Palo Volador   "Flying pole," an acrobatic performance that has been popular in Guatemala since Mayan times; men spin from ropes tied to their ankles as they descend from a tall pole.

RELIGIOUS

Anda   Float carried in Holy Week processions

Cofrade   Member of a cofradía

Cofradías   Indian religious organizations that oversee various rituals in villages around the country.

Maximón   Mayan god who is found in several towns around the highlands, dressed in jacket, pants, and hat with a wooden mask for a face; Indians believe he answers their prayers

Pascual Abaj   Another Mayan god whose shrine is on a hill near Chichicastenango

MENU SAVVY

Cak Ik   Mayan stew made with turkey or chicken, plantains, and vegetables

Licuado   Milk- or water-based drink made in a blender with fresh fruit

Pepian   Thick stew made with chicken, vegetables, and pumpkin seeds

Plátanos   Plantains, similar to bananas

sacrifices. When Spanish priests arrived preaching the worship of yet another god, the Mayas of Guatemala were amenable and readily accepted Catholicism but continued to worship their old gods. Over the years, the old gods became associated with Catholic saints, and today every village and town has its patron saint, whose feast day is cause for great celebration. An important part of many fiestas is masked dancing. Several of these dances depict historical events. See "Performing Arts and Evening Entertainment" in this chapter for more information on masked dances.

In several towns in the highlands, a strange cult holds sway over the people. In these villages, the Indians turn to a god known as Maximón, or San Simón, for intervention in their lives. Maximón, although he looks like little more than a mannequin wearing a hat, is a very real god to these people, and he may be derived from the ancient Mayan god Mam. The people come to him to solve their problems, to protect them, to find them a wife or husband, and to bring them wealth. It is the way in which they worship Maximón that is the strangest: Cigar smoke is blown into his face, and liquor is poured into the mouth of the mask that serves as his face. There are Maximóns in Santiago Atitlán and Zunil, among other places. Should you go looking for Maximón, be sure to bring a gift—money, liquor, and cigars are probably the safest offerings.

Guatemalans as a rule are extremely devout, and nowhere is their devotion to the Catholic church more evident than in Antigua during Semana Santa (Holy Week), the week prior to Easter Sunday. During this week, solemn processions march through the streets of the city. Intricate "carpets" made of colored sawdust, flowers, and pine needles are constructed in the streets, only to be trampled by men and women who march through the city carrying massive wooden floats atop which stand sculptures of Christ, the Virgin Mary, and various saints. Men dressed as Roman soldiers and mourners in black or purple robes commemorate the death and resurrection of Christ amid clouds of incense and doleful music played by marching bands. The pageantry of these processions is unsurpassed anywhere in Latin America, and the devout march through the streets from morning until late at night. Even though the processions in Antigua are the largest and draw immense crowds of spectators, nearly every town and village in Guatemala has similar processions during Holy Week.

PERFORMING ARTS & EVENING ENTERTAINMENT   The sound of the marimba, a large wooden xylophone played with rubber mallets, permeates Guatemala just as mariachi music prevails in Mexico. The instrument is often so large that it takes several people to play it. The rhythms that are produced are complex and hypnotic. You'll find marimba bands performing at nearly all celebrations, in restaurants, and on the radio.

Celebrations in Guatemala often include masked dances that have their basis in ancient Mayan customs. The most popular dance is the dance of the conquistadors, in which dancers dressed as Pedro de Alvarado and Tecún Umán symbolically reenact the battle that brought about the downfall of the Quiché people and the eventual conquest of Guatemala. By far the most famous "dance," if it can be called that, is the *palo volador* (the flying pole). In this breathtaking acrobatic display, two men climb to the top of a 60-foot pole, attach ropes to their ankles, and "fly" to the ground as the rope unwinds from the top of the pole. This ancient ritual is staged several times a year in different parts of the country, including Guatemala City and Chichicastenango.

Evening entertainment in Guatemala is pretty much restricted to going to the movies (U.S. movies dubbed in Spanish or with subtitles), hanging out in bars (a male-dominated activity), and going to discos.

SPORTS & RECREATION   The national sport of Guatemala is soccer (here known as *futbol*). Bicycle racing is also a very popular sport, and cyclists are frequently seen, especially on Sunday, puffing up the hill on the highway between Guatemala City and Antigua. Keep an eye out for cyclists when driving, especially if you are still on the road after dark, because some races go far into the night and the roads are not lit.

One favorite recreational activity among Guatemalans and tourists alike is volcano climbing. There are several volcanoes in the country that can easily be climbed in a day, and the views from the tops of these peaks can be spectacular if the weather is clear. Perhaps the most popular climb is up Pacaya Volcano, near Lake Amatitlán. It is possible to climb within about 100 yards of the cone of this active volcano (on a separate cone) and watch it erupt every few minutes.

4. FOOD & DRINK

FOOD Traditional Guatemalan cuisine is very similar to Mexican food in many ways. The staples are beans (here they are black beans) and corn in the form of tortillas. To these are added rice and perhaps a bit of stewed chicken. Such meals are not often found in restaurants, except in the simplest of *comedores* (basic food stalls most often found in or near markets). Restaurants throughout Guatemala lean heavily toward international food—with everything from chow mein to spaghetti showing up at nearly every meal.

Because the country has two coasts, it is not surprising that throughout Guatemala, good and inexpensive seafood is readily available. However, I suggest that you stay clear of any freshwater fish, which tend to have a muddy flavor, may come from very polluted rivers and lakes, and may even transmit cholera. Also avoid any type of *ceviche*, a raw seafood salad, which can also transmit cholera.

Pepian is the de facto national dish of Guatemala. It is a thick, often grainy stew made with chicken, vegetables, and toasted pumpkin seeds. *Cak ik* is a specialty of Cobán, a stew made with turkey or chicken, plantains (similar to bananas), and vegetables.

DRINKS Water and Soft Drinks Tap water in Guatemala is generally not safe to drink unless you treat it yourself. Hotels and restaurants often have large bottles of purified water on hand, from which they fill pitchers for their guests. If you have doubts about the water, it is best to avoid it. Tikal is one place where the water is notorious for making people sick. Bottled water, although relatively expensive, is readily available throughout the country, as is *agua mineral*, which is club soda. All major brands of soft drinks also are available. However, while in Guatemala you should take advantage of the delicious fresh juices and *licuados* (fruit juice blended with ice and water or milk), which are wonderful and very cheap. Some of my favorite licuados are those made with milk and papaya or mango. It is usually a good idea to get your licuado with milk and no ice to avoid consuming the water.

Beer, Wine, and Liquor Several brands of locally brewed beer are available at very reasonable prices throughout Guatemala. Virtually all the wines are imported and consequently are expensive; those imported from South America are the cheapest and often are quite good. All types of hard liquor are manufactured in Guatemala, with rum being the most popular.

IMPRESSIONS

The market at Guatemala is the only place where I have seen reality outdoing a Dutch still life.
—ALDOUS HUXLEY, *BEYOND THE MEXIQUE BAY*, 1934

5. RECOMMENDED BOOKS & FILMS

BOOKS The *Popol Vuh* (Simon & Schuster, 1986) is one of the only records we have of Mayan life before the Conquest. It provides fascinating insights into the history, culture, and religion of these pre-Columbian people.

If you're interested in learning more about Mayan art, I suggest *The Blood of Kings: Dynasty and Ritual in Maya Art* (George Braziller, Inc., 1986), by Linda Schele and Mary Ellen Miller, and *A Forest of Kings: The Untold Story of the Ancient Maya* (William Morrow, 1990), by Linda Schele and David Freidel, both of which are filled with excellent photos and in-depth information on specific sites and pieces of ancient art.

If you can find any English translations, or if you read Spanish, the novels and Indian legends translated into Spanish by Miguel Angel Asturias offer insight into Guatemalan life. Asturias won the Nobel Prize for Literature in 1967.

To learn more about the history of Central America, try *A Brief History of Central America* (University of California Press, 1989) by Hector Perez-Brignali, who is himself a Central American. If you want to gain a better understanding of the plight of Guatemalan Indians, *A Cry from the Heart* (Health Institutes Press, 1990), by V. David Schwantes, will certainly enlighten you. *Bridge of Courage* (Common Courage Press, 1994), by Jennifer Harbury, tells the life stories, through first-hand accounts, of Guatemalan peasants. *Guatemalan Women Speak* (EPICA, 1993), by Margaret Hooks, focuses on the lives of Guatemalan women and is told in their own words (translated into English). *I, Rigoberta Menchú* (Verso 1984), by Nobel Prize winner Rigoberta Menchú, also presents the struggle of Guatemala's indigenous people through the eyes of a Guatemalan Indian woman.

The classic travelogue to this region is Aldous Huxley's *Beyond the Mexique Bay,* a narrative of his travels through Guatemala, Belize, and Mexico in 1934; it's out-of-print, but your local library may have it. *Time Among the Maya* (Henry Holt, 1991), by Ronald Wright, is an interesting account of Wright's travels among the Mayas of Guatemala, Belize, and Mexico. Both contemporary and ancient Mayan life are explored.

The Long Night of White Chickens (Atlantic Monthly Press, 1992), by Francisco Goldman, is a critically acclaimed novel set in Guatemala and the United States. The book is the story of two men's love for a murdered Guatemalan woman.

FILMS *When the Mountains Tremble* (1983) is an excellent documentary about the struggle of Guatemala's Indian peasants. Directed by Thomas Sigel and Pamela Yates, the film depicts the experiences of the young Rigoberta Menchú. Gregory Nava directed *El Norte* (1984), a very moving portrayal of two Guatemalan youths who leave their country in search of a better life in the United States.

CHAPTER 10

PLANNING A TRIP TO GUATEMALA

Once you have decided to visit Guatemala, you're likely to have a lot of questions: How much is it going to cost? When should I go? Where in Guatemala should I plan to go? How do I get there? How do I get around once I get there? These are some of the many questions that this chapter will answer for you. In addition, you'll find information on health precautions that you should take before and during your visit, saving money on flights to Guatemala, studying Spanish in Guatemala, and finding more information before you leave home and after you arrive. In short, you'll find all the information that you'll need to make your visit as easy and enjoyable as you dreamed it would be. For information about travel insurance and any vaccinations or other health preparations you should make before coming to Central America, see "Health, Insurance, and Other Concerns in Chapter 2, "Planning a Trip to Costa Rica."

1. INFORMATION, ENTRY REQUIREMENTS & MONEY

SOURCES OF INFORMATION

For information on Guatemala before you leave home, you can contact the **Guatemalan Tourist Commission**, 299 Alhambra Circle, Suite 510, Coral Gables, FL 33134 (tel. 305/442-0651 or 442-0412; fax 305/442-1013). Within Guatemala, you will find **INGUAT** (Guatemalan Tourist Commission) offices or desks in Guatemala City (downtown and at the airport), Antigua, El Petén (Santa Elena Airport), Panajachel, and Quetzaltenango. See the appropriate chapters for details.

ENTRY REQUIREMENTS

DOCUMENTS To enter Guatemala, citizens of the **United States, Canada, Great Britain, Ireland,** and **Australia** will need a passport and either a visa or Tourist Card. (For information on getting a passport in the United States, see "Entry Requirements" in Chapter 2, "Planning a Trip to Costa Rica.") Visas are only available at embassies and consulates (free for United States citizens, $10 for all others), and are valid for 30 days per visit but can be used for multiple entries for up to three years. It is also possible to get a Tourist Card when you arrive in Guatemala. These cards cost $5 and are valid for a single entry of up to 90 days. If you are flying into Guatemala, get your Tourist Card from your airline or in the airport when you arrive. If you are arriving overland or by boat, you'll get your Tourist Card at the border. Citizens of **New Zealand** must have a visa. However, there is no Guatemalan embassy in New Zealand.

Guatemalan embassies and consulates include the following:

In the United States: Consular Section, 2220 R St. NW, Washington, DC 20008 (tel. 202/745-4952); 2500 Wilshire Blvd., Suite 820, Los Angeles, CA 90057 (tel. 213/365-9251); 870 Market St., Suite 667, San Francisco, CA 94102 (tel. 415/788-5651); 300 Sevilla Ave., Suite 210, Coral Gables, FL 33134 (tel. 305/443-4828); 180 North Michigan Ave., Suite 1035, Chicago, IL 60601 (tel. 312/332-3170); 57 Park Ave., New York, NY 10016 (tel. 212/686-3837); 10200 Richmond Ave., Suite 270, Houston, TX 77042 (tel. 713/953-9531).

In Canada: 130 Albert St., Suite 1010, Ottawa, Ontario K1P 5G4 (tel. 613/233-7188).

In the United Kingdom: 13 Fawcett St., London SW 10 (tel. 441/351-3042).

CUSTOMS When you enter Guatemala, Customs may or may not search your bags. You can legally bring in two bottles of liquor, two cartons of cigarettes, one still camera plus six rolls of film (rarely if ever enforced), and one movie camera.

MONEY

CURRENCY/CASH The unit of currency in Guatemala is the **quetzal (Q).** It's named after Guatemala's national symbol, the freedom-loving quetzal bird, which was revered by the ancient Mayas. One quetzal is divided into 100 centavos. There are 1-, 5-, 10-, and 25-centavo coins and bills in denominations of 50 centavos and 1, 5, 10, 20, 50, and 100 quetzals. At this writing, $1 U.S. will buy you Q5.80, so each quetzal is worth about 17¢.

THE QUETZAL, THE U.S. DOLLAR & THE BRITISH POUND

At press time, $1 was worth approximately Q5.80, and £1 was worth about Q9; these rates of exchange were used to calculate the dollar values given in this guide. This rate does fluctuate and may not be the same when you travel to Guatemala. Therefore the following table should be used only as a guide:

Q	U.S. $	U.K. £	Q	U.S. $	U.K. £
1	.20	.13	30	5.20	3.40
2	.35	.23	35	6.05	3.90
3	.55	.35	40	6.90	4.5
4	.70	.45	45	7.75	5.00
5	.90	.60	50	8.65	5.60
6	1.05	.70	75	12.95	8.40
7	1.20	.80	100	17.25	11.20
8	1.40	.90	200	34.50	22.40
9	1.55	1.00	300	51.75	33.60
10	1.75	1.10	400	69.00	44.80
15	2.60	1.70	500	86.20	56.00
20	3.45	2.20	750	103.45	84.00
25	4.35	2.80	1000	172.45	112.00

American dollars can be exchanged for Guatemalan quetzals ("quetzal*es*" in Spanish) easily and legally in many hotels as well as at banks. If a bank isn't open, ask at a hotel. However, banks always give a better rate. You will also get better rates of exchange the closer you are to Guatemala City. Ask around. The dollar-to-quetzal exchange rate began climbing late in 1989 and has been variable since, although from one week to the next there are only slight changes. It is a good idea not to change too much at one time just in case the rate changes to your benefit.

If you need to exchange other foreign currency (Canadian dollars, German marks, English pounds, and so forth), you'll find it most convenient to exchange it at a bank. Banks are found nearly everywhere that you are likely to go.

By the way, in Guatemalan villages you may hear the Maya words *pisto* for money (quetzals) and *leng* for centavos.

It's good to have $25 or so in U.S. dollars of small denominations with you at all times for emergencies (many places will take them if you don't have the proper local currency).

TRAVELER'S CHECKS Traveler's checks drawn in U.S. dollars are only slightly more difficult to change than cash dollars. You can change them at banks and hotels all over Guatemala, although hotel rates are usually not very good. Even bank rates vary considerably, so it is a good idea to shop around. It can take quite a while to change traveler's checks at a bank, so go as early in the day as possible, when the lines are shorter.

WHAT THINGS COST IN GUATEMALA CITY	U.S. $
Taxi from the airport to the city center	6.05
Local telephone call	.02
Double at Camino Real Hotel (deluxe)	140.00
Double at Hotel Pan American (moderate)	71.40
Double at Chalet Suizo (budget)	16.00
Lunch for one at Altuna (moderate)	5.00
Lunch for one at Cafetería el Roble (budget)	1.20
Dinner for one, without wine at Teppanyaki (deluxe)	22.00
Dinner for one, without wine at El Gran Pavo (moderate)	10.00
Dinner for one, without wine at Restaurant Ruby (budget)	5.00
Bottle of beer	.90
Coca-Cola	.45
Cup of coffee	.45
Roll of ASA 100 Kodacolor film, 36 exposures	6.40
Admission to the Popul Vuh Museum	1.75
Movie ticket	1.10
Theater ticket to the National Theater	1.75–20.00

CREDIT CARDS The international credit cards most widely accepted in Guatemala are MasterCard, VISA, Diners Club, and American Express. Very low-budget hotels and restaurants rarely accept credit cards, but moderate or expensive ones usually do. As in most places, it is very difficult to rent a car without a major credit card.

2. WHEN TO GO — CLIMATE, EVENTS & HOLIDAYS

CLIMATE

There are basically two seasons in Guatemala—the dry season (*verano* or summer) and the rainy season (*invierno* or winter). The rainy season lasts from May to October, and the dry season lasts from November to April. In the rainy season, it rains virtually every day, sometimes all day but sometimes only in the afternoon. It will also be chillier in the highlands and muggier in the lowlands during these months. During the dry season, the sun shines nearly every day, and there is almost never any rain. Days, even high in the mountains, are warm, but nights can be quite cold.

Average annual temperatures in Guatemala's highlands are 64° to 68°F; in Guatemala City, 68° to 72°F; in El Petén and along the Atlantic Highway, 77° to 86°F.

Average Monthly Temperatures & Rainfall in Guatemala City

	Jan	Feb	Mar	Apr	May	June	July	Aug	Sept	Oct	Nov	Dec
Temp °F	63	65	69	69	73	71	70	70	70	67	65	64
Days of Rain	2	2	2	5	8	20	17	16	17	13	6	2

HOLIDAYS

Official holidays in Guatemala include January 1, New Year's Day; Wednesday, Thursday, and Friday before Easter; May 1, Labor Day; June 30, Army Day; August 15, Assumption of the Virgin Mary; September 15, Independence Day; October 20, Revolution Day; November 1, All Saints' Day; December 24, Christmas Eve; December 25, Christmas; and December 31, New Year's Eve.

GUATEMALA CALENDAR OF EVENTS

FEBRUARY

☐ **Tecún Uman Day,** Guatemala City. The Dance of the Conquest is performed around at the entrance to Parque Aurora. February 20.

MARCH/APRIL

☐ **Semana Santa (Holy Week) Processions,** Antigua. Devout Roman Catholics, many dressed in robes, carry huge floats through the streets of the city. Streets are decorated with "carpets" made from flowers, colored sawdust, and pine needles. Make your hotel reservations months in advance and confirm often. The week before Easter.

☐ **Semana Santa,** Esquipulas. Pilgrims line up to kiss the foot of the Cristo Negro in the town's basilica. The week prior to Easter.

☐ **Semana Santa,** Zunil and Santiago Atitlán. During this time, these two towns parade their "evil" saint Maximón through the streets and crucify him. The week before Easter.

NOVEMBER

☐ **All Saint's Day.** In Santiago Sacatepequez, giant kites are flown from the graveyard; in Todas Santos Cuchamatán, there are horse races and the Dance of the Conquest. November 1.

DECEMBER

☐ **The Day of the Devil,** Guatemala City. Bonfires in the streets and lots of firecrackers are lit to burn out the spirit of the devil for the year. December 7.
☐ **Feast of St. Thomas,** Chichicastenango. Quiché Mayans gather to celebrate the feast day of their patron saint. The famous "flying pole" is erected during this festival. December 18–21.

3. WHAT TO PACK

CLOTHING Bring extra-warm clothes for the mountain towns, which can get quite cold at night at any time of year. Good walking shoes are an absolute necessity here—even sidewalks can be rough and uneven and streets are often cobblestone, which is hard on the feet no matter what kind of shoes you are wearing. Furthermore, a good pair of walking shoes is essential to enjoying the Mayan ruins of Tikal. You want good traction when climbing steep pyramids. An umbrella in the rainy season is much more useful than a raincoat, which will cause you to sweat in the heat.

OTHER ITEMS Bring plenty of insect repellent, especially when going to the lowland towns. It will help keep mosquitoes off you at night—very important, since malaria is still found in many parts of Guatemala. Sunscreen is necessary if you plan to spend a lot of time outdoors in the mountains, where the sun is much stronger. Although the water is supposedly safe to drink in cities and towns, I prefer not to take chances, especially in remote areas. I now carry a filter straw with me whenever I travel to places where the water is questionable. These straws are available in stores that sell camping equipment and are good for filtering about 30 gallons of water before they have to be thrown away. An alternative is to carry a bit of iodine, an eye dropper, and a water bottle for purifying your own water.

A few other items that have proven invaluable through countless trips all over the world are a Swiss army knife, a small flashlight, and a travel alarm clock or a watch with an alarm. In addition, I always wear a watch with a tiny built-in calculator, which can cost as little as $30 and is great for making quick exchange-rate calculations.

4. TIPS FOR THE DISABLED, SENIORS, SINGLES & STUDENTS

See "Tips for the Disabled, Seniors, Singles & Students" in Chapter 2 for more information.

FOR THE DISABLED Guatemala is not an easy country for the disabled to get around in. The streets are often narrow, with broken or nonexistent sidewalks, and in some cases they are even of cobblestone. Public transit is overcrowded, so a private vehicle is an absolute necessity. Few, if any, hotels or public buildings are accessible to the handicapped. However, don't be put off if you have your heart set on visiting Guatemala. I once met a man in a wheelchair on the remote Río Dulce. He had hired a boat to take him from Lvingston on the coast to the old Spanish fort of San Felipe, three hours up river.

FOR SENIORS You won't find senior-citizen discounts in Guatemala, but the prices are so low that they really aren't necessary.

FOR SINGLES Though single travelers are discriminated against in hotel pricing just as they are in so many other places, if you are traveling on a budget, you will find that room rates are surprisingly low.

FOR STUDENTS Students may want to look into studying Spanish for a while in Antigua (see "Language Programs," below) or Quetzaltenango. The courses are quite inexpensive and you can save more by staying with a local family.

5. ALTERNATIVE/ADVENTURE TRAVEL

LANGUAGE PROGRAMS

Every year, thousands of people come to Guatemala from Europe and North America to study Spanish in Antigua, Quetzaltenango, and elsewhere in Guatemala. There are literally dozens of schools offering courses and one-on-one tutoring at very reasonable prices. Some people make Antigua or Quetzaltenango their first stop in Latin America so that they can learn some Spanish before traveling on to other countries. Listed below are some of the better schools in Antigua and Quetzaltenango. When choosing a Spanish school, you should find out how many hours of study you will receive each day and whether this is one-on-one or group instruction, clarify whether you want to study grammar or conversation, have a look at the textbooks that will be used to see if they seem well written, and find out whether the price includes meals and accommodations with a local family. All rates listed below include room and board. Schools in Antigua usually offer anywhere from four to six hours of classes a day.

IN ANTIGUA

Academia de Español Tecún Umán, 6a Calle Poniente no. 34-A (apdo. 68), Antigua Guatemala 03901 (tel. 502-9/322-792). Weekly tuition: Q580 ($100) for 20 hours of one-on-one classes.

Centro Lingüístico Maya, 5a Calle Poniente no. 20, Antigua Guatemala (tel. 502-9/320-656). Weekly tuition: Q725 ($125) for 20 hours of classes.

Christian Spanish Academy, 6a Avenida Norte no. 15 (Apdo. 320), Antigua Guatemala 03001 (tel. 502-9/323-922; fax 502-9/323-760). Weekly tuition: Q812 ($140) for 20 hours of one-on-one classes. This is one of the larger schools in Antigua.

Proyecto Lingüístico Francisco Marroquin, 7a Calle Poniente no. 31 (Apdo. 237), Antigua Guatemala 03901 (tel. 502-9/323-777; fax 502-9/322-886; or tel. toll free in the U.S. 800/552-2051). Weekly tuition: Q1,015 ($175) for 30 hours of one-on-one classes. This is one of the largest, oldest, and most respected schools in Antigua.

Sevilla Spanish Academy, 6a Calle Oriente no. 3 (Apdo. 380), Parque La Union, Antigua Guatemala (tel./fax 502-9/323-609). Weekly tuition: Q580 ($100) 20 hours of one-on-one classes.

IN QUETZALTENANGO

Desarrollo del Pueblo Instituto de Español, Diagonal 12 6-28 (Apdo. 41), Quetzaltenango (tel./fax 502-9/61-4624). Weekly tuition: Q667 ($115) for 25 hours of one-on-one classes. This school also is involved with public health projects in various nearby villages.

Casa de Español Xelaju, 9a Calle 11-26, Zona 1 (Apdo. 302), Quetzaltenango (tel. 502-9/61-2628); or in the U.S.: 1022 St. Paul Avenue, St. Paul, MN 55116 (tel./fax 612/690-9471). Weekly tuition: Q754 ($130) to Q899 ($155) for 25 hours of classes (higher rate is for summer months). Weaving classes are also available.

Instituto Central America, 1a Calle 16-93, Zona 1, Quetzaltenango (tel./fax 502-9/63-1871); or in the U.S.: R.R. [–]2, Box 101, Stanton, NE 68779 (tel. 402/439-2943). Weekly tuition: Q580 ($100) to Q696 ($120) for 25 hours of classes (higher rate is for summer months). Various development projects are supported by this school.

Proyecto Lingüístico Quetzaltenango de Español, 5a Calle 2-40 (Apdo.

114), Zona 1, Quetzaltenango (tel./fax 502-9/63-1061); or in the U.S.: Hermandad Educativa, P.O. Box 205-337, Brooklyn, NY 11220-0006 (tel. 718/965-8522; fax 718/965-4643). Weekly tuition: Q580 ($100) to Q725 ($125) for 25 hours of one-on-one classes (higher rate is for summer months). This school also offers classes in the small village of Todos Santos Cuchumatán.

RIVER TRIPS

The ancient Mayas of El Petén had a far-flung empire that was connected by river routes, the old Mayan trade routes, that crossed El Petén and extended into Mexico. Trips on these rivers include days of river travel by outboard-powered boats through jungles, with stops at several remote Mayan ruins. **Ecoviajes Guayacán,** 11 Calle 3-49, Zona 1, Oficina no. 8, Guatemala City (tel. 502-2/513-753; fax 502-2/510-981), and **Tropical Tours,** 4a Calle 2-51, Zona 10, Guatemala City (tel./fax 502-2/323-748 or 345-893), are two companies offering such trips. If you're more interested in white-water rafting, contact **Maya Expeditions,** 15 Calle 1-91, Zona 10, Edificio Tauro, Loc. 104, Guatemala City (tel. 502-2/374-666), which offers rafting trips on the Cahabon and Usumacinta rivers. A 4-day trip costs Q864.20 ($149).

BICYCLE TRIPS

Montaña Maya Mountain Bike Tours, 6a Avenida Sur no. 12-B, Antigua Guatemala (tel. 502-9/322-768), offers trips ranging in length from half a day to a week or longer. Longer tours include 2- and 3-day rides between Antigua and Lake Atitlán and a week-long ride through the high plateaus of the Cuchumatán Mountains. Prices range from $100 for a 2-day, 1-night ride to $350 for a 7-day ride. Any of these rides will give you glimpses of Guatemala that you would not normally get while traveling by bus or car.

6. GETTING THERE

BY PLANE

Airlines serving Guatemala City from the United States include American Airlines (tel. toll free 800/433-7300), Aviateca (tel. toll free 800/327-9832), Continental (tel. toll free 800/231-0856), Lacsa (tel. toll free 800/225-2272), Mexicana (tel. toll free 800/531-7921), Taca (tel. toll free 800/535-8780), and United Airlines (tel. toll free 800/241-6522). Airlines serving Guatemala City from Europe include American Airlines and Continental from London, Iberia from Spain, and KLM from Amsterdam. Alternatively, you can fly British Airways or Delta Airlines to Miami and then transfer to another airline.

Flores Airport, which is the gateway to Tikal ruins, has service from Cancun, Mexico, on Aerocaribe and Aviateca, and from Belize City, Belize, on Tropic Air. See Chapter 11 for details.

BEST FOR THE BUDGET   These days there doesn't seem to be any particular airline that offers consistently lower prices. When rates at one airline go up, rates at all the other airlines follow, and vice versa. However, it pays to check the various Central American airlines, which tend to charge a bit less because their flights make more stops. In 1994 the lowest airfares to Guatemala City from most North American cities ranged from $450 to $650.

Bucket Shops   There is almost no reason to pay the regular full airfare for any international ticket. In nearly every major city in the United States and Britain, there are now discount ticket agencies known as bucket shops or ticket consolidators or brokers. These companies sell airline tickets on major carriers at a substantial discount over what you would pay the airline for the same ticket. In many cases, low-cost tickets that would be nonrefundable through an airline are refundable with a $100 penalty through a bucket shop. You'll find bucket shops advertised in major

FROMMER'S SMART TRAVELER: AIRFARES

1. Check the ads for discounted plane tickets in the Sunday travel section of major-city newspapers. These tickets can be $100 to $200 cheaper than the lowest standard airfare.
2. Consider getting a discounted ticket from your departure city to one of the Central American gateway cities (Miami, New Orleans, Houston, or Los Angeles), and combine this with a discount ticket from one of those cities on to Guatemala.
3. Check out the small Central American airlines that fly to Guatemala.
4. You'll usually save money if you take a "milk run" (flight that makes several stops) rather than a direct flight.
5. Always ask for the lowest-priced fare, which will usually be a midweek departure. Be flexible and you can save money.

newspapers (which are often available at your local library, even if you live in a small town). These ads often are misleading because the price listed may be available only to students and does not include taxes; but even when all the additional charges are included, you almost always save money at a bucket shop.

REGULAR AIRFARES   Regular, full-price airfares are often double the lowest fare ($900 to $1,000) and first-class fares are often triple the lowest fare ($1,200 to $1,600).

BY BUS

There are bus connections into Guatemala from Mexico, Belize, Honduras, and El Salvador. Buses leave San Cristobal de las Casas, Mexico, for the border station at Ciudad Cuauhtemoc, in the mountains. After border formalities, a Guatemalan bus heads for Huehuetenango and Guatemala City. The bus from the border will drop you at transfer points for Quetzaltenango, Chichicastenango, Panajachel, or Antigua if you wish. If you are coming from Tapachula, Mexico, you can take a bus from the downtown bus station or catch a minibus to the border crossing at either Talisman or Tecún Umán. There will be buses waiting on the Guatemalan side of the border. These buses are bound for Guatemala City with a connection to Quetzaltenango if desired. From Belize, you can catch a bus bound for the border town of Benque Viejo, Belize, in either Belize City or San Ignacio. Depending on which bus you catch, you may be taken all the way to the border station or may be dropped at the bus station in Benque Viejo, in which case you will need to take a taxi (inexpensive) the rest of the way. This route is favored by those wishing to visit the impressive Mayan ruins at Tikal. After border formalities, catch the waiting bus. You then continue, down a very rough dirt road, to the city of Flores. If you leave early enough in the morning, it is possible to get off this bus at El Cruce and catch a connecting bus directly to Tikal. You will be approached by money changers at all of these border stations; although these changers don't give very favorable rates (unless you have dollars or traveler's checks), they often are the only choice you have.

You can shorten procedures at the border a bit by getting your Tourist Card or visa in advance at a Guatemalan consulate, but don't spend a day doing it. If you're near a consulate (hours are usually 9am to 2pm weekdays) it's a good plan; if not, you can always get a Tourist Card at the border. The best place to get a Tourist Card or visa in advance is the Guatemalan Embassy in Mexico City or Belize City or the Guatemalan Consulate in Tapachula. Tourist cards cost $5.

BY CAR

The same routes that apply to buses also are available to cars. However, keep in mind that if you're driving from Belize, you're going to travel some of the worst roads that you have ever seen between the Guatemalan border and El Cruce 105 kilometers (65 miles) away. Even after you reach the city of Flores, you have an equally bad road to take to get to the rest of Guatemala. This route is nearly impassable in the rainy season and very difficult during the rest of the year. Only try it if your car has high clearance and, preferably, four-wheel drive. Armed robberies are frequent on the road from the Belize border to Flores or Tikal, so you may want to avoid this road. From Tehuantepec, Mexico, you can head either to Tapachula and the Pacific Slope road to Guatemala City or to Tuxtla Gutierrez and San Cristobal de las Casas for the high mountain road to Guatemala City. The low road along the Pacific Slope goes through lush tropical country and a few pretty towns. Straighter and faster than the high road, it still has several disadvantages: It's heavily trafficked (especially when the sugarcane harvest is on), hot and muggy all the time, and except for the lushness, there's not much to stop and see along the road. The high road, by contrast, is reached by going through San Cristobal, one of the prettiest places in Mexico; there is virtually no traffic for the first 161 kilometers (100 miles) into Guatemala; the mountain scenery is breathtaking; and interesting towns and villages abound all along the road. Perhaps you can see that I prefer the high road, despite its disadvantages: some landslides in the rainy season (late May to October), even though they are cleared away pretty quickly by road crews, and a curvy (but very good and safe) 40-m.p.h. mountain road.

The border-crossing procedures are the same at both posts. See the preceding section, "By Bus," for information on shortening border procedures.

The road from San Cristobal de las Casas, Mexico, is fairly fast. It's slightly over 161 kilometers (100 miles) from San Cristobal to Ciudad Cuauhtemoc, the border station, and you should be able to cover it in about 2½ hours. After winding through the mountains east of San Cristobal, you descend to a plain before heading into the mountains that mark the border. The first Customs post you'll come to is where you hand in your car papers and Tourist Card (you fill out a new one when you return from Guatemala). Go on to the border proper, about a mile down the road, and pass the barrier into Guatemala.

You must get a Guatemalan Tourist Card ($5) right across the border, if you don't already have a visa. After getting your card (have your passport), drive on for a mile or so to the Customs inspection station, where you'll get your car papers, usually after a fairly serious look at the car and its contents. You may have to open a few bags, but it's wise just to follow the inspector around and do exactly and only what he or she asks.

While you're getting your car papers, someone will wash your tires with a disinfectant solution. This fumigation is required and costs a few dollars—a bothersome but fairly minor nuisance. The entire border crossing takes about an hour, and the whole procedure is quite painless. The Guatemalan border stations keep regular business hours: 8am to noon and 2 to 6pm Monday through Friday, 8am to noon on Saturday. You can cross at other hours and on Sunday, but you'll end up paying a little extra. All in all, expect to pay around $25 to get across the border.

Note that Mexican auto insurance is not valid in Guatemala. Buy Guatemalan insurance through your agent at home, or through the AAA, or within Guatemala. It is usually available at border crossings.

Also note that your car permit is only valid for 30 days, though your Tourist Card is valid for 90 days. It is possible to get your car papers extended, but only in Guatemala City, and it is a time consuming and difficult process.

PACKAGE TOURS

Clark Tours, 9 Boston St., Suite 10, Lynn, MA 09104 (tel. 617/581-0844, or toll free 800/223-6764), has been organizing tours to Guatemala since 1929. This company is one of the biggest and best known in Guatemala, but it is also one of the most expensive. For less expensive tours, contact **Destination Miami,** 777 NW 72 Avenue, Lobby 21, Miami, FL 33126 (tel. toll free 800/226-TOUR).

If you are already in Guatemala, you can contact Clark Tours in the lobbies of the Hotel Camino Real, 14 Calle 0-20, Zona 10, Guatemala City (tel. 682-056), the Hotel Las Américas, Avenida Las Américas 9-08, Zona 13, Guatemala City (tel. 390-666), or the Hotel Princess Reforma, 13 Calle 7-65, Zona 9, Guatemala City (tel. 341-035). Another good tour operator to try is **Total Travel,** Avenida Reforma 1-50, Zona 9, Guatemala City (tel. 313-711 or 320-795).

7. GETTING AROUND

BY PLANE

Tikal is probably the only place in Guatemala that you will want to reach by air. Airfare between Guatemala City and Flores (the closest city to the Tikal ruins) is $65 to $90 one way. There are daily flights on Aviateca, Avcom, Tikal Jets, and Tapsa. If you are a very serious student of archeology, you may want to charter a plane to reach some of the remote Mayan sites. Such a charter flight, in a small plane, can work out to be fairly inexpensive if you have enough people to fill the plane.

BY BUS

Every town of any size in Guatemala has several bus companies that operate to surrounding towns and to the capital; minibus services connect the smaller villages or between towns a short distance apart.

BY CAR

CAR RENTALS Car rentals are available in Guatemala City, Antigua, Quetzaltenango, and Flores/Santa Elena. See Chapter 11, "Getting Around," for more information.

GASOLINE Unleaded gasoline is rarely available in Guatemala. Rental cars use regular gasoline. If you're from the U.S., expect gasoline to cost slightly more than you are used to paying.

DRIVING RULES The most important driving rule here is to stop for police and military checkpoints and blockades, which you will encounter frequently. Present the officer with your driver's license (international driver's licenses are best but not necessary), your vehicle registration papers, and perhaps your rental agreement. You should get everything back within a minute and be on your way. *Remember:* Never drive without your passport. Occasionally, it is not the police but leftist guerrillas who have barricaded the road. Should you encounter one of these barricades, do as you are instructed and you will likely be sent on your way unharmed. Otherwise, driving rules in Guatemala are basically the same as they are in the United States, except that you must be 18 years old to drive. Also keep in mind that if you see a pile of leaves, grass, or branches piled in the road, it is a signal that there is a vehicle stopped on the road ahead.

SAFETY Bandits are a bigger problem than guerrillas these days. During my last visit several carloads of tourists were robbed on the road from the Belize border to Tikal. No one was harmed by the armed bandits, but the incidents reinforced the fact that Guatemala can be a dangerous place, especially if you are driving your own car. Always ask in San Ignacio, Belize, if there have been recent robberies before heading out on this road. Though these armed robberies are mostly confined to remote areas of the country, they can happen almost anywhere. Just do as you are told and you won't be harmed. I suggest getting a good travel insurance policy that covers you for theft, and make sure that the company does not exclude Guatemala because of the guerrilla activity that has been going on there for decades.

MAPS Ask for a map when you rent a car. These maps are about the best that are readily available. If you want to get a map before you arrive, contact an INGUAT (Guatemalan Tourist Commission) office or visit a travel book store. See "Information, Entry Requirements & Money" in this chapter for addresses and phone numbers.

BREAKDOWNS If you should have a breakdown, immediately pile some branches in the road at least 100 feet on either side of your car. Wait for help from the national police or flag down a bus and ride to the nearest town in search of a mechanic.

BY FERRY

There are a few ferries in Guatemala that you should know about. It is possible to enter the country from Belize on a ferry that plies between Punta Gorda, Belize, and Puerto Barrios, Guatemala. The ferry makes the trip a couple of times a week. Another ferry also runs between Puerto Barrios and Lívingston, across the mouth of the Río Dulce. There are also boats that make regular runs between Lívingston and the town of Río Dulce, which is several hours up the river. There are also several ferries that operate on Lake Atitlán, providing service between Panajachel and several small villages on the shore of the lake. See the pertinent chapters for details on these ferries.

HITCHHIKING

Because buses in Guatemala are so cheap and go nearly everywhere in the country, you should not need to hitchhike. However, if you're driving a car, you will often notice hitchhikers. It is very common for hitchhikers to wait at toll booths and highway police check points. Often you will be asked by an officer if you can give someone a ride.

FINDING AN ADDRESS

The street-numbering system in Guatemala is logical, easy to use, and found in every town. In fact, the system is so good that there's almost no excuse for getting lost anywhere but in Guatemala City! Once you get the hang of it, you'll be on your way to the exact location of any hotel or restaurant. Here's how it works: Every town is planned on a grid with avenidas running roughly north to south and calles running east to west. Addresses are given in the following form: 2a. Av. 4-17, which means that the place you're after is on 2nd Avenue, at 4th Calle, number 17 (2a is "Spanish" for 2nd, 3a for 3rd, and so on). You can even tell what side of the street the building will be on. If the street number is even, it'll be on the right side; if the number is odd, it'll be on the left—as you walk along the avenida toward higher-numbered calles. You can guess, then, that 3a. Av. 5-78 will be on 3rd Avenue between 5th and 6th calles (closer to 6th, as the house number is a high one), on the right side. Once you get the hang of it, you'll see that it's a marvelous system.

One last note: Each town is also divided into zones, but in the small towns (everywhere but Guatemala City), almost every important place is in Zona 1. If a zone number does not appear as a part of any address given in this book, you can assume that the place you're looking for is in Zona 1.

8. SUGGESTED ITINERARIES

HIGHLIGHTS

The following are the top destinations to visit in Guatemala: 1) Antigua, 2) Chichicastenango, 3) Panajachel, 4) Quetzaltenango, 5) Tikal, and 6) Guatemala City.

PLANNING YOUR ITINERARY

IF YOU HAVE ONE WEEK

This is a rushed itinerary, but you will get an overview of Guatemala, its people, its history, and its landscape.

Day 1: Spend one day in Guatemala City visiting the museums.

Days 2 and 3: Settle into Antigua and explore this beautiful little colonial town for two days.

Day 4: Visit Chichicastenango if it is market day and spend the night there. If it is not market day, arrange your schedule accordingly.

Day 5: Return by way of Panajachel and beautiful Lake Atitlán, spending a day there.

Days 6 and 7: Spend your last two days visiting the Mayan ruins in Tikal.

IF YOU HAVE TWO WEEKS

With two weeks, you can spend more time in some of Guatemala's many beautiful locations.

Days 1 and 2: So that you won't have to carry your purchases around with you, head first to Tikal for two days. Don't buy anything here because prices are much lower in Chichicastenango and Panajachel.

Days 3 through 6: Make Antigua your base of operations for the next four days. Spend three days enjoying colonial Antigua, with perhaps a trip to climb a volcano or a visit to a nearby village. Take a day trip to Guatemala City to see the museums.

Day 7: From Antigua, head to Chichicastenango for market day and spend the night there.

Days 8 through 10: Continue on to Quetzaltenango, the heart of the highlands, the next day. Spend three days exploring the Indian villages near Quetzaltenango.

Days 11 through 14: By now you should be ready for a rest, so head to Panajachel and relax on the beach of this volcanic lake for four days, taking ferries to the little villages that ring the lake.

IF YOU HAVE THREE WEEKS

Days 1 and 2: Head first to Tikal for two days.

Days 3 and 4: After returning to Guatemala City, take a bus to Cobán for two days and visit the quetzal preserve and other natural wonders of this mountainous region.

Days 5 through 7: Continue toward the Caribbean Coast, but turn north to Río Dulce and take a boat down the river to Lívingston. You will probably have to spend the night in Río Dulce. Spend a day in Lívingston or Puerto Barrios.

Days 8 and 9: Head back toward Guatemala City, with stops at the ruins of Quiriguá and Copán.

Day 10: Spend a day visiting the museums of Guatemala City, then head for Antigua.

Days 11 through 13: Spend three days exploring Antigua.

Day 14: Go to Chichicastenango for market day and spend the night.

Days 15 through 17: Continue on to Quetzaltenango. Spend three days there visiting small villages on their market days.

Days 18 through 21: Head to Panajachel and Lake Atitlán for four days of rest and recreation.

THEMED CHOICES

Archeology buffs will want to take in Guatemala's many Mayan ruins, which include Tikal and several smaller and more remote sites in the Petén region. You might end up spending a week or more in this area. After flying back to Guatemala, you should head next for the ruins in Copán, Honduras, just over the border from Guatemala. This will probably take you another two or three days. Three much less impressive sites are Iximché near Lake Atitlán, Quiriguá near Puerto Barrios, and Zaculeu outside Huehuetenango. The huge carved-stone heads in La Democracia also are worth an excursion.

FROMMER'S FAVORITE
GUATEMALA EXPERIENCES

A Boat Ride Down the Río Dulce   Long narrow boats with outboard motors carry passengers between Río Dulce and Lívingston, stopping at a manatee preserve en route. Forested mountains rise up on either side of the river, and along its banks are the huts of fishermen for whom the river is the only link to the outside world.

Chichicastenango on Market Day   Guatemalan textiles are some of the most beautiful in the world, and Chichicastenango is the place to buy them. The local Indians wear colorful traditional costumes, and age-old rituals based on Mayan rites are performed in front of the town's main church and on a hillside just outside of town. There are great deals here late in the afternoon, when vendors are packing up their goods.

Antigua During Semana Santa   During the week prior to Easter, Antigua's cobblestone streets are the scene of religious processions in which thousands of people participate, carrying heavy religious floats on their shoulders as they march slowly through incense-filled streets.

Dawn and Dusk In Tikal   At the opening and close of each steamy day, the ruins come alive with the roar of howler monkeys, the chatter of spider monkeys, the squawking of parrots and toucans, and the songs of countless species of other birds. If you're lucky, you might even see a "herd" of coatimundis.

Climbing Pacaya Volcano   This is one of the few active volcanoes in the world that you can hike to the top of while it's exploding and spewing out molten rock, but hiking to the top of Pacaya is not for the faint of heart. The last bit of climbing to reach the peak of the volcano's quiet cone (it has two cones) can be extremely difficult when the winds are strong.

9. ENJOYING GUATEMALA
ON A BUDGET

SAVING MONEY ON ACCOMMODATIONS

Whether you are traveling on $10 a day or $100, you can almost always find a place to your liking in cities throughout Guatemala. However, when you start venturing off into small towns and villages, you can expect the quality of accommodations to be fairly low. Though it is possible to pay anywhere from $2 to $200 a night for a room in Guatemala, most hotels are in the $15-to-$60 range. Within this range of prices are some of the best hotel deals in the world, but there are also some overpriced losers. You can be sure that if it is recommended in this book it is the best that you can do in a given price range, unless a new hotel has opened since the book was updated.

Because maintenance of budget hotels is often minimal to nonexistent, what was a wonderful and clean new hotel two years ago could have become dirty and run down by the time you visit. Keep your eyes and ears open for new hotels, these are often the best deals around, because hotels frequently open with low prices in order to develop a word-of-mouth following. If you do stumble across some very fine new accommodations, please let me know by writing to the address in the front of this book.

To give you some idea of what to expect from Guatemalan hotels, in the lowest price range you'll likely get a bed and a bare light bulb, that's it. You'll also get a lot of free noise, so be sure to bring some earplugs. Cheap hotels tend to be near discos, bars, and bus stops. Moving up a bit, say to $15 a night for a double, you can expect a fairly clean bathroom, a fan, a window, and a bedside stand or table, and usually a quiet night's sleep. For $25 to $30, expect a spacious room with a bit of character, perhaps a bit of colonial-style furnishings or a good view. For $50 to $100, you might find antiques and a bit of thought given to interior decor. Above $100 you move into the domain of international standards, where a hotel room will look roughly like any other hotel room in the world and service will be just what you would expect from an international hotel chain. These high-priced hotels generally are not a very good value in Guatemala.

Best Budget Bets The cheapest accommodations in Guatemala are usually called *pensiónes*. *Albergue* and *posada* are other titles often attached to budget lodgings in place of the word "hotel." In Antigua, a very popular tourist town, there are a few apartment hotels that represent an excellent value since each apartment comes with a kitchenette that allows you to do your own cooking.

Seasonal Discounts Keep in mind that nearly everyone in Guatemala goes on holiday during Semana Santa (Holy Week), the week prior to Easter. Not only are rooms difficult to find, but room rates are nearly double. Rates are also higher at Christmas and New Year's.

Other Money-Saving Strategies Although our budget in Guatemala allows us the luxury of a private bath, if you're willing to forsake this and walk down the hall, you will save considerably on your hotel bills. Rooms with air conditioning are also much more expensive and rarely necessary. If there are two of you traveling together, getting one double room instead of two singles will save you money. Getting a *cama matrimonial* (double bed), instead of two twin beds, will also save you money in many cases. If there is a view from the hotel, you will pay for it; take a room without the view to save even more money.

SAVING MONEY ON MEALS

The *plato del dia* is the way to save money in Guatemala. This lunch special is usually a large three-course meal for much less than you would pay for just an entree at regular prices. These meals are served until the pot is empty. Breakfasts are usually surprisingly expensive, but if you stop by the market and buy some fruit and pick up some bread at a *panaderia*, you will need only a cup of tea or coffee to put together a tasty breakfast.

SAVING MONEY ON SIGHT-SEEING & ENTERTAINMENT

You won't find any special discount days at museums, and there aren't discount tickets to theaters. However, because the prices are so low in Guatemala already, it hardly matters.

SAVING MONEY ON SHOPPING

Best Buys Guatemala's best buy is in textiles. Most visitors come here because they are fascinated by the colorful cotton textiles woven by the highland Indians. Brilliant colors in bold stripes are the norm. These beautiful fabrics are sewn into a wide variety of traditional and modern fashions and are considerably less expensive than they are back home. The best place to buy textiles is often in the villages where they are manufactured. There are several villages near Quetzaltenango that are known for different textiles. You can make trips to the different villages on their respective market days and bargain for beautiful pieces of cloth. For ready-made fashions, the best places to shop are in Chichicastenango and Panajachel. The stores in Antigua tend to be expensive, although they sell contemporary designs.

Another good buy is jade, which was highly valued by the Mayas. Beautiful jade jewelry is available at several shops in Antigua. The prices are high, but the jade is of the highest quality.

Stay away from any pre-Columbian artifacts that are offered to you as being *originales*. It is against the law to buy, sell, or export original pre-Columbian art. It is also very doubtful whether anything offered to you truly is an original. High-quality fakes are common, and many people have been taken when they "got a great deal" on a piece of ancient Mayan pottery.

Markets Every town and village in Guatemala has its market day. Once or twice a week, people from all over the region will come into town to buy and sell their wares. The most famous market in the country, and now a major tourist destination, is the one at Chichicastenango. It takes place on both Thursday and Sunday; the Sunday market is larger and more colorful. You will always get a better deal in a market than you will in a tourist shop, and often they have the same items for sale. The market in Antigua is a prime example of this, so be sure to visit this market before making any purchases in Antigua. Calle Santander in Panajachel isn't really a market, but it is lined with vendors' stalls that offer those beautiful Guatemalan textiles at some of the best prices in the country.

Bargaining When making purchases in markets, especially when buying tourist items, be sure to bargain hard. The prices can be inflated several hundred percent if you look like you have the money to pay. Try to avoid looking "rich" and you'll save money; if you're wearing expensive jewelry and watches, you'll automatically be charged a high price. Bargaining is much easier late in the day when the vendors are packing up and will often lower their prices far below midday quotes. If you ask the price of something, you have expressed an interest in buying it and will be expected to negotiate for the item. This can be very frustrating if you're trying to do a little comparison shopping. If you ask the price and don't buy, you'll have to learn to live with the intimidating stares. It is much harder to bargain in shops, but it is possible, especially if you are buying several items. More and more shops are displaying "Fixed Prices" signs.

SAVING MONEY ON TRANSPORTATION

By Plane There is only one domestic flight of concern to visitors to Guatemala—the flight between Guatemala City and Flores, El Petén. Tapsa Tikal Jets, and Avcom all charge $65 each way, while Aviateca charges $90. The flights are often booked up by large tour groups, so try to reserve in advance. See Chapter 11 on El Petén for details.

By Bus Although cleaner and more comfortable, first-class buses are more expensive and run less often than the second-class buses known to travelers as "chicken buses." Whether this name derives from the livestock carried among the passengers or the disquieting passing habits of the drivers is a matter for speculation. Chicken buses almost always leave from the market of a town and are for those seeking adventure.

By Car To save money on a rental car, reserve at least one week ahead with a company in your home country. Once in Guatemala, the best way to save money on car rentals is to drive one with a stick shift and forsake air conditioning, which isn't really necessary in most of the country. Be sure to ask for a free road map when you pick up your car. When filling up the gas tank, ask for regular. *Lleno* means "full."

SAVING MONEY ON SERVICES & OTHER TRANSACTIONS

Tipping Bellhops: Q1 to Q2 (20¢ to 35¢) per bag. Waiters/waitresses: 10% to 15%, but only in more expensive restaurants. Taxi drivers: not necessary. Porters: Q1 (20¢) per bag.

Money Changing and Credit Cards Currency exchange rates vary from bank to bank in Guatemala, so it pays to check with a few banks before changing money. *Prensa Libre,* the daily newspaper, publishes a list of exchange rates at various Guatemala City banks. Although hotels will often change money, they tend to give very low rates. By using your credit card to pay hotel and restaurant bills, you will be locking in the bank exchange rate for the day the bill is submitted to a bank. This can work to your advantage and save you money if the value of the quetzal is falling rapidly against the dollar (that is, you're getting more quetzals for your dollar each day). However, make sure that you aren't charged a higher rate for using your credit card.

Telephones You'll save money on local phone calls by going to a phone booth rather than by calling from your hotel; budget hotels in Guatemala rarely have phones in the rooms anyway. For international calls, I suggest using a dial-direct service. However, only calling-card and collect calls can be made this way. You'll save time, money, and aggravation by making your call to the United States this way.

FAST FACTS GUATEMALA

American Express The only office is in Guatemala City at the Banco del Café at Avenida La Reforma 9-00, Zona 9 (tel. 340-040). Open Monday through Friday only.

Area Codes The area code for Guatemala City is "2," and the area code for the rest of the country is "9."

Business Hours Banks are generally open Monday to Friday from 9am to 3pm, with *ventanillas especialles* (special windows) open longer hours. Bars generally stay open until 2am, except on Sunday, when they close at midnight. Office hours are Monday to Friday from 8am to 4:30pm. Less expensive restaurants tend to be open all day, while more expensive ones tend to close for a couple of hours between meals. Shops are generally open Monday to Friday from 9am to 12:30pm and 3 to 7pm, Saturday from 9am to noon. Shops catering primarily to tourists usually have longer hours and stay open on weekends.

Camera/Film Color print, Ektachrome, and Fujichrome film are readily available, but usually more expensive than in the United States. It's best to bring your own. If your camera requires odd-size batteries, be sure to bring some spare ones with you. You can get a camera repaired in Guatemala City, but I can't vouch for the quality of service.

Climate See "When to Go" in this chapter.

Country Code The country code for Guatemala is "502."

Crime See "Safety," below.

Currency See "Information, Entry Requirements & Money" in this chapter.

Customs See "Information, Entry Requirements & Money" in this chapter.

Documents Required See "Information, Entry Requirements & Money" in this chapter.

Driving Rules See "Getting Around" in this chapter.

Drug Laws Although marijuana and cocaine are readily available, the drug laws are strict, and there is nothing your embassy can do to get you out of jail. If you take prescription drugs, play it safe and bring a good supply and your prescription with you. Most prescription drugs are actually available over the counter in Guatemala.

Drugstores Drugstores here are called *farmacias.*

Electricity The current is 110 volts.

Embassies and Consulates **Canada:** Embassy and consulate, 13 Calle 8-44, Zona 10, Edificio Edyma Plaza, Nivel 8 (tel. 336-102). **United Kingdom:** Embassy and consulate, 7a Avenida 5-10, Zona 4, Edificio Centro Financiero, Torre II, Nivel 7, (tel. 321-601).

United States: Embassy and consulate, Avenida La Reforma 7-01, Zona 10 (tel. 311-541 to 311-555).

Emergencies   Emergency phone numbers are different in each city. Check the appropriate chapter.

Hitchhiking   See "Getting Around" in this chapter.

Holidays   See "When to Go" in this chapter.

Information   See "Information, Entry Requirements & Money" in this chapter. Also see individual city chapters for local information offices.

Language   Spanish is the national language; many different Indian dialects derived from ancient Mayan languages also are spoken, primarily in the mountains. A good phrase book to take with you is the *Berlitz Latin-American Spanish for Travelers* (Berlitz Guides, 1992).

Laundry   For listings of laundromats, see individual city chapters.

Liquor Laws   Officially you must be 18 years old to buy alcoholic beverages in Guatemala.

Mail   Mail to the United States takes anywhere from one to two weeks. A postcard or letter to the United States costs 25 centavos (4¢). Stamps often are available at hotel desks; otherwise, you'll have to go to a post office. It is always a good idea to make sure that the stamps on your letter get canceled. If you want to ship a package home, it is best to use one of the shipping companies in Antigua or Panajachel; otherwise, you must go to the Central Post Office in Guatemala City. Don't close the package until after it has been inspected. Surface mail can be very slow (a month or more). Air mail is much faster.

Maps   Road and city maps are available from INGUAT offices, bookstores, and car-rental agencies (if you're renting one of their cars).

Newspapers/Magazines   You'll find several U.S. newspapers and magazines available at major hotels throughout the country, although these newspapers may be a day or two old and are expensive. *Prensa Libre* is Guatemala's most popular daily paper.

Passports   See "Information, Entry Requirements & Money" in this chapter.

Pets   Rabies is common in Guatemala, so it is best to leave your pet at home. If you must bring it, your dog must have vaccinations for rabies, distemper, leptospirosis, hepatitis, and parvovirosis, while your cat must have vaccinations against rabies, distemper, and hepatitis. Please do not buy any parrots that you are offered. These beautiful birds are disappearing in the wild due to hunting for the live bird trade.

Police   The phone number for the Policía Nacional is different in every town. You will find it in the phone book at the beginning of the section for each town or city. In Guatemala City, dial 120; in Antigua, dial 320-251; in Panajachel, dial 621-120; in Quetzaltenango, 612-569.

Radio/TV   There are plenty of AM and FM radio stations throughout the country. You're never far from a marimba or salsa music station. Most expensive hotels have satellite cable TV either in the rooms or in a TV lounge, so you can keep in touch with U.S. programming. A TV schedule is published daily in the newspaper *Prensa Libre.*

Restrooms   These are known as *servicios* or *servicios sanitarios*. Public toilets, rarely clean, are free or cost a few centavos. However, you will have to buy your own toilet paper from the restroom attendant at a table outside the door.

Safety   The government of Guatemala continues to wage a small-scale war against rebel guerrillas in the highlands. You will see gun-carrying soldiers almost anywhere you go in the country, but the main tourist areas are kept free of fighting; if I didn't tell you, you probably would not know that there was any fighting going on here at all.

Of greater importance is protecting yourself against pickpockets. I suggest getting a money pouch that you can wear under your clothes, either around your neck or around your waist. Be cautious with your bags when traveling by bus. Bags have been known to disappear from the roofs of buses, so try to keep your bag inside the bus with you.

Petty crime, armed robberies, and violent crime are all on the rise in Guatemala, especially in Guatemala City and El Petén. When planning a trip to Guatemala, be sure to contact the **U.S. Department of State's Citizens' Emergency**

Service (tel. 202/647-5225) in Washington, D.C., weekdays between 8:15am and 10pm for a recorded report of current travel advisories for Guatemala. If you are already in Guatemala, it is a good idea to ask about safety measures at your hotel or at your embassy. You should never hike alone in Guatemala, especially on the volcano trails. Hikers are frequently robbed on the trail up Pacaya Volcano, so if you make this hike, go with a group and don't carry any money. It is a good idea to carry as little cash as possible wherever you go in Guatemala, and if you are particularly concerned about theft, take out some travel theft insurance before you leave home.

Taxes The Guatemalan government levies a 17% room tax on each night you spend in a hotel. When a hotel receptionist quotes you the room price, the tax may or may not be included in the quotation. Ask to make sure. In this book I will quote room prices with the tax included, so that you'll know the total charge you will have to pay for a room.

Telephone The dial tone in Guatemala is a long, low tone similar to that heard in the United States. Telephone numbers vary in the number of digits that they have—usually four, five, or six digits. There is only one telephone book for all of Guatemala. You'll find several copies available at Guatel (the national telephone company) offices.

A pay phone in Guatemala is called a *telefono monedero,* but it is not very common. A 3-minute local call will cost you 10 centavos (2¢). Machines accept various coins but do not give change.

The best way to make a long-distance call is to call collect or to use a direct-dial operator. These numbers connect you directly to an English-speaking operator and are much faster than trying to make a call through a Guatel office. Guatemalan direct-dial numbers include the following: AT&T—190; Sprint—195; MCI—189; Canada Direct—198. If you must pay for the call yourself, you will need to go to a Guatel office and wait in line or pay a premium and call from your hotel. Calls have a tendency to go through better early in the morning.

Throughout this book, I have listed hotel phone numbers (and some other important numbers) with both their country code ("502") and area code (either "2" or "9"). When calling long distance within Guatemala, drop the country code, dial a "0" first, then the area code and the phone number.

Time Guatemala is six hours behind Greenwich Mean Time, which is the same as Central Standard Time.

Tipping See "Saving Money on Services & Transactions" in this chapter.

Tourist Offices See "Information, Entry Requirements & Money" in this chapter. Also see specific cities.

Visas See "Information, Entry Requirements & Money" in this chapter.

Water Consider all tap water unfit for drinking. Bottled water, although expensive, is readily available. I carry a filter straw that filters bacteria from water. These straws are available at stores that sell camping equipment. An alternative is to carry a little bottle of iodine, an eye dropper, and a water bottle for purifying water.

GUATEMALA CITY

The Guatemalan capital is a city of over two million people. It's the biggest and most modern city in the country—indeed, in all Central America—and is the headquarters for companies, airlines, and government. However, it is not a major point of attraction for anyone who visits Guatemala for pleasure rather than for business. After the spectacular beauty of the countryside and the clean air and relative quiet of the provincial towns, the capital almost puts you off: The decibel level and pollution index go up almost as soon as you leave Antigua and start on the Guatemala City road.

But since all roads lead to the capital, it's the transportation hub of the nation, and chances are you'll find occasion to pass through. Here's the information that you'll need to make a short visit pleasant.

1. FROM A BUDGET TRAVELER'S POINT OF VIEW

Budget Bests   There are plenty of hotels offering good value at moderate prices, and restaurant prices are still quite low. You can confidently walk into almost any restaurant in the city without having to worry about how much you are spending—and that includes major hotel restaurants. Taxis charge about what you would expect to pay in other major cities around the world, but public buses are a super deal at between 65 and 90 centavos (11¢ and 16¢).

Discount Opportunities   The only people who get any sort of discounts in Guatemala City are students and children, who get a reduction on museum admissions. However, admission fees are already so low that these discounts hardly matter.

What's Worth Paying For   The only thing that I can really say is worth paying for in Guatemala City is a plane ticket to Flores in El Petén, which is where the famous Mayan ruins of Tikal are located. The 1-hour flight costs around $60 and saves up to 18 hours of grueling bus travel over one of the worst roads I have ever traveled.

WHAT'S SPECIAL ABOUT GUATEMALA CITY

Museums
- ☐ The Museum of Archeology and Ethnology, Central America's finest collection of pre-Columbian artifacts.
- ☐ The Ixchell Museum, dedicated to the indigenous clothing of Guatemala.
- ☐ The Popol Vuh Museum, small but containing many beautiful terra-cotta artifacts.

Events/Festivals
- ☐ The ancient Indian dances performed several times a year.

Architectural Highlights
- ☐ The Centro Cultural Miguel Angel Asturias, which resembles a luxury cruise ship.

- ☐ The Centro Cívico, with high-rise buildings covered with murals.

Churches
- ☐ The Yurrita Chapel, a fascinating mixture of architectural styles.

Offbeat Oddities
- ☐ The Mapa en Relieve, a huge relief map of Guatemala.

Ancient Ruins
- ☐ Kaminal Juyú ruins on the outskirts of the city.

2. ORIENTATION

Guatemala City can be a confusing place, but with a little information, getting there and getting around can be quite painless and inexpensive.

ARRIVING

BY PLANE If you fly to Guatemala, you will arrive at the capital's La Aurora International Airport, in the southern part of the city only about 15 or 20 minutes from the center by taxi. La Aurora is small and rather dated but pleasant, and is equipped with a bank, dozens of interesting craft and clothing shops, several small cafeterias, and snack bars. Before you pass through Customs and Immigration, you will come to an INGUAT Tourism Information Desk, staffed by an English-speaking agent and open daily from 6am to 9pm. Guatemalan Tourist Cards ($5) can be obtained here or on board your plane before you arrive. Also available are a few brochures.

The Banco de Guatemala in the arrivals hall is open daily from 6am to 9pm. If it is closed when you arrive, ask at the souvenir shops to find someone who will change U.S. dollars into Guatemalan quetzals for you. There is another bank in the departures hall as well.

Outside the lower level of the terminal building are car-rental booths and taxi ranks. Taxi fare from the airport to Zona 9 or 10 is Q20 to Q25 ($3.45 to $4.35); to Zona 4 is Q30 ($5.20); and to Zona 1, the very center, is Q35 ($6.05). A small tip is appreciated but not required. You should have chosen your desired hotel by this time; examine the address and find its zone number so that you'll know what the taxi fare will be.

It is also possible to get into town on a public bus for only 90 centavos (16¢). There is a bus stop on the near side of the road directly in front of the terminal. The no. 83 and the black no. 5 (as opposed to the red no. 5, which runs a similar route but does

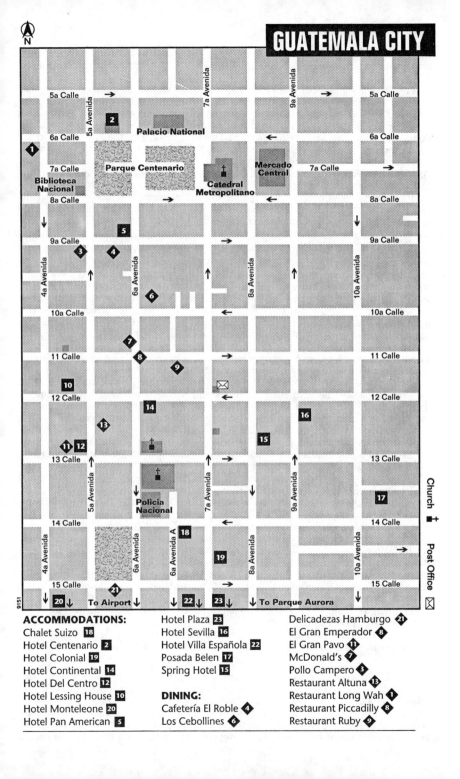

GUATEMALA CITY

ACCOMMODATIONS:
Chalet Suizo 18
Hotel Centenario 2
Hotel Colonial 19
Hotel Continental 14
Hotel Del Centro 12
Hotel Lessing House 10
Hotel Monteleone 20
Hotel Pan American 5

Hotel Plaza 23
Hotel Sevilla 16
Hotel Villa Española 22
Posada Belen 17
Spring Hotel 15

DINING:
Cafetería El Roble 4
Los Cebollines 6

Delicadezas Hamburgo 21
El Gran Emperador 8
El Gran Pavo 11
McDonald's 7
Pollo Campero 3
Restaurant Altuna 13
Restaurant Long Wah 1
Restaurant Piccadilly 8
Restaurant Ruby 9

not go all the way to the airport) "Aeropuerto" bus come by frequently. Other buses also head downtown to the *parque*, and you can take any of these. The trip downtown will take about 30 minutes.

For those going directly from the airport to Antigua, there is another option. You can take a minibus operated by **Turansa** (tel. in Antigua 9/322-664 or in Guatemala City 2/953-574), which makes two runs daily from the airport to Antigua and continues on Wednesday, Friday, and Sunday to Panajachel. Because their schedule is constantly changing, be sure to ask for a current schedule at the information desk inside the terminal. The trip takes about an hour. In Antigua, the minibus drops passengers at several of the top hotels. The fare of Q40.60 ($7) to Antigua is considerably more than that of a local bus leaving from downtown (see below) but is a third of the taxi fare to Antigua. The fare from Guatemala City to Panajachel is Q110.20 ($19). Minibuses are also operated by other companies and you can usually find several waiting outside the terminal when you arrive. If there are four of you, you might want to look into hiring a taxi. The official fare to Antigua is Q125 ($21.55).

BY BUS Unfortunately, because intercity bus routes are handled by dozens of bus companies, there is no single terminal at which you will arrive. You have to know which company you are traveling with to know where you will be arriving. The list of bus companies, routes, and times below should help you to figure out where you are when you arrive. Then you can walk to your destination (fairly easy in most cases if you're not carrying too much luggage and can find an intersection with both street names posted), catch a local bus (difficult because buses must use streets outside the main hotel and restaurant district), or hail a taxi (easiest). In the general chaos and disorientation of your first arrival in Guatemala, I suggest that you take a cab, even if you're on the tightest of budgets. It will save you much frustration and aggravation. Be sure to agree on a fare before getting into the cab. I have found that most taxi drivers in Guatemala City are pretty honest about their fares. Tipping is not necessary.

Following is a list of some of the more frequently used first-class bus lines in Guatemala City, along with their addresses and phone numbers. I have organized these by the cities or destinations each line serves. For more specific information, see the "Getting There" heading at the beginning of individual city sections.

Antigua: Transportes Unidos, 15 Calle between 3a and 4a Avenidas, Zona 1 (tel. 24-949 or 536-929). Buses also leave from the corner of 18 Calle and 4a Avenida.
Cobán: Escobar y Monja Blanca, 8a Avenida 15-16, Zona 1 (tel. 81-409).
El Carmen (Talisman and Mexican border) and Quetzaltenango: Galgos, 7a Avenida 19-44, Zona 1 (tel. 23-661 or 534-868).
Esquipulas (Copan): Rutas Orientales, 19 Calle 8-18, Zona 1 (tel. 536-714 or 512-160).
Huehuetenango: Los Halcones, 7a Avenida 15-27, Zona 1 (tel. 81-929).
La Mesilla (Mexican border): Transportes Velasquez, 20 Calle and 2a Avenida, Zona 1 (no phone).
Panajachel: Transportes Rebulli, 21 Calle 1-34, Zona 1 (tel. 513-521).
Puerto Barrios: Transportes Litegua, 15 Calle 10-42, Zona 1 (tel. 538-169).
Río Dulce: Fuentes del Norte, 17 Calle 8-46, Zona 1 (tel. 513-817).
Flores and Santa Elena (Tikal): Maya Express, 17 Calle 9-36, Zona 1 (tel. 21-914); La Petenera, 16 Calle 10-49, Zona 1 (no phone); and Transportes Fuente del Norte, 17 Calle 8-46, Zona 1 (tel. 513-817).
San Salvador: Melva International, 3a Avenida 1-38, Zona 9 (tel. 310-874).
Tecún Umán (Mexican border): Transportes Fortaleza, 19 Calle 8-70, Zona 1 (tel. 23-643 or 517-994).

BY CAR If you're driving into Guatemala City, you'll probably come in on the Carretera al Atlántico or the Pan American Highway. There are few signs when you come into town on the former: You suddenly find yourself no longer on a highway and surrounded by traffic. The heart of the city is to the south (left). Your best bet is to take 8a Avenida into downtown. If you're coming in on the Pan American Highway, just continue straight into town, following the signs, and you'll find yourself on 5a

Avenida. There is also a ring road (Anillo Periférico) that will help you avoid downtown if you just want to get around the city. To connect between the Carretera al Atlántico and Pan American Highway, take the ring road around the north side of the city.

Most of Guatemala is easy to drive in, with good, uncrowded roads and fairly courteous drivers. All that changes in the capital, where streets are narrow and crowded or wide and fast.

TOURIST INFORMATION

Contact **INGUAT**, the **Instituto Guatemalteco de Turismo** (Guatemalan Tourist Commission), 7a Av. 1-17, Zona 4 (tel. 311-333 or 311-347), in the Centro Cívico (Civic Center) complex. The entrance to the INGUAT building, marked by a blue-and-white sign bearing the letter *i*, is just south of the railroad viaduct on 7a Avenida. It's open Monday through Friday from 8:15am to 4pm, on Saturday from 8am to 1pm; closed Sunday.

CITY LAYOUT

MAIN ARTERIES AND STREETS Although Guatemala City is the largest city in all Central America, most visitors need to familiarize themselves with only a small portion of it. Plaza Mayor, between 5a and 7a avenidas and 6a and 8a calles, is the heart of the city. From here south on 6a Avenida, you'll find the city's greatest concentration of stores. The sidewalks are always jammed with pedestrians and vendors. Most of the buses you will want to use run on 7a and 10a avenidas. Avenida La Reforma, which is the most attractive avenue in the city, is a southern extension of 10a Avenida and divides Zona 9 and Zona 10.

FINDING AN ADDRESS The street-numbering system in Guatemala City, at least within the downtown area, is logical and easy to use. Once you get the hang of it, you'll be on your way to the exact location of any hotel or restaurant. Avenidas run roughly north to south, and calles run east to west. Addresses are given in the following form: 2a Av. 4-17, which means that the place you're after is on 2nd Avenida, at 4th Calle, number 17 (2a is "Spanish" for 2nd, 3a for 3rd; however, after 10, numbers are simply written 11, 12, and so on). You can even tell what side of the street the building will be on. If the street number is even, it'll be on the right side as you walk along the avenida toward higher-numbered calles; if the number is odd, it'll be on the left. You can guess, then, that 3a Av. 5-78 will be on 3rd Avenida between 5th and 6th calles (closer to 6th, as the house number is a high one) on the right side. Once you get the hang of it, you'll find that it's a marvelous system. Unfortunately, the city sprawls beyond the practical limits of the plan, so you find within the downtown area an address such as 14 Av. "A" 2-31, 14—"A" being a short street or alley between, and parallel to, 14th and 15th avenidas. Outside the downtown area of the capital, you'll also run into diagonales, rutas, vias, and other designations.

In an attempt to remedy this situation, all addresses in Guatemala City also have a "zona" designation. A zona is a section of the city. Most of downtown is within Zona 1. The system works well here, but when you cross into another zona, you may find that the numbering system has started all over again. Such is the case in Zona 10. Here you may find the address 4a Av. 16-27, Zona 10, but there may also be a 4a Av. 16-27, Zona 1. Always be sure that you are in the right zona.

NEIGHBORHOODS IN BRIEF **Zona 1** is the downtown shopping, hotel, and restaurant district. Starting at the Plaza Mayor in the north, Zona 1 extends to the Centro Cívico in the south.

Zonas 9 and 10 are the prettiest residential neighborhoods and flank Guatemala City's **Zona Viva,** the upscale hotel, restaurant, nightlife, and boutique district. The Zona Viva centers around the wide Avenida La Reforma, the capital's most attractive avenue and actually the southern continuation of 10a Avenida. Avenida La Reforma divides zonas 9 and 10, with Zona 9 to the west and Zona 10 to the east. It's here that you'll find most of the city's well-to-do residents, as well as the best hotels, the most important embassies, various corporate headquarters, and several of the city's finest museums.

Zona 13, in the southern part of the city, is where you'll find the large Parque Aurora, just west of the airport. The park holds Guatemala City's museums of modern art, archeology, and natural history, as well as its zoo, hippodrome (racetrack), and a government crafts market. There's also an amusement park amid towering, shady trees.

STREET MAPS   The tourist office, bookstores, and car-rental agencies have maps of Guatemala City.

3. GETTING AROUND

BY BUS

Public buses in Guatemala City are incredibly cheap—only 65 to 90 centavos (11¢ to 16¢). However, city buses are rolling wrecks, often without windows and desperately in need of paint, muffler work, seat cushions, and the like. At busy times they can be wall-to-wall human flesh. Bus stops are not well marked. But for all their discomforts and unsightliness, these buses do provide very cheap and quite convenient transportation up and down the long north-to-south avenidas.

To reach Parque Aurora, take bus no. 6, which leaves from 8a Calle across the park from the National Palace. The bus travels down 8a Avenida to 18 Calle, and you can pick it up anywhere along its route. Bus no. 5 ("Parque Aurora"), which travels up and down avenidas 5, 7, and 8, will also get you there. It's a 20-minute trip; get off the bus two stops after you pass the zoo, and you'll find the museums on your left. Keep in mind that there are two no. 5 buses—the red no. 5 and the black no. 5—and only the black no. 5 goes to Parque Aurora and the airport. Bus no. 101, which travels up 10a Avenida, continues along Avenida Reforma.

Bus routes are subject to change, so the best course is to ask a hotel clerk, shopkeeper, police officer, or passerby which bus to take to your destination.

BY TAXI

Taxis are fairly inexpensive in this city, with an average ride in town costing around $3 or $4. A taxi to the airport is Q35 to Q50 ($6.05 to $8.65).

ON FOOT

You will probably find yourself doing a lot of walking in Guatemala City—and it won't be easy. The sidewalks are crowded, the traffic is loud, and diesel exhaust fumes fill the air. Buses run primarily north to south and vice versa; if you're going east to west or vice versa, you'll have to hoof it. I have chosen hotels and restaurants for their proximity to one another so as to minimize your time on the streets. All the city's major sights are out along the Avenida La Reforma and in the Parque Aurora, which are both a long bus ride from downtown.

BY CAR

International car-rental agencies with desks at La Aurora Airport and in downtown Guatemala City include **Avis,** 12 Calle 2-73, Zona 9 (tel. 312-734; tel. toll free in the U.S. 800/331-1212); **Budget,** Avenida La Reforma 15-00, Zona 9 (tel. 316-546; tel. toll free in the U.S. 800/527-0700); **Dollar Rent a Car,** Avenida La Reforma 6-14, Zona 9 (tel. 348-285; tel. toll free in the U.S. 800/800-4000); **Hertz,** 7a Avenida 14-76, Zona 9 (tel. 322-242; tel. toll free in the U.S. 800/654-3131); and **National Car Rental,** 14 Calle 1-42, Zona 10 (tel. 680-175; tel. toll free in the U.S. 800/227-7368).

You will usually save a bit of money if you make your reservation in your home country at least two weeks ahead of time. Weekly rates for such advance bookings are between $300 and $400, including tax and insurance, for the smallest car available. This same car will cost you between $400 and $500 a week if you book it when you're already in Guatemala.

Daily rates are about $50 or $60 a day when you add in fees, insurance, mileage charges, and gas. Also, you cannot get insurance to cover all losses by collision or theft. You will usually be liable for something like $600 to $1,500 on any car, unless you take additional insurance at $2 to $4 per day. This extra insurance reduces your responsibilities to between $250 and $650. This is scary, but if you take precautions (park the car in a safe space at night and so forth) things should work out all right.

The minimum age for renting a car is usually 25 years; have a valid driver's license with you, as well as your passport and credit card.

If the big companies have no more cars, try calling **Tabarini Rent-a-Car,** 2a Calle "A" 7-30, Zona 10 (tel. 316-108), or **Tally Renta Autos,** 7a Av. 14-60, Zona 1 (tel. 514-113 or 23-327). The smallest vehicles these companies offer rent for around $40 including insurance and 100 free kilometers (62 miles).

FAST GUATEMALA CITY

Airlines   Remember to reconfirm your flight home. Following are the Guatemala City phone numbers of international airlines flying into Guatemala: American Airlines (tel. 347-379); Aviateca (tel. 81-479 or 81-415); Continental (tel. 353-341, 353-342, or 353-343); Iberia (tel. 320-911 or 323-914); KLM (tel. 370-222); Lacsa (tel. 310-906 or 323-907); Mexicana (tel. 336-001 or 336-012); Taca (tel. 322-360); and United Airlines (tel. 345-281 or 322-995).

American Express   The American Express office (the only one in the country) is located at Avenida La Reforma 9-00, Zona 9 (tel. 311-311 or 347-463). Open weekdays only.

Area Code   The area code for Guatemala City is 2.

Car Rentals   See "Getting Around" in this chapter.

Climate   See "When to Go" in Chapter 10.

Crime   See "Safety," below.

Currency Exchange   Many banks in Guatemala City are open Monday through Friday between 8:30 or 9am and 7 or 8pm, and on Saturday between 9 or 10am and 1 or 2pm. The Banco del Quetzal, also called Banquetzal, has an office at 10a Calle 6-28, Zona 1 (tel. 512-153 or 512-055), near the Hotel Ritz Continental—it is open Monday to Friday from 8:30am to 7pm, Saturday from 9am to 1pm.

Dentist   Contact your embassy for a list of English-speaking dentists in Guatemala City.

Doctors   Contact your embassy for a list of English-speaking doctors in Guatemala City.

Drugstores   Guatemala City uses a duty-pharmacy (*farmacia de turno*) system. Ask for directions to the nearest pharmacy, then look in the window for the address and telephone number of the nearby pharmacy that is open that day or night. Two conveniently located drugstores are the Pharmacia Klee, 6a Avenida and 12 Calle, Zona 1 (tel. 23-905 or 20-060); and the one at 6a Avenida and 14 Calle, Zona 1 (tel. 23-906).

Embassies and Consulates   See "Fast Facts" in Chapter 10.

Emergencies   For fire department call 123; for the national police call 120; for an ambulance call 125.

Eyeglasses   Get your glasses repaired or replaced at Optica Nacional, 6a Av. 14-55, Zona 1 (tel. 28-074).

Hairdressers/Barbers   Salon Ramiro, 5a Av. 140-02, Zona 1, is a conveniently located hairdresser.

Holidays   See "When to Go" in Chapter 10.

Hospitals   Two good private hospitals are the Centro Medico, 6a Av. 3-47,

Zona 10 (tel. 323-555), and Hospital de Amedesgua, 6a Av. 8-71, Zona 10 (tel. 345-0959 or 342-157). For the names and addresses of others, consult your embassy or consulate or the *Yellow Pages* of the telephone directory under "Hospitales."

Information   See "Tourist Information" in this chapter.

Laundry/Dry Cleaning   First check with your hotel—most offer laundry service and can tell you where the nearest dry cleaner (*lavanderia seca*) is located. If you still need to find someplace, try these two: Lavanderia Cisne, Ruta 7, 7-34, Zona 4 (tel. 316-756), is open weekdays from 8am to 7pm and Saturday from 8am to 6pm; Centro, 9a Calle 6-65, Zona 1 (tel. 24-641), is open weekdays from 8am to 1pm and 3 to 7pm, Saturday from 8am to 2pm.

Lost Property   You can contact the police or tourist office, but neither is really set up to handle lost and found.

Luggage Storage   Your only choice if you want to leave a bag is to ask at your hotel; if you need to leave the bag for only a few hours, ask at the INGUAT (Tourist Information Center), 7a Av. 1-17, Zona 4.

Newspapers/Magazines   Try the lobbies of major hotels for current editions of U.S. newspapers and magazines. They usually have *USA Today*, the *International Herald Tribune*, the *New York Times*, *Time*, and *Newsweek*. Guatemala's most popular daily newspaper is *Prensa Libre*, in which you'll find information on cultural events around town.

Photographic Needs   There are 1-hour to 24-hour film processing centers all over downtown, but I still recommend waiting until you get home to have your processing done. Film is expensive.

Police   See "Emergencies," above.

Post Office   The central post office is at the corner of 12 Calle and 7a Avenida in Zona 1—open Monday through Saturday from 8am to 4pm; closed Sunday. It has no sign to identify it. Look for the men selling postcards in large racks—that's the front door. Other post offices are generally open weekdays from 7:30am to 12:30pm and 1 to 2:30pm.

Radio/TV   Marimba is the national music and is heard on many radio stations. Many hotels now have satellites and offer U.S. programming.

Religious Services   Guatemala is a Roman Catholic country, in which there are dozens of Catholic churches, many of them old and beautiful. Some conveniently located churches include Catedral Metropolitana, 7a Avenida between 6a and 8a calles, Zona 1; Capuchinas, 10a Avenida and 10a Calle, Zona 1; and Nuestra Señora de la Merced, 11 Avenida and 5a Calle, Zona 1.

Restrooms   In Guatemala, public restrooms are called *servicios* or *servicios sanitarios*. Men are *caballeros* and women are *damas*. There aren't many public toilets around, but you will find them in restaurants and the lobbies of large hotels.

Safety   Guatemala City is very urban, with all the problems you would expect in a densely populated area. Petty crime and armed robberies are on the rise here so it's a good idea not to walk the streets alone after dark. Even daytime crime is on the rise, so don't carry large amounts of cash on your person. Take extra precautions with your money, credit cards, traveler's checks, and passport whenever you are out, especially if you are in a market or a crowded bus or on a busy sidewalk. It is best to wear a money belt large enough to hold your money and passport under your clothes. Carry only as much cash as you think you'll need when venturing out of your hotel and try to keep it in a buttoned pocket so you don't have to pull your money belt out in public. The areas around 7a Avenida and 18 Calle and 18 Calle between 4a Avenida and 8a Avenida are well known as haunts of pickpockets, so try to avoid these areas. If you are driving a car, never park it on the street. There are plenty of public parking lots available for only a few cents an hour. Look for signs reading *estacionamentos*.

Taxes   The 17% hotel tax is included in hotel room rates quoted in this book.

Taxis   See "Getting Around" in this chapter.

Telegrams   To send a telegram dial 127. International telegrams are handled by Guatel, the Guatemalan telephone company. The main office is at 7a Avenida 12-39, Zona 1 (tel. 20-498 or 519-298). All other telegrams are handled by post offices.

Telephones   Most telephone numbers in Guatemala City have six digits, but a few old ones have only five. Special information and emergency numbers have only three digits. For intercity long-distance calls, dial 121; for international calls, dial 171. Directory assistance is 124; the correct time is 126. A pay phone in Guatemala is called a *telefono monedero*.

Water   Although the tap water in the capital is chlorinated and presumably safe, it's probably a good idea to stick to bottled mineral water, soft drinks, wine, beer, and the like.

4. WHERE TO STAY

Just as you would expect in a large cosmopolitan city, Guatemala City has a wide variety of hotels in various price categories. Those at the low end of the budget tend to be concentrated in the area within a few blocks of 6a Avenida between 6a Calle and 16 Calle in Zona 1. You'll find a couple at the top end of your budget in Zona 4, but nearly all of the city's luxury hotels are in zonas 9 and 10. It is relatively safe (though street crime is on the rise), but Zona 1 is hardly what you might call an attractive neighborhood, and there is little of interest to see or do. Most visitors to Guatemala spend as little time as possible in the capital, and I suggest you follow suit. However, if you're forced to spend a night here, try these suggestions.

DOUBLES FOR LESS THAN Q145 [$25]

CHALET SUIZO, 14 Calle 6-82, Zona 1, Guatemala City. Tel. 502-2/513-786. 52 rms (13 with bath).

$ Rates: Q69.60–Q139.20 ($12–$24) single; Q92.80–Q162.40 ($16–$28) double; higher prices are for rooms with baths. No credit cards.

⭐ The Chalet Suizo is a longtime favorite of budget travelers. Though there are a few older rooms left in the hotel, most rooms are either new or remodeled. Shared bathrooms are large and clean, while private bathrooms are not quite so roomy. Street-side rooms can be a bit noisy; the quieter rooms with shared bath happen to be the oldest rooms. Though ventilation is lacking, the Chalet Suizo is still a good choice. There is a small café just inside the front door, and in the evenings, Indian women sell huipiles and traditional textiles.

HOTEL LESSING HOUSE, 12 Calle 4-35, Zona 1, Guatemala City. Tel. 502-2/513-891. 8 rms (all with bath).

$ Rates: Q35.10 ($6.05) single; Q58.50 ($10.10) double; Q81.90 ($14.15) triple. No credit cards.

💲 Located on one of the better streets in downtown Guatemala City, the tiny Lessing House is tucked into a narrow building that is easy to miss. The rooms here all sport a bit of local crafts for decoration, which helps the hotel seem a bit better than basic. Each room has two or three beds and a private bathroom with hot-water shower.

HOTEL MONTELEONE, 18 Calle 4-63, Zona 1, Guatemala City. Tel. 502-2/81-859, 82-600, or 513-073. Fax 502-2/539-205. 35 rms (25 with bath).

$ Rates: Q58.50–Q70.20 ($10.10–$12.10) single; Q81.90–Q93.60 ($14.15–$16.15) double; Q99.45–Q117 ($17.15–$20.20) triple; higher rates are for rooms with private bath. DC, MC, V.

This modern hotel is located right across the street from the Antigua bus station, and though the street is quite noisy, rooms at the back of the hotel are generally quiet. The rooms are small, basic, and lack character, but they are clean and most have windows to let in some light. Beds are new and comfortable. The shared bathrooms are usually quite clean also.

SPRING HOTEL, 8a Avenida 12-65, Zona 1, Guatemala City. Tel. 502-2/ 26-637, 514-207, or 514-876. Fax 502-2/20-107. 42 rms (23 with bath).
$ Rates: Q46.40–Q104.40 ($8–$18) single; Q69.60–Q133.40 ($12–$23) double; Q92.80–Q162.40 ($16–$28) triple. DC, MC, V.

A fairly good location, decent rooms in an old-style building converted for use as a hotel, and a sunny little courtyard make this a popular budget choice. The rooms are not fancy and might have a bit of peeling paint, but they are large. Higher prices are for rooms with private bathrooms.

DOUBLES FOR LESS THAN Q203 [$35]

HOTEL CENTENARIO, 6a Calle 5-33, Zona 1, Guatemala City. Tel. 502-2/80-381 or 80-383. Fax 502-2/82-039. 43 rms (all with bath). TV TEL
$ Rates: Q128.70 ($22.20) single; Q152.10 ($26.25) double; Q175.50 ($30.25) triple. AE, DC, MC, V.

Want to stay right near the National Palace? This old-fashioned hotel is right on the main square, almost next door to the National Palace. Built at least 50 years ago, the Centenario has been well maintained and recently redecorated. It's a modest place, but the staff is particularly helpful, providing carafes of drinking water, free ice, maps of the city, and pocket calendars. The carpeted rooms are simple but nice enough, and many have good beds (often there's a double and a single bed in a room). The bathrooms have showers that are well worn but tidy.

HOTEL COLONIAL, 7a Avenida 14-19, Zona 1, Guatemala City. Tel. 502-2/26-722, 22-955, or 81-208. 42 rms (36 with bath).
$ Rates: Q81.35 ($14.05) single without bath, Q108.60 ($18.75) single with bath; Q122.15 ($21.10) double without bath, Q149.30 ($25.75) double with bath; Q176.45 ($30.45) triple with bath. No credit cards.

If you'd like to stay in a grand old mansion converted into a hotel, try the Colonial. The pleasant interior court has been covered over with translucent plastic panels to let the sun in but to keep the rain out; the walls are of frighteningly tactile stucco; and the parlor is furnished in ponderous neocolonial pieces. The guest rooms gleam and shine—there is nothing tattered or worn here (except perhaps the aging mattresses). Carved bedsteads and huge old wardrobes, although not antique, are properly colonial. Most rooms have baths, and some rooms are more luxurious than others, so examine several before taking your pick.

HOTEL CONTINENTAL, 12 Calle 6-10, Zona 1. Tel. 502-2/518-251, 518-260, 518-261, or 518-262. Fax 502-2/518-265. 22 rms (all with bath). TV TEL
$ Rates: Q130 ($22.45) single or double; Q180 ($31.05) triple. AE, DC, MC, V.

This new, though rather basic, hotel is located in a restored building right on busy 6a Avenida. The brick building's facade features arches and frosted glass windows, giving it a turn-of-the-century appearance that is rarely encountered

---

IMPRESSIONS

I could see the volcanoes from the window of my hotel room . . . They were tall volcanoes and looked capable of spewing lava. Their beauty was undeniable; but it was the beauty of witches. The rumbles from their fires had heaved this city down.
—PAUL THEROUX, *THE OLD PATAGONIA EXPRESS,* 1979

here in Guatemala City. The rooms are all up on the second and third floors of the building and, though simply furnished, tend to be large.

WORTH THE EXTRA BUCKS

HOTEL DEL CENTRO, 13 Calle 4-55, Zona 1, Guatemala City. Tel. **502-2/25-980,** 81-519, or 80-639. Fax 502-2/300-208. 55 rms (all with bath). TV TEL
$ Rates: Q313.60 ($54.10) single; Q340.50 ($58.70) double; Q375.60 ($64.75) triple. AE, DC, MC, V.

If you can spend a bit more, this is perhaps the all-around best place to stay when considering its location, services, comforts, and price. A five-story building with colonial-inspired modern decor, the Del Centro has all the comforts and conveniences—from thick carpets and plush furniture to large, light, and airy guest rooms with two double beds, separate seating areas, big color TVs, and small but new and very clean tile bathrooms. Although there is a bit of street noise, this hotel offers one of the best values in the city and has been doing so dependably for several decades.

In the Del Centro's second-floor restaurant, a typical daily special meal might be soup, German-style pork chops, potatoes and fresh vegetables, dessert, and coffee for Q26 ($4.50), plus drink, tax, and tip.

HOTEL PAN AMERICAN, 9a Calle 5-63, Zona 1, Guatemala City. Tel. **502-2/518-709,** 518-713, 518-715, or 518-719. Fax 502-2/26-402. 60 rms (all with bath). TV TEL
$ Rates: Q366.60 ($63.20) single; Q414.15 ($71.40) double; Q461.70 ($79.60) triple. AE, DC, MC, V. **Parking:** Q10 ($1.75).

This is a colonial-style hotel in the very midst of Zona 1. The spacious interior courtyard is now covered, equipped with a fountain, decorated with framed huipiles, and set with tables and chairs to serve as a dining area. Waiters and waitresses are in traditional country garb. With the soothing sound of water from the fountain, it's a very enjoyable place for lunch. In keeping with the 1930s decor, there is one elevator, run by an operator, to take you upstairs. The rooms seem not to have changed much since the hotel's heyday and, although quite clean and tidy, are still furnished the same way. The clean private bathrooms have tubs and showers, and each room has a large cable color TV. Rooms facing the street can be noisy, but those overlooking the courtyard are quiet.

Even if you don't plan to stay here, come by for lunch, which might be a Guatemalan plate of chuchitos (tamales à la Chichicastenango), black beans, and fried bananas; a tropical fruit plate; or a beef pot roast. The portions are large, and the prices are a reasonable Q30 ($5.20) to Q60 ($10.35), plus drink, tax, and tip.

HOTEL PLAZA, Via 7, 6-16, Zona 4, Guatemala City. Tel. 502-2/316-**337** or 310-396. Fax 502-2/316-824. 64 rms (all with bath). TV TEL
$ Rates: Q295.80 ($51) single; Q319 ($55) double; Q348 ($60) triple. AE, DC, MC, V.

The Plaza is not downtown, but in Zona 4, south of the Civic Center. It's located just off busy 7a Avenida, but most of the rooms are quiet. This pleasant hostelry might best be described as a Spanish Bauhaus motel, with echoes of old Spain coming through the clean lines and curves of the Bauhaus idiom—you'll see what I mean. Two motel-style floors are arranged facing the enclosed parking lot or the courtyard's heated swimming pool. The guest rooms are comfy and well kept, with good baths. There's a nice restaurant and bar where a meal will run around Q30 ($5.20).

HOTEL SEVILLA, 9a Avenida 12-29, Zona 1, Guatemala City. Tel. **502-2/82-226,** 300-506, or 500-207. Fax 502-2/28-431. 80 rms (all with bath). TV TEL

$ Rates: Q203.60 ($35.10) single; Q251.10 ($43.30) double; Q298.60 ($51.50) triple. AE, DC, MC, V. **Parking:** Free.

This modern hotel is only a few years old and is one of the best values in Guatemala City. The clientele seems to be primarily Guatemalan businessmen. Rooms are carpeted and some are brightened by large windows (though others are quite dark). Bathrooms are small but clean. In the lobby, there is a small coffee shop and bar, and there is also room service. There's even a sauna.

POSADA BELEN, 13 Calle "A" 10-30, Zona 1, Guatemala City. Tel. 502-2/29-226 or 534-530. Fax 502-2/513-478. 10 rms (all with bath).
$ Rates: Q203 ($35) single; Q243.60 ($42) double; Q272.60 ($47) triple. AE, MC, V (add 8% surcharge).

This small family-run pension has long enjoyed an excellent reputation. Since the Belen is on a little downtown side street, its rooms are quiet, and the quiet is further encouraged by a policy of discouraging guests with children under five years of age. The pension has a charming, sunny courtyard with tropical plants; parrots; a fountain; much wrought-iron decoration; many fine examples of local textiles, including weavings and native blankets; a cozy breakfast room; and a rack of used books for exchange. The price is a bit high, but the Belen is certainly a unique place. The rooms are attractively appointed with lots of local arts and crafts. There are even skylights in the bathrooms.

HOTEL VILLA ESPAÑOLA, 2a Calle 7-51, Zona 9, Guatemala City. Tel. 502-2/317-417, 320-611, or 318-503. Fax 502-2/322-515. 67 rms (all with bath). TV TEL
$ Rates: Q324 ($55.90) single; Q371 ($64) double; Q488 ($84.15) triple. AE, DC, MC, V. **Parking:** Free.

This Spanish colonial–style motel, just south of downtown in Zona 9, could easily have been transported from a Texas interstate. All the expected amenities are here, except the swimming pool. Rooms are carpeted and have one or two double beds. You'll even find a tub in the bathroom, not just a shower. There is also laundry service. Down in the bright basement of the hotel, you'll find a large dining room decorated with colonial reproductions. The menu, which features both Guatemalan and international cuisine, is varied and reasonably priced—meals range from about Q25 ($4.35) to Q75 ($13). There is also a small bar down here.

5. WHERE TO EAT

For the best food at the best price in the most pleasant surroundings, the thing to do in Guatemala City is to dine at one of the better hotels. The Hotel Del Centro and the Hotel Pan American both have good dining rooms serving tasty food in large portions at surprisingly reasonable prices, usually around Q30 ($5.20) to Q60 ($10.40) for an entire meal. Refer to the descriptions of those hotels given above for details. For more reasonably priced meals, you might try the following.

MEALS FOR LESS THAN Q20 [$3.45]

CAFETERÍA EL ROBLE, 9a Calle 5-46, Zona 1. Tel. 516-642.
  Cuisine: GUATEMALAN.
$ Prices: Q3.25–Q13.50 (60¢–$2.35). No credit cards.
  Open: Mon–Fri 8:30am–8pm, Sat 8:30am–6pm.

If your budget is really low, take a look at this little place across from the entrance to the Hotel Pan American. A cafetería in Guatemala is an inexpensive eatery serving traditional fare. There are cafeterías all over town; they're where local office workers go when they're tired of fried chicken and burgers. This clean little café is nothing fancy, but you can get breakfast here for less than a dollar and lunch for only slightly more.

DELICADEZAS HAMBURGO, 15 Calle 5-34, Zona 1. Tel. 81-627.
    Cuisine: GUATEMALAN/GERMAN.
$ Prices: Breakfasts Q5–Q12 (90¢–$2.10); main dishes Q14–Q46 ($2.45–$7.95). No credit cards.
    Open: Daily 7am–9:30pm.
On the south side of the always busy Parque Concordia you'll find this typical Guatemalan diner. The lunch counter and the display case full of rainbow Jell-O may say small-town America, but the menu is sprinkled with German dishes—a reminder of old German coffee-growing days. Service is surprisingly good. Try the garlic soup if you're a fan of the fragrant cloves.

EL GRAN EMPERADOR, 14 Calle 6-74, Zona 1. No phone.
    Cuisine: VEGETARIAN.
$ Prices: Main dishes Q4–Q20 (70¢–$3.45). No credit cards.
    Open: Daily 8:30am–9pm.
Located right next door to the ever-popular Hotel Chalet Suizo, this hole-in-the-wall restaurant is always packed with budget travelers. There are pasta dishes, sandwiches, a few Chinese offerings, good soups, and great licuados. There are even a few chicken dishes on the menu. Breakfasts, at around Q7 ($1.20), are a filling bargain.

RESTAURANT LONG WAH, 6a Calle 3-70, Zona 1. Tel. 26-611.
    Cuisine: CHINESE.
$ Prices: Main dishes Q12–Q30 ($2.10–$5.20). No credit cards.
    Open: Daily 11am–11pm.
This noisy restaurant is in the midst of Guatemala City's tiny Chinatown district, a few blocks west of the Parque Central on 6a Calle at 4a Avenida, along with several other Chinese restaurants bearing names such as Felicidades, Palacio Real, and China Hilton. The five rooms at the Long Wah, done in the predictable gold lanterns, red booths, and black wainscoting, are often bustling with diners out for a change of pace. Adapt the Spanish transliterations on the menu slightly, and you'll see that "chaw mein" is chow mein, "wantan" is wonton, and so forth. The most expensive dishes are those with shrimp for Q30 ($5.20). Beer is served.

RESTAURANTE PICCADILLY, 6a Avenida 11-01, Zona 1. Tel. 514-268.
    Cuisine: ITALIAN.
$ Prices: Pasta Q8.50–Q11.50 ($1.50–$2); pizza Q13–Q24 ($2.25–$4.15); main dishes Q17–Q23 ($2.95–$4). V.
    Open: Daily 7am–midnight.
Watch for the take-out window at the corner of 11 Calle and 6a Avenida. You can grab a slice of pizza to go, or you can take a seat inside amid modern decor. A red neon sign glows on the wall of the first dining room, but the back room is more subdued. In addition to the Italian dishes, there are also shish kebabs and burgers. The spaghetti al pesto, though light on basil, is still quite good.

RESTAURANT RUBY, 11 Calle 6-56, Zona 1. Tel. 26-438.
    Cuisine: CHINESE.
$ Prices: Main dishes Q8.50–Q31 ($1.50–$5.35). No credit cards.
    Open: Daily 11:30am–8:30pm.
For Chinese food closer to the Chalet Suizo, try Ruby. The menu is suitably bewildering, running to 131 items, but the special plates (large or small) give you samplers of the best items. Ruby is one high-ceilinged corridor, a lunch counter, and several rear dining rooms that are always busy. The menu is in Spanish and English, and a number of new-world dishes make it into the list.

MEALS FOR LESS THAN Q30 [$6]

LOS CEBOLLINES, 6a Avenida 9-75, Zona 1. Tel. 27-750.
Cuisine: MEXICAN.
$ Prices: Appetizers Q7–Q20 ($1.20–$3.45); main dishes Q5.50–Q15.95 (95¢–$2.75). No credit cards.
Open: Daily 7am–11pm.

This restaurant, one of a popular chain, takes its name from the grilled green onions that are served with almost every dish. According to legend, cebollines were first served to Pancho Villa, who went nuts for them. My favorite way to dine here is to order from the appetizer list, trying whatever sounds different or unusual. When I'm full I stop trying new dishes. I've never gone wrong. More traditional diners will find a wide range of regional Mexican cuisines, including burritos, fajitas, and Mexiburguesas. The *caldo tlalpeño de pollo,* which should not be missed, is a large and delicious bowl of chicken soup made with chunks of avocado and lots of herbs and spices.

EL GRAN PAVO, 13 Calle 4-41, Zona 1. Tel. 510-933.
Cuisine: MEXICAN.
$ Prices: Main dishes Q21–Q58 ($3.65–$10). AE, DC, MC, V.
Open: Daily 9am–1am.
Plain but clean and cheerful, El Gran Pavo (the "big turkey") adjoins the Hotel Del Centro and is fairly large, with several dining rooms. A long menu tries admirably to cover every variety of Mexican cuisine, from Veracruz seafood and mole poblano through oaxaqueño quesos and cabrito al pastor. The antojito (appetizer) menu alone is enough to keep adventurous diners busy for weeks. A complete meal with drink, tax, and tip will cost about Q30 ($5.20). There's another branch on 12 Calle 6-54, Zona 9 (tel. 313-976).

RESTAURANT ALTUNA, 5a Avenida 12-31, Zona 1. Tel. 20-669.
Cuisine: SPANISH.
$ Prices: Main dishes Q23–Q37 ($4–$6.40). AE, DC, MC, V.
Open: Lunch Tues–Sun noon–4pm; dinner Tues–Sat 6–10:30pm.

Just a few steps north of the Hotel Del Centro is a big restaurant with lots of dining rooms done in European style—with dark-wood furniture, white tablecloths, and formal but pleasant and unobtrusive decor. The service is smooth and polished, and the specialties are Spanish cuisine and seafood, with fish and squid, shrimp, steaks, chicken, and even doves cooked in sherry on the menu. A full meal here, all included, will come to about Q50 ($8.65) per person. Altuna is quite popular with local businesspeople at lunch.

SPECIALTY DINING

FAST-FOOD CHAINS

Guatemala City has a full assortment of international fast-food restaurants. Downtown along 6a Avenida, you'll find **McDonald's** (also at 10a Calle and 5a Avenida), **Burger King,** and even **Taco Bell.** There are also plenty of local fast-food restaurants serving hamburgers, hot dogs, and fried chicken. The following is one of the most popular fast-food chains in Guatemala.

POLLO CAMPERO, 9a Calle and 5a Avenida, Zona 1. No phone.
Cuisine: CHICKEN.
$ Prices: Full meal Q7.20–Q12 ($1.25–$2.10). No credit cards.
Open: Daily 7am–10:30pm.
Imitations of Colonel Sanders' eateries can be found all over Guatemala. For a taste of fried chicken Guatemalan-style, look for a branch of Pollo Campero, which is bright and cheery with orange-and-yellow tables and burnt-orange floor tiles. You'll feel as though you're back home at your favorite chicken restaurant. There are branches at 6a Avenida and 15 Calle, Zona 1 and 8a Calle 9-29, Zona 1.

6. ATTRACTIONS

The largest city in Central America, Guatemala City, spreads across a narrow plateau cut by deep ravines. The old downtown section of the city, Zona 1, is centered on the Palacio Nacional (National Palace), the Catedral Metropolitana (Metropolitan Cathedral), and the Biblioteca Nacional (National Archives and Library), all of which face the Parque Central. Start your tour here, then head out to Parque Aurora, near the airport, where you'll find most of the city's other sights.

SUGGESTED ITINERARIES

IF YOU HAVE ONE DAY   Head first to the Museum of Archeology out near the airport. Then head over to the Avenida La Reforma area to visit the Popol Vuh Museum and the Ixchel Museum. These three museums should just about fill your day.

IF YOU HAVE TWO DAYS   On your second day, visit the Mapa en Relieve and the Parque Central, where you will find the Metropolitan Cathedral and the National Palace. After lunch, stroll down 6a Avenida for a bit of shopping. You might also hop a bus and visit the Yurrita Chapel.

IF YOU HAVE THREE DAYS   Visit the ruins of Kaminal Juyú on the outskirts of the city and perhaps the Museo de Artes e Industrias Populares.

IF YOU HAVE FIVE DAYS   If you have this much time, you should spend at least two days in Antigua, which is much more interesting than Guatemala City and is only an hour away.

THE TOP ATTRACTIONS

MUSEO DE ARQUEOLOGÍA Y ETNOLOGÍA, Building No. 5, Parque Auro-ra, Zona 13. Tel. 720-489.

The beautiful stark-white Moorish building in Parque Aurora is the Archeological and Ethnological Museum, which boasts the largest and most spectacular collection of Mayan carvings in the world. One of the more famous pieces now on display is the throne from Piedras Negras, which you should not miss.

As you wander through the archeological section of the museum, you'll see beautiful black ceramic vessels from excavations in Zaculeu (Preclassic Period, A.D. 200); an outstanding collection of clay masks (Postclassic Period, A.D. 925 to 1200), and artifacts of shell, alabaster, obsidian, and flint (Classic Period, A.D. 200 to 925).

There is also an ethnological section in the museum, with a textile room in which 150 native costumes are displayed. Moving through the other ethnological rooms, you'll see a glass rotunda exhibiting the types of dwellings the Indians used, and exhibits of nutrition (foods that originated in America) and industry (baskets, ceramics, weaving, and so on).

Admission: Q1 (20¢).
Open: Tues–Sun 9am–4pm. **Bus:** Black no. 5.

MUSEO POPOL VUH, EDIFICIO GALERIA REFORMA, 6th floor, Avenida La Reforma 8-60, Zona 9. Tel. 347-121.

In 1977 Jorge and Ella Castillo donated their personal collection of Mayan art to the Universidad Francisco Marroquin, which now cares for it in the Museo Popol Vuh, named for the sacred "painted book" of the Quiché Mayans, which is now known as the Dresden Codex. There is a copy of this unique book on display in the museum.

The immense collection of Mayan art is arranged by region and period, as is a smaller collection of colonial religious and secular art. Some of the Mayan pieces are simply gorgeous: polychrome vases, huge burial urns, incense burners, and ceramic figurines. The religious art, mostly of the 16th to 18th centuries, includes some handsome altars in wood with silver trim. You'll find folk art here as well: face masks, which are still made and used in many regions, and mannequins wearing regional costumes. This collection is perhaps the finest in the city.

There's a good museum shop here, with an excellent bookstore and a nice crafts collection.

Admission: Q5 (90¢) adults; Q3 (55¢) college students; Q1 (20¢) secondary-school students; 25 centavos (5¢) children under 12; Q5 (90¢) to take photos.

Open: Mon–Fri 9am–5pm, Sat 9am–4pm. **Bus:** Any Avenida La Reforma bus.

MUSEO IXCHEL DE TRAJE INDÍGENA (Ixchel Native Dress Museum), 6a Calle Final, Zona 10. Tel. 313-638 or 313-634.

Ixchel, wife of the Mayan sky god Itzamna, was goddess of the moon and protectress of women in childbirth, and the museum bearing her name is dedicated to the woven art of Guatemala's Mayan women and to their village lifestyle. Housed in a new building on the campus of the Universidad Francisco Marroquin, the Ixchel Museum is the most modern exhibit space in the country. Be sure to notice the facade of the museum, which is decorated with a traditional textile design.

The museum is filled with exquisite examples of Guatemalan traditional weaving from the various sections of the country. Artful use of mannequins has created lifelike situations that work well to give you a feeling for the creative, hardworking indigenous people of Guatemala. Several figures represent members of the cofradías, the traditional village socioreligious groups whose duties and beliefs bridge the gap between traditional Mayan and Roman Catholic religion. Other exhibits demonstrate the weaving process through the use of looms, diagrams, and photographs. There are also exhibits showing tie-dyeing, which is done in Huehuetenango and some other towns. Signs on the exhibits are in English as well as in Spanish.

On the ground floor, the museum has a nice shop selling books, crafts, and textiles.

Admission: Q10 ($1.75) adults.

Open: Mon–Fri 9am–5:30pm, Sat 9am–1pm. **Bus:** Any Avenida La Reforma bus.

PALACIO NACIONAL, Plaza Mayor, 6a Calle between 6a and 7a avenidas. No phone.

The heart of Guatemala's governmental power is here in the Palacio Nacional (National Palace), built at a cost of Q2,800,000—when that amount had a much higher exchange rate than today—by Gen. José Ubico, president from 1939 to 1943. The palace has three entrances you can use; the fourth, in the back, is for VIPs, whose darkened, bulletproof cars wait in readiness there. The main entrance facing the Parque Central is the site of exhibits that change from time to time; it's the two side entrances that will take you inside the palace. You will catch the mood of the palace as you climb the brass-and-wood stairways up through three levels of beautiful wood-beamed ceilings, hand-carved stone-and-wood columns, frescoed arches, large wrought-iron-and-glass lanterns, tile floors, and numerous murals by Alfredo Galvez Suarez. It's fascinating, with all the interest of a museum yet not so overpowering as to be an unlivable place. There's a sense of harmony about the palace which you don't often find in government buildings. The two side entrances lead up to symmetrical floors, both of which overlook separate courtyards on the ground floor.

Admission: Free.

Open: Mon–Fri 8am–4pm. **Bus:** Any bus that stops at Plaza Mayor.

MAPA EN RELIEVE, Parque Minerva, 11 Calle and 6a Avenida at the end of Avenida Simeon Cañas, Zona 2. No phone.

Guatemala City's Relief Map is a scale model of the entire country. It's 40 by 80 yards, with a depth of 2 yards; the proportions of the mountains (especially the volcanoes) have been exaggerated so that the topography of the country is readily apparent. You can observe the map from ground level or climb up one of the observation platforms for a look at Guatemala from the air. The major towns and features are marked by labels and little pennants. Francisco Vela, the engineer who created the map, had to traverse the country by donkey in 1904 to collect all the necessary information. The map is several dozen blocks to the north of the National Palace. To reach it, follow 7a Avenida north to its very end, where it joins Avenida Simeon Cañas near the Parque Minerva.

In recent years, visitors to the Relief Map have been the victims of robberies, so be sure to ask at your hotel or at the INGUAT information center if it is currently safe to visit the map. In particular, visitors are being told to avoid the observation tower.

Admission: Free.
Open: Daily 9am–5pm. **Bus:** Nos. 1 and 18.

MORE ATTRACTIONS

RUINS OF KAMINAL JUYÚ, Zona 7. Tel. 516-224.

Kaminal Juyú was a very early Mayan city (300 B.C. to A.D. 900), flourishing before the classic Mayan cities of Tikal and Palenque. The earliest people (the Miraflores) planted crops and made excellent ceramics and carved jade. They seem to have been dominated by the priestly class that held all the power. By A.D. 300 Kaminal Juyú had been conquered by the people of Teotihuacan (near Mexico City), but the rulers who came here from Mexico were "Mayanized" over the years. The remains of the Intermediate Period (the Esperanza Period), before the peoples were completely assimilated, show a strange mixture of Mayan and Teotihuacan art and culture.

The Spanish conquerors who came in the 1500s make no mention of Kaminal Juyú, probably because the city had been burned and destroyed when it was abandoned in A.D. 900. It wasn't until the late 18th century that mounds were discovered, and only in 1899 did Maudslay begin the first excavations. About 200 mounds have been found here—some from the Miraflores' time, when structures were built of adobe and pumice, others from the later Esperanza Period, when the inhabitants built pyramids and temples of limestone. Archeologists have found traces of Teotihuacan influence, such as stepped temple platforms called *tablero y talud* covered in red stucco, slit-eyed figurines, and three-legged pottery cylinders, as well as traces of influence from Monte Alban (Tlaloc figures with large headdresses). In the tombs here were the finest jade objects found in all Guatemala, and in fact, these people valued jade more than they did gold. The objects found in the tombs, which include precious stones, pottery, terra-cotta figurines, and incense burners, are in the Archeological Museum and the Museo Popol Vuh, as are the stelae carved with hieroglyphs, which date earlier than any stelae found in the Petén (before A.D. 290).

Urban development has covered or destroyed much of the ancient city, and what you see today are substructures of buildings from various periods, built mostly of ordinary clay and rubble. There are a few of limestone covered in a lime wash, which is not too impressive a sight.

Basically, there isn't much to see at Kaminal Juyú—a trip out here will likely be of interest only to serious archeology students.

Admission: Free.
Open: Daily 9am–4pm. **Bus:** Take bus BC, "Kaminal Juyú," to the intersection of Diagonal 24 and 24a Avenida; the entrance is just west of Diagonal 24.

CATEDRAL METROPOLITANA, Plaza Mayor, 7a Avenida between 6a and 8a calles. No phone.

Despite its look of antiquity, the Metropolitan Cathedral, on the east side of the Parque Central, was built between 1782 and 1815. The wrought-iron gates into the cathedral precincts are locked every day between 1 and 3pm (the caretaker's lunch, I suppose). Don't enter with expectations of seeing a gorgeous symphony of gleaming gold and flowery decoration. As with many Guatemalan churches, this national symbol is quite plain, even severe, inside. The Archbishop's Palace is next to the cathedral.

Admission: Free.
Open: Daily 8am–7pm. **Bus:** Any bus that stops at Plaza Mayor.

CAPILLA YURRITA, Ruta 6 8-52, Zona 4. Tel. 363-514.

Located in a newer section of town, amid car dealers and offices, this is one of the most architecturally unusual churches in Guatemala City. If you have been through this part of town already, you may have noticed the tall steeple and wondered what it was. The chapel, built in 1928, is a bizarre structure worthy of Bavaria's mad king Ludwig. It draws on numerous architectural styles, including Gothic and Russian Orthodox church architecture. Notice the work lavished on the front doors. This is a privately owned family chapel, but the public is welcome to visit.

Admission: Free.

Open: Tues–Sat 8am–noon and 3:30–6pm; Sun 8am–1pm and 4–7pm. **Bus:** Red or black no. 5.

MUSEO DE ARTES E INDUSTRIAS POPULARES, 10a Avenida 10-72, Zona 1. Tel. 80-334.

This small downtown museum is housed in an old colonial-style house. The collection includes naïve art paintings of processions and dances by Guatemalan artists. There are also examples of indigenous handcrafts, including carved and painted gourds, tin candle holders, and masks for the dances of the highland villages. There is also a large collection of antique musical instruments.

Admission: Q1 (20¢).

Open: Tues–Fri 9am–4pm; Sat–Sun 10am–noon and 2–4pm.

MUSEO NACIONAL DE HISTORIA, 9a Calle 9-70, Zona 1. Tel. 536-149.

To learn more about the history of Guatemala, stop by this museum. It has been undergoing renovation in recent years and is slowly taking on a modern appearance inside, although the exterior still looks quite decayed. The collection covers Guatemalan history from prehistory through the discovery, conquest, and colonization by Spain. Exhibits are more extensive for the period beginning after the country's independence in 1821. In these rooms you'll learn how the economic, social, and cultural life of the nation was shaped.

Admission: Free.

Open: Mon–Fri 9am–4pm.

MUSEO NACIONAL DE ARTE MODERNA, Building No. 6, Parque La Aurora, Zona 13. Tel. 720-467.

This small museum is located directly across the street from the Archeological Museum. The interior of the building is striking, with a high wooden rosette ceiling and white plaster walls. The museum was founded in 1934 and contains paintings and sculpture from the late 18th century up to the present. Some well-known Guatemalan painters, such as Carlos Merida and Garavito, are represented here. The historical section is smaller, the exhibit of greatest interest here being a collection of coins from the colonial period. There are sometimes temporary exhibits here that cause the permanent collection to be closed off. Call first.

Admission: Free.

Open: Tues–Fri 9am–4pm; Sat–Sun 9am–noon and 2–4pm. **Bus:** Black no. 5.

CENTRO CÍVICO, 21 Calle between 6a and 7a avenidas, Zona 1.

The central part of the city holds the Centro Cívico and Ciudad Olímpica, important complexes of buildings dedicated to city and national government, and to sports. This is the pride of Guatemala City because of its modern architecture. City officials claim that it is "the most advanced architecture in Latin America." The center includes the well-known (and always hopelessly crowded) Bank of Guatemala, the Social Security Building (IGSS), and Olympic City. Much of the exterior relief sculpture is the work of artists Efraín Recinos and Carlos Merida. As you enter the complex (at the intersection of 6a Avenida and Diagonal 2), you'll see a statue of a wolf with Romulus and Remus underneath; the statue is inscribed "From Eternal Rome to Immortal Guatemala." To the right as you face the statue is city hall and directly ahead of you in the distance is the Bank of Guatemala, constructed from 1962 to 1966. The high-relief murals in concrete are by Dagoberto Vasquez and depict the history of Guatemala. The Social Security Building behind city hall was designed by

Roberto Aycinena and Jorge Montes; the enormous mosaic, completed in 1959, is by Carlos Merida. On the hill behind you is the Fortress of San José and the National Theater, which looks a lot like a blue-and-white ocean liner. Olympic City, farther to the east, is an enormous building that houses the Mateo Flores Stadium (named after the athlete who won the Boston Marathon in 1952), the National Gymnasium, a swimming pool, tennis courts, and a Boxing Palace.

COOL FOR KIDS

If you have your kids with you, then you should definitely plan on spending a lot of time at Parque Aurora. The kids will definitely enjoy the amusement park and zoo and maybe even the Museum of Archeology.

7. SAVVY SHOPPING

The savvy shopper in Guatemala City should save every last penny to spend in the shopper's heavens of Chichicastenango and Panajachel. However, if for some reason you are not headed to either of these places but would still like to buy some of those beautiful Guatemalan textiles, head for the **Mercado Central**. Before the earthquake of 1976, the area directly behind the Catedral Metropolitana was the city's central market. It was ruined in the quake, and a new one was built that has most of its shopping space below street level (they're not going to let a quake "bring it down" again!). Walk through the huge market to see selections of cloth (both handwoven and machine-made), leather goods, wood carvings, metalwork, baskets, and other handcrafts. It's worth at least a stroll through. Be especially careful with your valuables: Pickpockets and purse slashers make a very good living here. Open Monday to Saturday from 9am to 6pm, Sunday from 9am to noon.

The **Mercado de Artesanía** (Handcrafts Market), located in Parque Aurora, has vendors' stalls, a small courtyard, and a modern restaurant. The products on sale represent a good portion of Guatemala, and the prices are not bad. They have leather goods, woven cloth, huipiles (blouses), ceramics, baskets, and hand-painted terracotta figurines. If you're traveling extensively throughout Guatemala, you'll find these products elsewhere, but it's probably worth a trip to see what they have here. Although prices are a little higher here than at the shops in Mercado Central, this is a very pleasant place, and you may even be entertained by a marimba band. Open Monday through Saturday from 9am to 6pm, Sunday 9am to 1pm.

If you're buying large quantities and want to ship things home, your best bet is to use one of the shipping companies in Antigua or Panajachel. This will save you the aggravation of dealing with the post office and all its paperwork.

8. EVENING ENTERTAINMENT

Although it is the largest city in Central America, Guatemala City has very little in the way of an entertainment scene. If you crave cultural programs or lively nightlife, you're out of luck here.

THE PERFORMING ARTS

CENTRO CULTURAL MIGUEL ANGEL ASTURIAS, 24 Calle 3-81, Zona 1. Tel. 24-041 or 24-044.

Perched high atop a hill overlooking the Centro Cívico is a dramatic blue-and-white building that looks strangely like a luxury cruise ship. Don't worry—the polar ice caps haven't melted; this is the city's cultural center, home to three theaters.

Inaugurated in 1978, the building is the work of Guatemalan artist Efraín Recinos. The Gran Teatro seats more than 2,000 people. The much smaller Teatro de Cámara is for chamber music concerts, while the Teatro al Aire Libre, an open-air theater, stages everything from music to dance to drama. Check *Prensa Libre,* the city's daily newspaper, for information on performances.

Prices: Q5–Q100 (90¢–$17.25), depending on performance and seat.

THE BAR, CLUB & MUSIC SCENE

The best place to look for active nightlife is in the Zona Viva, the area along Avenida La Reforma in Zona 9 and Zona 10. Here you will find the city's greatest concentration of expensive restaurants, bars, discos, and nightclubs. Your best bet will probably be to head to one of the major hotels in this area. Both the Hotel Conquistador Sheraton and the Westin Camino Real Hotel have popular discos frequented by locals and tourists.

9. AN EASY EXCURSION

LAKE AMATITLÁN

GETTING THERE   By Bus   Buses leave every 30 minutes from 20 Calle and 2a Avenida, Zona 1 in Guatemala City. Duration: 30 minutes. Fare: Q1.60 (30¢).

By Car   Take the Carretera al Pacífico south and watch for the turnoff to Lake Amatitlán.

DEPARTING   Catch a bus from the public beach back into Guatemala City. They run every 30 minutes throughout the day.

ESSENTIALS   Orientation   The lake, 28 kilometers south of Guatemala City, is 7½ by 2½ miles, with villas and vacation homes surrounding it. At the northwest end of the lake, near the highway, is one of the only public beaches on the lake.

Don't confuse this small lake with Lake Atitlán to the northwest; the latter is a spectacular sight, whereas this one, Lake Amatitlán, is not as interesting. If you're driving, after exiting from the highway bear left at the gas station, then left again at the T, then right down the wide, straight street to the lakefront.

WHAT TO SEE & DO

The government has built a park here on the shore with little stone thatch-roofed changing cubicles, picnic tables, and the like. The swimming at this beach is not great because the water tends to be dirty, so your best bet for a dip would be either to walk along the road to the left past the villas and cottages to a rock outcrop or to rent a rowboat for an hour, row out a short distance, and swim. Near the entry road where you came in are various little restaurants and soft-drink stands that will do nicely for lunch. The lake is mostly a place for denizens of the capital to cool off for a day. Don't plan an extended stay.

You may notice several *balnearios* (warm spring swimming pools) in the area. This is an area of much geothermal activity. There are hot springs at various places around the edges of the lake, and even the bottom of the lake itself is filled with hot springs. Perhaps this is why the ancient Mayas of this region used the lake for making offerings to the gods. The soft, hot mud of the lake bottom has preserved most of these offerings, and divers continue to recover amazing terra-cotta pots and urns, many of which are on display at the Popol Vuh Museum in Guatemala City.

Warning: Pollution from Guatemala City contaminates this small lake, and it is questionable whether you should swim here at all. Definitely do not eat any fish taken from the lake.

CHAPTER 12

THE GUATEMALAN HIGHLANDS & PACIFIC COAST

The Guatemalan highlands are a convoluted quilt of cultivated hillsides. The land has been turned on its side, but the tenacious Indians cling to the steep mountains and plant their corn as they have for thousands of years. Narrow roads wind through the mountains, and around nearly every bend is another breathtaking vista. Picture-perfect volcanic peaks, some sitting in silent grandeur, others providing explosive reminders of their presence, rise up above the surrounding mountains. However, it is the people of these mountains that capture the heart and imagination of the visitor to this country. Descended from the ancient Mayas, the indigenous people of the Guatemalan highlands pursue a way of life entirely separate from the life of the *ladinos,* the more Spanish inhabitants of this country's cities and towns. The Indians cling to their age-old traditions, many of which have been incorporated into Roman Catholic rituals. Most of the women (and some of the men) of this region continue to wear their very colorful traditional attire. In this often dry and dusty landscape, their skirts and huipiles (blouses), pants and jackets are bold splashes of unlikely colors—lime green and cherry red, indigo and purple, magenta and fuchsia. Every village has its own styles and colors, so that when people leave their village, they can be recognized wherever they go.

Among these mountains are three of Guatemala's most popular destinations—Antigua, Chichicastenango, and Panajachel. Antigua is a beautiful colonial city that has preserved its 17th- and 18th-century architecture amid the ruins of lavish Spanish churches, monasteries, and universities that have been destroyed by numerous earthquakes over the years. Chichicastenango is home to the country's largest and most famous market and is well known as the site of religious rituals that meld Mayan and Roman Catholic beliefs. Panajachel, a small resort town, sits on the shore of beautiful Lake Atitlán, a deep blue lake formed in a huge volcanic crater. Farther into the highlands are the cities of Quetzaltenango and Huehuetenango, which make good bases for exploring Indian villages.

The Pacific Coast is nearly the opposite of the highlands—flat, hot, humid, and populated primarily by people of Spanish, rather than Indian, descent. This is an agricultural region with few places of interest to visitors. The beaches of this coast are for the most part unmemorable, with black sand beaches and unkempt, impoverished fishing villages. Powerful waves make swimming along this coast difficult, if not impossible. The exception is the village of Monterrico, which has become

WHAT'S SPECIAL ABOUT
THE GUATEMALAN HIGHLANDS

Great Towns/Villages
- ☐ Antigua, one of Guatemala's colonial capitals, with beautiful architecture, atmosphere, and many ruins.
- ☐ Chichicastenango, famous for its shopping and rituals performed by local Indians.

Natural Spectacles
- ☐ Lake Atitlán, said to be the most beautiful lake in the world.
- ☐ Volcanoes, live or dormant, that you can climb.

Events/Festivals
- ☐ Holy Week (the week before Easter) in Antigua, celebrated with daily processions through the streets.
- ☐ Ancient Indian dances performed in towns and cities around the country.

Religious Shrines
- ☐ The Church of San Francisco, with the remains of Hermano Pedro, who is said to heal the sick.

Architectural Highlights
- ☐ Ruins of colonial churches, monasteries, convents, universities, and government buildings all over the town of Antigua.

Shopping
- ☐ The Chichicastenango market on Sunday and Thursday, flooded with vendors selling beautiful Guatemalan textiles at the best prices in the country.
- ☐ Panajachel's Calle Santander, lined on both sides with vendors selling "gringo" fashions in Guatemalan fabrics.
- ☐ Villages around Quetzaltenango, with colorful markets on different days of the week.

Guatemala's most popular gringo beach hangout. Along the narrow strip of the Pacific Coast lowlands, there are a few small archeological sites that adventurous types might want to seek out.

1. ANTIGUA

45 kilometers SW of Guatemala City; 100 kilometers E of Panajachel

GETTING THERE By Bus Buses leave Guatemala City from 15 Calle 3-65, Zona 1, every 30 minutes between 7am and 7pm. Duration: 1 hour. Fare: Q2.50 (45¢). If you are coming from anywhere in the highlands, your best bet is to catch any bus headed toward Guatemala and get off at Chimaltenango. Here you can catch a bus down to Antigua. Turansa (tel. 9/322-928 in Antigua or 2/953-574 in Guatemala City) operates a tourist van shuttle between Panajachel and Antigua on Wednesday, Friday, and Sunday. Fare: Q69.60 ($12). This company also operates a similar shuttle daily between Guatemala City and Antigua. You can catch this latter van at the airport at 7:15 am or 5:45pm. Fare: Q40.60 ($7).

By Car The road to Antigua heads northwest out of Guatemala City, climbing a long, steep hill. The junction for Antigua is in San Lucas Sacatepequez, which is a short distance over the hill.

DEPARTING Antigua's bus station is on the west side of town by the market. Buses to Guatemala City leave from here every 30 minutes between 7am and 7pm. To get to Panajachel, Chichicastenango, Quetzaltenango, or anywhere else in the highlands, you must first catch a bus to Chimaltenango and then transfer to a northbound bus.

Minibuses operate between Antigua and both Guatemala City and Panajachel. You'll see advertisements for these minibuses all over Antigua, so you can stop in at any travel agency or hotel and arrange your transportation.

ESSENTIALS Orientation Unlike most Guatemalan towns, Antigua has a street numbering system that includes compass designations; the central point for the plan is the city's main plaza, called the Parque Central. Calles run east to west, and so 4a Calle west of the Parque Central is 4a Calle Poniente; avenidas run north to south, and thus 3a Avenida north of the Parque Central is 3a Avenida Norte. Remember your directions here: *norte* (north), *sur* (south), *oriente* (east), *poniente* (west).

Information Antigua's tourist office is in the Palacio de Gobierno, at the southeast corner of the Parque Central, next to the intersection of 4a Avenida Sur and 5a Calle Oriente (tel. 320-763). It is open daily from 8am to 12:30pm and 2 to 6pm.

Fast Facts The **Banco g&t,** on the west side of the Parque Central, is open Monday through Friday from 9am to 8pm, and Saturday from 10am to 2pm. The **post office** (Correos)—open Monday to Friday from 8am to 4pm—is at 4a Calle Poniente and the Alameda de Santa Lucia, west of the Parque Central near the market. The Guatel **telephone office** is just off the southwest corner of the Parque Central, at the intersection of 5a Calle Poniente and 5a Avenida Sur, and is open daily from 7am to 10pm. **Car rentals** are available from Budget, 6a Avenida Norte no. 59-A (tel. 320-784); Avis, 5a Avenida Norte no. 22 (tel. 322-692); and Americana Internacional, 6a Avenida Norte no. 1-A (tel. 320-489). **Motorcycles** can be rented from Jopa Motorcycle Rental, 6a Avenida Norte no. 3 (tel. 320-794) for around Q125 ($21.55) per day. You'll find **laundries** at Calzada Santa Lucía Sur no. 3 and at 6a Calle Poniente no. 6. The **market** here is held daily (Saturday is most active). Feast day is the first Friday of Lent.

Officially called Antigua Guatemala, this well-preserved colonial city (alt. 5,020 feet; pop. 27,000) was the capital of the country from 1543 to 1773. Even before it was the capital, however, it was on the way to becoming the cultural and religious center of the country. Pedro de Alvarado encouraged the Dominican, Mercedarian, and Franciscan friars to come and teach here, and the church spent a great deal of money in subsequent centuries to make this the most impressive city in Central America.

As the capital of the Captaincy-General of Guatemala, Antigua's official name was La muy Noble y muy Leal Ciudad de Santiago de los Caballeros de Goathemala, or Santiago for short, and from here orders went out to all parts of the region (which included the present-day nations of Guatemala, Belize, Honduras, El Salvador, and Costa Rica). The city's population peaked at 55,000, and the citizens could boast that they lived in the third-oldest Spanish city in America (founded in 1542) and that they had the first Pontifical University in the hemisphere (founded in 1675). It remains impressive to this day, still beautiful and much-visited by tourists, even though the ravages of the earthquakes of 1773 and 1976 are plain to see, along with the effects of 14 smaller quakes, fires, and floods that damaged the city between 1540 and 1717. Some buildings have been in ruins since the quake of 1773; in the quake of 1976, some of the finest churches were badly damaged, but reconstruction efforts are now complete. The San Francisco church, virtually ruined in earlier quakes, was barely touched in the recent one. If you look at the photographs of the reconstruction work on display in the church, you'll see why: Modern construction methods using steel reinforcing rods kept everything in place.

Coming down into the valley of Antigua from Guatemala City, you'll see Antigua's impressive setting, surrounded by three magnificent volcanoes named Agua, Fuego, and Acatenango—Agua is the grand one to the south, visible throughout the town; Fuego is the middle one, which is always smoking.

Antigua is packed full during the week before Easter because of its unique pageantry during Holy Week, so if you plan to be here at that time be sure to reserve your room weeks (even months) in advance. At other times of year, Antigua is one of the most delightful towns to make your base, greatly preferable in all ways to Guatemala City, though Antigua does get crowded on weekends. I highly recommend that you settle in at Antigua and make day trips to the capital, rather than vice versa.

Antigua is almost as well known for its Spanish schools as it is for its ruins. There are dozens of large and small schools all over town and they vary greatly in the quality of their teaching programs. If you decide that you'd like to study Spanish in Antigua, you might want to first try one of the schools listed under "Alternative/Adventure Travel" in Chapter 10.

WHAT TO SEE & DO

Antigua has been declared a "Heritage of Humanity" site by UNESCO, and as such, the colonial city has been preserved much as it may have been in the 17th or 18th century. Streets are of cobblestone, and garish, modern signs are not permitted. Because buses are routed around the perimeter of the city, Antigua is one of the quietest and most smog-free cities in Guatemala (and consequently one of the best for exploring on foot). Stucco walls, wrought-iron window grills, and massive wooden doors studded with brass and iron are the street-side facades that hide old homes centered around flower-filled courtyards.

All over Antigua you'll see both restored and unrestored colonial buildings and ruins of old churches, monasteries, convents, and other buildings. The best way to take in these sights is simply to stroll the streets and follow your nose. Because the core of the old city covers an area of only six blocks by seven blocks, you can easily get to know the entire town in a matter of a few hours. However, to better guide you and so that you don't miss any important sights, I have incorporated the city's major points of interest into a walking tour that should allow you to see Antigua in a day. If you want to spend more time studying churches and ruins, you could split this tour into two days.

WALKING TOUR — ANTIGUA

Start: Parque Central
Finish: Parque Central
Time: 6 hours, including visits to museums and ruins.
Best Time: Tuesday through Friday, when the city isn't so crowded.
Worst Time: Monday, when some of the museums are closed.

Begin your tour on the:

1. **Parque Central,** also known as the Central Plaza or Plaza de Armas, which is Antigua's hub and a gathering spot for Guatemalans and gringos alike. The shade trees, flowers, and fountains make the park a very pleasant place to hang out. The square, originally used as a parade ground for the local military garrison, was the first block laid out when the Spanish platted Antigua in 1541. The fountain in the center of the park was originally built in 1738 and reconstructed in 1936. Across the street from the park to the south is the:
2. **Palacio de los Capitanes Generales,** which was the first seat of government

1. Parque Central
2. Palacio de los Capitanes Generales
3. Catedral Metropolitana
4. Casa de la Cultura
5. Museo de Santiago
6. Quinta Maconda
7. Posada de Don Rodrigo
8. El Arco
9. Convento y Iglesia de Nuestra Señora de la Merced
10. Convento de las Capuchinas
11. Hotel Casa Santo Domingo
12. Jades S.A.
13. Casa Popenoe
14. Iglesia de San Francisco
15. Escuela de Cristo
16. Casa de los Gigantes
17. Iglesia y Convento Santa Clara
18. Las Pilas
19. Museo Colonial

in Antigua and is one of the city's most beautiful buildings. This structure, with its two-story facade lined with arches, is currently home to the INGUAT tourist information office, the police station, and an army headquarters. The building was completed in 1764, destroyed by the earthquake of 1773, and finally partially restored in the early part of this century. On the east side of the park is the:

3. **Catedral Metropolitana,** which though large and imposing, is very unassuming. However, it is worth a visit simply for its distinction of being the church in which were buried such illustrious figures of Guatemalan history as Pedro de Alvarado, discoverer of the country; his wife Doña Beatriz de la Cueva, who succeeded him and became (though briefly) the first woman governor of New Spain; and Bernal Díaz de Castillo, whose day-to-day account of the conquest of Mexico and Guatemala has become a classic. Back in the 16th century, some 180,000 gold pieces went toward the construction of this cathedral. Inside are 68 vaulted arches carved with angels and coats of arms. The dome is 70 feet high; the altar is decorated with gold and lacquer. Unfortunately, very little remains intact of this once-opulent cathedral, but it is presently under reconstruction to repair the sections destroyed by various earthquakes. Right next door to the cathedral, you'll find the:

4. **Casa de la Cultura,** a small gallery space that presents changing exhibits on varying themes. On the north side of the park is the:

5. **Museo de Santiago,** which is housed in the former City Hall (Palacio de Ayuntamiento). With its stone arches, this building is nearly as impressive as the Palacio de los Capitanes Generales on the opposite side of the park. Though the earliest known City Hall to occupy this site was built in 1543, construction of this building did not begin until 1740. The museum houses a variety of artifacts pertaining to Guatemala's history. On display in the 16th-century building are cannons, guns, swords (including one that belonged to Pedro de Alvarado), religious articles, and other items from before and after the Spanish arrived. Note the barred rooms that were used as cells when the palace was converted to a prison in the 19th century. The museum is open Monday through Friday from 9am to 4pm and on Saturday and Sunday from 9am to noon and from 2 to 4pm. Admission is 25 centavos (5¢).

Leaving the park, head north on busy 5a Avenida, which is one of Antigua's main shopping streets. A few doors up you'll come to:

6. **Quinta Maconda,** an interesting little shop selling beautiful textiles. Continuing up 5a Avenida another block will bring you to the:

7. **Posada de Don Rodrigo,** one of Antigua's finest hotels. You can stroll around the courtyards and gardens and maybe listen to a marimba band performing for diners on the patio restaurant. Farther up the block is:

8. **El Arco,** Antigua's most famous landmark. This archway was supposedly built to prevent cloistered nuns living in Santa Catalina convent from seeing the outside world as they walked between the convent buildings on the east and west sides of the street. Atop El Arco is a clock tower that still chimes out the hours. From the north side of the arch, there is a breathtaking view of Agua volcano. Continuing up 5a Avenida, you will see straight ahead of you the south side of the:

9. **Convento y Iglesia de Nuestra Señora de la Merced,** which is called simply La Merced by local people. This church has the most elaborate facade of any church in Antigua. The exterior decorations are of stucco and are painted pale yellow and white. Though construction of this church began in the 1540s, it was not completed until more than 200 years later. Designed to be earthquake-proof, La Merced was inaugurated in 1767. In 1773, a massive earthquake destroyed Antigua, and though it left La Merced mostly intact, the capital was soon moved to present-day Guatemala City. A new La Merced was built in Guatemala City, and this building fell into disrepair. Over the past decade, the interior of the church has been restored. However, the simple style of the renovation in no way compares to the ornate exterior.

From La Merced, walk east on 1a Calle for three blocks, this will take you down one of the city's only tree-lined streets. Turn right onto 2a Avenida, and you will be at the:

10. **Convento de las Capuchinas,** which was built between 1726 and 1736 for Capuchin nuns. Earthquakes have destroyed a good part of the convent, but what remains is fascinating. You'll find a small museum of primarily religious artifacts on the right as you enter the convent. Here you can see tiles and ceramics from excavations done in 1974 and 1975 on several churches in Antigua; some of the relics found in these excavations date as far back as 400 B.C. Among the unusual features here are a bathroom with two stone tubs that seem to have been used for taking hot baths. A few steps away from this bathroom, steps lead down into a circular vault in the center of which is a huge concave pillar. Any sound echoes eerily in this chamber. No one has yet been able to explain the purpose of this chamber, but directly above it is another circular room off of which open 17 tiny cubicles. Presumably these were nuns' cells, and in one cubicle, there is a mock-up of a nun saying her vespers. In the central courtyard, two stairways lead to an upper level from which you can get a good idea of the layout of the convent and the surrounding area. The ruins are open daily from 9am to 5pm, and admission is Q1 (20¢).

From here walk south one block on 2a Avenida and then turn left on 3a Calle. In three blocks you will see on your left the nondescript entry to the:

11. **Hotel Casa Santo Domingo,** Antigua's most astounding hotel. Built among the ruins of a colonial convent, the Casa Santo Domingo incorporates the ruins into its fascinating design. You can stroll the grounds enjoying the gardens and fountains.

REFUELING STOP   The patio dining area at the **Casa Santo Domingo** makes the perfect spot to stop for lunch. Prices are a bit high, but the atmosphere can't be beat. You'll dine surrounded by flowering vines and centuries-old walls.

After lunch, head south one block to 4a Calle, turn right, and you will see:

12. **Jades S.A.,** Antigua's premiere jade store. Even if you can't afford to purchase any Guatemalan jade, you may enjoy looking at the display cases full of jewelry made from this precious stone. From here, turn left on 1a Avenida and in less than three blocks, you'll come to:

13. **Casa Popenoe.** Built in 1632 and destroyed in the earthquake of 1773, Casa Popenoe was restored in the 1920s and 1930s by Dr. Wilson Popenoe, who had come to Guatemala as a fruit and nut researcher for the United Fruit Company. It is Popenoe who is credited with introducing the avocado into cultivation in California. Popenoe and his wife were avid collectors of colonial antiques and filled their home with furnishings and artworks from the 17th and 18th centuries. Nowhere else in Antigua can you get such an insightful glimpse of what life was like in colonial Antigua. Among the more interesting pieces are several parchment lampshades made from Gregorian sheet music. Free guided tours of the house in English are available. Two of Popenoe's daughters still live on the grounds of this spacious compound. The museum is open Monday through Saturday from 2 to 4pm and admission is Q3 (55¢). Continue another block to the end of 1a Avenida and you will be at the entrance to the:

14. **Iglesia de San Francisco.** Over the years, earthquakes have destroyed a lot of the best work on the facade of this church, and a reconstruction during the 1960s failed to restore the church's interior to its original grandeur. However, because the Church of San Francisco contains the tomb of Pedro de Bethancourt, it has become the most visited church in Antigua. Better known as Hermano Pedro, this Franciscan father came to Antigua in about 1650 and later established a hospital where he cared for the sick and the poor. In life and in death he was credited with healing the sick, and people still come to solicit his help in curing their ailments. The walls around his resting place hold a fantastic array of testimonial plaques, letters, photos, and memorabilia. You may see someone

quietly praying before his crypt, gently knocking on it to let Hermano Pedro know that he's needed. Adjacent to the church are the ruins of the Franciscan monastery.

Leave the parking area by the gate diagonally across from where you came in and turn left. In three blocks, you will come to the:

15. **Escuela de Cristo,** a small church noted for its life-size wood statues of Christ carrying the cross and a second statue of Christ in a glass casket. If you walk back up to the Iglesia de San Francisco and turn left, you will see on your right the:

16. **Casa de los Gigantes,** one of Antigua's more interesting handcraft shops. Turn right on 2a Avenida, and you will come to the entrance to the:

17. **Iglesia y Convento Santa Clara,** which dates to 1734 and was destroyed in the earthquake of 1773. These ruins are open to the public. Directly across the street are:

18. **Las Pilas,** Antigua's old public clothes-washing sinks, which are still used today. The cement troughs stand at the end of a shady corridor of palm trees under which clothing and textile vendors display their wares. From here, walk up 3a Avenida and turn left on 5a Calle. Midway down the block is the:

19. **Museo Colonial,** which is located in the building that was once the University of San Carlos de Borromeo. This museum houses a collection of colonial art and antiques. The university was founded in 1676 and was the third university (after those in Mexico City and Lima) in Spanish America. Much of the existing building was built after the earthquake of 1773. As you step through the massive front door, you enter a beautiful and peaceful courtyard with a fountain. Surrounding this courtyard are rooms decorated in the colonial style of the 17th and 18th centuries, including period paintings and religious statuary. Though a bit run down, the museum succeeds in capturing the atmosphere of colonial Antigua. The museum is open Tuesday through Friday from 9am to 4:30pm and Saturday and Sunday from 9am to noon and from 2 to 4:40pm. Continue west on 5a Calle and you will arrive back at the Parque Central.

OTHER RUINS

Some of the city's other ruins worth seeking out include San José el Viejo on 5a Avenida Sur and 8a Calle Poniente; Compañia de Jesus, which was once the home of Bernal Díaz, author of the only first-hand account of Hernán Cortés's conquest of Mexico and Central America, and is now a *típico* market, at 4a Calle Poniente and 6a Avenida Norte; San Jerónimo, which is open to the public, at Santa Lucia and 3a Calle Poniente; La Recolección, also open to the public, at the end of 3a Calle Poniente; and San Agustín at 7a Avenida Sur and 5a Calle Poniente.

TOURS & RECREATION

If you'd like to have a knowledgeable guide take you around the sights of Antigua, contact Elizabeth Bell, 4a Calle Oriente no. 14 (tel. 320-228 or 323-768). Bell, the author of *Antigua Guatemala: An Illustrated History of the City and its Monuments,* offers tours daily at 9:30am and 4:30pm for Q58 ($10) per person.

If you'd like to get out into the countryside around Antigua you can rent a bike. They're available at several places around town and are quite inexpensive. Alternative-ly, you can go on a guided ride with Montaña Maya Mountain Bike Tours, 6a Avenida Sur no. 12-B (tel. 322-768). This company offers half- and full-day trips through coffee plantations, small towns, and countryside around Antigua. A half-day ride is $15 per person and a full-day ride (including lunch) is $29 per person. This company also offers multiday trips to and around Lake Atitlán and through the highlands. Any of these rides will give you glimpses of Guatemala that you would not normally get while traveling by bus or car.

There are also people around town who rent horses and lead guided horseback rides. Check bulletin boards around town for more information.

The trail up to Cerro de la Cruz, a hill on the north side of Antigua, used to be a

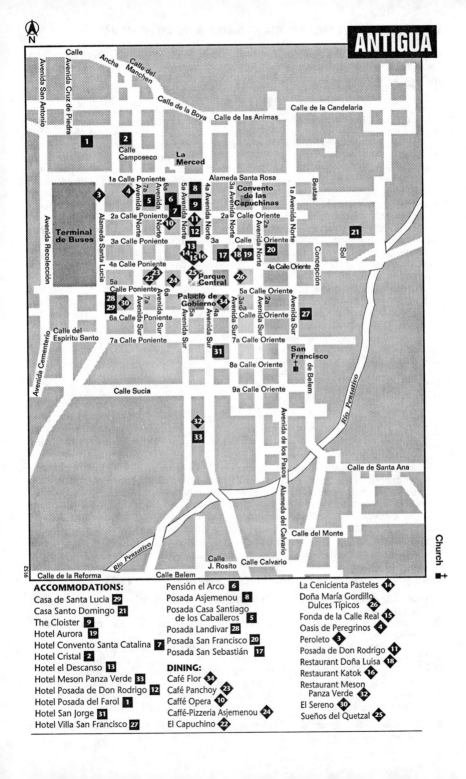

ANTIGUA

popular walk, but robberies and rapes have been all too frequent up here for quite a few years. Do *not* make the hike up here alone. If you have a group, you might be safe, but don't carry any valuables with you.

HOLY WEEK

The week between Palm Sunday and Easter Sunday, called Semana Santa throughout the Spanish-speaking world, is a time for solemn religious processions throughout Guatemala, but nowhere is this spectacle more elaborate than in Antigua. Throughout the week women and men dressed in purple robes carry massive carved wooden floats (*andas*) through the streets of the city. Atop these floats stand statues of Jesus, the Virgin Mary, and other saints. People pay for the privilege of carrying the heavy andas (through these payments the churches raise funds). Sign-up sheets are circulated months in advance and people usually are only allowed to help carry the anda for a block or two.

The andas can weigh several tons and are carried by as many as 40 bearers, who walk slowly and rhythmically. In front of each anda young boys swing censers that waft clouds of incense smoke into the streets. Marching brass bands play doleful hymns and the crowds of pilgrims from all over the world gaze with amazement and reverence. As Easter Sunday approaches, the stages of the Passion of Christ are reenacted. Men on horseback and on foot and dressed in the raiment of Roman soldiers march through the streets. Men in chains representing the thieves who were crucified with Christ are led through the town, and a criminal is even set free from the local jail.

On Good Friday, Antigua's cobblestone streets are blanketed with *alfombras,* carpets made of colored sawdust, flowers, pine needles, and the flowers of a particular palm tree. Neighborhoods, schools, wealthy families, and shops all try to outdo one another in creating the most beautiful alfombras, some of which are hundreds of feet long, take all night to create, and look like colorful cake decorations. This beauty is ephemeral, though, for within a few hours, the processions shuffle dolorously across the works of art, turning them into a tossed salad of bright colors.

The ritual continues on into the night, with andas illuminated by lights hooked up to gasoline generators. Each day, various churches parade different statues through the streets. Before and after the processions, the statues are placed on altars and surrounded by heaps of flowers and fruit.

Because of the large crowds of tourists and pilgrims, pickpockets and purse slashers are out in force during the processions. Do not leave anything of value in your pockets or purse. Be sure to wear a money belt or a neck pouch inside your clothing.

Again, this festival is very popular and packed with Guatemalans and foreigners who have come to enjoy the ceremonies. *You'll need hotel reservations well in advance.* A brochure listing the events during Holy Week can be obtained through the Tourism Office.

WHERE TO STAY

DOUBLES FOR LESS THAN Q87 [$15]

CASA DE SANTA LUCIA, Alameda de Santa Lucia Sur 5, Antigua Guatemala. No phone. 12 rms (all with bath).

$ Rates: Q50 ($8.65) single; Q60 ($10.35) double; Q90 ($15.55) triple. No credit cards.

⑤   The Casa de Santa Lucia is located in Antigua's busiest street, only two blocks from the bus station, but most of the rooms are quiet enough for sleeping and studying. The decor here is modern colonial with a lot of dark wood, much of it shaped on the lathe, creating a good atmosphere in the public rooms even though this is a very inexpensive pension. The guest rooms are quite plain and simple and have seen some wear, but the tiled showers always seem to have hot water.

HOTEL CRISTAL, Avenida el Desengaño no. 25, Antigua Guatemala. No phone. 13 rms (3 with bath).

$ Rates: Q35.10 ($6.05) single without bath, Q46.80 ($8.10) single with bath; Q46.80 ($8.10) double without bath, Q58.50 ($10.10) double with bath. No credit cards.

Spartan and dark but generally acceptable to hardy young travelers on a limited budget, the Cristal was undergoing a renovation when I last visited and was looking better than it had in years. Though it is on a busy street, if you get a room at the back, you shouldn't be bothered by noise. The rooms with private bathrooms that have been remodeled are the better deal. Try to get a room with a window.

HOTEL VILLA SAN FRANCISCO, 1a Avenida Sur No. 15, Antigua. Tel./fax 502-9/323-383. 9 rms (6 with bath).

$ Rates: Q35.10 ($6.05) single without bath, Q46.80 ($8.10) single with bath; Q52.65 ($9.10) double without bath, Q64.35 ($11.10) double with bath. MC, V.

Down at the very end of 6a Calle Oriente, you'll find a good budget choice that is popular with Peace Corps workers. Villa San Francisco is an imposing classical two-story building with wrought-iron balconies and a monstrously big front door covered with brass knobs. The guest rooms are a bit larger than you would expect for such prices, and though Spartan, are generally clean and have a bit of Guatemalan decor. On the premises, you'll find a video bar and bike rentals.

PENSIÓN EL ARCO, 5a Avenida Norte no. 32, Antigua Guatemala. No phone. 7 rms (all with shared bath).

$ Rates: Q24 ($4.35) single; Q35 ($6.05) double. No credit cards.

Located just north of the arch, this old colonial building has been divided up, and a smiling señora rents very plain rooms without baths. Some of the rooms are sort of claustrophobic, with no windows (but, oddly, there are screens on the doors), so it's a good idea to look at your room before you rent it.

POSADA LANDIVAR, 5a Calle Poniente no. 23, Antigua Guatemala. No phone. 11 rms (6 with bath).

$ Rates: Q30 ($5.20) single without bath, Q40 ($6.90) single with bath; Q40 ($6.90) double without bath, Q45 ($7.75) double with bath; Q45 ($7.75) triple without bath, Q50 ($8.65) triple with bath. No credit cards.

Good beds, clean tile bathrooms, and plenty of hot water make this a budget traveler's dream come true in Antigua. Though there is nothing in the way of decor here, most rooms are fairly bright and clean. You won't find better accommodations in this price range.

POSADA SAN FRANCISCO, 3a Calle Oriente No. 19, Antigua. Tel. 502-9/320-266. 15 rms (8 with bath).

$ Rates: Q20 ($3.45) single without bath, Q30 ($5.20) single with bath; Q35 ($6.05) double without bath, Q45 ($7.75) double with bath. No credit cards.

A good choice for those traveling on a very low budget, the Posada San Francisco offers basic, but clean, rooms with red-tile floors. You'll find the rooms down a hall and up a few steps from street level; they're on two floors and surround a small courtyard. Some of the double rooms are fairly large so ask to have a look before taking one. Bathrooms are functional but certainly not spacious.

DOUBLES FOR LESS THAN Q203 [$35]

HOTEL EL DESCANSO, 5a Avenida Norte no. 9., Antigua Guatemala. Tel. 502-9/320-142. 6 rms (all with bath).

$ Rates: Q100 ($17.25) single or double. No credit cards.

Waiting for you only a half block north of the Parque Central, in the building facing the restaurant called Café Café, is a little pension with only 6 rooms. This place is nothing fancy, just a place to rest, as the name implies. The rooms vary in size and the amount of light they get, but they are all fairly comfortable. This is a sort of Guatemalan homestay, and you'll feel like part of the family by the end of your visit. The hotel entrance is through a shop.

HOTEL MESON PANZA VERDE, 5a Avenida Sur no. 19, Antigua Guatemala. Tel./fax 502-9/322-925. 3 rms, 3 suites (all with bath).

$ Rates: Rooms Q133.40 ($23) single or double; suites Q185.60 ($32) single, Q290 ($50) double. MC, V.

The suites here at the Meson Panza Verde are, without a doubt, the best room deal in Antigua, and the regular rooms are a good value as well. The only drawback here is that it can be very difficult to get a room—they're almost always full. My favorite room is the upstairs suite with the modern decor (including elegant halogen floor lamps). The bathroom is absolutely huge, and the tiled bathtub is surrounded by a marble floor and has a dome above it. There are also two sinks and a coffeemaker. The other upstairs suite is not quite as luxurious, but it has a better view. The regular rooms are much smaller but have marble bathrooms and patios in a tiny back garden. The restaurant in the courtyard here is one of the best in Antigua, and there is also a very elegant bar.

HOTEL POSADA DEL FAROL, Calle los Nazarenos no. 17, Antigua Guatemala. Tel. 502-9/323-735. 7 rms (all with bath). TV

$ Rates: Q127 ($21.90) single; Q150 ($25.90) double; Q179.55 ($30.90) triple. MC, V.

Though this newer hotel is a bit out of the way, the artistic touches and quiet surroundings on the edge of an old coffee plantation make it a good choice. Owned by a German woman who also runs a local art gallery, the hotel is full of artworks, almost all of which are for sale. So, if you like the painting on the wall in your room, you can buy it and take it home with you. The rooms are all colorfully decorated with bright bedspreads, painted tables, and wicker headboards. There are also refrigerators in all the rooms. Bathrooms are, unfortunately, rather small and basic. You'll find the hotel two blocks north and three blocks west of La Merced church.

POSADA ASJEMENOU, 5a Avenida Norte (Calle del Arco) No. 31, Antigua. Tel. 502-9/322-670. 10 rms (6 with bath).

$ Rates: Q65 ($11.20) single without bath, Q89 ($15.35) single with bath; Q89 ($15.35) double without bath, Q116 ($20) double with bath. V.

A few doors past the arch on 5a Avenida you'll find one of the best deals in town. The hotel is situated in an old colonial home and the guest rooms surround two very tranquil courtyards. In one there is a fountain and colorful

---

ⓕ FROMMER'S SMART TRAVELER: HOTELS

1. Make your room reservations up to a year in advance if you want to be in Antigua for Semana Santa (Holy Week), which is the week before Easter. Rates then are as much as 50% higher than normal.
2. If you're coming here to study Spanish, check with your Spanish school about a homestay plan, the cheapest way to stay in Antigua. You'll also be able to practice your Spanish with the host family.
3. Check the bulletin board at Doña Luisa, 4a Calle Oriente no. 12, for information on apartments for rent.
4. Get a room close to the Parque Central so you'll be close to the best restaurants and can easily stroll the square after dinner.
5. Once you arrive in town, keep your eyes open for new lodges and hotels; they often offer excellent value.

garden, in the other a traditional clothes-washing basin (*pila*). Pale yellow walls, squeaky tile floors, and open porticoes all evoke Antigua's colonial heritage. On the other hand, there are very contemporary tables and chairs in the porticoes and even a television lounge. Decorative pottery braziers are replicas of Mayan urns. The rooms themselves are large and attractively decorated and the surroundings are serene.

DOUBLES FOR LESS THAN Q261 [$45]

HOTEL AURORA, 4a Calle Oriente 16, Antigua Guatemala. Tel. 502-9/ 320-217. 16 rms (all with bath).
$ Rates: Q191.40 ($33) single; Q220.40 ($38) double; Q249.40 ($43) triple. No credit cards.

⭐ An old favorite in the moderate range, even though it has become considerably more expensive in recent years, the Aurora is housed in a traditional colonial building. A grassy courtyard decorated with flowers and graced by a fountain is surrounded by a portico set with wicker furniture and paved in shiny tiles. For cool evenings, there's a snug parlor with a fireplace. The guest rooms are lofty and airy but a bit dark (as befits their colonial style), with odd bits of furniture both antique and not. All is in good condition. Moderately priced breakfasts are taken in an old-fashioned dining room.

HOTEL CONVENTO SANTA CATALINA, 5a Avenida Norte No. 28, Antigua Guatemala. Tel. 502-9/323-080. 18 rms (all with bath).
$ Rates: Q203 ($35) single; Q232 ($40) double; Q261 ($45) triple. No credit cards.
As its name implies, this hotel was once a convent—in fact it was the convent for which Antigua's famous arch was built. The arch was meant to hide the temptations of the world from cloistered nuns as they crossed the street between convent buildings. Today the hotel's rooms surround a garden courtyard in the center of which is a bubbling fountain. The wide porticoes are set with tables and chairs and serve as the hotel's dining room, although there is an indoor eating area as well. You'll have a strong sense of the history of Antigua if you stay here. Right next door, and blending into the hotel, are the ruins of the rest of the convent. The rooms, though dark, are high-ceilinged and spacious, with tile floors, old wooden wardrobes, and heavy wooden bed frames. Bathrooms are also quite large.

HOTEL SAN JORGE, 4a Avenida Sur (Calle del Conquistador) no. 13, Antigua Guatemala. Tel. 502-9/323-132. 8 rms (all with bath). TV
$ Rates: Q173 ($29.85) single; Q207 ($35.70) double; Q241 ($41.55) triple. V (add 7% surcharge).
Set on a long narrow lot south of the Hotel Antigua, the Hotel San Jorge offers very modern rooms at very reasonable prices. All the guest rooms are carpeted and have fireplaces, large windows, and reading lights. In the bathroom, you'll find a tub and plenty of counter space. Running the length of the rooms is a long veranda facing a narrow, though very lush, garden. For a small fee, guests here can use the pool at the Hotel Antigua.

POSADA CASA SANTIAGO DE LOS CABALLEROS, 7a Avenida Norte No. 67 (Calle San Sebastián), Antigua Guatemala. Tel. 502-9/320-465. 7 rms (all with bath).
$ Rates: Q203 ($35) single; Q237.80 ($41) double; Q266.80 ($46) triple. MC, V.
On a quiet street about 10 minutes from the Parque Central you'll find a tranquil little hotel. All the rooms have two double beds, some with Guatemalan blankets on them, and the bathrooms are modern and clean. The floors are of highly polished tile that squeaks when you walk across it. There's an old orange grove in back of the house and a sun deck on the roof.

POSADA SAN SEBASTIÁN, 3a Avenida Norte (Calle de la Princesa Xicotencalt) no. 4, Antigua Guatemala. Tel./fax 502-9/322-621. 8 rms (all with bath).
$ Rates: Q174 ($30) single; Q203 ($35) double; Q243.60 ($42) triple. MC, V.

⭐ The porticoes and rooms of this small hotel are overflowing with colonial antiques and handcrafts from around Guatemala, which makes a stay here a bit like a visit to a cluttered antique store. There is an overall feeling of faded glory here, but personally, I love the atmosphere. However, this hotel may not be for everyone. Most of the rooms are quite large and some have equally spacious bathrooms. The location only a block and a half from the Parque Central makes the Posada San Sebastian very convenient.

WORTH THE EXTRA BUCKS

CASA SANTO DOMINGO, 3a Calle Oriente no. 28, Antigua Guatemala. Tel. 502-9/320-140, 322-102, or 320-079. Fax 502-9/320-102. 17 rms, 7 suites (all with bath). TEL
$ Rates: Q780.40 ($134.55) single; Q848.25 ($146.25) double; Q950.05 ($163.80) triple; Q1,017.90–Q1,696.50 ($175.50–$292.50) suite. AE, DC, MC, V.

⭐ This is one of the most beautiful hotels I have seen anywhere in the world, and if you have some extra money to spend on a real splurge, this is the place to do it. Built amid the ruins of a colonial convent, the hotel combines the Spanish cultural heritage and atmosphere of Antigua with the service of an international luxury hotel. From the moment you step through the thoroughly nondescript front door, you are enveloped in another world—fountains bubble amid the flowers of the lush gardens, macaws squawk on their perches, and the coolness of a once grand edifice surrounds you. The front desk is an ornate altar, and everywhere you look there are colonial antiques. The modern guest rooms are beautifully decorated and furnished with the highest quality appointments. The dining room serves excellent international cuisine, and there is a tranquil garden terrace dining area. Out in the back garden, you'll find a cooling swimming pool.

THE CLOISTER, 5a Avenida Norte 23, Antigua Guatemala. Tel./fax 502-9/320-712 or (in the U.S.) 508/428-1156. 4 rms (all with bath).
$ Rates (including breakfast): Q290 ($50) single; Q319 ($55) double. No credit cards.

⭐ Owned and operated by transplanted American Barbara Leaver, The Cloister is
⭐ one of Antigua's most beautiful hotels and is surprisingly inexpensive. The restored colonial home is almost directly under the city's famous arch, which is visible from the hotel's courtyard. Guest rooms are huge and have soaring
Ⓢ ceilings that make the rooms seem even larger. All the rooms have fireplaces, shelves full of books, Guatemalan blankets on the beds, and colonial-style furnishings. There's a beautifully decorated and well-stocked library where guests can gather throughout the day or evening, and a courtyard garden that's a work of art. In fact, everywhere you look here, there are works of art. Several more rooms, in a new building, were under construction when I last visited.

HOTEL POSADA DE DON RODRIGO, 5a Avenida Norte (Calle del Arco) no. 17, Antigua Guatemala. Tel. 502-9/320-291 or 320-387. Fax 502-9/ 316-838. 34 rms (all with bath).
$ Rates: Q407.20 ($70.20) single; Q461.40 ($79.55) double; Q515.75 ($88.95) triple. AE, DC, MC, V.

⭐ Guests here can easily conjure up the lifestyle of the captains-general of Guatemala. The hotel is arranged around two courtyards, both very beautiful, the hind court having a tinkling fountain to entertain diners in the hotel's restaurant. The guest rooms have period furnishings: brass or carved-wood bedsteads, beamed ceilings, woven floor mats, and other antique or "antiqued" furnishings. The 24-hour hot water is sometimes little more than a warm trickle, but aside from this one drawback, the hotel is a rough-cut jewel. Rates are occasionally lower than those listed above, so be sure to ask for their best rates.

The main dining room and the bar of the open-air patio restaurant keep up the theme of colonial opulence, and marimba music entertains guests each afternoon.

READERS RECOMMEND

Hotel El Confort de Antigua, 1a Avenida Norte no. 2, Antigua Guatemala. Tel. 502-9/320-566. *"This Spartan, clean little hotel is a nicely renovated Spanish home just off busy 4a Calle and only four blocks from Parque Central. Security is excellent, as only guests have a key to open the massive wooden doors that open from a lovely courtyard onto the street."*—Irwin C. Richter, Holly Ridge, North Carolina

WHERE TO EAT

MEALS FOR LESS THAN Q29 [$5]

CAFÉ FLOR, 4a Avenida Sur no. 1. No phone.
   Cuisine: MEXICAN.
$ Prices: Main dishes Q12–Q20 ($2.10–$3.45). No credit cards.
   Open: Mon–Fri 7am–9:30pm; Sat 8am–9:30pm.
It is difficult to think of Mexican food as exotic and foreign when you are this far south of the border, but that is exactly what it is in Guatemala. Locals and tourists alike put away plates of tacos, burritos, and enchiladas. You can have yours made with beef, chicken, pork, or tofu. The restaurant is on two levels, with a couple of window tables that are sunny spots for lunch. The restaurant shows videos daily.

CAFÉ PANCHOY, 6a Avenida Norte no. 14a. Tel. 322-651.
   Cuisine: GUATEMALAN.
$ Prices: Appetizers Q6.50–Q12 ($1.15–$2.10); main dishes Q9–Q27 ($1.55–$4.65). No credit cards.
   Open: Wed–Mon 7am–10pm.
Authentic Guatemalan food is none too easy to find in Antigua, but in this little hole in the wall, you can order many of the same dishes you've seen for sale on the street (where you're likely to be hesitant to buy). My favorites are the corn tortillas topped with a meat-filled chili relleno or guacamole. You can also get good pepian and an excellent chicken soup.

CAFFÉ-PIZZERIA ASJEMENOU, 5a Calle Poniente no. 4. Tel. 322-832.
   Cuisine: PIZZA.
$ Prices: Pizzas Q12.50–Q44 ($2.15–$7.60). DC, MC, V.
   Open: Tues–Sun 8am–10pm.
Managed by the same people who run the popular Hotel Posada Asjemenou but located on the other side of town, this cozy little place serves up good pizzas amid an Italian café atmosphere. In addition to the pizzas, there are salads and excellent desserts, plus some of the best coffee in town. You can even get pizza to go.

FONDA DE LA CALLE REAL, 5a Avenida Norte no. 5. Tel. 322-696.
   Cuisine: GUATEMALAN/INTERNATIONAL.
$ Prices: Full meal Q14–Q40 ($2.45–$6.90).
   Open: Daily 7am–10pm.
Popular as a hangout and meeting place for Spanish students, the Fonda is known for its delicious *caldo real*—a delicious chicken soup that comes with tortillas and a condiment tray of oregano, cilantro, lime slices, chopped onions, and ground chili pepper—for Q17 ($2.95). Although the restaurant doesn't look very large from street level, upstairs there are 30 tables where you can sit comfortably and order roast chicken, fondues, steaks, and chops prepared by several busy señoras working hard in the downstairs kitchen. Steaks are the most expensive items.
   A newer annex is located at 3a Calle Poniente no. 7 (tel. 320-507) about a block away. This annex is much more elegant and relaxing than the original restaurant and

fairly sings with colonial memories. This branch also has an extensive wine list and serves a fabulous flan.

PEROLETO, Calzada de Santa Lucia No. 36. No phone.
   Cuisine: JUICE BAR/SNACKS.
   $ Prices: Licuados Q3.75–Q7.75 (65¢–$1.35), sandwiches Q3.50–Q7 (60¢–$1.20). No credit cards.
   Open: Daily 7am–8pm.

You're almost sitting in the street at this slightly sunken juice bar and snack shop just up from the market and bus terminal, and the noise of the buses roaring by can be a bit deafening. However, there's no place better for a quick, early breakfast or a cheap, fast lunch. If the noise is too much for you, they have an enclosed dining room right next door to the juice bar. Granola with yogurt and fruit salad, *ceviche*, burgers, and hot dogs are the staples on the menu here. The carrot cake is the best in town and the juices and licuados are excellent. Try the orange and carrot juice mix.

RESTAURANT DOÑA LUISA, 4a Calle Oriente no. 12. Tel. 322-578.
   Cuisine: INTERNATIONAL.
   $ Prices: Breakfast Q5–Q13 (90¢–$2.25); sandwiches Q8–Q18 ($1.40–$3.10). No credit cards.
   Open: Daily 7am–9:30pm.

This busy two-story café is the town's traditional and very popular meeting place, and it is not far off the main square. Enter the building, and you'll see a small central courtyard set with dining tables, but there are more dining rooms and porticoes on the upper level. Doña Luisa's is frequented almost exclusively by gringos; the newsy bulletin board bears messages in both Spanish and English, with a few notices in French and German thrown in for good measure. The menu is eclectic—with sandwiches of many varieties (made on good bread baked right here), yogurt, chili, cakes and pies, and also more substantial fare. Alcohol is served, as is excellent Antigua coffee.

SUEÑOS DEL QUETZAL, 5a Avenida Norte No. 3. No phone.
   Cuisine: VEGETARIAN.
   $ Prices: Main dishes Q12–Q25 ($2.10–$4.35). No credit cards.
   Open: Daily 7am–10pm.

With one of the only balconies in town, Sueños del Quetzal enjoys an enviable location. If you can manage to grab one of the two balcony tables while it is free, sit back for a leisurely meal and enjoy the view of the street activity below. An international vegetarian menu has made this restaurant a hit with young travelers and students staying in Antigua. On the menu, you'll find 15 different breakfasts, listed by nationality (including Australian). In addition to veggie standards such as tabouli, hummus, and veggie burgers, there are some local dishes cooked without the meat, and daily casserole specials.

 FROMMER'S SMART TRAVELER:
RESTAURANTS

1. Be sure to ask if there's a *plato del día*, which is always the best deal on the menu.
2. Some of Guatemala's best restaurants are in Antigua, so if you can afford a splurge or two, this is the place for it.
3. Check the opening time for a restaurant before heading off for your coffee and breakfast. Many restaurants don't open until fairly late in the morning.
4. You'll beat the dinner crowds, which can be particularly bad on weekends, if you eat dinner early, say between 5:30 and 6:30pm.

MEALS FOR LESS THAN Q58 [$10]

CAFFE OPERA, 6a Avenida Norte no. 17. Tel. 320-727.
Cuisine: SANDWICHES.
$ Prices: Sandwiches Q9–Q31 ($1.55–$5.35). No credit cards.
Open: Thurs–Tues 10am–9:30pm.

⭐ Modeled after a European café, Opera is a casually sophisticated place where you can listen to opera tapes while enjoying espresso and a pastry or a sandwich. The prices are high for Guatemala, but the atmosphere is great. There are autographed opera posters and photos all over the walls.

EL CAPUCHINO, 6a Avenida Norte no. 8. Tel. 320-613.
Cuisine: ITALIAN.
$ Prices: Main dishes Q16–Q70 ($2.75–$12.10). No credit cards.
Open: Tues–Sun 11am–10pm.
Between 4a and 5a calles Poniente, 1½ blocks from the Parque Central, you'll find one of Antigua's popular Italian restaurants. The facade of the restaurant doesn't look like much, but there is a covered interior court and arcade, with simple dining tables set out. Homey rather than fancy, the restaurant features a long menu of Italian food: pizzas, chicken cacciatore, lasagne, ravioli, spaghetti bolognese, and all the other favorites. Most meals here will not run over Q38 ($6.55). In the evening, the mariachi bands often stop by the restaurant; for a small tip, they will serenade you.

OASIS DE PEREGRINO, 7a Avenida Norte no. 96. No phone.
Cuisine: INTERNATIONAL.
$ Prices: Main dishes Q16–Q25 ($2.75–$4.35). No credit cards.
Open: Mon–Fri 5:30–10pm; Sat noon–10pm; Sun 10:30am–10pm.

⑤⭐ This is currently one of the best inexpensive restaurants in Antigua and is well worth the 10-minute walk to get here. Located in an old colonial building, the Oasis features classical music on the stereo and subdued lighting, candles, and fresh flowers on every table. On the menu, you'll find such varied dishes as nachos, vegetarian lasagna, bratwurst, and pasta with pesto sauce, and every dish is attractively presented. There is even a Sunday brunch. The foreign owners of the restaurant love their new country and show it by supporting educational programs for Guatemalan children.

POSADA DE DON RODRIGO, 5a Avenida Norte (Calle del Arco) no. 17. Tel. 320-291.
Cuisine: GUATEMALAN/INTERNATIONAL.
$ Prices: Main dishes Q47–Q79 ($8.10–$13.65); plato deldia Q53 ($9.15). AE, DC, MC, V.
Open: Daily 6am–9:30pm.

⑤ Although this is a splurge hotel, you can enjoy lunch here even if you're on a tight budget. You can order a filling platillo chapín (plate of Guatemalan specialties), including carne asada (grilled beef), guacamole, and frijoles refritos with rice and cheese, for Q53 ($9.15); with a drink, tax, and service, the bill may come to Q65 ($11.20). The menu also features a vegetarian plate, fish filets, chicken, pork, and steaks. Even a full à la carte meal will cost only Q70 ($12.10). The setting is pleasant, and the staff (dressed in traditional costumes) is accommodating and helpful.

RESTAURANT KATOK, 4a Avenida Norte no. 2. Tel. 320-524.
Cuisine: GUATEMALAN/INTERNATIONAL.
$ Prices: Main dishes Q26–Q46 ($4.50–$7.95). DC, MC, V.
Open: Daily 8am–10pm.
Located only half a block away from the Parque Central in a colonial-style building, Katok has several dining rooms plus a patio dining area. Fresh flowers grace every table, and waiters in bow ties make sure that everything is to your satisfaction. The plato típico especial Katok is a bounteous platter that includes two types of sausage, steak, beans, cheese, fried bananas, salad, potatoes, and fried green onion—all for Q39 to Q42 ($6.75–$7.25). The parrillada Katok is similar and costs Q41–Q44

($7.10–$7.60). Soups here are good and can be enough for a light meal. There's even a children's menu on Sunday. Also, there's a wide assortment of cocktails, beer, and wine.

SWEETS & PASTRIES

LA CENICIENTA PASTELES, 5a Avenida Norte no. 7. No phone.
Cuisine: PASTRIES.
$ Prices: Cake Q3.5–Q6.5 (60¢–$1.15) per slice. No credit cards.
Open: Daily 8:30am–8pm.
With its display case full of delectable and tempting cakes and pastries, Cenicienta is always jammed with young students indulging themselves. The daily menu includes quiche chapín (Guatemalan style), yogurt and fruit, New York cheesecake, and numerous licuados. Don't be discouraged by the crowd in the front room; there is another dining area in the courtyard out back. You also can get anything to go.

DOÑA MARÍA GORDILLO DULCES TÍPICOS, 4a Calle Oriente no. 11. No phone.
Cuisine: SWEETS.
$ Prices: 50 centavos–Q2.90 (10¢–50¢). No credit cards.
Open: Daily 9am–6pm.
Located across the street from the Hotel Aurora, this shop—filled with all sorts of sweets, desserts, and confections made from milk, fruit, eggs, marzipan, chocolate, and sugar—brings a bit of heaven to earth. Some local crafts are on sale as well. There is always a crowd of loyal customers filling the shop. Note that the treats here are for take-out only—there's no place to sit and munch. Since few if any of these sweets will be familiar to you, your best bet is to try a little of whatever looks good until you find the one that you can't live without.

WORTH THE EXTRA BUCKS

RESTAURANT MESÓN PANZA VERDE, 5a Avenida Sur no. 19. Tel. 322-925.
Cuisine: CONTINENTAL.
$ Prices: Appetizers Q22–Q48 ($3.80–$8.30); main dishes Q26–Q68 ($4.50–$11.75). MC, V.
Open: Tues–Sat noon–3pm and 6:30–10pm; Sun noon–4pm.
If you want to be pampered and surround yourself with elegance, head out 5a Avenida Sur to one of Antigua's classiest little restaurants. The European owner knows how to make his guests happy. You might start your meal with six snails for Q24 ($4.15), then order a perfectly done steak with béarnaise or green-pepper sauce for Q48 ($8.30). Top it off with chocolate mousse or peach Melba for Q18 ($3.10). There are also daily specials that include such tempting courses as cream of tomato soup, smoked salmon, and lobster thermidor. Your bill might come to around Q110 ($19), which is a fraction of what you would pay for this same meal back home.

EL SERENO, 6a Calle Poniente no. 30. Tel. 320-073.
Cuisine: INTERNATIONAL. **Reservations:** Recommended.
$ Prices: Appetizers Q15.50–Q22.50 ($2.70–$3.90); main dishes Q52–Q90 ($9–$15.55). AE, MC, V.
Open: Wed–Sun noon–3pm and 6:30–10pm; Mon 6:30–10pm.
Between the Alameda de Santa Lucia and 7a Avenida Sur, next door to the Tecún Umán School of Spanish, is one of Antigua's finest restaurants. Within this colonial house are several small dining rooms. There are corner fireplaces, original oil paintings (many for sale), a small open-air portico, and carefully tended plants here and there. A doorman will welcome you, and a barman awaits your order in the small old-fashioned bar. The service is as refined as the cuisine. You might start with fresh asparagus salad and go on to chicken tetrazzini followed by Kahlua-and-brandy cake. The menu changes weekly, with new items being added all the time. With a glass of house wine, a full dinner might cost as little as Q100 ($17.25)—but it

could be as high as Q150 ($25.90), or perhaps even a bit higher, depending on your wine selection. Whatever you pay, you won't soon forget your meal here.

READERS RECOMMEND

Quesos y Vino, 5a Avenida Norte no. 32. *"Run by an Italian, excellent and medium price. Best salads ever. Just above the arch on 5a Avenida."*—Madeleine A. Stone, Sebastopol, Calif.

EVENING ENTERTAINMENT

With so many Spanish students in town and the wealthy of the world discovering Antigua, it should come as no surprise that there are numerous bars in town. **Jazz Gruta,** Calzado Santa Lucia no. 17, is a cavelike bar/restaurant north of the bus terminal. The bar/restaurant has a Euro-Bohemian atmosphere about it, and the music on the stereo is great. Several nights a week there is live jazz. The **Maconda Pub,** 5a Avenida Norte no. 28, is located almost underneath the famous arch and is always full of gringos and Guatemalans, which makes for a very convivial atmosphere. The **Rainbow Reading Room,** 7a Avenida Sur no. 8, is a Generation X hangout that draws on the '60s for inspiration—it's a laid-back coffeehouse scene. There's also a video room and a bookshop here.

SAVVY SHOPPING

In the past few years, Antigua has become the upscale shopping center for Guatemala. Though you'll find a greater selection in Chichicastenango or Panajachel, nowhere will you find better quality merchandise, more contemporary fashion designs, or a more interesting assortment of jewelry, home furnishings, and quality craft items.

BEST BUYS

Art Galleries

GALLERIA DE ARTE ESTIPITE, Avenida el Desengaño 22. Tel. 320-469.
Owned by a German, this gallery showcases both Guatemalan artists and European and North American artists who live or work in Guatemala. There is a wide range of styles here in several rooms. Lectures are frequently held here.

Bookstores

CASA ANDINISTA, 4a Calle Oriente no. 5-A. No phone.
This store specializes on books about Guatemala and Central America and also has maps, postcards, and a bulletin board filled with interesting notices. The store is open daily from 8am to 7:45pm.

RAINBOW READING ROOM, 7a Avenida Sur no. 8. No phone.
With more than 4,000 used books in stock, this is the best place in Antigua to shop for a book to get you through the next bus ride. There's also a very popular café here.

UN POCO DE TODO, 5a Avenida between calles 4 and 5. No phone.
Located right on the Parque Central, this small shop has a good selection of new books in both English and Spanish, as well as magazines and newspapers from the U.S.

Fashions

KATZ, Casa de las Gargolas, 5a Avenida Norte no. 14. No phone.
This store is located in a shopping arcade just off the Parque Central and is filled with the most beautiful and most expensive women's and men's fashions in Antigua. The quality is high and the designs are out of the ordinary.

QUÉ BÁRBARA, 4a Calle Oriente no. 29-A. Tel. 320-602.
Attractive contemporary designs using colorful Guatemalan fabrics are the specialty of this shop which offers a quality above what you find in most shops.

Handcrafts

AL PIE DE VOLCAN GIFT SHOP, 3a Calle Poniente no. 3B. No phone.

This shop is filled with hand-made items including tablecloths, place mats, and napkins in primarily pastel colors. There are also beautiful pieces of hand-blown glassware made from recycled glass as well as attractive ceramics.

This store is open Monday through Saturday from 9am to 7pm and Sunday from 10am to 6pm. Branch shops are at the corner of Alameda de Santa Lucia (tel. 323-684) and at 5a Calle Poniente no. 13 (tel. 323-690). The store on Alameda de Santa Lucia specializes in fabric by the yard, while the 5a Calle shop sells ready-to-wear fashions in stylish designs.

AVIFAUNA, 3a Calle Oriente no. 31. No phone.

This store, which is located across from the entrance to the luxurious Casa Santo Domingo hotel, has an interesting collection of old wooden masks, contemporary wood carvings, interesting candle holders, *santos,* ceramics, and jewelry. The quality here is quite high.

CASA DE LOS GIGANTES, 7a Calle Oriente no. 18. Tel. 320-685.

Named for the two giant wood-and-cloth puppets that guard the entrance to the store, this place is as jam-packed as your grandma's attic. There are lots of rustic carved wood items for home decor, including towel racks, platters, knickknack shelves, and the like.

COLIBRÍ, 4a Calle Oriente no. 3-B. Tel. 320-280.

This store has long been popular for its attractive place mats and table runners.

QUINTA MACONDA, 5a Avenida Norte no. 11. Tel. 320-821.

Though most of the fabrics here are Guatemalan, they are not the standard garish colors and chaotic combinations. Instead, there are rich, though subdued, colors and lush textures. There are handbags, cosmetic cases, pillow covers, tablecloths, and even fabrics by the yard. Prices here reflect the quality of the materials.

Jade

When an ancient Mayan jade quarry was rediscovered in 1958, Guatemala once again became a center for jade jewelry. Unless you are very familiar with jade, I wouldn't advise buying any except from a very reliable dealer such as those mentioned here. Real jade is very expensive and even a simple little pendant can cost more than $100.

LA CASA DE JADE, 4a Calle Oriente no. 3. Tel. 320-834.

One-of-a-kind jewelry designs, superb craftsmanship, and high quality jade make the jewelry in this shop well worth a look. The store is open daily from 9am to 6pm.

JADES S.A., 4a Calle Oriente no. 34. Tel. 320-109. Also at 4a Calle Oriente no. 1 and 4a Calle Oriente no. 12 (tel. 322-613).

This was the first jade factory and store to open in Antigua and has now expanded to include three shops up and down 4a Calle. Though the stores sell much more than just jade jewelry, the jade jewelry is the main reason for a visit. The jade showroom is a large and elegant salon filled with jewelry in both traditional Mayan and more contemporary designs. The main store is open daily from 9am to 9pm.

Markets

The main market is located on the west side of town at the end of 4a Calle Poniente. Saturday is the main market day but there is plenty of activity here every day of the week. If you're looking for cheap clothes made from Guatemalan fabrics, this is your best bet in Antigua. However, quality is low. Beside the ruins of Compañia de Jesus at the corner of 4a Calle Poniente and 6a Avendia Norte, you'll find dozens of vendors selling *tipico* fashions, fabrics, jewelry, and handcrafts. Over on the opposite side of the Parque Central, at the corner of 3a Avenida and 6a Calle, in a palm-shaded park, you'll find a similar, though smaller, market.

ONE-DAY EXCURSIONS

Ambitious mountaineers can climb up **Agua,** the impressive volcano that rises just beyond the outskirts of town. Start by taking the bus from behind the Antigua market to Santa María de Jesus. After a 20-minute ride, the bus will drop you in the main square of the village of that name; from the square, a road leads out of town and up the volcano. It's a fairly easy hike (not a climb) to the top for someone who's used to hiking. The free bonuses are everywhere: lovely wildflowers, fragrant aromas, lots of forest, and more mist the higher up you get. You can reach the top in four hours if you push it, five hours if you don't. When you reach the top, you'll see the crater and a magnificent view (if it's a clear day and the clouds don't shut you off). Don't try this hike alone, however. As anywhere in Guatemala, to lessen your chances of being robbed, you should always hike in a group of at least three or four people.

If you've ever wanted to climb an active volcano, this is the place to do it. A 2½-hour drive from Antigua is **Pacaya,** a live volcano that can be climbed by anyone in good health. Every few minutes the volcano erupts, spewing red-hot rocks into the air. A nearby dormant cone serves as a perfect vantage point for observing the eruptions. Keep in mind that, although the hike up is strenuous, the last few hundred yards to the top of the crater, across loose lava rocks and up a steep slope, can be very difficult. Winds can be strong and the footing is always slippery. Also, keep in mind that for several years now bandits have been robbing people on the slopes of Pacaya. Do not carry any cash or other valuables with you if you climb this volcano. If you go with a guide from Antigua, the price of the trip should include security measures as well. Many companies and travel agencies around Antigua offer trips up Pacaya. The going rate is $7 or $8 for a day trip.

One more thing, if you're only interested in seeing the volcano erupt, be sure it's active before making the climb. Many adventurous types camp out near the peak to watch the eruptions at night; others simply make the hike a day trip.

Several tour companies also offer trips from Antigua to other parts of Guatemala, including Tikal, Lake Atitlán, Chichicastenango, Quirigua, Lívingston, and Copán (Honduras). Check with travel agencies around town for the current rates for such tours, many of which are quite economical. Aviatur, 5a Avenida Norte no. 35 (tel. 322-642) and Turansa, 5a Avenida Norte no. 22 (tel. 322-664) are two companies offering such tours.

2. LAKE ATITLÁN & PANAJACHEL

120 kilometers W of Guatemala City; 80 kilometers SE of Quetzaltenango; 40 kilometers S of Chichicastenango

GETTING THERE   By Bus   Rebuli buses from Guatemala City leave from 21 Calle 1-34, Zona 1 daily every hour from 6:30am to 4pm. Duration: 3 hours. Fare: Q8 ($1.40). From Antigua, first take a bus to Chimaltenango and then catch a north-bound bus as far as Los Encuentros, where you'll have to transfer again to reach Panajachel. Duration: 3 hours. Fare: Q12 ($2.10). From Chichicastenango, you may be able to catch a direct bus to Panajachel, otherwise take one to Los Encuentros and transfer there. Duration: 2 hours. Fare: Q6 ($1.05). From Quetzaltenango, you may be able to catch a direct bus, otherwise, transfer at Los Encuentros. Duration: 3 hours. Fare: Q10 ($1.75).

Turansa, 5a Avenida Norte no. 22, Antigua (tel. 322-664), operates a minibus service between Antigua and Panajachel on Wednesday, Friday, and Sunday. The one-way fare is Q69.60 ($12). You can also find other companies around Antigua offering minibus transport for about the same price or a little less. There are also minibuses that operate between Chichicastenango and Panajachel.

By Car   Lake Atitlán can be reached from either the north or the south, although the southern route is not recommended due to frequent rebel activity in that area. Coming from Guatemala City, take the Patzún turnoff and continue down to

Panajachel. Coming from Quetzaltenango, take the Sololá road. If you're coming from Chichicastenango, you must first turn west onto the highway before turning south a few miles later for Sololá and Panajachel.

DEPARTING Most buses out of Panajachel leave from the corner of Calle Principal and Calle Santander. Check at the INGUAT office for a current bus schedule.

There are also tourist vans that head up to Chichi for market days. Ask around in town for the name of a company offering these trips. Expect to pay around Q81.20 ($14) for the round-trip fare. Turansa (tel. 322-928 in Antigua or 953-574 in Guatemala City) operates a shuttle between Panajachel and Antigua on Wednesday, Friday, and Sunday. The shuttle van stops at the Hotel Regis on Calle Santander at 12:10pm. Fare: Q69.60 ($12).

ESSENTIALS Orientation Panajachel lies on the northern shore of Lake Atitlán, at the foot of the mountains. Coming into town from Sololá, you descend the mountainside along a serpentine road, and if you're driving, you might like to stop at the scenic overlook. Near the bottom of the hill, you pass the turnoff on the right for the deluxe Hotel Atitlán, then for the Hotel Tzanjuyu, and next for the Cacique Inn, before continuing into town along the Calle Principal, the main street. There's a grocery store on the right, then a Texaco service station. Finally you come to the heart of town: the intersection of Calle Principal, Calle Santander, and Calle Los Arboles, where you will see the Banco Agricola and the Hotel Mayan Palace. Calle Santander, on the right, goes down to the beach and the Hotel Monterrey.

Farther along, the Calle Principal holds several more hotels, restaurants, and shops and also the post and telegraph offices and the church. By the church is the town hall, the police station, and the marketplace, busiest on Sunday but with some activity on weekdays from 9am to noon.

Parallel to Calle Santander, going from the center of town to the beach at the Hotel del Lago, is the Calle de Balneario.

Fast Facts The INGUAT Tourism Office is in the center of town on Calle Santander near the Hotel Mayan Palace. It's open Friday to Tuesday from 8am to noon and 2 to 6pm, Wednesday from 8am to noon; closed Thursday.

Past Al Chisme on Los Arboles is the Gallery Bookstore, where you can find new and used books in English, Spanish, and other languages (open Monday through Saturday 9am to 6pm). It also has maps of Guatemala, local art, and Guatemalan coffee. If you've bought more stuff than you can carry, you can use the Get Guated Out shipping service here to send your purchases home.

The town's handiest bank is the Banco Agricola, on Calle Principal in the center of town—open Monday to Friday from 9am to 5pm and Saturday from 9am to 1pm, but note that currency-exchange hours are 9am to 4pm only! If the bank is closed, see if you can change money at your hotel or at some other hotel.

Bicycle rentals (Q5 [90¢] per hour) are available from a shop on Calle Los Arboles just around the corner from Calle Principal.

Market days are Thursday and Sunday. Feast days are October 2 to 6.

Panajachel (pronounced Pah-nah-hah-*chell*) lies on the shores of Lake Atitlán and is Guatemala's most popular resort town. The lake, which many people consider among the most beautiful lakes in the world, is almost a mile high and was formed when water filled a massive volcanic crater. Today the lake is more than 6 miles wide in places, and steep mountains and cliffs ring the waters. What makes Lake Atitlán so striking are the numerous cone-shaped volcanoes that lie around its shores. From Panajachel the view is absolutely breathtaking, especially at sunset when the volcanoes on the far side of the lake are silhouetted against a multihued sky.

There are several villages around the perimeter of the lake, but it is Panajachel that has become the most tourist oriented, with high-rise hotels, gringo-owned restaurants and bars, and streets lined with Guatemalan *típico* (local textiles and crafts) vendors.

Fishing, swimming, boating, waterskiing, and hang gliding are the most popular activities here, though as a mecca for budget travelers, Panajachel seems to be best known as a place simply to hang out.

Over the years, various villages around Lake Atitlán have been the scenes of fighting between rebels and the army. Before heading off to any little lakeshore village be sure to check in Panajachel to see if the village is currently safe to visit.

WHAT TO SEE & DO

It's only a 10- or 15-minute walk to the beach from any of the hotels mentioned below, and the beach is hardly ever crowded, perhaps because the water's a little chilly. There are beach cubicles for changing clothes, and several little eateries and soft-drink stands serve up snacks advertised on signboard menus. The one indispensable activity in Panajachel is sitting at one of the eateries along the beach, sipping a cool drink, and looking out over the water to the clouds scraping the tops of the volcanoes—you'll never forget the scene.

One of the main activities in Panajachel is shopping for clothes made from Guatemalan fabrics. All along Calle Santander, from Calle Principal to the beach, are vendors' stalls. After a while the riot of colors becomes overwhelming, so be sure to buy early in your stay before you get burned out on all the tipico clothing. Remember: Back home this stuff is twice as expensive.

WHERE TO STAY

Because Panajachel is one of Guatemala's major tourist destinations and is, in fact, the country's top beach resort, there is a wide selection of accommodations available.

DOUBLES FOR LESS THAN Q87 ($15)

Besides the hotels below, Panajachel abounds in very simple, extremely cheap family pensions. You'll see them all along the Calle Santander and in other parts of town. Bath facilities may consist of a cold-water tap and primitive shower, but the price per person is usually only Q15 ($2.60), which is about as cheap as you can find anywhere in the world these days.

HOSPEDAJE CABAÑAS COUNTRY CLUB, Calle Rancho Grande, Panajachel, Sololá. Tel. 502-9/62-2070. 23 rms (none with bath).
$ Rates: Q12.50–Q15 ($2.15–$2.60) single without bath; Q25–Q30 ($4.35–$5.20) double without bath. No credit cards.

Near the Rancho Grande Inn you'll find the most unusual of this type of rock-bottom pension. Despite its name, the Hospedaje Cabañas is a low-budget accommodation. The rooms are arranged along a central courtyard parking area and are built to resemble long cabins. Each is just large enough to hold two twin beds. Sheets and blankets are included in the price.

HOSPEDAJE SANTA ELENA, Panajachel, Sololá. No phone. 8 rms (none with bath).
$ Rates: Q17.65 ($3.05) single; Q23.50 ($4.05) double. No credit cards.
Here you get a bed, one sheet, no blankets, a light, and a small table—period. But the señora keeps it all tidy. There are little tables in the modest courtyard (which you share with banana plants and parrots) and there is a cold-water shower and toilet. The hospedaje is off Calle Santander on the road to the Hotel Monterrey.

HOTEL FONDA DEL SOL, Calle Principal, Panajachel, Sololá. Tel. 502-9/62-1162. 25 rms (15 with bath).
$ Rates: Q35 ($6.05) single without bath. Q50–Q75 ($8.65–$12.95) single with bath; Q50 ($8.65) double without bath, Q75–Q100 ($12.95–$17.25) double with bath; Q75 ($12.95) triple without bath, Q100–Q125 ($17.25–$21.55) triple with bath. AE, DC, MC, V.

The most expensive rooms are in a new wing that offers some of the most attractive rooms in town. Patchwork quilts cover the beds, and there are brick floors and stone walls that have been stuccoed over. The doorways are arched and there are marble bathrooms and big windows. The cheapest rooms benefit from modern, clean shared bathroom facilities. Laundry service is available. As you come into town on Calle Principal, this hotel is on the right just before you reach Calle Santander.

HOTEL JUCANYA, Callejón Chocruz Calle Los Salpores, Panajachel, Sololá. No phone. 12 rms (9 with bath).

$ Rates: Q60 ($10.35) single; Q65–Q85 ($11.20–$14.65) double. No credit cards.

This very unusual hotel is located on the far side of the river from Panajachel proper and is about a 10-minute walk from the corner of Calle Santander and Calle Principal. Set in a new residential area that still has quite a few small market gardens, the Jucanya is decorated with crafts and textiles from Asia as well as Central America, a reflection of the American owner's globe-trotting. All the rooms here have large windows and many have great views as well. There's a rooftop terrace, a great garden to hang out in, and a swimming pool and sauna as well. Vegetarian meals are occasionally served. To reach the hotel, take the road toward Santa Catarina Palopó, and after you cross the river, turn right down a gravel road that becomes a footpath. Watch for the hotel's sign.

HOTEL MAYA KANEK, Calle Principal, Panajachel, Sololá. Tel. 502-9/ 62-1104. 20 rms (15 with bath).

$ Rates: Q41.20 ($7.10) single without bath, Q58.85 ($10.15) single with bath; Q64.74 ($11.20) double without bath, Q88.28 ($15.22) double with bath; Q147.13 ($25.40) triple with bath. No credit cards.

Among this town's cheaper hotels is the Maya Kanek, just down from the church. It's a motel-style arrangement, with simple, fairly well used quarters facing a cement parking area. Twin beds, small showers, and dim light bulbs make this a fairly basic place to put up. One advantage is that you can park your car in the safety of the courtyard. Although there's more noise in the rooms above the reception desk, these are relatively new.

MAYAN PALACE HOTEL, Calle Principal, Panajachel, Sololá. Tel. 502-9/ 62-1028. 22 rms (all with bath).

$ Rates: Q80–Q90 ($13.80–$15.55) single; Q80–Q110 ($13.80–$19) double; Q100–Q130 ($17.25–$22.45) triple. DC, MC, V.

On the intersection of Calle Principal and Calle Santander at the heart of Panajachel you'll find another good choice. The rooms are fairly clean and were recently remodeled. They all have large windows looking out onto the open hallway that runs the length of the hotel. You'll have a nice view of the hills behind town from here, and you can watch the action in the street below. Several rooms have color TVs and most have some antique furniture.

HOTEL PRIMAVERA, Calle Santander, Panajachel, Sololá. Tel. 502-9/ 62-2052. 8 rms (all with bath).

$ Rates: Q75 ($12.95) single; Q95 ($16.40) double; Q115 ($19.85) triple. DC, MC, V.

Located near the corner of Calle Principal and Calle Santander, the Primavera is a German-owned hotel that offers a bit more comfort than most budget hotels in town. The two-story hotel has a pretty little garden in the courtyard out back. The rooms are simple but clean and very appealing because they are new. The bathrooms in some of the rooms have skylights. Run with German efficiency, this is an excellent choice. There's even a sauna here. Meals in the first-floor German restaurant range from Q20 to Q30 ($3.45 to $5.20).

DOUBLES FOR LESS THAN Q203 [$35]

HOTEL DOS MUNDOS, Calle Santander 4-72, Zona 2, Panajachel, Sololá. Tel./fax 502-9/62-2078. 10 rms (all with bath).

$ Rates: Q140 ($24.15) single; Q193.05 ($33.30) double; Q228.15 ($39.35) triple. MC, V.

⭐ This newer hotel is set back from Calle Santander down a long bougainvillea-lined driveway, and once you enter the compound, you leave the hubbub of the street behind. There are tranquil gardens set with tables and chairs and a thatched-roof dining room that serves Italian food. The guest rooms, which have high ceilings and red-tile floors, are spacious and attractively decorated with Guatemalan textiles. All in all, this hotel offers a very good value and pleasant surroundings.

HOTEL PARADISE INN, Calle del Río frente al lago, Panajachel, Sololá. Tel. 502-9/62-1021. 12 rms (all with bath).

$ Rates: Q149.30 ($25.75) single; Q176.45 ($30.45) double; Q203.60 ($35.10) triple. MC, V.

⭐ This hotel is located right behind the row of restaurants fronting Panajachel's main beach. The guest rooms have large windows and most have good views of the volcanoes (second-floor rooms get the best views). There are also fireplaces in all the rooms and attractive bent-wood furnishings. In front of the hotel, there's an attractive lawn, and the beach is only 100 yards away. Sunsets here are some of the best in town.

MINI HOTEL RIVA BELLA, Calle Principal, Panajachel, Sololá. Tel./fax 502-9/62-1353, 62-1348, or 62-1177. 11 rms (9 with bath).

$ Rates: Q81.20 ($14) single without bath, Q104.40 ($18) single with bath; Q104.40 ($18) double without bath, Q127.60 ($22) double with bath. MC, V.

Though this hotel is located right on busy Calle Principal, it is set back a bit from the road amid shady gardens. Most of the rooms are in little white bungalows with jalousie windows, tile floors, and small bathrooms. However, there are also a couple of smaller rooms that share a bathroom. You'll find the Riva Bella on the left just before the corner of Calle Principal and Calle Santander.

DOUBLES FOR LESS THAN Q261 [$45]

HOTEL MONTERREY, Panajachel, Sololá. Tel. 502-9/62-1126. 30 rms (all with bath).

$ Rates: Q169.65 ($29.25) single; Q210.60 ($36.35) double; Q239.85 ($41.35) triple. No credit cards.

Hidden away on a dirt lane a few hundred yards off Calle Santander is a rather stark blue-and-white, two-story motel-style establishment. Don't be put off by the dry and dusty parking lot. Facing the lake across its own lawns, which extend down to the beach, the Monterrey offers you clean and cheerful accommodations in pleasant surroundings.

HOTEL PLAYA LINDA, Calle Rancho Grande, Panajachel, Sololá. Tel. 502-9/62-1159. 18 rms (all with bath).

$ Rates: Q208.80–Q243.60 ($36–$42) single or double; Q208.80–Q307.40 ($36–$53) triple. DC, MC, V (a surcharge is added).

⭐ If you want to be as close to the lakeshore as possible, take a look at this hotel. A semi-modern building of brick, stone, white stucco, and dark wood, it has a small lawn, an aviary, lots of bougainvillea, and an assortment of guest rooms priced according to what sort of view they have. The one drawback here is that the

---

IMPRESSIONS

. . . you see Lake Atitlan . . . Nothing can ever come up to this first moment of seeing it below you at its widest expanse, two thousand feet down, unruffled, blue as a peacock's breast . . .
—SACHEVERELL SITWELL, *GOLDEN WALL AND MIRADOR,* 1961

area in front of the hotel is a large, noisy parking lot that gets very busy on weekends and holidays, spoiling the wonderful views. Meals in the open-air restaurant, with a fabulous view, cost around Q35 ($6.05).

MULLER'S GUEST HOUSE, Calle Rancho Grande 1-81, Panajachel, Solalá. Tel. 502-9/34-4293. Fax 502-9/34-4294. 5 rms (all with bath).
$ Rates (including continental breakfast): Q232 ($40) single or double; Q290 ($50) triple; Q348 ($60) quad. No credit cards.
Located on the street that runs parallel to Calle Santander, Muller's Guest House is another of Panajachel's German-owned hotels. Set amid attractive gardens, the guest house has the feel of a private residence. Each of the five rooms is decorated a bit differently from the others, but all have hardwood floors and ceilings, large bathrooms and closets—plenty of room to spread out in. There are tables in the garden and chairs on the veranda, which make this a great place for a bit of lounging and relaxing.

RANCHO GRANDE INN, Calle Rancho Grande, Panajachel, Solalá. Tel. 502-9/62-1554. In Guatemala City, tel. 502-2/764-768. Fax 502-9/62-2247. 16 rms (all with bath).
$ Rates (including breakfast): Q204–Q340 ($35.20–$58.65) single; Q234–Q351 ($40.35–$60.55) double. DC, MC, V.

Founded several decades ago, the Rancho Grande was conceived as an inn of German country-style architecture in a tropical Guatemalan setting. Since 1975 the inn has been owned by Marlita Hannstein, who has preserved the lovely white-stucco cottages with red-tile or thatched roofs and small sitting porches, all set in emerald lawns beneath towering palm trees. All the rooms are different and feature Danish modern furniture. It's a quiet place, equally convenient to town and to the beach, where you'll receive a warm welcome. The bungalows can hold as many as five people, which makes them an excellent choice for families. Rooms here tend to be in great demand, so reserve early.

WORTH THE EXTRA BUCKS

CACIQUE INN, Calle Embarcadero, Panajachel, Solalá. Tel. 502-9/62-1205. 33 rms (all with bath).
$ Rates: Q255 ($44) single; Q290 ($50) double; Q325 ($56) triple. No credit cards.
Another excellent, quiet choice, this hotel is off Calle Principal at the western edge of town. In its own walled compound not far from the lakeshore, the inn has a spacious court planted with tropical shrubs and trees and green lawns and furnished with a tidy little swimming pool. The guest rooms, dining room, bar, souvenir shop, and reception desk are in low, rustic-inspired buildings facing the court. Lots of rounded stone, tree trunks, and other country touches were used in construction. The rooms are large, each with a fireplace (with wood laid, ready to light), two double beds with locally made blankets, and odd sliding glass-and-wrought-iron doors that take some getting used to. Lunch or dinner in the simple dining room can be ordered à la carte; the table d'hôte dinner is about Q35 ($6.05).

HOTEL ATITLÁN, Panajachel, Solalá. Tel. 502-9/62-1416, 62-1441, or 62-1429. 65 rms (all with bath).
$ Rates: Q441 ($76.05) single; Q475 ($81.90) double; Q577 ($99.50) triple. AE, MC, V.

About 1½ miles (a 15- or 20-minute walk or a $2 taxi ride) from the center of town is one of Panajachel's more exclusive and expensive hotels. This is a fairly lavish Guatemalan-style establishment with spacious grounds and various tropical gardens filled with bougainvillea, ivy, and geraniums. The rambling three-story colonial-style hotel has gleaming tiled floors, antique wood carvings, and exquisite local craft pieces as decoration. The guest rooms have attractive baths, twin beds, local craft decorations, and shady balconies from which to enjoy the view of the grounds and the lake. The hotel's dining room has a splendid view of the lake and volcanoes, as does the patio dining area. In the cool months, a fire burns in a large fireplace in the dining room. In the evening, the cozy bar is the perfect place for a drink. Meals are in the Q40 to Q50 ($6.90 to $8.65) range.

There's also a swimming pool and private beach.

HOTEL REGIS, Calle Santander, Panajachel, Sololá. Tel. 502-9/62-1149. Fax 502-9/62-1152. 21 rms (all with bath).
$ Rates: Q251 ($43.30) single; Q285 ($49.15) double; Q319 ($55) triple. MC, V.
This attractive little hotel is opposite the Guatel office on Calle Santander. The colonial-style complex is set back from the street behind a row of vendors' stalls and is surrounded by lawns shaded by palm trees. The guest rooms are in long, low buildings and separate bungalows, each with a veranda facing the lawn. There are also two rooms that have kitchenettes. Some rooms have a TV and phone, as well as a small refrigerator. There is an attractively decorated dining room, a small gift shop, and in the garden, two hot tubs filled with water from a natural hot well.

WHERE TO EAT

The best dining is in the more expensive hotels. For more modest meals, Panajachel has numerous places to offer, many of which are run by foreigners looking for a way to stay in Panajachel. These restaurants often go out of business within a year of opening. Often some other foreigner moves in, renames the restaurant, changes the menu, and tries to make a go of it. Consequently, you might find that a restaurant recommended here no longer exists but another restaurant occupies the same location. Give it a try as long as you're there—it may be the next "in" restaurant, and you'll have helped discover it.

MEALS FOR LESS THAN Q29 ($5)

DELI RESTAURANT, Calle Principal. No phone.
  Cuisine: INTERNATIONAL/VEGETARIAN.
$ Prices: Main dishes Q10–Q20 ($1.75–$3.45); breakfast Q4.50–Q19 (80¢–$3.30). No credit cards
  Open: Thurs–Tues 7am–5:45pm.
Whole-wheat pancakes and waffles, tabouli, scrambled tofu and veggies. If these are the kinds of dishes you've been missing during your travels through Guatemala, you'll want to have quite a few meals here at the Deli. You'll find the Deli a block or so past the corner of Calle Principal and Calle Santander, on the right. There's also another Deli Restaurant down at the far end of Calle Santander.

LA HAMBURGUESA GIGANTE, Calle Santander. No phone.
  Cuisine: BURGERS/GUATEMALAN.
$ Prices: Main dishes Q5.50–Q27 (95¢–$4.65). MC, V.
  Open: Daily 8am–11pm.
This is a long-time favorite in Panajachel, a congenial place with dependably tasty burgers, steaks, shrimp, chicken, and fish at moderate prices. Try the barbecued chicken, for about Q21 ($3.65). Breakfast is served here as well.

MEALS FOR LESS THAN Q58 ($10)

AL CHISME, Calle Los Arboles. Tel. 62-2063.
  Cuisine: INTERNATIONAL.
$ Prices: Breakfast Q9–Q16 ($1.55–$2.75); main dishes Q10–Q36 ($1.75–$6.20). MC, V.
  Open: Thurs–Tues 7am–10:30pm.
With an excellent assortment of salads and pastries, it is no wonder this restaurant is such a hit in Panajachel. The menu includes all manner of European and American favorites, such as fajitas, pastas, salads, and lemon chicken. The music on the stereo is what you would expect if this restaurant were in Seattle or Miami. The narrow patio out front has a nice view of the steep hills outside town. You'll really get a sense of being inside a volcano when you gaze up at those walls.

EL BISTRO, Calle Santander. No phone.
   Cuisine: ITALIAN.
$ **Prices:** Appetizers Q11.50–Q16 ($2–$2.75); main dishes Q22.50–Q41 ($3.90–$7.10). No credit cards.
   Open: Wed–Mon noon–10pm.
Located on Calle Santander almost at the lake, El Bistro is one of Panajachel's better Italian restaurants. Pastas, such as fettuccine with four cheeses or spaghetti napoletana, are the specialties here, but they also do a good job with their local lake fish dinners. For dessert there are good sorbets and chocolate mousse. A modest wine list rounds out the menu. Most of the tables are out in the garden, but there are also a few inside. Classical music provides a pleasant evening atmosphere.

BOMBAY PUB & CAFE, Avenida de los Arboles. No phone.
   Cuisine: INTERNATIONAL/VEGETARIAN.
$ **Prices:** Main dishes Q15–Q25 ($2.60–$4.35). No credit cards.
   Open: Mon–Sat 11:30am–10pm.
Set at the back of the same shopping complex that houses the Get Guated Out shipping company and Gallery Bookstore, the Bombay Pub is more of a casual restaurant than drinking establishment. The food is the main emphasis, and, as the name implies, there are several Indian dishes available. There are also several pastas available each night. If you're a vegetarian, you'll find that eating here is just like eating at home.

EL PATIO, Calle Santander. No phone.
   Cuisine: INTERNATIONAL/GUATEMALAN.
$ **Prices:** Breakfast Q10–Q18.50 ($1.75–$3.20); lunch and dinner Q19–Q30 ($3.30–$5.20). DC, MC, V.
   Open: Sun–Fri 7:30am–9pm; Sat 7:30am–10pm.
As its name implies, this popular restaurant does indeed have a streetside patio for dining, plus a couple of interior rooms. Quiet music soothes your spirit as you order from the menu, which includes a good assortment of sandwiches and *platos fuertes* (main courses) such as pepian de pollo (Guatemala's national dish), Szechuan chicken, cassoulet, roast pork, Virginia-style ham, chicken à la king, and filet mignon. Drinks are served.

LA POSADA DEL PINTOR AND THE CIRCUS BAR, Calle Los Arboles. No phone.
   Cuisine: INTERNATIONAL.
$ **Prices:** Pizza Q19.50–Q41 ($3.40–$7.10); full meals Q13–Q32 ($2.25–$5.55). No credit cards.
   Open: Daily noon–midnight.
This is perhaps the most interesting place in the center of town. It's a rustic bar with stools, plus dining tables spread with blue-and-white-checked cloths. The walls are covered in old circus posters, and quiet jazz issues from speakers here and there, filling the dining rooms and the small courtyard with mellow music. In addition to pizza, there are many more interesting dishes on the menu, including shrimp thermidor, potato salad, ratatouille, and vegetables in béchamel sauce. If you drop by for just a drink, expect to pay Q6.50 ($1.15) for a straight drink and Q12 ($2.10) for a cocktail. There's live entertainment in the bar some evenings.

RESTAURANT EL DRAGON, Calle Santander. No phone.
   Cuisine: INTERNATIONAL.
$ **Prices:** Main dishes Q18.50–Q38 ($3.20–$6.55). MC, V.
   Open: Daily 1–10:30pm.
The international globe-trotters who have made their homes in Panajachel over the years have brought with them much that they've learned in their travels, including recipes for the cuisines of the world. Here at El Dragon, Indonesian dishes such as *nasi goreng* (fried rice) and *gado-gado* are two of the specialties. However, you'll also find German sausages, Caribbean soup, Hungarian goulash,

Szechuan chicken, and spaghetti. There's also good bread and great classical and blues music on the stereo.

TOCOYAL, Calle Rancho Grande. Tel. 62-1555.
   Cuisine: GUATEMALAN/INTERNATIONAL.
$ Prices: Main dishes Q21–Q53 ($3.65–$9.15). DC, MC, V.
   Open: Sun–Thurs 7am–9pm; Fri–Sat 7am–10pm.
Down at the end of Calle Rancho Grande, right on the beach, is this restaurant with one of the best views in the world. Take a seat on one of the restaurant's two terraces or inside the thatched-roof dining room with sliding glass walls and gaze across the lake at the volcanoes. It would be a crime not to have at least one sunset dinner here during your stay. With views like these, it doesn't really matter what the food is like, but luckily meals here are tasty, and the service is good. The menu includes fresh lake fish and seafood, international pasta dishes, sandwiches, and that Guatemalan carnivore's delight, the *parrillada*.

MEALS FOR LESS THAN Q87 [$15]

CASABLANCA, Calle Principal. Tel. 62-2025.
   Cuisine: INTERNATIONAL.
$ Prices: Soups and salads Q9–Q26 ($1.55–$4.50); entrees Q22–Q65 ($3.80–$11.20). DC, MC, V.
   Open: Daily noon–10pm (sometimes later).
Mellow jazz music plays on the stereo, and on the weekend this place has live jazz, reggae, and salsa. Contemporary art hangs from the walls, sunshine filters through skylights, and diners on two floors gaze out at pedestrians through the large windows. Young and hip waiters in bow ties hurry between the kitchen and the tables. Daily specials for about Q35 ($6.05) are the best deal here, but if you're in the mood for a splurge, you can dine on steak or lobster. Try the shrimp-stuffed avocado salad for a starter. If you aren't in the mood for a big meal, you can get a sandwich.

EXCURSIONS
SANTIAGO ATITLÁN

Around the shores of Lake Atitlán are several small villages, several of which can only be reached by boat or footpath. With the exception of Santiago Atitlán, these villages still seem very traditional and tranquil. However, many of these villages have been the scenes of violent fighting between guerrillas and the army. Before heading out to any lakeside village, check in Panajachel to see if it is currently safe to visit. However, many of the villages are now popular as day trips from Panajachel, and several have very basic hostelries frequented by backpack travelers.

However, the most popular day trip from Panajachel is to Santiago Atitlán, on the opposite shore of the lake from Panajachel. Santiago Atitlán lies on the shore of a small bay with volcanoes rising both behind the village and across the bay. In the bay, before you land, you will likely see local fishermen in the lake's unusual dugout canoes. If you are lucky, you might also catch a glimpse of a *poq*, a flightless waterbird that lives only in Lake Atitlán. Unfortunately, this bird is highly endangered because it is easy prey to a voracious gamefish that was introduced to the lake some years back.

Once your boat lands, head up the cobblestone street from the dock. Along the way, you will pass several art galleries selling paintings and woodcarvings by local artists. The paintings are done in a colorful naive style, while the wood carvings range from intricately realistic to stylishly contemporary. Displayed along this street, you will also see the ornately embroidered *huipiles* (women's blouses) and men's shorts that are the traditional attire of Santiago Atitlán.

A stroll through the market will show you the myriad of (mostly tiny) fish that are caught in this lake and then salted and dried. The aroma in the market is a bit heady, so be prepared.

Up the hill a bit farther is the town square, the town office, and the huge old church. Within the stark, echoing church are some surprising sights. Along the walls are wooden statues of the saints, each of whom gets a new shawl every year. On the carved wooden pulpit, note the figures of corn (from which humans were formed, according to Mayan religion); the quetzal bird reading a book; and Yum-Kax, the Mayan god of corn. There is similar carving on the back of the priest's chair. The walls of the church bear paintings, now covered by a thin layer of plaster. A memorial plaque at the back of the church commemorates Fr. Stanley Francis Rother, a missionary priest from Oklahoma who was beloved by the local people but despised by ultrarightist elements, who murdered him right here in the church during the troubled year of 1981. In the following years, much blood was shed in Santiago Atitlán, but the people of the town eventually rose up in protest and demanded the removal of the army from their town. The people were eventually successful, and the army was removed from Santiago Atitlán. Since that time, it has been fairly quiet here and tourism in the town has been growing.

Near the church, you are also likely to be approached by children offering to take you to see Maximón. Though the children will expect a tip, don't miss a chance to visit this Mayan god. Maximón is believed to be based on Judas, yet is worshipped as a god who can assist in times of need. Maximón is a life-size mannequin wearing a mask and he holds court in his home. He is usually dressed in *ladino* clothes, a cowboy hat, sun glasses, and many scarves. As outlandish as this visage sounds, he is taken very seriously by the local people. If you should visit Maximón, be sure to leave an offering of a few quetzales, or preferably some *aguardiente* (cheap white rum) and some cigars, which are the traditional offerings.

Other lakeside villages you might want to visit include San Pedro La Laguna, a dusty village on a rocky stretch of shoreline. Of interest here is an open-air coffee processing site. Santa Cruz La Laguna is actually high above the lake on a steep mountainside. Be prepared for a steep climb if you decide to visit. Sololá, which is not on the lake but instead on the road leading down to Panajachel, is also worth a visit for its old cathedral.

Several boats ply between Panajachel and Santiago Atitlán: The most convenient are those leaving from the main beach, which is down at the end of Calle Rancho Grande. Daily departures are at 8:35, 9, 9:30, and 10:30am and 3 and 4pm; the return trips from Santiago Atitlán leave daily at 6, 7, and 11:45am and 12:30, 1, 2, and 5pm. The round-trip fare is Q15 ($2.60). (There are also boats to San Pedro La Laguna, San Antonio Palopó, and San Lucas Tolimán with departures at various times between 5:30am and 5:30pm.) The outbound trip across the lake takes about 1¼ hours; the return trip takes 1¼ to 1½ hours, depending on the wind.

Where to Stay and Eat

HOTEL TZUTUHIL, Santiago Atitlán. Tel. 502-9/62-7174. 28 rms (20 with bath).
$ Rates: Q15–Q20 ($2.60–$3.45) single without bath, Q25 ($4.35) single with bath; Q30–Q40 ($5.20–$6.90) double without bath, Q50 ($8.65) double with bath. No credit cards.
Located two blocks downhill from the church in the middle of town, this budget hotel is easy to find—it's the tallest building in town. Economical and basic with small rooms, the Tzutuhil is above a restaurant, which is where you should go to ask about a room. Try to get room 17, which has a good view. If you can't get a room with a view, you can hang out on the rooftop patio and enjoy the views from there.

POSADA DE SANTIAGO, Santiago Atitlán. Tel./fax 502-9/62-7167. 6 bungalows, 2 suites (all with bath).
$ Rates (including continental breakfast): Q135 ($23.30) single; Q175 ($30.20) double; Q215 ($37.10) triple. No credit cards.
Built and owned by an American couple who have been living in Santiago Atitlán for a while, this cozy lodge is a great place to get away from it all. The bungalows are tucked amid a beautiful garden on a hillside above the lake. From the moment you open the intricately carved door to your room, you'll know that a lot of thought and care went into these rooms. There are stone walls and high ceilings, plenty of

windows, and hammocks on each individual patio. Fireplaces and Momostecan handwoven blankets will keep you warm on chilly winter nights. One bungalow even has a stone-sided platform bed. You can relax in the garden or just drink in the view from a thatch-roofed observation deck. The hotel's restaurant is furnished with rustic tables and chairs. The menu even features a bit of Mayan cooking (chicken pibil) and such dishes as Thai coconut shrimp. Entree prices range from Q8 to Q15 ($1.40 to $2.60) for lunch and Q24 to Q50 ($4.15 to $8.65) for dinner. This is one of my favorite hotels in the whole country.

READERS RECOMMEND

Arca de Noé, Santa Cruz La Laguna (Apdo. 22, Panajachel), Sololá. "Run by Karin, an American woman, [this small hotel] is unique. Electricity comes from a solar battery and you eat by candlelight. She and her friend cook for everyone and you eat excellent, organic food with a very international group of people at one table. We felt it had great charm, and it is right on the lake. Rates are about Q30 ($5.20) single, Q50 ($8.65) with a private bath; Q40 ($6.90) double, Q70 ($12.10) with a private bath."—Madeleine A. Stone, Sebastopol, Calif.

IXIMCHÉ

A short distance east of the Los Encuentros crossroads on the Pan American Highway, on the way toward Chimaltenango, there is a turnoff for the town of Tecpan, and signs point the way through the town to the ancient Mayan city of Iximché. If you have a car, make the detour to see this beautiful archeological site.

As you enter the site, you pass a small building, the museo, on your right. Then you enter the city itself, past some grass-covered mounds and into the main complex of plazas. On many of the pyramids here, the outer coating of plaster is visible in places. When you come to the first uncovered buildings, look for traces of painting on the low structure to the left.

Iximché was selected as the site for the capital city of the Cakchiquel Maya partly because of its natural defenses, as it is on a promontory surrounded on three sides by ravines. It was the Cakchiquel capital when the conquistadores came in the early 1500s, having been founded only a half-century before. The Cakchiquels formed an alliance with the Spaniards, who founded Tecpan nearby and who used Tecpan as their center of operations for the governing of Guatemala. But later these two warlike peoples had a falling out; in the ensuing battles, the Cakchiquels lost to the Spaniards. Still, the Cakchiquel capital city escaped massive destruction and stands today as a fascinating monument to that people.

3. CHICHICASTENANGO

120 kilometers NW of Guatemala City; 80 kilometers NE of
Quetzaltenango; 40 kilometers N of Panajachel

GETTING THERE By Bus Los Encuentros is the crossroads on the Pan American Highway from which frequent buses turn off for Chichicastenango (Chichi). From Panajachel, you can take a direct bus to Chichi on Thursday or Sunday morning at 6:45am. Duration: 2–2½ hours. Fare: Q6 ($1.05). There are also buses from Panajachel to Los Encuentros at frequent intervals throughout the day. From Antigua, first take a bus to Chimaltenango, then catch any north-bound bus to Los Encuentros. Duration: 3 hours. Fare: around Q12 ($2.10). From Quetzaltenango, take a bus bound for Guatemala City, and get off at Los Encuentros. Duration: 3 hours. Fare: around Q15 ($2.58).

On market days, there are also minibuses to Chichi from Antigua and Panajachel. From Antigua, Turansa (tel. 322-664 in Antigua) leaves at 7am, returning at 3pm, and charges Q69.60 ($12) each way. From Panajachel, Tourist Service Atitlán (tel. 622-075 in Panajachel) leaves at 8am, returning at 3pm, and charges $7 each way.

By Car   If you're coming from Guatemala City or Quetzaltenango, the turnoff from the highway is at Los Encuentros, where there's a small open market, a gas station, and a postal and telephone office.

The road to Chichicastenango is scenic, even dramatic, diving down into a deep ravine and then climbing steeply up the other side. Along the way are the inevitable cornfields and local women weaving beautiful clothes near their modest homes.

DEPARTING   Buses arrive and leave from various points around the market; several lines are based near the Hotel Santo Tomas. Just say the name of your destination to any bus driver or policeman and you'll be directed to the proper corner. There are direct buses to Quetzaltenango, Panajachel, and Guatemala City. If you can't find a direct bus that's headed in your direction, catch any bus out to Los Encuentros, and wait there for a bus that's going to the right place.

ESSENTIALS   Orientation   The center of town is, of course, the central square, where the market is held. Coming into town from Los Encuentros, you must turn left at the Hotel Santo Tomas and go down a few blocks. The square will then be two blocks or so over to your left. Note that Chichicastenango is a small town, with few street signs or numbers, so you have to ask around to find everything.

Fast Facts   The post office (correos) is at 7a Avenida 8–47, two blocks northwest of the Hotel Santo Tomas on the road into town. Very near it is the Guatel telephone office, at 7a Avenida 8–21, on the corner of 8a Calle. Market days are Sunday and Thursday. Feast days are December 18 to 21 and Holy Week.

Once a sleepy Indian village, Santo Tomas Chichicastenango (alt. 6,650 feet; pop. 6,800) is today one of Guatemala's most popular tourist destinations. They come for the same reason that Indians have come here for centuries—to shop at the market. Although the market is still where local women buy the necessities of life and local farmers sell their produce, it is also where foreigners come to get the best deals on Guatemalan textiles. Every Sunday and Thursday, the town's central square becomes a maze of stalls selling both traditional and modern textiles, machine- and handmade. This market has become so big and popular that Wednesdays and Saturdays are also pretty packed with vendors. However, it is on the main market days that busloads of tourists on excursions from Antigua and Guatemala City roar into town. You can avoid these crowds by visiting on a non-market day. Early morning, before the huge tour buses arrive, is also a good time to get your shopping in.

Facing the market square is the Santo Tomas Church, which figures prominently in the religion, both pagan and Christian, of the region. On the circular stone steps of the church, women sell flowers in the morning; throughout the day, Indians approach the massive doors of the church swinging censers made from old coffee cans. The fragrant incense smoke rises in clouds and drifts over the heads of the shoppers pushing their way among the stalls. Amid the chatter of vendors and shoppers, you can hear the chanting of a petitioner at the doors. The ritual is centuries old; the language is Quiché.

WHAT TO SEE & DO

Chichicastenango certainly isn't what you'd call an exciting place, except on market days, and that's its very fascination. Unless you're an anthropologist or a textile expert, you won't spend more than an afternoon looking over the marvelous handwoven and embroidered cloths for which the district is famous. Chichicastenango's other claim to fame, its much-vaunted paganism, involves things that you can't look for, although you may happen on them: A group of Indian men in colorful Spanish colonial garb and carrying a statue of a saint on their backs, burning incense, and lighting off deafening fireworks march through the street to the Church of Santo Tomas. The symbols, paraphernalia, and words are Christian, but the inspiration is clearly pagan.

On Sunday, the service in the Church of Santo Tomas presents a fascinating vignette: Within the church, Christian mass is in progress, while in front of the church, pagan rites are being held. The church dates from the mid-1500s, and its significance and power are not those of the Catholic church so much as of the local male groups known as **cofradías.** Each of these associations pays homage to its own patron saint and has religious and civic duties. In effect, the cofradías are as important as the local Catholic and municipal authorities; among the local people, they're more important. If you're in Chichicastenango on a major church holiday or on one of the cofradías' saints' days, you may see a cofradía procession, led by its alcalde (chief) and a ragtag band, winding through the town and the market.

For a look at more of this town's pre-Christian culture, take a short hike to the Shrine of Pascual Abaj, on a hill outside of town. To reach the shrine from Santo Tomas Church, turn right (as you face the church), walk down the hill on 5a Avenida to 9a Calle, and turn right. Go down the hill on 9a Calle, around the bend to the left; when the road turns sharply to the right, bear left and follow a path through the cornfields, keeping the ditch on your left-hand side. Proceed along the dirt path to the top of the hill covered in fragrant pines. At the very top is a clearing, and in it is the primitive carved-stone head of the idol, surrounded by little fireplace altars. Chances are good that a local man or woman will be chanting and praying at one or more of the altars and burning pungent incense. You can observe the rites without disturbing them, but don't try to take any photos. Before heading up here by yourself, ask at your hotel to make sure it is safe. In past years a number of people have been robbed when they ventured up here on their own. To be safe, you can hire a guide to bring you up.

Before heading up the hill to the shrine, stop in at one of the two mask makers' studios at the foot of the trail. At either studio, there are children who wait for tourists to pass by and then put on impromptu performances of traditional dances. A small tip is expected for the performance.

Chichicastenango has a museum facing the main square, the **Museo Regional.** The two large exhibit rooms have plain glass-fronted cabinets in best 19th-century museum style. In the left room are objects, figurines, and necklaces of jade, as well as clay incense burners, effigy pots and plainer vessels, metates (grindstones for corn), flint and obsidian arrowheads and spearheads, clay figurines, and copper axheads. In the right room are polychrome pots and those with relief work on them. Some of these are particularly nice. Admission is free.

WHERE TO STAY

DOUBLES FOR LESS THAN Q87 [$15]

HOTEL GIRON, 6a Calle 4-52, Chichicastenango. Tel. 502-9/561-156.
19 rms (all with bath).
$ Rates: Q45 ($7.75) single; Q60 ($10.35) double; Q75 ($12.95) triple.
You'll find this basic lodging behind the modern shopping center building that houses the Restaurante El Torito. Rooms are small and Spartan but usually clean, and you're right in the thick of things so you don't have far to walk when you become loaded down with purchases from the market.

POSADA BELÉN, 12 Calle 5-55, Chichicastenango. Tel. 502-9/561-244.
16 rms (7 with bath).
$ Rates: Q35 ($6.05) single without bath, Q50 ($8.65) single with bath; Q55 ($9.50) double without bath, Q70–Q150 ($12.10–$25.90) double with bath; Q75 ($12.95) triple without bath, Q90 ($15.55) triple with bath. No credit cards.
Basic but clean, the Posada Belén offers modest rooms, some of which have good views of the pine-covered hills surrounding town. The most expensive room is one that has a fireplace. There's a comedor on the ground floor. To find this hotel, stand facing the front of the Santo Tomas Church and then turn to your right. You should see the Posada Belén on the far side of town.

DOUBLES FOR LESS THAN Q203 [$35]

PENSIÓN CHUGUILÁ, Chichicastenango. Tel./Fax 502-9/561-134. 26 rms (21 with bath).

$ Rates: Q69.60 ($12) single without bath, Q139.20 ($24) single with bath; Q92.80 ($16) double without bath, Q162.40 ($28) double with bath; Q116 ($20) triple without bath, Q185.60 ($32) triple with bath. No credit cards.

✪ The budget traveler's version of the Mayan Inn is a charming old place a few blocks off the square. You enter from the cobbled street to find a cobbled courtyard (partly filled with parked cars) and a very pleasant portico paved in tiles and furnished with easy chairs, coffee tables, and tropical plants. The simple but pleasant dining room is to the left as you approach the reception desk and there's a patio café on the right. Some of the guest rooms have fireplaces; a few two-room suites have a bedroom and sitting room with fireplace. Furnishings are colonial in style, with accents of local cloth.

Breakfast in the dining room costs Q20 ($3.45). Lunch and dinner go for Q30 ($5.20).

MAYA LODGE, 6 Calle A 4-08, Chichicastenango. Tel. 502-9/561-167. 10 rms (all with bath).

$ Rates: Q117 ($20.20) single; Q152.10 ($26.25) double; Q187.20 ($32.30). No credit cards.

If you'd like to be right near the action on market day, this is the place for you. It's right on the main square where the market is held, and you'll have to weave your way through the maze of vendors to get in or out of the hotel. The rates are reasonable, and the accommodations are fairly comfortable. Try to get one of the cozy rooms with a fireplace (*chimenea*). Although rather bare compared to the town's other hostelries and perhaps a bit dark, this hotel is still a far cry from basic, though it is a bit overpriced. The clean, presentable rooms have their own tables and chairs in the long, narrow courtyard.

Breakfast in the simple little comedor costs Q20 ($3.45). Lunch and dinner go for Q25 ($4.35).

WORTH THE EXTRA BUCKS

Chichicastenango is an excellent place to let go of your budget and indulge yourself, because a little more money buys such an unforgettably beautiful experience.

HOTEL SANTO TOMAS, Chichicastenango. Tel. 502-9/561-061 or 561-316. Fax 502-9/561-306. 43 rms (all with bath).

$ Rates: Q373.25 ($64.35) single; Q441.10 ($76.05) double; Q542.90 ($93.60) triple. AE, DC, MC, V.

✪ The most luxurious hotel in town, the Santo Tomas is very popular with tour groups. You can't miss it as you come into town on the main road, but ask anyone to direct you if you have trouble. Colonial in style, it's modern in facilities. The rooms are arranged on two levels around two courtyards, each with its own fountain, gardens, and menagerie of parrots. Many of the rooms are filled by tour group participants, and the hotel is often abustle with guests arriving, leaving, heading out on shopping excursions, or returning from the same. If you want to stay here, you must reserve as far ahead as possible. The large, cheery rooms are decorated with local cloths and blankets and have private bathrooms and fireplaces. Most have twin beds. Throughout the hotel are pieces of local upper-class art—fancy robes, church statuary, antique altars, and so forth.

There is a large, attractive colonial-style dining room and also some tables set out under the arcade for courtyard dining. Lunch or dinner will cost between Q60 and Q100 ($10.35 and $17.25), with drinks, tax, and tip included. Facilities include a swimming pool, whirlpool tub, sauna, and exercise room on the terrace out back.

MAYAN INN, 8a Calle and 3a Avenida, Chichicastenango. Tel. 502-9/

561-176. Fax 502-9/561-212. In Guatemala City, tel. 502-2/310-213. Fax 502-2/315-919. 30 rms (all with bath).
$ Rates: Q441.10 ($76.05) single; Q508.95 ($87.75) double; Q610.75 ($105.30) triple. AE, MC, V.

This lovely old lodge on a quiet side street a few blocks from the bustling main market square was started in 1932 by Alfred S. Clark (of Clark Tours fame). It's composed of several colonial buildings, and the guest rooms are arranged under red-tile porticoes around courtyards planted with beautiful tropical gardens and lush grass. Parrots squawk and whistle here and there. The guest rooms are simple but charming, with antique furnishings, including carved-wood bedsteads, headboards painted with country scenes, heavily carved armoires, and rough-hewn tables. Each room has a little fireplace, with split logs laid ready to burn and a few sticks of *ocote* (fat wood) with which to kindle. Everywhere throughout the hotel are those gorgeous local textiles: window curtains, bedspreads, even shower curtains!

The hotel has its own cozy colonial bar with fireplace, and two dining rooms. A typical dinner might be cream of tomato soup; roast lamb, broiled beef, or beef tongue in a savory sauce; followed by salad; and rhum baba or ice cream for dessert, all for under Q100 ($17.25).

WHERE TO EAT

Meal possibilities are best in the above hotels, but if you want to save money, take a look at the little comedors (dining spots) around the market and near the post office and Guatel office on the road into town (7a Avenida). There are also several restaurants around town that cater almost exclusively to the tour-bus trade. Their menus are primarily international, with a few Guatemalan favorites thrown in for good measure.

RESTAURANTE EL TORITO, Comercial Giron, 2nd floor. Tel. 502-9/561-006.
Cuisine: GUATEMALAN.
$ Prices: Complete meal Q17–Q45 ($2.95–$7.75). No credit cards.
Open: Daily 7am–9pm.
"The Little Bull," as its name implies, is primarily a steak house; however, you can also get chicken, fish, shrimp, chorizo, and pork chops. All the meals come with soup, potatoes, rice, and bread or tortillas. It is on the second floor of a shopping arcade and has a few tables on the balcony overlooking the courtyard. The restaurant's main room is huge, obviously designed to accommodate busloads of diners. Light streams in through a wall of windows during the day.

RESTAURANTE LA FONDA DEL TZIJOLAJ, 2nd floor New Market Building, 6a Calle A. Tel. 561-013.
Cuisine: GUATEMALAN/INTERNATIONAL.
$ Prices: Complete meals Q15–Q45 ($2.60–$7.75). No credit cards.
Open: Thurs and Sun 7am–9pm, Fri–Sat and Mon–Wed 9am–noon.
Located upstairs from the new indoor produce market and overlooking the main outdoor market area, this restaurant provides a spot from which to observe the town's hustle and bustle. Meals include good chiles rellenos, vegetarian plates, and pizzas. Try to get a seat on the veranda.

RESTAURANTE TZIGUAN TINAMIT, 5a Avenida and 6a Calle. No phone.
Cuisine: GUATEMALAN.
$ Prices: Breakfast Q6–Q12 ($1.05–$2.10); main dishes Q7.50–Q30 ($1.30–$5.20). MC, V.
Open: Daily 7am–9pm.
Located on the corner just down from the Pensión Chuguilá, this simple restaurant serves good, inexpensive meals, especially breakfasts. For lunch and dinner there are steaks, fried chicken, fried fish, and pizza. Guatemalan textiles accent the Spartan dining room.

EXCURSIONS

Called simply **Quiché** by the natives, the provincial capital is only 20 miles farther along the road from Chichicastenango. A day trip will hold no great thrills, but you can take a look at its famous church and watch the local women weave straw hats as they walk. There are some ruins 2 miles from town at Ciudad Gumarcaan (no public transportation), once the royal city of King Quiché. Nothing's been excavated or rebuilt, and the grass-covered stone mounds give you the eerie feeling that you're walking in a dead city.

You can continue past Quiché by bus over a bumpy and dusty (or muddy) road for another three hours to **Nebaj.** The few *norteamericanos* who venture into Nebaj come to see the exquisitely beautiful costumes and headdresses of the Nebaj women, said by crafts experts to be the most beautiful in all of Guatemala. The area north of Nebaj, known as the Ixil Triangle has been one of the most devastated by the years of fighting between government forces and rebels demanding land reform in the highlands.

---

4. QUETZALTENANGO

79 kilometers S of Huehuetenango; 259 kilometers NW of Guatemala City; 155 kilometers NW of Panajachel

GETTING THERE By Bus Transportes Galgos buses from Guatemala City leave several times daily from 7a Avenida 19–44, Zona 1 (tel. 23-661). Duration: 4 hours. Fare: Q16.50 ($2.85). From Chichi or Panajachel, there are several direct buses daily to Quetzaltenango. However, buses to Los Encuetros run more frequently, and from Los Encuentros, you can take almost any north-bound bus to Quetzaltenango. If you're coming from Antigua, take a bus to Chimaltenango, and then catch a north-bound bus to Quetzaltenango. Watch for buses with "Xelaju"—the Indian name for Quetzaltenango—or its abbreviation "Xela" on the front.

By Car If you're coming from the Pacific Highway, take the Quetzaltenango toll road turnoff just past Mazatenango. Coming from Huehuetenango or Guatemala City, turn south at Cuatro Caminos, the intersection just north of Quetzaltenango.

DEPARTING At the main bus terminal on 13a Avenida and 4a Calle, Zona 3 (near Parque Minerva), there are second-class buses leaving regularly for cities and towns all over Guatemala. These buses are always very crowded. However, they leave much more frequently than the first-class buses of the companies mentioned below. Ticket prices are also slightly less. There are buses out here from the main plaza, or you can take a taxi for Q12 ($2.10). This is where to catch direct buses to Chichicastenango, Panajachel, Huehuetenango, Cobán, and La Mesilla. Alternatively, if you are heading to Panajachel or Chichi, you can take a south-bound bus and get off at Los Encuentros. First-class bus companies with service to Guatemala City and points along the Pan American Highway include Rutas Lima, 2a Calle 6-32, Zona 2 (tel. 614-134), which has three buses daily; Transportes Galgos, Calle Rodolfo Robles 17-43, Zona 1 (tel. 612-931), which has seven buses daily; and Lineas Americas, 7a Avenida 3-33, Zona 2 (tel. 614-587), which has five buses daily. These same companies have buses that go to the Mexican border.

ESSENTIALS Orientation The Parque Centro America is the center of town; most of the principal buildings face it, including the new municipal market, the Tourism Office and town hall, the church, the museum, and several hotels and restaurants. The streets are not well marked in this town, so keep track of where you're going.

Fast Facts Many of the city's banks face the Parque Centro America. Normal hours of operation are Monday to Friday from 8:30 or 9am to 2 or 2:30pm. The

Banco Industrial, on the Parque in the Palacio Municipal, at 11a Avenida and 5a Calle (tel. 61-2258 or 61-2288), is open Monday through Friday from 8:30am to 7pm and Saturday from 8:30am to 5:30pm.

Take your laundry to the Lavanderia Mini-Max, 14a Avenida C-47, at 1a Calle, next to the Taberna de Don Rodrigo.

The **Tourist Office** (tel. 61-4931) is in the Casa de la Cultura at the lower end of the Parque Centro America—open daily from 8am to noon and 2 to 5pm.

Market day is every day. Feast days are September 12 to 18.

Named by the Aztecs for what is now the national bird, Quetzaltenango is the country's second-largest town (alt. 7,800 feet; pop. 125,000). It was built on the site of the Quiché Maya Indian ancient capital of Xelaju, and the Indians still call it by this name. Quetzaltenango is a booming, growing city—but the countryside surrounding it is marvelously beautiful. In the marketplace, women (and a few men) wear traditional costumes of heavily embroidered cloth. These are not costumes in the sense that they're put on for special occasions, but rather they're the normal, everyday clothing in this traditional rural culture. The Indian garb contrasts strikingly with the Italianate columns and monuments in the main square, the Parque Centro America.

WHAT TO SEE & DO

Quetzaltenango itself does not have much to offer in the way of attractions, but the city does make a good base of operations for exploring the many market towns in the surrounding countryside. However, while you're here, check to see if there is an exhibit at the **Museo de Arte,** which is diagonally across the corner from the Tourist Office. This museum is open Monday through Saturday from 8am to noon and from 2 to 6pm. This combination art school and museum frequently has interesting exhibits of local art.

Also have a look in the **cathedral** and the **Palacio Municipal** (city hall). All three of these prominent buildings are on the Parque Centro America.

Walk north on 14a Avenida to 1a Calle, and you'll come face-to-face with the city's impressive neoclassical **Teatro Municipal.** If there's a performance, rehearsal, or meeting in progress when you visit, you'll have to be content with the view from the outside. Inside, however, are three tiers of seating, the lower two of which have private boxes for theatergoers. The boxes were once rented by prominent families by the season or the year; each is equipped with a vanity for women.

There is an indoor **market** to the left of the Tourist Office, at the southeastern corner of the Parque Centro America. You'll find produce vendors, food stalls, and shops selling everyday items on the lower level. However, some of the space here is also tourist oriented. It's definitely worth a walk through. To the right of the Tourist Office half a block you'll find the **Atitlán Shop,** 7a Calle 12–07, Zona 1, which has an interesting selection of local crafts and Guatemalan fashions. Another interesting shop here in town is **Vitra,** 13 Avenida 5-27, Zona 3 (tel. 63-5091), which sells unusual and attractive hand-blown glassware made from recycled glass. They also sell wrought-iron items. Prices here are very reasonable.

The city's large market is the **Mercado La Democracia,** in Zona 3, about ten blocks northwest of the Parque Centro America. To get there, walk along 14a Avenida to 1a Calle. Turn left, walk to 16a Avenida, then turn right. Walk along 16a Avenida, cross Calle Rodolfo Robles (the first major cross-street you encounter), and the market will be on your right. It extends for about two blocks. Here you'll find fruits, vegetables, tortillas, beans, chickens, shoes, children's clothing, and fabrics for sale. The selection of fabrics is not large, but the prices are fairly good.

Less than a mile west of the Parque Centro America is the **Parque Minerva** and its neoclassical **Templo de Minerva,** built to honor the classical goddess of education and to inspire Guatemalan youth to new heights of learning. There's yet another market here.

WHERE TO STAY

DOUBLES FOR LESS THAN Q87 [$15]

CASA KAEHLER, 13a Avenida 3-33, Zona 1, Quetzaltenango. Tel. 502-9/612-091. 7 rms (1 with bath).

$ Rates: Q40.95 ($7.10) single without bath, Q46.80 ($8.10) single with bath; Q46.80 ($8.10) double without bath, Q58.50 ($10.10) double with bath; Q52.65 ($9.10) triple without bath. No credit cards.

⑤ Before World War II, most of the coffee fincas (farms) on Guatemala's Pacific Slope were run by Germans, hence the German flavor of this city. It's very apparent in the name of this little place, which resembles a modest, old-fashioned European family pension. The guest rooms are very simple and plain but clean and quite cheap. For a bit more comfort, request room no. 7 (*cuarto numero siete*), which has a private bathroom and a double bed. Regardless of which room you stay in, you can make use of the beautiful sitting room with its rocking chairs and stained-glass windows. It's very homey and quiet here (and popular with young people studying Spanish in Quetzaltenango).

CASA SUIZA, 14a Avenida "A" 2-36, Zona 1, Quetzaltenango. Tel. 502-9/630-242. 12 rms (10 with bath).

$ Rates: Q29 ($5) single without bath, Q58 ($10) single with bath; Q41 ($7.10) double without bath, Q70 ($12.10) double with bath; Q53 ($9.15) triple without bath, Q80 ($13.80) triple with bath. No credit cards.

Swiss in name only, this very basic pension is located across the street from the Hotel Modelo (below). Walk through the street-side doors, and you'll find yourself in a colorfully painted courtyard. All the rooms here have high ceilings that make them seem very spacious. The bathrooms, which were obviously added on long after the building was constructed, are housed within glass-and-metal booths in the corners of the rooms.

HOTEL RÍO AZUL, 2a Calle 12-15, Zona 1, Quetzaltenango. Tel. 502-9/630-654. 19 rms (all with bath).

$ Rates: Q52.20 ($9) single; Q69.60 ($12) double; Q87 ($15) triple. MC, V.

⑤ The Río Azul is conveniently located close to the Parque Centro America and many good restaurants. The owner of the hotel, who speaks little English, is a wealth of information about the area and can help you organize your tour of Guatemala. The rooms are simple, and the red-tile floors give them a rustic appeal. Some rooms have nice views, and all have very clean bathrooms. Security is tight here, so you don't have to worry much about your belongings.

PENSIÓN ALTENSE, 9a Calle 8-48, Zona 1, Quetzaltenango. Tel. 502-9/612-811. 21 rms (all with bath).

$ Rates: Q25 ($4.35) single; Q50 ($8.70) double; Q75 ($13.05) triple. No credit cards.

Though the neighborhood around this budget hotel isn't very appealing, the pensión itself is quite acceptable. Housed in an older colonial-style building, the pensión has a covered courtyard filled with plants. The rooms, which open off of this courtyard, are a bit dark, but they do have private baths. There are usually quite a few notices for Spanish schools and various excursions posted in the entry hall.

DOUBLES FOR LESS THAN Q203 [$35]

HOTEL AMERICANO, 14a Avenida 3-43, Zona 1, Quetzaltenango. Tel. 502-9/618-219. 12 rms (all with bath). TV

$ Rates: Q81.90 ($14.15) single; Q93.60 ($16.15) double; Q105.30 ($18.15) triple. No credit cards.

⑤ In the middle of the restaurant district of Quetzaltenango, you'll probably hear the computerized cacophony of a video arcade. Don't rush by: Upstairs you'll find one of the better hotel deals in town. Luckily, the video games are shut off by 11pm, and upstairs you can barely hear them even when they are going full blast. All the rooms are carpeted, although few have windows. The bathrooms are tiny but adequate, and the beds are generally passable. This is a convenient place to get a good night's sleep before moving on. Downstairs there is a restaurant that serves excellent breakfasts.

HOTEL CASA FLORENCIA, 12 Ave. 3-61, Zona 1, Quetzaltenango. Tel. 502-9/612-326. 10 rms (all with bath). TV
$ Rates: Q122 ($21.05) single; Q146 ($25.20) double; Q176 ($30.35) triple. DC, MC, V.
This newer hotel is located right behind the Pensión Bonifaz and though the rooms lack Guatemalan character, they are rather modern in design. There's wall-to-wall carpeting, a TV, and wood paneling in all the rooms, and the beds are new and comfortable. The hotel is housed in an old building in which the central courtyard has been roofed over to create a skylit lounge area that is full of hanging plants. Though the Florencia seems a bit overpriced, it is convenient.

HOTEL DEL CAMPO, Km 224, Carretera a Cantel, Quetzaltenango. Tel. 502-9/618-082 or 631-665. Fax 502-9/630-074. 104 rms (all with bath). TV TEL **Bus:** No. 2 from 3 blocks behind the Tourist Office.
$ Rates: Q145 ($25) single; Q179.80 ($31) double; Q214.60 ($37) triple. AE, DC, MC, V.
Although it is a bit out of the way, on a side road off of the Pan American Highway, the del Campo is Quetzaltenango's largest, most modern, and most comfortable place to stay. Constructed in the 1970s, it has a decor that features natural wood and red brick. The guest rooms have private baths (showers) done in linoleum and most are generally bright and nice. Avoid the bottom-floor rooms because they can be dark; ask for a room numbered in the 50s.

The huge restaurant has large windows letting in lots of light. The prices are very reasonable, averaging Q14 to Q55 ($2.45 to $9.50). A small bar provides a comfortable gathering spot and there's a heated indoor swimming pool and game room.

HOTEL MODELO, 14a Avenida "A" 2-31, Zona 1, Quetzaltenango. Tel. 502-9/630-216 or 612-529. Fax 502-9/631-376. 32 rms (all with bath).
$ Rates: Q82.40–Q141.25 ($14.20–$24.35) single; Q106–Q164.80 ($18.30–$28.45) double; Q129.50–Q188.30 ($22.35–$32.50) triple. MC, V.
This solid, dependable, moderate-price hotel is located on a narrow, short street between 14a and 15a avenidas. An obliging family operates the hotel, and they will welcome you in the high-ceilinged lobby with its big fireplace. When they show you one of the guest rooms, you'll find it decorated with solid-color bedspreads, gaily colored Guatemalan huipiles (blouses) drawn on frames, and contemporary paintings. The rooms have hardwood floors and are equipped with small private bathrooms with tiled showers. Some rooms also have TVs and telephones. The cheaper rooms are in a nearby annex building.

There's a small but good restaurant located off the lobby. Breakfast will cost around Q10 ($1.75), and lunch and dinner may be had for Q25 ($4.35). You'll also find a small bar just off the lobby.

WORTH THE EXTRA BUCKS

HOTEL PENSIÓN BONIFAZ, 4a Calle 10-50, Zona 1, Quetzaltenango. Tel. 502-9/614-241 or 612-959. Fax 502-9/612-850, ext. 141. 63 rms, 2 suites (all with bath). TV
$ Rates: Q271.45 ($46.80) single; Q339.30 ($58.50) double; Q407.20 ($70.20) suite. AE, DC, MC, V.
The Bonifaz, the city's long-running favorite, is at the upper end of the Parque Centro America and is within walking distance of almost everything. Half of the rooms here (and these are preferable) are in the older, original building. They have French doors leading onto small balconies overlooking the street and are

quite spacious. The furnishings are fairly new, and the bathrooms are quite large. The rest of the rooms are in a modernized addition with wood paneling and Danish modern furniture. These rooms are large, and the bathrooms are done in tile (some with only showers). Facilities include a gift shop, swimming pool, and whirlpool tub. The hotel has two dining rooms, both of which serve the same excellent food—primarily continental with such offerings as stroganoff, filet mignon, spaghetti, and breaded shrimp. Prices are in the Q30 to Q50 ($5.20 to $8.65) range for entrees. Just inside the front door is a sedate but cheery bar.

WHERE TO EAT

The best place to dine is in the dining room of the Pensión Bonifaz, where you can start with a fruit cocktail or a bowl of savory black-bean soup; go on to filet mignon, smoked pork chops, or roast chicken; and finish up with cake or pie—for about Q80 ($13.80) per person, including tax, tip, and a beverage. Lighter fare, including a very substantial club sandwich, can be had, with a drink, for only half that much.

The dining room in the Hotel Modelo is also worth your consideration at mealtime. For a stroll past many of this city's better eateries, make your way to the corner of 14a Avenida and 3a Calle, then walk uphill along 14a Avenida.

MEALS FOR LESS THAN Q58 [$10]

CAFE INTERNACIONAL BAVIERA, 5a Calle 12-50, Zona 1. No phone.
   Cuisine: PASTRIES.
$ **Prices:** Q5.50–Q6 (95¢–$1.05). MC, V.
   Open: Daily 8am–8pm.

⭐ This cozy café is currently Quetzaltenango's most popular hangout with the Spanish-school crowd. They come for the convivial, European atmosphere, good coffee, and wide variety of delectable pastries. Be sure to take a look around at the many historic photos of old Quetzaltenango. For those with a larger appetite, there are also hot dogs.

PASTELERÍA BOMBONIER, 14a Avenida 2-20, Zona 1. Tel. 616-225.
   Cuisine: SANDWICHES/PIZZA/PASTRIES.
$ **Prices:** Q3–Q18 (55¢–$3.10). No credit cards.
   Open: Daily 9am–9pm.
This is a tiny family-run snack place with only a handful of tables—but with hamburgers priced at less than a dollar, it's a real bargain for a light meal. If you like sugary pastries, you'll definitely want to cruise past the pastry case here. It's full of unusual treats.

PIZZA RICCA, 14a Avenida 2-42, Zona 1. Tel. 618-162.
   Cuisine: PIZZA.
$ **Prices:** Pizzas Q10–Q36 ($1.75–$6.20). No credit cards.
   Open: Daily 11:30am–9:30pm.
This is a tidy little place with cozy booths and a busy wood-fired oven filled with pizzas bubbling and baking. The white-uniformed staff tends the fires and the pies. Order your pizza small, medium, or large; have a beer or soft drink; and the bill will come to about Q17 ($2.95) per person.

POLLO FRITO ALBAMAR, 4a Calle 14–16, Zona 1 and 4a Calle 13–84, Zona 3. Tel. 616-224.
   Cuisine: GUATEMALAN/INTERNATIONAL.
$ **Prices:** Q7–Q28 ($1.20–$4.85). No credit cards.
   Open: Daily 7am–10:30pm.

Ⓢ Primarily fried-chicken restaurants, these two family fast-food places also serve a variety of other meals, including filet mignon and some delicious típico favorites. And you can't beat the prices—even a steak will cost you only Q28 ($4.85). The one in Zona 3 is more family oriented than the one downtown. At the former, you'll find a huge slide to keep your kids entertained while you enjoy your meal. Meals are served either in a large dining room or on tables outside by the slide. The downtown restaurant is very conveniently located a block away from Parque Centro America.

RESTAURANTE EL KOPETIN, 14a Avenida 3-51, Zona 1. Tel. 618-381.
   Cuisine: GUATEMALAN/INTERNATIONAL.
$ Prices: Main dishes Q7.50–Q27.90 ($1.30–$4.85). DC, MC, V.
   Open: Daily 11am–10pm.

✪   In this dark, modern, family-run place with red tablecloths and natural wood, the specialty is outstanding appetizers. A person could make a meal on just an assortment of some of these delicious starters. Try the *quesos fundidos* (melted cheese) or one of the spicy *chorizo* sausage appetizers, both under Q10 ($1.75). The *parillada* for Q20 ($3.45) is a carnivore's delight that includes five different meats, potatoes, and vegetables. The menu also lists everything from shrimp and fish to filet mignon, all priced around Q20–Q28 ($3.45–$4.85), but there are burgers and sandwiches for much less. El Kopetin is only two blocks off the Parque Centro America.

RESTAURANT SHANGHAI, 4a Calle 12-22, Zona 1. Tel. 614-154.
   Cuisine: CHINESE.
$ Prices: Main dishes Q14–Q22.50 ($2.45–$3.90). No credit cards.
   Open: Daily 9am–10pm.

Chinese restaurants are common throughout Guatemala, and whenever you get tired of rice and beans and meat, you can always head to one for a big plate of steaming vegetables. The food at Shanghai is far from authentic and the staff seems to be 100% Maya (not Chinese), but the restaurant does add variety to your dining. The combination plates are priced even lower than most main dishes. And in very un-Chinese fashion, there is a tempting array of cakes displayed in the front of the restaurant, occasionally including Guatemalan-style cheesecake.

EL RINCON DE LOS ANTOJITOS, 5a Avenida and 15 Calle. No phone.
   Cuisine: GUATEMALAN/INTERNATIONAL.
$ Prices: Main dishes Q5–Q23.50 (90¢–$4.05). No credit cards.
   Open: Daily 8am–8pm.

Though burgers (including vegetarian bean burgers) and other sandwiches comprise the bulk of the menu here, there are also such traditional Guatemalan dishes as *pepian* and *pollo en jocón*. The former is the de facto national dish, and the latter is made with chicken in a flavorful green sauce. There are only four tables here, so arrive early if you want dinner. Breakfasts are also quite good. The walls here are usually covered with notices of interest to visitors.

TABERNA DE DON RODRIGO, 14a Avenida 47. Tel. 612-963.
   Cuisine: SANDWICHES.
$ Prices: Q6–Q19 ($1.05–$3.30). No credit cards.
   Open: Daily 10am–9pm.

Across the street from the plaza with the impressive Teatro Municipal you will find a place where local young people like to gather, chat, and consume hamburgers, cheeseburgers, hot dogs, cakes, Cokes, lemonade, coffee, and draft beer. To the local people it's a stylish place, but a light meal here will not cost more than a dollar or two. The specialty is a giant sandwich called the Don Rodrigo super sandwich. Order one of these and a beer for a total bill of less than Q25 ($4.35), and you've got a very filling and very cheap meal.

EXCURSIONS

There are dozens of Indian villages in the vicinity of Quetzaltenango, all of which have markets one or more days a week. These markets are excellent places to shop for local crafts and to see Indians in their colorful attire. On festival days you may also get to see traditional dances, such as the Dance of the Conquest, the Dance of the Moors, or the **palo volador** (flying pole). This latter dance, which dates back to pre-Columbian times, is a death-defying acrobatic event during which men swing from ropes tied to a tall pole.

The most famous market in the Quetzaltenango area is held each Friday in **San Francisco El Alto.** This town is perched on a ridge high above Quetzaltenango and has stupendous views of the surrounding highlands. However, what draws people here is the huge market that on Friday takes over nearly every street in town. On the central square, in front of the church, food vendors watch over bubbling clay pots filled with tamales and other campesino fare. Different streets tend to specialize in different goods, and it is on a field above the main square that you will find the livestock market area, which is one of the most fascinating areas of the market. Other streets are lined with produce vendors, cloth merchants, and vendors of used *ropa American*—American clothes. However, it is the locally made, hand-woven wool blankets that are the most popular item with tourists visiting San Francisco. You'll find stacks of these colorful blankets all over town. If you decide to buy, be sure to bargain. To reach San Francisco El Alto, take a bus either from the Parque Minerva bus park or from the corner of 2a Calle and 6a Avenida in Zona 2 (behind the Esso station).

The actual blanket-weaving center of this region is another 15 kilometers beyond San Francisco in the village of **Momostenango.** Because the road to Momostenango is unpaved, it's a rough ride out here. Few tourists bother to visit because the village's blankets can be had much more easily at the San Francisco El Alto market.

Only 5 kilometers out of Quetzaltenango on the road down to the Pacific lowlands, the climate and landscape change dramatically. Here, outside the town of **Almolonga,** market gardens have turned the valley floor into a lush green patchwork of vegetables. Among the most frequently grown crops here are carrots, radishes, and onions. These fertile fields are irrigated by a network of canals that wind through the valley. To get the water from the canals to the crops, farmers use wooden shovels to toss the water onto their fields. These vegetable fields continue down the valley to the town of Zunil, a much more interesting town than Almolonga. The market days for Almolonga are Wednesday and Saturday and the annual festival is held July 27 through 29.

For sheer eye-popping brilliance, no other traditional attire in Guatemala is as colorful as that worn by the women of **Zunil.** This small village is only a few miles south of Quetzaltenango on the road down to Retalhuleu, but it seems a world away. Built on a steep hillside above a little river, Zunil is in a fog zone and almost always cool and damp. To stay warm and dry, the women of the village cover themselves with cloaks of shocking pink, magenta, violet, and lavender. As they hurry down the cobblestone streets with their cloaks swaying behind them, they are like apparitions of a long-forgotten civilization.

Zunil is also home to one of the Maximón effigies that are found in a few villages here in the highlands. Maximón (also known as San Simón), is a thinly disguised Mayan god, Mam. He is revered by the local population for his powers to answer prayers and heal the sick. Maximón, who lives in a small house up the hill behind the church, consists of a mannequin wearing a mask, jacket and pants, hat, and dozens of scarves. He sits in state on a large chair, where he meets with those seeking his favors. The traditional way to worship Maximón is to blow cigar smoke in his face and pour liquor into his mouth. The Indians believe devoutly in Maximón, and if you should wish to meet with him, be sure to take him an offering (a few quetzales is acceptable, but some liquor and cigars are preferable).

Though Monday is market day for Zunil, there is a second and more interesting market here every Thursday as vendors from the big Friday market in San Francisco El Alto come to town to haggle over huge bundles of produce for their own market stalls. This colorful market takes place in front of Zunil's old whitewashed church. Zunil's annual festival is celebrated on November 25.

Before leaving town, be sure to stop in at Zunil's Cooperative de Tejadoras, a weavers' cooperative that sells those brilliantly colored traditional Zunil shawls, as well as blankets, clothes, and placemats.

Just past Zunil on the left is an alternate route into Quetzaltenango. If you turn up this road and then turn right on the first dirt road, you'll be heading for **Fuentes Georginas,** one of the most enchanting places in Guatemala. Several miles up this rough and muddy dirt road, at the head of a valley that begins on the flanks of Zunil Mountain, is a **hot springs complex** that feels at times like the most remote spot on earth. Clouds of steam rise from the pale-blue sulfurous waters and drift up a steep hillside that is draped with fronds of giant ferns. Beside the pool is a bar and tiny restaurant where you can order simple meals. There are a few basic cabins here, with tubs that can be filled with water from the hot springs. If you're looking for the ultimate low-budget spa, this is it. Cabins rent for less than $15 per night. Higueros Tours, 12 Avenida and 7a Calle (around the corner from the INGUAT office) in Quetzaltenango, offers day tours to Fuentes Georginas for around Q40 ($6.90).

Just up the road from Zunil toward Quetzaltenango, in the village of Los Baños (The Baths), are several dozen less appealing hot springs bathing facilities. If you want to warm up, hop off the bus and check out a few until you find one that meets your standards. My favorite is **Los Chorros** at the lower end of town. This place is open daily from 6am to 7pm and has private tub rooms and a warm-water pool. It costs Q5 (90¢) to use a big tub and Q1.50 (25¢) per person to use the pool. Best of all is the amazing paint job that's been done on the buildings surrounding the swimming pool. You have to see it to believe it!

There are also several more hot springs near Almolonga, which is between Zunil and Quetzaltenango. These include Los Vahos, Aguas Amargas, and El Rosario. Buses for Almolonga and Zunil leave from the corner of Avenida 9 and Calle 10 not far from the Tourist Office. Pick-up trucks also operate as taxis between Zunil and Almolonga.

Other area towns that you might want to visit include **Totonicapan,** which is 25 kilometers northeast of Quetzaltenango (past Cuatro Caminos) and is known for its ceramics, wooden masks, and textiles. However, there are few shops here selling the local crafts; most get shipped off to Chichi, Panajachel, and Antigua. Market days here are Monday, Tuesday, and Thursday, and the annual festival is held the last week of September.

Don't confuse Totonicapan with **San Cristóbal Totonicapan,** which is a little bit southwest of Cuatro Caminos and is best known for its 17th-century church, which has a silver-and-crystal altar, and convent. This latter town is down in the valley and has its market on Sunday and its annual festival on July 25.

If you have an interest in Guatemalan history, you might want to visit **Olintepeque,** which is 7 kilometers north of Quetzaltenango. It was near here, on a wide plain, that Tecún Umán, Guatemala's last Maya chieftain, was killed by the conquistador Pedro de Alvarado in 1524. Olintepeque's market is held on Tuesday and its festival is celebrated on June 24.

Between Cuatro Caminos and Quetzaltenango is the town of **Salcajá,** which has a colonial church that was among the first built by the Spanish. Salcajá's market is on Tuesday, and the town celebrates its festival on August 25. **Cantel,** 10 kilometers northeast of Zunil, is the site of large textile factories that make most of the machine-made fabrics you see here in Guatemala. Cantel's market day is Sunday and its festival is on August 15.

If you're looking for a natural excursion and would like to do a bit of hiking, head west 20 kilometers to the village of San Martin Chile Verde. This town is named for the chiles it grows, but it is **Chicabal Lake** on the volcano of the same name that has brought this town its fame over the years. Chicabal Lake, formed by an extinct volcanic crater, is considered sacred by the local Indians and consequently is surrounded by primitive altars. It is the chance to glimpse ancient Mayan rituals that makes a hike up here so worthwhile. It takes about two hours to hike from the village up to the lake, and along the way there are often great views. Ascension Thursday (40 days after Easter) is the lake's annual holy day, and on this day many pilgrims visit the lake.

Buses to the above-mentioned towns leave from the Parque Minerva bus park.

If you'd like to do some **guided touring,** contact the Santa María Project, 14 Avenida "A" 1-26, Zona 1 (tel. 618-281). This organization offers trips to nearby Santa

María volcano and Los Vahos hot springs ($25); Abaj-Takalik ruins, a pre-Maya site near Retalhuleu, and Playa Champerico ($46); San Francisco El Alto and Fuentes Georginas ($30); Chicabal Lake and Almolonga hot springs ($30). You can also find out about hiking up several nearby volcanoes by checking at the restaurant El Rincon de los Antojitos at the corner of 5a Avenida and 15 Calle. These trips range from a half-day to overnight (camping). Rates are very reasonable.

---

5. HUEHUETENANGO

258 kilometers NW of Guatemala City; 84 kilometers SE of La Mesilla (Mexican border); 82 kilometers N of Quetzaltenango

GETTING THERE By Bus Los Halcones buses from Guatemala City to Huehuetenango leave from 7a Avenida 15-27 daily at 7am and 2pm. Duration: 5 hours. Fare: Q19 ($3.25). If you're coming from the border, there'll be a bus there to meet your Mexican bus. From Quetzaltenango, you can either take one of the first-class buses heading to the Mexican border at La Mesilla or catch a second-class bus from Parque Minerva. Duration: 2½–3 hours. Fare: Q6–Q10 ($1.05–$1.75).

By Car From the Mexican border, it is a fairly easy 84 kilometers. Watch for the turnoff for Huehuetenango, which is about 6.5 kilometers off the highway. If you're coming from Guatemala City, continue going straight through the intersection known as Cuatro Caminos (Four Roads), which is the turnoff for Quetzaltenango. Watch for the Huehuetenango turnoff from the highway.

DEPARTING You can catch a bus to Quetzaltenango either near the market downtown or at the bus terminal, which is a mile or so outside town on the road to Quetzaltenango. First-class Los Halcones buses leave daily at 7am and 2pm from 7a Avenida across the street from the Hotel Casablanca in downtown Huehuetenango.

ESSENTIALS Orientation Huehuetenango's main square, reference point for everything in town, is bounded by 2a and 3a calles and by 4a and 5a avenidas.

Fast Facts Banco del Agro, located across the street from the relief map in the central park, is open Monday through Friday from 9am to 8pm and Saturday from 9am to 2pm. The Guatel telephone office and the post office are both located across the street from the Hotel Mary on 2a Calle.
    Market day is every day, and the Fiesta is July 22.

Huehuetenango, although it is miles from the Mexican border is the first major settlement on the road into Guatemala from Mexico and is the provincial capital of Huehuetenango (alt. 6,240 feet; pop. 40,000). There isn't much to keep you here, but the ruins of Zaculeu are only a few miles from town, and there's an assortment of hotels and restaurants, all within your price range. If you've taken a car or a bus from San Cristóbal, Mexico, this is the logical place to spend the night.
    This town might be your first glimpse of Guatemalan culture, and you'll be pleasantly surprised the farther you go into the country. The costumes seem to get more and more colorful and unusual as you head southeast through the highlands. Notice that throughout this region, it's traditional for women to wear aprons all the time—they come in all sizes, shapes, and colors. No matter what sort of apron she has, every woman must have one.
    On the road from Huehuetenango, the vistas continue: old men, young boys, teenage girls—literally everyone is on foot and carrying something. The men use a

"tump line" (a rope or strap from the backpack load to the forehead) to distribute the weight of the huge bundles they carry, or they put their packs in a large piece of cloth, tying the ends so that they can loop it over their foreheads and carry the load on their backs. It's a constant reminder that horses were not found in this hemisphere before the Conquest and that the Indian civilizations knew nothing about the wheel. It also shows how little Indian culture has changed from that day to this.

WHAT TO SEE & DO

You can visit the **market,** which is busy every day. It's located at 3a Avenida and 4a Calle, and its four great walls hold a busy collection of fruit stands, candle sellers, cloth shops, basket vendors, dried chile merchants, and even a bottle shop where you can purchase an old instant-coffee jar (nothing goes to waste in this town!). Shopkeepers are very obliging—most are friendly, all are curious—and they expect you to bargain for their merchandise. The best place to buy highland crafts and clothing made from Guatemalan fabrics is **Ixquil,** 5a Avenida 1-56, Zona 1, which is right next door to the Hotel Zaculeu and has identified displays of traditional clothing of this region.

Besides the market, you'll want to take a look at the **ruins of Zaculeu.** Avoid self-appointed "guides" and take one of the very battered minibuses that depart from 4a Calle between 7a and 8a avenidas. The bus fare is only 50 centavos (8¢). Alternatively, you can take a taxi for around Q35 ($6.05) for the round-trip. You can also walk—it's a pleasant hike of about 45 minutes.

If you drive, head out of town on 9a Avenida and keep following the signs on this 2½-mile ride, even though they seem to be leading you on a wild goose chase. You may have to ask directions a few times despite the signs. The ruins at Zaculeu date from the Postclassic Period just before the Spanish Conquest. The Postclassic Period began in A.D. 900, when the Mayan civilization began to fade out and become absorbed by the Mexican tribes that were moving down from the north. Out of this assimilation of Mexican and Mayan cultures arose three powerful nations, one of which was the Mam, who settled in the area around Huehuetenango and made their capital at Zaculeu. The Mayan culture had been greatly diffused by this time, so you will see very little similarity between the Mayan ruins of Yucatán and Petén and those at Zaculeu.

This site was restored in 1940 by the United Fruit Company "as a contribution to Guatemalan culture." The site is small, however, and there are several mounds that have not been uncovered; at present there are no plans for further excavation. The restoration was so complete, down to the coat of mortar that covered the temples, that it appears as a reconstruction rather than a restoration: "perfect temples" down to the manicured lawns. The surroundings are beautiful, and the ruins are worth a visit. There is a small but interesting museum on the premises. Entrance is free to the ruins and museum.

WHERE TO STAY

DOUBLES FOR LESS THAN Q87 [$15]

HOTEL MARY, 2a Calle 3-52, Zona 1, Huehuetenango. Tel. 502-9/64- 1618 or 64-1228. 25 rms (12 with bath).
$ **Rates:** Q22.25 ($3.85) single without bath; Q32.80 ($5.65) double without bath, Q46.80 ($8.10) double with bath; Q38.65 ($6.65) triple without bath, Q58.50 ($10.10) triple with bath. MC, V.

The Hotel Mary is a small hotel only a block from the main plaza and directly across the street from Guatel and the post office. The rooms are on four floors (no elevator), with open-air hallways that run the length of the building. It's very basic, but clean, and some rooms have views. You'll find a bit of off-street parking underneath the hotel by the reception desk. There is a small restaurant on the second floor, where meals average Q20 ($3.45).

HOTEL ZACULEU, 5a Avenida 1-14, Zona 1, Huehuetenango. Tel. 502-9/ 64-1086 or 64-1575. 40 rms (all with bath).
$ **Rates:** Q52.65–Q163.80 ($9.10–$28.25) single; Q76.05–Q210.60 ($13.15–$36.35) double; 99.45–Q257.40 ($17.15–$44.40) triple. No credit cards.

The long-time favorite of travelers passing through Huehuetenango is a colonial-style hotel a block away from the town's main plaza. Many of the rooms are decorated with local handcrafts—handwoven cloth, tin candlesticks, and clay water pitchers. Some rooms are truly charming, others are not. The older rooms at the front of the hotel open onto a courtyard filled with flowers and bordered by a colonial arcade. Although these rooms have more of a Guatemalan flavor to them, they are also closer to the street and therefore are noisier than the rooms in back. The newer rooms are done in a modern Spanish style—with bright bathrooms, carpets, and TVs. The higher prices are for these latter rooms. Additional facilities include a private parking lot and a good restaurant.

TODOS SANTOS INN, 2a Calle 6-74, Zona 1, Huehuetenango. Tel. 502-9/64-1241. 10 rms (all with shared bath).
$ **Rates:** Q25 ($4.35) single; Q40 ($6.90) double; Q60 ($10.35) triple. No credit cards.

Though the rooms in this economical hotel don't have private baths, they are still very comfortable and clean. All the rooms have tile floors, beamed ceilings, and colorful decor, and most have windows, some with nice views. The rooms are set back a bit from the street, so they are fairly quiet.

DOUBLES FOR LESS THAN Q145 [$25]

HOTEL CASABLANCA, 7a Avenida 3-41, Zona 1, Huehuetenango. Tel. 502-9/64-1173. 10 rms (all with bath). TV
$ **Rates:** Q87.75 ($15.15) single; Q128.70 ($22.20) double; Q152.10 ($26.25) triple. No credit cards.

This is the best of the convenient, downtown hotel choices. Though the central courtyard of this modern, colonial-style building is cemented over, there is a shady garden dining area in back. The rooms are large and are decorated with colorful Guatemalan bedspreads and paintings. The biggest drawback here is that the rooms are a bit dark, a vestige of colonial design. Meals in the dining room or out in the garden will run between Q30 and Q35 ($5.20 and $6.05).

WHERE TO EAT

Your best bet for a meal in Huehuetenango will likely be your hotel. If you should want to try someplace else, the following restaurants are convenient.

EBONY RESTAURANT, 2a Calle 5-11. No phone.
   Cuisine: GUATEMALAN/INTERNATIONAL.
$ **Prices:** Q3.50–Q12 (60¢–$2.10). No credit cards.
   Open: Daily 7am–11pm.

Around the corner from the main plaza you'll find a small, dark restaurant popular with the young generation in Huehuetenango. The walls and ceiling are made of split bamboo, and there are wicker baskets for lampshades. The overall effect is that of a tropical beach hangout, even though you're a long way from the ocean. On the menu are chicken, pork chops, steaks, and chorizo, and a variety of breakfasts for the same low price. Delicious fresh fruit licuados are only Q2.50 (45¢).

RESTAURANT CHURRASCOS LAS BRASAS, 4a Avenida 1-55, Zona 1. Tel. 64-2339.
   Cuisine: STEAKS/CHINESE.
$ **Prices:** Main dishes Q18–Q28 ($3.10–$4.85). MC, V.

Open: Mon–Sat 9am–9:30pm.

Located a block off the Parque Central and next door to the Hotel Mary, this combination steak house and Chinese restaurant is one of Huehuetenango's better restaurants. The steaks, though often chewy (as they are throughout Guatemala) are none-the-less quite cheap. Other menu items include chicken in wine and several shrimp dishes. At lunch, there are plenty of inexpensive sandwiches available.

EASY EXCURSIONS

Todos Santos Cuchumatán is a remote village three hours north of Huehuetenango by bus on a rough and dusty dirt road. I don't recommend this excursion unless you have a few days to spare and are very interested in visiting a small village with very basic accommodations. The village, which is situated in a long, narrow valley 8,060 feet high in the Cuchumatán Mountains, is one of the few places in Guatemala where the men still wear their traditional clothing, which consists of bright red striped pants; heavy, colorful, long-sleeved shirts with ornately woven collars and cuffs; and thick, round straw hats with narrow brims and low crowns. The ensemble is unmistakable.

The little village is worth a visit any time of year if you're interested in observing the campesino life of the highlands. However, the year's highlight is the annual fiesta in celebration of All Saints Day, for which the town is named. Between October 30 and November 1 (All Saints Day) the town indulges in a drunken bacchanal that includes all-night marimba music, dancing in the streets, and an outlandish horse race through town.

At other times of year, there is little to do here but observe the local life (this is a vegetable farming valley), hike out to the small Mayan ruins above the village, and spend a few minutes in the tiny local museum on the main square. However, you'll likely notice a surprising number of gringos hanging out here. Most are studying Spanish at the **Proyecto Lingüístico de Español/Mam Todos Santos,** which offers classes in both Spanish and Mam, the indigenous language of this region. Tuition here (for five hours of classes five days a week) ranges from $100 to $125 per week including room and board. To find out about studying here, contact the Proyecto Lingüístico Quetzalteco (See "Alternative/Adventure Travel" in Chapter 10).

Currently there are three very basic **pensions** in the village—Casa Familia, Hospedaje Tres Olguitas, and Hospedaje La Paz—none of which charge more than $2 per person for a room with a shared bath. All three pensions also serve meals, though you can also get a bite to eat at one of the simple comedors around town.

Buses from Huehuetenango to Todos Santos leave from behind the Pensión San Jorge at the corner of 1a Avenida and 4a Calle at 11:30am and 12:30pm.

---

6. RETALHULEU

182 kilometers W of Guatemala City; 52 kilometers S of Quetzaltenango; 121 kilometers E of Tapachula, Mexico

GETTING THERE   By Bus   A bus from the Mexican border into town takes about an hour and will cost about Q3.50 (60¢). Buses bound from Guatemala City to the Mexican border at either Tecún Umán or El Carmen stop at Retalhuleu en route. Galgos, 7a Avenida 19-44, Zona 1 (tel. 23-661), has six buses daily. Duration: 4 hours. Fare: Q24.15 ($4.20). Fortaleza, 19 Calle 8-70, Zona 1 (tel. 23-643), has four buses daily for about the same price.

By Car   Retalhuleu is 5 kilometers south of the crossroads of the highway to Quetzaltenango and the Pacific Highway. If you are coming from Antigua or Guatemala City, it's faster to go first to Escuintla and then take the Pacific Highway through the lowlands. If you are coming from Mexico, either from Ciudad Hidalgo/Ciudad Tecún Umán (31 kilometers away), or Talisman/El Carmen (80 kilometers away), just follow the main highway and you will see the turn off for Retalhuleu.

DEPARTING   There are several buses a day from Retalhuleu to Quetzaltenango, the Mexican border, and Guatemala City.

ESSENTIALS   Orientation   The town of Retalhuleu is 5 kilometers off the highway, but there are two hotels right on the highway that are better than those in town.

Retalhuleu is a quiet small town with little to recommend it other than a number of acceptable hotels that are the best for some miles around. Though the town is on the wide flat plain near the Pacific Coast, I include it in this chapter because it's a gateway to the highlands for travelers coming from or going to the lowlands of Mexico. There is no reason to stay more than a night. The three downtown hotel choices are close to the pretty main square in front of the church.

Just 5 kilometers out of town is the junction with the toll road to Quetzaltenango, an exciting drive that winds up 2 miles in altitude in only an hour's time. The road is good, and the scenery is exceptional: Four of the highest volcanoes in Guatemala flank the macadam strip, two on either side. Every now and then in the lower elevations an exceptionally beautiful ceiba tree will catch your eye, huge and of fine proportion, its bladelike roots standing as much as 20 feet high at its base.

About the only activity of interest around these parts is a visit to the nearby archeological excavations of **Abaj Takalik.** This is one of the few places where Olmecan and Mayan stone carvings are found at the same spot. At this active archeological site, more than 168 stone sculptures have been unearthed. Some of the buildings at Abaj Takalik, which means "standing stone," date to around 235 B.C. The best way to visit the site is on a tour arranged either in Retalhuleu or in Quetzaltenango. Check with your hotel or the INGUAT office in Quetzaltenango.

WHERE TO STAY & EAT

HOTEL ASTOR, 5a Calle 4-60, Zona 1, Retalhuleu. Tel. 502-9/710-475.
13 rms (9 with bath).
$ Rates: Q58 ($10) single without bath, Q69.60 ($12) single with bath; Q81.20 ($14) double without bath, Q92.80 ($16) double with bath. No credit cards accepted.

S This hotel is an old mansion in which the grand rooms have been split down the middle to make bedrooms for guests. Even so, the spaces are larger than those in most modern luxury hotels. The rooms are entered from a verdant courtyard surrounded by a colonnade. A small dining room looks onto the courtyard and provides very substantial meals. A typical dinner might be delicious black beans, potatoes, filet steak smothered in onions and tomatoes, plus fried bananas and mangoes (from the tree out back) for dessert, for only Q35 ($6.05) per person.

POSADA DE DON JOSÉ, 5a Calle 3-67, Zona 1, Retalhuleu. Tel. 502-9/710-180 or 710-841. 25 rms (all with bath). A/C TEL.
$ Rates: Q179.80 ($31) single; Q214.60 ($37) double. AE, DC, V.

A modern and luxurious downtown choice, the Don José is only a few blocks away from the Astor. This is the most comfortable downtown hotel, and you may feel that you owe it to yourself, if you've just made the arduous border crossing, to sit back and enjoy the air-conditioning or the swimming pool. Try to get a room on the second floor overlooking the plaza. These rooms are quite large, and the view is pleasant.

HOTEL MODELO, 5a Calle 4-53, Zona 1, Retalhuleu. Tel. 502-9/710-256. 7 rms (all with bath). TEL
$ Rates: Q35 ($6.05) single; Q50 ($8.65) double; Q65 ($11.20) triple. No credit cards.

This small hotel is directly across the street from the Astor, and although it is not as atmospheric, it is still a good choice. The rooms are set around a flowered courtyard, and all have hardwood floors, fans, and high ceilings. You might even find a small black-and-white TV in the room. Throughout the hotel there are framed huipiles (colorful blouses worn by Indian women) and contemporary paintings by local artists. The small restaurant and bar are just off the tile-floored lobby.

HOTEL SIBONEY, Cuatro Caminos, San Sebastián, Retalhuleu. Tel. 502-9/710-372. 48 rms (all with bath). A/C TV TEL
$ Rates: Q150 ($25.90) single; Q165 ($28.45) double; Q180 ($31.05) triple. DC, MC, V.

This is the first hotel that you'll come to near Retalhuleu, on the left at the intersection leading into town. Large trees shade the parking area. The rooms come with two double beds and color cable TVs so that you can watch all your favorite shows. There's a huge restaurant with screen walls that let in every least tropical breeze. Steaks and seafood are the specialties.

EN ROUTE TO GUATEMALA CITY
LA DEMOCRACIA

GETTING THERE   By Bus   In Guatemala City, Chatia Gomerana, Muelle Central, Terminal de Buses, Zona 4, has buses every 30 minutes from 6am to 6:30pm. Duration: 2 hours. Fare: Q6 ($1.05). You can also take a bus to Siquinalá and then get a local bus to La Democracia.

By Car   If you're coming from the west on the Pacific Highway, turn right in Siquinalá. From Guatemala City, take the Carretera al Pacífico to Siquinalá and turn left.

DEPARTING   You can catch a bus to Siquinalá and then transfer to a Guatemala City bus, or catch one of the less frequent buses that stop in La Democracia on their run from Sipacate to Guatemala City.

Located 57 miles southwest of Guatemala City, the tiny town of La Democracia is famous for strange, boulder-sized Preclassic Mayan (sometimes called Pre-Olmec) statues and artifacts found at a nearby farm, Finca Monte Alto. When you get to La Democracia, follow the signs for "El Museo." The museum is on the town's main square (two blocks east of the main road). The plaza is simple but has a pleasant cement gazebo built around a large ceiba tree, and several of the large stone sculptures decorate the square.

WHAT TO SEE & DO

La Democracia Museum was built in 1967 to house the numerous objects found during excavations at Finca Monte Alto and the smaller fincas of Río Seco, La Gomera, and Ora Blanca. The museum (open Tuesday to Sunday from 9am to noon and 2 to 5pm; closed Monday and holidays) is not large, so you should be able to see everything in an hour or so. Unfortunately, organization and classification are not the museum's high points, so you'll see primitive pottery and terra-cotta figurines (mostly female); obsidian blades, spears, and knives; and curious zoomorphic jars all mixed together, the primitive with the sophisticated. Some of the figurines have elaborate headdresses similar to those found in Zapotec Monte Alban (Mexico). There are several stone "yokes" and stone replicas of mushrooms, which immediately suggest that hallucinogenic mushrooms and their replicas were used in ceremonies by these people.

Outside the museum, in front of it, and in the plaza are the great Buddha-like stone figures and heads carved from boulders—11 of these have been found to date. Just what they represent is a mystery: Similar crude carvings have been found in El Salvador and as far north as Chiapas in Mexico—but are they deities, chiefs, or local dignitaries? Professor Edwin Shook, who headed the excavations here from 1968 to

1970 under the auspices of the National Geographic Society and Harvard's Peabody Museum, says that they were made during the period from 300 B.C. to the birth of Christ. He maintains that they were carved by a Mayan people, not "Pre-Olmecs" as many others thought; the Olmecs carved much more sophisticated heads, complete with headbands and ornaments, while these are really very crude images chipped out of the sides of boulders. His theory is that they were carved by a Preclassic Mayan people who settled at Monte Alto about 1000 B.C., reached the peak of their civilization from 300 B.C. to A.D. 1, and then declined by about A.D. 300. If this is so, these people would be very early Mayas, earlier than the people who settled at Tikal and Palenque, but so far no Mayan glyphs—which would be proof of their race—have been found at Monte Alto. Perhaps some will turn up, for glyphs were found at Kaminal Juyú (in Guatemala City) that predate those found at Tikal; therefore, it's thought that Mayan hieroglyphic writing may have started here on the Pacific Slope and then progressed north and east to the Petén and Yucatán.

The town of La Democracia itself is not what I'd call wildly interesting, unless you're an anthropologist who loves sticky heat, so plan on a quick visit to the museum and the plaza and then a quick retreat back up into the mountains to Guatemala City.

7. MONTERRICO

124 kilometers S of Guatemala City; 70 kilometers SW of Esquintla

GETTING THERE   By Bus and Boat   Transportes Cubanita buses leave Guatemala City for La Avellana from the Muelle Central, Terminal de Buses, Zona 4, at 10:30am and 12:30 and 2:30pm. Duration: 4½ hours. Fare: Q7 ($1.20). In La Avellana, arrange for a boat to take you the 3 kilometers through the mangroves to Monterrico Beach. A boat should cost around Q12 ($2.10).

By Car   Take CA-9, the Pacific Coast Highway from Guatemala, and at the circle in Esquintla, turn left toward Taxisco. Just past Taxisco, turn right toward La Avellana. In La Avellana, you'll have to park your car and take a boat down the canal to Monterrico.

DEPARTING   Be sure to ask at your hotel about arranging boat transportation back to La Avellana in time to catch a Guatemala City–bound bus.

ESSENTIALS   Monterrico is a small fishing village, and, because it is surrounded by waterways and the Pacific Ocean, is actually an island. There are no services to speak of here, so bring enough cash for your stay.

Monterrico is considered one of the best **beaches** on the Pacific Coast and has in the past few years become a magnet for budget travelers, especially those interested in nature. Though the black-sand beaches here are pleasant enough, it is the adjacent **Monterrico Nature Reserve** that makes a trip out here worthwhile. Biotopo Monterrico was created primarily to protect the nesting beach of endangered sea turtles. To that end, a captive hatching program has been implemented here, and each year between 5,000 and 8,000 newly hatched sea turtles are released back into the Pacific Ocean at Monterrico Beach. The nature reserve, which includes the mangrove forests behind the beach as well as the beach itself, also protects iguanas, caimans (a type of alligator), and many species of birds.

Other than visiting the turtle hatchery, touring the waterways of the preserve, and hitting the beach, there isn't much to do at Monterrico other than hang out. At The Pig Pen Beach Bar, you can find out about what's going on in Monterrico these days, rent a surfboard, or just have a drink. Great sunsets!

If you don't want to do all the travel planning yourself and want to learn more about the sea turtle conservation program, check at the ECO Training Center, 4a Avenida Norte no. 9-A, Antigua Guatemala (tel./fax 502-9/322-294). When I last visited, this company was offering two-night trips for Q174 ($30). The trips included transportation from Antigua and accommodations in Monterrico.

WHERE TO STAY

HOTEL BAULE BEACH, Aldea Monterrico. No phone. 16 rms (all with bath).
$ Rates: Q75 ($12.95) single; Q100 ($17.25) double; Q125 ($21.55) triple. No credit cards.
This hotel was opened by a former Peace Corps worker and was the first hotel at Monterrico. It is still one of the better places to stay and the clientele tends to be interesting young people who enjoy out-of-the-way places. Rooms are basic but comfortable. The restaurant serves good, inexpensive meals, and tours of the reserve are offered.

KAIMAN-INN, Aldea Monterrico. Tel. 502-9/826-513. 6 rms (all with bath).
$ Rates: Q110.20 ($19) single; Q121.80 ($21) double; Q147.90 ($25.50) triple. No credit cards.
This hotel is newer than the Baule Beach and is equally comfortable though still pretty basic. The restaurant here specializes in Italian food.

WHERE TO EAT

There are a couple of good and inexpensive restaurants on the beach that are popular with gringos. Try the **Restaurante Pez de Oro** or **Divino Maestro,** both of which serve good, inexpensive seafood.

CHAPTER 13

EL PETÉN

1. FLORES & SANTA ELENA

2. TIKAL

El Petén is Guatemala's vast, wild, low-lying jungle province—a land of dirt roads and four-wheel-drive vehicles, of mammoth Mayan ceremonial centers and towering temples. In its dense jungle cover you'll hear the squawk of parrots, the chatter of monkeys, and the rustling of strange animals moving through the bush. The landscape here is as different from Guatemala's highlands as night is from day.

There are two main reasons to penetrate El Petén. First and foremost is to visit Tikal, the greatest Mayan religious center yet uncovered (Caracol in Belize is said to be much larger but has not yet been fully excavated). The second is wildlife: The jungles of Petén are home to a wondrous variety of exotic animals, particularly birds. Some bird-watchers go to Tikal just to fill up their life lists.

---

1. FLORES & SANTA ELENA

450 kilometers NE of Guatemala City;
135 kilometers W of the Belizean border

GETTING THERE **By Air** Several airlines fly to Flores/Santa Elena from Guatemala City's La Aurora Airport. These include Avcom, Avenida Hincapié and 18 Calle, Zona 13, Hangar 21 (tel. 315-821 or 314-954); Tapsa, Avenida Hincapié and 18 Calle, Zona 13, Hangar 14 (tel. 314-860 or 319-180); and Tikal Jets Airlines, 4a Avenida 0-44, Zona 13, Hangar 8 (tel. 345-631 or 346-855). However, be aware that the above-mentioned airlines fly from terminals on the far side of the airport from the main terminal. To reach these terminals, you'll have to take a taxi, since there is no convenient bus service. Always remember to tell a taxi driver what airline you will be flying, so he'll know which terminal to take you to. Fares on any of these airlines are between Q377 and Q406 ($65 and $70) one way and between Q620.60 and Q678.60 ($107 and $117) round-trip. Aviateca, (tel. 328-027 or 318-227), the national airline of Guatemala, flies from the main terminal at La Aurora International Airport and charges around Q522 ($90) one way and Q928 ($160) round-trip.

You usually won't have any trouble booking one of these flights once you arrive in Guatemala, but if you have a limited amount of time, you should be sure to make a reservation well in advance.

By Bus There are several companies operating first-class buses from Guatemala City to Flores/Santa Elena. These include Transportes Fuentes del Norte, 17 Calle 8-46, Zona 1 (tel. 513-817); Transportes La Petenera, 16 Calle and 10 Avenida, Zona 1 (tel. 29-658); and Maya Express, 17 Calle 9-36, Zona 1 (tel. 21-914 or 539-325). Fare: Q45 to Q60 ($7.75 to $10.35). Duration: 12 to 14 hours. Each company has around four departures daily.

This is one of the most grueling bus rides I have ever experienced, and if you don't get on in Guatemala City, you aren't likely to get a seat. The first 200 kilometers from Guatemala City is paved and smooth, but then the pavement runs out and the buses bounce and swerve over a terminally potholed strip of mud or dust (depending on the season). You'll arrive in Santa Elena totally exhausted, especially if you take one of the night buses. Transportes La Petenera also operates an air-conditioned luxury video-equipped bus that costs around $25 each way. However, it isn't much quicker than the other buses.

If you're coming from Belize, you can take a bus from Belize City (or from San Ignacio) to the Guatemalan border. Here you'll find a bus waiting to take passengers onward from the border town of Melchor de Mencos to Santa Elena/Flores. Fare (from the border): Q10 ($1.75). Duration (from the border): 3 hours. If you plan to take this bus, you should get to the border by noon so that you can catch the early afternoon bus onward.

If you have a little more money to spend and can round up a few other travelers, I recommend taking a minibus from the border. These cost around Q290 ($50) for the vehicle and can carry seven passengers, so if you fill it up it will only cost each person around Q41.45 ($7.15). You can also hire a taxi or minivan in San Ignacio, but this will cost you a bit more than if you wait until you get to the border to arrange a ride.

By Car   The trip from Guatemala City or Belize is over the same roads the buses take, but you have the luxury of stopping along the way. For the trip from Guatemala City, I'd recommend spending the night at the Hotel Izabal Tropical near the Río Dulce bridge (see Chapter 12) and starting for Flores bright and early. An alternative is to make it along the bad road as far as Poptún and camp at the Finca Ixobel, where there are some services, including showers and meals.

The journey from the Belizean-Guatemalan border point at Benque Viejo (Belize) and Melchor de Mencos (Guatemala) to Flores takes about two hours by car. The road has lots of potholes and ruts from Melchor to El Cruce, and the average speed is probably 20 miles per hour. It's a rough trip, worse in the rainy season. After El Cruce (Ixlu), the road is paved and fast all the way to Tikal or Flores.

By Boat and Bus   It is also possible to travel from Palenque in Chiapas, Mexico, to Flores by bus and boat. It's an adventurous route for the hardy only, because you will have to endure long hours in beat-up buses on bad roads and spend the night in a jungle village short on services.

Take an early morning bus from Palenque to Emiliano Zapata, then another bus from Zapata to Tenosique. At Tenosique, catch a bus to La Palma, where a boat will be waiting. The boat will head down the Río San Pedro to El Naranjo, which is within Guatemala. There is one small, very basic hotel in El Naranjo where you can try to grab a little sleep. There may be little bedding provided and it can get cold here, so have some camping gear or warm clothes. A bus departs from El Naranjo for Flores at 3am, and this, too, can be a very chilly journey. The entire trip from Palenque to Flores can be done for under $35 per person, including your sleep break in San Pedro.

DEPARTING   By Air   Avcom (tel. in Guatemala City 315-821), Aviateca (tel. 501-238), Tapsa (tel. 500-596), and Tikal Jets (tel. 500-386) all return to Guatemala City in the late afternoon. Aerocaribe (tel. 501-477) and Aviateca fly to Cancún (Fare: $139 one way), and Tropic Air (tel. 500-386) flies to Belize City (Fare: $62 one way, $124 round-trip).

By Bus and Minivan   There are three companies operating first-class buses to Guatemala City. Transportes Fuentes del Norte is located on the far side of the Santa Elena market from the causeway, while Transportes La Petenera and Maya Express are both located on Calle Principal on the causeway side of the market. Each of these companies has four departures daily. Buses for Melchor de Mencos, on the Belize border, leave throughout the day from the market in Santa Elena and stop at the Hotel San Juan before leaving town. There are also two buses each morning to Naranjo for those heading to Palenque, Mexico. See the "Tikal" section for details on getting from Santa Elena/Flores to the ruins.

You can also book a seat on a minivan either to Melchor de Mencos (around Q58, $10) or all the way to Belize City (Q116, $20) or even Chetumal (Q203, $35). These minivans can be booked at the Hotel San Juan or almost any other hotel in Santa Elena or Flores.

ORIENTATION City Layout Now primarily known as Flores, this town actually consists of three smaller towns that have merged. Flores, on an island out in Lake Petén Itzá, is connected to the mainland by a long causeway. On the mainland are Santa Elena (nearest the airport) and San Benito (closer to the bus terminal and market). Whether you arrive by air or by bus from Guatemala City or Belize, you will come into town from the east. The road in from the airport leads straight through Santa Elena to the market and bus terminal, while the causeway to Flores is a turn to the right in the middle of Santa Elena. In Flores, all the hotels can be found on the road that circles the island.

Fast Facts There is a bank in Flores at the end of Calle 30 de Junio, open Monday to Thursday from 8:30am to 2pm (to 2:30pm on Friday). You may also be able to change money at your hotel.

The Flores post office is on the Pasaje Progresso just off the Parque Central, which is in front of the church. Santa Elena's post office is just down the street from the Hotel San Juan. Both are open Monday through Friday from 8am to 4:30pm. The Guatel office is in Santa Elena three blocks straight up the hill from the causeway.

GETTING AROUND By Car Rental cars, some of them four-wheel-drive Suzukis, are offered by several businesses in town, including **Auto Rental San Juan** (tel. 500-041). **Koka** (tel. 501-233) will rent you a car, minibus, four-wheel-drive vehicle, or pickup truck or will arrange for a taxi tour to Tikal or anywhere else. Basic rates for a four-wheel-drive car are about Q406 ($70) per day, including free mileage. Most hotels can also help you rent a Suzuki four-wheel-drive vehicle for about the same price.

El Petén has always been a remote region, and it was here, on the banks of Lake Petén Itza that the Itza people, descendents of the Mayas, resisted Spanish conquest until the end of the 17th century. Hernán Cortés had visited the Itza city of Tayasal, which once stood on the far side of the lake, in 1525 but had not tried to conquer the Itzas, who had a reputation for being fierce warriors. However, in 1697, the Spanish finally conquered the Itzas, and Tayasal became the last Indian city to fall under Spanish rule. Two years after taking Tayasal, the Spanish moved to Flores, an island that could easily be defended. They renamed this island Nuestra Señora de los Remedios y San Pablo de los Itzaes and between 1700 and 1701 built a fort here. In 1831, the island was once again renamed, this time being given the name Flores in honor of a Guatemalan patriot.

One of the most curious pieces of local history is the story of a sick horse left in Tayasal by Cortés when he passed through the area. The Itzas had never seen horses before and as soon as Cortés left, they began worshipping the horse. When the horse died, a stone statue of it was made, and the worship continued until Spanish missionaries arrived in Tayasal 100 years later. The missionaries, appalled by this idolatry, proceeded to pitch the blasphemous statue into the lake. To this day the legendary horse statue has never been discovered, though searches continue to be launched from time to time.

Seen from the air, Flores appears almost perfectly round and is connected to the shore by a long, narrow causeway. Buildings come right down to the water's edge. However, exploring the town at ground level, another picture emerges. It is not the buildings that come down to the water but the water that is coming up to the buildings. Flores is drowning. Since 1982, the water level of Lake Petén Itza has been steadily rising, and today, where once there were streets and houses, there are now several feet of water. A walk around the circumference of the island presents a sort of

Venetian experience. Streets and alleys are flooded, dugout canoes are beached in the middle of the street, houses rise straight up out of the water. Look around the perimeter of the island and you will see buildings that have had their first floors abandoned to the ever-deepening waters.

Why is the lake rising? No one is certain, but it is believed that a cave system that may have once drained the lake has been blocked off. With each passing rainy season, the lake grows deeper. Luckily the center of the island is a fairly large hill, topped with a church and park, so it will be quite a few years before the town is completely inundated. For now, the quiet town, with its colonial-style buildings and cobblestone streets, is one of the most fascinating little towns in Guatemala. Though most people spend time here only en route to or from the Tikal ruins, Flores is well worth exploring for a day or two.

Santa Elena, Flores' mainland counterpart, on the other hand, is a dusty, modern boom town with little at all to recommend it. However, Santa Elena is where you'll find the airport, the bus stations, and a good view of Flores.

WHAT TO SEE & DO

After first exploring this incipient Guatemalan Venice on foot, you should have a look at the island from the perspective of a boat. At the Hotel San Juan, you can arrange a 3-hour **boat tour** of the lake. These tours stop at La Guitarra Island, a small island with a few picnic tables and a swimming area (though I don't recommend swimming in this lake because of the raw sewage that flows into it); La Mirador, an unexcavated pyramid from which you get a fabulous view of Flores; a small and rather unimpressive zoo; and Petencito, a recreation center complete with water slide. This tour costs Q30 ($5.20) per person with a minimum of three passengers. Alternatively, you can arrange your own tour with one of the boatmen that moor their boats along the causeway. The more people you can get together for a tour, the less it will cost per person. If you'd rather propel yourself, ask around about **renting a dugout.** Be aware of the weather when you're paddling around the lake. Winds tend to pick up in the afternoon and whip up waves large enough to swamp a dugout.

To learn more about Flores and El Petén, visit the **Centro de Información sobre la Naturaleza, Cultura y Artesania de Petén** (CINCAP), which is located on the square in front of the church in Flores. CINCAP operates a museum with displays on the cultural and natural history of the region. Of particular interest is the exhibit on how chicle, the substance that once gave chewing gum its chewiness, is produced. There are also exhibits on the local ecology and on medicinal plants of the jungle. A gift shop here has locally made baskets, wood carvings, and carved bone reproductions of ancient Mayan artifacts.

If you're a spelunker, you might want to explore **Aktun Kan,** the Cave of the Serpent, a large cavern just outside of Santa Elena. The cave takes its name from a legend about a giant snake living there. But don't worry, it's only a legend. Yet another legend has it that this cave is connected to a cave beneath the church on Flores. To reach the cave, either walk out of Santa Elena on the road that crosses the causeway from Flores or ask a taxi to take you out there. The fare should be around Q10 ($1.75). Although there are lights in the cave, be sure to bring a flashlight just in case.

In the village of El Remate, about halfway to Tikal, you'll find **El Mirador del Duende,** where you can rent canoes for Q18 ($3.10) per person per day or bicycles for Q116 ($20) per day and arrange overnight guided jungle hikes for Q145 ($25) per day.

You can also arrange 1- to 3-day hikes and horseback rides with **Eco-Cultural Guides of Uaxactún,** which operate out of the Asociación de Rescate y Conservación de la Vida Silvestre (ARCAS) office on Calle Centroamérica in Flores (tel. 500-566). Trips cost between Q145 ($25) and Q261 ($45) per day depending on how many days you go for, how many are in your group, and whether you hike or ride horses.

WHERE TO STAY

DOUBLES FOR LESS THAN Q87 [$15]

HOTEL ALONZO, 6a Avenida 4-99, Zona 1, Santa Elena, Petén. Tel. 502-9/500-105. 21 rms (8 with bath).
$ Rates: Q15 ($2.60) single without bath, Q25 ($4.35) single with bath; Q30 ($5.20) double without bath, Q50 ($8.65) double with bath. No credit cards.
If you're looking for a clean, quiet place close to the bus station and you're on a rock-bottom budget, take a look at this place. It's very basic, with cement floors and no toilet seats, but otherwise it's clean.

HOTEL SAN JUAN, Santa Elena, Petén. Tel. 502-9/500-562. Fax 502-9/500-041. 55 rms (37 with bath).
$ Rates: Q23.20 ($4) single without bath, Q58–Q127.60 ($10–$22) single with bath; Q34.80 ($6) double without bath, Q69.60–Q139.20 ($12–$24) double with bath; Q81.20–Q174 ($14–$20) triple with bath. AE, DC, MC, V.
This modest hotel near the causeway to Flores has plain, clean, large rooms with two or three beds, rather large bathrooms with tile showers, cold water (hot on occasion), perhaps toilet seats, and—of all things—TVs! The two-story building is undistinguished but utilitarian. The more expensive rooms have air-conditioning. Keep in mind that the San Juan acts as a bus stop for buses to various other towns in El Petén, so buses begin leaving (with much shouting, revving of engines, and blowing of horns) around 5am. It's almost impossible to sleep through this cacophony, so you need to be a heavy sleeper to stay here (or you can plan to take an early bus yourself). There's a comedor (dining spot) off the courtyard parking lot, and in the lobby you'll find all sorts of information on getting around El Petén. This is also the place to book tickets on express minibuses to the Belize border and Mexico.

HOTEL VILLA DEL LAGO, Calle Centroamérica, Flores, Petén. Tel. 502-9/501-446. 8 rms (2 with bath).
$ Rates: Q40 ($6.90) single without bath, Q65 ($11.20) single with bath; Q50 ($8.65) double without bath, Q75 ($12.95) double with bath. No credit cards.
Located right next door to the very popular Posada El Tucan in Flores, the Villa Del Lago is a clean and homey place. The hotel is built out over the water and has its own little dock. Bathrooms are generally clean. Unfortunately some rooms are rather dark and have no views out their windows. Mosquitoes can be a problem here so bring a mosquito coil.

POSADA EL TUCAN, Calle Centroamérica no. 45, Flores, Petén. Tel./Fax 502-9/500-577. 4 rms (none with bath).
$ Rates: Q35 ($6.05) single or double; Q52.65 ($9.10) triple. No credit cards.
S This backpackers' haven is built on the water, with a pleasant garden and two little piers for sunning or swimming. There's a restaurant in the courtyard where you can relax over a cold beer and a good book. The rooms are spacious with double or twin beds, all sharing a single large bathroom which has hot water (something places in this price range rarely offer). If you're traveling on a shoestring budget, this should be your first choice. Meals at the restaurant are Mexican and American standards.

DOUBLES FOR LESS THAN Q203 [$35]

LA CASONA DE LA ISLA, Calle 30 de Junio, Flores, Petén. Tel. 502-9/500-662 or 500-692. Fax 502-9/500-163. 27 rms (all with bath).

$ Rates: Q116 ($20) single; Q174 ($30) double; Q232 ($40) triple. AE, DC, MC, V.

⭐ Owned by the same family that runs the Hotel Petén, La Casona shows the same attention to quality. The guest rooms here are all fairly small and lack much in the way of decor, but they do have hot water, ceiling fans, and large, though basic, bathrooms. Between the lobby and the lake, there is a pretty little garden with elephant ear plants and a terrace with a small swimming pool. There is also a good restaurant to one side of the lobby, though it doesn't have much in the way of a view. To find the hotel, just watch for the big pink building a few doors past the Hotel Petén.

HOTEL PETÉN, Calle Centroamérica, Flores, Petén. Tel./Fax 502-9/500-662. 19 rms (all with bath).
$ Rates: Q116 ($20) single; Q139.20 ($24) double; Q162.40 ($28) triple. AE, DC, MC, V.

From the street, this hotel looks like a very modest Caribbean town dwelling; enter the doorway, and you'll find a small courtyard with tropical plants and a nice brick-and-stucco building of several floors. The friendly manager will show you a comfy if plain room with a fan and an electric hot-water showerhead in the bathroom and perhaps a balcony overlooking the water. Most of the rooms here have been recently remodeled, but try to get a room on the top floor with a view of the lake. If you can't, be aware that the hotel's roof is actually a terrace that enjoys that same view. There's a restaurant on the ground floor.

HOTEL SABANA, Calle Centroamérica, Flores. Petén. Tel. 502-9/501-248. Fax 502-9/500-163. 28 rms (all with bath).
$ Rates: Q116–Q127.60 ($20–$22) single; Q127.60–Q145 ($22–$25) double; Q174–Q203 ($30–$35) triple. MC, V.

This comfortable hotel is located on the water on the far side of Flores from the causeway. Though the hotel is fairly basic, there are large windows in most rooms, and some rooms have good views of the lake. A two-story palapa bar/restaurant is a pleasant place for a meal or drink, especially at sunset. The more expensive rooms have air-conditioning.

HOTEL YUN KAX, Flores, Petén. Tel. 502-9/500-686. 32 rms (all with bath).
$ Rates: Q87–Q104.40 ($15–$18) single; Q110.20–Q133.40 ($19–$23) double; Q127.60–Q150.80 ($22–$26) triple. DC.

The Yun Kax (pronounced "yoon cash") was completely renovated a few years back and now offers some of the more comfortable accommodations in Flores. Rooms are fairly large and many have good views of the lake. Just outside the front door there is a small swimming pool and a sundeck overlooking the lake. There is also a small bar/restaurant just off the pool. The higher prices are for rooms with air-conditioning. Yun Kax, by the way, is the Mayan god of corn.

JAGUAR INN SANTA ELENA, Calzada Rodríguez Macal 8-79, Zona 1, Santa Elena, Petén. Tel./Fax 502-9/500-002. 18 rms (all with bath). TV
$ Rates: Q85.75 ($14.80) single; Q117 ($20.20) double; Q146.25 ($25.25) triple. MC, V.

This hotel is operated by the same people who run the Jaguar Inn at Tikal and is one of the best budget hotels in Santa Elena. Guest rooms all have high ceilings and tile floors and are decorated with Guatemalan textiles and art. Art deco wall sconces add a touch of class here in the wilderness. There's a garden in the courtyard and an open-air restaurant and lounge with a few comfortable sofas where guests can chat with other jungle explorers. Meals range in price from Q15 ($2.60) for breakfast to Q30 ($5.20) for dinner. To find the hotel, watch for the sign on the left as you come into town from the airport. The only drawback here is that it's a bit of a walk to Flores, which is where all the best restaurants are.

WORTH THE EXTRA BUCKS

HOTEL MAYA INTERNACIONAL, Santa Elena, Petén. Tel. 502-9/501-

276. Fax 502-9/500-032. In Guatemala City, 8a Calle I-75, Zona 10, Guatemala City. Tel. 502-2/348-136. Fax 502-2/346-237. 22 rms (all with bath).
$ **Rates:** Q290 ($50) single; Q324.80 ($56) double; Q348 ($60) triple. AE, DC, MC, V.

⭐ Built on the banks of the lake quite a few years ago, this hotel has had to contend with the rising lake waters. Several rooms have been abandoned over the years as they became inundated with water, while others built on stilts are still dry. The hotel's newest rooms are set back from the lake a bit and are slightly more substantial, though less romantic, than the older rooms. Still there are balconies and tile floors in the new rooms. The lakeside setting is excellent and a little bay full of water lilies has formed between the hotel's bungalows.

The hotel dining room is in a separate, larger thatched structure at the end of a short causeway out in the lake. Breakfast is around Q25 ($4.35) and dinner is about Q60 ($10.35).

HOTEL SANTANA, Calle 30 de Junio, Flores, Petén. Tel. 502-9/500-662. 12 rms. A/C TV
$ **Rates:** Q203 ($35) single; Q232 ($40) double; Q261 ($45) triple. MC, V.
Run by the same family that operates the ever-popular Hotel Petén, the Santana is similar in quality, with the addition of televisions and air-conditioning in all the rooms. The rooms are modern and comfortable and have bamboo headboards on the beds and big patios with their own couches and chairs. The patios all overlook the lake and even have little gardens. Bathrooms are large. On the ground floor, there is a restaurant/bar that also overlooks the lake and has a terrace dining area.

NEARBY PLACES TO STAY

In addition to the lodge mentioned below, there are some very basic bungalows (Q35 [$6.06] double) and a campground (Q10 [$1.75] per person) at El Mirador del Duende, which also operates hiking and bicycling trips around the area.

EL GRINGO PERDIDO, "THE LOST GRINGO," Flores, Petén. Tel. (in Guatemala City) 502-2/326-683 40 beds (none with bath).
$ **Rates:** Q87–Q104.40 ($15–$18) per person per night. No credit cards.

⭐ Three kilometers off the Tikal highway from the hamlet of El Remate (which is on the Tikal road 35 kilometers from Flores), you'll find one of Guatemala's only jungle lodges. It's a little offbeat paradise arranged along the lakeshore, with shady, rustic hillside gardens, a little restaurant, a bucolic camping area, and simple but pleasant guest quarters. A bungalow has four beds (two sets of bunks), a shower, a toilet, and a patio with palapa cover and hammock. A camarote is a smaller room with a toilet and washbasin and two sets of bunks; it's a little cheaper than the bungalow. Beds in the dormitory (eight beds to a room) are cheaper still. The very friendly staff will welcome you. El Gringo Perdido offers good swimming in the lake, 3 kilometers of nature trails, quiet times, and tranquillity. The Biotopo Cerro Cahui, a preserve for the endangered Petén turkey, is just across the road.

WHERE TO EAT

Though the menus at many restaurants in Flores include wild game such as deer and tepesquintle, I recommend sticking to meat from domesticated animals. The wildlife of El Petén is best observed in the forest rather than on a plate.

MEALS FOR LESS THAN Q58 ($10)

EL KÓBEN RESTAURANTE, Calle Centroamérica. No phone.
Cuisine: GUATEMALAN/MEXICAN.
$ **Prices:** Main dishes Q9–Q45 ($1.55–$7.75). MC.
Open: Daily 7am–10:30pm.

Located diagonally across the street from El Tucan, the Kóben is a small restaurant that opens right onto the street. The menu has the sort of Guatemalan favorites that you can usually only get from street vendors—garnachas, chiles rellenos—as well as good combination plates that include tacos, cheese, sour cream, rice and beans, and fried bananas.

RESTAURANT EL TUCAN, Calle Centroamérica no. 45. Tel. 500-577
   Cuisine: GUATEMALAN/MEXICAN
$ Prices: Main dishes Q15–Q35 ($2.60–$6.05). MC, V.
   Open: Mon–Sat 8am–9:30pm.

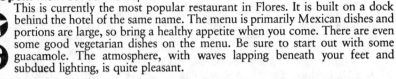

This is currently the most popular restaurant in Flores. It is built on a dock behind the hotel of the same name. The menu is primarily Mexican dishes and portions are large, so bring a healthy appetite when you come. There are even some good vegetarian dishes on the menu. Be sure to start out with some guacamole. The atmosphere, with waves lapping beneath your feet and subdued lighting, is quite pleasant.

RESTAURANT GRAN JAGUAR, Calle Centroamérica. No phone.
   Cuisine: GUATEMALAN/INTERNATIONAL.
$ Prices: Entrées Q20–Q50 ($3.45–$8.65). No credit cards.
   Open: Daily 11am–10pm.

Located not far from the Hotel Petén, this is an unusual restaurant with a bold jungle decor. The walls are made from rough-hewn slabs of wood with the bark still on them, and there are abundant plants, both real and artificial. The menu lists hamburgers, fish, steaks, spaghetti, and lots of drinks. This may be the most expensive place on the island.

Not to be missed is the Gran Jaguar's lakeside restaurant and swimming area across the lake from Flores. It's called Gran Jaguar del Lago, and a boatman will take you over for only Q5 (90¢). The ride back is free.

RESTAURANT LA JUNGLA, Calle Centroamérica. No phone.
   Cuisine: GUATEMALAN/INTERNATIONAL.
$ Prices: Entrées Q20–Q35 ($3.45–$6.05). No credit cards.
   Open: Daily 10am–10pm.

You have to fight your way through the dense wall of hanging plants in the doorway to enter this aptly named restaurant. Animal skins, including jungle cats, snakes, birds, turtles, and alligators, cover the walls here. There is even an out-of-place painting of a moose done on deerskin and a few dried giant mushrooms to complete the motif. Also included are a tiny street-side terrace with two tables and a standard Petén burgers/spaghetti/venison menu.

RESTAURANT LA MESA DE LOS MAYAS, Flores. Tel. 501-240.
   Cuisine: GUATEMALAN/INTERNATIONAL.
$ Prices: Q12–Q45 ($2.10–$7.75). MC, V.
   Open: Daily 7:30am–10pm.

This restaurant, just up a side street from La Jungla, is a popular place with two dining areas and plenty of tables. The menu is similar to those in other Flores restaurants, but it also includes a Mayan beef stew and some vegetarian dishes.

EXCURSIONS
EL CEIBAL & OTHER MORE REMOTE RUINS

If your life's passion is Mayan ruins or you simply crave more adventure than you have had so far on your visit to El Petén, maybe you should visit some of the more remote ruins of this region. In addition to exploring seldom-visited Mayan ruins, you'll be traveling by river through uninhabited jungles where you'll likely encounter a great deal of wildlife, which might include coatimundis, howler monkeys, anteaters, tapirs, and possibly even jaguars.

   El Ceibal is the most accessible of these other ruins. To reach El Ceibal, first take a bus the 65 kilometers from Flores to Sayaxché, which is a good-sized town for El

Petén (it even has a few basic hotels). From Sayaxché, you must hire a boat to carry you 18 kilometers up the Río de la Pasión. El Ceibal is a Late Classic ruin (A.D. 600 to 900) known for having the only circular temple in all of El Petén. There are also several well-preserved stelae arranged around one small temple structure on the central plaza. Many of the designs at El Ceibal indicate that the city had extensive contact with cities in the Yucatán, but whether this contact was due to trade or to warfare is unclear. An alternative to arranging a trip to El Ceibal on your own is to book a tour with Explore, Avenida Centroamérica, Flores (tel./fax 500-655). Day trips to El Ceibal cost Q174 ($30) and overnight camping trips cost Q551 ($95). These latter trips visit both El Ceibal and Aguateca, another Mayan ruin.

Uaxactún (pronounced "wah-shahk-toon"), 20 kilometers north of Tikal on a dirt road that is impassable in the rainy season, is another ceremonial center. Though many of the pyramids and temples here have been uncovered, they have not been restored as those at Tikal have been. If you'd like to visit these ruins, which are much less visited than those at Tikal, contact the Hotel San Juan, which offers day trips for Q116 ($20). Explore, mentioned above, offers a similar trip for Q174 ($30).

In order to visit ruins such as **Yaxchilan, Piedras Negras,** and **Altar de los Sacrificios,** you'll have to spend days camping on remote rivers. The best way to visit these would be on an organized trip; this way you would not have to leave anything to chance. See "Alternative/Adventure Travel" in Chapter 10 for information on companies that offer river trips to these ruins.

If you try it on your own, you'll have to rely on someone's recommendation to find a reliable boatman, arrange for several days' meals, bring your own tent, and make sure there is enough fuel to get you there and back. In short, you'll have to mount your own small-scale river expedition into the jungle. However, it can be done, and if you set out to try it, you'll certainly meet other like-minded adventurers with whom to share the costs.

---

2. TIKAL

544 kilometers NE of Guatemala City; 64 kilometers N of Flores.

GETTING THERE By Car   The ride from Flores to Tikal along a good paved road takes less than an hour by car. Head north out of Santa Elena, past the airport, and keep going straight. This road dead-ends at Tikal. Watch out for pedestrians and animals (both domestic and wild) on the roadway.

By Minibus   If you don't have a car, the best way to get to Tikal is by minibus. Minibuses from Flores and Santa Elena, and from the airport, leave at 4, 6, 8, and 10am and return at 2, 4, and 5pm. You can get a minibus at almost any hotel. If your hotel doesn't offer one, go to the Hotel San Juan in Santa Elena. Duration: 1 hour. Fare: Q20 to Q30 ($3.45 to $5.20) per person, one way.

By Bus   If you want to take the bus (slow and inconvenient), go to the Hotel San Juan in Santa Elena the night before you want to travel, buy your ticket, and be on the spot the next day at 6am or noon, which is when the buses leave. Duration: 2–3 hours. Fare: Q6 ($1.05).

By Taxi   A taxi from the town or the airport to Tikal costs Q150 ($25.90) or Q200 ($34.50) total, round-trip, for up to three people.

DEPARTING   If you come on a minibus, be sure to arrange your return time when you buy your ticket, especially if you plan to stay the night.

ESSENTIALS   The road from Flores ends in the parking lot of Tikal National Park. There are two museums, three hotels, a campground, a restaurant, and three little comedores (dining spots) here. The ruins are a 20- to 30-minute walk through the forest from the parking lot.

There is a post office and telegraph office on the left as you arrive at the parking area. You'll find a public phone in the new museum building. There is no bank here in Tikal, and only the Jungle Lodge will change traveler's checks (at an abysmal rate). Be sure you have enough quetzales to pay for your entire stay. Also, be sure to bring plenty of insect repellent with you. The bugs here are rapacious.

Admission to Tikal National Park is Q30 ($5.20) per day (24 hours), and the park is open daily from 6am to 6pm. If you'd like to stay in the park until 8pm (for sunset and nocturnal wildlife spotting), get your admission ticket stamped at the office behind the Stelae Museum. The best times to visit the ruins are in early morning and late afternoon, which are the least crowded and coolest times of day.

Tikal, one of the largest Mayan cities ever uncovered and the most spectacular ruins in Guatemala, ranks with Mexico's Chichen Itzá in pre-Columbian splendor. However, unlike at Chichen Itzá, the ruins of Tikal are set in the middle of a vast jungle through which you must hike from temple to temple. The many miles of trails through the park provide numerous opportunities to spot interesting birds such as toucans and parrots and such wild animals as coatimundis, spider monkeys, howler monkeys, and deer. Together, the ruins and the abundance of wildlife make a trip to Tikal an absolute must for anyone interested in Mayan history, bird-watching, or wildlife viewing.

Tikal is the largest of the Mayan ceremonial centers. So far, archeologists have mapped about 3,000 constructions, 10,000 earlier foundations beneath surviving structures, 250 stone monuments (stelae and altars), and thousands of art objects found in tombs and cached offerings. There is evidence of continuous construction at Tikal from 200 B.C. through the 9th century A.D., with some suggestion of occupation as early as 600 B.C. The Maya reached their zenith in art and architecture during the Classic Period, which began about A.D. 250 and ended abruptly about A.D. 900, when for some reason Tikal was abandoned. Most of the visible structures at Tikal date from the Late Classic Period, A.D. 600 to 900.

No one's sure just what role Tikal played in the history of the Maya: was it mostly a ceremonial center for priests, artisans, and the elite? Or was it a city of industry and commerce as well? In the 6 square miles of Tikal that have been mapped and

---

Note: When you are in El Petén, it is imperative that you sleep in an enclosed room with screens on the windows or beneath a mosquito net. This region is home to vampire bats that frequently carry rabies. The bats are nocturnal, and although they prefer cattle, they have been known to bite humans, especially on the toes and nose. The bite of a vampire bat is entirely painless, but an anticoagulant in the bat's saliva will cause a bite to bleed freely. The greatest risk is not from loss of blood, but from rabies. If not treated immediately, rabies is always fatal. Seek medical attention as soon as possible if you are bitten by a bat, or by any mammal for that matter.

Important Warning: Armed robberies take place with alarming frequency along the road between Tikal and Belize. Tourist minibuses and taxis seem to be singled out, so you may be safer riding the local bus. If you're returning to Belize, it might be a good idea to entrust your valuables to the management of your Belizean hotel before setting out on the road to Tikal.

These incidents may well have ceased by the time you read this. If you have doubts, you can call the **U.S. Department of State's Citizens' Emergency Service** (tel. 202/647-5225) in Washington, D.C., on weekdays from 8:15am to 10pm, for an up-to-date report. Or if you're already in Guatemala when you read this, inquire at your embassy in Guatemala City or ask the locals in Flores or San Ignacio, Belize, for news on the current situation.

excavated, only a few of the buildings were domestic structures; most were temples, palaces, ceremonial platforms, and shrines. Workers are excavating the innumerable mounds on the periphery of the mapped area and have been finding modest houses of stone and plaster with thatched roofs. Just how far these settlements extended beyond the ceremonial center and how many people lived within the domain of Tikal is still to be determined. At its height, Tikal may have covered as much as 25 square miles.

WHAT TO SEE & DO

Tikal is such an immense site that you will need several days to see it thoroughly, but you can visit many of the greatest temples and palaces in one day. To do it properly, you should have a copy of the excellent guidebook to the ruins—*Tikal*, by William Coe, written under the auspices of the University Museum of the University of Pennsylvania. Archeologists from the university, working in conjunction with Guatemalan officials, did most of the excellent excavation work at Tikal from 1956 to 1969. Pick up a copy in Flores or at Tikal Q50 ($8.65). One of the best features of the guide, and a real necessity given the size of the Tikal complex, is a very detailed map of the area. Don't take a chance on getting lost from site to site. Although you can buy a simple map at the park entrance when you pay your admission fee, Inguat (the Guatemalan Tourist Institute) also publishes a good map of the ruins.

Walking along the road that goes west from the museum toward the ruins, turn right at the first intersection to get to Twin Complexes Q and R. Seven of these twin complexes are known at Tikal, but their exact purpose is still a mystery. Each complex has two pyramids facing east and west; at the north is an unroofed enclosure entered by a vaulted doorway and containing a single stela and altar; at the south is a small palacelike structure. Of the two pyramids here, one has been restored and one has been left as it was found, and the latter will give you an idea of just how overgrown and ensconced in the jungle these structures had become.

At the end of the Twin Complexes is a wide road called the Maler Causeway. Turn right (north) onto this causeway to get to Complex P, another twin complex, a 15-minute walk. Some restoration has been done at Complex P, but the most interesting points are the replicas of a stela (no. 20) and altar (no. 8) in the north enclosure. Look for the beautiful glyphs next to the carving of a warrior on the stela, all in very good condition. The altar shows a captive bound to a carved-stone altar, his hands tied behind his back—a common scene in carvings at Tikal. Both these monuments date from about A.D. 751.

From Complex P, head south on the Maudslay Causeway to Complex N, which is the site of Temple IV, the Temple of the Two-Headed Snake. Temple IV is the tallest structure in Tikal and is 212 feet from the base of its platform to the top. The first glimpse you get of the temple from the Maudslay Causeway is awesome, for the temple has not been restored, and all but the temple proper (the enclosure) and its roof comb are covered in foliage. The stairway is occluded by earth and roots, but there is a system of steep stairways to the top of the temple. The view of the setting and layout of Tikal—and all of the Great Plaza—is magnificent. From the platform of the temple, you can see in all directions and get an idea of the extent of the Petén jungle, an ocean of lush greenery. Temple III (Temple of the Great Priest) is in the foreground to the east; Temples I and II are farther on at the Great Plaza. To the right of these are the South Acropolis and Temple V. The courageous and nonacrophobic can get even a better view by clambering up a metal ladder on the south side of the temple to the base of the roof comb.

Temple IV, and all the other temples at Tikal, are built on this plan: A pyramid is built first, and on top of it is built a platform; the temple proper rests on this platform and is composed of one to three rooms, usually long and narrow and not for habitation but rather for priestly rites. Most temples have beautifully carved wooden lintels above the doorways, but the one from Temple IV is now in a museum in Basel, Switzerland. The temple is thought to date from A.D. 740.

From Temple IV, walk east along the Tozzer Causeway to get to the Great Plaza, about a 10-minute walk. Along the way you'll pass the twin-pyramid Complex N, the Bat Palace (Palace of the Windows), and Temple III. Take a look at the altar and stela in the complex's northern enclosure—two of the finest monuments at Tikal—and also the altar in front of Temple III, showing the head of a deity resting on a plate. By the way, the crisscross pattern shown here represents a woven mat, a symbol of authority to the Mayas.

THE GREAT PLAZA

Entering the Great Plaza from the Tozzer Causeway, you'll be struck by the towering stone structure that is Temple II, seen from the back. It measures 125 feet tall now, although it is thought to have been 140 feet high when the roof comb was intact. Also called the Temple of the Masks, from a large face carved in the roof comb, the temple dates from about A.D. 700.

Temple I (Temple of the Great Jaguar), the most striking structure in Tikal, reaches 145 feet above the plaza floor. The temple proper has three narrow rooms with high corbeled vaults (the Mayan "arch") and carved wooden lintels made of zapote wood, which is rot resistant. One of the lintels has been removed for preservation in a museum. The whole structure is made of limestone, as are most others at Tikal. It was within this pyramid that one of the richest tombs in Tikal was discovered, containing some 180 pieces of jade, 90 bone artifacts carved with hieroglyphic inscriptions, numerous pearls, and objects in alabaster and shell.

The North Acropolis (north side of the Great Plaza) is a maze of structures from various periods covering an area of 21 acres. Standing today 30 feet above the limestone bedrock, it contains vestiges of more than a hundred different constructions dating from 200 B.C. to A.D. 800. At the front-center of the acropolis (at the top of the stairs up from the Great Plaza) is a temple numbered 5D-33. Although much of the 8th-century temple was destroyed during the excavations to get to the Early Classic Period temple (A.D. 300) underneath, it's still a fascinating building. Toward the rear of it is a tunnel leading to the stairway of the Early Classic temple, embellished with two 10-foot-high plaster polychrome masks of a god—don't miss these.

Directly across the plaza from the North Acropolis is the Central Acropolis, which covers about four acres. It's a maze of courtyards and palaces on several levels, all connected by an intricate system of passageways. Some of the palaces had five floors, connected by exterior stairways, and each floor had as many as nine rooms arranged like a maze.

Before you leave the Great Plaza, be sure to examine some of the 70 beautiful stelae and altars right in the plaza. You can see the full development of Mayan art in them, for they date from the Early Classic Period right through to the Late Classic. There are three major stylistic groups: the stelae with wraparound carving on the front and sides with a text on the back; those with a figure carved on the front and a text in glyphs on the back; and those with a simple carved figure on the front, a text in hieroglyphs on the sides, and a plain back. The oldest stela is no. 29 (now in the Tikal museum), dating from A.D. 292; the most recent is no. 11 in the Great Plaza, dating from A.D. 869.

If you head south from the Temple II, you will come to the area known as El Mundo Perdido (The Lost World). This plaza contains the Great Pyramid, which stands 114 feet high and is the oldest excavated building in Tikal. This pyramid is one of the most popular spots for watching the sunset. Directly east of the Great Pyramid is the Plaza of the Seven Temples, which dates to the Late Classic Period. Bordering this plaza on the east side is an unexcavated pyramid, and behind this is Temple V. This entire area is known as the South Acropolis.

If you cross through the South Acropolis to the east and then turn north in the general direction of the Great Plaza, you will come to the East Plaza. From here you can walk southeast on the Mendez Causeway to Temple VI (Temple of the Inscriptions), which contains a nearly illegible line of hieroglyphics that are the most extensive in Tikal. It's worth coming out this way just for the chance to spot some wild animals, which seem to be fairly common in this remote corner of the park.

THE MUSEUMS

There are two museums at Tikal. The Tikal Museum is located between the Jungle Lodge and the Jaguar Inn.

The museum contains a good collection of pottery, mosaic masks, incense burners, etched bone, and stelae that is chronologically displayed—beginning with the Preclassic objects on up to the Late Classic ones. Of note are the delicate 3- to 5-inch mosaic masks made of jade, turquoise, shell, and stucco. There is a beautiful cylindrical jar from about A.D. 700 depicting a male and female seated in a typical Maya pose. The drawing is of fine quality, and the slip colors are red, brown, and black. Also on exhibit are a number of jade pendants, beads, and earplugs as well as the famous stela no. 31, which has all four sides carved. On the two sides are spear throwers, each wearing a large feathered headdress and carrying a shield in his left hand; on the front is a complicated carving of an individual carrying a head in his left arm and a chair in his right. It is a most amazing stela from the Early Classic Period, considered one of the finest. The museum is open Monday through Friday from 9am to 5pm and Saturday and Sunday from 9am to 4pm. Admission is Q10 ($1.75).

The second museum is known as the Stelae Museum and is in the large new building on your left as you arrive at the parking area. This spacious display area contains a superb collection of stelae from around the ruins. Just outside the front door of the museum is a relief map that will give you an excellent perspective on the relationships between the different ruins here at Tikal. It's a good idea to have a look at this map in order to get your bearings before heading into the jungle. This museum is open the same hours as the other, but admission is free.

WHERE TO STAY

There are only three lodging places at Tikal in the national park. Rooms are often difficult to get, and making reservations is not easy. However, if you really want to stay at Tikal (an unforgettable experience), here are your choices.

JAGUAR INN, Tikal, Petén. Tel./fax 502-9/500-002. 6 bungalows (with bath), 3 tents.
$ Rates (including all meals): Q176 ($30.35) single; Q286 ($49.35) double; Q396 ($68.30) triple. Q50 ($8.65) single or double in tents (meals not included); Q30 ($5.20) to camp (meals not included); Q10 ($1.75) for hammocks. No credit cards.
Though this is the cheapest hotel at Tikal, it still is rather overpriced for what you get. The original rooms here are quite run-down, but there are several newer bungalows that are more modern and comfortable. If you're on a tight budget, you can stay in one of their tents or sling a hammock. Meals are generally worse than what you can get across the parking lot at one of the comedores, but they are included in the room rates, so you're stuck with what comes out of the kitchen.

JUNGLE LODGE, 29 Calle 18-01, Zona 12, Santa Rosa 2, Guatemala City. Tel. 502-2/770-570 or 768-675. Fax 502-2/760-294. 45 rooms (34 with bath).
$ Rates: Q87 ($15) single without bath, Q266.80 ($46) single with bath; Q116 ($20) double without bath, Q336.40 ($58) double with bath; Q406 ($70) triple with bath.
This is the largest and most comfortable of the three hotels here at the ruins, and consequently it stays full most of the time. If this is where you want to stay, make your reservation as early as possible. The rooms with shared bath, though very basic, are large and clean, and they open onto a veranda that looks into the forest. The rooms with private baths, though expensive, are very large and attractive, and most are in bungalows. Each has its own little porch with a couple of chairs so you can do some bird-watching without leaving your room. Meals in the large dining rooms are the best you can get here at Tikal. Meals are Q35 ($6.05) each. It's hot and

steamy here in the jungle, but after you've spent the day traipsing up and down pyramids, you can cool off in the hotel's pool.

TIKAL INN, Tikal, Petén. Tel. 502-9/500-065, or (in Guatemala City) 502-2/51-77-34. 11 rms, 11 bungalows (all with bath).

$ Rates (including breakfast and dinner): Q232–Q290 ($40–$50) single; Q261–Q377 ($45–$65) double; Q388.60–Q562.60 ($67–$77) triple. No credit cards.

Set back amid the trees, the Tikal Inn is the farthest hotel from the museum as you walk down the old airstrip. The accommodations are quite simple but clean. The bungalows have hardwood floors and are very nicely decorated with típico fabrics. To facilitate airflow, the walls of these rooms don't go all the way to the ceiling, and consequently these rooms don't have much conversational privacy. The smaller rooms in the main building have cement floors but the same attention to decor. All the rooms are airy and cool.

CAMPING

Just off the parking lot is a nice lawn with some trees for shade, marked and designated as the camping area. It has simple plumbing and cooking facilities and charges Q30 ($5.20) for use of the showers. If you have the gear, this is the place for you. You can also rent hammocks and pitch them under palapas for an additional Q10 ($1.75). Keep in mind, however, that in this area there are vampire bats, even though they don't often bite humans. Be sure to use a tent or mosquito net to keep the bats off while you sleep.

WHERE TO EAT

Besides the hotels above, there are several little eateries (comedores) between the main open area and the gate at the beginning of the road to Flores. As you arrive at Tikal from Flores, you'll see them on the right side: **Comedor Imperio Maya, Comedor Piramide,** and **Comedor Tikal.** All are similar in comfort and style (there is none), all are rustic and pleasant, and all serve huge plates of fairly tasty food at low prices. I had a huge piece of roast chicken, with rice, beans, and melon for Q20 ($3.45). If you have a friend with you, be sure to order a fruit plate for Q10–Q15 ($1.75–$2.60), the largest and most delicious fruit plate I've ever encountered.

Another choice is the restaurant behind the Stelae Museum, which is the big building on the left as you pull into the parking area. The restaurant is in a large covered area with several tables and is open daily from 6am to 8pm. A meal here will run you around Q30 ($5.20).

Within the area of the ruins there are picnic tables beneath shelters and itinerant soft-drink peddlers, but no snack stands. If you want to spend all day at the ruins without having to walk back to the parking area for lunch, take sandwiches.

CHAPTER 14

THE ATLANTIC HIGHWAY

Heading east from Guatemala City, you'll leave the cool highlands and descend first into dry rolling hills filled with cactus and then, as you approach the coast, into lush tropical vegetation. The roads branching off this highway tend to be in excellent shape. The Carretera al Atlántico (Atlantic Highway), leads to several interesting destinations, including the mountainous state of Alta Verapaz and its capital, Cobán; the Mayan ruins at Copán, Honduras; the great pilgrimage church at Esquipulas, famous throughout Central America; the marvelous Mayan stelae and zoomorphs at Quiriguá; the Río Dulce and Lake Izabal, on the road to Tikal; and Guatemala's Caribbean port and laid-back hideaway, Puerto Barrios and Lívingston.

---

1. COBÁN

215 kilometers NE of Guatemala City; 345 kilometers W of Puerto Barrios

GETTING THERE   By Bus   Escobar y Monja Blanca buses from Guatemala City leave from 8a Av. 15–16, Zona 1 (tel. 81-409), hourly between 4am and 5pm. Duration: 4 hours. Fare: Q12.10 to Q17.10 ($2.10 to $2.95).

By Car   Take the Carretera al Atlántico to El Rancho, then turn left for Cobán.

DEPARTING   Escobar y Monja Blanca buses for Guatemala City leave hourly throughout the day from 2a Calle 3-77, Zona 4 (tel. 511-952). To reach Puerto Barrios first take a bus to the junction with the Atlantic Highway at El Rancho and then catch one of the frequent buses bound for Puerto Barrios. If you are up for a grueling bus ride, you can head from Cobán to Huehuetenango, El Estor (on Lake Izabal), or Sayaxché (en route to Flores and Tikal).

ESSENTIALS   Orientation   Cobán is situated on a hill with the city sloping steeply away from the central plaza and cathedral. Some of the roads around town are one way so pay attention if you are driving.

Fast Facts   The Tourist Office is located next to the film processing store across the street from the Parque Central and is open Monday through Saturday from 8:30am to noon and from 2:30 to 6pm. The Banco del Agro, two blocks away from Hotel La Posada in the direction away from the Parque Central, is open Monday through Friday from 9am to 8pm and Saturday from 9am to 1pm. The Guatel office faces the Parque Central on the same side as the Tourist Office. The annual festival is the first week of August, and there is also a Folklore Festival the last Saturday in July.

WHAT'S SPECIAL ABOUT THE ATLANTIC HIGHWAY

Mayan Ruins
- Copán (actually in Honduras), nearly as impressive as Tikal.
- Quiriguá, known for its intricately carved stelae (record-keeping stones).

Natural Spectacles
- Semuc Champey cataracts and the quetzal preserve near Cobán.

Religious Shrines
- The basilica in Esquipulas, with a statue of Christ that is the object of a massive pilgrimage every year.

The Banco del Agro, where you can change money and traveler's checks, is two blocks from La Posada on the road leading to Guatemala City. The Guatel office is on the main plaza. Feast days are Holy Week and August 4.

Although the road east from Guatemala City rapidly carries you down to hot, dusty lowlands where cactus and other desert plants abound, a side trip north to the area of Alta Verapaz will take you into the most beautiful region of the country. High in these cloud-shrouded mountains, iridescent birds flit among trees draped with orchids, bromeliads, and ferns. The valleys are given over to pastures, and the lower mountain slopes are covered with coffee plantations (once owned by Germans) and farms that grow decorative tropical plants for export to colder climes as houseplants. These tropical-plant farms are often hidden under acres of shade cloth, which protects the plants from the burning rays of the tropical sun. It is shocking to see entire hillsides hidden beneath these sheets.

Even though Cobán (alt. 4,290 feet; pop. 18,000) has a long history, dating back to colonial times, it is the countryside surrounding the city that is the main attraction here. Alta Verapaz abounds in natural wonders, and Cobán is an excellent base for exploring the rest of the region.

WHAT TO SEE & DO

In Cobán itself there is very little to do. Activity focuses on the Parque Central and the market behind the cathedral. The Catedral de Santo Domingo, founded in 1687, is rather Spartan both inside and out. The cracked bell just inside the front door is not a Guatemalan Liberty Bell but a church bell that fell when the bell tower was struck by lightning. Also facing the central plaza is the art deco Palacio Municipal and another government office building with a two-story facade of long porticoes in the colonial style. In the plaza itself is a 1950s moderne band shell that is the site of occasional evening concerts in the dry season.

If you head out of town on the road to Guatemala City for a few blocks, you'll see a church high on a hill to your right. This is El Calvario, a small church in the middle of an old cemetery. The church is reached by a long flight of steps that lead up the hill. As you climb, you'll see little alcoves where offerings are made by the devout. At the top there are beautiful views of the surrounding valley and mountains. Behind El Calvario is a forest park that offers some good bird-watching.

If you have an interest in orchids, don't miss a chance to visit Vivero Verapaz, an orchid nursery a mile or so outside of Cobán. The owners have a huge private collection of orchids, as well as ones they raise for sale. The nursery is open daily, and a guided tour costs Q5 ($90¢).

Near the village of Tactic, about 32 kilometers before you reach Cobán, is an unusual natural phenomenon: the Pozo Vivo (Living Well), a pool of water formed by a spring that bubbles up from the ground in the middle of a beautiful green pasture. It derives its name from the way the sand at the bottom of the pool dances while the surface remains smooth as glass. It would hardly be worth stopping for, but it offers a chance to take a short stroll through this beautiful valley. Unfortunately, the well has not been very lively in recent years.

If you'd like to do a bit of walking, you can hike to the top of Chi-Ixim hill, just outside of town. From here there is an excellent view of Tactic and the surrounding fields. For an even more stunning view, you can climb nearby Mount Xucaneb. The hike, which begins in Aldea (village) Rocja on the road to El Estor between San Julian and Tamata, takes about four hours.

In Tactic itself, there is an attractive colonial church, and on the Cobán side of town, near Tactic's El Calvario chapel, you'll find the small Cooperativa Origen Maya-Pokom Ixoq aj Kemool, a local women's weaving cooperative. The shop is open Tuesday, Thursday, and Sunday from 9am to 5pm.

Nearby San Pedro Carchá, which is about 8 kilometers from Cobán, is famous for its silver filigree work. Unfortunately, you won't find any stores in town that sell this jewelry. However, San Pedro Carchá is a pretty little town and is worth a wander through. Situated atop a hill, the town has a large colonial church. During the town's feast days (June 24–29), masked dances are performed in the streets. If you'd like to go for a swim, visit Balnearios Las Islas, a nearby waterfall with a large pool at its base. There is also a small museum of local history to one side of the church here in San Pedro Carchá. It's open Saturday and Sunday from 9am to noon and from 2 to 5pm.

Both Tactic and San Pedro Carchá can be reached by frequent bus or minibus service from Cobán's bus-park market at the corner of 2a Calle and 2a Avenida.

WHERE TO STAY
DOUBLES FOR LESS THAN Q87 [$15]

HOSTAL DE ACUÑA, 4a Calle between 3a and 4a Avenida (Apdo. 10-16, 901), Zona 2, Cobán, Alta Verapaz. Tel./fax 502-9/511-547 or 511-268. 6 rms (all with shared bath).
$ Rates: Q17.55 ($3.05) per person. No credit cards.

This very inexpensive hostel may not have any rooms with private baths, but since rooms have only two or four beds, you won't be sleeping in a dorm full of strangers. This is one of the cleanest budget places I've run across in Guatemala, and the English-speaking owner is very helpful. There's a pretty garden out back, and to one side the original adobe building waiting to be restored. The hostel also offers rafting trips and guided camping trips through its Ultra-Ilimitada tour company. These trips visit caves, waterfalls, ruins, a macaw research area, remote lakes, and other interesting spots in the area. Trip prices range from $45 to $80 per person per day. You can also ask here about the peaceful guest house at nearby Aldea Chajaneb, which charges Q145 ($25) a night for a double with three vegetarian meals included.

HOTEL CENTRAL, 1a Avenida 1-79, Zona 4, Cobán, Alta Verapaz. Tel. 502-9/511-442. 13 rms (all with bath).
$ Rates: Q35.10–Q46.80 ($6.05–$8.10) single; Q46.80–Q58.50 ($8.10–$10.10) double; Q58.80–Q70.20 ($10.15–$12.10) triple. V.

Located across the street from Cobán's cathedral, the Central is an older courtyard-style building that has been undergoing renovation over the past few years. The more expensive rooms are those that have already been renovated, and these are very modern in design and decor. Try to get one of the rooms at the back, which have a nice view of the hills outside of town. The unrenovated rooms are a bit mildewed and dark, but will do in a pinch. In the courtyard, there's a glassed-in TV lounge, and at the front of the building, there is a good, inexpensive restaurant.

DOUBLES FOR LESS THAN Q145 [$25]

HOTEL EL RECREO, 10a Avenida 5-01, Zona 3, Cobán, Alta Verapaz. Tel. 502-9/512-160. Fax 502-9/512-333. 16 rms (all with bath).
$ Rates: Q93.60 ($16.15) single; Q126.40 ($21.80) double; Q140.40 ($24.20) triple. MC, V.
Though it is a 10-minute walk from the central square, this newer hotel is a very good value. Also, because it's out on the edge of town, it is a quiet location. All the guest rooms are carpeted (a rarity in this price range) and have good, new mattresses. The furnishings are surprisingly ornate, sort of budget Louis XIV reproductions. There's a dining room in the central skylit courtyard area that serves moderately priced meals. The people who run this hotel also operate the less-expensive Posada La Hermita, a small, rustic lodge about a mile out of town. This latter hotel has great views of the valley, but is not very convenient unless you have a car.

HOTEL LA POSADA, 1a Calle 4-12, Zona 2, Cobán, Alta Verapaz. Tel. 502-9/511-495. 14 rms (all with bath).
$ Rates: Q104.40 ($18) single; Q133.40 ($23) double; Q162.40 ($28) triple. No credit cards.
This rustic colonial hotel may be the best deal in all of Guatemala, perhaps because gringos as a whole have not yet discovered this beautiful region. Although the hotel is wedged between the two busiest streets in town and is consequently noisy, it still manages to maintain a rural atmosphere. You enter the hotel through a large gate and find yourself in a well-tended garden. Along the portico to the left is the office, where you can play table tennis if you like. The floors throughout are wood, and antique wooden benches line the portico. Traditional masks hang from the walls; and *santos,* little statues of saints, are seemingly everywhere. The guest rooms have beamed ceilings, old or antique furniture, and private baths with hot water. You'll spot signs for La Posada on your left just as you approach the Parque Central.
For meals, there is both a beautiful café on the veranda overlooking the square and a more formal dining room filled with antiques. Off the main dining room is yet another patio dining area that makes a great spot for breakfast. The fixed price dinner, which might be vegetarian lasagna or fried steak, will cost you less than Q40 ($6.90).

HOTEL MANSION ARMENIA, 7a Avenida 2-18, Zona 1, Cobán, Alta Verapaz. Tel. 502-9/512-284. 25 rms (all with bath). TV
$ Rates: Q90.10 ($15.55) single; Q122.30 ($21.10) double; Q154.45 ($26.65) triple. MC, V.
On the street leading to the base of El Calvario (The Calvary), Cobán's little chapel and cemetery, is this two-story neocolonial motel, which offers an excellent value. All the small rooms have arched windows facing onto a parking lot that is locked up at night. The tile floors are squeaky clean, and there are double beds, tables, and wardrobes in most of the rooms. Because of its location off the main street, it's a very quiet place for a good night's sleep. There is a small restaurant at the back of the hotel that serves three meals a day.

WHERE TO EAT

CAFÉ EL TIROL, 1a Calle 3-13. No phone.
Cuisine: COFFEE/SANDWICHES/BREAKFAST.
$ Prices: Coffee Q2.75–Q5 (50¢–90¢); sandwiches Q4–Q7.50 (70¢–$1.30). No credit cards.
Open: Tues–Sun 8am–8pm.
Directly across the street from the south end of the Parque Central is a café that is a showcase for locally grown coffees. Cobán is coffee-growing country, and you probably saw a great deal of it on your way up here. Don't miss the opportunity to tap

into it at its source. If you're a coffeeholic, you'll find the assortment here absolutely mouth watering: coffee "as black as midnight"; café americano; coffee with cocoa and whipped cream; espresso with cardamom; espresso with chocolate, sweet cream, and cinnamon; and even an assortment of coffees with different liquors. Tea and cocoa drinkers are not shunned either. To accompany your coffee, there are delicious pastries and some simple sandwiches. This is a great place for breakfast, lunch, or a late-night cup and cake. Have your repast on the portico surrounded by brilliantly colored bougainvillea vines.

CAFETERIA SAN JORGE, 1a Calle 1-79, Zona 4. Tel. 511-442.
  Cuisine: GUATEMALAN.
  $ Prices: Main dishes Q10–Q15 ($1.75–$2.60). No credit cards.
  Open: Daily 8am–8pm.
This is basically a Guatemalan diner, located in front of the Hotel Central. Meals are surprisingly inexpensive, which makes this place popular with locals. For less than $3 you can get a filling meal of perhaps fried chicken, a salad, corn on the cob, bread, and a bowl of soup. There is no written menu, just a couple of daily specials.

RESTAURANTE EL REFUGIO, 2a Calle and 2a Avenida, Zona 4. Tel. 511-338.
  Cuisine: GUATEMALAN/MEXICAN.
  $ Prices: Main dishes Q15–Q50 ($2.60–$8.65). AE, MC, V.
  Open: Daily 11am–11pm.
Located just across the street from the bus-park market and up a flight of steps from street level, El Refugio is a big open room that often fills up with lively diners. Steaks and Mexican dishes are the main draw here, but there are also daily specials and a full bar.

RESTAURANTE HACIENDA IMPERIAL, 1a Calle 4-11, Zona 1. Tel. 513-503.
  Cuisine: STEAKS/GUATEMALAN.
  $ Prices: Main dishes Q15–Q33 ($2.60–$5.70) DC, MC, V.
  Open: Daily noon–11pm.
This restaurant serves up excellent steaks in a thatched-roof building set back from the street. It is actually in the courtyard of an older building and is reached by a short hallway hung with contemporary local art. Other interesting paintings hang behind the bar in this softly lit restaurant. In addition to inexpensive steaks, the Hacienda Imperial also serves *cack' ik,* a local turkey stew, and a wonderful avocado salad with big scoops of avocado.

EXCURSIONS

MARIO DARY RIVERA BIOTOPO

Located at kilometer 163 on the road leading to Cobán (about an hour from Cobán), this nature reserve is one of the last places in the country where Guatemala's national bird, the resplendent quetzal, is still found. In pre-Columbian times, the most expensive garments, those worn by kings and princes, were often made from thousands of bird feathers. The most highly prized feathers of all were those of the quetzal, a pigeon-sized bird of the Central American cloud forests. Both the male and female quetzal sport iridescent green and brilliant red feathers. This beautiful coloring alone would be enough to label them the most beautiful birds in the world, but to add to this display of color, the male also has two willowy tail feathers that can reach almost a yard in length—the most highly prized feathers in pre-Columbian times.

The male quetzal's tail feathers resemble the fronds of epiphytic ferns that cling to the branches of trees in its cloud-forest habitat. Cloud forests, which form only at high elevations, are similar to lowland rain forests. They are perpetually damp, but the moisture here is not generally in the form of rain. The warm trade winds that pick up moisture as they cross the Caribbean Sea are forced up into colder elevations by

Guatemala's mountain ranges. As the moist air cools, it forms dense clouds that blanket the mountains for most of the year, keeping the forests damp. Thousands of species of plants have evolved to make the most of this damp environment. Branches of trees are covered with orchids, ferns, bromeliads, and other epiphytic plants. A stroll along the trails of this nature reserve is certain to elicit gasps from those unfamiliar with the dense tangle of vegetation that comprises a cloud forest. Among the most interesting plants are the tree ferns, which can grow up to twenty feet tall with huge feathery crowns.

Hundreds of species of birds call this forest home, and a sharp-eyed bird-watcher can easily spot several dozen, perhaps even a quetzal, in a hike through the reserve. Because of the density of the forest, the mammals that inhabit the reserve are much more difficult to spot. Among those that you might see, however, are monkeys and ocelots.

Where to Stay & Eat

HOSPEDAJE EL RANCHITO DEL QUETZAL, Km 163, Baja Verapaz. Tel. (in Guatemala City) 502-2/313-479. 4 rms (all with bath), 2 dorms.
$ Rates: Q23.50 ($4.05) per person in dorm; Q58.50 ($10.10) double with private bath. No credit cards.
Located only 200 yards from the entrance to the *biotopo*, this rustic lodge offers dorm space in rustic log cabins as well as much nicer rooms with private baths in a more modern building. The setting, though close to the road, is very peaceful, and you can get meals in the hospedaje's comedor.

LANQUÍN CAVES & SEMUC CHAMPEY

Northeast of Cobán 68 kilometers on a rough dirt road is the village of Lanquín and its nearby caves. The drive to this area is difficult and time consuming, so leave early in the morning. Don't even think about trying it in the rainy season. Even in the dry season, you'll need a four-wheel-drive vehicle if you want to go as far as Semuc Champey.

The mountains throughout this region are limestone and consequently are laced with caverns and sinkholes. Of the caves in the area, those at Lanquín are the most famous, extending for several miles into a mountain, with the Lanquín River running through immense halls. You can find a guide in the village who will turn on the lights in the caves and lead you through. The going is often slippery, so be sure to wear shoes with good traction. It's also a good idea to carry a couple of flashlights in case the power should go off. Admission is Q10 ($1.75).

Another 10 kilometers (a 3-hour hike) beyond Lanquín is Semuc Champey, a startlingly beautiful ravine that is also a result of the limestone of this region. Pools of icy water collect in bowls carved out of the limestone by torrents of water. Each pool is a different shade of turquoise, and all around are steep cliffs and lush vegetation. However, these jewel-like pools are only part of the magic of Semuc Champey. Just upstream from the pools, the Cahabón River cascades through a narrow gorge and suddenly disappears into a sinkhole. Further downstream, after passing under a natural bridge on top of which flows a stream, the river reemerges. After the difficult journey to reach this remote and rugged area, you'll certainly want to stay far longer than you had originally planned. If you have camping gear with you, there is a place here to pitch a tent. Admission is Q2 (35¢). If you don't have your own vehicle, you can take the bus to Lanquín from either Cobán (at 6am, 1pm, or 3pm) or San Pedro Carchá (at 1:30pm or 2:30pm). To reach Semuc Champey from Lanquín, you can usually get a ride in a pickup truck for around Q8 ($1.40) per person. Alternatively, you can arrange a tour at the Hostal de Acuña. If you can get six people together, the tour will cost you each Q127.60 ($22).

Where to Stay & Eat

HOTEL EL RECREO LANQUÍN CHAMPEY, Lanquín, Alta Verapaz. Tel. 502-9/512-160. Fax 502-9/512-333. 24 rms (all with bath).

$ Rates: Q93.60 ($16.15) single; Q126.40 ($21.80) double; Q140.40 ($24.20) triple. MC, V.

This rustic lodge offers very comfortable accommodations close to both Lanquín Caves and Semuc Champey. Set in a lush valley, the wooden lodge has simple rooms, most of which have nice views. There is a large, high-ceilinged dining room serving moderately priced meals.

---

2. COPÁN (HONDURAS)

180 kilometers E of Guatemala City; 109 kilometers S of Río Hondo

GETTING THERE   By Bus   You must first take a bus to Chiquimula, then take another to the border at El Florido. Chiquimula-bound buses leave Guatemala City from 19a Calle 8-18, Zona 1 (tel. 536-714), every 30 minutes from 5am to 6pm. Duration: 3½ hours. Fare: Q13.50 ($2.35). From the central park in Chiquimula, there are buses to the border at 7 and 10am and 12:30pm. Duration: 2 hours. Fare: Q6 ($1.05). If you leave Guatemala City at 7am or earlier, you can make the 11am bus and be at the Honduran border by 3pm (unfortunately the ruins close at 4pm). You can take a minibus or hire a pickup for 10 lempira ($1.30) to take you the remaining 15 kilometers to the ruins. Alternatively, you can hire a taxi in Chiquimula to take you to the border, but this will cost around Q116 ($20). If you'd like to leave all the planning to someone else, there are tours for around $200 that leave from Antigua or Guatemala City. Check the notice boards around Antigua for current information.

By Car   If you're driving, it'll take you five or six hours to reach Copán from Guatemala City. Turn off the Atlantic Highway at Río Hondo and take CA 12 south past Zacapa and Chiquimula. Just south of Chiquimula is a small sign pointing to a dirt road on the left. Take it—it may be a bad road, but it's all you've got. The distance to the border is 58 kilometers, over mountains and through streams and villages.

DEPARTING   Throughout the morning and on into the early afternoon, trucks and buses leave the town of Copán for the Guatemalan border. From El Florido, on the border, there are buses to Chiquimula several times between 8am and 4pm.

ESSENTIALS   If you needed a visa to get into Guatemala and are planning only to visit Copán and return to Guatemala, be sure your visa is good for multiple entries, otherwise, the nearest Guatemalan consulate is in San Pedro Sula. If you have a Tourist Card, you can get a temporary exit stamp for Q10 ($1.75) if you're just going to the ruins. This will allow you to reenter Guatemala without having to pay for a new Tourist Card. If you plan to continue on into Honduras, you'll pay Q5 (90¢) for an exit stamp. A temporary entry stamp for Honduras will cost you 10 lempiras ($1.30) and is good only for visits to Copán. The exchange rate currently is 7.8 lempiras to the U.S. dollar. You'll get a better exchange rate if you change your money on the Honduran side of the border rather than the Guatemalan side. Expect to pay between $10 and $20 each way to cross the border if you are driving your own car. The ruins are open daily from 8am to 4pm. Admission is 30 lempira ($3.85).

Though the Mayan ruins of Copán are across the border in Honduras, they are so close to Guatemala that I am including them in this book. Few people make the time-consuming journey to visit Copán, but it is certainly worth the effort if you have an interest in *El Mundo Maya* (The Mayan World). The temples and pyramids of Copán are not as impressive as those at Tikal, but the city's sculptural legacy is fascinating. The sculptors of Copán were perhaps the greatest in the Mayan realm, and many of their well-preserved works of art are on display here at the ruins.

To thoroughly explore Copán will take a full day or two. However, if you're short on time, it is possible to take in the highlights of Copán as a day trip from Chiquimula. To do so you must catch the first bus to El Florido in the morning. You can then spend several hours exploring the ruins and still get back to the border in time to catch a mid-afternoon bus back to Chiquimula. Always check on bus times before attempting such a day trip.

WHAT TO SEE & DO

THE RUINS AT COPÁN

Copán is in the valley of the Copán River, about 2,000 feet high in a hot, dusty desert region. The valley itself is, however, quite lush and fertile and is today primarily a tobacco-growing area. As with most early cities, Copán had several locations in its 1,500 years of existence. The first settlement (Early Classic, about A.D. 400) was where the town of Copán Ruinas is today. By the Late Classic Period (about A.D. 700), most of the area in the Copán valley had been occupied at one time or another. The ruins that have been excavated, and which make a visit to Copán worthwhile, are located about 1½ kilometers east of town and did not become the religious and governmental center until the middle of the 8th century A.D. It was at this time that the Mayan artisans of Copán reached their highest level of achievement.

Before heading out of town to the ruins, you may want to first visit the main museum, which faces the Parque Central in the center of town. The museum houses a collection of stelae, sculptures, many small jade and stone objects, and a complete tomb excavation. The artifacts on display here are among the finest to have been unearthed at the ruins.

To reach the ruins, you can take a taxi or walk. Should you choose the latter, note that there is a trail on the north side of the highway. At the ticket desk, you should pick up a copy of the well-written and informative booklet *History Carved in Stone*, which is a guide to the ruins (20 lempira [$2.60]). Alternatively, you can hire a guide for 100 lempira ($12.85).

The main ruins, known as the Principal Group, are in the center of the valley, north of the Copán River, 62 acres and are composed of five plazas surrounded by temples, pyramids, and platforms, all built at different times between A.D. 730 and 850. The largest complex, 130 feet high from the plaza floor, is at the southern end. Called the Acropolis, it was the center for religious life in the city. On the Acropolis's northeast corner (left as you face it from the plaza) is the famous Hieroglyphic Stairway, decorated with some 2,500 glyphs on the 63 stairs that lead up to Temple 26. (The stairs have been restored—a landslide in the 19th century toppled all but 15 of them.) Unfortunately, they won't let you get close enough to the stairs to have a good look at the glyphs.

The stairs on the north side of the Acropolis lead to the East and West Courts. Archeologists think the East Court was the most sacred spot at Copán because it contains Temple 22 (north side of the court), the most magnificent structure in Copán. Much of the work on the facade has been destroyed, but you can tell from the vestiges of mosaic and sculpture how grand it was. Note the two giant death's-heads intermeshed with squatting figures and grotesque monsters over the door to the

---

IMPRESSIONS

The only sounds that disturbed the quiet of this buried city were the noise of monkeys moving among the tops of the trees . . . It was the first time we had seen these mockeries of humanity and, with the strange monuments around us, they seemed like wandering spirits of the departed race guarding the ruins of their former habitations.
—J.L. STEPHENS, *INCIDENTS OF TRAVEL IN CENTRAL AMERICA, CHIAPAS AND YUCATAN*, 1841

sanctuary. The West Court is less impressive, although Temple 16, a stepped-platform type, is impressive enough. When Maudslay began excavations in 1885, he found fragments of sculpture that had once decorated this temple strewn all over the West Court.

The Great Plaza at the northern end of the Main Structure is similar in layout to the Great Plaza at Tikal and is where you will find Copán's famous carved stone altars and stelae.

From dates on the 20 stelae and 14 altars found here, archeologists think that the Great Plaza was the first complex built in the Main Structure. The center of life may have shifted to the Acropolis area once that part was finished. Be sure to notice the special artistry that Copán's sculptors exhibited in carving the glyphs here, for Copán's glyphs are the finest examples of this Maya "writing." Also, the unusual sculptures, unique in Mayan art, owe a lot of their beauty to the greenish volcanic stone found only at Copán.

WHERE TO STAY
IN COPÁN RUINAS

BRIZAS DE COPÁN, Copán Ruinas, Honduras. Tel. 504/98-3018. 18 rms (all with bath).
$ Rates: 80 lempira ($10.25) single; 120 lempira ($15.40) double or triple. No credit cards.

Located a block from the Parque Central on the corner of the road that leads out to the ruins, this newer hotel is a maze of rooms on several different levels. The guest rooms are simply furnished but very clean and have tile floors and hot water. Miniature reproductions of Mayan masks are used for lights throughout the hotel and add a touch of local character.

HOTEL MARINA COPÁN, Copán Ruinas, Honduras. Tel. 504/98-3070. Fax 504/57-3076. 38 rms (all with bath).
$ Rates: 500.75 lempira ($64.20) single; 585 lempira ($75) double; 667.70 lempira ($85.60) triple. MC, V.

Though this is a splurge, if there are three of you traveling together, it isn't much of a splurge. This is the best hotel in town and is frequented by large tour groups, so it stays full for much of the year. Built in the colonial style, the hotel has very comfortable rooms. In the bougainvillea-planted central courtyard there's a swimming pool, and a restaurant and bar provide slightly overpriced meals and libations. There's even an exercise room and sauna here. You'll find the hotel a half block off the Parque Central at the end of the park opposite the ruins.

IN CHIQUIMULA

HOTEL VICTORIA, 2a Calle and 10a Avenida, Zona 1, Chiquimula. Tel. 502-9/422-238. 30 rms (all with bath). TV
$ Rates: Q27 ($4.65) single; Q42 ($7.25) double; Q60 ($10.35) triple. No credit cards.

This simple hotel is only about two blocks from the bus stop for buses to the Honduras border, which makes it convenient if you are in transit to Copán or plan to do a day trip across the border to the ruins. Try to get a room on an upper floor; those on the ground floor can be a bit noisy. The restaurant downstairs is just about your best choice for meals here in Chiquimula.

WHERE TO EAT
IN COPÁN RUINAS

LOS GAUCHOS, 1½ blocks south of the Parque Central. Tel. 98-3402.
Cuisine: URUGUAYAN/STEAKS.
$ Prices: Main dishes 25–72 lempiras ($3.20–$9.25); lunch special 25 lempiras ($3.20). MC, V.

Open: Daily 11am–11pm.

This hotel on the edge of town is surprisingly sophisticated (white tablecloths, wine glasses, original art on the walls) for such a remote and dusty town, but with people from all over the world visiting the ruins, it isn't surprising that a first-class restaurant would open here. The restaurant is in an old house and has several separate dining rooms, a bar, and seating out on the veranda. The lunch special is the real deal here, but even in the evenings, you'll get great food at very reasonable prices. Try the paella a la Uruguaya or the plato típico.

3. ESQUIPULAS

222 kilometers SE of Guatemala City; 95 kilometers S of Río Hondo

GETTING THERE **By Bus** Buses leave Guatemala City from 19 Calle 8-18, Zona 1 (tel. 536-714) every 30 minutes between 4am and 6pm. Duration: 4 hours. Fare: Q17.50 ($3.05).

By Car From the Atlantic Highway, take the Esquipulas turnoff at Río Hondo.

ESSENTIALS **Orientation** Esquipulas centers around its famous basilica and its adjacent park.

There isn't much reason to come down to Esquipulas unless you are a Catholic pilgrim or simply have an interest in colonial churches and religious shrines.

WHAT TO SEE & DO

Esquipulas is not much different from any other Guatemalan town, except for its basilica—which is very special, indeed. Called by some the "Basilica of all Central America," it was ordered built by the first archbishop of Guatemala, Pedro Pardo de Figueroa, in 1759. The archbishop wanted such a grand place to house the sacred statue of Christ Crucified that had been made in 1594 by Quirio Cantano. The statue had had a long history of miraculous events connected with it even before the church was built: In 1740 it was said to have perspired profusely, a miracle authenticated by the then bishop of Guatemala.

Devout Catholics visit the basilica throughout the year, but the rites during Holy Week attract a larger-than-average crowd, as does the Festival of the Holy Name of Jesus (January 6 to 15). At times such as these, it's possible for visitors to file past the statue and even to kiss it, although the lines are unbelievably long.

Besides the statue, which is quite small and housed in the glass case above the altar, the church boasts the largest bell in Central America, installed in 1946. And the building itself is impressive, simple (for the style of the time) but harmonious, with four tall corner towers and beautiful grounds.

The market just outside the church is especially active during the two festivals mentioned; in fact, it takes on a carnival atmosphere: stalls selling snacks, such as fried banana slices; games of skill and chance; and the normal market activities of selling handwoven blankets and —here in Esquipulas—religious articles and trinkets. There are even fireworks displays during the festivals.

Because Esquipulas is a popular pilgrimage site, you will find dozens of economical hotels and restaurants around town should you decide to stay the night.

WHERE TO STAY & EAT

HOTEL LOS ANGELES, 2a Avenida 11-94, Zona 1, Esquipulas. Tel. 502-9/431-254 or 431-343. 35 rms (20 with bath).

$ Rates: Q50 ($8.65) single without bath, Q87 ($15) single with bath; Q75 ($12.95) double without bath, Q110 ($19) double with bath. V.

Located right across the street from the basilica, the Los Angeles is one of the best budget choices in town. The guest rooms, though basic, are fairly clean and are arranged around a small courtyard that now houses the hotel's restaurant. Consequently, first-floor rooms don't get much light. Meals here will run you around Q20 ($3.50).

HOTEL PAYAQUI, 2a Avenida 11-56, Zona 1, Esquipulas. Tel. 502-9/ 431-143 or 431-371. 40 rms (all with bath).

$ Rates: Q175 ($30) single; Q208.80 ($36) double. DC, MC, V.

Located right next door to the Los Angeles, the Payaqui is the fanciest downtown choice in Esquipulas, but don't expect much. The rooms are decent and there is a tiny swimming pool. Because of the location right across the street from the basilica, this hotel is very popular with wealthier pilgrims. The best rooms are the large family rooms, many of which have big windows.

4. QUIRIGUÁ

219 kilometers E of Guatemala City; 108 kilometers W of Puerto Barrios; 90 kilometers S of Río Dulce

GETTING THERE By Bus Any bus headed to Puerto Barrios will drop you off at the junction with the road to Quiriguá ruins or in the village of Quiriguá. From here it is possible to walk or hire a motorcycle to take you the remaining 4 kilometers to the ruins.

By Car The ruins of Quiriguá are 4 kilometers south of the Atlantic Highway at kilometer 205 on a dirt road that leads through a banana plantation.

DEPARTING Buses for Puerto Barrios and Guatemala City pass by on the highway frequently throughout the day. If you are heading to El Petén, you can catch a bus as far as the turnoff for Río Dulce or wait for one of the direct buses.

Though Quiriguá is not one of the more spectacular ruin sites in Guatemala, it is noteworthy for its well-preserved large stone carvings. These carvings, called stelae, were not just works of art but records of historic events. Through the study of such carvings much has been learned about Mayan culture and history. Though close to the Atlantic Highway, Quiriguá is not very convenient to visit unless you are traveling by car. If you are traveling by bus, you can stay in the village of Quiriguá and walk or hitchhike to and from the ruins. You almost have to stay overnight in the area, and to spend so much time on this small site may only be worthwhile to serious students of the Mayas. If you have your own car, however, it's much easier to visit and is certainly worth pulling off the highway for an hour or two.

WHAT TO SEE & DO

THE RUINS

Quiriguá is a Late Classic Mayan city, dating from A.D. 692 to 900. It was a dependency of Copán, and it was here that the Mayan methods of quarrying and carving great pieces of stone reached the height of excellence. The area around Quiriguá was once a dense forest of ceiba, mahogany, and palm, but at the turn of this century, the trees and bush were cleared to make way for the farms and plantations of the United Fruit Company. All that remains of the forest is the 75-acre park in which the ruins are set, about a mile south of the highway through the banana plantation.

The ruins were discovered in 1840, and Maudslay took an interest in them later

(1881–1894). After the turn of the century, several teams came and excavated at Quiriguá and the site was later restored by the University of Pennsylvania, sponsored by the National Geographic Society.

Quiriguá has three sites, but only the one most lately occupied (A.D. 751–900) is of interest. This is reached by crossing the railroad tracks, going through the parking lot, and then walking along a path to the southwest. The great plaza is about 1,500 feet long, north to south, and at the southern end of the plaza is the largest of the complexes, a temple plaza raised above ground level and surrounded by six temple-palace structures built at different times between A.D. 750 and 810. Take a look at the structure on the east side, which has two altars, designated Q and R by archeologists, in front of the west doorway. Both these altars represent human figures seated cross-legged. Also look at the 9-foot-high mosaic head over the doorway in the north facade of Structure 2, on the southwest corner of the plaza. Another sculpture mask with huge teeth is on the southwest corner of the same structure. And on Structure 1, at the far southern end of the plaza, look at the beautiful hieroglyphic inscriptions around the doors.

To me, Quiriguá is synonymous with the grand stelae the Mayas did so well. As you enter the park, you'll pass several of these, carved from brown sandstone, 13 to 35 feet tall. The most famous is 35-foot Stela E, the tallest stone shaft in Mesoamerica, which is about one-fourth of the way down the plaza as you walk south. (There are two stelae side by side here; facing south, Stela E is the one on your right.) Both the front and the back are carved with a man standing on a platform and holding in his right hand a manikin scepter (a Mayan ceremonial wand depicting a long-nosed god). The northern face is the best preserved. On the sides are glyphs that archeologists have used to date this stela at A.D. 771. Most of the other stelae here have similar figures, many having beards that seem to have come into fashion with the Maya for a 30-year period. Stela D, at the far north end of the plaza, has a figure with a beard; some of the glyphs on the sides have been deciphered, indicating that this figure is Two-armed Sky, a ruler of Quiriguá in A.D. 766 and a native of Copán.

Look also at the zoomorphs, huge boulders carved into monsters. Zoomorph B, behind Stela E, is one such monster who has a human torso and head protruding from (or, rather, disappearing into) his mouth. Another interesting one is at the far southern end of the plaza, on the east side: A crouched man is covered by a shield (looking like a human turtle); the shield, seen from the top, is clearly the face of a deity with two large earplugs, and the crouched figure has a face at each end. There are several more of these zoomorphs; to see them well you have to take your time and look at them from every possible angle.

A note on the sandstone used here: The Mayas were lucky in that the beds of this stone in the nearby River Motagua had cleavage planes good for cutting large pieces and that the stone, when freshly cut, was very soft and hardened only after some exposure to the air. No wonder the highly skilled Mayan craftsmen picked Quiriguá for their most impressive sculpture.

WHERE TO STAY & EAT

HOTEL ROYAL, Quiriguá, Izabal. No phone. 15 rms (2 with bath).
$ Rates: Q15 ($2.60) per person without bath, Q30 ($5.20) per person with bath. No credit cards.

The only place to stay in this little dirt-street hamlet several miles from the ruins is a short drive off the highway. It's a Caribbean-style wood structure with numerous large, high-ceilinged, well-ventilated rooms. Each room has a concrete floor on which are arranged four or five beds, a cold-water washbasin and, if you're lucky, a shower and a toilet, perhaps with a seat. Although severely plain, the rooms are clean, and the family who runs the place is friendly enough. A little comedor here is the only place in town for meals.

HOTEL SANTA MONICA, Km 200, Carretera al Atlántico, Los Amates, Izabel. No phone. 8 rms (all with bath).
$ Rates: Q50 ($8.65) single; Q65 ($11.20) double. No credit cards.

S Although it is located behind a Texaco gas station and a 24-hour convenience store, this small hotel is very clean and comfortable. The rooms are large, carpeted, and come with two beds each. There is a restaurant next door to the hotel where you can get inexpensive Guatemalan meals.

5. FRONTERAS (RÍO DULCE) & LAKE IZABAL

290 kilometers E of Guatemala City; 100 kilometers NW of Puerto Barrios; 90 kilometers N of Quiriguá

GETTING THERE By Bus Fuentes del Norte, 17a Calle 8-46, Zona 1 (tel. 513-817); Transportes La Petenera, 16 Calle and 10 Avenida, Zona 1 (tel. 29-658); and Maya Express, 17 Calle 9-36, Zona 1 (tel. 21-914 or 539-325) buses leave for Flores from Guatemala City several times daily and stop in Río Dulce about five hours later. Fare: Q25 to Q40 ($4.35 to $6.90).

By Car The turnoff for Río Dulce is just past the town of Morales.

DEPARTING If you plan to proceed from Río Dulce to Flores by bus, be aware that you are very unlikely to get a seat on the bus when it arrives in Río Dulce. In fact many people (usually backpacking travelers) end up riding on the roof because there isn't even any standing room on the bus. The road from Río Dulce to Flores is one of the worst in the country, and the trip is very uncomfortable even if you have a seat.

ESSENTIALS Orientation The town of Río Dulce is little more than a cluster of market stalls and shops located at the foot of the roll bridge over the mouth of Lake Izabal. The road to Castillo de San Felipe is a narrow muddy lane to the left after you cross the bridge. Boats for Livingston can be hired at the docks to the right after you cross the bridge.

Forty-eight kilometers northwest of the Atlantic Highway lie Lake Izabal and the Río Dulce, which connects the lake with the Gulf of Honduras and the Caribbean Sea. The lake and its jungle-and-forest setting are quite beautiful, but swimming is not recommended in the beaches near the road because the water's not very clean. It's very good for powerboating, however, and on weekends the wealthy citizens of the capital come to the lake and exercise the glittering craft stored on the shore. The lake was famous as a refuge for pirates in days gone by, and its entrance was protected by the picturesque fortress called the Castillo de San Felipe, on the northern shore, 4 kilometers from the bridge. In the past few years, Lake Izabal has become a refuge once again. This time for gringo sailors looking for an inexpensive place to moor their sailboats while they wait out the Caribbean hurricane season. Consequently, this area is taking on a very upscale feel—a sort of yacht-club-in-the-wilderness appeal.

WHAT TO SEE & DO

Ask down at the docks to find a boatman who's willing to ferry you to the **Castillo de San Felipe.** The minimum for a trip is two fares, and the boatman will rarely rush you to get through the castle. Plan to spend about an hour there, about two hours for the entire trip.

The castle was built in the 1600s by the Spaniards to keep pirates out of Lake Izabal, which was being used as a shipping point for gold that had been collected by the conquistadores. Restored in the 1950s, the fort is the only one of its kind in Guatemala. It is in a beautiful, tranquil setting on the banks of the lake, with palm trees waving in the breezes and clouds billowing overhead. You can play at fighting off marauding pirates as you wander through the maze of damp chambers that comprise the fort. Most budget travelers who make it to Río Dulce are either coming from or going to Livingston, a small town on the coast. The boat trip down the Río Dulce is reason enough to make this trip.

The trip will take between two and three hours. You first travel past luxurious vacation homes on the shores of El Golfete, another large lake that begins east of the bridge. Then, as you travel farther from the bridge, the houses disappear, and all you see are distant forested mountains. At the far end of El Golfete, the river narrows and passes between steep cliffs. Here and there along this section of the river are tiny huts that are the homes of local families who fish the river by night. The river is still their only link with the outside world, and you have a sense of being far from civilization as you motor past their simple huts.

An added bonus of going downriver is a chance to visit the Chocon Machacas Manatee Preserve. You aren't likely to see any manatees because of the motor on the boat, but there is a short trail through the forest where you are likely to see leaf-cutter ants, pacas (small rabbitlike rodents), and lots of birds.

If you want to hire a boat to take you down to Livingston, expect to pay Q50 ($8.65) per person with a five-person minimum. There is also a mailboat (charging the same fare) that makes this trip on Tuesday and Thursday mornings. However, this boat doesn't always stop at the manatee preserve.

If you'd like to do some sailing, there are usually people offering economical overnight boat trips out to the southern Belize cayes. *Las Sirenas*, a Polynesian catamaran, is one such boat operating sailboat trips out of Fronteras. A 2-night trip costs Q377 ($65) per person and a 6-night trip costs Q1,508 ($260) per person (these are double-occupancy rates. For more information, contact Aventuras Vacaciones, 7570 La Madre Way, Las Vegas, NV 89129 (fax 702/255-3641) or, in Guatemala, Viajes Tivoli, 5a Avenida Norte no. 10A, Antigua (tel. 502-9/323-041; fax 502-9/320-892).

WHERE TO STAY

Although there are a couple of small hotels near the bridge, your best low-budget choice in the area is out by the Castillo. You can hire a boat to take you there, or you can walk or drive the 4-kilometer road.

HOTEL DON HUMBERTO, Río Dulce. No phone. 12 rms (all with bath).
$ Rates: Q29.25–Q35 ($5.05–$6.05) single; Q35.10–Q40 ($6.05–$6.90) double; Q41–Q46 ($7.10–$7.95) triple. No credit cards.

A 5-minute walk down a quiet path from the Castillo de San Felipe you'll find this tranquil little budget hotel. This neighborhood was once the haunt of pirates, but today it is primarily given over to vacation homes for the wealthy of Guatemala City. The location is very quiet, and the park surrounding the Castillo is very pretty. The rooms are basic but have private bathrooms. The hotel even has its own little dock down on the lake shore, which is only about 100 yards away. The open-air restaurant serves inexpensive meals.

HOTEL IZABAL TROPICAL, Costado, Castillo de San Felipe, Lago de Izabal. Tel. 502-9/478-115. Fax (in Guatemala City 502-2/680-746. 16 rms (all with bath).
$ Rates: Q168.20 ($29) single; Q197.20 ($34) double; Q226.20 ($39) triple; Q261 ($45) quad. AE, DC, MC, V.

The Izabal Tropical is built on the edge of the lake and is very popular with boaters. Thatch bungalows with bamboo walls look out over the water, and the grounds are neatly manicured, with colorful tropical flowers in bloom year-round. By the two swimming pools (one for adults, one for children), there are thatched sunshades to save your skin from getting too burned. Beside the hotel's piers is a circular thatched-roof bar where rock music blares and young people gather.

Slightly higher than the bar is a circular open-air dining room that is much more sedate. You can enjoy spectacular views across the lake to the mountains in the distance while savoring delicious international meals at prices that range from Q30 to Q60 ($5.20 to $10.35).

WHERE TO EAT

RESTAURANT OLI MAR, dock on east side of road, Fronteras. No phone.
Cuisine: INTERNATIONAL.
$ Prices: Main dishes Q10–Q15 ($1.75–$2.60). No credit cards.
Open: Daily 7am–10pm.

This small open-air restaurant and bar caters primarily to the local gringo yachting community, but it also happens to be the best place in town and the spot where most boats from Lívingston dock. The menu, which changes regularly, includes such items as pizza, frittatas, salads, sandwiches, and coconut curry chicken. If you're dreaming of sailing off into the sunset, this is a good place to find a skipper looking for a crew.

---

6. LÍVINGSTON & PUERTO BARRIOS

298 kilometers E of Guatemala City; 108 kilometers E of Quiriguá;
100 kilometers SE of Río Dulce

GETTING THERE By Bus Transportes Litegua buses leave Guatemala City from 15a Calle 10-42, Zona 1 (tel. 538-169), frequently throughout the day. Duration: 5 hours. Fare: Q24 ($4.15) regular or Q32 ($5.55) express.

By Car Puerto Barrios is at the end of the Atlantic Highway. From here, it is necessary to take a boat to Lívingston.

By Boat The only way to get to Lívingston is by boat. From Puerto Barrios, the ferry takes about 1½ hours, leaving daily at 10am and 5pm and returning daily at 5am and 2pm. The one-way fare is Q8 ($1.35). For Q20 ($3.45), you can take a fast launch that will get you there in about half the time. These small boats leave only when they have at least five passengers, so you might have to wait for a while. If you don't feel like waiting or have a group, you can simply charter one of these boats for a little more than you would otherwise pay.

See the "Fronteras (Río Dulce) & Lake Izabal" section for information on boats between Lívingston and Río Dulce.

DEPARTING The ferry from Lívingston to Puerto Barrios leaves at 5am and 2pm daily.

Buses for Guatemala leave almost hourly from 6a Avenida between 9a and 10a calles.

A passenger ferry leaves on Tuesday and Friday at 7am for Punta Gorda in southern Belize. Duration: 3 hours. Fare: Q30 ($5.20). Be sure to buy your ticket the day before the ferry leaves because it is usually full by the time it departs and people sometimes get turned away. Also remember to get your passport stamped at the immigration office at the end of Calle 9, a couple of hundred yards down the dirt road to the right of the ferry dock as you face the water.

Boats leave Lívingston most days for the trip up the Río Dulce, and there is also a mailboat on Tuesday and Thursday. Duration: 3 hours. Fare: Q50 ($8.50). You can also hire a boat to take you upriver. The going rate is around Q200 ($34.50) for the boat.

ESSENTIALS Orientation Puerto Barrios, a fairly large city, is laid out in a grid similar to those used throughout Guatemala. Calles run toward the water, with the ferry to Lívingston located at the end of 12a Calle. The post office is at the corner of 7a Avenida and 6a Calle. The Guatel office is at 10a Calle and 8a Avenida. There is a Banco de Quetzal above the bus station at the corner of 6a Avenida and 9a Calle. It's open Monday through Friday from 8:30am to 7pm and Saturday from 9am to 10pm.

Lívingston is a small town with only a few streets. along either the street leading uphill from the ferry dock leave the dock. The Guatel office is at the top of the hi dock.

Guatemala's Atlantic shore is a narrow strip of land wedged
Belize on Amatique Bay. The main town on this coast is along with the nearby town of Santo Tomas comprises Guate facilities. These towns have very little to attract the foreign mountainous countryside outside of town sweeps down to th picturesque.

While Puerto Barrios is crowded, noisy, and busy, across the Dulce is the much quieter and more laid-back town of Lívingston. Guatemalan anomaly—a Caribbean town settled by people of Afric descent—but is similar to the other Creole and Garifuna towns along American coast from Belize to Panama. This black Caribbean culture, wit rhythms, has for many years attracted young travelers. However, thefts a robberies have been commonplace in Lívingston for so many years that it's recommend this town. The waters and beach are dirty, and it is a 3-mile walk nearest clean beach. The trip up the Río Dulce to the town of Fronteras is perha best reason to spend a night in Lívingston.

WHERE TO STAY & EAT
PUERTO BARRIOS

Doubles for Less than Q87 [$15]

HOTEL DEL NORTE, 7a Calle and 1a Avenida, Puerto Barrios. Tel. 502-9/480-087 or 482-116. 34 rms (16 with bath).
$ **Rates:** Q47.85 ($8.25) single without bath, Q61.50–Q82.10 ($10.60–$14.15) single with bath; Q68.45 ($11.80) double without bath, Q82.10–Q123 ($14.15–$21.20) double with bath. No credit cards.

My favorite place to stay in Puerto Barrios is this Caribbean classic, which will transport you into a Hemingway frame of mind. The huge cream-colored wooden building with green trim is right on the water, and long, wide verandas stretch the length of the building on both floors. You can sit out here and sip a beer and watch the banana boats sail away for northern ports. Inside, the high ceilings and the wide hallways help to keep the old building cool in the summer. The rooms, however, are small, with twin beds, but the high ceilings make them seem much larger than they really are. The dining room has a very old-fashioned air about it, with a huge old sideboard taking up most of one wall. Here you'll find a variety of seafoods, including lobster for Q55 ($9.50). Other seafood meals range from Q30 to Q50 ($5.20 to $8.65).

Doubles for Less than Q203 [$35]

HOTEL EL REFORMADOR, 16a Calle and 7a Avenida no. 159, Puerto Barrios, Izabal. Tel. 502-9/480-533. Fax 502-9/481-531. 36 rms (all with bath). TV
$ **Rates:** Q52.20–Q116 ($9–$20) single; Q104.40–Q150.80 ($18–$26) double. V.

In a very modern building near the center of town, the Reformador is just off the main road as you come into town from Guatemala City. The guest rooms are built around two small, sunny courtyards full of potted plants. Most rooms have air-conditioning, but the showers have cold water only, so you're better off sticking to a fan and saving some money. The small restaurant on the second floor gets a lot of sunlight and serves meals that range from Q15 to Q70 ($2.60 to $12.10).

HOTEL HEN..**ISFORD**, 9a Avenida and 17a Calle, Puerto Bar-
rios, Izal 2-9/481-557 or 481-030. Fax 502-9/481-557. 34 rms (all
$ Rates: (with bath $22) single; Q150.80 ($26) double; Q174 ($30) triple. DC, MC,
V.

About a bl.. from the Reformador is this slightly nicer hotel. The three-story
cement bu.. not very attractive, even though a balcony surrounds most of the
second an.. oors. However, in back of the main building, you'll find an unusual
covered re.. area that includes two pools, a bar, arcade games, and, of all things
to find in .. ltering climate, a hot tub. The rooms here are comfortable, and most
have larg.. ows so that they get plenty of sunlight. If you want a hot shower (rarely
necessar.. nd here), you'll have to ask for one of the rooms with hot water. The
hotel's r.. rant serves international, Guatemalan, and Caribbean meals at reasonable pri

LÍVINGSTON

Doubles for Less than Q87 [$15]

HOSEDAJE DOÑA ALIDA, Lívingston, Izabal. Tel. 502-9/481-567. 7 rms
(with bath), 3 bungalows (all with bath).
$ Rates: Q82 ($14.15) double without bath, Q140 ($24.15) double with bath;
Q175–Q300 ($30.20–$51.75) bungalow. No credit cards.

This quiet place is located down the road that runs along the side of the Hotel
Tucán Dugú and has its own private beach. Built on a high bluff overlooking the
bay, the Alida has great views from its grounds (and from the bungalows). The
rooms are in an older house and, though dark, are comfortable and very clean. If you
have a bit of money for a splurge, go for the Q300 bungalow, which is right on the
beach. You won't find anything nicer than this in this price range.

HOTEL AFRICAN PLACE, Lívingston, Izabal. No phone. 19 rms.
$ Rates: Q23.40–Q35.10 ($4.05–$6.05) single; Q35.10–Q46.80 ($6.05–$8.10)
double; Q46.80–Q58.50 ($8.10–$10.10) triple. No credit cards.

Though the African Place is on the far side of town from the ferry dock, it is
well worth the 20-minute walk if you are a fan of unusual lodgings. Housed in
a building that was designed along the lines of a Moroccan palace (tiles, arches,
heavy wooden doors, ramparts), the hotel is ultimately incongruous in this lush, green
environment. However, there is no place even remotely as fascinating in this price
range. Rooms are quite basic, but you can sit out in the garden during the day. The
restaurant here is the most popular in town and is open daily from 8:30am to
11:30pm, serving meals (mostly seafood) in the Q20-to-Q40 ($3.45-to-$6.90) range.

HOTEL HENRY BERRISFORD, Lívingston, Izabal. Tel. 502-9/481-568.
Fax 502-9/481-074. 40 rms (all with bath).
$ Rates: Q34.80–Q127.60 ($6–$22) single; Q69.60–Q150.80 ($12–$26) double;
Q104.40–Q174 ($18–$30) triple. DC, MC, V.
Affiliated with the hotel of the same name in Puerto Barrios, this is one of the largest
hotels in Lívingston, and though it is right on the water and has a pool, it is still
reasonably priced. The rooms are quite basic, but generally clean, and have good
mattresses. There is a nice view up the Río Dulce from the hotel's upper floors, and
also from the restaurant, which is at the back of the building. You'll find this hotel up
the road to the left as you leave the Lívingston dock.

Doubles for Less than Q145 [$25]

HOTEL CARIBE, Lívingston, Izabal. Tel. 502-9/48-1073. 26 rms (10 with
bath).
$ Rates: Q46.40–Q69.60 ($8–$12) single; Q87–Q116 ($15–$20) double;
Q127.60 ($22) triple. No credit cards.
One of the better budget choices in Lívingston, the Caribe is up the street to the left
when you get off the ferry from Puerto Barrios. The two-story building is set into a

shady hillside on the water, and if you get a room at the back, you can listen to the waves lapping on the beach. The rooms are very basic, with twin beds. The shared bathrooms are kept tolerably clean.

Worth the Extra Bucks

HOTEL TUCÁN DUGÚ, Lívingston, Izabal. Tel. 502-9/481-588 or 481-572. In Guatemala City, Avenida Reforma 13-70, Zona 9. Tel. 502-2/347-813 or 345-064. Fax 502-9/345-242. 45 rms, 5 suites, 4 bungalows (all with bath).

$ Rates: Q386.80 ($66.70) single or double bungalow; Q441.10 ($76.05)single, Q570.05 ($98.30) single suite; Q475.05 ($81.90) double, Q604.10 ($104.15) double suite. AE, DC, MC, V.

Although most accommodations in Lívingston are what you might anticipate based on the Caribbean lifestyle, the Tucán Dugú is quite different. This is Guatemala's only resort on the Caribbean Coast. Modern but still definitely Caribbean in style, it has many conveniences and comforts. You'll see the hotel on a low hill beside the ferry dock as your boat pulls into town. The two-story white building has a thatch-covered roof to give it a properly rustic appeal. My favorite rooms are the bungalows, even though these are the only rooms that don't have hot water. They are built into the hillside below the main building and are reached by wooden stairs and elevated walkways.

There are two restaurants here, one serving deluxe breakfasts and elegant seafood dinners for between Q20 and Q50 ($3.45 and $8.65) and another serving less expensive and more casual meals.

Possible activities here include scuba diving, waterskiing, sailboarding, sailing, boating, and sportfishing in both freshwater and saltwater.

CHAPTER 15

GETTING TO KNOW BELIZE

I f you learned your geography before 1973, you may never have even heard of this tiny country. Before that, Belize was known as British Honduras, a colony whose sole purpose was to supply hardwoods and other wood products throughout the British empire. Consequently, Belize is a Central American anomaly: It is an English-speaking nation surrounded by Spanish-speaking neighbors. With a population of only about 200,000 people, it is also the least-populated country in all Central America. The importance of this statistic is only now becoming significant as environmentalists discover the vast undisturbed wilderness of Belize, where jaguars still roam the jungle in search of tapirs, and macaws still screech in the treetops. Add to this the dozens of tiny islands set amid the world's second-longest barrier reef (which offers excellent diving and fishing opportunities) and a population that is more than 60% black Creoles and Garifunas (people of black and Indian ancestry), and you have what is ostensibly a Caribbean island nation on the Central American mainland. The most important British legacy left to Belize, however, is a stable political environment in a region of constant turmoil. To understand Belize, you have to go see it for yourself because, as the Belizeans say, "Seeing is Belizing!"

1. GEOGRAPHY, HISTORY & POLITICS

GEOGRAPHY

Belize is a narrow strip of land on the Caribbean Coast of Central America, located due south of Mexico's Yucatán Peninsula. It covers an area of 9,000 square miles, about the same size as the state of Massachusetts, and is bordered on the west and south by Guatemala and on the east by the Caribbean. Offshore from mainland Belize are hundreds of tiny islands, known as cayes (pronounced "keys"), that rise up from the world's second-longest barrier reef, which extends for more than 180 miles along the Belizean coast. From the wide, flat coastal plains, Belize rises up to mountain

WHAT'S SPECIAL ABOUT BELIZE

Beaches
□ Placencia, the longest and best beach in Belize.

Natural Spectacles
□ The barrier reef off the coast of Belize, the second longest in the world.
□ The Blue Hole on the Hummingbird Highway, a sinkhole filled with clear blue water.
□ Mountain Pine Ridge, a forest reserve with waterfalls and caves.

Zoo
□ The Belize Zoo, small but with an extremely well-treated menagerie.

Ancient Ruins
□ Xunantunich, a Mayan pyramid that is one of the tallest buildings in Belize.
□ Caracol, excavated though not restored, thought to be the largest Mayan city ever discovered.

□ Altun Ha Mayan ruins, with several excavated temples.

Islands
□ Dozens of small islands off the coast of Belize, including Caye Caulker and Ambergris Caye, which have small hotels.

Parks
□ The Cockscomb Basin Wildlife Preserve, the only jaguar preserve in the world.
□ The Community Baboon Sanctuary, an unusual program in which local farmers help protect howler monkeys.

Activities
□ Canoeing and horseback riding in the Cayo District.
□ Bird-watching anywhere in the country.
□ Scuba diving on the barrier reef.

peaks of more than 3,000 feet, the source of the many rivers that wind through the country, which were for years the only means of transport within Belize.

REGIONS IN BRIEF

The Cayes   Belize's offshore islands lie between the coast of the mainland and the protection of the 180-mile long Barrier Reef. The reef, easily visible from many of the cayes, offers some of the world's most exciting snorkeling, diving (visibility is up to 200 feet), and fishing. The more developed cayes offer various day and overnight trips to explore this lively underwater world.

For those whose main sport is catching rays, not fish, it should be mentioned that the cayes, and Belize in general, lack wide, sandy beaches. Although the water is as warm and clear blue as it's touted to be, most of your sunbathing will be on docks or on deck chairs.

Cayo District   This mountainous district near the Guatemalan border has become Belize's second most popular destination. Here you'll find some of Belize's most beautiful countryside and most fascinating natural and man-made sights. The limestone mountains of this region have produced numerous caves, sinkholes, jagged peaks, and waterfalls. There are clear flowing rivers that are excellent for swimming and canoeing as well as mile after mile of unexplored forest full of wild animals. This was also the site of several major Mayan settlements more than 1,000 years ago. Caracol is said to be the largest Mayan city known, but it has not yet been fully excavated. Xunantunich and Cahal Pech are smaller, but still impressive, pyramid-and-temple complexes not far from the town of San Ignacio.

HISTORY

Before the arrival of the first Europeans (shipwrecked English sailors), this was the land of the enigmatic Mayas. Although most people think of Mexico's Mayan cities in the Yucatán and Guatemala's Tikal when they hear the word "Mayas," recent discoveries suggest that what is today known as Belize was once the center of the Mayan Empire. River and coastal trade routes connected dozens of cities and small towns throughout this region to the now better known and more frequently visited cities of Mexico and Guatemala. Caracol, a Mayan ruin in the Cayo District of western Belize, may have been the largest Mayan city at one time. Unfortunately, very little of this amazing discovery has been excavated or is likely to be excavated. The funds for massive restorations, such as those done at Tikal and Chichén Itzá, simply are not available.

Corozal Town, in northern Belize, is built on the site of the last Mayan city still occupied when this area was discovered by a Spanish expeditionary force in the 1530s. By the time those first unlucky sailors washed ashore, the Mayan civilization was a mere remnant of its former glory.

Belize likes to play up the fact that it was founded by pirates and buccaneers, and, indeed, these unsavory characters were some of the first to make this region their base of operations, but they were hardly a civilizing influence. By the mid-17th century, British loggers were settling along the coast and making their way up the rivers and streams in search of mahogany for shipbuilding and other types of wood for making dyes. When it formally became the colony of British Honduras in 1862, it was firmly established as a major source of wood for the still-expanding British empire. The forests were exploited, but agriculture was never encouraged. The British needed their colony to remain dependent on the mother country, so virtually all the necessities of life were imported. Few roads were built, and the country remained unexplored and undeveloped with a tiny population, mostly clustered along the coast.

During the 18th and 19th centuries, African slaves were brought to British Honduras, and black Caribs also migrated here from the Caribbean Islands. They established their own villages and culture along the coast. In the mid-19th century, many Mexican and Guatemalan refugees fled across the borders into British Honduras and founded such towns as Corozal Town and Benque Viejo.

In the early 1960s, groundwork was laid for granting British Honduras independence. However, based on 16th-century Spanish claims to all Central America, Guatemala claimed that the territory belonged to them. Fearful of an invasion by Guatemalan forces, the British delayed granting independence until an agreement could be reached with Guatemala. Although the 1964 constitution granted self-government to the British colony, it was not until September 21, 1981, that Belize, which had changed its name in 1973, actually gained its independence. Thus Belize is Central America's newest nation.

BELIZE

50 km
31 mi

MEXICO

GUATEMALA

Chetumal
Santa Rita
Corozal Town

Orange Walk Town

San Pedro

Blue Creek

Crooked Tree

Uaxactún

Altun Ha

Tikal

Rio Bravo

Community Baboon Sanctuary

International Airport

Northern Highway

Spanish Lookout

Belmopan

Belize River

Hattieville

Ladyville
Belize City

San Ignacio

Santa Elena

Western Highway

Northern Lagoon

Southern Lagoon

Caracol

Hummingbird Highway

Mountain Pine Ridge

Gales Point

South Stann Creek

Maya Mountains

Cockscomb Range

Cockscomb Basin Wildlife Sanctuary

Dangriga

Hopkins

Monkey River

San Antonio

Blue Creek Village

Southern Highway

Placencia

Caribbean Sea

Punta Gorda

Mobo River

Temash River

Barranco

Gulf of Honduras

Sarstoon River

Livingston

Castillo de San Felipe

Lake Izabal

Fronteras

Puerto Barrios

Quiriguá

CA9

Morales

Rio Hondo

HONDURAS

9154

The British legacy in Belize is a stable government with a parliamentary system and regular elections that are contested by two major parties and several smaller parties. The country's small newspapers are mouthpieces for the various parties and are frequently filled with stories disparaging the actions of the other parties. They make fun reading.

2. CULTURAL & SOCIAL LIFE

ART AND ARCHITECTURE   Belize was set up as a colony to provide wood and wood products to the British empire. With its tiny population and isolation from the outside world, it did not develop any outstanding artists, writers, or architects. There are only one or two tiny natural history museums in the country and only a few colonial buildings of any interest in Belize City. Clapboard houses built on stilts were typical and quite a few of these buildings, often painted in the pastel colors that are so popular throughout the Caribbean, remain in small towns. There are, however, a number of excavated Mayan ruins scattered around the countryside. Xunantunich, near the town of San Ignacio, is a pyramid that is still one of the tallest artificial structures in the country.

THE PEOPLE   Modern Belize (pop. 200,000) is a very unlikely mixture of peoples and cultures: Although the descendants of the Maya still populate the western and southern jungle areas, the majority of Belizeans are black Caribs or Creoles, descendants of slaves shipwrecked in transit from Africa, who established their own African-type culture in the Caribbean. The first Europeans to settle in Belize were pirates turned loggers, but today they have been joined by Britons and North Americans, Chinese, Lebanese, and the adherents of a German Protestant sect called Mennonites. All these people live in apparent harmony and mutual respect, divided by no great differences in wealth or power. English is the official language of the country, but Mayan languages, Spanish, old German (by Mennonites), Arabic, Chinese, Garifuna (a language of African origin), and Creole patois also are spoken depending on the district.

EVENING ENTERTAINMENT   Nightlife is limited. There are only a handful of movie theaters in the country. Bars, which occasionally have live bands, are about the extent of the nightlife scene in Belize.

SPORTS AND RECREATION   Soccer is the national sport, but the two most popular recreational activities are scuba diving and sportfishing. Belize has the best of both. The offshore coral reef is the second-longest barrier reef in the world, while the waters, both offshore and inland, teem with such popular game fish as tarpon, snook, bonefish, barracuda, and snapper. Many companies in Belize offer fishing and diving trips.

3. FOOD & DRINK

FOOD   Don't expect gourmet food during your visit to Belize. Even the most basic meals in restaurants are much more expensive than they would be in Guatemala or Mexico. Belize has little in the way of its own cuisine, so you'll find burgers, pizzas, fried fish, and Chinese food—and, if you look hard, even a little local food. Because Belize only recently began to grow its own beef and crops, the country relied for a long time on wild game. A favorite is gibnut, a large forest rodent that looks like a cross between a rat and a deer. Another popular wild animal found prepared in restaurants is the sea turtle, endangered all over the world, including in Belize. It's not

❓ DID YOU KNOW . . . ?

- Belize has the second-longest barrier reef in the world.
- Belize is the newest nation in Central America. It gained its independence from the United Kingdom in 1981.
- Nearly 65% of Belize is uninhabited wilderness.
- Belize has the world's first and only jaguar preserve.
- English is the official language of this Central American nation.
- Belize has a sizable population of Mennonite farmers who speak an archaic form of German.
- Belize City has been destroyed by hurricanes several times.
- Belize was first settled by pirates.
- Belize has some of the best scuba diving in the world.

yet illegal to sell sea turtle within Belize, but international agreements prohibit its export. Please don't order gibnut, turtle steak, or other wild game. Belize is struggling to preserve its natural environment, and as long as people order wild game, it will show up on menus.

Belize has also been a major exporter of lobster for many years, but overfishing has caused the population to decline. It is still available and quite inexpensive, but there is a season on lobster (which is subject to change). Please do not order lobster between Feb 15 and July 14.

DRINKS Much of the **drinking water** in Belize is rainwater. People use the roof of their house to collect water in a cistern which supplies them for the year. Always ask for drinking water at your hotel. Tap water generally is not considered safe to drink. Most major brands of soft drinks are available as are fresh lime juice and orange juice.

Belikin beer and Belikin stout are local beers, but a few other imported brands also are available. Several commercially bottled fruit wines are produced in Belize using native fruits. These wines are very sweet and are more a novelty than anything else. In remote parts of the country, you'll find homemade fruit wines that are a bit like hard cider. Most restaurants serve mixed drinks, with a variety of domestic and imported liquors available.

4. RECOMMENDED BOOKS, FILMS & RECORDINGS

The history of Ixchel Farm, one of Belize's most popular eco-attractions, is chronicled in *Sastun: My Apprenticeship with a Maya Healer* (HarperSanFrancisco, 1994) by Rosita Arvigo, who spent years studying with a Mayan bush doctor. Along a similar line, *Jaguar* (Anchor Press, 1991) by Alan Rabinowitz, is an account of the author's time in Belize studying jaguars. Rabinowitz was a major force in the establishment of the Cockscomb Basin jaguar preserve.

Although it wasn't a box-office hit, you might want to rent a copy of *The Mosquito Coast* (1986), which was filmed in Belize. Starring Harrison Ford and directed by Peter Weir, the film is about an inventor who relocates his family to the Central American jungle. Another film shot in Belize is *Dogs of War* (1980), which features Christopher Walken.

If you're taken by the pounding beat of soca music (a Caribbean music akin to calypso) and Belize's own punta rock (a kind of reggae-rock fusion), you can pick up cassette tapes in Belize City.

CHAPTER 16

PLANNING A TRIP TO BELIZE

More and more intrepid explorers are discovering Belize's natural and historic wonders: bird, monkey, and jaguar sanctuaries; Mayan ruins; mahogany forests; and huge limestone caves. The interior does not give itself up easily, though, and that's why it has remained so special and undeveloped. Belize is probably the most expensive country in Central America, but there are still bargains to be had. This chapter will tell you all you need to know about your trip, including how to snag the cheapest airfares, how to map your itinerary, what things cost, and how to stretch your dollars without cramping your style.

For information on travel insurance or to find out what health preparations (such as vaccinations) you should make before coming to a Central American country, see "Health, Insurance & Other Concerns" in Chapter 2, "Planning a Trip to Costa Rica."

1. INFORMATION, ENTRY REQUIREMENTS & MONEY

SOURCES OF INFORMATION

The **Belize Tourist Board,** 8 Haven Avenue, Port Washington, NY 11050 (tel. 516/944-8554, or toll free 800/624-0686; Fax 516/944-8458) will send you a package of information about the country. You can also contact the **Belize Tourist Board,** 83 North Front St., P.O. Box 325, Belize City (tel. 77213 or 73255)—open Monday to Friday from 8am to noon and 1 to 5pm. Whether your interest is pirate lore or bird identification, you'll find books of interest in the shops on Ambergris Caye.

ENTRY REQUIREMENTS

DOCUMENTS If you are a citizen of the United States or a Commonwealth country, you need only a valid passport to enter Belize. (See "Entry Requirements" in Chapter 2, "Planning a Trip to Costa Rica," for information on getting a passport.) All other visitors must also have a visa, available from a Belizean consulate. Visas and entry stamps are issued for up to 30 days. To extend your visa, apply at the Immigration Office, Barrack Road, Belize City, with B$25 ($12.50).

The Belize Embassy in the United States is at 2535 Massachusetts Avenue NW, Washington, D.C. 20008 (tel. 202/332-9636); in England it is at 10 Harcourt House, 19A Cavendish Square, London W1M 9AD (tel. 71/499-9728).

CUSTOMS   Visitors may bring 200 cigarettes (one carton) and a fifth of liquor into Belize.

MONEY

CASH/CURRENCY   The unit of currency in Belize is the Belizean dollar, abbreviated B$. Denominations of B$1, B$5, B$10, B$20, B$50, and B$100 are available. Coins come in 1B¢, 5B¢, 25B¢, 50B¢, and B$1 denominations. On the black market, $1 U.S. equals B$2. Although it is officially illegal, the black market is where everyone changes money because the banks charge a 2% to 3% commission. Never change money with someone who approaches you on the street. Always ask at your hotel where you can change money. If they can't make the transaction themselves, they'll tell you who will.

It's good to have at least $25 in U.S. dollars with you for emergencies (most places will take them if you don't have Belize dollars).

TRAVELER'S CHECKS   Traveler's checks are almost as readily convertible as cash dollars anywhere in Belize, so it pays to take the precaution of carrying your money in this more secure form.

CREDIT CARDS   Credit cards are generally not accepted at the low-end hotels and restaurants, however, there are exceptions to this rule on Ambergris Caye. American Express, MasterCard, and VISA are the most readily accepted cards in Belize.

WHAT THINGS COST IN BELIZE	U.S. $
Taxi from the airport to the city center	15.00
Local telephone call	0.15
Double at Ramon's Reef Hotel (deluxe)	121.90
Double at Barrier Reef Hotel (moderate)	68.90
Double at Ruby's Hotel (budget)	26.00
Lunch for one at Elvi's Kitchen (moderate)	10.00
Lunch for one at The Pizza Place (budget)	5.50
Dinner for one, without wine, at Paradise Hotel (deluxe)	30.00
Dinner for one, without wine, at Lily's (moderate)	15.00
Dinner for one, without wine, at Ambergris Delight (budget)	7.00
Bottle of beer	1.15
Coca-Cola	0.65
Cup of coffee	0.50
Roll of ASA 100 Kodacolor film, 36 exposures	5.00
Admission to the Xunantunich ruins	1.50

2. WHEN TO GO — CLIMATE & HOLIDAYS

CLIMATE   The climate of Belize is very similar to that of southern Florida. In the summer months, it is very hot (temperatures in the shade can approach 100°F), with rain almost daily from June to December. The amount of rainfall varies considerably with the regions. In the south, there may be more than 150 inches per year, while in the north there is rarely more than 50 inches per year. The dry season extends from January to May, with temperatures dipping down as low as 40°F in the mountains of the Cayo District. There is also a brief dry period in August. Although temperatures on the coast can climb quite high in the summer, the constant trade winds offer a bit of relief.

Average Monthly Temperatures & Rainfall in Belize

	Jan	Feb	Mar	Apr	May	June	July	Aug	Sept	Oct	Nov	Dec
Temp °F	73.4	76.1	77.9	79.7	81.5	81.5	81.5	81.5	80.6	78.8	75.2	74.3
Temp °C	23	24.5	25.5	26.5	27.5	27.5	27.5	27.5	27	26	24	23.5
Days of Rain	12	6	4	5	7	13	15	14	15	16	12	14

HOLIDAYS   Official holidays in Belize include January 1, New Year's Day; March 9, Baron Bliss Day; Good Friday; Holy Saturday; Easter Monday; May 1, Labor Day; May 24, Commonwealth Day; September 10, St. George's Caye Day; September 21, Independence Day; October 12, Columbus Day; November 19, Garifuna Settlement Day; December 25, Christmas; December 26, Boxing Day; December 31, New Year's Eve.

3. WHAT TO PACK

See Chapter 2, "Planning a Trip to Costa Rica," for information on what to pack. Bring a bathing suit, plenty of sunscreen, and an analgesic gel for soothing bug bites. If you have your own snorkeling or scuba-diving equipment, you should bring this as well.

4. TIPS FOR THE DISABLED, SENIORS, SINGLES & STUDENTS

FOR THE DISABLED   Few streets in Belize have sidewalks, and on the cayes there are really no streets at all, only sandy lanes and paths. Consequently, disabled visitors to Belize have a difficult time.

FOR SENIORS   Don't expect to find senior-citizen discounts here. The tourism industry is still a fledgling in Belize, and seniors are treated the same as anyone else. But you may be able to save 10% on your airline ticket. If you don't think you have the energy required for a visit to a jungle lodge, think again. The jungle lodges of Belize offer a wide variety of activities that people of all ages will find enjoyable. You're never too old to explore the jungles!

FOR SINGLES   As in most places, the single traveler is at a disadvantage in Belize. Some hotels do have single rooms though they usually do not have private baths and are generally quite small. If you don't plan to spend much time in your room, you can save money with one of these. Unfortunately, single room rates are usually higher than what each person would pay in a double room. In San Ignacio, Eva's Restaurant serves as a meeting ground for lone travelers seeking other adventurers to help cut the cost of taxis, canoe rentals, and tour rates. Tell Bob behind the counter what you're interested

THE BELIZEAN DOLLAR, THE U.S. DOLLAR & THE BRITISH POUND

At press time, $1 was worth approximately B$2, and £1 was worth about B$3; these rates of exchange were used to calculate the dollar values given in this guide. This rate does fluctuate and may not be the same when you travel to Belize. Therefore the following table should be used only as a guide:

B$	U.S.$	U.K.£	B$	U.S.$	U.K.£
1	.50	.33	7	3.50	2.30
2	1.00	.65	8	4.00	2.60
3	1.50	1.00	9	4.50	2.90
4	2.00	1.30	10	5.00	3.20
5	2.50	1.60	50	25.00	16.00
6	3.00	2.00	100	50.00	32.00

in doing, and he'll put your name on a list with other people interested in the same activity.

FOR STUDENTS   Check with the airlines when purchasing a ticket; there are sometimes special fares for students.

5. ALTERNATIVE/ADVENTURE TRAVEL

ECOTOURS

Much of Belize is still unspoiled forest inhabited by hundreds of species of birds and rare animals, including the world's largest population of jaguars. There are several tour companies that operate natural history tours to Belize. These trips usually include visits to wildlife preserves, hikes in the jungle, bird-watching, and visits to Mayan ruins, and, just to balance things out, spending a few days on the beach. **Great Trips,** P.O. Box 1320, Detroit Lake, MN 56501 (tel. 612/890-4405, or toll free 800/552-3419), offers several different tours. **International Expeditions,** One Environs Park, Helena, AL 35080 (tel. 205/428-1700, or toll free 800/633-4734), and **Sea & Explore,** 1809 Carol Sue Ave., Suite E, Gretna, LA 70056 (tel. 504/366-9985, or toll free 800/345-9786; Fax 504/366-9986), also operate similar nature tours to Belize. In Canada, try **EcoSummer Expeditions,** 1516 Duranleau Street, Vancouver, BC V6H 3S4 (tel. toll free in Canada 800/465-8884 or in the U.S. 800/688-8605).

If you're a member of the Sierra Club, Smithsonian Institution, or Audubon Society, you might look into their programs—all three offer trips to Belize.

KAYAK & BICYCLE TRIPS

If you're interested in an active vacation, consider sea kayaking through the cayes with **Island Expeditions Co.,** 368-916 W. Broadway, Vancouver, B.C. V5Z 1K7, Canada (tel. 604/325-7952 or toll free 800/667-1630). Prices begin around $695 for an 8-day trip. If you'd rather sea kayak up a jungle river, contact **Monkey River Expeditions,** 1731 44th Avenue SW, Suite 100, Seattle, WA 98116 (tel. 206/660-7777), which offers a 7-day trip for $1,295.

If bicycling is more your speed and you can tolerate heat and humidity, contact

Paradise Bicycle Tours, P.O. Box 1726, Evergreen, CO 80439 (tel. 303/674-2816 or toll free 800/245-2229).

6. GETTING THERE

BY PLANE

Even though it is only two hours by air from Miami, Belize is relatively expensive to reach—one reason it has not yet been overdeveloped. Daily flights to Belize City run from New York, Los Angeles, Miami, Houston, and New Orleans, with additional flights from Mexico City, Mérida, Guatemala City, and Flores (Tikal). Carriers flying from the United States include **TACA** (tel. toll free 800/535-8780), **Continental** (tel. toll free 800/231-0856), and **American** (tel. toll free 800/433-7300). Tropic Air (tel. toll free 800/422-3435), a small Belizean airline, has flights from Flores (Tikal).

BEST FOR THE BUDGET Airfares to Belize are generally abysmal. For some reason, it is almost always more expensive to fly to Belize than to Guatemala City or Cancún. Consequently, when checking airfares, consider flying to one of these cheaper destinations and then continuing to Belize another way. If you live on the West Coast of Canada or the U.S., you may be forced to either fly all night or spend a night in Houston both coming and going, neither of which is very appealing to me. One other thing to keep in mind is that flights in the off-season (late spring through early fall) are sometimes cheaper.

REGULAR AIRFARES At the time of this writing, the regular airfares, which have no restrictions, are between $650 and $750 in coach and around $1,200 in first class.

BY BUS

There are only two land routes into Belize—from Chetumal, Mexico, and from Flores, Guatemala. Both routes offer daily service, although the road from Guatemala can become impassable in the rainy season. Buses from Mexico cross the border and proceed into Corozal Town. From Corozal Town, you can catch a bus to Belize City or fly to San Pedro on Ambergris Caye.

Buses from Flores, Guatemala, drop passengers in Melchor de Mencos at the bridge that separates Guatemala and Belize. You must then cross the bridge and catch a Belizean bus or take a taxi. The first town in Belize is Benque Viejo, which has few services or accommodations and is less than a mile from the border. Your best bet is to continue another 8 miles into San Ignacio by either bus or taxi. If you arrive early in the day, you can share a taxi for only B$4 ($2) per person; otherwise, you'll have to pay about B$20 ($10) to hire a taxi to San Ignacio. The bus from the border to San Ignacio is B$1.50 (75¢). From San Ignacio, you can catch a bus to Belize City.

See "By Car" below for details on crossing the border.

BY CAR

If you're driving from Chetumal, you must hand in your Mexican Tourist Card (and/or car papers, if you have them) at the Mexican border station. You'll be issued new ones if you reenter Mexico. If you have Mexican auto insurance, get the policy stamped by an official so that you can get a rebate for the days you're outside Mexican territory. Cross the bridge over the Río Hondo and you're in Belize.

Both Mexican and Belizean border stations seem to be open during daylight hours all week, with no breaks for lunch.

Your entry permit is the rubber stamp put on your passport (other forms of identification are not accepted), and it will show how long you're allowed to stay. To be on the safe side, ask for a few more days than you think you'll need; the cayes can be very enticing.

FROMMER'S SMART TRAVELER: AIRFARES

1. Check the Sunday travel sections of major-city newspapers for companies selling discounted airline tickets that can be $100 to $200 less than the lowest standard airfare.
2. See if you can get a discounted ticket from your departure city to a Central American gateway city (Miami, New Orleans, Houston, or Los Angeles), and combine this with a discount ticket from one of those cities to Belize City.
3. Check airfares to Cancún, including air-and-hotel packages, which are often substantially less than flights to Belize City, which is only a day's bus ride away from Cancún.
4. Shop all the airlines that fly to Belize, including the small Central American airlines that travel agents don't usually check.
5. Even if you are on a tight budget, don't overlook the flights from Belize City to Caye Caulker and Ambergris Caye; these flights are almost as cheap as going by boat.
6. Always ask for the lowest-priced fare, which will usually be a midweek departure.
7. If you're a senior citizen, check to see if you can get a discount.

Be sure to get a Temporary Import Permit for your car, even if no one tells you a thing about it. Ask for the Customs official if he's not there and get the permit, or you'll be held up at the border when you leave the country. Also required is Belizean auto insurance, which you can buy in the restaurant across the road from the border station.

After they've stamped your passport, issued your auto permit, and inspected your car (a process that ranges from a glance through the window to a good search), and after you've bought auto insurance, you're on your way. The money changers at the border will give the standard two-to-one for your U.S. dollars. *However, don't change pesos here because you'll lose a tremendous amount.* There are banks in Corozal Town (open Monday to Thursday from 8am to 1pm, Friday from 8am to 1pm and 3 to 6pm) 7 miles down the road, where you'll get a better rate on pesos but a worse rate on dollars.

BY SHIP

For adventurous travelers, there's a ferry from Puerto Barrios, Guatamela, to Punta Gorda, Belize, on Tuesday and Friday at 7am. The one-way fare for the 3-hour trip is Q32.10 ($5.55). You can buy your ticket at the Immigration Office on 9a Calle, where you should be sure to get your passport stamped before leaving. Secure a ticket the day before your departure. After arriving in Punta Gorda, take the bus north (along a rough dirt road) or fly to Belize City.

PACKAGE TOURS AND CRUISES

U.S. companies specializing in package tours to Belize are **Great Trips,** P.O. Box 1320, Detroit Lake, MN 56501 (tel. 612/890-4405, or toll free 800/552-3419); **International Expeditions,** One Environs Park, Helena, AL 35080 (tel. 205/428-1700, or toll free 800/633-4734); **Sea & Explore,** 1809 Carol Sue Avenue, Suite E, Gretna, LA 70056 (tel. 504/366-9985, or toll free 800/345-9786); and **Accent on Travel,** 1865 NW 169th Place, Beaverton, OR 97006 (tel. 503/645-7323, or toll free 800/288-8646).

Small cruise ships also ply the turquoise waters of Belize; this may be the best way to see the country's underwater wonders. **American Canadian Caribbean Line,**

Inc. (tel. toll free 800/556-7450) offers 12-day cruises for as little as $1,622, which include lots of snorkeling and visits to Mayan ruins. **Belize Tradewinds,** 8715 W. North Avenue, Wauwatosa, WI 53226 (tel. toll free 800/451-7776) specializes in scuba-diving trips.

7. GETTING AROUND

BY PLANE Because of the lack of decent roads in most of Belize, flying is recommended as a means of getting around. There are flights between Corozal Town and San Pedro and between Belize City and Corozal Town, San Pedro, Caye Caulker, Caye Chapel, Dangriga, Big Creek, Placencia, and Punta Gorda. Except for the flights to the Cayes, the flights are not cheap, but they will save you many hours of travel over very bad roads. The following small Belizean airlines have toll free numbers in the United States: **Island Air** (tel. 800/521-1247), **Tropic Air** (tel. 800/422-3435), and **Maya Airways,** represented by a tour company (tel. 800/552-3419). On occasion, Maya and Tropic airlines have not honored reservations, even with paid tickets. If you should be left with a ticket and no plane, you may want to consider chartering a plane from the international or municipal airport. However, charters are not cheap.

BY BUS Buses run between all the main towns in Belize, with Belize City acting as the hub for most routes. However, the bus service is not always frequent. The fares are low, and the buses are generally in good condition.

BY CAR Most roads in Belize are not paved, and so you must have a very sturdy vehicle, preferably with four-wheel drive (especially in the rainy season). There are really only two paved highways—the Northern Highway and the Western Highway. The Hummingbird, or Southern, Highway was partially paved at one time, but now it is a battlefield of potholes that is slowly being repaved. You'll be thankful for plain old dirt after driving this road. If you're driving your own car, install heavy-duty shocks. Also keep your eyes peeled for "sleeping policemen"—speed bumps (usually unmarked)—that can be found as you enter any populated area.

BY RV There are a few campgrounds scattered around Belize. You can also camp at the Cockscomb Basin Jaguar Preserve. You'll need an overnight permit, available at the preserve headquarters.

BY FERRY Boats make regular runs to Caye Caulker and Ambergris Caye from Belize City; others operate between Big Creek and Placencia, which is not an island but a long spit of land.

HITCHHIKING You can hitchhike in Belize, but the buses are easier and quite cheap. The only time you might wish to hitchhike is if you're trying to get to some of the remote parks and preserves without taking a tour or hiring a car. Remember there is little traffic on Belize's back roads.

8. SUGGESTED ITINERARIES

HIGHLIGHTS

The following are Belize's most important destinations: 1) Ambergris Caye (scuba diving, snorkeling); 2) Caye Caulker (snorkeling, scuba diving); 3) San Ignacio (Cahal Pech, Xunantunich, Caracol, Mountain Pine Ridge); 4) Placencia (beach); 5) Commu-

FROMMER'S FAVORITE BELIZE EXPERIENCES

A Sailboat Trip to Hol Chan Marine Reserve   The barrier reef off the coast of Belize is the second longest in the world, and the wooden sailboats that sail from Caye Caulker will take you to the protected waters of the Hol Chan Marine Reserve off Ambergris Caye. After a couple of hours of sailing, you can snorkel or scuba dive, then visit San Pedro on Ambergris Caye before sailing back to Caye Caulker.

Canoeing on the Macal River   Three-foot-long iguanas bask along the rocky banks and skitter for cover as canoes float past. Women wash their laundry while standing knee-deep in the river, and children swing from ropes and splash into the water. A day spent paddling quietly along the course of the Macal River is a day well spent.

A Visit to the Cockscomb Basin Wildlife Preserve   This preserve was created to protect the world's largest concentration of jaguars. Trails lead through the jungle, and it's even possible to camp or rent a bunk here.

A Day Trip to the Mountain Pine Ridge   Deep in the mountains of western Belize's Cayo District is a rugged forest reserve of pine forests and jungles with spectacular 1,000 Foot Falls, the Río Frío caves, and the Río On pools. A day spent exploring caves and swimming in mountain rivers is unforgettable.

Remote Cayes   If you are really looking for a Robinson Crusoe adventure, then keep your eyes open whenever you see a bulletin board or a notice pinned on a wall and you will find advertisements for the tiniest of cayes—places where there may be three palm trees, a hut, and nothing else. Maybe there won't even be the palm trees. Such island getaways are popping up all over, and I've seen notices for little huts on cayes off Ambergris Caye, Caye Caulker, Long Caye, and Placencia. What they all have in common is a small hut where you'll be the only guests. You do your own cooking and stay for a prearranged number of days. If you decide a 30-foot-long island is just too quiet even for you, tough luck, the boat won't be back until the day you told it to return!

A Visit to the Community Baboon Sanctuary   This unusual howler monkey preserve includes several villages and has involved the villagers directly in preserving these endangered primates. With a local guide, you can often get within a few feet of the vociferous creatures.

nity Baboon Sanctuary (howler monkeys); 6) Cockscomb Basin Wildlife Preserve (jaguar preserve); 7) Punta Gorda (Mayan ruins, Mayan villages); 8) Altun Ha; 9) Lamanai; and 10) Crooked Tree Wildlife Refuge.

PLANNING YOUR ITINERARY

IF YOU HAVE ONE WEEK

Days 1 through 3: Fly directly to Ambergris Caye or Caye Caulker and relax on the beach, go snorkeling or scuba diving at Hol Chan Marine Reserve, and sail between Ambergris Caye and Caye Caulker.

Day 4: Take a boat to Belize City and continue west to San Ignacio in the Cayo

District, stopping at the Belize Zoo on your way. Visit Xunantunich or Cahal Pech ruins in the afternoon.

Day 5: Take a canoe trip on the Macal River, visiting the Panti Medicine Trail.

Day 6: Spend the day in the Mountain Pine Ridge, visiting waterfalls and caves and enjoying the tropical scenery.

Day 7: Head back to Belize City, stopping at Guanacaste Park and making a side trip to the Blue Hole.

IF YOU HAVE TWO WEEKS

Days 1 through 4: Your first four days should be spent in the mountainous Cayo District. Use your first day to reach San Ignacio, with a stop at the Belize Zoo. Spend one day canoeing the Macal River and visiting the Panti Medicine Trail. Spend another day in Mountain Pine Ridge visiting waterfalls and caves. On the fourth day go horseback riding in the morning and visit Xunantunich and Cahal Pech ruins in the afternoon.

Days 5 and 6: Journey into Guatemala to visit the impressive ruins of Tikal, spending the night either at Tikal or in Flores.

Days 7 and 8: Travel to Placencia on the southern coast, with stops at Guanacaste Park, the Blue Hole, St. Herman's Caves, and the Cockscomb Basin Wildlife Preserve. Spend a day lazing on the beach and snorkeling, perhaps hiring a boat to take you to the cayes.

Day 9: Go back up the coast to Belize City.

Days 10 through 12: Catch the early boat to Caye Caulker. Hang out and/or go snorkeling, scuba diving, or fishing. Sail to Ambergris Caye on your third day.

Days 13 and 14: Enjoy more fun in the sun (perhaps on a Tobacco Caye) until you have to fly back to the mainland to catch your flight.

IF YOU HAVE THREE WEEKS

Days 1 through 4: Explore the Cayo District by foot, horse, canoe, or Jeep. During your time here, you should visit the Xunantunich ruins, the Panti Medicine Trail, and Mountain Pine Ridge. On your way here from Belize City, stop at the Belize Zoo and Guanacaste Park.

Days 5 through 7: Spend two days exploring Tikal ruins in Guatemala, returning to San Ignacio on your third day.

Days 8 through 11: Continue on to Placencia, stopping at the Blue Hole, St. Herman's Caves, and the Cockscomb Basin Wildlife Preserve. Spend the next two days relaxing on the beach, swimming, snorkeling, scuba diving, and fishing. On the eleventh day, proceed back up the coast to Belize City.

Day 12: Using Belize City as a base, make a trip to Altun Ha and the Community Baboon Sanctuary.

Days 13 through 16: Catch the early boat to Caye Caulker and spend the next three days enjoying the laid-back atmosphere. Snorkel, scuba dive, or go fishing. Read a good book. On your last day, sail to Ambergris Caye and stop at Hol Chan Marine Reserve to go snorkeling.

Days 17 through 21: Relax in the sun. If you didn't visit the Altun Ha ruins already, you can do so by boat from here. Try an excursion to the Mexican Rocks for snorkeling or rent a sailboard. Fly back to Belize City to catch your flight home.

THEMED CHOICES

Although many people see Belize as just another Caribbean resort, it has much more to offer, especially to naturalists and bird-watchers. A trip focusing on the natural parks would include stops at the Cockscomb Basin Wildlife Preserve, the Community Baboon Sanctuary, the Crooked Tree Wildlife Sanctuary, Mountain Pine Ridge, Guanacaste Park, the Hol Chan Marine Reserve, and the Belize Zoo.

Would-be archeologists and those fascinated by the Mayas can see ruins as well as present-day Mayan villages. Among the ruins that can be easily visited are Cahal Pech, Xunantunich, Pacbitun, Chechem Hah, Altun Ha, Lamanai, Lubaantun, Nim Li Punit, and Santa Rita. With a bit more effort and money, it is possible to visit Caracol, which is thought to have been one of the largest Mayan cities. Down in southern Belize, there are several villages that are populated by latter-day Mayas whose lifestyle has changed little with the passing of time.

9. ENJOYING BELIZE ON A BUDGET

SAVING MONEY ON ACCOMMODATIONS

The best way to save money on accommodations in Belize is to travel during the off-season, which is roughly June to October. Not all hotels offer discounts during the off-season but many do, and some start offering discounts as early as May. Taking a room with a shared bathroom will also save you quite a bit. Avoid staying in Belmopan, where all the hotels are relatively expensive. You'll also save money on your beach visit if you choose to stay someplace other than Ambergris Caye. Generally speaking, the smaller and more remote coastal villages and inhabited cayes tend to have less expensive (though likewise less luxurious) accommodations. One of the best ways to save money is to read bulletin boards. The newest budget hotels (those that haven't gotten into any guidebooks yet) often have the best rates and tend to post notices on any bulletin boards they can find.

SAVING MONEY ON MEALS

The cheapest food in Belize is found on the street. In almost every town, women cook up their specialties such as coconut buns, chicken tacos, or tamales wrapped in banana leaves and sell them on the street. Often Mom will set up her food stand in a park or near a bus terminal, and the kids will walk around with buckets full of baked goodies. Never let one of these bun boys pass you by without finding out what he's selling. Tacos in Belize are a breakfast dish and consist of a chicken stew rolled in a steamed corn tortilla. You can usually get three tacos or two buns for B$1 (50¢).

SAVING MONEY ON SIGHT-SEEING

Check bulletin boards for notices advertising inexpensive tours. Enterprising folks are always setting up their own little tour companies in Belize, and often their prices are lower than the established competition. You can be sure that if you go to a travel agent in Belize, you will be paying top price for a tour. The walls of Eva's restaurant in San Ignacio are covered with posters and notices for various tours, many of which are surprisingly economical (at least for Belize). You'll almost always save money by getting a group of people together to share taxi or boat expenses.

SAVING MONEY ON SHOPPING

One of the best buys in Belize is Marie Sharp's hot sauce, which comes in three degrees of spiciness and is made with the eye-watering habanero pepper. A small bottle can be had for less than B$2 ($1). If you've developed a taste for reggae and soca music, the record and tape stores in Belize City have very reasonable prices.

SAVING MONEY ON TRANSPORTATION

Taxis, especially those in the Cayo District, are ridiculously expensive. Likewise, the rental cars here are the most expensive that I have encountered anywhere in the world. A 15-year-old gas-guzzling Detroit tank rents for almost $100 per day. Add to this gasoline at $2.50 per gallon. Save money by taking very inexpensive local buses, or, if you absolutely must hire a taxi, try to get together with several other people and share the expense. Eva's Restaurant in San Ignacio is a good place to meet people with whom to share a cab to some of the more interesting sites in the area. Just tell Bob at the counter what you're interested in doing.

SAVING MONEY ON SERVICES AND OTHER TRANSACTIONS

Tipping   Bell hops: B$1 per bag. Waiters/waitresses: 10% to 15%, but only in better restaurants. Taxi drivers: none. Porters: B$1 per bag.

Money Changing and Credit Cards   Although it is officially illegal, changing money on the black market (at a hotel or with someone recommended by your hotel manager) will save you the bank service charge. Credit cards are not widely accepted at restaurants, but they are accepted at hotels. Using your credit cards will get you the official two-to-one rate without having to pay a service charge.

Telephone Calls   There are direct-dial AT&T phones at the Belize International Airport and at the main phone office in downtown Belize City. A few phones in San Pedro also offer this service.

FAST FACTS: BELIZE

American Express   Belize's only American Express office is in Belize City, upstairs from Belize Global Travel Services, 41 Albert St. (tel. 77363). Open Monday to Friday from 8am to noon and from 1 to 5pm, Saturday from 8am to noon.

Business Hours   Banks are open Monday through Thursday from 8am to 1pm and Friday from 8am to 1pm and 3 to 6pm. Offices are open from 8am to noon and 1 to 5pm. Restaurants are generally open daily from 11am to 2pm and again from 6 to 10pm. Stores are open daily 8am to noon, 1 to 4pm, and 7 to 9pm (many are only open in the morning on Wednesday).

Camera/Film   Film is available in Belize, but it's very expensive. Bring plenty from home. Remember to bring spare camera batteries also.

City Codes   Belize City 2, Belmopan 8, Benque Viejo 93, Blue Creek 3, Burrell Boom 28, Caye Caulker 22, Corozal 4, Dangriga 5, Independence 6, Ladyville 25, Orange Walk 3, Placencia 6, Punta Gorda 7, San Ignacio 92, San Pedro 26, Spanish Lookout 6. When dialing long distance from within Belize, you must first dial a zero.

Climate   See "When to Go" in this chapter.

Country Code   The country code when dialing Belize is 501.

Crime   See "Safety," below.

Currency   See "Information, Entry Requirements & Money" in this chapter.

Documents Required   See "Information, Entry Requirements & Money" in this chapter.

Driving Rules   See "Getting Around" in this chapter.

Drug Laws   Although marijuana is grown in Belize, it's illegal, and the penalties for its possession are stiff. The same goes for cocaine. Be sure to bring along copies of prescriptions for any regulated medicine that you might need because this can save you problems with Customs officials and help you get prescriptions filled while you're here.

Drugstores   You'll find licensed pharmacies in most towns in Belize.

Electricity   Current is 110 volts.

Embassies and Consulates   United States Embassy, 29 Gabourel Lane, Hutson Street, Belize City (tel. 77161); Canada Consulate, 83 North Front St., Belize City (tel. 31060); British High Commission, Embassy Square, Belmopan (tel. 8/22146 or 8/22147); Guatemalan Embassy, 6A St. Mathews St., Belize City (tel. 2/33150 or 33314).

Emergencies   Fire and ambulance, dial 90; police emergency, dial 911 or 72210 in Belize City, 22222 in Belmopan, 2022 in San Ignacio, Benque Viejo, or San

Pedro, 23199 in Placencia, 2120 in Caye Caulker, 22022 in Dangriga, Orange Walk, or Corozal Town.

Hitchhiking   See "Getting Around" in this chapter.

Holidays   See "When to Go" in this chapter.

Information   See "Information, Entry Requirements & Money" in this chapter. Also see individual city chapters for local information offices.

Language   English is the official language, although Spanish, several Indian dialects, Garifuna, and Creole also are spoken.

Laundry   For listings of laundromats, see individual town and island chapters.

Liquor Laws   You must be 18 years old to purchase alcoholic beverages in Belize.

Mail   Letters take about a week to reach the United States. A postcard to the United States costs 30B¢ (15¢) and a letter costs 60B¢ (30¢). You can usually buy stamps at your hotel and in stores selling postcards as well as at the post office. Post offices are open from Monday to Thursday from 8am to 5pm, Friday from 8am to 4:30pm. It is best to ship parcels from the Parcel Post Office, North Front Street, in Belize City. Open Monday to Thursday from 8am to noon and 1 to 5pm, Friday from 8am to noon and 1 to 4:30pm. If you are a member of American Express, you can have mail sent to you care of (c/o) American Express, Belize Global Travel Services, 41 Albert Street, Belize City.

Maps   The Belize Tourist Bureau in Belize City has several different maps—some free, others for a few dollars. They sell a very good, but expensive, map of the entire country for B$30 ($15), but it is probably more economical to buy a map at home and bring it along with you. If you plan to drive, I recommend Emory King's *Driver's Guide to Beautiful Belize*, a small book that takes you mile by mile down every road with many small maps. It's available at bookstores and gift shops.

Newspapers/Magazines   The *Miami Herald* and *USA Today* are the most readily available international newspapers in Belize and can be found at larger hotels throughout the country. The Belizean newspapers are profoundly lacking in hard news, being primarily mouthpieces for the many political parties in the country.

Passports   See "Information, Entry Requirements & Money" in this chapter.

Pets   If you want to bring your pet along, you must have a recent veterinarian's certificate of good health and inoculation against rabies.

Police   See "Emergencies," above.

Radio/TV   There are three radio stations in Belize. Programming consists of talk shows and plenty of soca and reggae music. TV offerings include two national TV stations, satellite, and cable TV.

Restrooms   In hotels and restaurants only.

Safety   Belize City has a reputation for being a dangerous place. Whenever you're traveling in an unfamiliar city or country, stay alert. Be aware of your immediate surroundings. Wear a money belt and keep a close eye on your possessions. Be particularly careful with cameras, purses, and wallets—all favorite targets of thieves and pickpockets.

Taxes   There is a B$22.50 ($11.25) departure tax when you leave the country by air. The hotel room tax is 5%, which I have included in the rates listed in this book.

Telephone   Pay phones can be found on the street. They accept coins of different denominations but do not give change; a local phone call is B25¢ (13¢). The dial tone is similar to that in the United States. The main telephone office in Belize City is at 1 Church Street, open Monday through Saturday from 8am to 9pm and Sunday from 8am to noon. You'll find direct-dial AT&T and Sprint phones here, also UK and Canada direct. A 3-minute call to the U.S. costs B$9.60 ($4.80). There's only one phone book for all of Belize.

The country code for Belize is 501, and this number must be used when dialing Belize from a foreign country. Phone numbers in Belize differ in the number of digits they have, and each town has its own area code. When dialing long distance within Belize, you must always dial a zero before the area code, but when calling from outside Belize, you don't use the zero. When making local calls, do not use the area code.

Time   Belize is on Central Standard Time, or six hours behind Greenwich Mean Time.

Tipping   See "Saving Money on Services and Other Transactions" in this chapter.

Tourist Offices   See "Information, Entry Requirements & Money" in this chapter. Also see individual city chapters.

Visas   See "Information, Entry Requirements & Money" in this chapter.

Water   On the cayes, avoid tap water, which is often from shallow wells. In Belize City and other towns tap water is heavily chlorinated and safe to drink. Throughout the country people rely on cisterns to collect rainwater for drinking. At your hotel, ask for a pitcher of drinking water; otherwise, bottled water is available.

CHAPTER 17

NORTHERN BELIZE

Belize City is no longer the capital of Belize, but as the largest city in the country, it is the business and transportation hub. Sooner or later you're going to have to spend some time here, unless you do all your in-country traveling by air or have a very well-planned itinerary. Whether you are just passing through or spending a day or two here, this chapter will make Belize City a breeze for you.

The cayes, on the other hand, are hard to leave. With their trade winds and coral reefs, cheap lobster and rum punch, they can seduce the most hardened of tropical travelers. The Belizean cayes epitomize life in the slow lane and offer everything from kicked back to laid back to flat on your back soaking up the sun.

---

1. BELIZE CITY

103 miles S of the Mexican border; 82 miles E of the Guatemalan border

GETTING THERE By Air Continental, American, TACA, and several local airlines serve Belize City's two airports. See Chapter 16, "Planning a Trip to Belize," for details.

By Bus Belize City is well served by about half a dozen different bus lines that run to all corners of the country that have roads. See Chapter 16, "Planning a Trip to Belize," for more details.

By Car There are only two highways into Belize City—the Northern Highway, which leads to the Mexican border, and the Western Highway, which leads to the Guatemalan border.

By Boat The *Andrea* and *Andrea II* make the run between San Pedro, Ambergris Caye, and Belize City Monday to Saturday. There also are boats that run between Caye Caulker and Belize City daily.

DEPARTING Belize City's bus stations are about ten blocks from the Swing Bridge. From Albert Street between the Swing Bridge and the Central Park, walk up Orange Street, cross a canal, continue to the far side of the next canal, and turn left for Novelos, located on West Collet Canal (tel. 2-77372); Batty Bros., on Mosul Street (tel. 2-72025), is to the right one block before you cross the second canal. The last two companies, Venus (tel. 2-73354) and Z-Line (tel. 2-73937), are farther away, off Orange Street; turn right onto Magazine Road to find them.

Batty Bros. runs several buses a day to San Ignacio: only certain buses go to Melchor de Mencos, Guatemala. The trip takes 1½ hours to Belmopan, where there's a brief stop, then another 1½ hours to San Ignacio. Novelos buses leave for San Ignacio every hour on the hour from 11am through 7pm. The schedule is pared down a bit on Sunday. Venus and Z-Line serve Dangriga, Mango Creek, Placencia, and Punta Gorda. Batty Bros. and Venus split the northern route to Chetumal; between the two of them, a bus runs every hour.

The stereo speakers are as big as houses" exclaimed a recent visitor to Belize City (pop. 50,000), and even though that is a bit of an exaggeration, Belize City does rock to a Caribbean beat. Maybe all the rocking is due to the city's shaky foundations. Legend has it that the city was founded 300 years ago by pirates and built out of the marshes on a foundation of empty rum bottles. Whether that is true or not, Belize City is surrounded on three sides by water, and at high tide it is nearly swamped. Several hurricanes have inundated the city over the years, causing extensive damage each time and affecting the creation of two other towns—Belmopan and Hattieville. Belmopan, at the geographical center of the country, may be the capital of Belize, but Belize City is the cultural and commercial center. It's a strange, fascinating warren of narrow streets and canals (the latter being little more than open sewers and pretty pungent in hot weather), modern stores, dilapidated shacks, and quaint wooden mansions. It's not the kind of place that you want to hang around any longer than necessary, but if you happen to be stuck here for a day or two, explore a bit—you might be surprised by what you find.

ORIENTATION

ARRIVING When you fly into Belize, you'll land at the Philip S. W. Goldson International Airport, which is located 10 miles northwest of the city on the Northern Highway. At the airport you'll find a bank, open daily from 8 to 11am and from 12:30 to 4:30pm, just outside the terminal entrance. There are also car-rental desks and an information desk, open 8am to 9:30pm daily, that is actually more of a travel agency providing reservations at the more expensive hotels and lodges around the country. A taxi into town will cost B$30 ($15). There is now shuttle bus service from the international airport to Belize City, charging B$5 ($2.50) each way. Buses in from the airport are scheduled for 8am, and 1 and 4pm. Phone 2/73977 or 2/77811 for additional information. If you fly in from somewhere else in Belize, you'll land at the Municipal Airport, which is on the edge of town. A taxi from here should be no more than B$8 ($4).

If you arrive in town by bus, you'll be somewhere on the west side of town, depending on where you came from and which bus line you used. All the bus stations are within 10 blocks of Albert Street, which is an easy walk in the day, but it is not recommended after dark. A taxi from the bus station to any hotel in town will cost B$4 ($2) for one person or B$5 ($2.50) for two people.

If you arrive by car from the north, keep on the road into town, paying close attention to one-way streets, and you'll end up at the Swing Bridge. If you're arriving on the Western Highway, stay on it after it becomes Cemetery Road, and you'll end up at the intersection with Albert Street, a block away from the Swing Bridge.

INFORMATION The **Belize Tourist Board,** 83 North Front St. (tel. 77213 or 73255) is open Monday to Friday from 8am to noon and 1 to 5pm. Travel agencies are another good source of information.

CITY LAYOUT Belize City is surrounded on three sides by water, with the murky waters of the Haulover Creek dividing the city in two. The Swing Bridge, near the mouth of Haulover Creek, is the main route between the two halves of the city. At the south end of the bridge is the market and the start of Regent Street and Albert Street, where you'll find most of Belize City's shops and offices. To the east of these two major roads is a grid of smaller roads lined with dilapidated wooden houses. On the north side of the bridge and to the right, you'll find a pleasant neighborhood of old mansions. This is where you'll find the U.S. embassy, a couple of guest houses, and several expensive hotels. Cemetery Road heads out of town to the west and becomes the Western Highway, and Freetown Road becomes the Northern Highway.

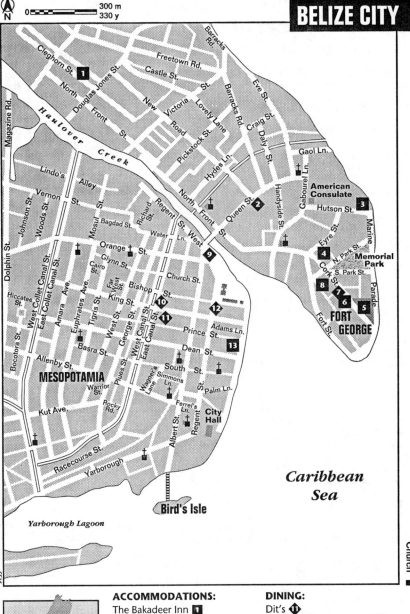

BELIZE CITY

Caribbean Sea

Yarborough Lagoon

Bird's Isle

MESOPOTAMIA

FORT GEORGE

American Consulate

Memorial Park

City Hall

0   300 m
     330 y

Belize City

BELIZE

ACCOMMODATIONS:
The Bakadeer Inn **1**
Belize Guest House **3**
Colton House **6**
Eyre Street Guest House **4**
Fort Street Restaurant
  & Guesthouse **8**
Hotel El Centro **5**
Seaside Guest House **13**

DINING:
Dit's **11**
Guang Zhou Restaurant **7**
Kadel's **9**
Macy's **10**
Pop 'N Taco **12**
Sea Rock Indian Restaurant **2**

Church

GETTING AROUND

The only way to get around town is on foot or by taxi, unless you have your own car.

BY TAXI   A taxi is B$4 ($2) for one person, B$5 ($2.50) for two people, and B$6 ($3) for three people between any two points in town. You'll find taxis waiting on the Market Square near the Swing Bridge, or you can call **Caribbean Taxi Garage** (tel. 72888) or **Cinderella Plaza Taxi** (tel. 33340).

BY CAR   Car Rentals   I don't know of anyplace in the world where it is more expensive to rent a car. It seems that anyone who can get a couple of old Detroit eight-cylinder bombs down here from Texas can open up a car-rental agency. You can count on these cars guzzling expensive gas and breaking down at some point (not my idea of a fun way to spend my vacation).

A much better bet is to rent a small four-wheel-drive vehicle that will likely get better mileage and be reliable even though it costs a bit more per day. International car-rental agencies with offices in Belize include **Avis** (tel. toll free in the U.S. 800/331-1212), with branches at 50 Vernon Street (tel. 70729) and Philip S.W. Goldson International Airport (tel. 52385); **Budget Rent-a-Car** (tel. toll free in the U.S. 800/527-0700), 771 Bella Vista (tel. 32435); and **Hertz Rent A Car** (tel. toll free in the U.S. 800/654-1831), Philip S.W. Goldson International Airport (tel. 32981). Local companies you might try are **Lewis Auto Rental,** 23 Cemetery Rd. (tel. 2/74461) and **Ace Auto Rental,** 6 North Front St. (tel. 2/31650).

The most economical four-wheel-drive vehicles (Suzuki Samurais) rent for around $85, taxes and insurance included. Try to make a reservation several weeks in advance with one of the international companies. You'll be glad you did.

 BELIZE CITY

American Express   The office is located upstairs from Belize Global Travel Services, 41 Albert St. (tel. 77363). Open Monday to Friday from 8am to noon and 1 to 5pm, Saturday 8am to noon.

Area Code   The area code for Belize City is 2.

Bookstores   The Book Center, 144 North Front St. (tel. 77457), sells magazines and classic books and is open Monday to Friday from 8am to noon, 1 to 5pm, and 7 to 9pm; Saturday 8am to noon, 1 to 4:30pm, and 7 to 9pm.

Business Hours   See "Fast Facts: Business Hours" in Chapter 14.

Car Rentals   See "Getting Around" in this chapter.

Climate   See "When to Go" in Chapter 14.

Crime   See "Safety" below.

Currency   See "Information, Entry Requirements & Money" in Chapter 14.

Currency Exchange   Most banks are around the Central Park, though few people use banks for changing money because they charge a commission. Ask your hotel manager about changing money. If the hotel can't help you, they can point you in the right direction. The Belize Bank is open Monday to Thursday from 8am to 1pm, and Friday 8am to 1pm and 3 to 6pm.

Dentist   Contact your embassy for the name of a reliable dentist.

Doctors   Contact your embassy for the name of a reliable doctor.

Drugstores   Brodie's Pharmacy, Regent and Albert Sts. (tel. 77070, ext. 266), is open Monday through Thursday 8:30am to 7pm, Friday 8:30am to 9pm, Saturday from 8:30am to 5pm; and Sunday 9am to 12:30pm.

Embassies and Consulates   See "Fast Facts" in Chapter 16.

Emergencies   Fire and ambulance call 90; police call 911 or 72210.

Eyeglasses   The Belize Vision Center, 9 Daly St. (tel. 45038), can repair or replace your glasses. Open Monday to Friday 8am to noon and 4 to 7pm, Saturday 8am to noon.

Holidays   See "When to Go" in Chapter 14.
Hospitals   The two major medical care facilities are Belize City Hospital (tel. 2/77251) and Medical Associates (tel. 2/30303).
Information   See "Information" in this chapter.
Laundry/Dry Cleaning   Your best bet is to ask at the front desk of your hotel. If the hotel doesn't do laundry, the staff should be able to refer you to a place nearby.
Luggage Storage/Lockers   Ask at your hotel or try a bus station; otherwise, there's no place to leave luggage in Belize City.
Lost Property   The best you can do is contact the police.
Newspapers/Magazines   The *Miami Herald, USA Today, Time,* and *Newsweek* are available at bookstores and other shops.
Photographic Needs   Spooner's, 89 North Front St. (tel. 2/31043) sells film and photographic supplies and processes film.
Police   See "Emergencies," above.
Post Office   The main post office is on North Front Street at the north end of the Swing Bridge (tel. 72201). Open Monday to Thursday from 8am to 5pm, and Friday from 8am to 4:30pm. The parcel post office next door is open Monday to Thursday from 8am to noon and 1 to 5pm, Friday 8am to noon and 1 to 4:30pm.
Radio/TV   Local radio stations primarily play reggae, soca, and rap music. Satellite cable TV is what most people here watch.
Religious Services   Among the denominations with churches in Belize City are Anglican, Baptist, Presbyterian, Jehovah's Witness, and Seventh Day Adventist. Check the Belize telephone book for addresses and phone numbers.
Restrooms   You'll find them in restaurants and hotels, but that's about it.
Safety   Like any big city, Belize City has its share of criminals and dangers, although with a bit of caution and common sense, you shouldn't have any problems. You'll hear that you shouldn't go out alone at night in Belize City, but there's nothing that should prevent you from walking from a restaurant to your hotel in pairs, down well-lit main streets. Look like you know where you're going and don't flash money. If someone tries to engage you in conversation not to your liking, excuse yourself politely. Invariably, people who get ripped off are participating in illicit exchanges. You certainly won't have any problems on the cayes, where life never exceeds a snail's pace, but it's still a good idea not to leave valuables in your room.
Taxes   There is a 6% tax on hotel rooms.
Taxis   See "Getting Around" in this chapter.
Telephone   For all your long-distance needs, head to the Belize Telecommunications Ltd. office at 1 Church St. Open Monday to Saturday from 8am to 9pm, Sunday 8am to noon. You'll find direct-dial AT&T and Sprint phones here, as well as UK and Canada direct phones.

WHAT TO SEE & DO

A walk around town is all that you need to entertain you in Belize City because the fascination never seems to end. Turn right as you come off the northeast end of the Swing Bridge, before the post office, and follow the street southeast to the Fort George Lighthouse and Baron Bliss Memorial. Baron Bliss, who visited Belize on his yacht in the 1920s, left Belize City most of his fortune (a few million dollars, in fact) when he died on the yacht in the harbor, and many of the city's public buildings derive from his bequest.

The Supreme Court building, off the small Central Park, is a real prize of English colonial architecture (à la Caribbean). If you walk down to the end of Regent Street, you'll come to Government House, built in 1814 by the British, who ruled Belize for many years. Across the street is the Anglican Cathedral of St. John the Baptist. In the

19th century, three kings of the Mosquito Coast were crowned here. Also along Regent Street are several old buildings that were once slave quarters.

WHERE TO STAY

Accommodations in Belize City can be a problem: The cheapest hotels are not recommended because of the danger of theft, and the expensive hotels often commit a similar offense by charging too much for what you get. I've listed only safe choices. Remember: When dialing the following phone numbers from within the country of Belize but outside Belize City, drop the country code and dial 0 before the first digit.

DOUBLES FOR LESS THAN B$50 ($25)

EYRE STREET GUEST HOUSE, 7 Eyre St., Belize City. Tel. 501-2/77724. 9 rms (2 with bath).

$ Rates: B$31.80 ($15.90) single without bath; B$42.40 ($21.20) double without bath, B$63.60 ($31.80) double with bath; B$68.90 ($34.45) triple without bath, B$84.80 ($42.40) triple with bath. No credit cards.

Secure, quiet, and reasonably priced, this guest house has three of the qualities difficult to find in a hotel in Belize City. It's located in a good neighborhood around the corner from the U.S. embassy. The old-style house is in the process of being restored, and has some nice features such as a veranda and a bit of grass in front. Some of the rooms are dark and stuffy, but the staff is very friendly and will cook you breakfast in the morning.

SEASIDE GUEST HOUSE, 3 Prince St., Belize City. Tel. 501-2/78339. 6 rms.

$ Rates: to be determined. No credit cards.

⑤ One of Belize City's most popular low-budget lodgings, the Seaside is located on a very quiet street just off Southern Foreshore. Unfortunately, the Seaside was slated to be sold the last time I visited, and its future as a guest house was uncertain. This typical Caribbean wood-frame house has been a haven for the backpack crowd, and it's very difficult to secure space on the first day that you're in town. If you want to stay here, call and make a reservation. There are only two singles, three doubles, and a five-bed dorm here—but they're all clean. And there are lots of maps of Belize on the walls for those interested in exploring the interior. Breakfasts are served at an additional cost, and there is a coffee shop upstairs.

DOUBLES FOR LESS THAN B$90 ($45)

BELIZE GUEST HOUSE, 2 Hutson St., Belize City. Tel. 501-2/77569. 4 rms (2 with bath).

$ Rates: B$50 ($25) single or double without bath; B$70 ($35) single or double with bath. MC, V.

This guest house is in my favorite Belize City neighborhood, in which the shady streets are lined with stately old homes that once housed the British officials who governed Belize. Today, the neighborhood is home to embassies, doctors, and lawyers. Although this is not one of the more attractive homes in the neighborhood, it is the closest to the water. In fact, the Belize Guest House claims that it is only 5 feet from the water. The rooms are large but not well furnished. The best feature of this guest house is the veranda, which looks out over the Caribbean and catches the nearly constant trade winds. Ask for a room that faces the sea. There is a bar and restaurant downstairs and a large lounge with dark wood-paneled walls upstairs. Laundry service is available.

COLTON HOUSE, 9 Cork St., Belize. Tel. 501-2/44666. 4 rms (2 with bath).

$ Rates: B$63.60 ($31.80) single without bath, B$74.20 ($37.10) single with bath; B$74.20 ($37.10) double without bath, B$84.80 ($42.40) double with bath; B$90.10 ($45.05) triple without bath, B$100.70 ($50.35) triple with bath. No credit cards.

Located in Belize City's most attractive historic neighborhood, Colton House is directly across the street from the much pricier Radisson Fort George Hotel. A lushly planted yard, a wide veranda, hardwood floors, shuttered windows, and big rooms with high ceilings and overhead fans all add up to a tropical colonial atmosphere, although the furnishings lack the tropical style of the building. If you can afford to spend a bit more, you can't do much better than this. It's easy to forget you're in Belize City.

HOTEL EL CENTRO, 4 Bishop St., P.O. Box 2267, Belize City. Tel. 501-2/72413, 77739, or 78101. Fax 501-2/74553. 13 rms (all with bath). TV TEL

$ Rates: B$79.50 ($39.75) single; B$90.10 ($45.05) double; B$100.70 ($50.35) triple. AE, MC, V.

This is a bit of a splurge, but the rooms are fairly new, generally clean, and air-conditioned. Some are quite large and all are comfortable by Belize City standards. There is even a lawn in back of the hotel, which is a rarity around here. The hotel is right in the heart of the business and shopping district, with several restaurants within a few blocks. At street level is an air-conditioned restaurant where you can get breakfast, lunch, and dinner.

WORTH THE EXTRA BUCKS

THE BAKADEER INN, 74 Cleghorn St., P.O. Box 512, Belize City. Tel. 501-2/31400. Fax 501-2/31963. 12 rms (all with bath).

$ Rates: B$106 ($53) single; B$116.60 ($58.30) double. AE, DISC, MC, V.

Built in 1990, this inn has a pleasant Tudor exterior, and the rooms, although furnished in a chain-motel style, are clean and have air-conditioning, telephones, cable TV, and refrigerators. A restaurant is conveniently located downstairs. If you are driving a car, you'll be glad to know that the parking area is very secure. Rates here are lower between May 1 and October 31.

FORT STREET RESTAURANT & GUESTHOUSE, 4 Fort St., P.O. Box 3, Belize City. Tel. 501-2/30116. Fax 501/2-78808. 6 rms (none with bath).

$ Rates (including full breakfast): B$95.40 ($47.70) single; B$127.20 ($63.60) double. DISC, MC, V.

⭐ There aren't too many old homes left in Belize City—repeated hurricanes have made sure of that—so it is a special treat to stay in this, one of the city's old gems. Even though all the rooms here share one bathroom (a definite drawback), you won't find accommodations like these anywhere else in town. Situated on a triangular corner lot with a grassy front yard, the lovely, restored 1928 house has a long flight of steps leading up to the first floor, where you'll find a gift shop selling many Guatemalan típicos. The guest rooms are located on the second floor, where you'll also find two wicker sitting areas. The table settings of crystal goblets and linen cloths set a very romantic mood in the first-floor dining room. The woodwork is dark and rich; it's right out of an old New England village, with a dash of Caribbean thrown in. You place your breakfast order the night before by leaving a note in a bottle outside the door of your room. Lunch, served from 11am to 2pm, is a good value at B$7 ($3.50) to B$13 ($6.50). Dinner is pricey at B$27.50 ($13.75) to $32 ($16).

WHERE TO EAT

MEALS FOR LESS THAN B$20 ($10)

DIT'S, 50 King St. Tel. 73330.
  Cuisine: CAKES.
$ Prices: Slice of cake 75–B$1.50 (40¢–75¢); meals B$2.50–B$8 ($1.25–$4).
  Open: Mon–Sat 7am–9pm, Sun 8am–4pm.

When a cake craving strikes you in Belize City, search out this little place. A tempting assortment of cakes and pies are displayed in a glass case at the counter, with many

Central American specialties that you may never have encountered before—such as cow pie, raisin pie, three-milks cake, and coconut tarts. Dit's also serves simple meals.

MACY'S, 18 Bishop St. Tel. 73419.
   Cuisine: BELIZEAN.
   $ Prices: B$9–B$14 ($4.50–$7). No credit cards.
   Open: Mon–Sat 11:30am–9:30pm.
For authentic Belizean cooking, try this tiny local place. The food is consistent, the service is friendly, and the dining room is cool and cozy. Order a fish filet with rice and beans for B$9 ($4.50), or be more daring and try one of their daily chalkboard specials. You may want to skip the wild game to help preserve Belize's wildlife. A tall glass of cold, fresh-squeezed orange juice is a bargain in the Belizean heat at B$2.50 ($1.25).

POP 'N TACO, 24 Regent St. Tel. 73826.
   Cuisine: CHINESE.
   $ Prices: B$2–B$19 ($1–$9.50). No credit cards.
   Open: Lunch Mon–Sat 9am–3pm; dinner Mon–Sat 5–9:30pm.
Despite its Mexican name, this is primarily a Chinese restaurant popular with folks from the surrounding neighborhood (which happens to house several budget hotels). There are a few tables in the simple restaurant, or you can get your food to go. Most dishes are priced at around B$10 ($5).

MEALS FOR LESS THAN B$25 [$12.50]

GUANG ZHOU RESTAURANT, 3 Cork St. Tel. 35179.
   Cuisine: CHINESE.
   $ Prices: Main dishes B$8–$B19.50 ($4–$9.75). No credit cards.
   Open: Lunch daily 11:30am–2:30pm; dinner 5:30–10pm. Dim Sum Sun 10am–2:30pm.
Lots of wall fans keep it cool, and except for some little chandeliers near the tables, it's nothing fancy, but the food is actually quite good by local standards. Try Dou Fu Potage, satay kabobs, or sweet potato dumplings. Baked shrimp with ginger and green onions is B$19.50 ($9.75). Also on the menu (in season) is that melding of Belizean and Chinese cuisines, lobster chow mein. Beer and liquor are served here, as is Dim Sum on Sundays.

KADEL'S, Second floor, Commercial Center. Tel. 70103.
   Cuisine: BELIZEAN/MEXICAN. **Reservations:** Accepted
   $ Prices: Main dishes B$7.50–$B20 ($3.75–$10). No credit cards.
   Open: Mon–Sat 7am–10pm.
Located in the new Belize City market, Kadel's is named after the restaurant's chef, who worked in Los Angeles and New York before opening this restaurant. The menu is fairly standard, with the exception of a couple of items such as shrimp scampi or Belizean spicy shrimp, but the atmosphere is clean and pleasant. From the big windows there are great views of the boats in the river, and the bamboo walls are covered with photographs. Breakfast at Kadel's will run you about B$7 ($3.50).

SEA ROCK INDIAN RESTAURANT, 35 Queen St. Tel. 34105.
   Cuisine: INDIAN.
   $ Prices: Main dishes B$10–B$18 ($5–$9). No credit cards.
   Open: Mon–Sat 11:30am–11pm, Sun 5–11pm.

IMPRESSIONS

If the world had any ends British Honduras [Belize] would certainly be one of them.
—ALDOUS HUXLEY, *BEYOND THE MEXIQUE BAY*, 1934

✪ This place is run by an Indian family, so you know the food is delicious and authentic, as the local people, gringoes, and video enthusiasts here will attest. Tandoori chicken for B$10 ($5) and chicken in yogurt and spices B$12 ($6) are tender and well flavored. Choices include dhal kashmiri, lentils and spinach, and crunchy vegetable samosas—in fact, a vegetarian can dine nicely here.

EVENING ENTERTAINMENT

The numerous bars in Belize City can be rough places and are not recommended unless you have a local guide to take you to places he knows. If you just want to relax over a drink, try the second-floor bar at the **Bellevue Hotel** on Southern Foreshore. It looks over the water and occasionally has live bands on the weekends.

The **Baron Bliss Institute,** 1 Bliss Promenade. Tel. 02-77267, named for and financed by Belize City's benefactor, is the city's cultural center, where you'll find a public library, three Mayan stelae, and occasional cultural performances, including the annual Festival of the Arts.

EXCURSIONS
THE BELIZE ZOO

By the time you finally get around to visiting the **Belize Zoo,** you'll already be familiar with the zoo's most famous resident—April the tapir—because her picture appears on posters all over the country. April is just one of dozens of species of animals native to Belize that are housed in this zoo. Among the most popular are a variety of indigenous Belizean cats and other wild animals in natural surroundings. The animals here are some of the liveliest and happiest looking that I've ever seen in a zoo. It's obvious that they're well cared for. All the exhibits have informative signs accompanying them.

The entrance is a mile in from the Western Highway. Any bus traveling between Belize City and Belmopan or San Ignacio will drop you off at the zoo entrance. Do a bit of calculating as to when the next bus will be coming by, or plan on hitching to your next destination.

Admission is B$10 ($5). Open daily 9:30am to 4pm, the zoo is at mile 28 Western Highway.

ALTUN HA RUINS

About 30 miles north of Belize City on the Old Northern Highway are the ruins of Altun Ha, an ancient Mayan city thought to have existed here since about A.D. 250. Watch for the turnoff to the right just past Sand Hill. Once you're on the Old Northern Highway, watch for a small and rather inconspicuous sign for the Maruba Resort on the right side of the road. From the highway, it's a bumpy 2¼ miles to the ruins. About 1½ miles in, the road forks—take the right fork.

Altun Ha flourished during the Classic Period of Mayan civilization, up to the 800s. It was an important trading center linking the coastal and interior settlements. Only a few of the most imposing temples, tombs, and pyramids have been uncovered and rebuilt; hundreds more lie under the jungle foliage. The unique jade-head sculpture of Kinich Ahau (the Mayan sun god), the largest well-carved jade from the Mayan era, was discovered here. Today, it's kept in a bank vault in Belize City out of public view. The site was named after the village in which it's situated—Rockstone Pond, the literal Mayan translation meaning "stone water." The archeological work was done principally by the Royal Ontario Museum beginning in 1964, and although restoration has resulted in some anachronistic juxtapositions, it's a beautiful ruined city, well worth the visit. Open daily from 8am to 5pm, admission is B$3 ($1.50), children under 12 are free. There is no public transport to Altun Ha, so you'll need to take a tour, a taxi, your own wheels, or hitchhike.

A soft-drink stand and picnic area are available. Don't go too far off the beaten track in this area. (You wouldn't want to stumble on someone's private marijuana plantation.) If you're an intrepid explorer of lost ruins, get a guide.

COMMUNITY BABOON SANCTUARY

No, there aren't really baboons in Belize, this is just the local name for the black howler monkeys who reside in this innovative sanctuary. The sanctuary is a voluntary program run by local landowners in eight villages to preserve the local population of these endangered and vociferous primates. There is a visitors' center and natural history museum in the village of Bermudian Landing, and it is here that you can pay your minimal admission fee. The admission fee includes the services of a guide, so don't bother hiring one of the local guides. There are several trails through the preserve and as you walk along, you will undoubtedly hear the whooping and barking of the howler monkeys as they make their way through the treetops feeding on fruits, flowers, and leaves. Most visitors also see a few monkeys, though they are often quite high in the trees. Carry binoculars. Many other species, especially birds, make their homes in this preserve.

Bermudian Landing village, site of the preserve's visitor center, is about 20 miles west of Belize City. If you are driving, head north on the Northern Highway and watch for the Burrel Boom Road turnoff. Buses to Bermudian Landing leave Belize City Monday through Saturday at 12:30pm from the corner of Orange and Mosul streets and at 12:30, 1, 3:30, and 5pm from the corner of Orange and George streets. Buses return to Belize City at 5:30 and 6am. The fare is around B$2 ($1). Accommodations are available with local families for B$15 ($7.50) single and B$20 ($10) double. Three meals will cost an additional B$15 ($7.50) per person. For more information or to make a reservation for accommodations, contact the Belize Audubon Society, 12 Fort St. (P.O. Box 1001), Belize City, (tel. 501/2-35004). Be sure to bring mosquito repellent and/or mosquito coils if you plan to stay overnight.

CROOKED TREE WILDLIFE SANCTUARY

Crooked Tree Wildlife Preserve is a swampy lowland that serves as a resting spot for dozens of species of migratory birds, including kites, hawks, ducks, grebes, pelicans, ospreys, egrets, and herons. However, the preserve was established primarily to protect Belize's main nesting site of the endangered jabiru stork, the largest bird in the western hemisphere. Crooked Tree has rapidly become known as an excellent place to spot other endangered wildlife as well. Crocodiles, iguanas, coatimundi, and howler monkeys are all frequently sighted. The best way to explore the preserve's swamps, lagoons, and waterways is by dugout canoe. Ask in town or at the sanctuary's visitor center and administrative building for a local who will paddle you around in a dugout for a few hours.

Crooked Tree is located 33 miles northwest of Belize City. If you are driving, head up the Northern Highway and watch for the turnoff to Crooked Tree. Buses leave for Crooked Tree Village from the Batty Bros. bus terminal on Mosul Street (one block before West Collet Canal) Monday through Friday at 4pm, returning at 7am the following day; Saturdays at noon, returning at 4pm; and Sundays at 9am, returning at 4pm.

Jex bus company leaves from the same terminal Monday through Saturday at 10:55am and 5:15pm, returning from Crooked Tree at 5:30 and 7am and 2:15pm. The fare is around B$4 ($2). If you'd like to spend the night, accommodations can be arranged with a local family for B$15 ($7.50) single or B$20 ($10) double. Meals are an additional B$15 ($7.50) per person. For more information or to make a room reservation, contact the Belize Audubon Society, 12 Fort St. (P.O. Box 1001), Belize City (tel. 501-2/35004).

2. AMBERGRIS CAYE

36 miles N of Belize City; 40 miles SE of Corozal Town

GETTING THERE By Plane   There are dozens of daily flights between Belize

City and San Pedro on Ambergris Caye. Flights leave from both the Philip S. W. Goldson International Airport and the Belize City Municipal Airport. If you're coming in on an international flight and heading straight for San Pedro, you should book a flight from the international airport. If you're already in Belize City it's cheaper to fly from the municipal airport, which is also cheaper to reach by taxi. Tropic Air (tel. 2/45671 in Belize City, 26/2012 in San Pedro), Island Air (tel. 2/31140 in Belize City, 26/2435 in San Pedro), and Maya Airways (tel. 2/72312 in Belize City, 26/2611 in San Pedro) are the three main airlines flying to San Pedro. Duration: 20–30 minutes. Fare (from the municipal airport): B$39 ($19.50) one way and B$70 ($35) round-trip. Fares from the international airport are higher. Because a taxi into Belize City from the international airport costs B$30 ($15) and the boat to San Pedro costs B$20 ($10), it is only slightly more expensive to fly if you are heading directly to San Pedro after arriving on an international flight.

Island Air (tel. 022/2013 on Caye Caulker) has several flights each day between Caye Caulker and Ambergris Caye. Duration: 15 minutes. Fare: B$35 ($17.50) one way, B$60 ($30) round-trip.

There are two flights a day between Corozal Town and San Pedro on Tropic Air. Duration: 20 minutes. Fare: B$60 ($30) one way, B$120 ($60) round-trip.

By Boat   The *Andrea* and *Andrea II* (tel. 2/74988 in Belize City; 26/2578 in San Pedro) ply from Belize City to San Pedro Monday through Saturday, departing from a pier near the Bellevue Hotel on Southern Foreshore at 3pm. Duration: 75 minutes. Fare: B$20 ($10) each way.

If you're going to Ambergris Caye from Caye Caulker, the fastest boat is the *Triple J* (tel. 2/33464 in Belize City) at 10am daily. Check at one of Caye Caulker's travel agencies to make a reservation and find out where the *Triple J* stops. Duration: 45 minutes. Fare: B$12 ($6) each way.

You can also sail over from Caye Caulker on one of the sailboats that go out to Hol Chan Marine Reserve. These boats usually stop for lunch on Ambergris Caye, and there is nothing to stop you from staying in San Pedro. Fare: B$30 ($15). Departures from Caye Caulker are around 10am. Find out about trips by asking in front of the Reef Hotel.

DEPARTING   The *Andrea* and *Andrea II* leave San Pedro Monday through Saturday at 7am. Their dock is toward the north end of San Pedro on the reef side of the town. The *Triple J,* which leaves from a dock on the reef side of the island toward the north end of town, departs daily at 3pm for Caye Caulker and Belize City. Flights leave throughout the day for Belize City's two airports and Caye Caulker. Boat and plane reservations can be made at any of the travel agencies along Barrier Reef Drive. For plane reservations, you can also walk to the airport and make a reservation in person.

ESSENTIALS Orientation   San Pedro (the only town on the island of Ambergris Caye) is three streets wide. The streets, from seaside to lagoonside, are Barrier Reef Drive (Front Street), Pescador Drive (Middle Street), and Angel Coral Street (Back Street). The airport is at the south end of town.

Fast Facts   Belize Bank, across from the Spindrift Hotel on Barrier Reef Drive, is open Monday to Thursday 8am to 1pm and Friday 8am to 1pm and 3 to 6pm. Lopez Drugs is in a shopping center on Barrier Reef Drive toward the north end of town—open daily 8am to noon, 2 to 5pm, and 7 to 9pm. Emergency numbers: police 2022; fire 2372; medical 2234. The post office is located on a cross street near the Atlantic Bank and just around the corner from Barrier Reef Drive. It's open Monday through Thursday from 8am to noon and from 1 to 5pm and on Friday from 8am to noon and from 1 to 4:30pm. The B.T.L. telephone office is at the north end of town on Pescador Drive and is open Monday through Friday from 8am to noon and 1 to 4pm and on Saturday from 8am to noon. There are two laundries on Pescador Drive toward the south end of town.

Long before the British settled Belize, and long before the sun-seeking vacationers and zealous reef divers discovered Ambergris Caye, the Mayas were here. In fact, the Mayas created Ambergris Caye when they cut a channel through the long thin peninsula that extended down from what is now Mexico. The channel was cut to facilitate coastal trading and avoid the dangerous barrier reef that begins not too far north of San Pedro. Today Ambergris Caye is 25 miles long and only half a mile wide.

For many years now the town of San Pedro has been Belize's main sun-and-fun community and it is here that you'll find the country's largest concentration of tourist developments. Though San Pedro once attracted primarily scuba divers and fishermen, it is today popular with a wide range of folks who like the slow-paced atmosphere. People compare the island to the Florida Keys 30 or 40 years ago, though San Pedro is rapidly catching up. The town still has no paved streets, but automobiles are proliferating and wooden Caribbean houses have given way to concrete and cinder-block buildings. Unfortunately, in the process, the town has lost almost all of its shade trees, so be sure to bring a good sun block and sunglasses.

Most of Ambergris Caye is still uninhabited, but nearly all of it has been subdivided and sold to developers. Despite the fact that much of the island is seasonally flooded mangrove forest, and despite laws prohibiting the cutting of mangroves, developers continue to clear this marginal land. Indiscriminate cutting of the mangroves is already having an adverse effect on the nearby barrier reef: Without the mangroves to filter the water and slow the impact of waves, silt is formed and carried out to the reef where it settles and kills the coral. Hopefully, before it is too late, something will be done to stop the destruction of the coral reef—the very reason people come to Ambergris Caye.

WHAT TO SEE & DO

This is a beach resort, so you can expect to find most of the standard activities (on a limited scale). There are no submarine rides, but you can rent a sailboard; there are no sunset dine-and-dance cruises, but you do get a rum punch when you go out on a glass-bottomed boat. Sorry golfers: There are no golf courses here—yet.

First, you should be aware that there really isn't any beach to speak of on Ambergris Caye: There is a narrow strip of sand where the land meets the sea, but even at low tide it isn't wide enough for you to unroll a beach towel on in most places. The widest section of sand happens to be right in the middle of town, where all the boats dock (not a pleasant place to hang out). Try walking north or south from town along the water to find a more secluded spot where you can sit and stare out to sea. Otherwise, the beachfront (read "expensive") hotels create their own beaches by building retaining walls and filling them in with sand.

Likewise, swimming is not what you might expect. For 100 yards or more out from shore, the bottom is covered with sea grass. Beneath the grass is a layer of spongy roots and organic matter topped with a thin layer of white sand. Walking on this spongy sand is most unnerving, and it's easy to trip and stumble. Swimming is best off the pier at the Paradise Resort Hotel, where the management has created a sort of swimming pool in the sea by scooping out a deep spot and clearing away all the grass. All the beaches on the caye are public, and you can probably use the hotel's lounge chairs if it's a slow day. The best swimming is from boats anchored out in the turquoise waters between the shore and the reef.

So why do people bother to come here if there is no beach and you can't go swimming right off the shore? They come for the turquoise waters and the coral reef. Less than a quarter mile offshore is the longest coral reef in the western hemisphere. Only Australia's Barrier Reef is longer than this one.

For reliable scuba diving service and reasonable rates, contact **Out Island Divers,** P.O. Box 7, San Pedro (tel. 2151), which is across from the Spindrift Hotel on Barrier Reef Drive. This company leads dives to popular nearby sites and also offers a day trip to the famous Blue Hole, a huge offshore sinkhole (collapsed cavern) made famous by Jacques Cousteau. A 1-day dive trip to the Blue Hole is pricey and will run you between B$330 ($165) and B$390 ($195) depending on whether you take the boat or a small plane out to the dive site. These trips include three dives. For nearby dives and rental equipment, try **Bottom Time Dive Shop,** at the Sunbreeze Hotel on the south end of Barrier Reef Drive (tel. 2348) where two dives with all equipment included will cost B$130 ($65). The **Holiday Dive Shop,** at the Holiday Hotel (tel. 2437) charges around B$100 ($50) for two dives, including equipment. There's a diving school at Ramon's Reef Hotel, where you can practice in the pool before going out. Snorkeling equipment is available at several locations in town for about B$12 ($6). If you're an independent type, just rent your own snorkeling gear and hop off one of the docks. However, you really need to go out to the reef to see much of anything other than sand and sea grass.

The best snorkeling is at the **Hol Chan Marine Reserve,** which is about four miles southeast of San Pedro. *Hol chan* is a Mayan term meaning "little channel," which is exactly what you'll find here—a narrow channel cutting through the shallow coral reef. The walls of the channel are popular with divers, and the shallower areas are frequented by snorkelers. Some of the exciting residents of the area are several large green moray eels (friendly but dangerous), stingrays (don't touch), and nurse sharks (harmless). The reserve covers 5 square miles and is divided into three zones: the reef, the sea-grass beds, and the mangroves. There is a B$3 ($1.50) charge for diving at Hol Chan, which is usually not included in the price of boat excursions to the reserve.

There are several boats offering trips out here. The *Reef Seeker* **Glass-Bottom Boat** tour for B$25 ($12.50) includes a 1-hour trip, an hour of snorkeling (snorkel gear not included), and a complimentary rum punch. Unfortunately, Hol Chan seems to be getting too many visitors and the coral seems to be dying and there are fewer and fewer fish here each year. You may want to consider visiting a different snorkeling site, such as Mexico Rocks Coral Gardens, Tres Cocos, or Mata Rocks. **Island Adventures** (tel. 2697), on the pier at Fido's, and **Amigo Travel** (tel. 2180), on Barrier Reef Drive, both offer snorkeling trips to other sites outside the marine reserve. These trips range in price from B$25 ($12.50) to B$36 ($18), but snorkel gear is not included.

Another trip that has recently become popular is a day trip to see manatees and do some snorkeling at remote cayes. These trips are offered by several companies around San Pedro and cost around B$80 ($40).

You can also make arrangements at Amigo Travel for a full day on the catamaran *Me Too.* For B$80 ($40), you get snorkeling equipment and instruction, a guide, drinks, and bathroom facilities. The *Winnie Estelle,* a 66-foot island trader sailboat operated by **Heritage Navigation** (tel. 2394) does a similar trip for B$90 ($45) and leaves from the Paradise Hotel dock. Alternatively, Island Adventures offers a sunset cruise for B$30 ($15).

The local windsurfing school is housed at Ramon's Village resort. Rental rates are B$30 ($15) per hour. At Island Adventures, you can also rent kayaks and canoes for B$10 ($5) per hour and powerboats for between B$30 and B$40 ($15 and $20) per hour.

Sportfishing for tarpon and bonefish is among the best in the world around these cayes, and over the years a few record catches have been made. At Ruby's Hotel you can arrange a half day of angling for bonefish, tarpon, or reef fish for B$200 ($100) or a full day for B$300 ($150). If you prefer deep-sea fishing, contact **Hustler Tours** (tel. 2279 or 2538), which charges B$500 ($250) for a half-day fishing trip and B$700 ($350) for a full-day trip.

If you'd like to explore Ambergris Caye itself, you can rent a bike for around B$5 ($2.50) per hour, a motor scooter for around B$16 ($8) per hour, or golf cart for between B$25 ($12.50) and B$30 ($15) per hour at several places around town (rates are lower by the half day or full day). If you'd like to explore the island on horseback, stop by **Equestrian Stables** (tel. 2895) at the north end of Pescador Drive. However, horses rent for a whopping B$40 ($20) per hour.

WHERE TO STAY

DOUBLES FOR LESS THAN B$30 [$15]

MILO'S, P.O. Box 21, San Pedro, Ambergris Caye. Tel. 501-26/2033. Fax 501-26/2463 16 rms (2 with bath).
$ Rates: B$21.20 ($10.60) single without bath; B$26.50 ($13.25) double without bath, B$63.60 ($31.80) single or double with bath; B$37.10 ($18.55) triple without bath. MC, V.

Milo's are among the cheapest rooms on the island for a few reasons: You'll share a bathroom with someone else, the rooms are rather dark, and there's no atmosphere to speak of. Some people swear by Milo's, though. The question you must answer for yourself is: How much time will I be spending in my room? At least the shared bathrooms here are clean. You can find out about rooms here in the general store downstairs. Milo's is just before the Paradise Hotel on Front Street. There are also a couple of more expensive rooms with private bathrooms and air-conditioning (B$5 extra per person).

RUBY'S HOTEL, Barrier Reef Dr., P.O. Box 56, San Pedro, Ambergris Caye. Tel. 501-26/2063. Fax 501-26/2434. 19 rms (15 with bath).
$ Rates: B$26.50–B$31.80 ($13.25–$15.90) single or double without bath; B$53–B$74.20 ($26.50–$37.10) single or double with bath. No credit cards.

⭐ Down at the airport end of town, you'll find a place called Ruby's. Most of the rooms overlook the water. In fact, this is definitely the cheapest place on the island with a water view. The floors are wooden, the rooms are simply furnished with a couple of beds and little else, and the showers are generally clean.

SEYCHELLES GUEST HOUSE, San Pedro, Ambergris Caye. Tel. 501-26/2649. 4 rooms (all with shared bath).
$ Rates: B$20 ($10) single; B$25 ($12.50) double. No credit cards.

This older house on stilts is just south of the airport and is operated as a sort of casual bed-and-breakfast by Sandra Cooper, a young Belizean woman. The rooms are small and quite Spartan, but all have fans. There is a combination living room and dining room where guests can hang out, and a kitchen that they can use. From the front porch, there is a view of the water.

DOUBLES FOR LESS THAN B$70 [$35]

HOTEL SAN PEDRANO, Barrier Reef Dr. San Pedro, Ambergris Caye. Tel. 501-26/2054. Fax 501-26/2093. 7 rms (all with bath).
$ Rates: Nov–Apr B$57 ($28.50) single, B$68.40 ($34.20) double, B$85.50 ($42.75) triple; May–Oct B$45.60 ($22.80) single, B$57 ($28.50) double, B$68.40 ($34.20) triple.

Although few of the rooms here have ocean views, they do have nice wooden floors and well-maintained blue patio furniture. There are a single and a double bed in every room and clean baths with tubs. What views you do have from the wide veranda are over the rooftops of adjacent buildings. The hotel is upstairs from a small gift shop toward the northern end of Front Street.

MARTHA'S, Pescador Dr. (P.O. Box 27), San Pedro, Ambergris Caye. Tel. 501-26/2053. Fax 501-26/2589. 13 rms (all with bath).
$ Rates: Nov–Apr B$46 ($23) single, B$69 ($34.50) double, B$92 ($46) triple; May–Oct B$30 ($15) single, B$55 ($27.50) double, B$75 ($37.50) triple. AE.

It's hard to believe that a hotel located upstairs from a grocery store could be so expensive, but here in San Pedro, nothing is cheap. At least the new rooms here are larger than those at most other hotels. There are reading lights over the two double beds, ceiling fans, and big verandas at either end of the building so that you can watch the sunrise or sunset. You'll find Martha's about halfway down Pescador Drive.

FROMMER'S SMART TRAVELER: HOTELS

1. Consider renting a house for your stay if you're coming here with your family or a group of friends. Most rental houses are in the more attractive parts of the island away from San Pedro. Check with Amigo Travel (tel. 26/2180) on Barrier Reef Drive.
2. If you're on a tight budget, get a room without a private bath. There are only a few of these left on the island, so be sure to make a reservation.
3. Visit the island during the summer (June through Aug), if you can stand the heat, and you'll pay lower rates at most hotels.
4. If you crave peace and quiet, try to get as far away from the airport as possible (though luckily flights only operate during daylight hours).

TOMAS HOTEL, Barrier Reef Dr., San Pedro, Ambergris Caye. Tel. 501-26/2061. 8 rms (all with bath).
$ Rates: B$53 ($26.50) single; B$53 ($26.50) double, B$74.20 ($37.10) double with A/C; B$63.60 ($31.80) triple, B$84.80 ($42.40) triple with A/C. MC, V.
Toward the north end of Front Street, directly across the street from an old blue wooden house with flower designs on it, you'll spot the sign for the Tomas Hotel. The modern cement building is one of the better budget hotels on the island. All the rooms have tile floors, very clean bathrooms, and fans. There's a deck on the second floor where you can get a bit of sun.

DOUBLES FOR LESS THAN B$90 [$45]

LILY'S, on the beach, San Pedro, Ambergris Caye. Tel. 501-26/2059. 10 rms (all with bath).
$ Rates: Nov–May B$53 ($26.50) single, B$74.20 ($37.10) double; May–Nov B$42.40 ($21.20) single, B$58.30 ($29.15) double. MC, V.
If you want a private bath and a water view, you'll have to pay for it. Lily's is on the beach, right behind the Tomas Hotel, which is toward the north end of Front Street. The rooms are large and have ceiling and table fans, wood paneling, and typical fluorescent lighting. Get your money's worth by watching the sun rise every morning and listening to the waves lap at your doorstep after the sun sets. You'll find a seating area on the front veranda and lounge chairs on the beach for the guests' use. Don't forget your mosquito repellent. Not all of the rooms here have a water view—be sure to ask.

PIRATE'S LANTERN GUEST HOUSE, P.O. Box 28, San Pedro, Ambergris Caye. Tel. 501-26/2146. Fax 501-26/2726. 5 rms (all with bath).
$ Rates: B$50 ($25) single; B$70 ($35) double; B$90 ($45) triple. MC, V.
Though it is a bit of a walk south from the airport, this small guest house benefits from being outside of town. There are trees and shrubs out here, and the second-floor rooms overlook a shrubby area that attracts several different species of birds. Rooms have hardwood floors and wicker furniture and there's a veranda across the second floor. There's a restaurant and bar on the first floor. If you're paying by credit card, add 5% to your bill.

SANDS HOTEL, Barrier Reef Dr., San Pedro, Ambergris Caye. Tel. 501-26/2040, or in the U.S. 713/723-6171. Fax 501-26/2618.
$ Rates: B$80–B$120 ($40–$60) single or double. AE, MC, V.
Owned and operated by an American couple who moved down here years ago, the Sands Hotel is right in the middle of town and has one of the only gardens (albeit a bit cluttered) in San Pedro, which makes it a pleasant choice. There are several different styles of rooms, which vary in size and decor. Some rooms have kitchenettes, while others have king-size beds, but all have clean tiled bathrooms. There is a barbecue in

the garden and a sun deck up on the roof. You can rent bikes, canoes, and golf carts here.

WORTH THE EXTRA BUCKS

BARRIER REEF HOTEL, Barrier Reef Dr. (P.O. Box 34), San Pedro, Ambergris Caye. Tel. 501-26/2075. Fax 501-26/2719. 11 rms (all with bath). A/C

$ Rates: B$101.80 ($50.90) single; B$137.80 ($68.90) double; B$159 ($79.50) triple (lower off-season rates). AE, MC, V.

This pricey little hotel is my favorite building in San Pedro. Directly across the street from the town square, the Barrier Reef is a blindingly white building designed to resemble a traditional Caribbean wooden house. On the second floor is a long veranda, and on the third floor is a small balcony. Three gables extend seaward from the roof to complete the picture. Each room has a double and a single bed with a built-in headboard, tile floors, a fan, and air-conditioning. The nicest rooms are those facing the water, for the view and for access to the best section of veranda. On the first floor, the Navigator restaurant and bar is a very casual place serving pizza for B$16 to B$38 ($8 to $19). Daily specials include such fare as shrimp scampi and fish filet in lemon sauce.

HIDE-A-WAY HOTEL, P.O. Box 484, San Pedro, Ambergris Caye. Tel. 501-26/2141 or 2269. 30 rms (all with bath).

$ Rates: B$74.20 ($37.10) single; B$95.40 ($47.70) double; B$159 ($79.50) triple. AE, DISC, MC, V.

Located just south of the airport, the Hide-A-Way is the cheapest hotel you'll find in San Pedro with a pool, and though it's a small pool, it does give you an easy place to go swimming. The hotel has a bit too much cement around it (and walls in the rooms are cinder block), which tends to make the rooms a bit hot. However, if you spend your days in the water, it shouldn't matter too much. The Hide-A-Way is fairly comfortable, though very basic. What you're paying for here is the pool. The bar can get a bit noisy at night, so ask for a room toward the back.

HOTEL CASABLANCA, Pescador Drive, San Pedro, Ambergris Caye. Tel. 501-26/2327. Fax 501-26/2992. 5 rms (all with bath). A/C

$ Rates: B$100 ($50) single, double, or triple. MC, V.

This hotel, owned and operated by a former nightclub designer from Britain, is a refreshingly contemporary hotel that diverges from the San Pedro norm. Instead of bamboo furnishings and tropical motifs, you'll find a sort of merger of Miami Beach modern and Marrakesh Moorish. There are bright, primary colors everywhere, unusual cement corner shelves, and contemporary furniture designs (even stylish steel chairs). The guest rooms have king-size beds and are comfortably stark. On the ground floor, there's the best restaurant on the island, and up on the roof, there's the Sunset Bar, with a great view of San Pedro and the waters all around.

OASIS DE MAR, P.O. Box 89, San Pedro Town, Ambergris Caye. Tel. 501-26/2695. Fax 501-26/2254. 6 cabins (all with bath).

$ Rates: B$78–B$130 ($39–$65) single, double, triple, or quad. MC, V.

Located just south of the airport on the outskirts of town, this collection of tropical cabins really lives up to its name. Though the frequent flights make this place noisy during the day, the shade trees, flowers, and shrubs make it a genuine oasis in barren San Pedro. The cabins sleep up to four people and are all quite spacious. High ceilings, louvered windows, and ceiling fans help keep the rooms cool, and there are kitchenettes. Though the price is high for one or two people, this is a deal for three or four. Lower rates are in summer.

WHERE TO EAT

Seafood is, of course, the most popular food on the island, and there's plenty of it around all year. However, please keep in mind that there are seasons for lobster, conch, shrimp, and sea turtles (sea turtles are endangered, and turtle should never be ordered). Lobster is available from July 15 to February 14, conch is available from October 1 to June 30, and shrimp is available from August 15 to April 14. When lobster is in season, it's the best deal on the island, and you can order it for three meals a day and not go bankrupt. However, it is rock lobster and is not as flavorful as northern, cold-water lobster.

MEALS FOR LESS THAN B$10 [$5]

AMBERGRIS DELIGHT, Pescador Dr. No phone.
Cuisine: BELIZEAN.
$ Prices: B$7–B$12 ($3.50–$6). No credit cards.
Open: Lunch daily 11am–2pm; dinner daily 6–10pm.
Located a block north of Elvi's, Ambergris Delight is popular with locals and offers excellent and inexpensive burgers and seafood. A big blackboard serves as menu and includes occasional specials such as conch soup. The best deals are the combination dinners of rice and beans served with a fish filet, whole fried fish, broiled fish, or chicken for B$10 ($5). There are always a few cakes and pies on the counter.

THE PIZZA PLACE, Fido's Courtyard, Barrier Reef Dr. No phone.
Cuisine: PIZZA.
$ Prices: Whole pizza B$11–B$38 ($5.50–$19). No credit cards.
Open: Dinner Sun–Thurs 6:30–9pm, dinner Fri–Sat 6:30–10pm.
For a quick meal any day of the week, try this walk-up window. Sit at bar stools under a palapa hut, or take your meal away. Juices and shakes are B$3 ($1.50) but aren't very big. A large pizza here is plenty for four people.

MEALS FOR LESS THAN B$20 [$10]

ELVI'S KITCHEN, halfway down Pescador Dr. Tel. 2176.
Cuisine: SEAFOOD/INTERNATIONAL.
$ Prices: Seafood dinners B$10–B$35 ($5–$17.50). AE, MC, V.
Open: Lunch Mon–Sat 11am–2pm; dinner Mon–Sat 5:30–10pm.
Elvi's is the most popular restaurant on Ambergris Caye, and it may be the only restaurant in all of Belize that ever has a waiting line. Even after they enlarged the dining room, they still couldn't handle the dinner crowds who came for the substantial servings, good prices, and food cooked to order. The restaurant is a thatched, screened-in building with picnic tables, a tree growing up through the roof, and a floor of crushed shells and sand—very tropical. Fans cool the place nicely. A typical dinner here might include squid, scallops, and shrimps in red sauce with spaghetti, okra, and cream of vegetable soup. Be sure to have a fruit shake (*licuado*) while you're here. Surprisingly, there is also a very formal entry and bar area.

ESTEL'S DINE BY THE SEA, oceanside behind Atlantic Bank. Tel. 2019.
Cuisine: INTERNATIONAL.
$ Prices: Main dishes B$8–B$23 ($4–$11.50). No credit cards.
Open: Wed–Mon 6am–8pm.
If you want to dine right by the water, it's hard to get much closer than Estel's. This casual place has a sand floor and thatch roof and a sand terrace outside. The food, though pretty standard, gains from its proximity to the water. There's a Mexican plate, as well as barbecued chicken and grilled fish. In general, it's a mellow scene, with great music on the stereo.

JADE GARDEN, ¼ mile south of airstrip. Tel. 2126 or 2506.
Cuisine: CHINESE.
$ Prices: Appetizers B$10–B$14 ($5–$7); main dishes B$9–B$36 ($4.50–$18). AE, MC, V.
Open: Daily 11am–2pm, 6–10pm.
Located in a large contemporary house south of the airport, Jade Garden has long

been San Pedro's most popular restaurant. Wicker chairs, overhead fans, high ceilings, and a balcony overlooking the sea and garden create the atmosphere, and the kitchen serves up a long menu of well-prepared Chinese standards with the emphasis on seafood. There are also several non-Chinese specialties such as surf-and-turf kebabs, broiled lobster, and T-bone steak. After a big dinner, you can walk back to your hotel and burn up a few calories.

MEALS FOR LESS THAN B$30 ($15)

COCONUTS, one block south of Elvi's on Pescador Drive. Tel. 2184.
  Cuisine: INTERNATIONAL.
  $ Prices: Main dishes B$19.50–B$20.50 ($9.75–$10.25). No credit cards.
  Open: Tues–Sun 7am–midnight.
With appetizers such as smoked fish with curry salad and entrées such as breast of chicken served with plantain dumplings and curry sauce and brochettes of red snapper and shrimp served with lime-butter sauce, Coconuts has one of the more original menus in San Pedro. The small restaurant is very casual and has a sand floor (in classic Ambergris style), and the adjacent bar is full of beach balls. Lunches are quite a bit less expensive than dinner but aren't quite as imaginative, and breakfast is served as well.

LAGOON RESTAURANT, Pescador Dr. Tel. 2327.
  Cuisine: INTERNATIONAL.
  $ Prices: Appetizers B$5–B$6 ($2.50–$3); main dishes B$15–B$35 ($7.50–$17.50). MC, V.
  Open: Daily 6–10pm.
Located below the Hotel Casablanca, the Lagoon is an equally sophisticated place that brings contemporary North American restaurant decor to Belize. Custom-made steel chairs and candelabras, track lights, a deep blue ceiling painted with stars, and blue glass blocks in the bar spell out an urban chic that has never before been seen on Ambergris Caye. The menu here changes regularly, but instead of the standard Belizean fried fish dishes, you might find such offerings as chicken and pork satay; orange, onion, and radish salad; chilled cucumber soup; black bean lasagne; lobster anise; and cajun shrimp. Don't miss the watermelon granita with blackberry brandy.

LILY'S, on the beach in the middle of town. Tel. 2059.
  Cuisine: SEAFOOD. **Reservations:** Recommended.
  $ Prices: Main dishes B$25–B$30 ($12.50–$15); lunch B$15–B$20 ($7.50–$10). MC, V.
  Open: Daily, breakfast 6:30–11am, lunch 11am–2pm, dinner 5:30–9pm.
Lily's Hotel, on the waterfront, is also home to one of the best restaurants in San

Pedro. You don't get much choice here, but if you like seafood, you'll love this place. A fish, lobster, conch, or fish/shrimp combo dinner costs B$25 to B$30 and is served family style so that you can eat your fill. The delicious food is cooked to order and comes with french fries, cole slaw, and a vegetable. The restaurant itself is brightly lit, but there are candles on the tables and wicker chairs for atmosphere.

LITTLE ITALY RESTAURANT, Spindrift Hotel, Barrier Reef Drive. Tel. 2866.
Cuisine: ITALIAN.
$ Prices: Appetizers B$8–B$20 ($4–$10); main dishes B$13–B$35 ($6.50–$17.50). AE, MC, V.
Open: Lunch Thurs–Tues 11:30am–2pm; dinner Thurs–Tues 5:30–9pm.

At the back of the Spindrift Hotel, you'll find San Pedro's best Italian restaurant. It's located right on the water and has a terrace dining area as well as an indoor dining room. Though the decor is more tropical than Italian, the food is certainly authentic. Regular menu items include the likes of manicotti and spaghetti with shrimp or snapper, while the daily special might be something slightly less familiar such as fresh shrimp with linguine, sweet peppers, olives, and feta cheese. Desserts include ice cream with liqueur. There is a good wine list, as well as a full bar.

EVENING ENTERTAINMENT

THE TACKLE BOX BAR, off Barrier Reef Dr. near the south end of town. No phone.
The first thing to do is drop in for beer (B$3, $1.50) or a piña colada (B$7, $3.50) here at San Pedro's most famous bar, out at the end of a short pier. Local fishermen and sailors gather here to exchange information. If you want a boat to another caye, the folks behind the bar will be able to set you up with a ride. Nautical motifs decorate the interior, and out behind the back terrace is an enclosed tank full of sharks and giant sea turtles. Don't miss it!

BIG DADDY'S, across from the Barrier Reef Hotel and behind the church. No phone.
Nowhere have I ever seen a bar or disco located so close to a church. The saints and sinners seem to be in a competition to see who can play the loudest music. The church often throws its doors open and cranks up the volume on its organ, but there always seems to be more people in the disco. The dress is casual, and the drinks are not overpriced.

EXCURSIONS

If you've been on the island for a while and want to see more of Belize contact **Amigo Travel** (tel. 2180) or **Travel & Tour Belize** (tel. 2031), both on Barrier Reef Drive. They offer excursions to various locations—including Altun Ha, Xunantunich, Mountain Pine Ridge, and Tikal. The popular day trip to the Mayan ruins at Altun Ha begins on a powerful little boat that will whisk you over to the mainland. You'll then take a taxi to the ruins and have lunch before returning to San Pedro for B$116–B$120 ($58–$60) per person.

---

3. CAYE CAULKER

20 miles N of Belize City; 10 miles S of Ambergris Caye

GETTING THERE By Air Island Air (tel. 2/31140 in Belize City) has daily flights to Caye Caulker from both the international and municipal airports in Belize City. Duration: 20–30 minutes. Fare: B$35 ($17.50) one way from municipal airport,

B$60 ($30) one way from international airport. Island Air (tel. 26/2435 in San Pedro) also flies between Ambergris Caye and Caye Caulker. Duration: 15 minutes. Fare: B$35 ($17.50) one way, B$60 ($30) round-trip. If you just flew in to Belize from another country and are heading directly to Caye Caulker, you might consider flying, because the combination taxi into Belize City and boat to Caye Caulker cost B$41 ($20.50), only B$19 ($9.50) less than the plane.

By Boat   High-speed launches leave from behind the Texaco gas station on North Front Street. You'll find the gas station about 50 yards west of the Swing Bridge, downtown Belize City's main reference point. Several boats a day leave between 10am and 3pm. Duration: 50 minutes. Fare: B$10–12 ($5–6). You pay when you arrive at Caye Caulker. Unsavory street guides will offer to take you to the boat to Caye Caulker; these guides are not to be trusted, so don't wander off with one to negotiate any deals.

DEPARTING   There are daily flights to both Belize City airports and to Ambergris Caye. The boats heading back to Belize City charge between B$10 and B$15 ($5 and $7.50). Most boats leave Caye Caulker between 6 and 7am. It's a good idea to buy your ticket the day before you plan to leave. The *Triple J* speedboat makes the trip to Ambergris Caye daily at 10am.

You can also sail over to Ambergris Caye on one of the sailboats that go out to the Hol Chan Marine Reserve; these boats usually leave Caye Caulker around 10am and stop for lunch in San Pedro in the afternoon. Instead of sailing back, you can just stay in San Pedro.

ESSENTIALS   Orientation   Most boats dock at the Front Bridge, so named because this is the front side of the island facing the reef (east). The town extends north and south from here. As you debark, you'll be able to see the western side of the island and the Back Bridge/dock. Caye Caulker consists of two main sand roads, a few cross streets, and numerous paths.

Fast Facts   You can change money and traveler's checks at the Atlantic Bank, open Monday through Friday from 8am to noon and 1 to 2pm, and Saturday from 9am to noon, or at most hotels, though you'll probably get a better rate at the hotels. Several women on the island take in laundry; watch for their signs around town. The telephone office is about midway along Front Street and is open Monday to Friday 8am to noon and 1 to 4pm, Saturday 8am to noon. If you are calling somewhere else in Belize, remember to dial 0 before the phone number. Though Caye Caulker is still a relatively safe place, it is not advisable to leave money or valuables in your hotel room.

For more than 20 years Caye Caulker was the preferred destination of young backpackers traveling on a very low budget. Rooms and meals were cheap and the atmosphere was truly laid back. Though many new hotels and restaurants and even a few gift shops have sprouted over the years, the island remains basically the same. This may all be changing now that Caye Caulker has its very own airstrip and is connected to both Belize City and San Pedro by air. There are no resorts yet, but hotels on the island have been renovating in anticipation of more well-to-do guests.

On the other hand, some locals and resident foreigners have been trying to enact building codes and establish a nature and marine reserve here. However, pressures from developers are intense. Hopefully the island will not become as overbuilt and shadeless as San Pedro.

One more thing you should know about Caye Caulker—it's home to nasty sand fleas, a tiny insect with a vicious bite that leaves an itchy welt. These sand fleas come out whenever the trade winds die. When this happens, the best solution is to put on socks and long pants, since they tend to bite feet and ankles. Sitting out at the end of a long pier also offers some relief.

WHAT TO SEE & DO

The main activity on Caye Caulker is swimming and sunbathing off the docks. The water is very calm off Back Bridge, making it a good place to practice if you're an inexperienced snorkeler. Take care if you're swimming off a dock. After a swimmer was killed by a boat, a designated swimming area was set aside off the Front Bridge.

Several boats leave from the front-side docks on half-day trips to the reef. For safety's sake, the boat should be in good condition, with a working motor (even on sailboats) in case the seas become rough or in the rare event that a quick rescue is needed. Your guide should be attentive and aware of your experience or inexperience.

Ellen McRae, resident marine biologist and founder of Cari Search, Ltd. (a group dedicated to research and protection of Belize's natural environment), advises that "you'll be safe with just about any of the residents who take people out, but it's still best to find out about the recent experiences of fellow tourists on the island." If you want to know more about what you'll see at the reef, Ellen offers a Reef Ecology Tour that includes a 1-hour lecture in the morning before an afternoon of guided snorkeling for B$24 ($12) with gear rental extra. She also offers 3-hour bird/cayes ecology hikes for B$10 ($5). Bring binoculars if you have them. You can find Ellen at the **Galeria Hicaco** (tel. 2178 or 4/4307 ext. 104) gift shop, near the Tropical Paradise, which features original artwork made in Belize.

Sea-ing is Belizing (tel. 2189, open daily from 9am to 5pm) is a gallery that specializes in underwater photography by co-owner James Beveridge, who has been photographing Belize since 1969. Besides selling photographic postcards and framed and unframed prints, the gallery offers slide shows illustrating the reefs and cayes. Programs are held regularly at 8pm. It costs B$4 ($2) per person. They also offer guided sailboat trips to explore the barrier reef ecosystem, as well as T-shirts, books about Belize, and film processing.

Right beside Sea-ing Is Belizing is **Belize Diving Services** (tel. 2143), Caye Caulker's only full-service dive center. Open Monday to Saturday from 8am to 5pm; Sunday from 10am to 4pm. A two-tank dive will cost you B$80 ($40). They also offer cave diving to certified cave divers, scuba-diving courses, and equipment rental.

Sunrise Boat Tours and Charters (tel. 2195), located on the north end of the island near the Sandbox Restaurant, takes people out to Goff's Caye to snorkel and see manatees (if you go, please don't touch the manatees). An all-day trip is B$50 ($25), but doesn't include lunch or gear. Another trip they make is to Half-Moon Caye, the Blue Hole, and Turneffe Islands for B$135 ($67.50) which includes lunch but not gear. You can also ask around for **Chocolate,** who also does boat trips to visit the manatees and charges the same price.

Benjie Smith (tel. 501-22/2250) runs his small sailboat **Answer** on extended trips as far south as Placencia, stopping at different cayes to explore and camp. Call him or ask around for additional information.

Kayak rentals are available at Daisy's Hotel. A 4-hour rental of a one-person kayak costs B$30 ($15); for a double kayak the cost is B$40 ($20). Look around for places to **rent a bicycle;** Island Rentals (tel. 2229 or 2111) rents **golf carts** for B$15 ($7.50) an hour.

In terms of shopping, there are only a few shops on the island: a couple of general stores, a few gift shops, and **Jan's Deli,** a good place to pick up bread, cheese, yogurt, drinks, and other staples, open Monday to Saturday from 7am to 1pm and 3 to 7pm, Sunday from 8am to noon. Nearly all general stores are closed between 1 and 3pm, so be sure to buy your lunch supplies before then.

For evening entertainment, you can stargaze, go for a night dive, or have a drink in one of the island's handful of bars. That's about it for nightlife on Caye Caulker.

WHERE TO STAY

Accommodations on Caye Caulker have improved in recent years, but they're still far from luxurious. In the off-season (May through Aug), it's possible to get substantial discounts. However, you'll have to put up with biting flies in May and mosquitoes in

June, July, and August. Besides the hotels listed below, there are furnished houses for rent on Caye Caulker—just walk around, and you'll see signs for them.

DOUBLES FOR LESS THAN B$50 [$25]

THE ANCHORAGE, south of the Front Bridge, Caye Caulker. No phone. 4 rms (all with bath).
$ Rates: B$30 ($15) single or double. No credit cards.

A 10-minute walk south of the Front Bridge, the Anchorage is the sort of place tropical travelers on a very low budget dream about—white sand, coconut palms rustling in the trade winds, turquoise water, and the distant murmur of waves crashing on the barrier reef. There are four whitewashed adobe huts with palm-thatch roofs, each with its own bath (cold-water showers only). American Jo Ann Wilson is the owner here.

DAISY'S, Front Street near Tropical Paradise Rest...rant, Caye Caulker. Tel. 501-22/2150. 12 rms (1 with bath).
$ Rates: B$21.50 ($10.75) double without bath, B$42.40 ($21.20) double with bath; B$37.50 ($18.75) triple with bath. No credit cards.

Located on Front Street, the rooms are situated in a sort of courtyard. Even though the rooms have fans, the ones on the first floor are stuffy and have little air circulation, but the larger rooms upstairs are much roomier and, because they catch the ocean breezes, cooler. Get one of these if you can. Furnishings are rather stark, with a single flourescent light in the middle of the ceiling. The bathrooms have cold water only.

IGNACIO'S BEACH CABAÑAS, south of Front Bridge, Caye Caulker. No phone. 17 rms (all with bath).
$ Rates: B$30 ($15) single, double, or triple (old cabañas) B$45 ($22.50) single, double, or triple (new cabañas). No credit cards.

S These are currently the accommodations most popular with the backpack set. Located next to the Anchorage, the cabañas here are brightly painted little wooden boxes that sit right on the sand or up a bit on stilts and give the appearance of a shanty town, but the groups of young people relaxing in hammocks strung between the palm trees indicate that this is a low-budget tropical paradise. The owner, Ignacio, is one of the island's more colorful characters.

JIMENEZ CABAÑAS, Caye Caulker. Tel. 501-22/2175. 4 rms (none with bath), 6 cabañas.
$ Rates: B$10 ($5) single; B$15 ($7.50) double; cabañas B$30 ($15) single, B$46 ($23) double, B$58 ($29) triple, B$63 ($31.50) quad. MC, V.

★ Across the island from the Tropical Paradise Hotel (below) is this very attractive little grouping of cabañas set in a sunny garden with conch shell–lined walkway. The cabañas are peaceful and secluded and have palm-trunk walls, thatched roofs, and little porches. Each contains one or two double beds, or a double and single bed, and a very basic bathroom with hot water. The other four rooms are not nearly as nice, so hold out for a hut. The owner was a lobster fisherman for years until the lobster harvest began to decline.

LENA'S HOTEL, on water near Tropical Paradise Hotel, Caye Caulker. No phone. 16 rms (8 with bath).
$ Rates: B$31.80 ($15.90) double without bath, B$53–B$63.60 ($26.50–$31.80) double with bath; B$74.20 ($37.10) triple with bath. No credit cards.

Lena's is right on the water, and if you have an ocean-front room, you will also have a veranda for sitting and gazing out at the Caribbean. Unfortunately, the other rooms aren't nearly as pleasant. Even though the building looks run-down, the rooms are clean and well kept (and have firm foam mattresses with good sheets). Rooms with a shared bath are definitely within the budget, and as prices are creeping up in Caye Caulker, the price for a double with a bath is competitive as well. Rooms have fans and hot water, and some have a small closet area in the bathroom.

TOM'S HOTEL, south of Front Bridge. Tel. 501-22/2102. 29 rms (none with bath), 5 cabañas (all with bath).

$ Rates: B$25 ($12.50) single without bath; B$45 ($22.50) double without bath, B$55 ($27.50) triple in cabaña. No credit cards.

The rooms here are tiny and can get hot and stuffy, but if you spend all your time snorkeling or hanging out elsewhere, you won't mind very much. There is a veranda overlooking the water and a private dock for tanning. The cabañas, with private baths, are much roomier than the rooms in the main building. Consider the rooms last resorts if none of the cabañas are available.

DOUBLES FOR LESS THAN B$70 [$35]

RAINBOW HOTEL, north of Front Bridge, Caye Caulker. Tel. 501-22/2123. 17 rms (all with bath).

$ Rates: B$47.70–B$58.30 ($23.85–$29.15) single; B$58.30–B$68.90 ($29.15–$34.45) double; B$68.90–B$79.50 ($34.45–$39.75) triple; lower rates May–Oct. MC, V.

Located next door to the Reef Hotel, the Rainbow is very similar in appearance to the Reef, both inside and out. Only a few feet from the water it has a veranda and a private dock for guests. The rooms are clean, with tiled showers, ceiling fans, and louvered windows that let in the breezes; double and twin beds are available.

Upstairs rooms are more expensive and have cable TV and better furniture. It may be difficult to find the manager; sometimes there's someone around and sometimes there isn't.

SHIRLEY'S GUEST HOUSE, close to the airstrip, Caye Caulker. Tel. 501-22/2145. Fax 501-22/2264. 10 rms (7 with bath).

$ Rates: B$65 ($32.50) double without bath, B$85 ($42.50) double with bath. MC, V.

Just about the first accommodations you'll see as you walk north along the water from the airstrip are these picturesque white cabins with green trim. They're set on stilts and are shaded by coconut palms. The setting is idyllic, safe, and quiet. Although they are a little on the expensive side, it is worth it for the location and the fairly large and comfortable rooms.

TROPICAL PARADISE HOTEL, Caye Caulker. Tel. 501-22/2124. Fax 501/22-2225. 5 rms, 6 cabañas, 5 air-conditioned suites (all with bath).

$ Rates: Rooms B$53 ($26.50) single, B$58.30 ($29.15) double; cabañas B$68.90 ($34.45) single, B$74.20 ($37.10) double; suites B$127.20 ($63.60) double. DISC, MC, V.

Proprietor Ramon Reyes runs a tight ship: The rooms are very clean and paneled, with a little bit of storage space for your things and a narrow front porch for catching the breeze. The hot water is a bit finicky, however. The cabins and suites are the most expensive and are quite a bit larger than the rooms. But the cabins aren't as breezy as the rooms at the back of the complex behind the restaurant that bears the same name. They even have a hot tub.

WORTH THE EXTRA BUCKS

SEA BEEZZ, Caye Caulker. Tel. 501-22/2176 or (in the U.S.) 516/668-9212. 6 rms (all with bath).

$ Rates: B$84.80 ($42.40) single or double. MC, V (additional charge).

Gray buildings with white trim give this place a bit of Cape Cod styling, but the iron bars on the windows remind you that you are in Central America. Although the guest rooms are modern and clean and have ceiling fans and hot water, they are situated in such a way that they don't catch the breezes. To make up for this, there is a pretty garden with tables in the sand only steps from the water. Sea Beezz also has its own small restaurant and bar that serves excellent (though expensive) margaritas. This hotel is open only from November to April.

READERS RECOMMEND

Caye Caulker Guest House, *Caye Caulker. "We liked the Caye Caulker Guest House on the third street off the beach. Much cleaner and quieter than the four other places we looked at. It also doesn't fill up as fast."* —Judy and Rick Galliher, Mounds View, MN

WHERE TO EAT

As on Ambergris Caye, seafood is popular and plentiful all year but cheaper than in San Pedro. Do remember to abide by the seasons on lobster, conch, shrimp, and don't order turtle steaks (sea turtles are endangered). The seasons are the same for Ambergris Caye. Restaurants are not supposed to serve lobster in the off-season, when the lobsters are breeding. If it's on the menu off-season, please don't order it.

Caye Caulker has a thriving cottage industry of snack bakers. Wander the streets and you're sure to see signs offering yogurt and granola, freshly squeezed juices, hot lobster pie, sweet rolls, chocolate or cheese pie—each B$1–B$2 (50¢–$1). Don't be bashful: Just step right up and knock on the door for a homemade treat. You won't be disappointed. (It's also a chance to get a glimpse into a few Belizean homes.) For more substantial meals, try one of the restaurants listed below.

MEALS FOR LESS THAN B$15 [$7.50]

GLENDA'S, in back of Atlantic Bank, Caye Caulker. Tel. 2148.
    Cuisine: BELIZEAN.
$ Prices: Breakfast B$5 ($2.50); lunch B$1–B$5 (50¢–$2.50). No credit cards.
    Open: Daily 7am–3pm.
Run by Glenda and her daughter, this establishment is one of Caye Caulker's little home bakeries gone upscale. They specialize in cinnamon rolls, pastries, *garnaches,* and fresh juices. Locals and tourists alike say the burritos and other lunch items are great home cookin'.

SAND BOX RESTAURANT, north end of Front St. Tel. 2200.
    Cuisine: SEAFOOD/INTERNATIONAL.
$ Prices: B$9–B$16 ($4.50–$8). No credit cards.
    Open: Thurs–Tues noon–2:30pm and 6–10pm.
The old wooden building isn't very big and with sand on the floor of the dining room and a few tables in the sand out front, it is appropriately named. The menu here is rather eclectic and is posted on a little bulletin board that is brought to your table. There are crunchy conch fritters and nachos. Shrimp shows up in curried shrimp and shrimp salad; other dishes include jerk chicken, snapper almondine, a delicious vegetarian lasagna, and seafood chowder rich with fish, shrimp, and potatoes. We made a regular nightly pilgrimage here for the awesome chocolate cake topped with coconut ice cream. You might have to wait for a table.

TROPICAL PARADISE HOTEL RESTAURANT, south of Front Bridge. Tel. 2124.
    Cuisine: BELIZEAN.
$ Prices: Breakfast B$3–B$8 ($1.50–$4); dinner B$6–B$17 ($3–$8.50). No credit cards.
    Open: Mon–Sat 8am–2pm and 6–9pm; Sun 8am–2pm.
The Tropical Paradise stays packed for all three meals, because it serves consistent food at good prices. Inside, it has the feel of a small-town diner. Try one of the dinner specials, such as curried lobster or fried chicken. In front of the restaurant, there's a coffee shop/bar that is open for most of the day.

MEALS FOR LESS THAN B$25 [$12.50]

CASTAWAYS RESTAURANT, north end of town, Caye Caulker. Tel. 2294.

Cuisine: BELIZEAN/INTERNATIONAL.
$ Prices: Main dishes B$9–B$25 ($4.50–$12.50). No credit cards.
Open: Wed–Mon 6am–10pm.

Inside this traditional red-trimmed white Belizean cottage, you'll find such international favorites as Thai chicken, chicken Korma, lasagna, curries, chow mein, and delicious stone crab when it's available. The British owner (who also rents rooms) has lived in Belize for many years and is a good person to search out for a convivial chat. If you're looking for an early breakfast, this is the place.

MARIN'S RESTAURANT & BAR, located a block west of the Tropical Paradise. Tel. 2104.
Cuisine: BELIZEAN/INTERNATIONAL.
$ Prices: Complete dinner B$6.50–B$17 ($3.25–$8.50). MC, V.
Open: Daily 8am–2pm and 5:30–10pm.

There's plenty of local atmosphere here, with soca music playing all day long. Marin's serves fresh seafood in its outdoor garden or in its mosquito-proof dining room. In lobster or shrimp season, try the shrimp or lobster with pineapple (Belizean style, sweet-and-sour) for B$14.50 ($7.25) or jerk or barbequed lobster. Vegetarians can order a pile of vegetables with rice. If you're starving, go for the Marin's special, a platter of fried shrimp, conch, and fish.

4. COROZAL TOWN & THE NORTHERN HIGHWAY

96 miles N of Belize City; 31 miles N of Orange Walk;
8 miles S of the Mexican border

GETTING THERE **By Air** Island Air (tel. 26/2435 in San Pedro) operates two flights daily from San Pedro. Duration: 20 minutes. Fare: B$60 ($30) each direction. Tropic Air (tel. 26/2012 in San Pedro) flies mornings and afternoons from San Pedro to Corozal. Duration: 20 minutes. Fare: B$108 ($54) round-trip.

By Bus Both Batty Bros. and Venus bus lines run several buses daily from Belize City. Duration: 3 hours. Fare: B$7.50 ($3.75). Buses originating from Chetumal, Mexico, go into town daily every hour from 4am to 6pm.

By Car Corozal Town is the last town on the Northern Highway before you reach the Mexican border. Take Freetown Road out of Belize City to connect with the Northern Highway. If you want to visit the Altun Ha ruins, take the Old Northern Highway. The turnoff is 22 miles from Belize City, on the right. If you're driving in from Mexico, you'll reach a fork in the road 3 miles from the border; bear left to reach Corozal Town.

DEPARTING Buses leave throughout the day for both Chetumal, Mexico, and Belize City. The fare for the 9-mile trip to Chetumal is B$2.50 ($1.25). Expect to spend 30 to 45 minutes going through border formalities.

ESSENTIALS The bus station is located two blocks west of the town's central park. Three of the four hotels listed here are at the south end of town where the Northern Highway runs alongside the bay.

Nine miles from the Mexican border, Corozal Town (pop. 8,700) is for many people their first glimpse of Belize. There isn't much to see or do in Corozal. It's mostly just a stopping point for weary travelers. However, it sits on the shores of the **Bay of Chetumal,** which has the most amazing turquoise-blue water. The town was settled in the mid-19th century by refugee Mestizos from Mexico, and Spanish is still the principal language spoken here. Before the 1850s, the area had been one of the last centers of the Mayan civilization.

WHAT TO SEE & DO

If you've just come from Mexico, swim in the bay, or walk around town and marvel at the difference between Mexican culture and Belizean culture. The countries are so close and yet worlds apart. Belize is truly a Caribbean country, with frame houses built on high stilts to provide coolness, protection from floods, and shade for sitting. Farming and growing sugarcane are what Corozal survives on, plus a little fishing.

If you haven't yet had your fill of Mayan ruins, there are a couple to visit in the area. If you look across the water from the shore in Corozal Town, you can see **Cerros** or **Cerro Maya** on the far side of the Bay of Chetumal. It's that little bump in the forest, but up close it seems much larger. Cerros was an important coastal trading center during the Late Preclassic Period. Some of the remains of this city are now under the waters of the bay, but there's still a 65-foot-tall **pyramid** that you can visit. By asking around town, you should be able to find someone willing to take you by boat to the ruins.

Right in town is another small ruin called **Santa Rita.** Corozal Town is actually built on the ruins of Santa Rita, which was an important Late Postclassic Mayan town and was still occupied at the time of the Spanish Conquest. The only excavated building is a small temple across the street from the Coca-Cola bottling plant. To reach it, head north past the bus station and, at the curve to the right, take the road straight ahead that leads up a hill. You'll see the building one block over to the right.

WHERE TO STAY & EAT

Three of the listings below are at the southern end of the town. Ask the bus driver to drop you off or take a taxi from the bus station. You'll find good and inexpensive food at the market, three blocks south of the central square.

DOUBLES FOR LESS THAN B$25 [$12.50]

CARIBBEAN MOTEL, Cabins and Trailer Park, south end of town on Belize Highway, Corozal Town. Tel. 501-4/22045. 6 rms (all with bath).
$ **Rates:** B$25 ($12.50) single or double. No credit cards.

On the bay, in an idyllic location shaded by lofty palms and with a swimming dock across the street, this is the traditional place to stay. Even though it has seen better days, the Caribbean is still a great deal and may provide the cheapest room with private bath that you'll find in Belize. Quaint and primitive thatched bungalows are built according to traditional Mayan designs and are almost identical (from the outside) to the ones that you see all over the Yucatán. The bungalows are being renovated, so expect prices to go up.

The restaurant is open every day except Tuesday (try to time your stay accordingly, other choices for food aren't as good) and serves all three meals. It's possible to camp here, also.

NESTOR'S HOTEL, 123 Fifth Ave., Corozal Town. Tel. 501-4/22354. 18 rms (all with bath).
$ **Rates:** B$20 ($10) single; B$25–B$35 ($12.50–$17.50) double. No credit cards.

The cheapest prices in town are to be found here, on the corner of Fifth Avenue and Fourth Street. Rooms are basic, with solar-heated showers and fans, and the plumbing tends to act up now and then in the back rooms.

DOUBLES FOR LESS THAN B$50 [$25]

HOTEL MAYA, P.O. Box 112, Corozal Town. Tel. 501-4/22082. 15 rms (all with bath).
$ **Rates:** B$37.10 ($18.55) single; B$58.30 ($29.15) double; B$63.60 ($31.80) triple. MC, V.

Located on the shore road south of town, the Maya is probably your best bet. The rooms are very clean and basic, and all have private showers with hot and cold running water. This place tends to be popular with American businesspeople who come to negotiate deals, so you may find no rooms available. Unfortunately, it can also get a little bit noisy. You can get a big breakfast for B$9.50 ($4.75), including meat, beans, orange juice, coffee, and toast or johnnycakes. Dinner runs B$8–B$11 ($4–$5.50).

WORTH THE EXTRA BUCKS

TONY'S INN & BEACH RESORT, south end, Corozal Town. Tel. 501-4/ 22055. 29 rms., all with bath.

$ Rates: B$42.40–B$127.20 ($21.20–$63.60) single; B$53–B$148.40 ($26.50–$74.20) double. Cheaper in summer months; children under 12 stay free in parents' room. AE, DISC, MC, V. 5% surcharge added.

The rooms here are newer and larger than those in the above hostelries, and consequently this place is popular with group tours and conferences. Tony's is on the left just past the Caribbean Motel on the shore road south of town. The grounds are nicely landscaped, with lawn chairs that overlook the ocean. There's even a little beach. The rooms come with mahogany furniture, tile floors, attractive floral-print bedspreads, and potted plants. The rooms with air-conditioning also come with cable color TVs. Although the prices in the restaurant here are high, especially if you've been traveling in Mexico, it's certainly a welcome oasis of cool air during the summer.

EN ROUTE TO BELIZE CITY

Between Corozal Town and Belize City, the only other town of any size is Orange Walk. There's nothing much of interest here to tourists, but it can make a good base for visiting several surrounding attractions if you have your own car. Sites that could be visited include the Altun Ha and Lamanai ruins and the Crooked Tree Wildlife Sanctuary. For information on Altun Ha and Crooked Tree, see the "Excursions" section of Chapter 15. There really isn't any convenient way to visit Altun Ha by public transportation from Orange Walk, but you could hitch a ride. If you're driving, be sure to take the turnoff for the old Northern Highway as you head south toward Belize City.

Lamanai is an even more difficult ruin to visit—time and money are required to rent a boat to take you down the New River from either Guinea Grass or Shipyard, two small villages near Orange Walk. Ask around in Orange Walk before heading out and you might be able to arrange a tour straight from Orange Walk. Expect to pay around B$60 ($30) per person for a boat to take you upriver to the ruin. During the dry season it's possible to drive to Lamanai if you have a four-wheel-drive vehicle. From Orange Walk, take the road to San Felipe.

Lamanai (submerged crocodile in Mayan) is one of the largest Mayan sites in Belize; it was occupied from around 1500 B.C. until the Spanish arrived in the 16th century. In addition to the numerous pyramids and temples, there are also ruins of two churches built by the Spanish. Lamanai's most striking feature is the 12-foot-high stone-and-mortar face set into the side of one of the temples. Most of the ruins here have not been cleared and are surrounded by dense rain forest. The trails leading between temples offer excellent bird watching.

WHERE TO STAY

D'❂ VICTORIA HOTEL, Belize-Corozal Rd., Orange Walk. Tel. 501-3/ 22518 or 22847. 31 rms (all with bath).

$ Rates: B$44.40 ($22.20) single; B$50 ($25) double, B$74.25 ($37.15) double with A/C, TV. No credit cards.

Spacious, clean rooms with tile floors and hot and cold water await you here, a surprisingly nice hotel on an otherwise dreary section of road, if you just can't go any farther. You'll also find a cool swimming pool with a tiled patio around it. The restaurant serves Belizean and Chinese food at reasonable prices.

CHAPTER 18

SOUTHERN & WESTERN BELIZE

As is often the case in places blessed with beautiful islands, warm waters, and colorful coral reefs, areas away from the water can be overlooked. When you've had enough sunshine and swimming out on the cayes, spend some time exploring the rest of Belize. Once the heart of the Mayan Empire, Belize has many excavations scattered throughout the country.

In western Belize's Cayo District, a densely forested region of limestone mountains and clear-running rivers, Caracol is the largest Mayan city yet discovered. Though Caracol has not been turned into a major tourist destination like the Mayan ruins in Mexico or Guatemala, it's worth seeing for serious students of Mesoamerican cultures. The mountains here are laced with caves, several of which can be explored.

Wildlife abounds throughout Belize, though it is increasingly endangered. The Belize Zoo, near the capital city of Belmopan, is dedicated to educating the public about the benefits of preserving Belize's wild heritage. South of Belmopan is the Cockscomb Basin Wildlife Preserve, the world's first jaguar preserve. North of Belmopan are the Community Baboon Sanctuary (a howler monkey preserve) and the Crooked Tree Wildlife Sanctuary, another preserve that is home to many rare species of tropical birds.

If you find yourself in need of another dose of beach life, Placencia, in southern Belize, offers the best beach in the country. Miles of sand stretch northward from this tranquil little village at the tip of a long peninsula.

And way down at the isolated southern end of the country, near the town of Punta Gorda, there are numerous villages where Mayan Indians farm the land much as they did 1,000 years ago. If you're interested in staying in a Mayan home to learn more about these indigenous people, this chapter will tell you how.

1. BELMOPAN

52 miles W of Belize City; 30 miles E of San Ignacio; 90 miles N of Placencia

GETTING THERE **By Bus** Batty Bros., Novelos, Z-Line, and Venus all run buses to Belmopan frequently throughout the day. Duration: 1½ hours. Fare: B$2.75–B$3 ($1.38–$1.50).

By Car From Belize City, take Cemetery Road to the Western Highway.

DEPARTING Buses run frequently to San Ignacio, Belize City, and Dangriga. From Dangriga you can get a bus to Placencia if you arrive before 3pm on Monday, Wednesday, Friday, or Saturday. It's about 1½ hours to either Belize City or San Ignacio and 3 hours to Dangriga.

ESSENTIALS Orientation Belmopan is a planned city with a ring road and wide deserted streets. There is only one road in or out of the city. It branches off the Hummingbird (Southern) Highway 2½ miles south of the Western Highway.

Conceived as the dynamic center of a growing Belize, Belmopan (pop. 4,000), the capital of Belize, is actually a sleepy place 2½ miles in from the Western Highway. Modest government buildings are laid out according to a master plan, and small residential areas are enclosed by a ring road. Business seems limited to a gas station, a few little food shops, and three modest hostelries. The facilities here that you may find useful are a bank, post office, hospital, and microwave telephone installation.

Belmopan is a model city designed and built from scratch in the jungle at the geographical center of the country. Unfortunately, the planners who designed it didn't count on the people's resistance to moving here. Belmopan has yet to see any substantial growth, and Belize City remains the country's largest city.

WHAT TO SEE & DO

Since Belize doesn't yet have a museum, the many Mayan artifacts found at sites around the country are displayed in the basement of the **Archeology Department** (tel. 8/22106). It is open Monday, Wednesday, and Friday from noon to 4pm, and you must give two days advance notice if you wish to visit; admission is free. It is located on the ground floor of the building at the far side of the quadrangle that is adjacent to the bus-depot market.

What follows are several possible excursions that can be made with Belmopan as a base.

Guanacaste Park, a 50-acre park located where the Hummingbird Highway turns off of the Western Highway, about 2½ miles north of Belmopan, is an excellent introduction to tropical forests. The park is named for a huge old guanacaste tree that is found within the park. Guanacaste trees were traditionally preferred for building dugout canoes, but this particular tree, which is about 100 years old, was spared the boat-builders' ax because it has a triple trunk that makes it unacceptable for canoe building. More than 35 species of epiphytes (plants that grow on other plants), including orchids, bromeliads, ferns, mosses, lichens, and philodendrons cover its trunk and branches.

There are nearly 2 miles of trails in the park, with several benches for sitting and observing wildlife. The park is bordered on the west by Roaring Creek and on the north by the Belize River. Among the animals you might see are more than 100 species of birds, large iguanas, armadillos, kinkajous, deer, agoutis (large rodents that are a favorite game meat in Belize), and jaguarundis (small jungle cats). A map and a brochure about the park are available from the Belize Audubon Society in Belize City.

The Maya Mountains are primarily limestone and consequently laced with caves—that's why this region of Belize is known as Cave Branch. About 11 miles from Belmopan on the Hummingbird Highway, you'll come across a dirt road to the right. About half a mile down this road is the entrance to **St. Herman's Cave,** one of the largest and most easily accessible caves in Belize. You'll need at least two good flashlights and sturdy shoes to explore this undeveloped ½-mile long cave.

Equally fascinating is the **Blue Hole,** a collapsed cavern just off the Hummingbird Highway, 12½ miles south of Belmopan. After locking your car and placing any valuables in the trunk, walk down the cement steps. Dense jungle surrounds a small natural pool of deep turquoise. A limestone cliff rises up from the edge of the pool on two sides. The water flows for only about 100 feet on the surface before disappearing into a cave. This is a great place for a quick dip on a hot day because the water is refreshingly cool and clear. You can clearly see fish swimming around the edges of the Blue Hole.

WHERE TO STAY & EAT

BANANA BANK RANCH, Box 48, Belmopan. Tel. 501-8/23180. Fax 501-8/23505. 5 rooms, 5 cabañas with bath.

$ Rates: In lodge B$74.20 ($37.10) single without bath, B$116.60 ($58.30) single with bath; B$106 ($53) double without bath, B$137.80 ($68.90) double with bath. In cabanas B$137.80 ($68.90) single; B$159 ($79.50) double; B$180.20 ($90.10) triple; B$201.40 ($100.70) quad. Meals extra B$56 ($28) per day. No credit cards.

The turnoff for this fascinating lodge is at Mile 47 on the Western Highway, not far past the turnoff for Belmopan. From here it is about 1¼ miles to the ranch.

Owners John and Carolyn Carr moved to Belize from the United States about 17 years ago. Carolyn is an artist and John is a cowboy from Montana. Together, they operate one of the oldest cattle ranches in Belize and for several years have been taking in paying guests. The guest quarters are on the banks of the Belize River. Each of the 5 cabins comes complete with a sleeping loft, room for six people, a private bathroom, two bedrooms, queen-size beds, and plenty of space to spread out and make yourself at home. These cabins also have their own private patios overlooking the river. On the property you can visit a Mayan ruin and meet the Carrs' pet jaguar, Tika. Horseback riding, canoeing, and day and overnight trips can be arranged at additional cost. Meals are served in a small dining room. The house specialty is barbecued pork spare ribs, served with all the trimmings.

EL-REY INN, 23 Moho St., Belmopan. Tel. 501-8/23438. Fax 501-8/22682. 12 rms (all with bath).

$ Rates: B$36 ($18) single; B$46 ($23) double. No credit cards.

This small hotel is located in a residential neighborhood a short walk, drive, or taxi ride from the bus station. The rooms are fairly basic, but the rates are quite reasonable for Belmopan. There's a restaurant serving reasonably priced meals, and tours and horseback riding can be arranged.

CAMPING

MONKEY BAY WILDLIFE SANCTUARY, Mile 32 Western Highway, P.O. Box 187, Belmopan. No phone.

About 1½ miles down a dirt road off the Western Highway, four miles west of the Belize Zoo, is a tranquil spot where you can park your RV or pitch a tent. There are no monkeys and no bay, but there are beautiful big trees, acres of pasture, a creek, a river nearby, and plenty of solitude. The privately owned sanctuary is only just being developed and so the facilities are primitive. Register with the caretaker, Pedro Reyes, who lives in the little house on the other side of the fence. The fee for camping is B$5 ($2.50) per night.

2. DANGRIGA

72 miles S of Belize City; 64 miles SE of Belmopan; 48 miles N of Placencia

GETTING THERE By Plane Maya Airways (tel. 2/72312 or 44032) has flights Monday through Saturday from Belize City to Dangriga. Duration: 20 minutes. Fare: B$50 ($25) one way, B$90 ($45) round-trip.

By Bus Z-Line (tel. 73937 in Belize City) buses leave from the Belize City's Magazine Road bus station several times daily (only twice on Sundays). Duration: 4 hours. Fare: B$10 ($5).

By Car From Belize City, head west on Cemetery Road, which becomes the Western Highway. Just past the Belize Zoo, at around Milepost 30, turn left (south) on the New Belize Road. This road is shorter, faster, and smoother than the old Hummingbird Highway route through Belmopan. Follow this road, turn left and head into Dangriga. You'll arrive at the south end of town.

DEPARTING   There are flights to Belize City, Big Creek (Placencia), and Punta Gorda. The airport is at the north end of town. Buses leave daily for Belize City, Belmopan, and Punta Gorda. There are also buses to Placencia on Monday, Wednesday, Friday, and Saturday. The bus ticket office is at the north end of St. Vincent Street near the new bridge over Stann Creek, and there is also a station at the south end of St. Vincent Street.

Boats to Tobacco Caye leave from Southern Foreshore on the Gumaragu River near the new bridge (around the corner from the Z-Line ticket office of St. Vincent Street). There is also a small boat that operates between Dangriga and Puerto Cortez, Honduras. The trip takes between 3 and 10 hours and costs B$70 ($35).

ESSENTIALS   The main street through Dangriga is called St. Vincent Street south of the new bridge and Commerce Street north of the new bridge. The Scotia Bank on Commerce Street (just north of the new bridge) is open Monday through Friday from 8am to 1pm (also 3 to 6pm on Friday). The B.T.L. phone office is across from the police station about halfway up Commerce Street from the new bridge and is open Monday through Friday from 8am to noon and 1 to 4pm and on Saturday from 8am to noon.

Dangriga is one of Belize's larger towns and is located about midway down the coast. As the capital of the Stann Creek District, which is one of the main citrus-growing regions of Belize, Dangriga is a bustling community. However, despite its agricultural-boomtown air, it lacks the seaminess that characterizes Belize City. The town fronts right on the Caribbean and has several waterfront parks, which are surrounded by attractive residential neighborhoods. There isn't much to see or do here, but it certainly can be a pleasant town simply to walk around in.

Dangriga is also the center of Belize's Garifuna culture. The Garifuna people are descendants of Africans who were bound for New World slave auctions but who managed to avoid enslavement when their ship wrecked off St. Vincent Island (in the Windward Islands) in the early 1600s. The Africans eventually intermarried with the local Carib Indians, who had a reputation as cannibals. Becoming known as Black Caribs, the Garifuna were feared by Europeans and eventually forced off St. Vincent. They eventually settled on the Caribbean Coast of Central America and today can be found from Belize to Costa Rica. Each year on November 19, Garifuna Settlement Day is celebrated in Dangriga with much music and dancing in the streets. The Garifuna have their own traditional music, which is based on wooden drums and has become quite popular throughout Belize in recent years.

If you'd like to have a look at some Garifuna paintings, visit the studio of Benjamin Nicholas, 25 Howard Street (tel. 22785). Using a Caribbean naive style, Nicholas paints scenes of traditional Garifuna village life. You'll find the studio a couple of blocks south of Stann Creek and a block east of St. Vincent Street.

There are several excursions that can be made out of Dangriga or using Dangriga as a starting or ending point. See below for details.

WHERE TO STAY

PAL'S GUEST HOUSE, 868A Magoon St., Dangriga. Tel. 501-5/22095. 14 rms (11 with bath).

$ Rates: B$15 ($7.50) single without bath, B$30–B$40 ($15–$20) single with bath; B$25–B$30 ($12.50–$15) double without bath, B$40–B$60 ($20–$30) double with bath.

This hotel is down at the south end of town near the bus station (at the mouth of Havana Creek) and is clean and quiet. The rooms with shared bath are small and basic, but are otherwise fine. If you have a bit more money to spend, you should opt for one of the beachfront rooms, which have air-conditioning, hot water, and TVs.

RIO MAR HOTEL, 977 Southern Foreshore, Dangriga. Tel. 501-5/ 22201. 7 rms (all with bath).
$ Rates: B$27.50–B$43 ($13.75–$21.50) single; B$33–B$53 ($16.50–$26.50) double. No credit cards.

This small, basic hotel takes its name from the fact that it is at the mouth of the Gumagurugu River (*rio*) flowing into the sea (*mar*). Rooms are a bit run-down and are starkly furnished, but the location is good. There is a restaurant on the ground floor.

WORTH THE EXTRA BUCKS

BONEFISH HOTEL, 15 Mahogany St. (P.O. Box 21), Dangriga. Tel. 501-5/22165. Fax 501-5/22296. 10 rms (all with bath). A/C TV
$ Rates: B$74.20–B$95.40 ($37.10–$47.70) single; B$95.40–B$127.20 ($47.70–$63.60) double. MC, V.

Located a block from the water and across the street from a park, the Bonefish provides the best all-around value in Dangriga. Though it is out of our price range, it is significantly more comfortable than other hotels listed here. The guest rooms are generally quite large and are carpeted. If you don't want the air conditioner on, there are jalousie windows that let in the breezes. There are even tubs in the bathrooms. There is a TV lounge in the lobby, and a sunny dining room. This is a convenient place to stay if you are headed out to Tobacco Caye.

WHERE TO EAT

Up and down the main street through town (St. Vincent Street/Commerce Street), you'll find numerous very basic (and usually very noisy) restaurants. Your best bet, though expensive (between B$20 and B$30 [$10 and $15]), is the dining room at the Bonefish Hotel. The Burger King Restaurant (not affiliated with *the* Burger King) is a local favorite serving simple Belizean meals heavy on the grease. There are also several Chinese restaurants along the main street.

EASY EXCURSIONS
TOBACCO CAYE

Located 12 miles east of the town of Dangriga, Tobacco Caye sits right in the middle of the barrier reef and surrounds a shallow lagoon, so the snorkeling is always good. The island is only about 200 yards by 350 yards, so you'd better bring a few good books if you head out here. Despite the island's small size, it manages to support several modest lodges. A boat out here from Dangriga costs B$25 ($12.50) per person if there are two or more people and can be arranged by asking at the fish market near The Hub or at the guest house at the last Z-Line bus stop in Dangriga. If there is only one person, the fare is B$50 ($25). The ride out to Tobacco Caye takes about 30 minutes.

FAIRWEATHER & FRIENDS TOBACCO CAYE GUEST HOUSE, Tobacco Caye. No phone. 10 rms (all with bath).
$ Rates (including three meals): B$25–B$30 ($12.50–$15) per room. B$25 ($12.50) meals. No credit cards.

Elwood Fairweather's place is sort of a motel-style hotel that seems a bit out of place on this tiny island, but the low rates do make it attractive. Rooms are very basic.

OCEAN'S EDGE, Tobacco Caye, P.O. Box 265, Belize City. Tel. in U.S. 713-894-0548. 4 cabins (all with bath).
$ Rates (including three meals): B$137.80 ($68.90) single; B$212 ($106) double. No credit cards.

Operated by Mr. Lincoln, the Ocean's Edge offers the most interesting accommodations on the island. The four cabins are all about seven feet off the ground and are attached to one another by an elevated walkway. There are fans to keep you cool and screens to keep out the insects. Water for showers is provided by a rainwater cistern. The room rates here also include snorkeling and fishing equipment.

REEF'S END LODGE, Tobacco Caye, P.O. Box 10, Dangriga. Tel. 501-5/ 22171. Fax same as phone. 4 rms (all with bath); 2 cabins.
$ Rates (including three meals): B$84.80 ($42.40) single; B$137.80 ($68.90) double. No credit cards.

Operated by a former lobsterman, the Reef's End Lodge is a small place with a Caribbean feel. The rooms are in a wooden building with a long veranda across the front. Electricity is provided by photovoltaic cells. The lodge's dining room is built on a pier on the lagoon side of the island, and there's even a ladder leading down from the kitchen into the water. The room rates here also include use of snorkeling equipment, fishing gear, and canoes to the reef.

GALES POINT

Gales Point is a small Creole fishing village about 30 miles north of Dangriga. It is a peaceful little village where you can get in tune with one of Belize's traditional cultures and its slower pace of life. However, what brings most people to Gales Point are the manatees that inhabit the water of the lagoon that surrounds the village. For B$60 ($30) you can hire a dory to take you out to where the manatees are usually seen. A dory will hold up to eight people, so the more people you can line up, the less it will cost each of you. You can also ask around in the village about renting a dugout canoe to paddle yourself out to where the manatees feed. Other possible trips from Gales Point include visits to the beach or the caves and nighttime turtle walks. All of these trips cost between B$60 ($30) and B$100 ($50) for a boat.

Gales Point is one of several villages in Belize to have a community-based ecotourism homestay program. Rooms in local villagers' homes are very basic and usually do not have running water or flush toilets. The rates are B$10 ($5) for a single and B$15 ($7.50) for a double. You can also camp in Gales Point for B$5 ($2.50) per person. Breakfast and lunch are B$5 ($2.50) each and dinner is B$10 ($5). To arrange a homestay in Gales Point, call the community phone (tel. 5/22087) and ask for Josephine or Alfias Smith. If you should arrive in the village without a reservation, go to the homestay coordinator's home and arrange your night's lodging.

There is no regular bus service to Gales Point, so from Dangriga you will have to take a Belmopan-bound bus and get off at the Gales Point Road. From here, you will have to hitchhike. From Belize City, you can take a boat on Wednesday or Saturday at 10am from the Bolton Bridge pier. The fare is B$20 ($10). These boats return to Belize City Wednesday and Friday at 4am.

HOPKINS VILLAGE, SITTEE RIVER VILLAGE & GLOVER'S ATOLL

Hopkins, a large Garifuna village 20 miles south of Dangriga, is a picturesque place with lots of colorfully painted clapboard houses. There isn't much to do here but wander around the village talking with children, fishermen, and elderly folks hanging out in front of their homes. If you stick around long enough, you may be able to learn a bit about traditional Garifuna lifestyles. Fishing is still the main employment of many of the villagers, who head out to the barrier reef in large dugout canoes. From this large boat, smaller, one-man canoes are launched, and the fishermen spread out in search of good fishing.

Hopkins is on a long curving swath of beach, and because of its isolation, is rarely visited by tourists. Unfortunately, the beach right in the village is too polluted with garbage and human waste for swimming, but if you head north or south, you'll find cleaner sand and water. There are a couple of small restaurants around the village. My favorites are Over the Waves, which is built on a pier over the water, and the Lebeha Bar, a rasta place with a beautiful garden, cheap meals, and fresh juices.

Buses to Hopkins leave Dangriga Monday, Wednesday, Friday, and Saturday at noon, returning the same days at 7am. There is also a truck that carries passengers between Dangriga and Hopkins. Ask at the Z-Line bus station in Dangriga to find out about this alternative. If you are heading south, you can take the bus, truck, or hitchhike out to the Southern Highway and wait for a south-bound bus.

Sittee River Village is a few miles south of Hopkins and is the staging site for trips out to Long Caye. This caye has only one accommodation on it, and consequently is one of the most remote budget accommodations in Belize. If you are looking to get away from it all and don't mind very rustic accommodations, Glover's Atoll Resort is definitely the place.

Where to Stay

SANDY BEACH HOTEL, Hopkins. Tel. 501-5/22033. 9 rms (3 with bath).
$ Rates: B$15 ($7.50) single without bath, B$23 ($11.50) single with bath; B$23–B$30 ($11.50–$15) double without bath, B$32 ($16) double with bath. No credit cards.
This small hotel is located right on the beach at the south end of Hopkins and is operated by a local women's cooperative. The cooperative was formed and the hotel opened so that the women could have some sort of employment here in Hopkins and not have to go work on the orange plantations. The rooms are very basic, but the setting is great. There's a big, screen-walled dining room serving inexpensive meals.

GLOVER'S ATOLL RESORT, P.O. Box 563, Belize City. Tel. 501-8/22149 or 23180. Fax 501-8/23505 or 23235. 8 cabins (all with shared bath).
$ Rates: B$110 ($55) per person for a week in cabin, B$204 ($102) per person for 2 weeks in cabin; B$60 ($30) per person for a week camping. Meals about B$30 ($15) per day; boat trip B$40 ($20) per person one way. MC, V (additional charge).
Located on Long Caye, off the central coast southeast of Dangriga, Glover's Atoll Resort is a very rustic sort of place that should appeal to hardy travelers accustomed to camping. Each of the cabins sleeps two and has its own kitchenette. You can either buy meals or bring your own food for the duration of your stay (a small store stocks only the basics), although you should be able to catch or buy fish while you are here. You'll also have to carry water from a well. The cabins have their own showers and outhouses. The reef here is within swimming distance of the shore, the snorkeling is excellent, and the scuba diving is said to be the second best in Belize—the Blue Hole is considered the best.

Long Caye is reached by a private boat that leaves from Sittee River Village every Sunday at 8am; the boat ride takes about five hours. The best way to catch the boat is to spend the night in Sittee River Village at the Glover's Atoll Guest House, where a bed is only B$5 ($2.50). To get to Sittee River Village, take any Saturday bus that leaves for Punta Gorda or Placencia and be sure to tell the driver that you want to get off 1½ miles past the Sittee Road. From here a truck will take you the rest of the way to Sittee River Village. The bus fare is about B$8 ($4) and truck fare is about B$10 ($5).

---

3. PLACENCIA

150 miles S of Belize City (120 miles by New Belize Road);
100 miles SE of Belmopan; 55 miles NE of Punta Gorda

GETTING THERE   By Plane   Maya Airways (tel. 2/72312 or 77215 in Belize City) has flights from Belize City to Placencia in the morning and afternoon, Monday through Saturday; flights on Sundays and holidays are less frequent. Fare: B$120 ($60) one way. Tropic Air (tel. 2/45671 in Belize City) has three flights daily. Fare: B$110 ($55) one way.

By Bus   On Monday, Wednesday, Friday, and Saturday there is bus service between Dangriga and Placencia. Buses depart Dangriga around 2:30pm and from Placencia at 6am. Fare: B$8 ($4). Alternatively, there are several buses daily that operate between Dangriga and Mango Creek (Z-Line and Williams Bus) and between Belize City and Mango Creek (Williams Bus Service from the Pound Yard Bridge and Z-Line from Magazine Road). Fares: from Belize City B$15 ($7.50), from Dangriga B$6 ($3). From Mango Creek, you must take a boat across Placencia Lagoon—see "By Boat" below for details.

By Car Take the Western Highway from Belize City. Around Mile 30, watch for the New Belize Road turnoff for Democracia and points south. This good dirt road now has a bridge where it was once necessary to ford a river, which was possible only in the dry season. The road cuts 30 miles off the drive to Placencia but bypasses Belmopan, the Blue Hole, St. Herman's Cave, and Guanacaste Park. At the end of the New Belize Road turn left onto the Hummingbird Highway. In 1½ miles, you'll come to the turnoff for the Southern Highway (Dangriga is 6 miles farther). After 22½ miles on the Southern Highway, turn left onto the road to Riversdale and Placencia. From this turnoff it's another 20 miles to Placencia. Be sure to fill your tank in Dangriga.

By Boat Outboard-powered skiffs, which can carry up to six people, can be hired for the trip across Placencia Lagoon from Big Creek or Mango Creek for B$25–B$45 ($12.50–$22.50), one way, for one or two people. For three or more, it's about B$10 ($5) per person.

DEPARTING The bus for Dangriga leaves Monday, Wednesday, Friday, and Saturday at 6am from Placencia. Buses also leave from Mango Creek several times daily for Dangriga, Belize City, and Punta Gorda. There are daily flights from Big Creek to Belize City.

ESSENTIALS Orientation There's only one road in Placencia, and it ends at the dock and gas station at the south end of town. The town's main thoroughfare is the Sidewalk, a narrow cement path that parallels the beach beginning at the Fishermen's Co-op by the dock.

The post office is upstairs from the Fisherman's Co-op at the south end of town. Open Monday to Friday from 8am to noon and 1 to 4pm, Saturday from 8am to 1pm. The village's public phone is midway down the Sidewalk in the BTL building. There is no bank in Placencia, so finding a business that will take travelers' checks is a good way to get Belize dollars.

Located at the southern tip of a long, sandy peninsula that is separated from the mainland by a narrow lagoon, Placencia is a tiny Creole village of pastel-colored houses on stilts. The town's main thoroughfare is a sidewalk, which will give you some idea of how laid-back and quiet this place is; the people here are still friendly to tourists. If you're looking for lots to see and do, you're better off going to Ambergris Caye. Best of all is that Placencia has one of the only "real" beaches in Belize—16 miles of white sand backed with dense vegetation, although at high tide the beach disappears.

WHAT TO SEE & DO

There isn't much to do in Placencia, which is exactly why people come here. You just can't help slowing down and relaxing. Sit back, sip a seaweed punch, and forget your cares. Nobody ever seems to get up early (except maybe the fishermen), and most people spend their days reading books and eating seafood. The beach, although narrow, is just about the only real beach I know of in Belize. You can walk for miles and see hardly a soul. North of town a mile or two, there's good snorkeling right off the beach.

If you're serious about diving or snorkeling, you'll want to get a group together and hire a boat to take you out to the dozens of little offshore cayes. It's between 10 and 25 miles out to the reef here, so a snorkeling or dive trip is not cheap. At **Placencia Dive Shop** (Kitty's Place), north of town (tel. 23227), scuba divers pay between

B$130 and B$150 ($65 and $75) for a two-tank dive; snorkelers B$70 to B$90 ($35 to $45) for trips including equipment, food, drinks, and a guide. Bring sunscreen and a T-shirt to cover your back. Another company specializing in diving is **Rum Point Divers** (tel. 23239 or in the U.S. toll free 800/747-1381), where a two-tank dive to Laughing Bird Caye will cost B$130 ($65). Other adventurous types can organize overnight boat trips to remote rivers where the wildlife is said to be spectacular. These trips are B$80 ($40) per person at Placencia Dive Shop, although less expensive day trips also are available. If you ask around town, you can probably arrange a trip out to the reef or cayes for much less than what Kitty charges. Trips for scuba diving and snorkeling, and tours to Monkey River and Mayan ruins are also offered by **Belize EcoAdventures** (tel. 23250).

Snorkeling trips (including equipment, lunch, and drinks) can be arranged at the Flamboyant Restaurant for about B$30 ($15). Kayaks can be rented at Kitty's for B$70 ($35) per day.

Fishing around here is some of the best in Belize. A day's fishing expedition will cost B$400 to B$450 ($200 to $225) for a boat. Grouper, tarpon, bonefish, and snook are the popular gamefish.

WHERE TO STAY

DOUBLES FOR LESS THAN B$50 [$25]

PARADISE VACATION HOTEL, Placencia. Tel. 501-6/23118 or 23179. 12 rms (4 with bath).
$ Rates: B$20 ($10) single without bath; B$27.25 ($13.65) double without bath, B$36.25–B$47.50 ($18.15–$23.75) double with bath. No credit cards.

S Although it hardly lives up to its glorious name, the Paradise Vacation Hotel is Placencia's best and most popular true budget hotel. You'll find everyone from backpackers to vacationing lodge owners here. The ground-floor rooms have private baths and are slightly more spacious than the rooms without baths. The eight rooms on the second floor get more breezes and share two moderately clean bathrooms downstairs and at the back of the building. The calm waters of the bay lap at your doorstep, and there's a pier that is great for sunning and swimming. You can rent fins and masks here for B$10 ($5) or a sailfish for B$10 ($5) per hour.

Tentacles restaurant next door serves good seafood and is a popular place to hang out and meet interesting people. Meals range from B$6–B$40 ($3–$20).

SEASPRAY, Placencia. Tel. 501-6/23148. 6 rms (4 with bath).
$ Rates: B$21 ($10.50) single without bath, B$26.25–B$42 ($13.15–$21) single with bath; B$31.50 ($15.75) double without bath, B$36.75–B$52.50 ($18.40–$26.25) double with bath; B$47.25 ($23.65) triple without bath, B$63 ($31.50) triple with bath. No credit cards.

The rooms here are small and lack any semblance of style, but they're inexpensive and conveniently located in the middle of town. Fans help you stay cool at night, and if you're traveling in a group, you might appreciate the bunk beds. The rooms are arranged on either side of a wide hallway, which serves as the lounge and library.

DOUBLES FOR LESS THAN B$90 [$45]

THE VILLAGE INN, Placencia. Tel. 501-6/23217. Fax 501-6/23267. 5 rms (3 with bath), 2 cabanas (both with bath).
$ Rates: B$63.60 ($31.80) single without bath; B$84.80 ($42.40) double with bath; B$159 ($79.50) triple with bath. No credit cards.

One of the cabanas here is a trailer, and one is a newly constructed wooden plank house with a corrugated roof. Everything is new and works well, although you have to hand pump pressure into your water in the new cabana. The rooms are in a cement building and are modern and fairly comfortable; however, they can get hot during the day. Mercy, the owner, will cook a good Cuban dinner on request for B$18 ($9). You can rent kayaks here, too, for B$100 ($50) per day for two people.

WORTH THE EXTRA BUCKS

RANGUANA LODGE, Placencia. Tel. 501-6/23112. Fax same number. 5 cabins (all with bath).

$ **Rates:** B$120 ($60) per cabaña (triple). DISC, MC, V.

Although the five cabins here are packed together on a tiny piece of sand in the middle of town, they're still very attractive inside. The water is only a few steps away. Nearly everything in these cozy cabins is made of hardwood—walls, floors, ceilings, even the louvered windows. Each has a little refrigerator and coffee maker, porch, tub, and table.

Just outside your door, you'll find a little thatch-roofed open-air bar where folks (both local and foreign) love to sit around all day gabbing and drinking and soaking up the sun. The Kingfisher serves as the restaurant for the Ranguana Lodge. It's a big screened-in room right on the water, where a meal will cost anywhere from B$8 to B$20 ($4 to $10).

SONNY'S RESORT, Placencia. Tel. 501-6/23103. 11 rms (all with bath).

$ **Rates:** B$47 ($23.50) single; B$94 ($47) double; B$122 ($61) single or double cabaña. MC, V.

One of the older hotels in Placencia, Sonny's was started with a couple of mobile homes that had been divided into three guest rooms each. Over the years, screened porches were added to them, giving them a more permanent feel, and although they have seen better days, they still suffice. However, there are also eight spacious wooden cabins raised up on stilts. Each has a large porch and is situated to make the most of the prevailing trade winds. They also have small refrigerators, coffee makers, reading lamps, and high ceilings with fans.

The hotel's restaurant is a casual diner-style place with a small bar where fishermen swap stories in the evening. It's open 7am to 10pm daily. Prices range from B$6 to B$15 ($3 to $7.50).

NEARBY PLACES TO STAY

RANGUANA REEF RESORT, Ranguana Caye. Tel. 501-6/23112. 3 cabanas (all with shared bath).

$ **Rates:** B$60 ($30) single; B$80 ($40) double; B$120 ($60) triple; B$120 ($60) quad. DISC, MC, V.

Ranguana Caye is located 22 miles offshore from Placencia, and everything you ever wished for on a remote island retreat is here: peace, quiet, good snorkeling, fishing, a sand beach, sunrise on one side of your cabana and sunset on the other. The charming wood cabanas are beautifully maintained. Showers and drinking water are supplied by rain water, and electricity by wind and solar power. Bring your own groceries, as no meals are included. Camping is possible for about B$5 ($2.50) per person. Unfortunately, a big expense here is a water taxi from Placencia, which will cost you about B$150 ($75) one way for up to four people. However, if you can arrange to come out with Eddie Leslie, the lodge owner, you may be able to negotiate a cheaper boat fare.

WHERE TO EAT

BJ'S RESTAURANT, on main road at north end of town, Placencia. No phone.
Cuisine: BELIZEAN.

$ **Prices:** Breakfast B$3–$10 ($1.50–$5), dinner B$7–$25 ($3.50–$12.50). No credit cards.
Open: Daily 7am–10pm.

As you sit on benches in a thatched porch, try a seaweed shake; BJ's makes one of the best around. For breakfast, try the fry cakes. The service is on Belizean time, so don't be in a hurry. If you want to go on a trip to Cockscomb Wildlife Preserve, ask for Ellis Burgess, a naturalist tour guide who frequently hangs out here.

THE FLAMBOYANT (also called Jene's Restaurant), across from Seaspray Hotel. Tel. 23112.

Cuisine: BELIZEAN/INTERNATIONAL.
$ Prices: B$8–B$30 ($4–$15). No credit cards.
Open: Tues–Sun 7:30am–11pm.

Jene's is a long-time favorite in Placencia, a central location for meeting people. The small dining room has hardwood paneling, floors, and ceiling. Paper money from countries all over the world adorns one wall—a testimonial to the diverse backgrounds of visitors who've discovered Placencia. A sign on the large "Flamboyant" tree outside features a map of Belize—it's most pleasant to sit under this tree and dine on conch fritters, barbecued chicken, shrimp, or veggie burgers while you plan your upcoming jungle expedition. Refreshing fresh juices are sometimes available.

THE GALLEY, across the soccer field from the main road, Placencia. No phone.

Cuisine: BELIZEAN/SEAFOOD.
$ Prices: B$8–$18 ($4–$9). No credit cards.
Open: Daily 7:30am–10pm.

The owner of this restaurant is a retired musician and usually has good jazz and Calypso playing on the stereo. Menu offerings include burgers and sandwiches, a full range of local seafood, and an exotic shake called craboo, made with a slightly bitter berry that looks like a miniature apple. Though the four-table atmosphere is slightly austere, as in all the restaurants in Placencia, shoes are optional. Beware of the habañero sauce here. It's made with fresh homegrown habañero chiles and is hot enough to peel paint.

KINGFISHER RESTAURANT, behind Ranguana Lodge. No phone.

Cuisine: BELIZEAN/SEAFOOD.
$ Prices: B$8–B$20 ($4–$10). No credit cards.
Open: Lunch Mon–Sat 8am–2pm; dinner Mon–Sat 6–10pm.

Situated on the beach, the Kingfisher is a large, open room with screen walls that let in the sea breezes. The big porch out front is a great place to relax with a drink and meet fellow travelers. Inside, the decor is typically rustic, with a sportfish nailed to the wall. Fish, shrimp, conch, and lobster make up the bulk of the short menu, with pork chops, fried chicken, and steaks also available. There are daily seafood specials for around B$15–B$18 ($7.50–$9), which make this one of the best places to find inexpensive seafood.

O'MAR'S FAST FOOD, near The Flamboyant, east of the sidewalk, Placencia. No phone.

Cuisine: BELIZEAN.
$ Prices: B$3.50–B$15 ($1.75–$7.50). No credit cards.
Open: Daily 8am–9:30pm.

This is not your typical "fast food"—in fact, it really isn't very fast at all. But it's good food from a one-man kitchen. On the menu are shrimp, chicken, vegetable, or fish burritos, chow mein of shrimp or conch, and garnaches, which are tiny crisp tortillas with beans, cheese, cabbage, and tomato. You order at a window and eat on a screened porch.

TENTACLES, next door to Paradise Vacation Hotel. Tel. 23156.

Cuisine: SEAFOOD.
$ Prices: B$6–B$40 ($3–$20). MC, V.
Open: Breakfast Mon–Sat 7:30–9:30am; lunch Mon–Sat 11:30am–1:30pm; dinner Mon–Sat 5:30–9pm.

It's hard to beat the view from the second-floor deck of this restaurant at the very southern end of Placencia. There are more tables outside than there are inside, but no matter where you sit, you'll be among friendly locals, tourists, businesspeople, and boaters in from the sailboats moored offshore. The conversation is usually lively. You'll find all the Belizean standards on the menu. If the food isn't

memorable, the setting certainly is: The mangrove swamps begin a few
while several little islands dot the far horizon; sailboats rock gently at
skiffs race back and forth to the mainland. It's positively bewitching wh
sparkles on the waves. They have a fairly decent full bar.

A NEARBY PLACE TO EAT

KULCHA SHACK, Seine Bight Village. No phone.
   Cuisine: GARIFUNA/CREOLE.
$ Prices: Main dishes B$10–B$30 ($5–$15). No credit cards.
   Open: Daily 8am–10pm.

The name is a play on words and conjures up images of Belizean culture shock, but
what you'll find here is actually some of the best down-home cooking and traditional
entertainment in Belize. Seine Bight is a Garifuna village and the menu here includes
several local specialties such as *hudut,* a fish stew made with coconut milk, herbs, and
plantains; *tapow,* a similar stew made with vegetables and served with rice and casava
bread; and *bundegah,* which is similar to tapow but is made with patties made from
grated bananas. The Kulcha Shack also does traditional Garifuna drumming and
dance performances if enough people are interested, though the charge for this
entertainment is a rather steep B$20 ($10) per person.

AN EXCURSION

Weighing up to 200 pounds and measuring more than six feet from nose to tip of tail,
jaguars are king of the new-world jungle. Nocturnal predators, jaguars prefer to hunt
peccaries (wild piglike animals), deer, and other small mammals. The **Cockscomb
Basin,** a wildlife sanctuary established in 1986 as the world's first jaguar reserve,
covers nearly 150 square miles of rugged forested mountains and has the greatest
density of jaguars in the world. It is part of the even larger Cockscomb Basin Forest
Reserve, which was created in 1984.

The forests within the preserve are home to other wild cats as well, including
pumas, ocelots, and margays, all of which are very elusive, so don't get your hopes of
seeing them too high. Few people do. Other mammals that you might spot if you're
lucky include otters, coatimundis, kinkajous, deer, peccaries, anteaters, and armadillos.

The largest land mammal native to Central America—the tapir—is also resident.
Locally known as a "mountain cow," the tapir is the national animal of Belize. A tapir
can weigh up to 600 pounds and is related to the horse, although its protruding upper
lip is more like an elephant's trunk.

Much more easily spotted in the dense vegetation surrounding the preserve's trails
are nearly 300 species of birds, including the scarlet macaw, the keel-billed toucan,
the king vulture, and the great curassow.

Great caution should be exercised when visiting the preserve—in addition to
jaguars, which can be dangerous, there are also poisonous snakes, including the
deadly fer-de-lance. Always wear shoes, preferably boots, when hiking the trails here.

Ellis Burgess (tel. 23186) is an excellent naturalist (formerly a bush guide for the
British army) who offers guided trips to the Cockscomb Basin for about B$45 ($22.50)
per person. Many mornings he can be found at BJ's Restaurant.

Visitors' facilities include an information center, picnic area, campground, and a
few primitive cabins costing B$15 ($7.50) per person per night. Drinking water is
available. For more information on the preserve, contact the **Belize Audubon
Society,** P.O. Box 1001, 12 Fort St., Belize City (tel. 2/35004).

4. PUNTA GORDA

205 miles S of Belize City; 100 miles S of Dangriga

GETTING THERE   By Plane   Maya Airways (tel. 2/72312 or 2/77215 in ze City) flies several times a day from Belize City to Punta Gorda. Duration: 1 hour. Fare: B$150 ($75) one way. Tropic Air (tel. 2/45671 in Belize City; tel. 7/22008 in Punta Gorda) flies to Punta Gorda three times daily. Fare: B$140 ($70) one way.

The Punta Gorda airport is on the west edge of town within walking distance of the town's hotels and guest houses.

By Boat There is a ferry between Puerto Barrios, Guatemala, and Punta Gorda, Belize, every Tuesday and Friday leaving Puerto Barrios at 7am. Buy your ticket the day before departure at the green ferry ticket office. Duration: 2–3 hours. Fare: Q32.10 ($5.55). When you arrive, be sure to get your passport stamped at the immigration office just up from the dock.

By Bus Z-Line buses leave from the Magazine Road bus terminal in Belize City Monday to Saturday at 8am; Monday, Wednesday, and Saturday at 3pm; and Sunday at 10am. Duration: 8 hours. Fare: B$22 ($11).

By Car It is a long and grueling road to Punta Gorda. The Southern Highway, which starts in Dangriga, is unpaved for 100 miles and, though fairly good in the dry season, can get very muddy in the wet season. Any time of year you'll have to take it slowly. Coming from Belize City, you can take the Manatee Road turnoff just past the Belize Zoo or continue on to Belmopan and turn south on the Hummingbird Highway. Neither road is very good, but the Hummingbird Highway is infamous for its killer potholes (though it's supposed to be repaved). Avoid it if you can.

DEPARTING Buses for Mango Creek (Placencia), Dangriga, Belmopan, and Belize City leave once or twice a day. Planes depart daily for Mango Creek, Dangriga, and Belize. The ferry to Puerto Barrios, Guatemala, leaves Tuesday and Friday at noon. Be sure to buy your ticket the day before at the office next to the Maya de Indita store half a block north from the northwest corner of the central park. Duration: 2–3 hours. Fare: B$13 ($6.50). Launches also make the trip across to Puerto Barrios on an irregular basis. They usually leave between 8am and noon from the main wharf and charge around B$20 ($10). Ask around at the wharf for a boat.

ESSENTIALS Punta Gorda is a small coastal town, and the road into town runs right along the water before angling a bit inland. There is a Belize Bank on the town's central park; it's open Monday to Thursday 8am to 1pm, Friday 8am to 1pm and 3 to 6pm. The post office is on Front St. across from Immigration and is open Monday through Thursday 8:30am to noon and 1 to 5pm, and Friday 8:30am to noon and 1 to 4:30pm.

The central park is also where you can catch buses to nearby Mayan villages.

Punta Gorda, Belize's southernmost town, is a quiet place with clean paved streets, lush vegetation, and hardly a soul about after the sun goes down. Although it is right on the Caribbean, there is no beach and the water is rather murky. However, the surrounding scenery is as verdant as you'll find anywhere in Belize (due to nearly 200 inches of rain a year). The surrounding Toledo District is home to several Mayan ruins and numerous villages that are still peopled by Maya Indians who migrated here from Guatemala during the last century.

Settled by Black Caribs in 1823, Punta Gorda was only accessible by boat for many years, and even though the Southern Highway now connects the town with points north, the 100 miles of bad gravel road ensure that the town is still isolated. As the administrative center for the Toledo District, Punta Gorda has an active market and bus services to the many surrounding Mayan villages, although connections are not very good. Most travelers do little more than pass through Punta Gorda on their way to or from Guatemala by way of the Puerto Barrios ferry. However, there is plenty to keep the adventurous traveler busy for several days.

WHAT TO SEE & DO

A stroll through Punta Gorda is the best way to enjoy the Caribbean atmosphere. If you've come down from the north, you'll likely be surprised at what a clean and quiet town Punta Gorda is compared with Dangriga or Belize City. It's a welcome relief and worth savoring for a day or two.

Most people who spend any time in Punta Gorda are interested in learning more about Mayan village life or sustainable agriculture, although there are also several Mayan ruins that attract a few hardy Mayaphiles. For information on a nearby permaculture (sustainable agriculture) farm and how to arrange staying in a Mayan village, see the listings below for Dem Dats Doin and Nature's Way Guest House.

The largest of the nearby Mayan ruins is **Lubaantun** (Place of Fallen Rock), which is about 20 miles from Punta Gorda and about 1 mile from the village of San Pedro Columbia. From the main road it is a 20-minute walk to the ruins. This Late Classic Maya ruin is unusual in that the structures were built using a technique of cut-and-fitted stones rather than the usual limestone-and-rock construction technique used elsewhere by the Mayans. Lubaantun is perhaps most famous as the site where a crystal skull was discovered by a Canadian woman in 1926. Kept in a vault in Canada, the skull has been surrounded with controversy. What was it used for? How could such a hard stone have been carved in such a detailed manner? Where did it come from? Some stories claim a light emanates from the skull, others attribute magical powers to it.

Nim Li Punit (Big Hat), off the Southern Highway 25 miles north of Punta Gorda, is the site of the largest Maya stela (carved record stone) known in Belize. It measures almost 30 feet tall and is one of more than two dozen stelae found here.

Other ruins in the area include **Uxbenka** near Santa Cruz and **Pusilha** near Aguacate. There is no charge to visit any of these ruins, yet, and the resident guards will even give you free guided tours.

Though the ruins were abandoned centuries ago, Maya Indians still live in this region. The villages of the Toledo District are populated by two groups of Maya Indians—the Kekchi and the Mopan—who have different languages and agricultural practices. The Mopan are upland farmers, while the Kekchi farm the lowlands. Both groups are thought to have migrated into southern Belize from Guatemala less than 100 years ago. San Antonio, the largest Mopan Maya village, is in a beautiful setting on top of a hill, with an old stone church in the center of the village. Steep streets wind through the village, and there are both clapboard houses and traditional Mayan thatched huts. San Antonio is known for its annual festival on June 13th in honor of the village's patron saint. The festival includes masked dances similar to those performed in the Guatemalan highlands. In San Antonio, you can stay at Bol's Hilltop Hotel, a very basic place with great views that charges B$15 ($7.50) for a single and B$30 ($15) for a double.

Beyond San Antonio is the more traditional village of Santa Cruz, where the homes are all in the traditional style, with thatched roofs and plank walls. There is a small village guest house here that is part of the Toledo Ecotourism Association, which is headquartered at Nature's Way Guest House (tel. 501-7/22119) in Punta Gorda, which is where you should check to find out about staying here or at any of the other village guest houses in this region. Rates at the 10 member guest houses are B$16 ($8) per person per night and meals are an additional B$18 to B$20 ($8 to $10) per person per day. You can also arrange guided hikes through the forest; visits to ruins, waterfalls, and caves; and traditional music, dancing, and storytelling performances.

Mayan culture, past and present, may be the main attraction of Punta Gorda, but it also boasts natural attractions. About 2½ miles before the village of San Antonio is one of the most beautiful swimming holes in all of Belize. Flowing out of a cave in a limestone mountain, the aptly named **Blue Creek** is a cool stream with striking deep turquoise water. Lush rain forest shades the creek, creating an idyllic place to spend an afternoon. You can cool off by swimming up into the mouth of the cave from which the stream flows. Blue Creek is a privately owned park charging a B$4 ($2) admission.

Near the village of Big Falls, which is near a waterfall on the Rio Grande, there is a natural **hot spring** that's a popular weekend picnic spot. You can have a refreshing swim in the river at the falls and then warm your muscles in the hot spring. There are also some attractive small waterfalls near the village of San Antonio.

There are buses from Punta Gorda to San Antonio, Big Falls, and Blue Creek, and buses headed north to Belize City pass by Nim Li Punit. However, some of these buses only run every other day, so making connections can take time. It's also possible to hitchhike, though not always reliable. Check at Nature's Way Guest House or with the Toledo Visitor Information Center at the wharf in Punta Gorda to find out about current bus schedules.

WHERE TO STAY

DEM DATS DOIN, P.O. Box 73, Punta Gorda. Tel. 501-7/22470. 1 rm.
$ Rates: B$30 ($15) single; B$40 ($20) double. No credit cards.
Dem Dats Doin bills itself as an energy sufficient low-input organic minibiosphere, in other words, it's a self-sufficient organic farm. As part of the farm, owners Alfredo and Yvonne Villoria have a single bedroom available as a bed-and-breakfast (lunch and dinner also available for B$10 to B$12 [$5 to $6] per person per meal). The farm is primarily visited by people fascinated by sustainable agriculture (permaculture). Electricity and cooking fuel come from the sun and biogas, and there are more than 1,000 varieties of tropical plants as well as a collection of butterflies and insects on the farm. The farm is within walking distance of the Kekchi Maya village of San Pedro Columbia and Lubaantun ruins.

If you'd just like to visit and see what's doin', 2-hour tours are available for B$10 ($5). The Villorias also help promote a homestay program in several of the nearby Maya villages. There is a B$10 ($5) registration fee and the room and board cost B$22 ($11) per person. If you're interested in spending a night with a Mayan family, register at the Villoria's Toledo Visitors Information Center on Front Street at the main wharf (where the Puerto Barrios ferry docks). The information center is open Monday through Wednesday and Friday and Saturday from 8am to noon.

GOYO'S INN, Main Middle St., Punta Gorda. Tel. 501-7/22086. 9 rms (all with bath).
$ Rates: B$31.80 ($15.90) single; B$37.10 ($18.55) double. No credit cards.
Located right on the central park, Goyo's is convenient if you arrive in town after dark and don't want to wander around an unfamiliar town looking for a room. Light sleepers beware. There is a small restaurant on the first floor, and behind this is a TV lounge. All rooms have hot water and cable TV, but otherwise vary considerably; some are large and clean, while others are smaller, darker, and not as clean.

NATURE'S WAY GUEST HOUSE, 65 Front St., Punta Gorda. Tel. 501-7/ 22119. 6 rms (none with bath).
$ Rates: B$16 ($8) single; B$26 ($13) double; B$35.50 ($17.75) triple. No credit cards.

S Located three blocks south of the central park and across the street from the water, Nature's Way is a longtime favorite of budget travelers and should be your first choice in Punta Gorda. Even though the rooms do not have private bathrooms, the shared baths are large, clean, and modern. The guest house is operated by an American named William "Chet" Smith who moved down here more than 20 years ago to promote sustainable agricultural practices. Chet is a wealth of information about the area and helped start a village guest house program which allows visitors to stay in the nearby Mayan villages.

PUNTA CALIENTE HOTEL & RESTAURANT, 108 José María Nunez St., Punta Gorda. Tel. 501-7/22567. 8 rms (all with bath).
$ Rates: B$43 ($21.50) single, B$53 ($26.50) double. B$15 ($7.50) for extra bed. No credit cards.
Inexpensive for Belize, this place has some nice features such as plants in the hallway and a restaurant on the ground floor. Located next to the Z-line bus station, the

building is of modern cinder-block construction. There are, surprisingly, no doors on bathrooms; they are separated by a partition only. Rooms have fans, and some even have a queen-size bed.

ST. CHARLES INN, 23 King St., Punta Gorda. Tel. 501-7/22149. 15 rms (all with bath).

$ Rates: B$30 ($15) single; B$40 ($20) double. No credit cards.

Located two blocks north of the central park, the St. Charles is part of a small general store, which is where you should go to ask about a room. The guest rooms are in two buildings, and the second floor is a bit nicer since it has a veranda and overlooks a small green yard. The small rooms have louvered windows, fans for cooling, hot water, and cable TV.

WORTH THE EXTRA BUCKS

INTERNATIONAL ZOOLOGICAL EXPEDITIONS LODGE AT BLUE CREEK, 35 Lemon St., Dangriga. Tel. 501-5/22119. Fax 501-5/23152. In the U.S. 508/655-1461, fax 508/655-4445. 6 cabins (all with shared bath).

$ Rates: B$159 ($79.50) per person including meals, 3-day minimum stay. No credit cards.

This lodge is located in the jungle near the Mayan village of Blue Creek, about 22 kilometers northwest of Punta Gorda. The comfortable cabins overlook the beautiful Blue Creek River, while the lodge houses the bathrooms and dining area and is also a meeting place for scientists and students doing ecological studies in the forest. Guided trips to caves in the area are included in the room price, and if you want to do further exploration, Indian guides can be hired for day hikes to the Moho River and other places. The IZE's tree canopy observation platforms are located across the river, and although access is limited, it's interesting to watch the activity from below.

WHERE TO EAT

KOWLOON RESTAURANT, 35 Main Middle St., Punta Gorda. Tel. 22692.

Cuisine: CHINESE/AMERICAN.

$ Prices: B$8–B$18 ($4–$9). No credit cards.

Open: Mon–Sat lunch 11am–2pm, dinner 6:30–10:30pm; Sun 5:30–10:30pm.

There are several Chinese restaurants in Punta Gorda, but currently this is the best one. You can get all the regular Chinese dishes such as chow mein, chop suey, and fried rice fixed with Belizean conch, fish, shrimp, and lobster. It's located a block off the square and three blocks over from the water.

MAN MAN'S 5 STAR RESTAURANT, no address. No phone.

Cuisine: BELIZEAN.

$ Prices: Full meal B$8–B$10 ($4–$5). No credit cards.

Open: Breakfast daily 7:30–10:00am; dinner daily 6–9pm.

This is Punta Gorda's most famous eating establishment, and if you're lucky, Man Man will still be cooking up a storm when you pass through town. To find the restaurant, walk two blocks east (away from the water) from the north side of the central park and then turn right. In the middle of the block you should see a sign for the restaurant hanging in a tree. Behind the sign is a tiny shack: inside there is one table to the side of the tiny kitchen. Man Man does the cooking and the menu is whatever he happens to be fixing that night, which is frequently delicious fresh fish. Portions are huge, and if he isn't busy, Man Man will sit and chat with you over your meal. Don't miss this rare dining experience.

SHAIBA TROPICAL RESTAURANT, 6 Front St. Tel. 22370.

Cuisine: CREOLE.

$ Prices: Main dishes B$5–B$20 ($2.50–$10). No credit cards.

Open: Daily 7am–2pm and 6–11pm.

Owned by "Pino" Sierra, a competent artist, and his wife Lila, who runs a Creole dance company, Shaiba is another Punta Gorda gem. Lila does the cooking—the menu changes daily but usually includes the likes of conch soup, pork chops, fish filet, and butter conch. She intends to expand the menu, adding more Creole standards like boiled casava, sweet potato, and yam pea, in addition to the jams and wines she already makes from local fruits and ginger. If you'd like to try some, ask what's available. Don't miss the seaweed punch either; it's a bit like eggnog.

5. SAN IGNACIO & THE CAYO DISTRICT

72 miles W of Belize City; 40 miles W of Belmopan; 9 miles E of the Guatemalan border

GETTING THERE By Bus Novelos and Batty Bros. buses leave frequently from their Collet Canal stations in Belize City (the station is actually one block before the canal down a side street to the right. Duration: 3 hours. Fare: B$4 ($2). There's also frequent daily service from Belmopan. Duration: 1½ hours. Fare: B$2 ($1).

By Car Take the Western Highway from Belize City.

DEPARTING Novelos and Batty Bros. operate buses to Belmopan and Belize City daily between 4am and 4pm.

If you are heading for Tikal in Guatemala, get an early start. Batty's buses leave for the border at 8:30 and 9:30am (B$1.50 [75¢]), although there are buses throughout the day to Benque Viejo, which is only a mile from the border. You can also take a taxi from San Ignacio to the border for B$20 ($10) or from Benque Viejo B$4 ($2).

Be sure to leave at least an hour for border formalities. Leaving Belize, you'll have to fill out a departure card and turn in your temporary entry permit if you're driving your own car. Entering Guatemala, you will have to pay Q25 ($5) for a Tourist Card (if you don't have a visa), and you may also be asked to pay a few quetzales to have your bags cursorily inspected. If you're driving a car, expect to pay around $25 depending on the whims of the border guards. This payment covers required papers, fumigation of your tires and possibly the inside of your car, and most likely a bribe. You can keep border-crossing costs to a minimum by crossing during regular business hours, which are Monday through Friday 8am to noon and 2 to 6pm. Outside these hours, and especially after dark, you can expect to be asked for additional unexplained payments (bribes). There are always several money changers working here at the border, so be sure to change your Belize dollars for quetzales (usually a bad exchange rate) and 50 to 100 U.S. dollars to see you through Tikal where the lodges offer notoriously bad exchange rates.

Once you've passed through Guatemalan border formalities, cross the bridge and walk up the hill to the gas station to find out when the next bus leaves for Flores. There are usually five or six buses a day between 3am and 4pm. If you're in a hurry to reach Tikal, take the bus to El Cruce (also called Ixlu), which is the turnoff for Tikal and is about two hours away over a horrendously rutted road. Unfortunately, buses headed to Tikal pass fairly early in the morning, so your only option may be to try hitchhiking. A safer plan is to take the bus all the way to Flores, spend the night there, and continue to Tikal the next day.

ESSENTIALS Orientation San Ignacio is on the banks of the Macal River, on the far side of an old metal bridge. Just across the bridge is a traffic circle. Downtown San Ignacio is to the right on Burns Avenue, and the San Ignacio Hotel is to the left on Buena Vista Road. Most of the hotels and restaurants are on or within a block of Burns Avenue.

See Bob at Eva's Restaurant on Burns Avenue for information about the area. He can help you arrange tours and accommodations.

Fast Facts   There is a drugstore downstairs from the Venus Hotel on Burns Avenue. The police emergency phone number is 2022. The telephone office is across from the Venus Hotel on Burns Avenue, open Monday to Friday 8am to noon and 1 to 4pm, Saturday 8am to noon.

The Belize Bank is open Monday through Thursday 8am to 1pm and Friday 8am to 1pm and 3 to 6pm. The post office is located on the traffic circle upstairs from the police station and is open Monday through Thursday 8:30am to noon and 1 to 4:30pm, and Friday 8:30am to noon and 1 to 4pm.

In the foothills of the mountains, close to the Guatemalan border, lie the twin towns of Santa Elena and San Ignacio (pop. 7,100) on either side of a beautiful, calm, clear river (good for a swim). San Ignacio is the administrative center for the Cayo District, a region of cattle ranches and dense forests, of clear rivers and Mayan ruins. If you've come from Guatemala, you'll sense immediately that you are now in a Caribbean country. If you've come up from the coast, you might be surprised by how cool it can get up here in the mountains. Cayo and the cayes are worlds apart. While the cayes cater to those looking for fun in the sun, Cayo caters to those interested in nature. This area makes a good first stop in Belize; you can get in a lot of activity before heading to the beach to relax.

WHAT TO SEE & DO

High on a hill to the southwest of downtown San Ignacio are the Mayan ruins of **Cahal Pech.** This former royal residence was recently restored with the help of the United States Agency for International Development and San Diego State University. The restoration has created a bit of controversy in town because parts of the ruins were restored to the way they looked when they were first built, which is a bit more polished and modern-looking than most people like their ruins. However, the setting is beautiful, with tall old trees shading the site's main plaza and pyramid/castle. The name Cahal Pech means the "Place of the Family of Pech" (Pech means tick in Mayan). The name was given to the site in the 1950s when there were quite a few ticks in the area. The ruins date back to between A.D. 650 and 900, though there are indications that the site was used prior to this time as well.

A **museum** displays a collection of artifacts recovered from the site and provides insight into the Cahal Pech social structure. Admission to the museum and ruins is B$3 ($1.50), open 8am–5pm daily. Be sure to ask for a copy of the very informative guide to the site. To reach Cahal Pech, walk up toward the San Ignacio Hotel continuing on around the curve for a few hundred yards until you see the sign pointing up a dirt road to the ruins. The entrance to the ruins is near the large thatched building on top of the hill. It's about a 20-minute walk.

After a visit to the ruins, or any time for that matter, nothing feels better than a swim in San Ignacio's **Macal River.** Though you can join the locals right in town where the river is treated as a free laundry, car wash, horse and dog wash, and swimming hole, you'll do better to head upstream a few hundred yards above the bridge to a swimming hole complete with rope swing and cliffs for high divers.

Another alternative is to head downriver about 1½ miles to a spot called **Branch Mouth,** where the different-colored waters of the Macal and Mopan rivers converge. Branch Mouth is a favorite picnic spot, with shady old trees clinging to the river banks. There's even a rope swing from one of the trees. The road is dusty, so you'll be especially happy to go for a swim here.

For much of Belize's history, the rivers were the highways. The Mayans used them for trading, and British loggers used them to get mahogany. If you're interested, you can explore the Cayo District's two rivers by canoe. In fact, you can paddle as far as the coast if you're so inclined. The waters in these rivers have a few riffles, but you don't need white-water experience. The trips are leisurely, with stops for swimming or land excursions. **Tony's Adventure Tours** (tel. 2267) offers regular day-long guided canoe trips up the Macal River as far as Chaa Creek Cottages and the Panti Medicine Trail. These trips cost B$25 ($12.50) per person. Along the way, you're likely to see iguanas, snakes, toucans, and other wildlife. There are always plenty of stops to cool off in the water, and you can have lunch at Chaa Creek and then tour the Panti Trail (both of these cost extra).

If your preferred activity is **mountain biking,** you can rent bikes at **B & M Mountain Bike Hire** (tel. 22457), 119 George Price Avenue, Santa Elena. However, let me warn you that the hills here are steep and the heat and humidity can be overwhelming. Take (and drink) lots of water, and try to avoid pedaling during the middle of the day. Rental rates when I last visited were B$5 ($2.50) per hour.

If you enjoy horseback riding, contact **Mountain Equestrian Trails,** Mile 8 Mountain Pine Ridge Road, Central Farm P.O., Cayo (tel. 8-23180). Although not cheap, they provide excellent horseback tours of the area, including visits to caves and waterfalls. A half-day trip including lunch costs B$120 ($60) per person; a full-day trip costs B$160 ($80).

Easy Rider (tel. 23310) offers jungle, valley, and ruins trips for B$40–B$60 ($20–$30). Call them for free pickup in San Ignacio. Also, keep in mind that most lodges in the area also offer horseback riding.

WHERE TO STAY

Good accommodations in San Ignacio are scarce: There are lots of choices that are outside your budget and several that are more basic than you'll probably want, but little in between. Still, there are a few options in this beautiful neck of the Belizean woods.

DOUBLES FOR LESS THAN B$30 [$15]

HI-ET, 12 West St., San Ignacio, Cayo. Tel. 501-92/2828. 5 rms (none with bath).
$ Rates: B$10 ($5) single; B$20 ($10) double. No credit cards.
The water is cold and you have to share a bathroom, but the Hi-Et is family run, clean, and secure. This is the best of the bottom-of-the-budget hotels in San Ignacio. Unfortunately, it's almost always full.

DOUBLES FOR LESS THAN B$50 [$25]

BELMORAL HOTEL, 17 Burns Ave., San Ignacio, Cayo. Tel. 501-92/2024. 11 rms (all with bath).
$ Rates: B$35–B$75 ($17.50–$37.50) single; B$45–B$85 ($22.50–$42.50) double; B$63–B$100 ($31.50–$50) triple. AE, MC, V.
Located right beside the bus station on the main street through town, the Belmoral is one of San Ignacio's better deals (and most outlandish hotels). Walls throughout the hotel are covered with one-inch square mirrors and have been painted with a thick, combed paint. You have to see it to believe it. The lower priced rooms are those with fans instead of air conditioners, which are all you really need most of the time. The rooms vary considerably in size and comfort, but most are acceptable. There is morning coffee available, and continental breakfast can also be arranged.

MARTHA'S GUEST HOUSE, 10 West St., San Ignacio. Tel. 501-92/2276. 3 rms (all with shared bath).
$ Rates: B$26 ($13) single, B$30 ($15) double. No credit cards.
S This small guest house is a bit like a Belizean homestay and is located in a modern apartment above a general store. Guests can hang out in the high-ceilinged living room, which has couches and plaited mats for rugs. Out front, there's a large balcony. There is also a kitchen for the use of the guests, although you can also arrange to have breakfast prepared for you. Tours and a laundry service

are available. This is San Ignacio's newest and cleanest budget hostelry and as such is a very good deal.

PLAZA HOTEL, 4A Burns Ave., San Ignacio, Cayo District. Tel. 501-92/ 3332. 12 rms (all with bath).
$ Rates: B$37.10–B$58.30 ($18.55–$29.15) single; B$47.70–B$74.20 ($23.85–$37.10) double. No credit cards.
The Plaza, which is located right on San Ignacio's main street about a block from the bus station, is a basic Belizean business hotel. Though the hotel is fairly modern, there's no Belizean character. There are, however, TVs and ceiling fans in the rooms, as well as air conditioners in the more expensive rooms. Bathrooms are small and the rooms aren't always spotless, but in Belize, you don't ask too much of a budget hotel.

WORTH THE EXTRA BUCKS

ROSE'S GUEST HOUSE, by Cahal Pech ruins, San Ignacio. Tel. 501-92/ 2282. 5 rms (all with shared bath).
$ Rates (including breakfast): B$68.90 ($34.45) single; B$84.80 ($42.40) double (lower rates in off-season). No credit cards.
Located on a hill above San Ignacio and adjacent to the Cahal Pech ruins, Rose's is an attractive house with stucco walls and a red-tile roof. The guest rooms are large, modern, and comfortable and some have a good view. There always seems to be a cooling breeze up here and the lawn is a great place to sit out and enjoy the views.

SAN IGNACIO HOTEL, P.O. Box 33, San Ignacio, Cayo. Tel. 501-92/ 2034. 25 rms (all with bath).
$ Rates: B$91.16–B$137.80 ($45.60–$68.90) single; B$106–B$159 ($53–$79.50) double; B$127.20–B$180.20 ($63.60–$90.10) triple. AE, MC, V.
The San Ignacio Hotel is up the steep hill just past the police station, at the west end of the bridge into town. Because it's situated on Buena Vista Road, it has magnificent views of the jungle. The hotel is a welcome oasis in this country of generally substandard accommodations, but it's often full by sundown. Although it's a bit expensive, it's clean and comfortable.
There's a good restaurant and bar with decent food and great views from its terrace. A full breakfast costs B$12 ($6); dinner is about B$30 ($15).

CAMPING

Cosmos Camping is a campground on the road leading out toward Branch Mouth and Las Casitas, where you can park your van or pitch your tent for B$10 ($5) per day. It has a cold-water shower and an outhouse, but there isn't much other than that. The river is just across a field, which makes this a rather nice spot.

WHERE TO EAT

EVA'S RESTAURANT & BAR, 22 Burns Ave. Tel. 2267.
Cuisine: BELIZEAN/INTERNATIONAL.
$ Prices: B$6–B$9 ($3–$4.50). No credit cards.
Open: Daily 7am–midnight.
S Although it's short on atmosphere, Eva's is long on information—and the conversation is lively. Owner Bob Jones is a wealth of information about the area and acts as the local branch of the tourist board. If you want to get a group of people together to rent a taxi or canoe or to defray the costs of a tour, let Bob know—he'll try to put you in touch with other like-minded folks. Rice, beans, and chicken cost B$6 ($3); fish and fries cost B$9 ($4.50). There are daily specials (usually local dishes) such as escabeche or chilemole for B$7 ($3.50) that are always good choices.

MAXIM'S CHINESE RESTAURANT, 23 Far West St. Tel. 2233.
Cuisine: CHINESE.
$ Prices: B$5.50–B$16 ($2.75–$8). No credit cards.
Open: Lunch daily 11am–3pm; dinner daily 5:30pm–midnight.
For delicious Chinese food, try this casual place. Various plates of fried rice range from B$5.75 ($2.90) to B$10 ($5), and sweet-and-sour dishes cost B$8 ($4) to B$10 ($5). There's also a host of vegetarian dishes. Try the Belikin Stout if you like dark beer with a bite. The owner goes into Belize City once a week to secure fish and other ingredients. (The owner will also change traveler's checks as a favor.) Take-out is available.

SERENDIB RESTAURANT, 27 Burns Ave. Tel. 2302.
Cuisine: SRI LANKAN.
$ Prices: B$7.50–B$15 ($3.75–$7.50). No credit cards.
Open: Mon–Sat 9:30am–3pm and 6:30–11pm.
This pleasant little restaurant is an unexpected surprise in the tiny town of San Ignacio. Owner Hantley Pieris is from Sri Lanka and came to Belize years ago with the British army. He now runs a restaurant serving excellent curries in the style of his native country. You can get beef or chicken curry with yellow or fried rice and potato salad for B$9.50 ($4.75). In addition, there are sandwiches, burgers, chow mein, and fried fish on the menu for B$3 to B$15 ($1.50 to $7.50). Mr. Pieris also operates a coffee shop, serving ice cream and pastry, to the left of the restaurant.

SHAL'S DINER, Mile 67½ Western Highway, Santa Elena. Tel. 23856.
Cuisine: BELIZEAN.
$ Prices: Main dishes B$2.50–B$12 ($1.25–$6). No credit cards.
Open: Daily 6am–10pm.
For some good Belizean cooking, take a 10-minute walk from the metal bridge through Santa Elena to Shal's Diner. This restaurant has tables both inside and on the porch outside. A breakfast of corn tortillas, refried beans, and eggs costs B$6 ($3), rice and beans with chicken, salad, and fried plantain is B$6.50 ($3.25), and a large glass of fresh-squeezed orange or grapefruit juice is B$1.50 (75¢). The restaurant, (as well as the bathrooms here) is spotlessly clean. You'll find Shal's on the south side of the highway.

NEARBY PLACES TO STAY & EAT

If you've made it this far, you're probably the adventurous type, and I'm sure you'd like to know about some wonderful splurges in the Cayo District. Within a few miles of San Ignacio are several **jungle lodges** where you can canoe down clear rivers past 4-foot iguanas sunning themselves on the rocks, ride horses to Mayan ruins, hike jungle trails, and spot dozens of beautiful birds and, occasionally, other wild animals. I highly recommend that you stay at one of the jungle lodges listed below while you're in the area. A few of the lodges can be reached by public bus from San Ignacio though you may have a 20-minute walk after getting off the bus. All the lodges will arrange trips to various sites in the area—such as Mountain Pine Ridge, Xunantunich, and Tikal. You can also hire a taxi, though this is quite expensive: B$50 ($25) to Chaa Creek and B$60 ($30) to duPlooy's.

DOUBLES FOR LESS THAN B$90 [$45]

BLACK ROCK, P.O. Box 48, San Ignacio, Cayo District. Tel. 501/92-2341. 6 tent cabanas (3 with bath).
$ Rates (including three meals): B$120 ($60) single without bath, B$162 ($81) single with bath; B$178 ($89) double without bath, B$227 ($113.50) double with bath. MC, V.
So, you *really* want to get away from it all? Well, this is the place. To reach Black Rock, you travel six miles down a dirt road and then hike for a mile along the Macal River. What do you do at Black Rock? Why, nothing of course! Just enjoy the river, with its rapids, waterfalls, and cliffs. The only electricity out here is from photovoltaic cells, so

at night it's just you and the stars and all those strange noises. Transportation out here will set you back B$40 to B$60 ($20 to $30), but, if you ask me, it's worth it.

CLARISSA FALLS COTTAGES, P.O. Box 44, San Ignacio, Cayo. Tel. 501-92/3916. 3 cabins (none with bath).

$ Rates (without meals): B$15.90 ($7.95) per person. B$5.30 ($2.65) per person to camp. No credit cards.

Clarissa Falls and the jade green waters of the Mopan River are the backdrop for this, my favorite budget lodging in Cayo. Situated on an 800-acre working cattle ranch, these three cottages are quite basic, with cement floors and beds and little else. However, the spartan decor is more than compensated for by the beautiful surroundings of hilly pastures and river.

When we last visited, Chena, the friendly and helpful owner, was planning to build an additional six rooms.

An open-air restaurant serving excellent Belizean/Creole–style meals for between B$10 ($5) and B$15 ($7.50) sits atop a Mayan ruin. Boats and inner tubes can be rented and horseback riding is available. If you'd like to just visit for the day, you can swim in the river and picnic for B$2 ($1), which is a very popular activity on weekends (if you crave peace and tranquility, visit on a weekday). Clarissa Falls Cottages are about 1½ miles off the highway about 4 miles west of San Ignacio. The bus to Benque Viejo will drop you at the turnoff.

MIDA'S RESORT, Branch Mouth Rd., San Ignacio. Tel. 501-92/3172, 92/2101, or 92/2737. Fax 501-92/3845. 4 cabins (2 with bath).

$ Rates (without meals): B$31.80 ($15.90) single without bath, B$42.40 ($21.20) single with bath; B$42.40 ($21.20) double without bath, B$47.70 ($23.85) double with bath. B$7 ($3.50) per person to camp. MC, V.

Though Mida's is just a short walk from downtown San Ignacio, it feels a world away. The round Mayan-style cottages are set in a sunny garden but have thatch roofs and screen walls so they stay cool, and there is also lawn space for camping. The Macal River is only a stroll away down a grassy lane, and you can spend the day lounging on the little beach on the river bank. There's no restaurant here, but it only takes a few minutes to walk into San Ignacio. To reach Mida's, walk out of town across the fields behind San Ignacio's combination bus terminal and public park. A dirt road leads past Mida's toward Branch Mouth.

PARROT'S NEST, Bullet Tree Falls, c/o General Post Office, San Ignacio, Cayo. Tel. 501-92/3702. 4 rms (all with shared bath), 1 guest house (with bath).

$ Rates: B$35 ($17.50) single or double; B$60 ($30) guest house. No credit cards.

Located three miles from San Ignacio and operated by Fred Prost, who once ran the popular Seaside Guest House in Belize City, the Parrot's Nest is a unique accommodation for backpack travelers. Set on a 5-acre tropical plant farm on the banks of the river, the rustic lodge consists of four very basic treehouses and the more comfortable guest house. Though there is a bit of noise from traffic passing on the adjacent road, this is otherwise a great place to spend a few days. Meals are available, but alcoholic beverages are not, so bring your own. Guided hikes and horseback rides are available.

RANCHO LOS AMIGOS, San José Succotz Village. Tel. 501-93/2483. 4 cabins (none with bath).

$ Rates (including breakfast and dinner): B$50 ($25) single; B$100 ($50) double; B$150 ($75) triple; B$30 ($15) per person to camp. No credit cards.

If you don't mind using a pit toilet and bathing in a spring-fed pool, Rancho Los Amigos may just be your idea of paradise. This rustic retreat is an economical place to experience all the best of the Cayo District. Xunantunich ruins and the Mopan River are only a mile or so away, and if you have more energy, you can walk to Black Rock on the Macal River. The cabins here are rustic but comfortable and the Jenkins family, refugees from Southern California, will make you feel right at home. Excellent meals (including vegetarian) are cooked up in an open-air kitchen atop a Mayan ruin. The lack of electricity here adds to the rustic appeal. If you happen to have any aches or pains, you might even get Ed Jenkins to perform a bit of acupuncture on you.

WORTH THE EXTRA BUCKS

CHAA CREEK COTTAGES, P.O. Box 53, San Ignacio, Cayo. Tel. 501-92/ 2037. Fax 501-92/2501. 19 rms (all with bath).

$ Rates: B$201.40 ($100.70) single with bath; B$243.80 ($121.90) double with bath. Meals are an additional B$80 ($40) per person per day. AE, MC, V.

Much loving care has gone into creating the beautiful grounds and cottages here; if you decide to spend the extra money, I'm sure you'll be glad you did. This is one of the oldest of the jungle lodges in the Cayo District and is located on the Macal River. To reach the cottages, drive 5 miles west from San Ignacio and watch for the sign on your left. It's another couple of miles down a very rough dirt road from the main highway. All of the thatched-roof cottages are artistically decorated with Guatemalan textiles and handcrafts and have private baths with hot water. The Panti Medicine Trail is located nearby, as are a butterfly breeding farm and a natural history center. There are canoes available at an additional charge, and horseback rides can always be arranged. For those seeking a real jungle experience, several-day hiking trips through the jungle can be arranged. Mick and Lucy Fleming are the engaging hosts here.

A separate bar and dining room provide plenty of space for socializing.

DUPLOOY'S, San Ignacio, Cayo District. Tel. 501-92/3301. Fax 501-92/ 3301. In the U.S. 803/722-1513. 17 rms (8 with bath).

$ Rates (without meals): B$74.20 ($37.10) single without bath, B$95.40 ($47.70) double without bath; (including meals) B$212–B$275.60 ($106–$137.80) single with bath, B$307.40–B$402.80 ($153.70–$201.40) double with bath. MC, V.

You'll certainly think that you're lost long before you reach this remote lodge, but keep following the rutted road. When you finally top a very steep hill and gaze down into the pastured valley below, you won't ever want to leave. The lodge is situated overlooking the Macal River, with jungle-covered limestone cliffs opposite. Jungle covers the surrounding hills. Ken and Judy duPlooy, who moved here a few years ago from South Carolina, are your hosts. Their lodge is a bit more luxurious than the others in the area; this, combined with the stunning location, make duPlooy's my favorite of Cayo's jungle lodges. The nine rooms are in three stone-and-stucco buildings with tile roofs. Each has a screened porch and a private bath. They have also added luxury bungalows and budget accommodations in the Pink House, where meals can be purchased separately.

There's a beach on the river, and canoes and snorkeling and fishing equipment are available for rent. If you're paying by credit card, add 5% to your bill. Follow the directions for Chaa Creek Cottages. DuPlooy's is a bit farther on the same dirt road, but be sure to take the right fork and follow the signs.

EXCURSIONS
XUNANTUNICH

Although you may not be able to pronounce it (say "Shoo-nahn-too-nitch"), you can visit it. Xunantunich is a Mayan ruin 6½ miles past San Ignacio on the road to Benque Viejo. The name translates as "maiden of the rocks." Open daily from 8am to 4pm. The admission is B$3 ($1.50).

At 127 feet, this pyramid is one of the tallest structures in Belize, despite the new glass-tower addition to the Fort George Hotel in Belize City. The panorama from the top is amazing. Don't miss it. On the east side of the pyramid, near the top, is a remarkably well-preserved stucco frieze.

Down below, under the protection of a thatched palapa in the temple forecourt, are three magnificent stelae portraying rulers of the region. Xunantunich was a thriving Mayan city about the same time as Altun Ha, in the Classic Period, about A.D. 600 to 900.

Take a bus bound for Benque Viejo and get off in San José Succotz. To reach the ruins, you must cross the Mopan River aboard a tiny hand-cranked car-ferry in the village of San José Succotz. You're bound to see colorfully dressed women washing clothes in the river as you are cranked across by the ferryman. After crossing the river, it is a short walk to the ruins. You can also take a taxi, but it's very expensive—unless you share one for about B$4 ($2) per person to the border and ask the driver to drop you off at the ferry.

IX CHEL FARM & THE PANTI MAYAN MEDICINE TRAIL

Located adjacent to Chaa Creek Cottages, Ix Chel Farm is a tropical plant research center operated by Drs. Rosita Arvigo and Greg Shropshire. Rosita studied traditional herbal medicine with Don Eligio Panti, a local Mayan medicine man. Here on the farm she has built a trail through the forest to share with visitors the fascinating medicinal values of many of the tropical forest's plants. You can tour the trail with a guide for B$15 ($7.50) per person or use Rosita's guidebook to the trail available for B$10 ($5). Contact your lodge owner or Bob at Eva's Restaurant for information on scheduling a visit.

Ix Chel Farm also produces a line of herbal concentrates called Rainforest Remedies that can be purchased at the farm or at the gift shop at Eva's, among other places. Dr. Arvigo has organized the Belize Association of Traditional Healers, which in turn has helped to create **Terra Nova,** an old-growth-forest reserve to be managed for the preservation and study of medicinal plants. If you are interested in supporting this project, you can speak with someone at the farm or write to the Belize Association of Traditional Healers, c/o Dr. Rosita Arvigo, Ix Chel Farm, San Ignacio, Cayo, Belize, C.A.

MOUNTAIN PINE RIDGE & CARACOL

Few people think of pine trees as being a tropical species, but you'll see plenty of them in Belize, especially in these rugged mountains. This 3,400-foot ridge is complete with a secret waterfall, wild orchids, parrots, keel-billed toucans, and other exotic flora and fauna. Mountain Pine Ridge, Hidden Valley Falls (also called Thousand Foot Falls), and the Río On and Río Frío Caves are off the Western Highway near Georgeville.

These roads are nearly impassable in the wet season and are pretty bad even in the dry season, so don't even think about attempting the trip in anything less than a four-wheel-drive vehicle. All the lodges offer tours to the area, with prices ranging from B$60 to B$90 ($30 to $45) per person if you have a group of four or five people. You can arrange a trip for B$50 ($25) through Bob at Eva's Restaurant. He'll put your name on a list with other people who are interested in going.

Caracol is believed to be the largest of the Mayan ruins, and as important as Tikal. It's not set up as a tourist sight, but if you have the interest, stamina, and vehicle to make it, you can visit. It's on the same road as Mountain Pine Ridge, several very rough miles farther south. Don't try it in the rainy season.

CHECHEM HAH

Ten miles south of Benque Viejo, on a dirt road that is recommended only for four-wheel-drive vehicles, is the cave of Chechem Hah, which was only rediscovered a few years ago. When the cave was explored, a cache of Mayan artifacts was discovered within the cave. The Mayas believed that caves were a direct avenue to the underworld gods; caves filled with offerings have been found throughout Mayan territory. Chechem Hah is privately owned and there is an admission charge of B$50 ($25) per group for a tour of the cave, where you can see many of the Mayan relics just as they were found. It is also possible to stay on a farm near the cave. Also in the vicinity is **Vaca Fall,** a beautiful and remote waterfall that's a popular day trip with horseback riders. Check at Eva's for more information on visiting Chechem Hah.

INDEX

COSTA RICA

GUATEMALA

BELIZE

Now Save Money on All Your Travels by Joining
FROMMER'S ™ TRAVEL BOOK CLUB
The World's Best Travel Guides at Membership Prices

FROMMER'S TRAVEL BOOK CLUB is your ticket to successful travel! Open up a world of travel information and simplify your travel planning when you join ranks with thousands of value-conscious travelers who are members of the FROMMER'S TRAVEL BOOK CLUB. Join today and you'll be entitled to all the privileges that come from belonging to the club that offers you travel guides for less to more than 100 destinations worldwide. Annual membership is only $25 (U.S.) or $35 (Canada and foreign).

The Advantages of Membership

1. Your choice of *three* free FROMMER'S TRAVEL GUIDES (any *two* FROM-MER'S COMPREHENSIVE GUIDES, FROMMER'S $-A-DAY GUIDES, FROMMER'S WALKING TOURS *or* FROMMER'S FAMILY GUIDES—plus *one* FROMMER'S CITY GUIDE, FROMMER'S CITY $-A-DAY GUIDE *or* FROMMER'S TOURING GUIDE).
2. Your own subscription to **TRIPS AND TRAVEL** quarterly newsletter.
3. You're entitled to a **30% discount** on your order of any additional books offered by FROMMER'S TRAVEL BOOK CLUB.
4. You're offered (at a small additional fee) our **Domestic Trip-Routing Kits.**

Our quarterly newsletter **TRIPS AND TRAVEL** offers practical information on the best buys in travel, the "hottest" vacation spots, the latest travel trends, world-class events and much, much more.

Our **Domestic Trip-Routing Kits** are available for any North American destination. We'll send you a detailed map highlighting the best route to take to your destination—you can request direct or scenic routes.

Here's all you have to do to join:

Send in your membership fee of $25 ($35 Canada and foreign) with your name and address on the form below along with your selections as part of your membership package to **FROMMER'S TRAVEL BOOK CLUB, P.O. Box 473, Mt. Morris, IL 61054-0473.** Remember to check off your *three* free books.

If you would like to order additional books, please select the books you would like and send a check for the total amount (please add sales tax in the states noted below), plus $2 per book for shipping and handling ($3 per book for foreign orders) to:

FROMMER'S TRAVEL BOOK CLUB
P.O. Box 473
Mt. Morris, IL 61054-0473
(815) 734-1104

[　] **YES.** I want to take advantage of this opportunity to join FROMMER'S TRAVEL BOOK CLUB.
[　] **My check is enclosed.** Dollar amount enclosed_____ *
　　　　　　　　　　　　　　(all payments in U.S. funds only)

Name_____
Address_____
City_____ State_____ Zip_____
　　　　　　　　All orders must be prepaid.

To ensure that all orders are processed efficiently, please apply sales tax in the following areas: CA, CT, FL, IL, NJ, NY, TN, WA and CANADA.

*With membership, shipping and handling will be paid by FROMMER'S TRAVEL BOOK CLUB for the three free books you select as part of your membership. Please add $2 per book for shipping and handling for any additional books purchased ($3 per book for foreign orders).

Allow 4–6 weeks for delivery. Prices of books, membership fee, and publication dates are subject to change without notice. Prices are subject to acceptance and availability.

Please Send Me the Books Checked Below:

FROMMER'S COMPREHENSIVE GUIDES
(Guides listing facilities from budget to deluxe,
with emphasis on the medium-priced)

	Retail Price	Code		Retail Price	Code
☐ Acapulco/Ixtapa/Taxco 1993–94	$15.00	C120	☐ Japan 1994–95 (Avail. 3/94)	$19.00	C144
☐ Alaska 1994–95	$17.00	C131	☐ Morocco 1992–93	$18.00	C021
☐ Arizona 1993–94	$18.00	C101	☐ Nepal 1994–95	$18.00	C126
☐ Australia 1992–93	$18.00	C002	☐ New England 1994 (Avail. 1/94)	$16.00	C137
☐ Austria 1993–94	$19.00	C119	☐ New Mexico 1993–94	$15.00	C117
☐ Bahamas 1994–95	$17.00	C121	☐ New York State 1994–95	$19.00	C133
☐ Belgium/Holland/ Luxembourg 1993–94	$18.00	C106	☐ Northwest 1994–95 (Avail. 2/94)	$17.00	C140
☐ Bermuda 1994–95	$15.00	C122	☐ Portugal 1994–95 (Avail. 2/94)	$17.00	C141
☐ Brazil 1993–94	$20.00	C111	☐ Puerto Rico 1993–94	$15.00	C103
☐ California 1994	$15.00	C134	☐ Puerto Vallarta/Manzanillo/ Guadalajara 1994–95 (Avail. 1/94)	$14.00	C028
☐ Canada 1994–95 (Avail. 4/94)	$19.00	C145	☐ Scandinavia 1993–94	$19.00	C135
☐ Caribbean 1994	$18.00	C123	☐ Scotland 1994–95 (Avail. 4/94)	$17.00	C146
☐ Carolinas/Georgia 1994–95	$17.00	C128	☐ South Pacific 1994–95 (Avail. 1/94)	$20.00	C138
☐ Colorado 1994–95 (Avail. 3/94)	$16.00	C143	☐ Spain 1993–94	$19.00	C115
☐ Cruises 1993–94	$19.00	C107	☐ Switzerland/Liechtenstein 1994–95 (Avail. 1/94)	$19.00	C139
☐ Delaware/Maryland 1994–95 (Avail. 1/94)	$15.00	C136	☐ Thailand 1992–93	$20.00	C033
☐ England 1994	$18.00	C129	☐ U.S.A. 1993–94	$19.00	C116
☐ Florida 1994	$18.00	C124	☐ Virgin Islands 1994–95	$13.00	C127
☐ France 1994–95	$20.00	C132	☐ Virginia 1994–95 (Avail. 2/94)	$14.00	C142
☐ Germany 1994	$19.00	C125	☐ Yucatán 1993–94	$18.00	C110
☐ Italy 1994	$19.00	C130			
☐ Jamaica/Barbados 1993–94	$15.00	C105			

FROMMER'S $-A-DAY GUIDES
(Guides to low-cost tourist accommodations and facilities)

	Retail Price	Code		Retail Price	Code
☐ Australia on $45 1993–94	$18.00	D102	☐ Israel on $45 1993–94	$18.00	D101
☐ Costa Rica/Guatemala/ Belize on $35 1993–94	$17.00	D108	☐ Mexico on $45 1994	$19.00	D116
☐ Eastern Europe on $30 1993–94	$18.00	D110	☐ New York on $70 1994–95 (Avail. 4/94)	$16.00	D120
☐ England on $60 1994	$18.00	D112	☐ New Zealand on $45 1993–94	$18.00	D103
☐ Europe on $50 1994	$19.00	D115	☐ Scotland/Wales on $50 1992–93	$18.00	D019
☐ Greece on $45 1993–94	$19.00	D100	☐ South America on $40 1993–94	$19.00	D109
☐ Hawaii on $75 1994	$19.00	D113	☐ Turkey on $40 1992–93	$22.00	D023
☐ India on $40 1992–93	$20.00	D010	☐ Washington, D.C. on $40 1994–95 (Avail. 2/94)	$17.00	D119
☐ Ireland on $45 1994–95 (Avail. 1/94)	$17.00	D117			

FROMMER'S CITY $-A-DAY GUIDES
(Pocket-size guides to low-cost tourist accommodations and facilities)

	Retail Price	Code		Retail Price	Code
☐ Berlin on $40 1994–95	$12.00	D111	☐ Madrid on $50 1994–95 (Avail. 1/94)	$13.00	D118
☐ Copenhagen on $50 1992–93	$12.00	D003	☐ Paris on $50 1994–95	$12.00	D117
☐ London on $45 1994–95	$12.00	D114	☐ Stockholm on $50 1992–93	$13.00	D022

FROMMER'S WALKING TOURS
(With routes and detailed maps, these companion guides point out the places and pleasures that make a city unique)

	Retail Price	Code		Retail Price	Code
☐ Berlin	$12.00	W100	☐ Paris	$12.00	W103
☐ London	$12.00	W101	☐ San Francisco	$12.00	W104
☐ New York	$12.00	W102	☐ Washington, D.C.	$12.00	W105

FROMMER'S TOURING GUIDES
(Color-illustrated guides that include walking tours, cultural and historic sights, and practical information)

	Retail Price	Code		Retail Price	Code
☐ Amsterdam	$11.00	T001	☐ New York	$11.00	T008
☐ Barcelona	$14.00	T015	☐ Rome	$11.00	T010
☐ Brazil	$11.00	T003	☐ Scotland	$10.00	T011
☐ Florence	$ 9.00	T005	☐ Sicily	$15.00	T017
☐ Hong Kong/Singapore/			☐ Tokyo	$15.00	T016
Macau	$11.00	T006	☐ Turkey	$11.00	T013
☐ Kenya	$14.00	T018	☐ Venice	$ 9.00	T014
☐ London	$13.00	T007			

FROMMER'S FAMILY GUIDES

	Retail Price	Code		Retail Price	Code
☐ California with Kids	$18.00	F100	☐ San Francisco with Kids		
☐ Los Angeles with Kids			(Avail. 4/94)	$17.00	F104
(Avail. 4/94)	$17.00	F103	☐ Washington, D.C. with Kids		
☐ New York City with Kids			(Avail. 2/94)	$17.00	F102
(Avail. 2/94)	$18.00	F101			

FROMMER'S CITY GUIDES
(Pocket-size guides to sightseeing and tourist accommodations and facilities in all price ranges)

	Retail Price	Code		Retail Price	Code
☐ Amsterdam 1993–94	$13.00	S110	☐ Montréal/Québec		
☐ Athens 1993–94	$13.00	S114	City 1993–94	$13.00	S125
☐ Atlanta 1993–94	$13.00	S112	☐ Nashville/Memphis		
☐ Atlantic City/Cape			1994–95 (Avail. 4/94)	$13.00	S141
May 1993–94	$13.00	S130	☐ New Orleans 1993–94	$13.00	S103
☐ Bangkok 1992–93	$13.00	S005	☐ New York 1994 (Avail.		
☐ Barcelona/Majorca/Minorca/			1/94)	$13.00	S138
Ibiza 1993–94	$13.00	S115	☐ Orlando 1994	$13.00	S135
☐ Berlin 1993–94	$13.00	S116	☐ Paris 1993–94	$13.00	S109
☐ Boston 1993–94	$13.00	S117	☐ Philadelphia 1993–94	$13.00	S113
☐ Budapest 1994–95 (Avail.			☐ San Diego 1993–94	$13.00	S107
2/94)	$13.00	S139	☐ San Francisco 1994	$13.00	S133
☐ Chicago 1993–94	$13.00	S122	☐ Santa Fe/Taos/		
☐ Denver/Boulder/Colorado			Albuquerque 1993–94	$13.00	S108
Springs 1993–94	$13.00	S131	☐ Seattle/Portland 1994–95	$13.00	S137
☐ Dublin 1993–94	$13.00	S128	☐ St. Louis/Kansas		
☐ Hong Kong 1994–95			City 1993–94	$13.00	S127
(Avail. 4/94)	$13.00	S140	☐ Sydney 1993–94	$13.00	S129
☐ Honolulu/Oahu 1994	$13.00	S134	☐ Tampa/St.		
☐ Las Vegas 1993–94	$13.00	S121	Petersburg 1993–94	$13.00	S105
☐ London 1994	$13.00	S132	☐ Tokyo 1992–93	$13.00	S039
☐ Los Angeles 1993–94	$13.00	S123	☐ Toronto 1993–94	$13.00	S126
☐ Madrid/Costa del			☐ Vancouver/Victoria 1994–		
Sol 1993–94	$13.00	S124	95 (Avail. 1/94)	$13.00	S142
☐ Miami 1993–94	$13.00	S118	☐ Washington, D.C. 1994		
☐ Minneapolis/St.			(Avail. 1/94)	$13.00	S136
Paul 1993–94	$13.00	S119			

SPECIAL EDITIONS

	Retail Price	Code		Retail Price	Code
☐ Bed & Breakfast Southwest	$16.00	P100	☐ Caribbean Hideaways	$16.00	P103
☐ Bed & Breakfast Great American Cities (Avail. 1/94)	$16.00	P104	☐ National Park Guide 1994 (avail. 3/94)	$16.00	P105
			☐ Where to Stay U.S.A.	$15.00	P102

Please note: if the availability of a book is several months away, we may have back issues of guides to that particular destination. Call customer service at (815) 734-1104.